RICHARD MULCASTER

Positions Concerning the Training Up of Children

RICHARD MULCASTER

Positions Concerning the Training Up of Children

edited by William Barker

UNIVERSITY OF TORONTO PRESS
Toronto Buffalo London

Toronto Buffalo London
Printed in Canada
Reprinted in 2018
ISBN 0-8020-2987-6
ISBN 978-1-4875-7906-7 (paper)

Printed on acid-free paper

Canadian Cataloguing in Publication Data

Mulcaster, Richard, 1530?–1611
Positions concerning the training up of children

Includes bibliographical references and index.

ISBN 0-8020-2987-6

1. Education – Early works to 1800.
I. Barker, William (William Watson), 1946–
II. Title.

LB475.M8P67 1994 370 C94-931007-7

This book has been published with the help of a grant from the Canadian Federation for the Humanities, using funds provided by the Social Sciences and Humanities Research Council of Canada.

❧ Contents

Preface / vii

Introduction / xi

1 *Positions* / xiii

2 The Style of *Positions* / xlv

3 Richard Mulcaster / lix

4 Date and Text / lxxix

Positions Concerning the Training Up of Children / 1

Textual Notes and Variants / 295

Commentary / 305

Bibliography / 457

Index / 493

❧ Preface

Positions Concerning the Training Up of Children – to use Richard Mulcaster's own short title – is a thoughtful book that argues for changes in the education of Elizabethan England. It was written to its own historical moment, and in the introduction to this edition I have sketched out some of the main issues in Renaissance education as we perceive them today. Some readers have found the style of *Positions* obscure or inelegant; I have also in the introduction tried to explain how the stylistic method expresses a politics of education. And I have given a short life of the author, concentrating on his work as a teacher and writer at the time he wrote this book.

There is a dimension to *Positions* other than its purely 'historical' importance. Many working teachers have been drawn to this book for the way it addresses a perennial classroom problem. Like most books on education, *Positions* is utopian in impulse. Yet Mulcaster struggles with this utopianism. He argues throughout for 'certaintie' or 'one right waye' in education. Yet at the same time he argues for a careful attention to the specific 'circumstances' of the conditions of schooling. Of course, these 'circumstances' – the details and compromises of daily life – always conflict with 'certaintie.' So there is an unresolved tension in *Positions*. On the one hand, there is a striving towards an ideal system and, on the other, there is a recognition of the messiness of the everyday. Though Mulcaster is alert to the problems of his own ideological situation and speaks repeatedly of the kind of learning and teaching required of the subject in a monarchy, his emphasis on 'circumstances' leads him away from the absolute uniformity he espouses from the very first pages onwards. Ultimately, what seems so interesting in *Positions* is this struggle to balance the claims of uniformity and order with the conditions of the moment. Mulcaster's book is ambitious – far more, in its way, than the better-known *Scholemaster* of Roger Ascham.

This is the first edition of *Positions* based on a full consideration of the textual evidence. This is more than a straightforward reprint of the 1581 edition. Such a reprint already exists. In 1887 a teacher and historian of education named Robert Hebert Quick sent a copy of the 1581 *Positions* to a printer and simply had the book typeset; to this he added a short afterword. This widely distributed text became the standard edition for modern readers who wished to read the book and had no access to the old text in a scholarly library. But Quick's edition did not take into account something that scholars have long known about early printed books: namely that printers then regularly sold all the printed sheets together, so that an old book is a mix of corrected and uncorrected gatherings. My work has been to consult as many copies of the book as possible and to compare them in detail, looking for changes. Thus, on page 69, line 23, of this edition you will find the phrase 'natural heat.' In all but one of the twenty-seven copies of the book that I consulted, the passage reads 'natural health.' In Mulcaster's vocabulary of medicine, the phrase makes no sense. But 'natural heat' does make sense and that was how the phrase was corrected by the printer, probably quite late in production. Quick's edition does not show this correction. This is a small point, of course, but it is representative. For this edition I have tried to take into account a broader range of evidence than have editors in the past.

At the end of my introduction, I explain the editorial procedures in greater detail. I have retained the old spelling of the original, despite an increasing tendency among present-day editors to modernize. Although the spelling for non-specialist readers may seem to be very eccentric and at times initially confusing (where 'to' can also mean 'too' or 'two,' or 'too' can be spelled 'two'), old spelling often reveals meaning through puns and other devices of rhetoric (in one of Mulcaster's favourite wordplays, 'travell' means 'travel' and 'travail' at the same time). Rather than erase this playfulness of language, I have instead tried to explain how it works in my introduction and commentary, where I provide a literary and historical context to the work. For a work that is so concerned with 'circumstances' this context is especially important. Of course no reader will be entirely satisfied with the commentary. In one of his essays (3.13), Montaigne describes how he always stumbles over the passages that the commentator never annotated, that were supposed to be obvious.

A modern edition is in many ways unlike the artefact of the past. It serves – one hopes – not to entomb the older text within a fixed and final form, but to mediate between the textual practice of the past and the needs of readers of the present. For readers of the future, a digital version of the Mulcaster text (but not my introduction and commentary) is available at the Oxford University Text Archive.

During the preparation of this published form of my work, I received assistance from many individuals. My most grateful thanks go to William Blissett, James Butrica, David Carlson, Patricia Cavanagh, Jacqueline Cousin, J.M. Davie, Richard DeMolen, Nancy Earle, Jean Guthrie, A.C. Hamilton, John Henderson, Natalie Johnson, James McConica, Randall (M)(c)L(e)(o/ou)d, Frank Mantello, the late Peter Marinelli, Craig Monk, Jeff Monk, Peggy Ann Parsons, Mark Philpott, Kurt Pritzl, Erika Rummel, Andrew Skinner, William Stoneman, George Story, Sr Geraldine Thompson, Frank Tompa, Fred Unwalla, Sharon Wall, John Warden, Germaine Warkentin, Peter Wegemer, and two anonymous readers for University of Toronto Press. Yet I wish above all to thank Desmond Neill, who, as an advisor and reader, helped me in many ways during a difficult time. Mulcaster has already dedicated *Positions* to Elizabeth I. I dedicate my work on this edition to Mr Neill; word for word, he comes out about even with the first recipient of the book, though he will note his share is generally set in smaller type.

I am grateful to scores of librarians at dozens of libraries, chiefly the Bodleian Library, the British Library, the Folger Shakespeare Library, and the Robarts Library of the University of Toronto (especially Mr Albert Masters and the Count).

The Vice-President's Research Fund of Memorial University of Newfoundland gave assistance for the revision of the work, and at an earlier time I received support from American Associates of the University of Toronto, from A.G.S. Griffin, and from Mrs W.J. Veitch.

At University of Toronto Press, the late Prudence Tracy encouraged me to submit the book and I am thankful for her support; Suzanne Rancourt helped the book along; Beverly Johnston provided invaluable support; and Judy Williams corrected a number of inconsistencies, for which I am especially grateful. In an unusual arrangement with University of Toronto Press, Matthew Church and I typeset this book (following the specifications of the publisher), and I am grateful for Matthew's informed enthusiasm. Babs and Evan Church provided a pleasant home for our cottage industry.

For always encouraging me, while engaged herself in work of greater magnitude, I thank my wife, Elizabeth Church. Anthony, Madeleine, Lucy, and Elinor have each, in his or her own way, been amused or bored with their father, and old Mulcaster in his various manifestations.

William Barker
St John's, Newfoundland

INTRODUCTION

1 *Positions*

Richard Mulcaster's *Positions Concerning the Training Up of Children* is one of the best-known English treatises on education from the latter half of the sixteenth century. At the time of publication (1581), Mulcaster was headmaster of Merchant Taylors' School, the largest school in London. *Positions* expresses some of the frustration he felt with the condition of schools and schooling at the time. Because of its deeply political orientation, the book serves also, and more importantly, as an introduction to the ideological debates over pedagogy in the English Renaissance.

From early in the century, under the new order of Tudor education, many schools were founded or refounded under secular patronage. A stricter classical curriculum, brought to England by humanist reformers, was now available to a cross-section of the population that increasingly included the gentry or well born as well as those of poorer background. Of course, most people in England worked in agriculture and manual trades and in absolute numbers few young men ever went to school. Nevertheless, the educational opportunity was considerable. There was informal instruction by local clerics, educated relatives, village dames, and others who taught reading and writing to youngsters in their community. And there was a wide, and expanding, network of local grammar schools for older boys to begin their training in Latin, under masters who were often graduates of Oxford and Cambridge. This grammar school education had by the 1580s become stable, though not yet what we today would call a system, for the schools were all locally run and the curricula subject to the interests of their founders, supporters, and teachers. Yet despite its many restrictions (especially for women), formal education was surprisingly open: proportionally more boys were then in school than in the eighteenth or even nineteenth centuries.[1]

The educational resources of the country expanded because of a range of social pressures. For the religious community, guided in the early years of Elizabeth's reign by a small number of enthusiastic Protestant reformers, widespread education and literacy were means for a direct encounter with God's Holy Word – and a way of ensuring uniformity of doctrine. For those in secular power, state control could be enforced by education if it could to a certain extent be regularized and directed centrally; that this control was to be increased through the religious hierarchy through the licensing of schools and schoolmasters reflected the intimate relations between politics and religion. And for the commoners who founded many of the schools, who sent their children to them, who themselves (by the end of the reign) may have been taught in them, the schools provided access to a social order which placed a new premium on classical learning for prestige or for practical affairs of government or church. Behind the changes in the schools and their expansion lies a whole cluster of historical changes in the English economy, status, and organization of government, as well as in cultural fashion.

Mulcaster writes to this shifting and conflicted moment in English social history. His work is a struggle to make sense of what is taking place, a series of proposals that argue for a more systematic development of the institutional and curricular structure. Around him, Mulcaster sees a lack of order in the way schools are organized locally and the way the young proceed through them at the whim or self-interest of the parents. The 'positions' (posited statements for discussion or argument) are intended to introduce a much longer work of many volumes outlining a formal institutional education from the child's beginning at the elementary school possibly up to his completion of grammar school.[2] This longer work was to have included detailed analyses of curriculum and pedagogical technique. Mulcaster completed only one subsequent volume, *The First Part of the Elementarie* (1582), and how many more parts he had in mind is never made explicit. From what we do have, however, we can see the completed edifice would have been vast, even grander than the *Institutes* of the great Roman teacher Quintilian, whose work seems to have inspired him.

In *Positions* Mulcaster presents a general outline of his principles, gives a close discussion of physical education, and discusses aspects of institutional structure. In the *Elementarie* he begins with an outline of his 'elementary' program and proceeds directly to a highly detailed analysis of 'right writing' (or orthography). Thus, in these two books, he takes us from a preliminary discussion of schooling in the broadest terms to a detailed outline of English spelling, and in nearly six hundred pages presents matter Quintilian handles in only fifty.

Positions is above all a book of advice. Though these 'postulates or preliminary maxims' (as C.S. Lewis has defined the title)[3] arise out of contemporary practice, they are an introduction to what the author would like to see happen in the schools, presented in the particular style of a deliberative orator. Mulcaster touches on an extraordinary range of specific topics in the midst of his more general reflections on society and education. He comments on the age of the pupil's entry to school, the parents' role in teaching manners and morals, the location of school buildings, the use of the left and right hands in the young, the advantage of anthologies of the classics in the classroom, the personal qualities needed of the teacher, and so on. Indeed, for readers interested in Elizabethan education, these asides on the details of curriculum and behaviour may be the most attractive parts of the book. Yet ultimately, all of the wide range of comments on many aspects of schooling bear down on a single proposition, the most significant of his positions, which is that uniformity and the pre-eminence of the state lie at the heart of any educational theory. As he says to Elizabeth at the beginning, 'the very ende of my whole labour ... is to helpe bring the generall teaching in your Majesties dominions to some one good and profitable uniformitie' (4.37–5.2).

UNIFORMITY

For Mulcaster, education is a branch of politics, and all learning is directed ultimately to the public good: '*Education* is the bringing up of one, not to live alone, but amongst others, (bycause companie is our naturall cognisaunce) whereby he shall be best able to execute those doings in life, which the state of his calling shall employ him unto, whether *publike* abrode, or *private* at home, according unto the direction of his countrie whereunto he is borne and oweth his whole service' (186.13–19). In *Elementarie* he reminds the reader that 'publik use ... is the naturall use of all learning' (sig B2v). The state should have the power to control all learning, direct the individual into particular callings, even indeed control the private desires of the citizen (145.30ff).[4]

In his emphasis on the political nature of education, Mulcaster follows Plato (*Republic* and *Laws* 7), Aristotle (*Politics* 7 and 8), and Xenophon (*Cyropaedia*), each of whom sees education as subordinate to the interests of the state, no matter if democracy, oligarchy, or monarchy. Acquiescence to central authority is, of course, especially necessary in a monarchy. Thus, for Mulcaster, one of the chief signs of a child's aptness to learn is his capacity to submit to commands and punishment: 'That child therefore is like to prove in further yeares, the fittest subject for learning in a *monarchie*, which in his tender age sheweth himselfe obedient to scholeorders, and eitheir will not lightly offend, or if he do, will take his punishment gently: without either much repyning, or great stomaking' (154.21–5). The classroom is a monarchy *in parvo*, as is emphasized a number of times: 'is not his maister his *monarche*? and the scholelawes his country lawes?' (155.20–1). Indeed, 'the *rod* may no more be spared in schooles, then the *sworde* may in the *princes* hand' (270.2–3).

Mulcaster emphatically argues for the importance of the state. In his consistently secular view, he is unlike other Elizabethan pedagogical writers, who present themselves as concerned principally with the Christian faith. Of the 'three speciall pointes' to which Ascham writes his *Scholemaster*, 'trothe of Religion' precedes 'honestie in Living' and 'right order in learning.' Likewise, Gnomasticus, the schoolmaster in Gascoigne's *Glasse of Governement*, teaches his boys that their 'first chapter and lesson shall then be, that in all your actions you have an especiall eye and regard to almighty God.' In his *Education of Children* William Kempe divides educational history into three eras, calling his own the 'Schoole of Christianitie' which 'was not onely instituted by the authoritie of our gratious God, but also the first Doctor therein was his only deere Sonne our Saviour Jesus Christ.'[5]

Such beliefs are echoed by almost every other English writer of the period except Mulcaster, who strictly separates the orders of nature and grace, and chooses nature as the proper sphere of education. At one point he declares that 'the end of our being here is to serve God and our country' (132.5–6) but elsewhere he modifies the claim. For Mulcaster, God is 'the *Lorde* of *nature*, which created that motion to continue the consequence of all living creatures' (173.24–5). Yet God's ways are mysterious and unknowable: 'probabilities be our guides' (145.20). The secular quality of his approach is best seen in his definition in the peroration of *Elementarie* of the 'end of everie particular mans doings.' Here, following Aristotle, he claims that 'everie privat man traveleth in this world to win rest after toil, to have ease after labor' (sig 2F4v). For Mulcaster, the end of doing and hence of learning is 'rest.' We may contrast this view with Milton's famous declaration in his tract *Of Education*: 'The end then of learning is to repair the ruins of first parents by regaining to know God aright, and out of that knowledge to love him.'[6] Milton attempts to bring learning and faith together; Mulcaster appears content to keep them apart.

Of course Mulcaster cannot remain entirely secular in his views; in *Elementarie*, for instance, he explains that 'Christianism maie furnish the matter, tho prophanism yeild the form' of learning in school (sig B1v) and in a short passage speaks of bringing the child 'unto Christ' (sig C4r). His two later textbooks, the *Catechismus Paulinus* (1599?) and the *Cato Christianus* (1600), promised in *Elementarie* (sig G4r), are both oriented toward the state religion and suggest that the secularity of *Positions* and *Elementarie* is part of a theoretical stance.

Perhaps we may account for the lack of direct emphasis on religion as Mulcaster's attempt to remove religious factionalism from the arena of educational debate. Religious life in England was an unsettled mixture of radical Puritanism, barely suppressed Catholicism, and a state religion which we now call Anglicanism. For each faith a different form of education was appropriate. By separating education and religion, Mulcaster neatly avoided a loaded issue, while still promoting the central authority of the state. Of course, to a Puritan or Roman Catholic, strong endorsement of uniform state control of education would be seen as an acceptance of the Elizabethan settlement in religion.

THE SOUL

Though Mulcaster favours the public over the private in education, he does not limit his discussion solely to problems of administration and curriculum, but here and there attempts to acquaint his reader with some explanation of the working of the learner's mind. His psychology follows the conventional Aristotelian theories, although certain of the terms to describe the process of learning (such as 'nature' and 'art') may have come to him through the standard educational or, more strictly speaking, rhetorical works of Cicero, Quintilian, and their humanist inheritors.[7]

Mulcaster's psychology begins with the division of body and soul, in which the soul is 'the fountaine of life, and the quickner of the bodie' (51.25) and 'in nature more absolute, and in value more precious' than the body (38.22–3). He does not explore the nature of the soul in its relation to God (except at one point where he recommends the '*Divine*' as the best doctor for the soul [129.22ff]) or as it exists prior and subsequent to the body. Such theological issues were of great importance to Renaissance theorists such as Vives and Melanchthon who had provided relatively recent syntheses of classical psychology with Christian doctrine.[8] Instead, he holds closely to the more strictly Aristotelian notion of the 'natural' soul as it is known in relation to the body. In Aristotle's treatise *On the Soul*, the soul is the informing principle of the body, 'the first actuality of a natural body possessed of organs,' and although the soul is not actual substance, 'it is substance in the sense of formula,'[9] in other words substance as idea. Aristotle shows at length how the soul may receive information through the senses, so that it is capable of being influenced by physical events, just as it in turn influences the body. Mulcaster agrees with this principle of reciprocity: 'The soule and bodie ... having generally a common sympathie, and a mutuall feeling in all passions: how can they be, or rather why should they be severed in traine?' (51.8–11).[10] Education should instruct the entire being, body and soul, though like his predecessors Elyot and Ascham, Mulcaster gives greater emphasis to the training of the soul (ie, the intellect).

Despite his unwillingness to linger over the definition of the soul and its divisions ('meane I not to make any anatomie, or resolution of the soule his partes and properties' 38.29–30), the whole of Mulcaster's pedagogical theory rests on a single assumption, that the soul may indeed be taught. According to Aristotle, the transmission of knowledge is through the senses via the imagination (*phantasia*) to the mind, which receives the information into memory where it is examined and acted upon by the senses of opinion and intellect.[11] In his *Elementarie* Mulcaster follows this analysis closely: 'we have also a perceiving by outward sense to fele, to hear, to se, to smell, to tast all sensible things, which qualities of the outward, being received in by the *common sense*, and examined by *fantsie*, ar delivered to *remembrance* and afterward prove our great and onelie grounds unto further knowledge' (sig D4v). The soul, then, is not a passive receptacle of knowledge, but has the innate capacity to perform tasks of 'understanding beyond sense, of judging by reason' (sig E1r). The act of learning is both the receipt of the information and the exercise of the understanding and reason upon it. And education is the training of the mental functions: 'those abilities in their first naturall kinde concern but the being of a rude man, but when theie ar fashioned to their best by good education, theie procure the being of a perfit and an excellent man' (sig E1r).

Now what is needed for 'good education'? According to Mulcaster, two things: 'naturall abilities' and 'artificiall principles.' The former are those qualities 'which natur planteth in our mindes and bodies' (sig D3r). 'Artificiall principles' are the rules of art, the ordering principles, which act to 'take sure hold of all naturall inclinations and abilities, and bring them to perfection' (sig D3v). The pupil brings to his education his 'natural abilities,' which are acted upon by 'artificiall principles'; art makes manifest the universals inherent in the learner's nature. If the nature of the child is not apt, or if the art of the master is wanting (that is, it does not match the nature of the child), then there will be no improvement of mind. Finally, to secure the fruitful combination of nature and art, a third quality – 'practice' or 'habit' – is needed. Education must be 'confirmed by use, perfited with continewance, which crouneth the hole work' (sig E1v).

'Nature,' 'art,' and 'habit' or 'use' are terms conventionally mentioned together in the educational doctrine of classical and Renaissance writers. Plato is perhaps the earliest to give expression to this tripartite theory of learning. In the *Phaedrus*, Socrates claims that 'to become a perfect orator ... is probably, perhaps must be dependent on conditions, like everything else. If you are naturally rhetorical, you will become a notable orator when to your natural endowments [*physis*] you have added knowledge [*episteme*] and practice [*melete*]; at whatever point you are deficient in these you will be incomplete.' Aristotle in his analysis of education in book 7 of the *Politics* likewise stresses the need for 'nature, habit and reason [*physis, ethos, logos*].' These same terms appear in Cicero, Quintilian, the pseudo-Plutarchan essay 'On the Education of Children,' Aeneas Sylvius Piccolomini, Mapheus Vegius, Johann Sturm, and Peter Ramus. They are the cornerstone of Erasmus' pedagogical psychology in the *De pueris instituendis*, where *natura, ratio,* and *usus* must be in perfect harmony: 'Nature is realized only through method, and practice, unless it is guided by the principles of method, is open to numerous errors and pitfalls.' These three terms are found in English writers too, either as a brief commonplace in More, Cheke, and Sidney, or more elaborately, as in Ascham's *Toxophilus*, where 'aptness,' 'knowledge,' and 'use' are developed into a full theory of education.[12]

Mulcaster is making use of an important commonplace when he says: 'the end of education, and train is to help natur unto hir perfection, which is, when all hir abilities be pirfited in their habit, whereunto right Elements [ie, the parts of the elementary program that comprise the 'art'] be right great helps' (sig D2v). Most often, though, he omits 'habit,' and in *Positions* especially we note that for him education is primarily bipolar, consisting of 'nature' and 'nurture' (or 'art'). These two aspects of learning are proverbial, English Renaissance proverbs (coming from the Latin) declaring that 'nature surpasses nurture' or 'nurture surpasses nature';[13] as is common with many proverbs, the meaning is found more in the opposition of the two terms than in the actual precedence of one over the other.

If education consists of nature and art, then the nature of the learner must be closely examined in the same way as the art of the curriculum, so that the two may fit together well. Mulcaster offers his readers few specific signs by which a child's academic aptness could be noted. His contemporaries were perfectly aware that great differences existed among children; Montaigne put the problem most wittily when he recommended for the unresponsive pupil, 'qu'on le mette patissier dans quelque bonne ville, fust-il fils d'un duc, suivant le precepte de Platon qu'il faut colloquer les enfans non selon les facultez de leur pere, mais selon les facultez de leur ame.'[14] A bold attempt was made by Juan Huarte de Navarro, Spanish author of *The Examination of Mens Wittes* (1575; translated 1594), to sort out the particular qualities of mind needed for different intellectual tasks. Although Mulcaster is sensitive to the differences among pupils ('some be hastinges and will on, some be hardinges, and draw backe' 31.24–5), his method of differentiating abilities is presented in general terms. In *Elementarie* (sig B4r) he lists the character traits necessary for learning: intelligence ('sharpnesse of wit to perceive soon'); perseverance ('an invincible and laborious courage to go thorough with al paines'); curiosity ('a desire to be asking, and demanding of others'); capacity for work ('Never to be idle, but ever well occupied, tho it be in plaie'); memory ('a fast memorie to kepe well, and a good foresight to continew it well'). He especially dwells on the student's sense of shame and 'vertew' (sig C1r), effectively moving from intellectual abilities to moral (and political) malleability and docility. Chapter 37 of *Positions* especially stresses the suitability and circumstances of the individual child to continue on in school. Nor does he forget the physical strength of the child: in *Positions* he classifies the types of pupils in four categories, weak body with weak mind, weak body with strong mind, strong body with weak mind, and (inevitably most 'worthy the wishing') 'a strong witte, in as strong a bodie' (33.11). Such attempts to define the qualities of the student recall Ascham's 'seven plaine notes to choise a good witte in a childe for learninge,' borrowed in large part from Plato, that offer a similar reading of the learner's psychology.[15] There is, however, an important point in Mulcaster not made so emphatically by Ascham: that a child not be rushed into school at the earliest possible age and that more of the child than his intellectual capacity be considered.

Yet Mulcaster may be less interested in the individual psychology of the child than he is in the politics of that psychology. He has set out to tell the Queen and his other readers which children shall be allowed to move on in schools, and which ones shall be refused the benefits of formal schooling. Those who are not 'apt' or receptive to learning are not to continue on. As a practising schoolmaster, Mulcaster is aware that individual difference and the practical politics of their situation must be acknowledged by parents and teachers. Certain types are just not cut out for schooling. In both *Positions* and *Elementarie* he argues that all must accede to the central authority of the monarchical state, and his rudimentary psychology is a means for achieving a harmony between the private and the public. In both works he articulates a public 'art' that is to take precedence over the private 'nature' of the pupil.

THE ELEMENTARY

Thus, though he acknowledges the importance of 'nature,' Mulcaster's two books are principally about 'art,' the methodical program of teaching. *Positions* is the analysis of the social and political framework of this program; *Elementarie* is the beginning of a long and closely detailed description of the program that he would like to see uniformly established in the schools. Because *Positions* looks ahead to this program and refers to it repeatedly, we should consider it here.

The elementary curriculum (described in chapters 5 of *Positions* and 11 of *Elementarie*) is meant for children up to about the age of twelve, and is in five parts – reading, writing, drawing, music for voice, and music for instrument. Reading is the 'first and fairest principle' (41.25). It is to precede grammar and begins with English, not Latin, for English reading 'is most naturall to our soile, and most proper to our faith' (42.4–5) and has the added benefit of being more difficult than Latin reading and therefore a better training.[16] Writing comes next, when the child is physically capable of holding the pen; again, is is better 'to write English before Latin, as a thing of more hardnesse' (45.20–1); by this Mulcaster means the child is to learn English secretary before an Italic script. 'Writing' has a secondary sense as well; it is orthography as well as penmanship. The *Elementarie* treats of 'right writing' or standardized orthography as a preliminary to reading; in the work Mulcaster sets down certain basic principles followed by a list of some eight thousand spellings. As elsewhere in his educational theory, he attempts in his orthography to mediate between a systematic ideal and the haphazard practice; following Quintilian, 'reason' and 'custom' are the two poles between which his theory is situated.

The remaining three subjects, drawing and the two kinds of music, are barely touched on in the two treatises. If he had continued his work, however, he would have written extensively about them. In regard to drawing, for instance, we have a letter to the Dutch geographer Abraham Ortelius in which Mulcaster, perhaps showing off a bit, mentions that he owns what he calls Dürer's *De humani corporis fabrica libri quatuor* and a Vitruvius edited by Daniele Barbaro, and that he has consulted Pliny the Elder, Polydore Vergil, Caelius Rhodiginus, Aelian, Quintilian, 'et eius generis autores omnes' (and all other authors of the kind). He now desires of Ortelius information of other books not yet known to him 'in qua voles lingua' (in whatever language you wish).[17] This is an impressive enough list for a subject normally considered to be a manual art. Mulcaster sees drawing less as a vocational skill, however, than as a part of a child's general education in 'the proportion and seemelines of all aspectable thinges' (46.2–3), though (and this is where he and a writer for gentlemen like Elyot part company), 'if any dexterity that waye do draw the child on, it is an honest mans living' (46.34–6).[18] Music, likewise, is a 'double principle both for the soule, by the name of learning, and for the body, by the waye of exercise' (48.14–15).

The form of this 'elementary' is, as Mulcaster acknowledges, drawn mainly from books 7 and 8 of Aristotle's *Politics* and from the first two books of Quintilian's *Institutes*. Even so, the program he proposes would not have been foreign to the contemporary education of England. Reading, writing, and music were traditional subjects of the medieval and Tudor schools.[19] This is the standard curriculum too of Elyot's young governor. Mulcaster's unusual approach comes in his desire to see the program institutionalized for *all* children, independent of status and sex, and brought under the control of the state. This 'elementary' will become established through laws, more thorough regulation of teachers, standardized texts and curricula, and, most important, the universal obedience of all citizens in education to the authority of the state.

THE BODY

Many English writers before Mulcaster had included physical education in their curricula. Elyot enthusiastically recommended a full range of sports for the governor. Ascham's scholarly Toxophilus argued that archery is good for both body and soul of the archer. In the interpenetrating worlds of fiction and actual practice, the 'shepherd-knight' Astrophel (Sir Philip Sidney) was accounted to be expert in field sports: 'wrestling nimble ... renning swift ... shooting steddie,' and above all hunting.[20] By the early Stuart period there were many books about fencing, swimming, hunting, hawking, riding, and so on, all directed to the young gentleman, or would-be gentleman.[21] Standard schoolbooks took notice of sports for children; the dialogues of Erasmus, Cordier, and Vives all have sections on sports.[22]

Unlike most earlier and contemporary writers, who consider sports to be extra-curricular in that they are normally unconnected with the formal academic curriculum, Mulcaster wishes them to be brought within the school. In his long section on physical education, Mulcaster looks at what he calls sports for 'within dores' and 'without dores.' Some of these activities are the conventional games and exercises of the English gentleman, now to be brought to students of all social degrees. Others are familiar as English village games, such as wrestling or scourging the top.[23] A few might strike the modern reader as unusual, even ridiculous, such as laughing, weeping, or holding the breath (though for the orator, control of the breath and emotion is essential to *pronuntiatio* or delivery). And as he shows, all his sports are entirely defensible in the traditional framework of ancient medicine, especially as articulated in the writings of Galen, the second-century AD medical philosopher whose writings were so vastly influential in the Renaissance.

Mulcaster wishes to see all the traditional sports as part of a regular school program, under the supervision of his 'training master.' As he progresses sport by sport he carefully analyses each one for its benefits and drawbacks, and subjects each to the scrutiny of the Galenic categories. Everyone knows a child is hot and moist in his physical complexion, but if a child sits for long hours in study, his body will suffer. Will the sport sufficiently excite the natural heat of the body in order to overcome the coldness brought on by too many hours in the classroom and the library? Or will it too suddenly dry out the body that by its nature must retain a great deal of this youthful moisture? Will the sport improve the appetite? Or will it cause the student to feel unwell and to fall off his food? Every aspect of the sport is considered in the light of the humoral balance of the child or scholar practising it.

Now and then it is all too clear, from his limited enthusiasm and information, that Mulcaster has never practised some of the sports he describes. Furthermore, it is clear that although he speaks about a sport within the context of schools and education, he has not a clue how to bring that sport into the general curriculum of a school, certainly not into the understaffed schools of Elizabethan England. It is all quite theoretical. And yet he is able to admit that he is describing a theoretical ideal, not a standard for regular day-to-day practice. His reform is not to be absolute, but to be set within the 'circumstances' of the time, place, habits, and so on of his fellow Englishmen. By his application of 'circumstances' he tries to set his theoretical program within a contemporary context.

Nevertheless, despite this attention to circumstances, there seems something remarkably bookish about Mulcaster's discussion of sports for English schools. He talks about the English situation and tries to orient his suggestions to the English scene, and yet most of his authorities are classical. Despite the remarkable attempt to argue for sports and the principle of 'a wise minde, and a healthfull bodie' (53.9–10), the chapters seem curiously second-hand. An exception is the lively and anecdotal chapter 'Of Shooting'; Mulcaster, like Roger Ascham, was a known enthusiast, a member of the famous knights of Prince Arthur who annually gathered in patriotic tribute to celebrate the traditional English longbow. Yet he does little justice to other sports, and his arguments for them seem pale.

There is an explanation for the thinness of his arguments, and he provides it himself near the end of the section on physical education. In chapter 35 of *Positions*, almost in an aside, he says: 'for the professed argument of the whole booke, I know not any comparable to *Hieronymus Mercurialis*, a verie learned *Italian Physician* now in our time, which hath taken great paines to sift out of all writers, what so ever concerneth the whole *Gymnasticall* and exercising argument, whose advice in this question I have my selfe much used, where he did fit my purpose' (134.10–15). Most of his many pages on physical education are borrowed, adapted from, or sometimes directly translated from the *De arte gymnastica libri sex* by the Italian physician Girolamo Mercuriale. The extent of Mulcaster's debt was first analysed in 1892 by Georg Schmid.[24] Even so, few subsequent readers of *Positions* seem to know that what they are reading in chapters 6 through 35 is a digest and reorganization of a treatise first published in Venice in 1569.[25]

Mercuriale's treatise is almost entirely concerned with ancient sport – 'exercitationum omnium vetustarum genera' as the title page emphasizes – and is an extraordinarily well documented survey of the Greek and Latin sources for the study of physical exercise. The first book treats of definitions and of the early history of gymnastics, goes on to discuss the various locations where ancient sports were practised (*palaestra*, *gymnasium*, baths, and so on), and finally establishes the matter of the rest of the volume – medical gymnastics, as opposed to martial exercise and athletics or the professional sports of the gladiator. Books 2 and 3 are a detailed analysis of the history and practice of the many sports the author classifies under 'gymnastica medica' – leaping, various forms of ball games, dancing, wrestling, throwing of the discus, walking, running, riding, swimming, hunting, and the like. Included among these are a few of the less well known sports, however famous among the ancients, such as pancreatic wrestling, the use of the *halterus*, and a few activities which we today would call exercise of a kind if not sport as such – holding the breath, loud speaking, and drills for the voice. Books

4 through 6 are more specifically medical than those preceding. Book 4 presents the effect of exercise on different physical types (chapter 7 wonders, for instance, 'An corpora aegra ullò pacto exerceri conveniat' [whether it is appropriate for weak bodies to be exercised in any way]). Books 5 and 6, following the same order as books 2 and 3, re-examine each of the sports, this time analysing their benefits and harms from a medical point of view. The chapter 'De cursus natura' at book 5, chapter 7, for instance, completes the discussion of running begun in 'De cursu' at book 2, chapter 10. Together these two chapters provide a history and analysis of running as a sport of 'gymnastica medica,' including all the benefits and harms that the sport induces. As one may well imagine, the author's double approach to each of his sports does not provide the book with much continuity.[26] Yet the work is immensely learned, with references to at least 122 ancient authorities – principally Hippocrates, Galen, Aristotle, Celsus, Oribasius, and Aetius, as well as the Arabs Avicenna, Averroes, and Rhazes. Mercuriale reads these sources critically, and often places differing opinions side by side to allow the reader to see how sound medical advice may be obtained through the weighing of apparently contradictory authority.

We do not know how Mulcaster came across Mercuriale's *De arte gymnastica*; perhaps it was through the same kind of network he used when he sought advice on drawing from Ortelius. Nor do we know on which edition he relied.[27]

Mulcaster followed a consistent method of reading and borrowing for most of his chapters. For instance, Mulcaster's chapter 21 'Of Running' is based on the chapters 'De cursu' (Of running; 2.10) and 'De cursus natura' (On the nature of running; 5.7) mentioned above. Mulcaster begins his little essay on running by proving its utility. The first paragraph is an extended paralipsis, in which he tells the reader that 'To polishe out this point with those effectuall reasons [regarding the necessity of running] ... were to me nothing needefull' (95.33–96.7). As part of this circumlocutory device he maintains that it is not necessary to tell 'what *Alexander* the *Macedonian*, nor what *Papyrius* the *Romain* did by swift foote, nor that *Homere* gave *Achilles* his epithete of his footmanship' (96.8–10); he need only state 'that *running* is an exercise for health, which if reason cannot winne, whereof every one can judge, sure historie will not' (96.11–12). In other chapters, the historical proof is often taken from the early chapters of *De arte*; this time, however, Mulcaster has gone elsewhere, to Sir Thomas Elyot, who refers to Alexander, Papirius, and 'swifte foote Achilles' in his observations on the benefits of running in book 1, chapter 16, of his *Boke Named the Governour*. Mulcaster then proceeds from his preliminary historical proof to a division of running by type: two kinds 'vehement swift' and 'gentle and moderate' he analyses at some length, and he concludes his chapter with the 'other kindes of *running*' (98.5ff), namely 'long outright,' 'streight backward,' 'round about,' 'uphill,' 'downhill,' 'in ... clothes,' 'out of ... clothes,' 'in winter,' 'in sommer.' All this is from Mercuriale, and is a condensation of five pages of *De arte* in which running is divided into 'uelocius, atque uehementius' (faster and more violent), 'remissius & placidius' (more relaxed and gentle), 'in rectum' (forwards), 'in retro' (backwards), 'circulariter' (round about), 'per accliuia' (uphill), 'per decliuia' (downhill), 'tecto corpore' (clothed), 'nudi corporis' (unclothed), 'in hyeme' (in winter), and 'in aestate' (in summer), in the same order followed by Mulcaster.

The English follows the Latin closely, although a great deal has been omitted. Most of the references to ancient authorities, for instance, have been passed over – 'a Celso' (from Celsus), 'credidit Rufus Ephesius' (Rufus Ephesius believed) 'secundum Antyllum' (following Antyllus) – and similar formulae are dropped. Also left out are debates on the harms of running to those with what Mulcaster translates as 'an ill heade, or a weake bulke, or burning and hoat urine' (97.34–5) and on running in and out of clothes. Throughout this chapter Mulcaster is intent on providing sure opinion, not debate. To argue points pro and con would vitiate his deliberative style, which must be strong and positive; moreover he would lose the avowed central train of his topic, which is education, not medicine. The only debate he gives in the chapter is at the very end, where he mentions contrasting views on running in summer and winter, and provides a simple resolution. In the second half of the chapter there is only one observation added to the material from Mercuriale, and that is the image of a 'chafed [ie, vexed, irritated] deare' (97.37–8) who must run from the hunter but who would dearly like the hunter to 'give him leave to pisse' – a fanciful image to show the danger of running with a full bladder, and quite in keeping with Mulcaster's style, which throughout *Positions* now and then plays with intrusively amusing digressions to give relief to purely technical discussion. Likewise, his alliterations continue sound-patterns used all the way through *Positions*: examples are 'defluxions and distillings' (97.17, combining definition and alliteration for Mercuriale's simple 'defluxiones'), 'cooleth the flesh & furthereth not the feeding' (97.32–3, for 'carnem refrigerat, nec alimenti reddit capaciorem,' itself a chiastic alliteration), and 'as the fore warning of some forreine disease' (98.15, for 'quibus morbus forinsecus immineat').

Overall, as an analysis of chapter 21 of *Positions* shows, and as a close reading of other chapters would also demonstrate, Mulcaster condenses his source by omitting debate and authorities. He adds to Mercuriale a few historical examples and images, and he transforms the fairly straightforward medical jargon of the *De arte gymnastica* into his own 'close' style of writing. These chapters on sports may be the least successful in *Positions* – heavily studded with authorities most of whom are borrowed directly from Mercuriale, less concerned with students and parents, and often lacking in personal observation and experience. Yet they do show us Mulcaster attempting to work in as full a manner as he could with a subject seemingly unfamiliar to him, and the chapters on dancing, archery, ball games, and the training master do show a concern with contemporary practice which is not found in the *De arte gymnastica* of Girolamo Mercuriale.

The fact that Mulcaster relied on Mercuriale as he does and the manner in which he modifies his source are directly related to the ideological direction of his argument. Unlike his two predecessors Elyot and Ascham, Mulcaster is not specifically concerned with the education of the gentleman. His program considers all social groups. In a sense, his recommendations reflect an important shift in late sixteenth-century schooling. The education of the gentleman, formerly undertaken under the guidance of a tutor in a great house, was still in practice, but in decline. Mulcaster is resolutely in favour of a public education, and brings forth all the ancient authorities to attack the notion of private instruction. He is a supporter of a strong central state that retains hierarchy but that does not give undue worth to any degree except for the monarchy itself. The whole program of sports fits into his more general claims. The schools will retain the best of the older education of the gentleman, but they will not be just for gentlemen or the wealthy. Yet how can he present his argument? He cannot argue that horseback riding and fencing must be taught because they are *socially* correct. This would undercut his argument that they should be open to all. So he has undertaken a different approach. These sports will be practised, along with many others, because they are *scientifically* sound. The whole social aspect of sports is obscured by an apparently medical argument in their favour. Yet this scientific – or perhaps one should say pseudo-scientific – argument for sports is really part of Mulcaster's rhetorical method. Thus, everything the medical humanist Mercuriale says about a sport is intended to disseminate and increase medical knowledge; everything the educational propagandist Mulcaster says – no matter how scientific or how well supported by authorities – is used as part of a defence of uniformity in public schooling.

GENTLEMAN AND COMMONER

Earlier sections of *Positions* allude to the problem of education for various classes, but in chapter 39 of *Positions* Mulcaster turns specifically to 'the training up of yong gentlemen.' Most earlier sixteenth-century treatises were concerned solely with the private education of the gently born. In *Positions*, however, Mulcaster sees the instruction of the gentleman as a topic subsidiary to public education as a whole.

In *Positions*, Mulcaster witnesses and seeks to relieve the public discontent caused by unusual social mobility. Steady growth in population, especially in London, rapid changes in prices, increased activity in real estate and other commercial ventures all tended to increase movement in the old hierarchy. City merchants and successful artisans sought to rise in status; some families of relatively humble origin had become established in the aristocracy by the end of Elizabeth's reign. The ancient problems of status and social privilege were therefore coming under scrutiny as members of various classes were being shifted around in the hierarchy, indeed as the hierarchy itself was being re-examined.[28]

Like any writer discussing the gentleman's education, Mulcaster attempts a definition of status. 'What is it,' he asks, 'to be a *nobleman* or a *gentleman*?' (197.39). Society consists of two large general categories, the '*commonalty*' and the '*gentilitie*,' the former being '*marchauntes* and *manuaries*' (those who buy and sell and those who work with their hands), the latter gentlemen (confusingly described as 'the *creame* of the common' 198.11), noblemen, and the prince. The difference in the levels of the hierarchy lies in the 'authoritie' of power of each. And it also consists in certain qualities: '*gentility* argueth a courteous, civill, well disposed, sociable constitution of minde in a superiour degree' (201.2–4). Such qualities may be taught, though Mulcaster also holds that in their finest degree the qualities are inborn and somewhat mysterious (and therefore unattainable by the outsider).

Mulcaster's descriptions of the social order and of the gentleman are in accord with those of other writers. Sir Thomas Smith, for instance, in his *De republica Anglorum* (written c 1565 but not published until 1583, posthumously), writes of the division of the parts and persons of the commonwealth, and finds 'four sortes, gentlemen, citizens and yeomen, artificers[,] and laborers.' Gentlemen consist of 'nobilitas major,' 'nobilitas minor,' 'esquiers,' and plain 'gentlemen.' Like Mulcaster, Smith is especially anxious about the line of status separating the citizen and the gentleman; he wonders 'whether the maner of England in making gentlemen so easily is to be allowed.'[29] Smith sees nothing wrong with flexibility; Mulcaster seems somewhat more conservative, and is especially suspicious of those who have climbed up the ladder by virtue of wealth: 'for of all the meanes to make a gentlemen, it is the most vile, to be made for money' (194.35–6), even if that is how the system usually worked.

Certainly all authorities insisted that learning be joined with wealth where good birth was lacking; as Smith (who owed a political career to initial success as a scholar) argued, anyone who has studied the law or in the university and can live 'idly and without manuall labour ... he shall be called master ... and shall be taken for a gentleman.'[30] Education and class were intimately connected. Even the nobly born, generally a very conservative group in any society, had fully embraced the new learning by the end of Elizabeth's reign, the radical impulse of Protestant humanist learning now having been domesticated in a new status quo.

English writers before Mulcaster generally favoured the private instruction of the gentleman. Elyot's *Governour*, Ascham's *Scholemaster*, Humphrey's *Nobles*, the anonymous *Institucion of a Gentleman*, and such literary works as Hoby's popular translation of Castiglione's *Courtier* and Lyly's *Euphues* all present a largely aristocratic ideal of education in which a young man of good birth is trained up privately by tutors in physical and intellectual skills before he is ready for a life of service to the crown as a soldier-administrator. These works, however, suggest only a limited aspect of what was actually practised. There were, of course, tutors in many households – Ascham taught both Elizabeth and Lady Jane Grey, Samuel Daniel instructed the future earl of Pembroke, Thomas Blundeville worked in the household of Sir Nicholas Bacon – but only the wealthy and very highly placed could afford to hire an 'auncient and worshipfull man, in whom is aproved to be moche gentilnes, mixte with gravitie,' as Elyot described the ideal private tutor.[31] In actuality the lower gentry sent their young to nearby public grammar schools or to the better-known larger schools outside their county, such as Eton or Winchester. Even those of higher status went to public schools; Philip Sidney and Fulke Greville were educated at Shrewsbury (the largest school in England, with 450 boys) under Thomas Ashton.[32] The schools were seen increasingly as an acceptable alternative to tutoring at home or service in a great man's household (as Thomas More much earlier had known in the household of Cardinal Morton).

In acknowledgment of this great shift in schooling, Mulcaster argues that the education of the gentry should be public, not private. Only the young nobleman of the highest rank should be treated exceptionally. The very nature of education is public, he says (following Quintilian),[33] and the term 'private education' is for him very nearly a self-contradiction. He sees no need for the gentry to be treated any differently from the 'common':

> What exercises shall they have? The verie same. What maisters? The same. What circunstance else? All one and the same. (193.39–194.1)

There is only one area of exception, that they be given lessons 'which do appertaine to governement, to direct others well, and [which] belong to obedience, to guide themselves wisely' (193.29–31). Other than this special 'matter,' gentlemen are to have the same education as the 'common,' even to the point of attending the schools of divinity, law, and medicine at the end. Mulcaster works hard to show how these clerkly and professionally bookish activities are suitable to the status of a gentleman – a point few writers would have made fifty years earlier. He makes no mention of training for the court, and he is openly hostile to the military life: 'I do not hold *Tamerlane,* or any barbarous, and bloody invasions to be meanes to true nobilitie' (218.2–4). Even travel, by the 1580s already considered to be part of the young gentleman's education, he largely discommends ('I say young *gentlemen* may learne better at home, as her *Majestie* did' 212.17–18) and regards voyages abroad solely in the light of their benefits to the commonwealth, an interpretation which follows Plato's *Republic* closely.[34]

Mulcaster is intent on assimilating the education of the gentry into a larger system, in which 'common' and 'gentle' both owe their training and obedience to the state. To a modern reader, Mulcaster might appear to be democratic in the way he would allow all children to start in a common training. Yet above all he is a monarchist – the continuance of pupils in the system is determined as much by brains as by social status, wealth, and the ultimate vocation of the child as a servant to the crown.

THE SCHOOLING OF WOMEN

'The bringing up of young *maidens* in any kynd of learning, is but an accessory by the waye' to the education of young men (138.14–16). So argues Mulcaster. In chapter 38 of *Positions* he shows it to be an important accessory.

The chapter begins with proofs that women should be taught – arguments from contemporary practice, from the duty that men owe to women, from the 'naturall towardnesse' that women show for learning, and from examples of women who have been successfully taught. These points are set forth as a challenge to a prevailing attitude – that women are ignorant by nature and by custom, and that no time should therefore be spent on their instruction. Indeed, though he does not say so, Mulcaster is arguing against a tradition of misogyny which in his day found expression in philosophical commentaries, medical and legal treatises, and popular works of anti-feminist vilification.[35] The counter-arguments he uses are, however, as conventional as those of the anti-feminists, and are found in many earlier humanist works that seek to defend the fame of good women or which propose instruction for women, such as the writings of Vives, Agrippa, and Elyot.[36] And despite his attempt to defend women's right to learn, he sees women always in terms of their relationship to men; women are to men as 'pupilles unto tutours, as bodies unto heades, nay as bodies unto soules' (171.26–7).

Keeping his eye on what he sees as the limited vocation of women, Mulcaster outlines the particular circumstances of their learning: which, when, what, how much, where, and under whom. Such details of curriculum as he gives are interesting. Girls are to begin schooling at about the same age as boys, and are to study to the same degree the subjects of the elementary, including the physical training. Mulcaster is not interested in the practical aspects of their vocational training ('I medle not with *nedles*, nor yet with *housewiferie*' 180.2). He does call for some academic training beyond the elementary, some 'skill of languages' and a bit of geometry, musical theory, law, medicine, divinity, and philosophy. He approves of drawing (in spite of his earlier statement, he claims 'it would helpe their nedle' 182.32–3). For him, the young woman who is 'thoroughly furnished' is able to 'reade plainly and distinctly, write faire and swiftly, sing cleare and sweetely, play wel and finely, understand and speake the learned languages, and those toungues also which the time most embraseth, with some *Logicall* helpe to chop, and some *Rhetoricke* to brave' (183.3–7).

Although the program he proposes may be thought to be unusually advanced for the day, it seems likely that it was found typically in women of a certain status in mid-Elizabethan England, as indeed is suggested by his concluding comment that 'such there be, and such we know' (183.13–14). There were of course the paragons – the Cooke sisters, Mary Sidney, Queen Elizabeth herself, and others – who were hard at work translating the Greek and Latin classics or preparing metrical versions of the Psalms. Yet there were other less distinguished women who read learned books and were engaged in a life of the mind. Grace Sherrington (or Sharington), married at fifteen to Sir Walter Mildmay's son Anthony, was not taught by an Ascham, Foxe, or Daniel, but by a female cousin who started her in reading and writing, and who encouraged her in the composition of music and in the study of herbs and medicine. Her diary presents evidence that she was skilled in most of the things Mulcaster wrote about, except for the classical languages and geometry, and that she also knew some law and philosophy.[37] Mulcaster sets down in formal terms no more of a curriculum than a Grace Sherrington would have already known. Again, he is claiming for the public a practice already inscribed in private.

Although his belief in women's education is strongly stated, it is nonetheless limited. Education for Mulcaster is always 'our owne traine,' that is, developed by and belonging to men, given as a special concession to women. Women are not to be entered in the grammar school or the university ('a thing not used in my countrie' 170.19–20). Their tutors are ideally men. And whereas he has no doubts about their ability to attain an advanced level, he gives them no status to return the learning to the state. Women may be taught divinity, but are certainly allowed no 'pulpittes to preach in' (182.19). In other words, there is a contradiction at the heart of his arguments in favour of women's education. His whole notion of education is public and oriented towards the state; his idea of women is that they are not to serve the state except indirectly. And he barely mentions one way in which a woman could use her learning at that time, namely in the instruction of her children. Classical writers and Protestant theorists encouraged women to seek learning and to teach their offspring manners and religion.[38] Of course, this would be a form of the private instruction that he seems committed to overturning.

The contradiction in *Positions* regarding the education of women appears inevitably in other writers of the time. For these writers, to resolve it would have meant redefining education or the nature of woman, or both. In his low view of women in the public sphere, Mulcaster holds to a social attitude then prevailing. Women were meant to be wives, whose place in the scheme of things was determined by the place of the husband. 'He for God only, she for God in him,' as Milton succinctly put it.[39] Wives were perceived as a form of 'absolute property,' that is as legal extensions of men, not legal beings in their own right.[40] It is perhaps not surprising, then, that a general ambivalence towards women is found in many humanist treatises, even those that praise women extensively, and not just in Mulcaster's *Positions*.

Nevertheless, Mulcaster is 'toothe and nail' in favour of women's learning, and that he is so may be due to his seeking of patronage from Queen Elizabeth. She is mentioned several times in the chapter, always as the finest example of the learned lady – 'our diamond at home,' the tenth muse who, like the number ten, contains 'al perfections in nature' (175.18–23). His grandiloquent compliments, found here and elsewhere, indicate a willingness to please which may have induced him to include a chapter of special interest to his sovereign, and to speak so enthusiastically of the education of women.

THE SCHOOLMASTER

Although the medieval church had tried to organize English education according to a few central principles, 'the sixteenth century saw more attempts than before to legislate for education, to supervise schoolmasters, to control their work and to introduce a desirable uniformity into their classrooms.'[41] Uniformity was increasingly enforced by government-approved textbooks such as Lily's *Grammar*, Nowell's *Catechism*, and Ocland's *Anglorum praelia* (to which Mulcaster wrote prefatory verses), by the licensing of schoolmasters by episcopal authority, and by the codification of school statutes often modelled on those of earlier foundation.[42] Despite all this activity, it was felt by many observers that a desirable uniformity had not yet been established. In *Positions*, Mulcaster is emphatic that 'there is to much variety in teaching, and therfore to much ill teaching (bycause in the midst of many bypathes, there is but one right waye)' (260.2–4). Whether or not his contemporaries agreed with the assumption that in teaching 'there is but one right waye,' certainly Elizabethan schools lacked a highly consistent order. Because the curricula of the schools were established locally, often by individual teachers themselves (who would necessarily have to leave off from statutory programs because of an inadequate supply of textbooks or because of their own interests and training), there was considerable variation from school to school in what the young were taught. Even the three texts just mentioned were not used universally; indeed, it is doubtful if Ocland's poem was ever read much at all. There was tremendous difference among the academic achievements of the teachers, who might range from the village dame to the Master of Arts. High turnover among teachers was a further problem; a recent graduate might teach for only a few years before moving on to an easier life as a beneficed clergyman. Because of poor pay, many teachers had to support themselves by other work, such as preaching or farming, and were therefore unable to give their pedagogical duties full attention.[43]

Mulcaster's solution to what he sees as the disorganization of teaching is to turn schoolmastering from a vocation into a profession.[44] He suggests several ways to do this. The first is the training of teachers. His reform of the universities, outlined in chapter 41, recommends that the old system of colleges and faculties be replaced by seven new colleges organized around professions, somewhat like the Inns of Court. They would be for the study of languages, mathematics, philosophy, divinity, law, medicine, and teaching. A college of mathematics is most unusual of the seven, though Gresham College with its orientation towards the scientific and practical was to be founded not much later in London. The last of these, the college for 'training maisters,' is, however, for Mulcaster the most significant part of the reorganization. Although such a proposal might seem very forward-looking, Mulcaster was actually calling for the reinstatement of the medieval grammar faculty which had trained masters of grammar from the fourteenth through to the early sixteenth century. The collapse of this program had occurred in his own lifetime (the last Masters of Grammar had graduated at Cambridge in 1548, at Oxford in 1568). Mulcaster seeks to rehabilitate the old professional school, and to set it up on the same level and importance at the schools of medicine, law, and divinity.[45] By having its own faculty, the teaching of grammar will gain in dignity.

Mulcaster has a few other suggestions for the revaluation of teaching as a profession. Schoolmasters should be paid more (a universal complaint in all places and times, surely).[46] And they should be given more respect: 'The teachers life is painfull' for he 'wrastles with unthankfullnesse above all measure' (276.15–18). One way for this respect to be gained is through 'conference' or meeting between teacher and parents. Often the child by 'shed of teares, and some childish passion' (279.35–6) will work the parents against the teacher; conference eliminates misunderstanding. It also promotes the teacher as a formal adviser of the parents. Conference among equals (for in Mulcaster's scheme, the teacher is not a servant) leads to consensus, which with '*certainetie* of *discipline*' and 'constancie' is the basis of proper and uniform education.[47]

Finally, though Mulcaster does not say this explicitly, *Positions* itself is a sign of the professional status of the schoolmaster. By insisting on the political nature of education and by venturing to advise his Queen, Mulcaster is asking to be taken seriously as a counsellor of state. In his view, the teacher has an important political function that extends beyond (or through) the classroom to public affairs and the general uniformity and political well-being of the commonwealth.

THE CONTEMPORARY REPUTATION OF *POSITIONS*

As many later commentators have pointed out, *Positions* seems to point the direction of what was to come in English education. In its own time, however, the book did not get the enthusiastic reception one senses the author had hoped for, though certainly the book was known to contemporary readers.

The earliest published comment may have been that of Thomas Nashe, who wrote at the end of his *Anatomie of Absurditie* (1589):

I know the learned wil laugh me to scorne, for setting down such Rams horne rules of direction, and even now I begin to bethinke me of *Mulcasters Positions*, which makes my penne heere pause as it were at a full point; which pause hath changd my opinion, and makes me rather refer you to Aschame the antienter of the two ...[48]

Nashe's comment picks up on Mulcaster's authorial bossiness, perhaps only by reputation. There is no sense here that Nashe had actually read the book (Mulcaster shows no direct debt to Pierre de la Ramée's 'rules of direction,' to which there seems to be a playful allusion, though the section on sports does use a branching method to set out its argument). But that Nashe should refer to *Positions* in this offhand way suggests that the book may have been known to his readers. His preference for the *Scholemaster* of Roger Ascham was also shared by them – that book had already gone through five editions by the time Nashe wrote – though Nashe's own bias is perhaps better explained by his sentimental attachment to his old Cambridge college, St John's, which Ascham and his circle had made famous. Yet the comparison, which leaves Mulcaster at such a disadvantage, must have seemed inevitable to his contemporaries. Even Mulcaster tried to forestall such a comparison when he regretted that Ascham or his assigns had called his book 'the *scoolemaister*, bycause myselfe dealing in that argument must needes sometime dissent to farre from him, with some hasard of myne owne credit, seeing his is hallowed' (238.39–239.2). And when *Positions* was entered in the Stationers' Register, Thomas Chard, who had obtained the licence to print, had to promise that *Positions* would not cut into the sales of Ascham's book.[49]

If Nashe disliked Mulcaster's *Positions*, it seems inevitable that Nashe's arch-rival Gabriel Harvey should have enjoyed it. He quotes extensively from *Positions* in the margins of other books, and in 1593 he complimented Mulcaster extravagantly as a stylist.[50]

Another well-known contemporary certainly knew *Positions*. Yet the only mark Ben Jonson made in his copy is a signature. Nowhere in his published writing does he refer to *Positions*; nor, indeed, does he even mention the *Elementarie*, which was the single most extensive source for his *English Grammar*.[51]

Indeed, if citation of the text is any evidence, *Positions* does not seem to have made much of an impression on contemporary readers. Mulcaster is not cited as are Elyot and Ascham. He is not mentioned in any of the principal educational writings of the day. His absence in the writings of the schoolmaster John Brinsley, who flourished about thirty years later, is especially noteworthy, though Brinsley is less of a theoretician and inclines only to codify and restate contemporary practice. A much later figure sometimes mentioned as successor of Mulcaster is John Locke.[52] Yet Locke never refers to Mulcaster in *Some Thoughts Concerning Education*, nor does he seem to have had a copy of *Positions* in his quite extensive library. Mulcaster and Locke can be read in the light of a shared tradition of practical pedagogy and, rather than read Locke to find the influence of Mulcaster, one would do better to examine their shared models – the classical writers, especially Quintilian, and the humanists, above all Erasmus.

Mulcaster does receive notice in at least two treatises of the seventeenth century, Charles Hoole's *A New Discovery of the Old Art of Teaching Schoole* and John Newton's *School Pastime for Young Children*.

Hoole's *New Discovery* was published in 1660, though its plan was first outlined, according to the title page, around 1637.[53] Hoole (1610–67) was a schoolmaster who drew up a complete picture of the program of studies from the elementary level through the grammar school. The emphasis is practical and directly related to the daily work of the teacher, though Hoole did ground his work on a reading of such earlier authorities as Quintilian, Erasmus, Ascham, Brinsley, and, here and there, Mulcaster. *A New Discovery* is divided into 'four small Treatises' which cover 'A Petty-Schoole,' 'The Ushers Duty,' 'The Masters Method,' and 'Scholastick Discipline,' the last three pertaining to grammar school. Mulcaster is referred to, both directly and indirectly, in the first, second, and fourth parts, and although Hoole mentions only *Positions* by title, he is obviously familiar with *Elementarie*, which he quotes from twice. Most of the references to Mulcaster are in the form of simple citations: 'Latin *Grammar*, (which *of it selfe is but a bare rule*, and a very naked thing, as Mr. *Mulcaster* hath well observed),'[54] quoting *Elementarie*: 'For grammar of it selfe is but the bare rule, and a verie naked thing' (sig G1v). In his discussion of school foundations in part 4, Hoole relies heavily on chapter 40 in *Positions*, as well as on what he has been 'informed touching Mr. *Farnabies* improvement of a private Grammar Schoole in *Gold-Smiths Alley*' and on what he himself has 'experienced for about fourteen years together.'[55] He follows Mulcaster for the historical observations that more schools were built in Elizabeth's reign 'then there were before in all her Realm'[56] (a claim that is not correct, for so many of the schools were refoundings of older institutions, but a claim that to a seventeenth-century observer might have appeared to be true). His general description of the ideal school and of its financial maintenance is derived straight from Mulcaster, though some of the specifics (such as the amounts to be paid to the ushers) are derived from later practice. He concludes his chapter on this topic by reciting 'some *remarkable passages of Mr. Mulcasters* out of his *Positions* (*Ch.* 40) which I leave to the consideration of others, to think how far they concurre with what I have said, as well concerning the foundation of a Petty, as a Grammar-Schoole.'[57] Judging from the ease with which Hoole quotes Mulcaster, he has studied his source with some care. It is significant that he read Mulcaster for the practical aspects of public education and not for any larger political reforms.

The second reader is John Newton (1622–78), author of numerous mathematical and educational treatises. His *School Pastime* (1669?) is an instructional guide to the reading, writing, and grammar of English.[58] In his introductory letter 'to the Reader' the author, not a schoolmaster himself but concerned with the way the young are being readied for the trades, complains of the poor instruction and suggests that the principal flaw is improper grounding at the start. He quotes briefly from chapter 5 of *Positions* and chapter 11 of *Elementarie*. Although Newton may have come to Mulcaster through Hoole, he has clearly read the two books independently.[59] That Hoole and Newton quote Mulcaster and other English authors rather than classical or continental humanist authorities shows an interesting shift. A new curriculum, imported from abroad and fully institutionalized by teachers like Mulcaster in the middle to late sixteenth century, is now seen to be English.

It is not entirely surprising that Mulcaster's books did not capture much interest beyond a few pedagogical specialists. They are written specifically for the 'circumstances' of schooling in his own time. They are closely written in a style the author consciously chose to be 'hard.' They did not attempt to flatter the gentry. Nor, and this may be the deeper reason, did they appeal to the notion of an individuality of the learner, to the private self, which became the focus of much educational theory during the great epistemological shift in the seventeenth and eighteenth centuries. Mulcaster's notion of education is deeply public.[60] *Positions* is difficult to remove from the historical practices and institutional discourses of late sixteenth-century England.

NOTES

1 Lawrence Stone 'Educational Revolution'; see also Simon *Education and Society*, which has a bibliography at 404–36, and for the vast range of material published on Tudor education, see also Simon's bibliography on cols 2381–418 of G. Watson comp *New Cambridge Bibliography of English Literature*. The argument that schools expanded under the Tudors is in direct opposition to the late nineteenth and early twentieth-century work of A.F. Leach (who found the Tudor period one of marked decline); see Moran *The Growth of English Schooling 1340–1548* 3–20 who summarizes the various positions and who finds, in agreement with Nicholas Orme (*English Schools in the Middle Ages*), that earlier periods show a parallel, if not such a persistent, growth. Spufford 'The Schooling of Peasantry in Cambridgeshire, 1575–1700' gives a detailed glimpse into the opportunities available in one area.

2 That *Positions* and *Elementarie* were to be parts of a much longer series is shown at *Elementarie* sig 2F1r, where Mulcaster promises to 'deal with grammer, next after mine elementarie.' At *Positions* 287.2 he refers to 'this whole booke' as a 'preface.' See also *Elementarie*, chapter 11.

3 Lewis *English Literature* 348

4 It has been argued that domestic relationships in the sixteenth and seventeenth centuries, especially those of parents to children, tended to be more formal than in later periods (Lawrence Stone *The Family, Sex and Marriage* esp 105ff), though this argument has been modified by later writers (eg, Pollock *Forgotten Children* and Thomas 'Children in Early Modern England').

5 Ascham *Scholemaster* in *English Works* ed Wright 180; Gascoigne *Glasse of Governement* in *Complete Works* 2:19; Kempe *Education of Children* sig D2r in Pepper ed *Four Tudor Books* 207

6 Aristotle *Politics* 7.15 (1334a); Milton 'Of Education' 366–7

7 The tradition of Renaissance psychology is introduced by E. Ruth Harvey *The Inward Wits*. Useful summaries of English material are given by Cruttwell 'Physiology and Psychology' and Babb *The Elizabethan Malady* chapter 1. See also Schüling's *Bibliographie der psychologischen Literatur*.

8 See Vives *De anima et vita libri tres* (1538), especially the section 'De discendi ratione' 86–93, and Melanchthon *Liber de anima* (1553) in *Werke* 3:303–72. For an account of the Protestant psychology of learning, see Strauss *Luther's House of Learning* 71–84.

9 Aristotle *On the Soul* 2.1 (412b)

10 Compare Montaigne: 'Ce n'est pas une âme, ce n'est pas un corps qu'on dresse: c'est un homme; il n'en faut pas faire à deux' *Essais* 1.26, in *Oeuvres complètes* 164.

11 Aristotle *On the Soul* 3.3 (428a) and Vives *De anima* 87

12 Plato *Phaedrus* 269D; cf Isocrates *Against the Sophists* 15 and *Antidosis* 186ff where 'imitation' is added to the list; Aristotle *Politics* 7.12 (1332a–b); Cicero *De oratore* 1.4.14 and 2.57.232; also in *Ad Herennium* 1.1.1 and 1.2.3; Quintilian *Institutes* 1.Pr.26–7 and 2.19.1–3; pseudo-Plutarch 'On the Education of Children' in Plutarch *Moralia* 2Aff; Aeneas Sylvius Piccolomini (Pius II) *De liberorum educatione* 96–7; Mapheus Vegius *De educatione liberorum* 1:72; Johann Sturm *Nobilitas literata* trans T. Browne as *A Ritch Storehouse* fol 38v (and see also Gilbert *Renaissance Concepts of Method* 78); for Ramus on 'natura, doctrina, exercitatio' see his *Dialecticae partitiones* [or *institutiones*] (1543) commented on by Ong *Ramus and Talon Inventory* 46ff. Some background is given in Close 'Commonplace Theories' and 'Philosophical Theories' and Shorey '*Φύσις, Μελέτη, Ἐπιστήμη*' presents the early Greek history of the commonplace.

Erasmus *De pueris instituendis* in LB 1:496E–497A trans CWE 26:311 and see also ed Margolin 401 with note 280 and Margolin 'L'Idée de nature dans la pensée d'Erasme.'

More *Utopia* in *Complete Works* 4:58–9, on Cardinal Morton; Sir John Cheke 'A Letter ... to His Loving Frind Mayster Thomas Hoby' in Castiglione *The Book of the Courtier* trans Hoby 7; Sidney *Apology* ed Shepherd 133 and note on 217; Ascham *Toxophilus* in *English Works* ed Wright 58ff and *Whole Works* ed Giles 1:168. See also Thomas Wilson *Arte of Rhetorique* ed Mair 16–17 and, on Gabriel Harvey's *Rhetor*, H.S. Wilson 'Gabriel Harvey's Orations on Rhetoric.'

13 Tilley N47 and N357

14 Montaigne *Essais* 1.26 in *Oeuvres complètes* 162

15 Ascham *Scholemaster* in *English Works* ed Wright 193–7; for the source in Plato see *Schoolmaster* ed Ryan 27 note 29.

16 Reading as a part of religion is further emphasized in *Elementarie* (sig G4r); see also Nelson 'The Teaching of English.' Davies *Teaching Reading in Early England* has an undifferentiated mass of material on the subject. For the social context of Mulcaster's program see Cressy *Literacy and the Social Order*.

17 Mulcaster to Ortelius, 24 April 1581, in Hessels et al ed *Ecclesiae Londino-Batavae archivum* 1:250; on microfilm in British Library, Department of Manuscripts (M/457); the original is privately owned. See note to 45.8g. Dürer's *Four Books on the Symmetry of the Human Body* had been published in the Latin translation of Camerarius (1534, 1537, 1557) and the French of Meigret (1557) as well as the original German (1528).

18 'Nowe ... I intende nat ... to make of a prince or noble mannes sonne, a commune painter or kerver'; Elyot *The Boke Named the Governour* 1.8 ed Croft 1:48.

19 For a survey of the traditional subjects in an earlier period, see Orme *English Schools in the Middle Ages* chapters 2, 3, and 7.

20 Edmund Spenser 'Astrophel' lines 73–84 in *Minor Poems* 339–40.

21 There is no thorough study of sport for the period. Surveys are given in Lilly C. Stone 'English Sports and Recreations,' Brailsford *Sport and Society, Shakespeare's England* 2:334–483, Strutt *Sports and Pastimes* ed Cox. The only separate study on Mulcaster and sport is Stelvio and Alda P. Dal Piaz *Un ginnisiarca dell'età elisabettiana.*

22 An unusual anthology of these dialogues on sports is the anonymously compiled *Varij lusus pueriles* published in Paris in 1555 (copy in Folger Shakespeare Library).

23 Rowse 'Parish and Sport' in his *Elizabethan Renaissance* 166–99

24 Georg Schmid 'Richard Mulcaster' in Karl Adolf Schmid ed *Geschichte der Erziehung vom Anfang an bis auf unsere Zeit* 3/1 (1892), 372–81, with discussion of Mercuriale at 373–6. The material following is condensed from Barker 'Richard Mulcaster's *Positions* and Girolamo Mercuriale's *De arte gymnastica libri sex.*'

25 Girolamo Mercuriale was an almost exact contemporary of Mulcaster. He was born in Forlì in 1530, studied at Bologna and Padua, and worked as a physician and teacher. He wrote many books – on the nursing of children, skin diseases, diseases of women, and so on – as well as commentaries and lectures. He was a successful practitioner. From 1562 to 1569 he was physician to Cardinal Alessandro Farnese, to whom he dedicated the first edition of the *De arte gymnastica*. He became very famous in 1573 when he cured Maximilian II from a deadly illness. That same year he also rededicated the *De arte gymnastica*, now in a second illustrated edition, to the Emperor. In later years he taught in Bologna and in Pisa; he died in 1606, a celebrated practitioner and an important humanist scholar of medicine. See Busacchi 'Girolamo Mercuriale nel 350° anniversario della morte'; the translator's introduction to Mercuriale *Arte ginnastica* trans Galante xix–xxvi; the entry on Mercuriale in Michaud *Biographie universelle* sv; Paoletti *Gerolamo Mercuriale e il suo tempo*. On the contents of *De arte gymnastica* there are the two not entirely satisfactory articles by Brunoni and by Terzi and Ronchi in a volume of *Romagna Medica* 8 (1956). There are two curious attempts to turn Mercuriale into a precursor of the Fascist doctrine of physical culture: Mazzini *Jeronimo Mercuriale (1530–1606) y su 'De arte gymnastica'* and Suaudeau and Suaudeau-Deterne *La Renaissance de la gymnastique médicale du XVe au XVIIe siècle et le 'De arte gymnastica' de Mercurialis.*

De arte gymnastica libri sex went through five editions in the author's lifetime: Venice: Giunta 1569; Venice: Giunta 1573; Paris: Du Puys 1577; Venice: Giunta 1587; Venice: Giunta 1601. Paris 1577 was a reprint of Venice 1573. For reasons explained in note 27, we follow the edition of 1569.

26 Jacques Ulmann: 'préoccupations médicales et historiques interfèrent'; *De la Gymnastique aux sports modernes* 99; 97–114 on *De arte gymnastica*. Ulmann does not seem entirely sympathetic to the historical project implicit in much of humanist thought, including its science.

27 Mercuriale's text went through revisions in succeeding editions. Though I have analysed their relation to *Positions*, I have been unable to determine which edition Mulcaster used. Because he never makes mention of the very striking illustrations, found from 1573 onwards, he may have been using the 1569 edition. On the woodcuts in 1573 and later editions, see Mortimer *Catalogue of Books and Manuscripts Part II: Italian 16th Century Books* no 302.

28 See Lawrence Stone 'Social Mobility in England, 1500–1700' and Siegel 'English Humanism and the New Tudor Order.' For general studies on the education of the gentleman, see Lawrence Stone *The Crisis of the Aristocracy 1558–1641* chapter 12 'Education and Culture' 672–724, Hexter 'Education of the Aristocracy in the Renaissance,' Kelso *The Doctrine of the English Gentleman in the Sixteenth Century*, and Simon *Education and Society* chapter 14 'The Institution of the Gentleman' 333–68.

29 Sir Thomas Smith *De Republica Anglorum* 18ff

30 Ibid 27

31 For the actual practice of instruction, see Lawrence Stone *Crisis of the Aristocracy* 672–724 and Simon *Education and Society* 333–68; Elyot *The Boke Named the Governour* 1.6 ed Croft 1:36.

32 Lawrence Stone *Crisis of the Aristocracy* 683–7; Hexter 'Education of the Aristocracy' 50ff; Cliffe *The Yorkshire Gentry* 68–73

33 *Institutes* 1.2

34 In his attitude towards travel, he shares the hostile view of Ascham's *Scholemaster* in *English Works* ed Wright 222ff, even though in this period 'travel abroad was now an essential aspect of the institution of the nobleman' (Simon *Education and Society* 346), as Philip Sidney's trip abroad from 1572 to 1575 most dramatically illustrates.

35 Maclean *The Renaissance Notion of Woman*; Kelso *Doctrine for the Lady of the Renaissance* especially chapter 2 'Women in the Scheme of Things' 5–37; Powell *English Domestic Relations* especially chapter 5 'Contemporary Attitudes to Women' 147–78; Carroll Camden *The Elizabethan Woman* 15–35, 241–71. For education of Elizabethan girls, see Camden 39–58 and Gardiner *English Girlhood at School* 141–205; also, for higher status, McMullen 'The Education of English Gentlewomen 1540–1640.' On books for women, Hull *Chaste, Silent*

and Obedient. On the ambivalence found in humanist programs for women, Friedman 'The Influence of Humanism on the Education of Girls and Boys in Tudor England' esp 65.

36 Cornelius Agrippa *A Treatise of the Nobilitie and Excellencye of Woman Kynde* (first published in Latin in 1529; English trans 1542); L. Vives *A Very Frutefull and Pleasant Boke Called the Instruction of a Christen Woman* (first published in Latin in 1523; English trans 1529, rpt, slightly condensed, in Foster Watson *Vives and the Renascence Education of Women*); Sir Thomas Elyot *The Defence of Good Women* (1540).

37 Weigall 'An Elizabethan Gentlewoman'; portions of her diary (in Northampton Central Library) as well as extracts from her other papers have been published by Linda Pollock *With Faith and Physic*, especially 25–7 for her education.

38 On the problem of the status of women's learning, there is an interesting parallel in the situation of a fifteenth-century Veronese scholar; Jardine 'Women Humanists – Education for What?' in Grafton and Jardine *From Humanism to the Humanities*. Contemporary reflections on the education of mothers are reported in Travitsky 'The New Mother of the English Renaissance,' citing especially Bucer and Bullinger, though most of the books she lists are specifically about marriage. See also Charlton '"Not Publike Onely But Also Private and Domesticall": Mothers and Familial Education in Pre-Industrial England.'

39 Kelso on page 1 of her *Doctrine for the Lady of the Renaissance* begins by saying that 'the lady, shall we venture to say, turns out to be merely a wife. Most of this book will serve for proof of this conclusion.' Milton *Paradise Lost* 4.299 in *Poems* ed Carey and Fowler; see Siegel 'Milton and the Humanist Attitude toward Women.'

40 Keith Thomas 'The Double Standard' 216

41 Orme *English Schools in the Middle Ages* 253

42 On the licensing of teachers and the general trend towards uniformity see Wood *The Reformation and English Education* chapter 2 'Schoolmasters' 51–79; Tate 'Episcopal Licensing of Schoolmasters in England' with responses in the same journal by G. Jenkins (159 [1958] 78–81) and J. Addy (160 [1959] 251–2).

43 Feyerharm 'The Status of the Schoolmaster and the Continuity of Education in Elizabethan East Anglia'; Orpen 'Schoolmastering as a Profession in the Seventeenth Century' especially 186. The situation has a parallel in sixteenth-century Germany, where 'most teachers pursued other trades as well' (Strauss *Luther's House of Learning* 186). Cressy 'A Drudgery of Schoolmasters' looks at the problems of low pay and low status; Orme 'Schoolmasters' looks at the late medieval period.

44 Orpen 'Schoolmastering as a Profession' examines the background to this shift at length. See also Charlton 'The Teaching Profession in Sixteenth- and

Seventeenth-Century England' and his earlier discussion in his *Education in Renaissance England* 123–8; also Morgan *Godly Learning*, chapter 10. DeMolen 'Richard Mulcaster and the Profession of Teaching in Sixteenth-Century England' is a brief summary of Mulcaster's ideas.

45 Dr John Bathurst made a similar proposal in 1649 for a 'College for making and training up of schoolmasters by the State'; Charlton 'The Teaching Profession' 46. No such institution was founded in England until the nineteenth century; Tempest 'Some Sources for the History of Teacher-Training in England and Wales' 61. An exception, of course, was the grammar college of the medieval university. God's House, Cambridge, was founded c 1439 for training grammar masters, but its character was altered significantly with its refoundation as Christ's College early in the sixteenth century; Charlton *Education in Renaissance England* 132–3. On the background for the Master of Grammar, see Bartlett 'The Decline and Abolition of the Master of Grammar' and, for a fuller picture, Leader 'Grammar in Late-Medieval Oxford and Cambridge.'

46 In comparing the wages of the horse-trainer and the schoolmaster, Ascham says of parents that 'to the one, they will gladlie give a stipend of 200. Crounes by yeare, and loth to offer to the other, 200. shillinges'; *Scholemaster* in *English Works* ed Wright 193. For general working conditions of schoolmasters see Stowe *English Grammar Schools in the Reign of Queen Elizabeth* 55–103. Stowe lists salaries (180–3) though he neglects to add gifts from pupils and friends, for which see Feyerharm 'The Status of the Schoolmaster' 109–11. Schoolmasters were traditionally exempt from taxes (Prothero *Select Statutes* 23, 36); in *Elementarie* sig 2K2r Mulcaster describes an abortive attempt to remove this ancient privilege.

47 The low opinion of schoolmasters is suggested by Thomas Morrice's *An Apology for Schoolmasters* (1619) sigs C2rff, which very seriously offers 'Certain Reasons Demonstrating the Prioritie of Place of the Schoolmaster, before the Steward' in a nobleman's household. Book 5 of Geoffrey Fenton's *Forme of Christian Pollicie* offers a praise of schoolmasters. Conferences among the teachers, though not with parents, were also suggested by Vives in his *De disciplinis* (1531): 'Four times a year let the masters meet in some place where they may discuss the natures of the pupils and consult about them' (*On Education*, trans Watson 62).

48 Nashe *Works* ed McKerrow 1:48

49 Arber ed *Transcript* 2:178b

50 See the end of the following section with accompanying note 26 for the passage in Harvey. In *Marginalia* ed Smith 147, 182, 185, 187, Harvey quotes Mulcaster on the reform of the university, exercise, the use of testimonies, and the good body.

51 Copy in the Folger Shakespeare Library. For Jonson's use of the *Elementarie*

see the notes to his *The English Grammar* in his [*Works*] ed Herford and Simpson 11:165ff.

52 For an argument connecting Locke and Mulcaster, see DeMolen 'Richard Mulcaster and the Profession of Teaching' 129; Locke had more than a dozen educational treatises in his library (Harrison and Laslett *The Library of John Locke* appendix sv 'Education').

53 *A New Discovery of the Old Art of Teaching Schoole, in Four Small Treatises ...* (1660). References here are to the Scolar reprint; the pagination of the 1660 edition is in two series, 1–41 and 1–309; for the following references, the series number precedes the page number. For 1:15 in Hoole, see *Elementarie* sig O4v; 2:9–11 is from *Positions* 21.17ff; 2:11 is from ibid 42.29; 2:13 from *Elementarie* sig G1v; 2:14 from *Positions* 41.34–6; 2:217 from ibid 221.23ff; 2:220 ('Queen *Elizabeths* dayes') from ibid 226.16–19; 2:227 perhaps from ibid 222.39ff; 2:228 top from ibid 223.4; 2:228 bottom from ibid 236.27–32; 2:232–3 from, in order of quotation, ibid 222.32–9, 229.2–5, 229.5–8, 226.35–227.1. For a short life of Hoole, see *DNB* 9:1193–4.

54 *New Discovery* 2:13

55 Ibid 2:217–18

56 Ibid 2:220; see note 53 above.

57 Ibid 2:232; see note 53 above.

58 *School Pastime for Young Children: Or the Rudiments of Grammar, in an Easie and Delightful Method, for Teaching of Children to Read English Distinctly, and Write it Truly. In Which, by Way of Preface, a New Method is Propounded for the Fitting of Children First for Trades, and then for the Latin, and Other Languages ...* (nd; Wing N1068–9 suggests ?1669). The collation of the work is in two series A–E and A–E, and Mulcaster is mentioned only in the first series, sigs A4v–5r and B1v. Newton was a doctor of divinity from Oxford and chaplain to Charles II; see *DNB* 14:394–5 for a short biography and a list of his unusual range of publications. I have examined many – though not all – of his other works, and found no other references to Mulcaster. I am indebted to Mr John Henderson for telling me about Newton's *School Pastime*.

59 Hoole is mentioned in the first series, sig A4r, just before Mulcaster, but Newton quotes material not found in *New Discovery*.

60 One should note that the book has had for the past few hundred years a small but persistent audience. It was known and in fairly constant circulation during the seventeenth, eighteenth, and nineteenth centuries, as can be seen by the signatures and other marks of ownership in the fairly large number of extant copies. I have listed these copies at the end of the textual notes; the provenance of the copies is outlined in summary form in appendix 1 of Barker PH D diss (1982). There are thirty-eight copies in public collections, and from various sales catalogues of this century others are known to exist.

2 The Style of *Positions*

MULCASTER'S 'DELIBERATION'

Near the end of *Positions*, Mulcaster says he 'might have set downe my Positions aphorismelike' but he does not wish 'with precisenesse to aliene, where I might winne with discourse' (287.21–2).[1] Here, briefly, is a clue to the rhetorical method of the book. Rather than set his positions down as a series of injunctions, he has opted to argue the reader to his point of view by 'discourse.' Such 'discourse' requires that he interest his readers, show them that problems do exist, offer them solutions to the problems, and sway them to accept the solutions – everything that Cicero summed up in his succinct charge to the orator, 'docere, delectare, permovere,' to instruct, to please, to move.[2]

Mulcaster has written discourse using a formal technique now unfamiliar to modern readers. Though *Positions* is no speech, its discourse is a written representation of a specific oratorical style. According to classical rhetoricians and their humanist successors, there were three types of oration, the forensic, the epideictic, the deliberative. The forensic is where one argues a case for or against, such as Philip Sidney did in his *Defence of Poetry* (written in the early 1580s, though first published in 1595). The epideictic is the oration of praise (or dispraise) for a person, a thing, even an idea, as in the praise of music or *Apologia musices tam vocalis quam instrumentalis et mixtae* sometimes attributed to the Oxford philosopher John Case (1588). The deliberative is, as Aristotle says, 'either hortatory or dissuasive; for both those who give advice in private and those who speak in the assembly either exhort or dissuade.'[3] Often one finds these three kinds mixed together. *Positions* does show aspects of forensic and epideictic oratory, but it is overwhelmingly deliberative in style.

The first sign of this special style of deliberation is a regular reference to the speaker's own self. This isn't from simple vanity. 'For,' Aristotle says, 'it makes a great difference with regard to producing conviction –

especially in demonstrative ... oratory – that the speaker should show himself possessed of certain qualities and that his hearers should think that he is disposed in a certain way towards them; and further, that they themselves should be disposed in a certain way towards him.' As Quintilian notes, the speaker must build himself up, so that he can be perceived as 'possessing genuine wisdom and excellence of character.'[4] Thus, the many references to Mulcaster's own experience: we are told that this is his first book (3.13; 288.18–19), that he is a 'scholer' (18.26), that he has taught for 'two and twentie yeares' (16.3), 'twenty yeares' of which have been at Merchant Taylors' (228.23–9), that he has taught 'thousandes' of pupils (275.7), and that he has personally encountered many of the problems he discusses (corporal punishment, 36.13–16; taking of boarders, 226.30; etc). As he spins out his discourse, he is creating an image of himself as full of both authority and good will. For he is always making generous nods to his 'loving countriemen, and friendly readers' (269.4–5).

Yet despite the abundant expressions of solicitude, Mulcaster sometimes forgets the good will of the audience when he decides to take charge:

> But how may the publike in the *poore*, and the private in the *riche*, make their owne market in the education of those whom they preferre to learning? I will tell ye how. (143.35–8)

In a book of advice, it is a fine line to advise without being bossy, and at the end Mulcaster apologizes for being 'dictatorlike,' for appearing to be 'like a *Caesar* to offerre to make lawes' (288.20–1).

Indeed, some of the confusion in the speaker's persona (one moment he is telling the reader what to do, and the next requesting the reader's indulgence) is due to his multiple audiences. As Quintilian noted, 'it makes a considerable difference whether' you are addressing 'the senate or the people, the citizens of Rome or Fidenae, Greeks or barbarians.'[5] Mulcaster is speaking to 'my good and curteous countriemen' generally, but this large and indefinite audience is broken down at various places into 1) the Queen and her counsellors of state ('Epistle Dedicatorie'), 2) the learned ('I make the learned my judges' 16.24–5), 3) fellow schoolmasters ('nowe must I saye somwhat of him, and to him, which is to direct the exercise' 128.26–7), and 4) the 'unlearned' who be 'mostwhat no latinistes' (16.26–38). To some of these he is a supplicant, to others he must be the voice of authority. To the Queen he advises basic reforms in education; to parents he makes proposals on the level of what age the child is ready for school. Even though the audience is always 'my countrymen,' it is a shifting audience, and it is hard to tell how contemporary readers would situate themselves in relation to the advice in the text.

The ancients often analysed an oration in terms of speaker, audience, and matter. It is over the third that Mulcaster has greatest command. In a short table in his *Rhetorique*, Thomas Wilson outlines the basic 'reasons' on which deliberative arguments are based. Principally, in deliberation, the oration is structured around arguments from 'honour' or 'expediency.' Thus, under 'honour' you can argue that 'The thing is honest. Profitable. Pleasaunt' or that it is 'Lawfull and meete. Praise worthie. Necessarie.' Under 'expediency' the arguments will be that the thing is 'Saufe. Easie. Hard.'[6]

Honour and expediency are the two points to which the deliberative speaker (or writer, as Wilson admits) must direct his arguments. The former is shown by analysing any course of action into its virtues, that is, by examining it in the light of morality. For the latter, one examines the circumstances surrounding the course of action. These circumstances are defined by Quintilian as being concerned with 'time (for example, "it is expedient, but not now") or with place ... or with particular persons ... or with our method of action ... or with degree.'[7]

Circumstances are very important in Mulcaster's form of argument, and he refers to them repeatedly. In chapter 38, for instance, we can see how he uses these circumstances to present the position 'that young maidens are to be set to learning.' He begins to argue from 'foure speciall reasons': 'the *manner* and *custome* of my countrey,' 'the *duetie*, which we owe unto them,' 'their owne *towardnesse*,' and 'the excellent *effectes* in that sex' (169.28–170.3). These four points could be classified in Wilson's scheme as 'lawfull and meete,' 'honest,' 'praise worthie,' and 'profitable.' But then he proceeds to argue from the 'expedient' aspects of the position: 'Wherefore in directing of that traine, which I do assigne unto young maidens, I will follow this methode, and shew which of them be to learne, and when, what and how much, where and of whom' (177.16–18). These circumstances ('which ... when, what and how much, where and of whom') show how the position may be effected immediately in the commonwealth; they purport to relate the education of women directly to current practice.

In *Positions* Mulcaster's arguments move regularly from honour to expediency. On the whole, arguments from honour seem stronger. In a discussion of the four kinds of school conference, for instance, Mulcaster reasons from the nature of 'conference' as a human activity in a series of enthymemes which prove that it 'is the cognisance of humanitie, and that of the best humanitie' (281.27–8). But he does not go on to show how school conferences may be made to happen on a day-to-day basis in the schools. The same is true for his grand scheme of university reform in chapter 41. In deliberative oratory, one of the first steps in an argument for expediency is to show whether or not the matter proposed may indeed be enacted.[8] Mulcaster is usually good at showing why a change is 'necessary' (that is, honourable or virtuous), but in some of his positions he neglects to address himself to the all-important claims of expediency.

Near the beginning of *Positions* he claims that he is going to speak to 'that mediocritie, which furnisheth out this world, and not to that excellencie, which is fashioned for an other' (28.29–31). Nevertheless, in the way he frames his arguments, he is often speaking to the 'excellencie' of another world. In other words, despite his repeated concern about 'circumstances,' in his rhetoric he shows himself to be a moralist, not a politician. Of course, to the modern reader it is hard to overlook the political drift of his moral discussion. His emphatic loyalty to the crown and his insistence on a moral 'uniformity' shows his allegiance to the state, even while he argues and entertains by his 'discourse.' Indeed, one experiences a strange kind of split in reading his prose – he argues for uniformity, order, and a kind of social sobriety, yet he works at winning his readers over by a remarkable range of stylistic devices, some of them extraordinarily, even wilfully, playful.

STYLE

Many readers dislike Mulcaster's style. Typical is the terse assessment of Spenser's biographer, A.C. Judson: 'Mulcaster lacked a clear and graceful style, so that his books are little read today.' C.S. Lewis is perceptive, yet hardly more generous: 'At his best Mulcaster is Hooker's precursor in English prose. But of course he is not always at his best.'[9] For readers trained to the virtues of a straightforward and unambiguous plain style, Mulcaster's highly rhythmical and highly figured discourse requires an effort to work through. Yet this effort is exactly what he wished from his readers, as several comments in his books clearly indicate.

The peroration to *Elementarie* contains a defence of the English language culminating in the famous claim 'I love *Rome*, but *London* better, I favor *Italie*, but England more, I honor the *Latin*, but I worship the *English*' (sig 2H1v).[10] Part of this lively defence of the language is an apology for his own style. Mulcaster willingly admits that his 'to careful penning maie perhaps offend som, as seming too obscure' (sig 2H4v). He acknowledges that he comes from 'the students forge,' that he is 'still acquainted with strong stele,' that he 'cannot but resemble that metle' in his own style (sig 2I2v). In any intellectual task worth undertaking, there should be effort on the part of the student: 'If easie understanding be the rediest learning, then wake not my Ladie, she learns as she lies' (sig 2I3v). Thus, for Mulcaster a hard style is an outward sign of worthwhile and challenging matter; difficult thoughts should be set forth in such a way to make readers think about them carefully, even forcing them to reread passages. Indeed, 'a litle hardnesse yea in the most obscure, and philosoficall conclusions, maie never seme tedious to a conquering mind' (sig 2K1v).

In a brief passage in the same peroration, Mulcaster describes the four qualities of English that make it a particularly strong stylistic medium. The first is 'daliance,' the ability of the language to carry repeated sound patterns. Rhetoricians had a large vocabulary to describe the techniques of repeated sound, which they called schemes.[11] These would include alliteration and rhyming sounds (homoioteleuton), repetition of words (ploce), repetition of the same roots in different forms (polyptoton). Punning (allusion) was generated from words that sound the same (paronomasia) or from a single word with several meanings (antanaclasis). The second quality of English praised by Mulcaster, 'staie of speche, and strong ending,' acknowledges the large number of monosyllables and stressed final syllables in English, from words naturally of that order or from words artificially contracted (by such devices as acope, aphaeresis, and syncope). 'Fine translation,' the third quality, refers to the capacity of the language for metaphor and related figures (metonymy, synecdoche, personification, and the more extended allegoria), all of which permit the fourth, which is 'close delivery in few words' found especially in the similitude and the proverb. All these techniques are found abundantly in Mulcaster's style. Indeed, *Positions* is a showpiece of studied rhetoric.

In his use of the figures of sound Mulcaster favours alliteration, rhythmically balanced clauses, some end rhymes, and word repetitions. Usually the alliteration is most concentrated in proverbs or proverb-like expressions ('that foolish fellow, was fretished for cold, which followed the fond *swallow*, that flew out to timely, and to farre before her fellowes' 262.9–11). Or one finds it at the end of a particular line of reasoning, for emphasis ('In such pointes, as be intelligible to both, I must praie them both to waie me well, and ever to have before them, that my will wisheth well, howsoever I perfourme, wherin will deserves well, and weaknes prayeth excuse' 27.13–16). Though it is concentrated in such passages, it is used throughout, and there is scarcely a sentence in *Positions* in which some kind of vigorous repetition is not present, sometimes perhaps 'to often,' to 'bewraie affectation not sound but followed' as Mulcaster himself warned against.

This repetition is more than just a surface quirk, but is worked into the very syntax. The device is called isocolon, a balancing of clauses; often this isocolon is accompanied by antithesis, in which two ideas are set against each other ('For if one neede not to beat children to have them do ill, wherunto they are prone, we must needes then beat them for not doing wel, where nature is corrupt' 75.37–76.1). Antitheses are sometimes made stronger by the use of alliteration, and again these are brought together in isocolon. Such alliterative antitheses as 'nature/nurture' or 'public/private' are common in sixteenth-century English and are made to echo throughout *Positions*. Indeed some alliterations are played with in the most elaborate fashion: 'foreign/fit' (meaning 'strange or inappropriate' and 'appropriate') are found also as 'forreine ... unfit' (20.22), 'forraine ... unfitnesses' (159.3–5), 'with forreine fashions? they wil not fit' (210.36–7), 'Forreine matters fit us not' (212.2), and so on, with the meaning of the original antithesis being twisted and turned at every use. Less common, though still found often, are the rhyming words such as 'lawe ... awe' (76.16), 'skill ... will' (158.28–9), 'rarer and fayrer' (236.5), or 'reft of goodnesse, and left goodlesse' (255.33–4). Rhyme of adjoining words, a device that may strike the modern reader as the most bizarre aspect of this close style, results in unusual collocations such as 'offall of all' (162.29) and 'noting nothing' (188.20). Word repetition (to which the rhyming is closely related) is also found throughout *Positions*: 'Of *conference* I must needes say this, that it is the cognisance of humanitie, and that of the best humanitie, being used for the best causes that concerne humanitie, and all humaine societie' (281.27–9). Such repetition is an aspect of the close style that might lead the unsuspecting modern reader to conclude that Mulcaster was an impoverished stylist. If anything, the opposite is true. There is not a sentence in *Positions* that does not strive for some kind of stylistic effect.

These schemes of repetition give Mulcaster's style its closeness, and in some places the reader must proceed slowly to pick out the refracted meanings of words. Indeed, at times the only way to proceed is to read such prose aloud. Rhymes and repetitions often give the reader a clue to the structure of the longer sentences far faster than the organization of literal sense. And the original punctuation (retained in this edition) is there to enhance sound, which is inextricable from sense.

The principle of varied repetition applies also to sets of images to which we are often returned. The language of building recurs, and throughout the text the words 'foundation,' 'plat,' 'ground,' 'groundwork' regularly appear. Closely affiliated is the language of planting: 'ripe,' 'plant,' 'reap,' 'spring,' 'fruit,' 'root,' and 'soil' are found in a great variety of forms from beginning to end. Other important image clusters are those of flying ('ascent,' 'rise,' and references to birds) and riding or driving ('bridle,' 'post,' 'rein,' and references to horses). All four main image groups are appropriate to education, three of the four combining pictures of movement and growth, and the fourth suggesting directed movement. The constant play in the text of 'travel' and 'travail' and the many uses of the words 'course' and 'train' help to reinforce the imagery of movement as well as to suggest the forward sweep of the book's argument. These images are, of course, largely conventional. The imagery of planting, for instance, is found in many ancient and contemporary books on education, for instance in the pseudo-Plutarchan essay 'On the Education of Children,' Cicero, Quintilian, Erasmus, and Ascham; in some authors the image is presented in three parts, where the child's nature is the fertile (or not so fertile) soil, the educational program the seeds, and the necessary practice the careful supervision of the growing plant by the farmer.[12] The relationship of riding and education is as old as the image of the driver controlling the horses of reason and appetite in Plato's *Phaedrus*.[13] Yet Mulcaster shows considerable ingenuity in the way he has spread the images throughout the text, so that at times one is scarcely aware of their presence. He has in a sense played with his main tropes as though they too are schemes of repetition.

Repetition, rhythmical balance, internal rhyme, recurring images – all these create for the reader a sense of restless yet controlled abundance in the representation of the author's voice. Such abundance is also apparent in Mulcaster's use of 'testimony' – the proverbs, similitudes, anecdotes, and quotations from famous people that are part of an extra-textual authority which helps in turn to make the author appear more 'authoritative.'

One of Mulcaster's favourite devices is what the modern reader would call 'proverb' but what in Renaissance rhetoric was often divided into two devices, adage (paroemia) and sentence (apophthegm or gnome).[14] The former is the pithy saying, usually of anonymous popular origin, which contains a lively image, such as 'beares the bell' (61.36), 'marres the ... market' (255.17), or 'a clowdy day ... when all shrews have dined' (158.1–2). The latter may usually be ascribed to an author and often have a more obvious moral content, such as 'labour is the conquerour' (240.16–17) from Virgil's 'labor omnia vicit' (*Georgics* 1.145). Yet even proverb and 'sentence' are often indistinguishable in many instances, for both are used in the same way, that is as extrinsic testimony where the appeal is to common understanding (even when the proverb itself may be obscure in its origins). Although such proverbs and sayings may impart a homely air to sixteenth-century writing, they were actually rather sophisticated, often culled directly or indirectly (via Erasmus' *Adagia*) from classical antiquity. Thus Mulcaster's 'the rowling stone doth gather mosse' (159.27–8) is an ironic rewording of what appears in Erasmus as 'saxum volutum non obducitur musco.'[15]

In addition to the recognizable proverbs, there are a number of proverb-like expressions in *Positions* which Mulcaster himself may have composed or taken from contemporary language; examples are 'repairers get the pence' (134.23), 'If ye shew a child an apple, he will crye for it' (162.32–3), 'If the chancell have a minister, the belfray hath a maister' (246.13–14), 'make not all priestes that stand upon the bridge as the *Poope* passeth' (166.37–8), and so on. Whether or not such proverbial-sounding expressions were known to his readers, they do have a ring to them that would contribute to the tone of authority and allusion (and elusiveness) he is always striving for in his deliberation.

Closely related to the proverbs are similitudes. Mulcaster uses them less often, and rather than present them in a short form as they are usually found in contemporary collections such as Erasmus' *Parabolae* (1514) or William Baldwin's *Treatise of Moral Philosophy* (1547), he builds the image up quite fully. An example is the revolting description of the lazy young lady who refuses to wash and look after her hair, so that it becomes 'a cluster of knottes, and a feltryd borough for white footed beastes' (211.20–3). This image appears in the context of an argument against travelling for purely selfish reasons; the unusualness and apparent unsuitability of the comparison account for its forcefulness.

Finally, we should look at Mulcaster's use of citation, one of the principal branches of 'testimony.' As a logical proof, quoting a famous author has no weight at all ('It is not so, bycause a writer said so, but bycause the truth is so' 26.34–5); nevertheless, Mulcaster knew that citations of classical and other authorities bore great emotional power to convince one's listeners. Thus, although 'it is no proufe, bycause *Plato* praiseth it, bycause *Aristotle* alloweth it, bycause *Cicero* commendes it, bycause *Quintilian* is acquainted with it,' 'those that be learned know that witnesses, and wise mens names be verie good ware ... and that *Rhetorick* takes testimonies for a principall proofe' (24.38–25.1; 26.22–5). In *Positions*, Mulcaster on the whole prefers to argue by 'the greatest weight of most apparent reasons,' and repeatedly expresses his reluctance to use 'the best authoritie of most allowed writers.' As he says, 'to avoide length therby, I will neither use authoritie, nor example, seeing matter is the maine, and not the mans name' (25.30–2). Indeed, in contemporary writing, there is too much needless citation: 'we heape but up witnesses ... wheras the naturall use of testimonies is, to prove where doubt is, not to cloye, where all is cleare' (26.5–9). Both *Positions* and *Elementarie* are consequently free of much of the heavy cluster of citation which hangs on the structures of so many Renaissance treatises.

Mulcaster is opposed to the more extreme form of reference and quotation indulged in by his contemporaries, yet he does not eschew testimony altogether. Many classical authors are quoted or mentioned in *Positions*: Mulcaster gives evidence (obtained either first or second hand) from the ancient historians (Xenophon, Aelian, Plutarch, Dionysius of Halicarnassus, Josephus, Livy, Suetonius), the scientists (Euclid, Galen, Pliny the Elder, Celsus), the writers of comedy (Menander, Aristophanes, Lucian, Terence), the poets (Hesiod, Homer, Musaeus, Virgil, Horace, Juvenal), and the rhetoricians (Isocrates, Cicero, Quintilian). Most of these references are given in passing, with the understanding that a classical name is 'verie good ware.' A few authors, however, are referred to more persistently. These are Plato, Aristotle, Xenophon, Cicero, and Quintilian. For each he has turned to only a limited part of their complete work. Of modern authors he makes little mention: Erasmus, Melanchthon, Vives, Boccaccio, Ariosto, Pico della Mirandola, Linacre, Cheke, and Ascham are present in *Positions* as famous names, but the use he makes of their writings is tangential, at least in so far as they might have affected his educational doctrine, though Erasmus, Vives, and Ascham certainly had an important indirect effect. Although Mulcaster refers directly to him only once, the Italian humanist physician Girolamo Mercuriale is, as we have noted in the previous section, the key source for his ideas on sports; rather than refer to Mercuriale, Mulcaster will give references to Hippocrates and Galen that he has picked up second-hand from *De arte gymnastica*. This was acceptable practice, and indicates how important the name was, as it was shifted from one context to another in the underground world of second-hand scholarship.

In *Positions* there are many more devices besides those outlined here. There is a self-consciousness to the style which one might expect from a teacher of rhetoric, and the book is meant to be a display of the possibilities of English prose. The style is closely allied to the argument of deliberation, indeed at times is the argument. In *Positions* most of the proofs are rhetorical, being based on enthymeme and extrinsic testimony – appeals to witnesses, examples from the past and present, projections to the future, and so on, much of this testimony conveyed by similitudes, proverbs, personal experience (martyria), experience of others (chria), fictionalization of dialogue (prosopopoeia), and historical example. Mulcaster certainly uses structures from logic to support and structure his arguments, but their direction is determined by the rhetorical concern for the audience. Even Mulcaster's 'method' is really a non-scientific method based on the rhetorical circumstances, not on the Aristotelian categories. The overall effect is one of relentless playfulness, strenuousness, and willed energy.

CICERO AS INFLUENCE

To a modern classicist, Mulcaster's style will not seem terribly Ciceronian. Yet as principal model for the rhetoric of *Positions* and *Elementarie* Mulcaster specifically names Cicero, 'the *Romane* paragon, while he was alive, and our best patern now' (*Elementarie* sig 2H2r). Indeed, he notes with approval Cicero's reliance on 'artificiall and strange' words and the 'newnesse' of his arguments (see especially sig 2I3r).

The 'Ciceronian' style Mulcaster has in mind is only one of Cicero's three, the *tertium dicendi genus*. In his *Orator* Cicero describes the plain, middle, and ornate styles, and attempts to justify his own use of the third of these, a style which he claims was largely of his own devising though based on Greek models. Each of the three styles is appropriate to its own ends. Although the third ornate style is much to be despised if badly applied, when used well it is by far the most effective:

> The orator of the third style is magnificent, opulent, stately and ornate; he undoubtedly has the greatest power. This is the man whose brilliance and fluency have caused admiring nations to let eloquence attain the highest power in the state; I mean the kind of eloquence which rushes along with the roar of a mighty stream, which all look up to and admire, and which they despair of attaining.[16]

This ornate style, then, is characterized by its richness and its embellishments 'both in the use of single words and in their combinations.'[17] In a remarkable passage, Cicero describes some of the devices at the disposal of the speaker in the third style:

> words are redoubled and repeated, or repeated with a slight change, or several

successive phrases begin with the same words or end with the same, or have both figures, or the same word is repeated at the beginning of a clause or at the end, or a word is used immediately in a different sense, or words are used with similar case endings or other similar terminations; or contrasting ideas are put in juxtaposition (antithesis), or the sentence rises and falls in steps (climax); or many clauses are strung together loosely without conjunctions; or sometimes we omit something and give our reason for doing so; or we correct ourselves with a quasi-reproof; or make some exclamation of surprise or complaint; or use the same word repeatedly in different cases.[18]

The same variety is to be found in the figures of thought, and Cicero goes on to list further techniques which make up this third style:

[The orator] will seem to consult the audience, and sometimes even with the opponent; he will portray the talk and ways of men; he will make mute objects speak; he will divert the attention of the audience from the point at issue; he will frequently provoke merriment and laughter; he will reply to some point which he sees is likely to be brought up; he will use similes and examples; he will divide a sentence, giving part to a description of one person, part to another; he will put down interrupters; ... he will take the liberty to speak somewhat boldly ...[19]

and so on. The passage, here quoted only in part, is a convenient inventory of the devices also employed by Mulcaster.

Another quality of prose treated in *Orator* is rhythm, the subject of the last third of the treatise. Cicero is emphatic in his support of the highly rhythmical and symmetrical sentence:

The arrangement of words in the sentence has three ends in view: (1) that final syllables may fit the following initial syllables as neatly as possible, and that the words may have the most agreeable sounds; (2) that the very form and symmetry of the words may produce their own rounded period; (3) that the period may have an appropriate rhythmical cadence.[20]

Symmetry, or *concinnitas*, is the principal recommendation for prose rhythm in *Orator*. Cicero is not, however, describing his climactic period, but a more balanced structure, such as he uses in his *Pro Milone*, where he even goes so far as to employ full rhymes ('instituti ... imbuti').[21]

From what we have set out above, it should be apparent that Mulcaster is giving us almost a textbook representation of the *tertium dicendi genus* described by Cicero in *Orator*. In doing so, he is following an experiment in English prose which had begun with Roger Ascham.

Ascham follows this Ciceronian third style, especially in the devices of alliteration, isocolon, parison, and antithesis.[22] Other authors of the middle half of the sixteenth century, especially the 1570s, who also spoke in the measures of the Ciceronian *concinnitas* included John Rainolds and Gabriel Harvey. Lyly's euphuistic style is closely related to the Latin writings of the time, especially those of Rainolds.[23] The imitation of Cicero (though not necessarily of this ornate style) had been a major issue in the theory and practice of prose composition, especially as it was taught in the schools, since the early part of the century. Yet the direction in English prose towards Ciceronian balance as it was defined in the *Orator* was a comparatively new movement at the time Mulcaster was writing and was to culminate in the extravagant pulpit oratory of a few years later.[24] His mastery of this style is the reason for his election by Gabriel Harvey as one of the best writers of his day. For, as Harvey asks, 'how few may wage comparison with Reinolds, Stubbes, Mulcaster, Norton, Lambert, and the Lord Henry Howarde? whose severall writings the silver file of the workeman recommendeth to the plausible interteinement of the daintiest Censure?'[25]

The approval of Harvey, who was sensitive to the shifting tides of received literary fashion, suggests that Mulcaster had successfully worked his style towards a representation in English of 'hardness.' Such a style represented him before his readers as an intellectually demanding, perhaps rather sophisticated orator in print. He could be read as a worthy counsellor, one fully familiar with the gestures of an academic manner, one who is even to a certain extent setting this stylistic agenda. At times one is tempted to apply Gertrude's words to Polonius – 'more matter with less art.' For even Mulcaster admits towards the end of *Positions* that 'I am to long in talking of to litle' (257.35–6). Yet succinctness would contradict the point of the display. A Polonius without his artful discourse no longer resembles a counsellor of state.

NOTES

1 By 'aphorism' Mulcaster seems to mean 'closely rendered truth'; at *Positions* 260.13–14 he sets it parallel with 'sure *oracle*.' The most striking use of aphorism in the English Renaissance is Bacon's *New Organon*; see Vickers *Francis Bacon and Renaissance Prose* 60–95, especially Vickers' comment that 'Mulcaster's brief distinction between the "preciseness" of aphoristic delivery which might "aliene", and the greater persuasive power of "discourse" is the only reference I have found – and it is a very shadowy one – to an aspect of the genre which increasingly occupies Bacon: the relationship between the

bare truth of the aphorism and the more connected but equally more distorting form of systematic communication' (72). See 47.30 note.

2 Cicero *De optimo genere oratorum* 1.3; cf *De oratore* 2.28.121 and *Orator* 69. Thomas Wilson says in his *Arte of Rhetorique* (1560) 'Three thinges are required of an orator. To teach. To delight. And to perswade' (ed Mair 2).

3 Aristotle *Rhetoric* 1.3.3 (1358a). Aristotle considers deliberation at 1.4–8 (1359a–66a); see also Cicero *De oratore* 2.81.333–83.340 and *De inventione* 2.155–76; *Ad Herennium* 3.2.2–6.9; Quintilian *Institutio* 3.8. Some of the main points are summarized in Lausberg *Handbuch der literarischen Rhetorik* nos 224–38. The only Elizabethan analysis of any weight is Wilson *Rhetorique* ed Mair 29–60.

4 Aristotle *Rhetoric* 2.1.3 (1377b)and see also 2.1.5 (1387a); Quintilian 3.8.12–13

5 Quintilian 3.8.37; cf Cicero *De oratore* 2.82.337–9

6 Wilson *Rhetorique* ed Mair 29. The division of topics in this manner is analysed at length by Quintilian 3.8.22ff; see also Cicero *De oratore* 2.82.335 and especially *De inventione* 2.51.155ff, which may be Wilson's source.

7 Quintilian 3.8.35; also Cicero *De partitione oratoria* 27.95. The circumstances are neatly defined in verse by Wilson *Rhetorique* ed Mair 17: 'Who, what, when, and where, by what helpe, and by whose: / Why, how, and when, doe many things disclose.' See Baldwin *William Shakspere's Small Latine* 2:311–12 for the circumstances as used in narrative.

8 Cicero *De oratore* 2.82.336: 'all debate is at once cut short by the realization that a thing is impossible or if it is proved to be inevitable.'

9 Judson *The Life of Edmund Spenser* 17; Lewis *English Literature in the Sixteenth Century* 348.

10 On this defence, see R.F. Jones 'Richard Mulcaster's View of the English Language' and for background his *The Triumph of the English Language*.

11 There are a number of standard handbooks that define the following terms: one of the best is still Sr Miriam Joseph *Shakespeare's Use of the Arts of Language*; others are Lanham *A Handlist of Rhetorical Terms* and Sonnino *A Handbook to Sixteenth-Century Rhetoric*.

12 'On the Education of Children' in Plutarch *Moralia* 2B, E; Cicero *De oratore* 2.21.88; Quintilian 1.Pr.26 and 1.2.26; Erasmus *De pueris instituendis* ed Margolin 383 note 75 (LB 1:496F trans CWE 26:311); Ascham *Toxophilus* in *English Works* ed Wright 58–9. Cf also Kempe *Education of Children* (sigs E3r–v) in Pepper ed *Four Tudor Books on Education* 217–18.

13 Plato *Phaedrus* 246A–C

14 On proverbs, see Erasmus' preface to his *Adagia* (at the beginning of LB 2 trans CWE 31); for background see Archer Taylor *The Proverb* and Weinstock *Die Funktion elisabethanischer Sprichwörter und Pseudosprichwörter bei Shakespeare* especially 18–25.

15 Erasmus *Adagia* in LB 2:821A; this is Tilley s885.
16 Cicero *Orator* 97
17 Ibid 134
18 Ibid 135
19 Ibid 138
20 Ibid 149
21 Ibid 165
22 Vos 'The Formation of Roger Ascham's Prose Style'; Vos argues against the influence of Isocrates, a view put forward by Ryan *Roger Ascham* 280ff. The most extensive work on the Ciceronian movement in Elizabethan England is that of Morris Croll in his *Style, Rhetoric and Rhythm: Essays*. Croll was unsympathetic to Ciceronianism; for an excellent review of his work and the whole issue of balanced prose, see Vickers *Francis Bacon and Renaissance Prose* 96–140. For some of his argument, Vickers follows the still influential treatise of Norden *Die antike Kunstprosa* 2:773ff for Ciceronianism and 2:786–8 for Euphuism.
23 For Rainolds, see Ringler 'The Immediate Source of Euphuism'; for Harvey, see Duhamel 'The Ciceronianism of Gabriel Harvey.'
24 Scott *Controversies over the Imitation of Cicero* which includes a translation of Erasmus' *Ciceronianus* (a better trans is CWE 28); see also Gabriel Harvey *Ciceronianus* trans Forbes. On the development in preaching, see Shuger *Sacred Rhetoric*.
25 Harvey *Pierces Supererogation* sig 2B1r; the references are to John Rainolds, Philip Stubbes, Thomas Norton, William Lambarde, and Henry Howard, first earl of Northampton, whose *A Defensative against the Poyson of Supposed Prophecies* was published in 1583. As was noted in the previous section, note 49, Harvey seems to have read *Positions* quite carefully.

3 Richard Mulcaster

Richard Mulcaster was born about 1532 in the northern city of Carlisle, the eldest son of William and Margaret Mulcaster.[1] The family were landowners, long prominent in the county. William Mulcaster became an alderman and a member of Parliament. Much later in his life Mulcaster alluded proudly to his being 'by ancient parentage and linnial discent, ann esquier borne.'[2] His gentle birth should be remembered when reading his comments on the social aspects of education in chapter 39 of *Positions*; most of the boys he taught at Merchant Taylors' came from families socially inferior to his.

The earliest documented date for Mulcaster's education is 1548, the year he matriculated at King's College, Cambridge, at the age of sixteen.[3] His schooling probably began in Carlisle, but rather than finish at the local grammar school he was sent to Eton as a King's Scholar.[4] There he may have studied under one or more of the masters of the 1540s, a man named Smyth, Robert Cater, and William Barker.[5] Many of his fellow students also went on to become schoolmasters: Thomas Browne, headmaster of Westminster (1564–72), Christopher Holden, sur-master at St Paul's (1561–78), William Malim, headmaster of Eton (1561–71) and high master of St Paul's (1573–81), Thomas Reeve, headmaster of Durham School (1558–68), and Ralph Waddington, master of Christ's Hospital (1564–1612).[6] These men, none of them scholars of the first rank yet all of them highly competent teachers, were influential in spreading the new learning of the humanist curriculum throughout the schools of England.

As was usual for King's Scholars, Mulcaster began university at King's College, Cambridge. Afterwards, however, he began to move about. Some time during his undergraduate years he transferred to Peterhouse, from which he graduated BA in 1553/4, a year later than his class of fellow matriculants. Moreover, rather than remain at Cambridge to complete the MA, he went to Oxford; in May 1556 he applied for admission to Christ Church, on 5 June he was incorporated, and on 17

December he received the MA.[7] There is no sure reason for this peripatetic scholarship. Perhaps during the period 1554–6 he lived in London, for there is a record of a Richard Mulcaster accused of stealing from Dr John Caius, the famous physician and later founder of Gonville and Caius College, who was in London in the 1550s.[8] Maybe the removal to Oxford was to escape the influence of Caius, who was a very powerful figure in Cambridge.

From school and university, Mulcaster would have become a competent Latinist (though by the less demanding standards of our own era we would consider him outstanding in his ability to read and write the language) and been at home in Aristotle and other Greek authors, and he may have had some Hebrew. He seems to have followed the usual statutory curriculum of the day. In the only report of his own education, he tells in *Positions* how Sir John Cheke (one of the principal humanist scholars of his day and Provost of King's while also tutor to Edward VI) presented undergraduates of King's and St John's with copies of Euclid and Xenophon 'to encourage them ... to the greeke toungue' (239.22). Yet despite Mulcaster's long training and his apparent love for the classics, he was no Roger Ascham. Hugh Broughton, a famous Hebrew scholar for whom Mulcaster once did a favour, described him as 'the best learned in the world in his owne conceit, reasonably in Heathen Greeks in deed,' a back-handed compliment, yet one which helps to explain the familiarity with Greek authors so openly displayed in *Positions*.[9] Although Mulcaster is often said to have been a first-rate Hebraist, there is no evidence for the claim, for it is certain that Broughton would have mentioned it.[10]

After Oxford, or possibly before if he had worked for Dr Caius, Mulcaster moved to London. We have no record of his first years there, but by 1559, about the time of his marriage to Katherine Ashley, a grocer's daughter, he had become active in several aspects of city life. In that year he served in Elizabeth's first parliament as one of the two members from Carlisle. He also participated in the pageant welcoming the new Queen into the city of London, and wrote out its narrative in a book that was probably the original of a pamphlet entitled *The Quenes Majesties Passage*, which appeared in the same year under the imprint of Richard Tottel.[11] And according to Mulcaster in *Positions* (16.2–3), this was also the year he began teaching.

Although he says he started his career in 1559, Mulcaster's first known appointment as a schoolmaster was on 24 September 1561, when the Court of the Company of Merchant Taylors made him head of their new school (228.27–9). He remained there for twenty-five years. That he was the only man considered for the job was probably due to the influence of the principal founder of the school, Richard Hilles, whom Mulcaster could have met in Parliament or during his work on the pageant. Hilles was a devout Protestant, a successful businessman and an important member of the Company (he was Master in 1561). He put up £500 of the £566 13s 4d for the building cost (half of the Manor of the Rose, built in the reign of Edward III and located in the parish of St Laurence Pountney), and he supplemented Mulcaster's low annual salary of £10 with an additional £10.[12]

Although we may assume that a zeal for learning and a desire to propagate the faith were uppermost in his mind, Hilles left no statement regarding his motives for founding the school. Neither do the statutes of the school explain why he and the Merchant Taylors were willing to undertake such a large commitment. Indeed, a close reading of the statutes suggests that the school was begun with some trepidation.[13] In establishing the foundation, the Merchant Taylors did what was quite common; they borrowed their statutes from an already functioning institution. John Colet's injunctions to the Mercer's Company for the refounding of St Paul's School (1509)[14] provided the actual wording for almost all the statutes of Merchant Taylors' School. Earlier writers have commented on the similarity of the two documents; one should, however, also consider an interesting difference. Colet's school was to be entirely free for all 153 boys. Merchant Taylors' was free for 100; of the remaining 150, 50 had to pay 2s 2d a quarter, and 100 5s a quarter. The surprising total from student payments alone is £121 15s a year, only £40 of which was marked for the salaries of the four teachers (one master and three ushers). Even if some of the boys were not required to pay full fees (Thomas Lodge, the son of a Lord Mayor, went to the school at reduced fees),[15] the school still should have returned a tidy profit to the Merchant Taylors.

If the school was turning a profit, Mulcaster had good reason for the annoyance he showed towards the Company during his last years in their employ, and his complaints in *Positions* (chapter 41 especially) about the low pay of schoolmasters no doubt reflect his own situation. Even with the supplement from Hilles, he was earning considerably less than the high master of St Paul's. By the 1580s, his official relations with the Merchant Taylors had degenerated into a continuous sparring over wages. One gets the impression that Mulcaster was not an easy man to deal with in matters of finance, and throughout his life he had problems with money. In 1586, after some strong words had been exchanged on both sides, Mulcaster resigned. The breach was not final, however, for he was asked back as an examiner on several occasions in later years.[16]

The twenty-five years at Merchant Taylors' School were his best years as a teacher. Although when he retired from the school, he may have looked forward to advancement in the church or as a schoolmaster elsewhere, his greatest work was behind him. His later years, first at his own schools (one somewhere outside of London and another in the city, on Milk Street),[17] and then at St Paul's, where he was high master from 1596 until his final retirement in 1608, may have been distinguished, but they were not so full and productive as those at Merchant Taylors'.[18]

Throughout *Positions* Mulcaster refers to his own experience as a teacher. To a certain extent, as has been noted, he is using a rhetorical technique as well as following his model Quintilian. Nevertheless, one feels that personal experience does underlie much of what he says in *Positions*.

We know very little about the daily operations of Merchant Taylors' School during its first twenty-five years. Whereas the Statutes are very specific about the hours (from seven to eleven in the morning, and from one to five in the afternoon, not quite the hours in *Positions* 224.3–4 and 229.37ff), holidays (Sundays, and either Tuesday or Thursday afternoon in those weeks in which no religious holiday was being celebrated),[19] and the number of boys, there is no mention of curriculum, the heart of the school's program. The statutes for St Paul's contain Colet's famous injunction against the study of 'blotterature,' by which he meant the pagan authors of antiquity; Colet would have had his boys read Augustine, Ambrose, Prudentius, and Lactantius instead of Cicero and Ovid. The statutes of Merchant Taylors' have nothing to say on this subject.

Probably Mulcaster followed a variation of what is now recognized as a more or less standard curriculum, a form of which he would have encountered at Eton. A pupil on entry to Merchant Taylors' was expected to know 'the catechism in English or Latyn' and to be able to 'read perfectly and write competently.'[20] Perhaps even these basic requirements were not insisted on, for Mulcaster complains in *Positions* (19.2ff) that too often the child is rushed through his elementary course and begins his grammar ill prepared. The pupil would start his Latin studies with the *Shorte Introduction of Grammar* which was, as Mulcaster points out in his 'Epistle Dedicatorie,' one of the few uniform texts in English education at the time. After the grammar, taught no doubt by one of the ushers, the pupil started the first readers: the heavily moralistic *Disticha* ascribed to Cato (a Christian and radically un-Cato-like version of which was composed in later years by Mulcaster himself), Aesop in Latin, and dialogues by Erasmus, Vives, Cordier, or a Latin translation of Lucian. He read through and memorized the longer catechism by Alexander Nowell, also by the 1570s a standard text (Mulcaster later wrote a versified *Catechismus Paulinus*). By the end of his third year, still under the guidance of one of the three 'ushers' or assistant masters, the pupil was ready for the letters of Cicero, and might also have read parts of Mantuan's *Eclogues* or Palingenius' *Zodiacus vitae*. If Mulcaster followed his own advice in *Positions*, much of the preliminary instruction would have been in English; there was also much training in the translation of English to Latin, though one doesn't know if the method of double translation commonly associated with Ascham was used. Then, on to a full-length play, such as Terence's *Andria*, and poetry by Ovid and Virgil. Prose would be continued with more of Cicero, perhaps by now his *De senectute* or *De amicitia*. By the last two years of school, now probably under the guidance of Mulcaster himself, the pupil was ready for detailed work in Cicero, rhetoric (the text was often Susenbrotus), Greek grammar with preliminary readings in Homer, and possibly some Hebrew. There were endless variations in this kind of curriculum, which has been analysed in detail by T.W. Baldwin.[21] The lack of uniformity in the higher forms must have played havoc with the education of students forced to change school, and Mulcaster comments on this problem (259.36ff).

Examinations held in the early years of the school give more specific evidence of what Mulcaster was teaching the boys.[22] On 9 June 1572, boys were examined for the new fellowships founded by Sir Thomas White at St John's, Oxford. The outside examiners, all very eminent, were Alexander Nowell, dean of St Paul's, Dr Watts, archdeacon of Middlesex, Gabriel Goodman, dean of Westminster, and Robert Horne, bishop of Winchester. After determining which books the boys of the seventh form had been studying, Nowell began with a book in Horace, 'comaundinge the lowest of that order to begyn to declare the sence and construction therof w.ch from one to another he p(ro)secuted throughe the whole number untill the capteyn, requiringe diversytie of phrases and varietie of wordes and fynally obmyttinge nothinge w.ch mighte seme neadfull for the tryall of their lerninge in the latyn tonge.' Nowell, a former schoolmaster,[23] was testing the boys in the way the Mulcaster might have reviewed a section of their work – that is, by checking not only their command of the material but also their 'copiousness,' their ability to paraphrase and rework the language of the original. Dr Watts examined the boys in their Homer, and the bishop tested their Hebrew by quizzing them on the Psalms. Finally the senior boys were dismissed, and the dean of Westminster examined the sixth-form boys in Cicero.

Most of Mulcaster's life at Merchant Taylors' was spent in drilling the boys in their classics. There can be no doubt that at this job he was supremely competent. The only contemporary account of Mulcaster's teaching was written by Sir James Whitelocke, who became a Judge of the Court of King's Bench under James I and who was also an important antiquarian scholar:

> I was brought up at school under mr. Mulcaster, in the famous school of the Marchantaylors in London, whear I continued untill I was well instructed in the Hebrew, Greek, and Latin tongs. His care was also to encreas my skill in musique, in whiche I was brought up by dayly exercise in it, as in singing and playing upon instruments, and yeerly he presented sum playes to the court, in whiche his scholers wear only actors, and I on among them, and by that meanes taughte them good behaviour and audacitye.[24]

From this all too brief passage, we get a glimpse of a richer life at the school than is conveyed by the minutes of the Court of Merchant Taylors. The emphasis on music, both 'singing and playing,' shows an accord between practice and Mulcaster's written statements in *Positions*. Perhaps acting too was justified as 'loud speaking'; Mulcaster never included any thoughts on acting in *Positions*. Acting was often done in the larger schools of the day; what is unusual about the program at Merchant Taylors' is that the boys were trained well enough for performance at court.[25]

There is no record of any other extra-curricular activities in the school. Above all, considering how extensively the subject is discussed in *Positions*, it would be interesting to know if there was any physical education. That seems unlikely.

Another important aspect of life in the school for which we have no evidence is religion. Compared with Mulcaster's own education at Eton or with the statutory requirements at St Paul's, Merchant Taylors' School seems to have been a somewhat more secular organization. There were prayers three times a day and study of the catechism, but there is no evidence of any more extensive religious training in the school.

Because of the rigour of the academic program and the probable lack of sports, proper discipline must have been difficult to maintain in a school in which the ratio of teacher to student was just over one to sixty. Mulcaster is emphatic that parents and friends are to enforce right behaviour outside of the classroom, whereas the teacher must enforce it within (40.9ff). The way to achieve proper behaviour is through discipline and control, attained in unruly or 'negligent' children by punishment. In some places in *Positions* Mulcaster speaks highly of affection, and claims that boys should proceed 'never fearing the rod' (39.30), yet in others he argues for the necessity of beating, which must be used 'to expell the contagious humours of negligence' (74.32). In the end, 'the *rod* may no more be spared in schooles, then the *sworde* may in the *Princes* hand' (270.2–3). All this seems to be far removed from the advice of Mulcaster's model Quintilian, who rejects beating (except that the practice is 'fit only for slaves'), and who argues that 'children are helpless and easily victimized, and therefore no one should be given unlimited power over them.'[26]

The following anecdote, reportedly from an early seventeenth-century manuscript, has the facetious air of the jest-book about it, but that Mulcaster is named as the master suggests that Thomas Fuller's description of him as '*Plagosus Orbilius*' (the hard-hitting schoolmaster in Horace)[27] may have some truth:

Of Monckaster, the famous Paedagogue.
Monckaster was held to be a good schoolemaster, and yet he was somewhat too severe, and given to insult too much over children that he taught. He beeinge one day about whippinge a boy, his breeches beeinge downe and he ready to inflict punishment uppon him, out of his insultinge humour he stood pausinge a while over his breech: and there a merry conceyt taking him he sayd, 'I aske the banes of matrymony between this boy his buttockes, of such a parish, on the one side, and Lady Burch, of this parish on the other side: and if any man can shewe any lawfull cause why they should not be joyned together, let them speake, for this is the last time of askinge.' A good sturdy boy, and of a quicke conceyt, stood up and sayd, 'Master, I forbid the banes.' The master, takinge this in dudgeon, sayd, 'Yea, sirrah, and why so?' The boy awnswered, 'Bycause all partyes are not agreed;' whereat Monkaster, likinge that witty awnswer, spared the one's fault and th'other's presumption.[28]

In *Positions*, Mulcaster claims that he taught 'thousandes' of pupils during his twenty-two years so far as a schoolmaster (275.7). Even though Merchant Taylors' was the second largest school in England (only Shrewsbury was larger), and the largest in London, this number is most likely an exaggeration.[29] By the time he finished at the school, he may have taught somewhere around 1,500 to 2,000 boys. Of these, 859 are recorded in the printed register of the school, which in turn is based on the Minute Books of the Company and other miscellaneous sources.[30] Of this group, we are given the occupations of the fathers of 692 boys.

Many of Mulcaster's pupils had formal connections with the Merchant Taylors, and almost 50 percent had fathers who worked in some area of the cloth trade. Only a tiny 3 percent of the fathers were professional men, such as doctors, lawyers, or clergymen. The remaining 47 percent of the fathers worked in an amazing variety of trades – there were shoemakers, innkeepers, fishmongers, scriveners, plasterers, carpenters, chandlers, pewterers, goldsmiths, plumbers, bakers, grocers, and many more. A large number of the young men left the school to go to university or the Inns of Court. Of the 859, 160 had some education beyond the school. The others would have gone on to apprenticeship. Many would have died young. *Positions* seems to have been written with the background and subsequent careers of these pupils in mind; Mulcaster argues on behalf of these boys and directs his arguments towards their 'parentes and freindes' who at the best might be literate tradesmen, but were 'mostwhat no latinistes' (16.37–8). In his work as teacher, as in his book, Mulcaster bridges the social strata of tradesman and gentleman; a boy might come to him from a relatively poor and even illiterate family; by virtue of a university education that the school opened up for him, he could become a gentleman. In part this work merely confirmed the social order; but for the individual boys and their families, the chance for social elevation would be valuable.

Many of Mulcaster's students were very successful, surprisingly so in purely intellectual achievement.[31] The school produced scientists, writers, churchmen, academics, and lawyers. Matthew Gwynne, Thomas Heath, Nicholas Hill, Thomas Hood, Thomas Moffett, and William Paddy were precursors of a scientific revolution in the next century, some of them through connections with Gresham College. Edmund Spenser is the most famous of the writers, but Thomas Lodge and Thomas Kyd also went to Merchant Taylors'. Seven translators of the 1611 Bible studied under Mulcaster: Lancelot Andrewes, Thomas Dove, Ralph Huchenson, John Peryn, Ralph Ravens, John Spencer, and Giles Thompson. Although Mulcaster himself cannot be given full credit for the careers of these and the many other men of similar though lesser accomplishments, he may have influenced them, perhaps encouraging them to continue on in academic studies. Certainly he and his school were significant gatekeepers in Elizabethan culture. Whitelocke's memoir quoted above suggests that many of the men Mulcaster taught looked back to him as an important figure in their lives. Bishop Andrewes, for instance, kept a portrait of his old master over his study door and remembered Mulcaster's family in his will.[32]

During his years at Merchant Taylors', Mulcaster did not confine his activities to the classroom. He wrote verses for the Lord Mayor's pageants of 1561 (attributed) and 1568 and for the Queen's reception at Kenilworth.[33] As mentioned above, he brought his boys to court to act before the Queen on five different occasions.[34] In 1573 he wrote commendatory verses for John Baret's polyglot *Alvearie, or Triple Dictionary,* and in 1575 for Tallis and Byrd's *Sacrae cantiones*.[35]

During the 1570s, or perhaps earlier, Mulcaster became acquainted with Emmanuel van Meteren (1535–1612), a leader of the Dutch community in London and a businessman who was also something of a scholar. His history of the Low Countries went through many editions both authorized and unauthorized from the 1590s onwards. Mulcaster knew van Meteren very well; in 1578 he was godfather to one of the van Meteren children.[36] A number of writers have suggested that van Meteren may have introduced van der Noot, the Dutch poet, to Mulcaster, who in turn may have arranged for the young Edmund Spenser to prepare the English version of the verses in what is traditionally called *A Theatre for Worldlings*.[37] All this is premised on Mulcaster's having known van Meteren as early as 1569, the year the *Theatre* was published. Perhaps they met this early, though the earliest record of their friendship is a poem dated 1577 from Mulcaster to van Meteren in the latter's *Album amicorum*, a manuscript of 120 leaves with greetings from some very impressive friends (Abraham Ortelius, William Camden, Justus Lipsius, Count Egmont, Robert Cotton, Christian Huygens, and others). That Mulcaster was especially close to van Meteren is shown by his signature and greeting on the flyleaf of the book.[38]

Through van Meteren, Mulcaster made contact with several influential humanists from the Low Countries who were passing through London: Janus Gruter, Abraham Ortelius, Janus Dousa, and Carolus Utenhovius.[39] For our immediate purposes, the most interesting contact was with Ortelius, the geographer, to whom Mulcaster addressed a letter that is still extant, asking him for advice about good books for the teaching of art, one of the subjects Mulcaster intended to discuss in a later part of the unfinished *Elementarie*.

Thus, by the end of the 1570s, Mulcaster was headmaster of the second largest school in England, the largest in London; he had access to the court and to the merchant community of London; he was known as an author of occasional verse in Latin and English; and, through van Meteren, he had met some of the leading intellectual figures of the continent. His educational writings seem to arise quite naturally from this background. *Positions* (1581) and *The First Part of the Elementarie* (1582) were bids for further notice from the court (as is evidenced by the dedicatory letters to Elizabeth and Leicester and by the many compliments to Elizabeth throughout *Positions*); they are addressed as well to his boys' parents, most of whom were members of the merchant community; and they display the kind of learning, in some places quite recondite, which would impress the more learned of his audience (who of course would first have to forgive him for writing in English and not in Latin). *Positions* especially is directed to all three groups. Much of the *Elementarie*, with its detailed observations on 'right writing,' is written for a more professional audience of teachers and other humanist scholars (across Europe some of the most advanced scholars of the classics had also turned their attention to the problems of the vernacular, especially spelling).

Mulcaster wrote in part as a bid for royal patronage, and it has been argued that his books were recognized by the Queen in her gift of several livings.[40] Perhaps so, but such gifts were slow in coming. Although in 1584 he was given a lease of lands in Middlesex and Devon, he did not receive his first benefice until eight years after *Elementarie*, and then it was a contemporary from Peterhouse, Archbishop Whitgift, who proferred the vicarage of Cranbrooke, Kent. (There is no record of Mulcaster's ordination, which may have followed his retirement from Merchant Taylors'.) In 1593, Mulcaster received a further living, becoming prebendary of Yatesbury in the Church of Sarum, but for this he had to fight, as several extant letters attest. In 1596 he received another and more important benefice, the rectorship of Stanford Rivers in Essex, a gift of the Queen. Despite these various livings, there is evidence that Mulcaster was short of money even after his appointment in 1596 as high master of St Paul's. During the 1570s, as church warden of St Laurence Pountney, Mulcaster had claimed various sums for himself as a stipend, and the suit of the parish to regain this money dragged on until 1599.[41] Thus, if he wrote his books for some kind of direct patronage from the crown, he must have been disappointed, for what gifts he did receive seem to have been reluctantly bestowed.

During the ten years following his resignation form Merchant Taylors' School in 1586, Mulcaster's career as a teacher and writer had come to a crisis. He stopped writing. He quarrelled with the Merchant Taylors over an old unpaid loan. His attempt to start a school outside London only got him further into debt. Besides trying to gather the benefices mentioned above, he was not above preaching occasionally at Lincoln's Inn, at ten shillings a sermon.[42] All in all, it was not a happy period, certainly not for a man in his late fifties and early sixties.

In the mid-1590s, his fortunes took a sudden turn. The new living at Stanford Rivers must have been especially welcome. But even better was his installation as high master of St Paul's. Before 1596, the Mercers Company had been having difficulties with the then high master, John Harrison, who had been charged with neglect and incompetence, who refused to resign, and who was finally removed by process of law. During the wrangling before Harrison's dismissal, the Mercers went to the extraordinary length of sending the boys to a temporary school a few hundred yards away in Milk Street, where they studied under Mulcaster and two assistants. When Harrison was finally ousted, Mulcaster was made the new high master, perhaps because of the influence of his old pupil Lancelot Andrewes, now prebendary of St Paul's and a regular examiner at the school. So, about the age of sixty-five, Mulcaster was able to begin twelve years as head of another excellent school. And as a matter of some practical gratification, the salary and emoluments were generous, and provision was made for support after his retirement.

Although he was able to restore something of the old image of the school after the disastrous administration of Harrison, Mulcaster does not seem to have had the same success in nurturing young scholars as he had at Merchant Taylors'. Though it is surmised that Mulcaster, an experienced director of boy-actors, must have supported the theatrical activities associated with the school, the revival of the 'children of Paul's' was the work of Edward Pearce, master of the Cathedral choir school, which was quite separate from Colet's foundation.[43]

During his years at St Paul's, Mulcaster began writing again. *Poemata* (now lost) and a copy of the first edition of *Catechismus Paulinus* were perhaps published in 1599 or early 1600 (what may be the first edition of the *Catechismus*, in the St Paul's School library, lacks a title page). *Cato Christianus*, an elementary textbook in verse, appeared in 1600. This work has an important preface that recapitulates many of the themes of *Positions*. At the death of Elizabeth, Mulcaster wrote a long poem in Latin entitled *In mortem serenissimae reginae Elizabethae, Naenia consolans*, and with it an English version, *The Translation of Certaine Latine Verses*, both published in 1603. It seems appropriate, if his first writing had indeed been for Elizabeth's entry into London in 1559, that his last might be a 'latine Oration' in the entry pageant for James '*Viva voce* delivered by one of maister *Mulcasters* Schollers, at the dore of the free-schole fownded by the Mercers.'[44]

Mulcaster retired in 1608. He had been granted a pension by the Mercers, and he spent his last few years as rector of Stanford Rivers.[45] He died in 1611, after a full and active life. Though a man not of the utmost rectitude or patience in his social relations, he appears to have been a gifted and original teacher.

NOTES

1 For date of birth, see note 3 below. The earliest and most persistently quoted life is by Thomas Fuller in *The History of the Worthies of England* (1662), here quoted in full, under 'Westmerland,' 3rd sequence of pages, 149–50:

> RICHARD MULCASTER was born of an ancient extract in the *North*, but whether in this *County* [i.e., Westmoreland] or *Cumberland*, I find not decided. From *Eaton-school* he went to *Cambridge*, where he was admitted in **Kings-colledge* 1548. but before he was graduated, removed to Oxford. Here such his proficiency in learning, that by general consent he was chosen the first Master of *Merchant-Tailors-School* in *London*, which prospered well under his care, as by the flourishing of Saint *Johns* in *Oxford* doth plainly appear.
>
> The *Merchant-Tailors*, finding his Scholars so to profit, intended to fix Mr. *Mulcaster*, as his Desk to their School, till death should remove him. This he perceiv'd, and therefore gave for his Motto,
>
> *Fidelis servus, perpetuus asinus*.
>
> But after *twenty five* years he procured his freedome, or rather exchanged his service, being made Master of *Pauls-school*.
>
> His method in teaching was this. In a morning he would exactly and plainly construe, and parce the lessons to his *Scholars*, which done he slept his hour (custome made him critical to proportion it) in his desk in the School, but wo be to the Scholar that slept the while. Awaking he heard them accurately, and *Atropos* might be perswaded to pity, as soon as he to pardon, where he found just fault. The prayers of cockering Mothers prevailed with him as much as the requests of indulgent Fathers, rather increasing then mitigating his severity on their offending child.
>
> In a word, he was *Plagosus Orbilius*, though it may be truly said (and safely for one out of his School) that others have taught as much learning with fewer lashes. Yet his sharpness was the better endured, because unpartiall, and many excellent Scholars were bred under him, whereof Bishop *Andrews* was most remarkable.
>
> Then quitting that place, he was presented to the rich Parsonage of *Stanford-rivers* in *Essex*. I have heard from those, who have heard him

Figure 1 Bateman *A Christal Glasse* (1569)

> preach, that his Sermons were not excellent, which to me seems no wonder; partly, because there is a different discipline in teaching children and men; partly, because such who make Divinity (not the choice of their youth, but) the refuge of their age, seldome attaine to eminency therein. He died about the middle of the reign of Queen *Elizabeth*.

Though this short biography is correct in some of its details, Fuller's uncertainty over the place of birth and the inaccurate guess at the date of death (actually 1611) show how little he really knew his subject. The personal details – Mulcaster's parting shot at the Merchant Taylors, his punctual snooze, his severity, and the dullness of his sermons – may be based less on any ascertainable facts than on Fuller's self-confessed intention to amuse his readers. The dozing schoolmaster may be a trope: in Bateman's *Christal Glasse* (1569), sig F4r, the chapter 'Of Sloth,' the master sleeps while his charges play foolishly about (see figure 1).

There is also Anthony à Wood in *Athenae Oxonienses* (1691) ed Bliss 2:93–5. H[enry] E[llis] 'Biographical Anecdotes of Richard Mulcaster' (1800) depends very heavily on Fuller and Wood. H.B. Wilson *The History of Merchant-Taylors' School* (1814) in a long note on 85ff follows Ellis closely but elsewhere gives much valuable information on Mulcaster's years at the school. Nothing new is added to the record by Quick's biography appended to his edition of *Positions* (1887–8), Foster Watson in *Richard Mulcaster and his 'Elementarie'* (1893), or J.H. Lupton's 1894 life in *DNB* 13:1172–3 (though this latter has a useful bibliography). The best summary of information to the end of the nineteenth century is Klähr *Leben und Werke Richard Mulcaster's*

(1893). New information is given in Cooper and Cooper *Athenae Cantabrigienses* (1913) 3:40–3. All this, and much more, is gathered together in DeMolen 'Richard Mulcaster: An Elizabethan Savant' (1975) based on preliminary research in his PH D dissertation (University of Michigan 1970); this in turn appears in chapter 1 of DeMolen *Richard Mulcaster*. I am heavily indebted to DeMolen for what follows, though I disagree in a number of details and have added new material to the facts of the life.

2 From the brass plate in the church of Stanford Rivers, Essex, erected by Mulcaster in memory of his wife, Katherine, quoted in full by DeMolen *Richard Mulcaster* 40–1

3 Mulcaster's matriculation is also the only source for his date of birth; he was entered 14 August 1548 in the King's College Protocollum Book (1500–78) at sixteen years; reproduced in DeMolen PH D diss appendix A–3 and translated, with some detailed notes, in his *Richard Mulcaster* 187–8.

4 Perhaps through the influence of Robert Aldridge, who for a time was both bishop of Carlisle and provost of Eton; *DNB* sv 'Aldrich, Robert' and *Contemporaries of Erasmus* 1:27–8

5 Maxwell-Lyte *A History of Eton College* 140ff for a description of the school at the time; on the headmasters, 598. The William Barker who was headmaster there from 1546 to 1555 has never been properly identified. There were at least five of that name who graduated MA from Cambridge during the period 1538–40 (Venn *Alumni Cantabrigienses ... Part I* 1:88). See also George B. Parks 'William Barker, Tudor Translator.'

6 Based on the names and dates in Sterry *The Eton College Register 1441–1698*

7 Following the dates in Cooper and Cooper *Athenae Cantabrigienses* 3:40. Foster *Alumni Oxonienses* 3:1044 has the MA awarded 17 June. At Peterhouse, Mulcaster was a fellow commoner, according to Walker *A Biographical Register of Peterhouse Men* 181; Walker also identifies a John Mulcaster and a Christopher Mulcaster who he claims are related to Richard.

8 By order of the Privy Council, 4 December 1555, Sir Henry Bedingfield, lieutenant of the Tower of London, was to 'receive the bodie of Richard Mulcaster servaunt to Doctor Caius vehemently suspecte for robbing his Mr. and by the best meanes he can to examyn hym hereof and to bring him to the racke and put him in feare of the Torture if he will not confesse/' (Public Record Office PC 2/7 fol 326, as reproduced in DeMolen *Richard Mulcaster* 189). The Coopers were the first to point out this document (which was transcribed 'Canis' in *Acts of the Privy Council* ed Dasent ns 5 [1554–6] 198), but they simply note 'the coincidence of name is remarkable.' DeMolen (*Richard Mulcaster* 6) takes the same document and weaves around it an unsupportable fiction: 'Mulcaster acted as Latin secretary to Dr. Caius' and 'From his daily contacts with the learned physician, he was inspired to continue his

classical studies.' For Caius's stay in London, see *DNB* sv 'Caius, John.'

9 Hugh Broughton *An Explication* (1605) 40. Broughton and John Rainolds were arguing over scriptural chronology; by a letter of 4 November 1591 Broughton referred the matter to the arbitration of Archbishop Whitgift; Mulcaster was the bearer of the letter (Mulcaster had been a classmate of Whitgift's at Peterhouse). Broughton was guilty of the same vice of self-conceit that he imputes to Mulcaster: 'I will suffer no scholar in the world to crosse me in Ebrew and Greek, when I am sure I have the truth' (*Works* 663); no wonder he was called 'Braggadoccion Broughton' (in the anonymous *Master Broughtons Letter* [1599] 24).

10 The claim is repeated in Wood, Ellis, DeMolen and almost all the other biographies. Though the boys were examined in Hebrew at Merchant Taylors', James Whitelocke, who has left the only record of studies with Mulcaster (*Liber Famelicus* 12–13, quoted below), was tutored in the subject by one Hopkinson, 'an obscure and simple man for worldly affayres, but expert in all the lefthand tongs' (13). Mulcaster may have known some Hebrew, but we cannot say how much.

11 For his term in Parliament, see Hasler *The House of Commons 1558–1603* 3:108–9, with a short biography by A.M. Mimardière, and DeMolen *Richard Mulcaster* 7 and note 34. He served before his father, who was MP in 1566. *The Quenes Majesties Passage* was published in two issues by Tottel in 1558; C.R. Baskervill, in 1935, discovered that a Richard Mulcaster had received 40s from the Court of Aldermen of the City of London 'for makyng of the boke conteynynge and declaryng the historyes set furth in and by the Cyties pageauntes at the tyme of the Quenes highnes commyng thurrough the Cytye to her coronacion ... which boke was geuyn vnto the Quenes grace' (quoting from Repertory Book XIV fol 143, for 4 April 1559; document reproduced in DeMolen *Richard Mulcaster* 189). Whether Mulcaster composed the text himself or merely copied out its contents in manuscript for presentation to the Queen hinges on one's interpretation of 'makyng of the boke.' So we cannot be sure that Mulcaster was actually the author of the 'boke' or indeed that the 'boke' printed by Tottel was the same as that given to the Queen. Mulcaster himself declares *Positions* to be 'my first travell, that ever durst venture upon the print' (3.13; cf 288.18–19); moreover, this declaration was made to the very person who was the recipient of *The Quenes Majesties Passage*.

12 On the beginning of his teaching career, Mulcaster made some conflicting statements; see note 44 below. On the founding of the school, on Mulcaster's appointment, and on Hilles, see Draper *Four Centuries of Merchant Taylors' School* chapter 1, Clode *The Early History of the Guild of Merchant Taylors* part II 58–239; H.B. Wilson *History of Merchant-Taylors' School* 1ff. Hilles had been a merchant in the cloth trade for the whole of his working life. He was also

in his youth a fervent puritan who had spent ten years (1539–49) at Strasbourg in exile. By Mary's reign his faith had weakened to a state of reluctant compromise (Haugaard *Elizabeth and the English Reformation* 84 note 3). His letters show him to be a keen, though self-taught, reader and stylist in Latin (Robinson ed *Original Letters* 230, 196; Robinson ed *The Zurich Letters* 171).

13 Printed in Draper *Four Centuries* 241–51

14 Printed in Lupton *A Life of John Colet* 271–84

15 Paradise *Thomas Lodge* 13

16 The arguments are outlined in Draper *Four Centuries* 15 and 19–20 and H.B. Wilson *History of Merchant-Taylors' School* 73–5. Thomas Fuller reports that his parting shot to the school was a little epigram: '*Fidelis servus, perpetuus asinus*' (see note 1 above for full text). On his later role as an examiner, see Draper 20. A family connection was also maintained with the school; his grandson Richard was there from 1616 to 1618. There are also Mulcasters in the eighteenth and nineteenth centuries. For the names and dates see Hart *Merchant Taylors' School Register*.

17 DeMolen 'Richard Mulcaster: An Elizabethan Savant' 54–5

18 Mulcaster's years at St Paul's are discussed in detail by McDonnell *The Annals of St Paul's School* 164–82.

19 On hours and days, see Draper *Four Centuries* 246, 248.

20 Ibid 246

21 Baldwin *William Shakspere's Small Latine* 1:418ff. To round out an idea of the curriculum, see also Sayle 'Annals of Merchant Taylors' School Library'; the long list of 1662 covers books purchased during the first one hundred years of the school and still in its possession by that year, but does not indicate when the books actually entered the school library. There is also a list of of 1599, but these were books given to the school by Hugh Hendley, master in 1590.

22 Draper *Four Centuries* 16–17

23 Nowell had been master of Winchester from 1543 to 1555; Churton *The Life of Alexander Nowell* 10.

24 Whitelocke *Liber Famelicus* 12

25 The boys under Mulcaster's direction performed on five occasions; see Draper *Four Centuries* 252–3 and DeMolen 'Richard Mulcaster and the Elizabethan Theatre.' See also note 34 below.

26 1.3.13–17

27 See above, note 1; Horace *Epistles* 2.1.70–1

28 Sheppard 'Flowers of Anecdote' 260, where the compiler is identified as Thomas Wateridge of the Middle Temple in the reign of James I. The tale is retold in Rev Wm. Cooper (pseudonym for James Glass Bertram) *Flagellation and Flagellants* 430 (for this I consulted the copy of A.E. Housman in the Bodleian Library). Bertram notes the 'same story is related of Dr. Busby of

Westminster' (430). There is no record of a Thomas Wateridge in the Middle Temple, or in the other inns of court, or in either university. I have been unable to trace this notebook, though another anecdote quoted by Sheppard mentions Ellis Swayne, who entered the Middle Temple in 1607, was called to the bar in 1614, and was confirmed barrister in 1616 (Venn *Alumni Cantabrigienses*; Sturgess *Register of Middle Temple* 1:89). So the document may have been genuine but now is lost.

29 If the school started from the first day and had a subsequent annual turnover of 50 boys, he would have had the care of 1,450 boys by 1586; with a turnover of 70 boys (that is, with their average time at the school under four years) he would have taught 1,930. In 1569 Mulcaster was taking in over the number of boys allowed by the school statutes, but was stopped by the overseers of the school (Draper *Four Centuries* 15).

30 Hart *Merchant Taylors' School Registers*; Natalie Johnson, whose work has never been published, compared the printed register with the company records and with university and other registers, and believes that the printed register is accurate except that sometimes Hart does not tell the full record of a boy's further education; that is, the MA will be listed, but not the BD if he got one (I am grateful to Ms Johnson for her assessment of Hart). The figures break down as follows: 859 boys are listed in Hart's *Register* as having entered the school from its beginnings to 1586. Of these, occupations or guild affiliations are given for fathers of 692. Of these 692, 199 were sons of Merchant Taylors, 145 sons of men associated in some way with the cloth trade (drapers, mercers, and so on), 21 were sons of professional men (doctors, ministers, lawyers), and 329 were sons of men engaged in other occupations. Of the total of 859, 160 went on to Oxford, Cambridge, or the Inns of Court, or studied abroad. The number of Oxford and Cambridge entrances is of course not completely sure because many common names cannot be traced in Venn or Foster. Mention should be made of an earlier register by Charles J. Robinson, which is much less full, but which shows annual entrances; Hart's register is less conveniently arranged as a massive alphabetical list up to the year 1934.

31 Based on Hart *Register* and, where available, on *DNB*

32 DeMolen *Richard Mulcaster* 37 following John Buckeridge 'A Sermon' in Andrewes *XCVI Sermons* ed Laud and Buckeridge, 5th ed (1661) 791; the portrait has not been traced.

33 The anonymous speeches for 1561 are reprinted in Robertson and Gordon eds *A Calendar of Dramatic Records* 38–9 and the authorship is examined at 42–3; Mulcaster's for 1568 are in ibid 48–9 and also in Sayle *Lord Mayors' Pageants* 53–5. The Kenilworth pageant with Mulcaster's speech had been printed by 1576 by the London printer Richard Jones but is now extant only

in two editions of 1821: Gascoigne *Princely Pleasures* (published by Burn) 10 and Gascoigne *The Princelye Pleasures* (published by Marshall) 4; the text in Gascoigne *Works* ed Cunliffe 2:95 is based on a comparison of the two.

34 See note 25 above and Feuillerat *Documents Relating to the Office of the Revels* 174, 206, 213, 350, and 355; also Motter *School Drama* 105ff.

35 Baret *An Alvearie or Triple Dictionarie* (1573) sig *4v and Baret *An Alvearie or Quadruple Dictionarie* (1580) sig A4v. Later dedications are found in Ocland *Anglorum praelia* (1582) at the beginning of the second part *Εἰρηναρχία sive Elizabetha* sig A4v (the poem is left out of John Sharrock's English translation of 1585); Claude Holiband (Desainliens) *Campo di Fior or Else the Flourie Field of Foure Languages* (1583) sig *3v; Strigelius *A Third Proceeding in the Harmonie of King Davids Harp* trans R. Robinson (1595) sig A4v (a commendation in English prose); Hakluyt *The Principal Navigations* (1598) sig 2*3r–v, two poems, with others by Camden and Broughton et al (Mulcaster did not write for the first edition of 1589).

Cooper and Cooper *Athenae Cantabrigienses* 3:42 lists a distich 'on the death of Henry Dow, 1578.' Henry, son of Robert Dowe, an eminent Merchant Taylor, studied under Mulcaster at Merchant Taylors', entered Christ Church, Oxford, in 1576 and died there in 1578. There were two brass plaques erected in his memory. The upper brass survives in the Cathedral today, though not in its original place. On the lower brass, now lost, were distichs by Dowe's three brothers, by his two tutors (John Rainolds and John Horden) and by Mulcaster (named as his 'Praeceptor'). Anthony à Wood (*History and Antiquities* ed Gutch [1786] 3:484) transcribed Mulcaster's poem some time before 1695: 'Qualis in Autumno judex Academia, certe / Nobilis in primo palmite gemma fuit' (Just as he was in his Autumn, o judging Academy, so to be sure as a bud in his first blossoming he was noble). See also Wilson *History of Merchant-Taylors' School* 1163–4.

36 Nevinson 'Emanuel van Meteren, 1535–1612,' especially 143

37 Pienaar 'Edmund Spenser and Jonker Jan van der Noot' and Forster 'The Translator of the "Theatre for Worldlings"'

38 [Van Meteren] *Album amicorum Emanuelis de Meteren mercatoris Antuerpianj* fol *1r; the poem is on fol 38r.

39 For Gruter see Forster *Janus Gruter's English Years* 57; Gruter sends greetings to Mulcaster, Alexander Nowell, and others in a letter to William Camden of 21 June 1590 (Camden *Epistolae* ed Smith 43). Mulcaster's letter to Ortelius, now in private possession, is printed in Hessels *Ecclesiae Londino-Batavae Archivum* 1:249–52. Dousa and Mulcaster are discussed by van Dorsten *Poets, Patrons, and Professors* 81; Mulcaster signed Dousa's *Album amicorum* (now in University Library of Leiden) on 26 August 1584; two years later Dousa mentioned Mulcaster in his Ode on the Queen's birthday in *Odarum Britanni-*

carum liber (see van Dorsten *Poets* 92). On Utenhovius and Mulcaster, see van Dorsten *The Radical Arts* 126 note 38. Gruter, Ortelius, and Utenhovius were all related to van Meteren, according to the genealogical tree in van Dorsten *Poets* 21.

40 Quick in appendix to his edition of Mulcaster *Positions* 303

41 On the gifts in Middlesex and Devon, see Cooper and Cooper *Athenae Cantabrigienses* 3:41; on Cranbrooke, ibid 3:41; on Yatesbury, Le Nève *Fasti ... 1541–1857* ed Horn 88, British Library Harleian Ms 6996 fols 33 and 35 and Additional Ms 4160 fol 201 (97), and DeMolen *Richard Mulcaster* 26; on Stanford Rivers, DeMolen ibid 39–41. The rectory of Stanford Rivers was a generous living; the buildings and surrounding property c 1610 are described in Newcourt *Repertorium* 2:546–7. Mulcaster had some trouble with this benefice; the parishioners complained about the general disrepair of the church buildings (Emmison *Elizabethan Life* 135; see also 203). DeMolen, who surveyed the documents for these various livings, does not mention another that Mulcaster may have received in St Clement, Eastcheap, according to Foster *Alumni Oxonienses* 3:1044 but not in Newcourt *Repertorium* 1:327. On the suits, see DeMolen ibid 19.

42 His debts to Thomas Tyrrell, a London grocer, totalled £300 and were never completely paid; DeMolen *Richard Mulcaster* 25. In the accounts of Lincoln's Inn for 1593 to 1594 there is record of a payment of '20s. to Mr Mulcaster, clerk, for 2 sermons preached in the Chapel'; *Records of the Honorable Society of Lincoln's Inn: The Black Books Vol. II* 38 and see also DeMolen ibid 26–7.

43 On Mulcaster at St Paul's, see note 18 above. Though Mulcaster himself may not have been directly associated with the acting, his name was; in Fletcher's *The Knight of the Burning Pestle* (1.1.93–4 in Beaumont and Fletcher *Dramatic Works* ed Bowers 1:17) the Grocer's Wife asks Master Humphrey 'I pray you brother, with your favor, were you never none of Maister *Monkesters* schollars?'; Zitner, in his edition of Fletcher *Knight*, suggests that the Wife shows her ignorance because she confuses the boys of St Paul's School (where Mulcaster is now teaching, but not training actors) with the boys of Merchant Taylors' (where Mulcaster had trained boy actors some twenty years earlier).

44 The *Poemata* is listed in the catalogue of the Bright sale at Sotheby's, March/April 1845, item 4611, bound after an edition of P. Porcius (pseud) *Pugna porcorum*, Antwerp 1533, an extraordinary Neo-Latin poem whose every word begins with 'p.' There is a chance this lost work might still be found. For the late writings, see DeMolen 'Four of Richard Mulcaster's Last Publications'; the actual history of *Catechismus Paulinus* seems more complicated than what DeMolen describes. See Barker and Chadwick 'Preface to *Cato Christianus*' for a detailed account of the two textbooks. Because of the way the two books join so neatly with his plans in *Positions* and *Elementarie*,

they may have been begun years earlier, but revised and seen through to publication after Mulcaster came back to a formal teaching position at St Paul's. The entry of James was written out by Thomas Dekker as *The Magnificent Entertainment Given to King James ... 1604* (in *Dramatic Works* ed Bowers 2:291–2 in Latin and 2:293–4 in English). This speech claims that Mulcaster has taught for 'more than 50.4 yeeres' ('annos iam quatuor supra quinquaginta'); in the dedication to *Catechismus Paulinus* (dated 1599) sig A5r he says he has taught for forty-eight years. Both have him starting his career some time around 1551 to 1553.

45 On his pension, see McDonnell *Annals* 177. Mulcaster left no will; letters of administration of his estate were granted on 26 April 1611 and the value of the inventory was £89 17s 7d (DeMolen *Richard Mulcaster* 191 reproduces and transcribes the document).

4 Date and Text

PUBLICATION AND DATE

Positions was published at London in 1581. There is no contemporary evidence that the book was ever republished during the author's lifetime.[1]

The book was entered in the Stationers' Register on 6 March 1581 to Thomas Chard, with an interesting proviso: 'That yf this booke conteine any thinge preiudiciall or hurtfull to the booke of maister Askham that was printed by master Daie / Called *the Scolemayster* That then this Lycence shalbe voyd.'[2] Roger Ascham's *Scholemaster* had first been published posthumously in 1570, and new editions appeared in 1571, 1573, and 1579, all under the imprint of John Day, who must have felt that the sales of his successful property would be threatened by another book on the same subject by a prominent London teacher.[3] Some kind of agreement was struck, and Mulcaster ruefully mentions his predecessor's book: 'I wish he had not himselfe, neither any other for him entitled the *scoolemaister*, bycause myselfe dealing in that argument must needes sometime dissent to farre from him, with some hasard of myne own credit, seeing his is hallowed' (238.38–239.2).

Although 'Thomas Chare' is named as the publisher of *Positions*, the book went for printing to Thomas Vautrollier. We know the manuscript was in his shop on 24 April 1581, because that is the date of the letter Mulcaster wrote to Ortelius asking for information about books on drawing. In the letter, Mulcaster mentions that he has in hand (completed? or in progress?) a book which he has called his *Elementarie* ('Habeo iam in manibus libellum, quem Elementarium nomino') and that Vautrollier has in his workshop another book (ie, *Positions*) which Mulcaster has written in English ('Habet Vautrollerius typographus iam sub praelo librum, quem Anglice conscripsi').[4]

Positions appeared for sale within the next few months. The earliest date of purchase in an extant copy is 11 September 1581, accompanying the signature of one John Laughton.[5] This early date gives us sure proof that the book was indeed published in 1581. And that it was written, or at least revised, just before publication is shown by Mulcaster's claim in the book that he had taught at Merchant Taylors' for 'twenty yeares' (228.29); the School was founded (as the title page conveniently reminds us) in '*anno.* 1561.' Evidence both external and internal shows that *Positions* refers to exactly contemporary events and practice.

Thomas Chard is named as the publisher of *Positions* in the Stationers' Register, but the rights seem to have been controlled jointly by Chard and Vautrollier.[6] Chard's name (in a common variant spelling) appears on the title page of about half of the extant copies (*STC* 18253 'Imprinted at London by Thomas Vautrollier / for Thomas Chare. / 1581'); the other copies name only Vautrollier (*STC* 18253a 'Imprinted at London by Thomas Vautrollier / dwelling in the blacke Friers by Ludgate / 1581'). Earlier and later connections between the two bear out the impression that Mulcaster first approached Vautrollier with the manuscript. Mulcaster's first published poem appeared in Tallis and Byrd's *Sacrae cantiones*, which came out under Vautrollier's imprint in 1575; the *Elementarie* was published by Vautrollier in 1582; in 1583, Claude Holiband's *Campo di Fior*, also from Vautrollier, had a congratulatory poem by Mulcaster.

Vautrollier's busiest year ever was 1581, so it seems that to spread out the volume of the work he went into some kind of partnership with Chard.[7] Indeed, in 1581 the only books produced by Chard have imprints shared with Vautrollier. The relationship between the two remained close for several years. When Vautrollier, for religious reasons, was forced to leave London for Edinburgh, it was perhaps Chard who kept the London operation going, for books continued to be issued in London with Vautrollier's imprint.[8]

Whatever the respective interests held in *Positions* by Chard and Vautrollier, two years after publication Chard still held copies of the book and was promoting them eagerly. In 1583 he sent a shipment of books to Cambridge, including eleven copies of *Positions* (at 14s 8d, or 1s 4d each), more copies than of almost any other of the nearly five hundred titles forwarded.[9] Perhaps Chard was just trying to get rid of a book that was not selling. Despite the author's sanguine prediction that if his series were issued in small parts the printer's 'sale will be quik' (*Elementarie* sig *4v), it seems that neither *Positions* nor *Elementarie* was a big seller, for there was no contemporary reissue of either book.

THE EDITION OF 1581

The extant copies of *Positions* show the book to be a single printing with a variant title page. A complete examination of the whole text, based on a full collation of one incomplete and seven complete copies and further detailed comparisons with nineteen others, indicates that though individual formes go through one or more progressive changes, the copies may not be sorted into two families of distinctive variants.[10]

An analysis of the variants of the first gathering (sig *) proves that the shared imprint (Vautrollier and Chard) actually followed the single imprint (Vautrollier), even though Chard had entered the copy. Of the thirty-eight extant copies, eighteen have the double imprint (*STC* 18253) and twenty have the single (*STC* 18253a).[11]

Positions is an attractively and on the whole accurately printed book. Unlike most Tudor books on education, and somewhat in contrast with the avowed Englishness of its contents, it is printed not in black-letter but in roman (very much in the general style of a Garamond, though manufactured by a Protestant typesetter named Haultin), Greek (again, like a Garamond), and italic (like a Granjon), all in the continental style favoured by Vautrollier. The roman face has an unusual peculiarity; the lower case 't' is cast on a body that is just a bit short, and in many places the letter is only faintly visible. This same 't' is found in other books printed by Vautrollier that year. Of even greater interest, it is also found in a book printed by Chard for Vautrollier (Whitaker's *Ad Rationes ... responsio*). Thus, we see that Vautrollier printed for Chard and Chard printed for Vautrollier; yet the books are all made from the same type used in Vautrollier's workshop. The working arrangements of the two men are close.[12]

By contemporary standards, *Positions* is carefully set and there seem to be few apparent misprints. The book was corrected in press; of the total of eighty quarto formes, twenty-one have been altered at least once.[13] All variants are listed in the textual notes, along with corresponding line numbers for this edition and for 1581. The three most error-ridden formes, Q outer in two copies (British Library c.175.1.10 and Folger Shakespeare Library 18253a 2), and 2B outer and inner in one copy (Folger 18253), have totals of twelve, five, and seven errors respectively. Of these twenty-four changes only two might be called substantive, at 134.12–13 where 'sift of out' is corrected to 'sift out of') and 195.16 where the phrase 'where the great welth' is altered to 'which greate wealth.' The only other corrections in the whole book which might be said to affect the actual sense of the text are those at 60.31 ('suppected' to 'suspected' to 'supported'), 69.23 ('naturall health' is corrected in only one copy to 'naturall heat'), 224.30 ('heauenly' should read 'homely' according to the errata list and has been so corrected in a few copies), and 273.39 ('*impuritie*' in one copy has been corrected to '*impunitie*'). There is one remaining oddity in the text, a one-word sentence found in all copies reading simply 'And' (204.38). This may either be an error or – more likely – an intentionally surprising device of elocution.

Of the total of sixty-three press-corrections found in the collated copies of *Positions*, then, the great majority are changes in punctuation and spelling. Most of them are rather minor. Yet taken as a group, they show an interesting pattern. In his *Elementarie* Mulcaster sets forth a theory and practice of English spelling. Although this reform of spelling, he says, is limited to the 'pen' and not the 'print' (printers have their own systems of orthography, he suggests in *Elementarie* sig 2K2v), the proof corrections in *Positions* show a tendency to move towards his recommended spelling. Thus, when 'Phisicall' is changed to 'Physicall,' 'scrapt' (our 'scraped') to 'scrapte,' 'gentility' to '*gentilitie*,' 'il' to 'ill,' 'trane' to 'traine,' and 'sequell' to 'sequele,' the orthography is being shifted, however slightly, towards Mulcaster's own system. There are a very few spellings that contradict this drift, but there is enough evidence, I believe, to suggest that Mulcaster may have corrected his own proofs. This is normal enough for the time; what is unusual is that the evidence is typographical. Usually the evidence for such corrections comes from an extant authorial proof-sheet or by documentary evidence from a letter or other historical testimony; here it comes from a small number of changes made in the text that correspond to the kind of spelling we know the author approved. Ironically, the smallness and the fussiness of the changes suggest the author's hand; a thoroughgoing correction of the full book would probably not have been accepted by a printer because of the cost.

Thus, a tiny but most suggestive piece of evidence that the author may have corrected these proofs is found in the change at line 60.31 from 'suppected' to 'suspected' to 'supported.' The first is an obvious error accounted for by the apparent misreading of the 'or' in the copy as 'ec,' a simple confusion in secretary hand. The second is the first attempt at correction and tries to make the word into a recognizable English form; it has the appearance of a rationalizing correction by the proof-reader, who fails to consult his copy. The third and final change has the authority of the errata list which in both style and the use of the first person appears to have been written by Mulcaster. The change, at line 35 of the same page, of 'Phisicall' to 'Physicall,' made with the final correction to 'supported,' could only have been introduced by someone interested in spelling style. The 'y' corresponds perfectly with Mulcaster's theory of 'enfranchisement' outlined in *Elementarie* and may have been substitituted at the last minute as his eye roved over the page looking for other errors.

If Mulcaster had a hand in the proofs, then the 1581 printing is probably, within the context of contemporary publishing, an adequate public form of his work. We of course do not know if he saw all of the proofs, nor indeed can we be completely positive that he indeed did read them. Yet the evidence seems strong that the text that we have is what Mulcaster wrote, with the usual contemporary compositorial interventions, and therefore needs minimal adjustments by the modern editor. Indeed, in many ways the original 1581 printing is a 'definitive' edition of *Positions*.

THIS EDITION

This text is a lightly modified old-spelling edition. The spelling is not in any way difficult or unusual; the difficulty in reading Mulcaster for some readers will be found in his syntax and plays on words which sometimes are, as has been argued above, quite complex. The only changes to the text have been in the modernization of i/j, u/v, and long s, the expansion of all contractions (including &), the correction of obvious errors, and the adjustment of the few errors discovered in the collation of texts (all changes, except the expansion of contractions and modernization of the letter forms, are recorded in the section of textual notes). I have added to my text the page numbers in square brackets of the 1581 text (but I have not broken words at the page breaks, as is often the practice). I have also, in the preliminary list of contents, added the page number for each chapter. With perhaps half a dozen alterations, I have retained the original punctuation which is organized more around the rhythms of speech than logical partitions of thought. The Greek also is unchanged, even though some accents will seem incorrect or misplaced to a modern classicist. In other words, little obvious editing has been done and the text remains quite similar to that presented to the reader in 1581. The reader should know, however, that this text is the result of thorough investigation, as is not the case in the century-old edition of Quick.[14] Other commonly cited editions are, unfortunately, inadequate for a historical reading of the text: the selections from Mulcaster prepared by James Oliphant and the abridged *Positions* by Richard DeMolen both distort the text radically in their well-meaning attempts to modernize the morphology and syntax, not just the spelling, of the original.[15] In this edition I have attempted to present, with as few compromises as possible, a text satisfactory for present-day readers.

NOTES

1 Ames and Herbert *Typographical Antiquities* 2:1073 reports an edition of 1587; Lowndes *The Bibliographer's Manual* ed Bohn 1628 reports one of 1591, but both seem to be ghosts perhaps based on erroneous transcriptions of '1581.' McKerrow, in his edition of Nashe *Works* 4:41, claims that *Positions* was several times reprinted after 1581, but like his predecessors gives no evidence for the claim.

2 Arber *Transcript of the Registers of the Company of Stationers* 2:178b (checked against a microfilm of the original in Robarts Library, University of Toronto).

3 Ryan *Roger Ascham* 250–4; Ascham is also mentioned at *Positions* 108.16 in relation to archery. There is a copy of *Positions*, Cambridge University Library Syn 7.57.29[2], bound with the first edition of *The Scholemaster* in possibly late seventeenth-century calf (the copy bears the signature of 1672 of 'Charles Warnes' and the verso of the title leaf has the book plate of George I, hence it was possibly part of the collection of Bishop Moore, as in De Ricci 34–5).

4 Hessels *Ecclesiae Londino-Batavae archivum* 1:249–52 (British Library, Department of Manuscripts, microfilm M/457 [825–8]); the letter is in private possession.

5 Bodleian Library, Douce M M 484. The signature and date, partly cropped, have been independently verified by David Rogers of the Department of Printed Books. There is a John Laughton who matriculated as a pensioner at Pembroke College, Cambridge, in 1559; a John Laughton was rector of Drayton, Beauchamp, Bucks, 1572 until his death in 1584 (Venn *Alumni Cantabrigienses ... Part I* 3:50).

6 Chard's career is briefly described in McKerrow *Dictionary*, Jahn 'Letters and Booklists of Thomas Chard (or Chare) of London, 1583–4,' Paige 'An Additional Letter and Booklist of Thomas Chard, Stationer of London,' Lloyd E. Berry 'Thomas Charde, Printer and Bookseller.' For Vautrollier, there are McKerrow *Dictionary*, Clair 'Thomas Vautrollier,' and Pepper 'Francis Clement's *Petie Schole* at the Vautrollier Press, 1587.'

7 For Vautrollier's output, see the index in vol 3 of the revised *STC*. Chard/Vautrollier imprints are William Whitaker *Ad rationes decem E. Campiani, responsio* (*STC* 25358); ibid, 2nd ed (*STC* 25359), and Whitaker's *Responsionis ad decem illas rationes quibus fretus E. Campianus defensio* (*STC* 25361 = 25362). Chard's only extant work of 1578 is Whitaker's translation into Latin of John Jewel's *Adversus T. Hardingum*; like *Positions* it has variant

title pages, one naming Chard and Vautrollier (*STC* 14608), the other naming only Vautrollier (*STC* 14607.5), and a third, now dated 1588, again naming Chard and Vautrollier (*STC* 14609; *STC* rev ed under 14607.5 hypothesizes that this date is a misprint). Greg *Companion to Arber* 31 mentions the relationship of Chard and Vautrollier.

8 Clair 'Thomas Vautrollier' 226; for background see F.S. Ferguson 'Relations between London and Edinburgh Printers and Stationers (–1640).'

9 Jahn 'Letters and Booklists of Thomas Chard' 219–37; for *Positions* see 231 (no 425). Johnson assumes that this price is retail in 'Notes on English Retail Book-Prices, 1550–1640' 107 (no 359). A copy of 'i mulcaster deposition' is found in a Shrewsbury booklist of 1585; see Rodger 'Roger Ward's Shrewsbury Stock' 251 (no 37).

10 Any differences in formes are simple press-corrections; there is no evidence of the resetting of any complete forme.

11 In the first state, the combined imprint is found with a number of errors in the outer forme: *3r headline reads 'THE EPISTLE.' (later 'DEDICATORIE'); *4.10 'heltfull' (later 'healthfull'); and 'Your Maiesties most humble and / obedient subiect RICHARD MVLCASTER' ('Your Maiesties most humble and / obedient subiect / *Richard Mulcaster*'). In the second state these are all corrected. In the third state the imprint is altered with the addition of Chard's name. The inner forme has only one variant, a turned parenthesis at *3v.23 ('labour) if'); of a group of twenty-seven copies examined personally, this error is found in twelve of the thirteen of the single imprint and in none of the fourteen of the double imprint, suggesting that the inner and outer formes of sig * were corrected at the same time.

12 Clair 'Vautrollier' 224; Isaac *English Printers' Types of the Sixteenth Century* plate 70 has a close approximation, a Garamond 70. In addition to discussion in Isaac, see W. Craig Ferguson *Pica Roman Type in Elizabethan England* 31–2 and figure 145; the type, in Ferguson's classification, is Vautrollier's 1b, derived from the matrices of Jerome Haultin, in the general style of a Garamond. Sample books of the same year with the odd 't' are Théodore de Bèze *Confessio Christianae fidei* (*STC* 2006.2) and the Whitaker *Ad rationes ... responsio* (*STC* 25358).

13 Noting always that this information is not based on full collation of all copies.

14 *Positions* ed Robert Hebert Quick has the imprint London and New York: Longmans, Green, and Co 1888, though some half-titles have the date 1887 at the bottom. The text is a simple reprint of the University of London copy: (Q.M.L.) K. (Mulcaster) (2nd issue of first edition). A note by Quick, dated 1886, on the verso of the first flyleaf says this was the copy used by the printer.

15 The procedure of modernization used in the Oliphant 'edition' is such a distortion of usual editorial practice that it has some interest as a curiosity. It is a shame that it is still used as a source by some historians (eg, Lawrence Stone *Family* 203). DeMolen, whose work on Mulcaster's biography has been very helpful in this edition, is an enthusiastic modernizer: in his 1971 edition of *Positions* he quite openly states that 'certain obsolete words, such as "train" and "president," have been changed to their modern equivalents, "training" and "precedent"' (xi).

POSITIONS VVHERIN THOSE PRIMITIVE CIRCVMSTANCES BE EXAMINED, WHICH ARE NECESSARIE FOR THE TRAINING vp of children, either for skill in their booke, or health in their bodie.

VVRITTEN by RICHARD MVLCASTER, *master of the schoole erected in London anno.* 1561. *in the parish of Sainct Laurence Povvntneie, by the vvorshipfull companie of the merchaunt tailers of the said citie.*

Imprinted at London by Thomas Vautrollier
for Thomas Chare.
1581

To the most vertuous ladie, his most deare, and soveraine princesse, Elizabeth by the grace of God Queene of England, Fraunce, and Ireland, defendresse of the faith &c.

My booke by the very argument, most excellent princesse, pretendeth a common good, bycause it concerneth the generall traine and bringing up of youth, both to enrich their minds with learning, and to enable their bodies with health: and it craves the favour of some speciall countenaunce farre above the common, or else it can not possiblie procure free passage. For what a simple credit is myne, to perswade so great a matter? or what force is there in common patronage, to commaunde conceites? I am therefore driven upon these so violent considerations, to presume so farre, as to present [*2v] it, being my first travell, that ever durst venture upon the print, unto your majesties most sacred handes. For in neede of countenaunce, where best abilitie is most assurance, and knowne vertue the fairest warrant, who is more sufficient then your excellencie is, either for cunning to commend, or for credit to commaunde? And what reason is there more likely to procure the favour of your majesties most gracious countenaunce, either to commende the worke, or to commaunde it waie, then the honest pretence of a generall good, wherein you cannot be deceived? For of your accustomed care you will circumspectlie consider, and by your singular judgement, you can skillfully discerne, whether there be any appearance, that my booke shall performe so great a good, as it pretendeth to do, before you either praise it, or procure it passage. In deede it is an argument which craveth consideration, bycause it is the leader to a further consequence: and all your majesties time is so busily employed, about many and maine affaires of your estate, as I may seeme verie injurious to the common weale, besides some wrong offered to your owne person, to desire your Majestie at this time to reade any [*3r] part therof, much lesse the whole, the booke it selfe being very long, and your Majesties leasure being very litle. And yet if it maye please your most excellent Majestie of some extraordinarie grace towardes a most obsequious subject in way of encoraging his both toilsome and troublesome labour, to take but some taste of any one title, of smallest encumbraunce, by the very inscription, the paw of a Lion may bewraie the hole body in me by the proverbe, in your highnesse by the propertie, as who can best judge, what the Lion is. For the rest, which neither your Majesties time can tarie on, neither my boldnesse dare desire that you should: other mens report, which shall have time to read, and will lend an officious countrieman some parte of their leysure, will prove a referendarie, and certifie your highnesse how they finde me appointed. I have entitled the booke POSITIONS, bycause entending to go on further, for the avauncement of learning I thought it good at the first, to put downe certaine groundes very needefull for my purpose, for that they be the common circunstances, that belong to teaching and are to be resolved on, eare we begin to teach. Wherin I crave consent of my countrey, [*3v] to joyne with me in conceit, if my reasons prove likely, that therby I may direct my whole currant in the rest, a great deale the better. Now if it maye stand with your Majesties most gracious good will to bestow upon me the favourable smile of your good liking, to countenance me in this course, which as it pretendeth the publike commoditie, so it threatneth me with extreme paines, all my paine will prove pleasant unto me, and that good which shall come thereby to the common weale shall be most justly ascribed to your Majesties especial goodnesse, which encoraged my labour, and commended it to my countrey. Which both encoragement to my selfe, and commendacion to my countrey, I do nothing doubt but to obtaine at your Majesties most gracious handes, whether of your good nature, which hath alwaye furthered honest attemptes: or of your Princely conceit, which is thoroughly bent to the bettering of your state, considering my travell doth tend that way. For the very ende of my whole labour (if my small power can attaine to that, which a great good will towards this my cuntrey hath deepely conceived) is to helpe to bring the generall teaching in your Majesties dominions, [*4r] to some one good and profitable uniformitie, which now in the middest of great varietie doth either hinder much, or profit litle, or at the least nothing so much, as it were like to do, if it were reduced to one certaine fourme. The effecting wherof pretendeth great honour to your Majesties person, besides the profit, which your whole Realme is to reape therby. That noble Prince king HENRY the eight, your Majesties most renowned father vouchesafed to bring all Grammers into one fourme, the multitude therof being some impediment to schoole learning in his happie time, and thereby both purchased himselfe great honour, and procured his subjectes a marveilous ease. Now if it shall please your Majestie by that Royall example which otherwise you so rarely exceede, to further not onely the helping of that booke to a refining: but also the reducing of all other schoole bookes to some better choice: and all manner of teaching, to some redier fourme: can so great a good but sound to your Majesties most endlesse renowne, whose least part gave such cause of honour, to that famous King, your Majesties father? By these few wordes your highnesse conceiveth my full meaning I am well assured, [*4v] neither do I doubt, but that as you are well able to discerne it, so you will very depelie consider it, and see this so great a common good thoroughly set on foote. I know your Majesties pacience to be exceeding great in very petie arguments, if not, I should have bene afraid, to have troubled you with so many wordes, and yet least tediousnesse do soure even a sweete and sound matter, I will be no bolder. God blesse your Majestie, and send you a long, and an healthfull life, to his greatest glorie, and your Majesties most lasting honour.

Your Majesties most humble and obedient subject

Richard Mulcaster [2*1r]

Author Ipse ad Librum Suum.

Insita naturae nostrae sitis illa iuuandi
   Ignauum vitae desidis odit iter.
Parca cibi, saturata fame, deuota labori,
   Prodiga nocturni luminis vrget opus.
Quod, simul ac lucis patiens fore viderit, edit,
   Inde licet multo plena timore gemat.
Poenitet emissam per mille pericula prolem,
   Quae poterat patriae tuta latere domi.
Iudiciumque timens alieni pallida iuris
   Omine spem laedit deteriore suam.
Sed sine sole nequit viui, prodire necesse est,
   Curaque quod peperit publica, iura vocant.
Fortunae credenda salus, quam prouida virtus,
   Quam patris aeterni dextera magna regit.
Sic sua Neptuno committit vela furenti
   Spem solam in mediis docta phaselus aquis.
Sed mihi spes maior, cui res cum gente Deorum,
   Quae certo dubiis numine rebus adest.
Perge igitur, sortique tuae te crede, parentis
   Tessera parue liber prima future tui.
Et quia, quà perges, hominum liberrima de te
   Iudicia in mediis experiere viis, [2*1v]
Quidnam quisque notet, quidnam desideret in te,
   Quo possim in reliquis cautior esse, refer.
Interea veniam supplex vtrique precare,
   Nam meus error erat, qui tuus error erit.

Qui neutrius erit, cum, quis sit, sensero, quippe
 Nullum in correcto crimine crimen erit.
Ergo tuae partes, quae sint errata, referre:
 Emendare, mei cura laboris erit.
Namque rei nouitas nulli tentata priorum
 Hac ipsa, qua tu progrediere, via,
Vtrique errores multos, lapsusque minatur,
 Quos cum resciero, num superesse sinam?
Cui tam chara mei lectoris amica voluntas,
 Vt deleta illi displicitura velim.

R. M.

THE ARGUMENTES HANDLED IN EVERY PARTICULAR TITLE.

Cap. 1
The entrie to the positions, conteining the occasion of this present discourse, and the causes why it was penned in English. 15

Cap. 2
Wherefore these positions serve, what they be, and how necessarie it was to begin at them. 17

Cap. 3
Of what force circunstance is in matters of action, and how warily authorities be to be used, where the contemplative reason receives the check of the active circunstance, if they be not well applyed. Of the alleadging of authors. 21

Cap. 4
What time were best for the child to begin to learne. What matters some of the best writers handle, eare they determine this question. Of lettes and libertie wherunto the parentes are subject in setting their children to schoole. Of the difference of wittes and bodies in children. That exercise must be joyned with the booke, as the schooling of the bodie. 27

Cap. 5
What thinges they be, wherin children are to be trained, eare they passe to the Grammar. That parentes, and maisters ought to examine the naturall

abilities in their children, wherby they become either fit, or unfit, to this, or that kinde of life. The three naturall powers in children, Witte to conceive by, Memorie to retaine by, Discretion to discerne by. That the training up to good manners, and nurture, doth not belong to the teacher alone, though most to him, next after the parent, whose charge that is most, bycause his commaundement is greatest, over his owne child, and beyond appeale. Of Reading, Writing, Drawing, Musick by voice, and instrument: and that they be the principall principles, to traine up the minde in. A generall aunswere to all objections, which arise against any, or all of these. 36 [2*2v]

Cap. 6
Of exercises and training the body. How necessarie a thing exercise is. What health is, and how it is maintained: what sicknesse is, how it commeth, and how it is prevented. What a parte exercise playeth in the maintenaunce of health. Of the student and his health. That all exercises though they stirre some one parte most, yet helpe the whole bodie. 51

Cap. 7
The braunching, order, and methode, kept in this discours of exercises. 59

Cap. 8
Of exercise in generall and what it is. And that it is Athleticall for games, Martiall for the fielde, Physicall for health, praeparative before, postparative after the standing exercise: some within dores, for foule whether, some without for faire. 60

Cap. 9
Of the particular exercises. Why I do appoint so manie, and how to judge of them, or to devise the like. 63

Cap. 10
Of lowd speaking. How necessarie, and how proper an exercise it is for a scholler. 65

Cap. 11
Of loude singing, and in what degree it commeth to be one of the exercises. 68

Cap. 12
Of loude, and soft reading. 69

Cap. 13
Of much talking and silence. 71

Cap. 14
Of laughing, and weeping. And whether children be to be forced toward vertue and learning. 72

Cap. 15
Of holding the breath. 76

Cap. 16
Of daunsing, why it is blamed, and how delivered from blame. 79

Cap. 17
Of wrastling. 83

Cap. 18
Of fensing, or the use of the weapon. 85 [2*3r]

Cap. 19
Of the top and scourge. 87

Cap. 20
Of walking. 89

Cap. 21
Of running. 95

Cap. 22
Of leaping. 98

Cap. 23
Of swimming. 100

Cap. 24
Of riding. 102

Cap. 25
Of hunting. 104

Cap. 26
Of shooting. 106

Cap. 27
Of the ball. 109

Cap. 28
Of the circumstances which are to be considered in exercise. 113

Cap. 29
The nature and qualitie of the exercise. 114

Cap. 30
Of the bodies which are to be exercised. 115

Cap. 31
Of the exercising places. 119

Cap. 32
Of the exercising time. 120

Cap. 33
Of the quantitie that is to be kept in exercise. 123

Cap. 34
Of the maner of exercising. 126

Cap. 35
An advertisement to the training maister. Why both the teaching of the minde, and the training of the bodie be assigned to the same maister. The inconveniences which ensue, where the bodie and soule be made particular subjectes to severall professions. That who so will execute anything well, must of force be fully resolved [2*3v] *of the excellency of his owne subject. Out of what kinde of writers the exercising maister may store himselfe with cunning. That the first groundes would be laid by the cunningest workeman. That private discretion in any executor is of more efficacie then his skill.* 128

Cap. 36
That both young boyes, and young maidens are to be put to learne. Whether all boyes be to be set to schoole. That to many learned be to burdenous: to few to bare: wittes well sorted civill, missorted seditious. That all may learne to write and read without daunger. The good of choice, and ill of confusion. The children which are set to learne, having either riche or poore freindes: what order and choice is to be used in admitting either of them to learne. Of the time to chuse. 137

Cap. 37
The meanes to restraine the overflowing multitude of scholers. The cause why everie one desireth to have his childe learned, and yet must yelde over his owne desire to the disposition of his countrie. That necessitie and choyce be the best restrayners. That necessitie restrayneth by lacke and lawe. Why it may be admitted, that all may write and read that can, but no further. What is to be thought of the speaking and understanding of Latine, and in what degree of learning that is. That considering our time and the state of religion in our time, lawe must needes helpe this restraint: with the answere to such objections as are made to the contrary. That in choice of wittes, which must deale with learning, that wit is fittest for our state, which answereth best the monarchie, and how such a wit is to be knowne. That choice is to helpe in scholing, in admission into colledges, in proceeding to degrees, in preferring to livinges, where the right and wrong of all the foure pointes be handled at full. 145

Cap. 38
That young maidens are to be set to learning, which is proved, by the custome of our countrey, by our duetie towardes them, by their naturall abilities, and by the worthy effectes of such as have bene well trained. The ende wherunto their education serveth, which is the cause why and how much they learne. Which of them are to learne, when they are to begin to learne. What and how much they may learne. Of whom and where they ought to be taught. 169

Cap. 39
Of the traning up of yong gentlemen. Of private and publike [2*4r] *education, with their generall goods and illes. that there is no better way for gentlemen to be trained by in any respect then the common is being well appointed. Of richmens children which be no gentlemen. Of nobilitie in*

generall. Of gentlemanlie exercises. What it is to be a nobleman, or a gentleman. That infirmities in noble houses be not to be triumphed over. The causes and groundes of nobilitie. Why so many desire to be gentlemen. That gentlemen ought to professe learning and liberall sciences for many good and honorable effectes. Of travelling into forraine countries: with all the braunches allowance and disallowance thereof: and that it were to be wished, that gentlemen would professe, to make sciences liberall in use, which are liberall in name. Of the trayning up of a yong Prince. 184

Cap. 40
Of the generall place, and time of education. Publike places, Elementarie, Grammaticall, Collegiate. Of bourding of children abroad from their parentes houses, and whether that be best. The use and commoditie of a large, and well situate training place. Observations to be kept in the generall time. 221

Cap. 41
Of teacher and trainers in generall, and that they be either Elementarie, Grammaticall, or Academicall. Of the Elementarie teachers abilitie, and entertainement. Of the Grammer maisters abilitie and his entertainment. A meane to have both excellent teachers, and cunning professors in all kindes of learning, by the division of colleges according to professions: by sorting like yeares into the same roumes: by bettering the studentes allowance and living: by providing and maintaining notable well learned readers. That for bringing learning forward in his right and best course, there would be seven ordinarie ascending colleges for Toungues, for Mathematikes, for Philosophie, for Teachers, for Physicians, for Lawyers, for Divines, and that the generall studie of Lawe would be but one studie: Every of these pointes with his particular proofes, sufficient for a position. Of the admission of teachers. 230

Cap. 42
How long the childe is to continue in the elementarie ear he passe to the toungues, and grammer. The incurable infirmities which posting hast worketh in the whole course of studie. How necessarie a thing sufficient time is for a scholer. 253 [2*4v]

Cap. 43
How to cut of most inconveniences wherwith schooles and scholers, mais-

ters and parentes be in our schooling now most troubled. Wherof there be two meanes, uniformitie in teaching and publishing of schoole orders. That uniformitie in teaching hath for companions dispatch in learning, and sparing of expenses. Of the abbridging of the number of bookes. Of curtesie and correction. Of schoole faultes. Of friendlinesse betwene parentes and maisters. 258

Cap. 44
That Conference betwene those which have interest in children: Certainetie of direction in places where children use most: and Constancie in well keeping that, which is certainely appointed, be the most profitable circumstances both for vertuous manering and cunning schooling. 277

Cap. 45
The peroration, wherin the summe of the whole booke is recapitulated and proofes used, that this enterprise was first to be begon by Positions, and these be the most proper to this purpose. A request concerning the well taking of that which is so well ment. 286

[1]

Positions Concerning the Training Up of Children.

First Chapter.

The entrie to the positions, conteining the occasion of this present discourse, and the causes why it was penned in English.

Whosoever shall consider with any judgement the maner of training up children, which we use generally within this Realme cannot but wish, that the thing were bettered, as I my selfe do: though I do not thinke it good here to displaie the particular defectes, bycause I am in hope to see them healed, without any so sharp a rehersall, (for the error being once graunted and well knowen straight way craveth helpe without aggravation, and that way in helping must needes be most gracious, which the partie helped confesseth least greivouse.) If I should discover all those inconveniences, wherby parentes and maisters, teachers and learners, do but enterchaunge displeasures, if I should rip up those difficulties, wherby the traine it selfe, and bringing up of children is marvellously empeached, I might revive great gaules, and even therby worse remedie the greifes. And though I remedied them yet the partie pacient might beare in minde, how churlishly he was cured, and though he payed well for the healing, [2] yet be ill apayd for the handling. Wherfore in helping thinges, that be amisse I do take that to be the advisedest way, which saveth the man, and sowreth not the meane. If without quoting the quarrelles, I set down that right, wherunto I am led, upon reasonable grounds, that it is both the best, and most within compasse, the wrong by comparison is furthwith bewraied, and the chek given without anie chiding.

The occasion of this discourse.

I have taught in publike without interrupting my course, now two and twentie yeares, and have alwaie had a very great charge under my hand, which how I have discharged, they can best judge of me, which will judge without me. During which time both by that, which I have seene in teaching so long, and by that which I have tryed, in training up so many, I do well perceive, upon such lettes, as both my selfe am subject unto, and other teachers no lesse then I, that neither I have don so much as I might, neither any of them so much as they could. Which lettes me thinke I have both learned, what they be, and withall conceived the meane, how to get them removed. Wherby both I and all other maie do much more good, then either I or anie other heretofore have don. Wherin as I meane to deale for the common good, so must I appeal to the common curtesie, that my good will maie be well thought of, though my good hope do not hit right. For I do but that, which is set free to all, to utter in publike a private conceit, and to claime kindnes of all, for good will ment unto all: as I my selfe am ready both freindly and favorably, to esteme of others, who shall enterprise the like, requiring every one, which shall use my travell, either as a reader, to peruse, or as a reaper to profit, that he will think well of me, which may cause him allow: or if he do not, that yet he will be sorie for me, that so good a meaning had so meane an issue.

Why it is penned in English.

I do write in my naturall English toungue, bycause though I make the learned my judges, which understand Latin, yet I meane good to the unlearned, which understand but English. And better it is for the learned to forbeare Latin, which they neede not, then for the unlearned to have it, which they know not. By the English both shall see, what I say, by Latin but the one, which were some wrong, where both have great interest, [3] and the unlearned the greater, bycause the unlearned have not any but only such English helpes, the learned can fetch theirs from the same fountaines, whence I fetch mine. My meaning is principally to helpe mine owne countrie, whose language will helpe me, to be understood of them, whom I would perswade: to get some thankes of them, for my good will to do well: to purchace pardon of them, if my good will do not well. The parentes and freindes with whom I have to deale, be mostwhat no latinistes: and if they were, yet we understand that tounge best, wherunto we are first borne, as our first impression is alwaie in

English, before we do deliver it in Latin. And in perswading a knowen good by an unknowen waie, are we not to cal unto us, all the helpes that we can, to be thoroughly understood? He that understands no Latin can understand English, and he that understands Latin very well, can understand English farre better, if he will confesse the trueth, though he thinke he have the habite, and can Latin it exceading well. When mine argument shall require Latin, as it will eare long, I will not then spare it, in the degree, that I have it, but till it do, I will serve my countrie that waie, which I do surely thinke will prove most intelligible unto her. For though the argument, which is dedicate to learning, and must therfore of force use the termes of learning: which be mysteries to the multitude, maie seeme to offer some darknes and difficultie in that point: yet it is to be construed, that the thing it selfe must be presented in her owne colours, which the learned can discry, at the first blush, as of their acquaintaunce, who must be spoken to in their owne kinde: as the unlearned must be content to enquire, bycause we straine our termes to have them intitled. And yet, in all my drift, for all my faire promise, I dare warrant my countrie no more, then probabilitie doth me, which if it deceive me, yet I have it to leane unto, and perhaps of such pith, as might easely have beguiled a wiser man then me. But till I prove beguiled, I will dwell in hope, that I am not, to deliver my minde with the better courage, and therby to shew that I thinke my selfe right. For the greatest enemy, that can be to any wel meaning conceit is, to mistrust his own power, and to dispaire of his good speede where happy fortune makes evident shew. [4]

Chapter 2.

Wherfore these positions serve, what they be, and how necessarie it was to begin at them.

My purpose is to helpe the hole trade of teaching, even from the very first foundation: that is, not only the Grammarian, and what shall follow afterward, but also the Elementarie, which is the verie infantes train, from his first entrie, untill he be thought fit to passe thence to the Grammar schoole. My labour then beginning so low, am I not to follow the president of such writers, as in the like argumentes, have used the like methode? The maner of proceding which the best learned authors do use, in those argumentes, which both for the matter be of most credit, and for the maner of best accompt, kepeth alwaie such a currant, as they at the first laie downe certaine groundes, wherin both they and their readers, whether scholers onely, or judges alone, do resolutely agree. Which consent enureth to this effect, that they maie therby either directly passe thorough to their ende without empeachment: or else if any difficulty do arise in the way, they may easely compound it, by retiring themselves to those primitive groundes. The Mathematicall, which is counted the best maister of sound method, of whome all other sciences do borow their order, and way in teaching well, eare he passe to any either probleme or theoreme, setts downe certaine definitions, certaine demaundes, certaine naturall and necessarie confessions, which being agreed on, betwen him and his learner, he proceedeth on to the greatest conclusions in his hole profession, as those which be acquainted with *Euclide* and his freindes, do verie wel know. Wil the naturall philosopher medle with his maine subject, before he have handled his first principles, matter, forme, privation, motion, time, place, infinitie, vacuitie, and such other, wherunto *Aristotle* hath dedicated eight whole bookes? What shall I neede to take more paines in rehersall of any other writer, whether Lawyer, Physician, or any else, which entreateth of his peculiar argument learnedly, to proove that I am first to plant by positions, seeing the verie divine himselfe, marcheth on of this foote and groundeth his religion upon [5] principles of beleefe? I professe my selfe to be a scholer, wherby I do know this methode, which the learned do kepe, and I deale with an argument, which must needes at the first be verie nicely entertained, till proofe give it credit, what countenaunce soever hope maie seeme to lend it, in the meane while. I maie therfore seeme to deale against mine owne knowledge, if I do not fortifie my selfe with such helpes, as upon probable reason, maie first purchace their owne standing, and being themselves staid in place of liking maie helpe up all the reste.

I am specially to further two degrees in learning, first the Elementarie which stretcheth from the time that the child is to be set to do any thing, till he be removed to his Grammar: then the Grammarian, while the child doth continew, in the schoole of language, and learned tounges, till he be removed for his ripenes, to some Universitie: which two pointes be both of great moment.

For the Elementarie: Bycause sufficiency in the child, before he passe thence, helpes the hole course of the after studie, and insufficiencie skipping from thence to soone, makes a very weake sequele. For as sufficient time there, without to much hast, to post from thence to timely, draweth on the residew of the schoole degrees, in their best beseeming time, and in the ende sendeth abroade sufficient men for the service of their countrie: so to hedlong hast scouring thence to swiftly at the first, (for all that it seemeth so petie a thing,) in perpetuall infirmity of matter, procureth also to much childishnes in yeares to be then in place, when judgement with skill, and ripenes with grayhaires should carie the contenaunce. And is not this pointe then to be well proyned, where hast is such a foe, and ripenes such a freind? Where pushing forward at the first before maturitie bid on, will still force that, which followeth till at the last it marre all?

For the Grammarian: As it is a thing not unseemely for me to deale in, being my selfe a teacher, so is it verie profitable for my countrie to heare of, which in great varietie of teaching doth seeme to call for some uniforme waie. And to have her youth well directed in the tounges, which are the waies to [6] wisdome, the lodges of learning, the harbours of humanitie, the deliverers of divinitie, the treasuries of all store, to furnish out all knowledge in the cunning, and all judgement in the wise, can it be but well taken, if it be well perfourmed? or can it but deserve some freindly excuse, yea though good will want good successe? If occasion fitly offered by the waie, cause me attempt any further thing then either of these two, though I may seeme to be beside my schoole, yet my trust is that I shal not seeme to be beside my selfe.

Now then dealing with these matters which appertaine to men, and must be allowed of men, if they deserve allowance, or wilbe rejected by them if they seeme not to be sound, whether have I neede to proceede with consent or no? For what if some shall thinke their penny good silver, and will not admit mine offer? neither receive teaching at the hand of so meane a controwler? what if some other graunt, that there is some thing amisse in deede, but that my devise is no meane to amend it? what if disdaine do worke me discredit, and why should he take upon him? A petie companion, I confesse, but till some better do deale, why may not my petinesse fullwell take place? And if the ware which I do bring, prove marchandable, why may I not make shew, and offer it to sale? Such instances and objections wilbe offered, with whom seeing I am like to encounter, why ought I not at the first to resolve those, which will relent at the voice of reason? and so entreat the other, which make more deintie, to be drawen on, as my deutie being discharged towardes the thing, by argumentes, towardes them, by curtesie, if there be any strayning afterwardes themselves may be in fault?

But bycause I must applie my positions to some one ground, I have chosen the Elementarie, and him rather then the Grammarian: for that the Elementarie is the verie lowest and first to be dealt with, and the circunstances being well applyed unto him, may with very small ado, be transported afterward to the Grammarian or anie other else. And under the title of the particular circunstance, (though it seeme peculiarly to appertaine to the Elementarie, by waie of mine example, which I do applie unto him primitively) yet I do travell commonly with [7] the generall considerations in all persons which use the same circunstance, in anie degree of learning, as the places themselves hereafter will declare. Which I do both to ende these positive arguments at once, and to make the precept also somwhat more pleasant to the reader, having the entertainement of some forreine, but no unfit discourse.

The positions.

The positions therfore which I do meane, be these and such other. At what time the child is to be set to schoole. What he is to learne when he is at schoole. Whether all be to be set to schoole. Whether exercise be to be used as a principle in trayning. Whether young maidens be to be set to learne. How to traine up young gentlemen. How to procure some uniformitie in teaching. Of curtesie and correction. Of private and publike education. Of choise of wittes, of places, of times, of teachers, of schoole orders. Of restrayning to many bookish people, and many other like argumentes, which the nature of such discourses useth to hale in by the waie. Wherin I require my countreymens consent, to thinke as I do, and will do mine endevour to procure it, as I can, before I deale with the particular praeceptes, and schooling of children. Which while I do, as I follow the praesident of the best writers, for the methode, which I chuse, so for the matter it selfe I will use no other argument, then both nature and reason, custome and experience, and plaine shew of evident profit shall recommend to my countrie, without either manifest appearaunce, or secrete suspicion of a fantasticall devise: considering it were an argument of verie small witte knowing fantasticallnes to disgrace the man, and impossibilitie to displace the meane: in so necessarie a thing as I pretend this to be, to entermingle either fantasticall matter, for all men to laugh at, or impossible meane, for as many to muse at. If earnest desier to have some thing bettered, do cause me wishe the amendement, I hope that will not be accounted fantasticall, unles it be to such, as do thinke themselves in health when they are deadly sicke, and feeling no paine, bycause of extreme weaknes, do hold their freindes halfe foolish, which wishe them to thinke upon alteration of life. [8]

Chapter 3.

Of what force circunstance is in matters of action, and how warily authorities be to be used, where the contemplative reason receives the check of the active circunstance, if they be not well applyed. Of the alleadging of authors.

Some well meaning man, when he will perswade his countrie to this or that thing, either by penne or speache, if he find any good writers authoritie, which favoreth his opinion, he presumeth streight waie therby both his owne perswasion to be sufficiently armed, and his countries execution to be strongly warrranted. Which his assuraunce is sometime chekt by wisdome, sometime by experience: By wisdome, which forseeth, that the circunstance of the countrie will not admit that, which he would perswade: by experience, which giving way at the first to some probability, is in the end borne back by unfitting circunstance. So that in those cases, where authorities perswade, and circunstances controwle, such as use writers for their credit, must feare circunstance for her chek. Bycause the misse in circunstance makes the authour no authour, where his reason is altered, and the alledger no alledger, where discretion wanteth. Seeing therfore my selfe deale with these two pointes of authoritie and circunstance, both to confirme mine owne opinion the surer, and to confute the contrarie sounder, where difference in opinion, shall offer to assaile me, I thought it good in the verie entrie to say somwhat of both, considering their agreement doth promise successe, and their disagreement doth threaten defeat.

I do see many very toward wittes, of reasonable good reading, and of excellent good utteraunce, both forreine abroad, and freindes at home marveilously overshoot themselves by overruling the circunstance, and overstraining authoritie. For upon some affiaunce in their owne wittes, that they see all circunstances, and some small assuraunce, that the authours which they reade, do soothe all that they say: they will push out in publike certaine resolute opinions, before either their wittes be setled, or their reading ripe: which is then to be thought wisely ripe, when after the benefit of many yeares, after much [9] reading of the most and best writers, after sound digesting of that, which they have red, and applying it all to some certaine ende: time hath fined their judgement, and by precise observing and comparing, both what others have said, and what themselves have seene, hath made them maister the circunstance. Which mastering of the circunstance, is the only rule, that wisemen live by, the only meane, that wisedome is come by, the only ods betwen folie and witte. The marking wherof is of so great a force, as by it eche countrie discovereth the travellour, when he seeketh to enforce his forreine conclusions, and clingeth to that countryman, which hath bettered her still, by biding still at home. It discrieth the young student, which is ravished with the object, eare he can discern it, and honoreth the wise learned, whose understanding is so staied, as he may be a leader. The consideration of circunstance is so strong in all attemptes, where man is the subject, as it maketh of all nothing, and of nothing all. The skill to judge of it is so lingring, and so late, bycause man is the gatherer, and so long eare he learne it, as it seemes to be reserved, till he be almost spent. It is not enough to rule the world, to alleadge authorities, but to raunge authorities, which be not above the world, by the rule of the world, is the wisemans line.

I am to deale with training, must I entreat my countrey to be content with this, bycause such a one commendes it? or to force her to it, bycause such a state likes it? The shew of right deceives us, and the likenes of unlike thinges doth lead us, where it listeth. Differences and ods discover errors, similitude and likenes lead even wise men awrie. The great philosopher *Aristotle* in fining of reason, maketh the abilities to discerne these two pointes, where thinges like be unlike, and where the unlike be like, two of his prin-

1. Topic. de 4. instrumentis Dial.

cipall instrumentes to trie out the trueth. Which skill to discern so narrowly, as it is not in all, so where it is, there is great discretion, there will nothing be brought from authoritie to practise, but that circunstance will praise, and yet hardly winne. For though circunstance in our countrie and others do seeme verie like, nay rather almost one, yet if our countrie do admit, where any ods appeareth, though it offer the relenting, when it comes to proufe, she aventureth [10] her selfe, and we which perswade, have great cause to thanke her, that she will harken unto us, as she also will thanke us, if she praise at the parting. Wherfore seeing the ground is so slipperie to deale by authoritie, and therfore to approve it, bycause such a one sayth it, till judgement have subsigned, and circunstance sealed, I thought it good, as I said before, to speake somwhat therof, that I may therby stay my selfe the better, marching by them, and thorough them: and also remove some scrupulouse opinion, that I use them not strangely, when I use them so, as they wishe themselves to be used.

But for the better understanding, with what warynes authoritie is to be used, may it please you to consider, that there be two sortes of authours wherwith we deale in our studie: wherof the one regardeth the matter only, and by inevitable argument enforceth the conclusion. In this kinde be the Mathematicall sciences, and all such naturall philosophie, as proceedeth by necessitie of a demonstrable subject. The other joyneth the circunstance with the matter, as Morall, and politike Philosophie, as the Professions, as Poetes, as histories do, when they enforce not the necessitie of their conclusion, by necessitie of the matter, though by the fourme of their argument, which concludeth of force, in matters of least force. The argumentes of those Artes and Professions, which be in this second kinde, do depende upon apparence in probable conjecture, and be creatures to circunstance, wherin as man is the mainest subjecte, so the respectes had to man have the raine in their hand.

Hence commeth it that lawes in severall landes do differ so much, that Phisicke in severall subjectes is so severall in cure, that Divinitie in ceremonies admitteth change, where the circunstance is observed, and yet the truth not tainted.

Hence it commeth that in diversitie of states, there be diversities of staie, whereby men governe, bycause circunstance commaundeth. Wherunto, he that affirmes, must still have an eye, bycause it sheweth, what is seemely and convenient, not in great states alone, but also in the meanest thinges of all: bycause it moderateth both what soever men do: and in what soever respect they do. In the first kinde of authours and authorities, [11] the truth of the matter maintaines it selfe, without he said or he did: bycause it is true by nature, which staied it, not by authour which said it. And being so setled, it ministreth of it selfe no matter to debate, or at the least verie litle. For in pointes of necessitie, naturally inferred, the difference of opinion is no proufe at all, that the matter is debatable, but it is a sufficient argument of an insufficient writer, if he penne his opinion, or of an ungrounded learner, if his error be in speeche, which harpeth still about some outward accident, and never perceth the inward substance. So that in such conclusions there is but one currant, what forceth the matter, and not what sayeth the man: what commandes the immutable truth, and not what commendes the changeable circunstance. All the controversie is in the second kinde, where circunstance is prescription, wherin the writers credite oftimes authoriseth the thing, and the truth of the thing doth make the man an authour: wherin unles he take verie good heede, which is the alleadger, he may do his writer exceeding great injurie, by bringing him to the barre, and forcing that upon him, which he never dreamed on, and harme himselfe to, who mistaking his ground, misplaceth his building, and hazardeth his credit.

Hence commeth it, that so many fantasticall devises do trouble the world, while everie man being desirous to breede somwhat worthy of commendacion either for shew of learning, or for shield of opinion, bringeth in the poore writers, and enjoyneth them speach, where in deed they be mute: and if they could speake, they would aske the alledger why he did so abuse them. A generall and a verie hard case in these our dayes, when the most erronious opinions be fathered upon the most honest writers, which meant nothing lesse, then that which is threpte upon them. In matter of Pollicy this man wrote thus, and was verie well thought of, an other in some schoole pointes gave his censure in this sorte, and became of account. Transport the circunstance the allowance is misliked, the alleadger laughed at: and yet the worthinesse of the writer not empayred at all, when he is rightly weyed, bycause he was forced: In this kinde of argument wherin I presently deale, it is no proufe, bycause *Plato* praiseth it, bycause *Aristotle* alloweth [12] it, bycause

Cicero commendes it, bycause *Quintilian* is acquainted with it, or any others else, in any argument else, that therfore it is for us to use. What if our countrey honour it in them, and yet for all that may not use it her selfe, bycause circunstance is her check? Nay what if the writers authoritie be alledged without consideration of their owne circunstance? who then offereth his countrey the greatest wrong? is it not he which wringeth the writer, and wreasteth his meaning? And yet such alledgers there be, which passe it over smoothly, till they be espyed, where then their owne weaknes appeareth, the writers worthinesse is evident, and his wrong revénged, by discovering the wreaster. Wherfore he that will deale with writers so, as to derive their conclusions to the use of his countrey, must be verie well advised, and diligently marke, that their meaning, and his applying be both of one ground, and also how much of their opinion his countrey will admit, which, as she will not be forced by idle supposalles, so pronounceth she him to be but a fleeter, who so ever shall offer to force her that waye. If the matter be well pikt, and properly applyed, she embraceth it forthwith, and gives it the growing. Whether I shall perfourme so much my selfe, as I require in others, I dare not warrant, but I will do my best, to use my authour well, and to observe the circunstance, and not once to profer any thing to my countrey, which shall not have all those foundations, that I promised before, so much as I can, *Nature* to lead it, *reason* to back it, *custome* to commend it, *experience* to allow it, and *profit* to preferre it.

For alledging of Authours.

But here by the waye, I must advertise my reader thus much, that I thinke a student ought rather to invest himselfe in the habite of his writer, then to stand much upon his title, and authoritie, in proofe or disproofe, seeing who knoweth not, that all our studies be generally detters to the first devise, and fairest deliverie? Therfore to avoide length therby, I will neither use authoritie, nor example, seeing matter is the maine, and not the mans name, saving onely where one mans deposition upholdes or overthrowes: and the ground of the example is so excellent in that kinde, as it were to much unkindenesse, not to let the person be knowen, where the fact [13] is so famous. I wil reste upon reason the best, where I finde it, the next where that failes, and conjecture is probable, to prove such thinges, as reason must paterne. If the triall be in proofe, and experience must guide it, I will binde upon proofe, and let triall be the tuche.

For with the alledging of authours, either to shew, what I have read or to tuche common concordes, where any thing is to much, and nothing is enough, I meane not at all to buisie my selfe. Bycause we heape but up witnesses, which be nothing needefull, in such cases, as be nothing doubtfull, when we use many gaie names all agreeing in one, and none saying but so: wheras the naturall use of testimonies is, to prove where doubt is, not to cloye, where all is cleare. In such cases for want of sound judgement, a catalogue of names, and a multitude of sentences, which say but that is soothed, and no man denyes, are forced to the stage, to seeme to arme the alleadger, which fighteth without foe, and flyeth without feare.

In pointes of learning, which be wonne from quarrell, or resolute groundes, which be without quarrell, and neede no assurer, I referre my dealing to the judgement of those, which can trace me, where I tread, and shall finde my truth, without the authours name, whom they will confesse to be well alleadged, when I saye, as he sayeth, and prove as he proveth, either by habite got by reading, or by likenesse in judgement, though I never red.

If controversie arise, and be worth the recounting the matter shall not sleepe: if it hange of the man, and without him be lame, the man shall not slyp: but otherwise, no. Those that be learned know that witnesses, and wise mens names be verie good ware, where the question is, whether such a thing be done, and they be said to know it, and that *Rhetorick* takes testimonies for a principall proofe, and verie neare the harte, as *Logick* placeth them in the outmost of her argumentes, being themselves of small pith, though their stuffe be worth praise, and both bind and loose, where reason beares the swaie, and probabilitie is to purpose. I do honour good writers but without superstition, nothing addicte to titles. But for so much as *Reason* doth honour them, they must be content [14] to staie without them selves, and use all meanes to preferre her to presence, as their ladie and mistresse, whose authoritie and credit procures them admission, when they come from her. It is not so, bycause a writer said so, but bycause the truth is so, and he said the truth, the truth gives him title, and that is it, which must passe, strong enough of it selfe, and oftimes weakned in the hearers opinion, though not in it selfe, by naming the writer: which commonly proves so when the hearer is wedded unto names, and sworn to authoritie, not so much eying the thing which is uttered, as the persons title by whom it is uttered. If truth did depend upon the person, she would oftimes be brought into a miserable plighte, and looke rufully upon it, being constrained to serve fansie, and to alter upon will, wheras she is still one, and should be bent unto, neither will her selfe bend, howsoever opinative people do perswade them selves.

This the learned and wise know, whose curtesie I crave, as I wish them well: for whose helpe and health, I undertooke this paine, whose wisedom I appeal to, if either diffidence do wrangle, or ignoraunce do quarrell. As for the unlearned, I must needes overtreat them, not to stand with me in pointes, where they cannot judge themselves, if not for mine owne, yet for their sakes, which beleve me themselves, and will give their word for me. In such pointes, as be intelligible to both, I must praie them both to waie me well, and ever to have before them, that my will wisheth well, howsoever I perfourme, wherin will deserves well, and weaknes prayeth excuse.

Chapter 4.

What time were best for the child to begin to learne. What matters some of the best writers handle, eare they determine this question. Of lettes and libertie wherunto the parentes are subject in setting their children to schoole. Of the difference of wittes and bodies in children. That exercise must be joyned with the booke, as the schooling of the bodie.

The first question that of any necessitie commeth in place, seemeth to be at what yeares children be to be put to schoole: for neither would they be differred to long for leasing [15] of their time, nor hastened on to soone, for hindering of their health. The rule therfore must be given according to the strength of their bodies, and the quiknes of their wittes joyntly.

The auncient antecedents.

Such of the auncient writers, both Greek and Latin, as either picture us out the platfourmes of the best framed common weales: or do lend us the looking on of some such a paragon as in some particular kinde, they devise to be peerelesse, before they call it in question, when their youth shall begin to learne, they do fetch the ground of their traine exceeding farre of. As, what regard is to be had to the infante, while he is yet under his nurse. Where they moile themselves sore, with the maners and conditions of the nurse, with the fines or rudenes of her speeche: with the comelynes of her person and favour of her face. And in controversie about milkes, sometime they preferre the mother, if her health, her complexion, her kinde of life, will best fit for her owne: sometime they yeeld: but with great choice to the forreine nurse: if any just circunstance do discharge the mother, whom nature unletted seemes to charge most. Againe they examine what companie is to be choosen for him, when he doth begin first to crepe abroad, wherby that good may begin betimes, which must continew longe, and is greatly furthered by choice of companie, that pikked and choice play fellowes may succede after a fine and well fitted nursery. Againe, they debate in good sadnes, what an exquisite traine is to be devised for him, when he is to go to schoole, either private, or publike, though they still preferre the publike as most beseeming him, which must live among many and never be recluse. And such other considerations they fall into, which do well beseeme the bringing up of such a one, as they did but wishe for: and we may not hope for: but by no meanes can be applyed to our youth, and our education, wherin we wishe for no more, then we hope for to have. Nay they go further, as whether may not wishers? and appoint the parentes of this so perfect a child, to be so wise and so well learned, as is in verie deede most consonant with their platte, but to farre surmonting the modele of my positions. Wherfore leaving those meanes, which they do but devise, to bring up those people, which they do but patterne, I meane to proceede [16] from such principles, as our parentes do build on, and as our children do rise by, to that mediocritie, which furnisheth out this world, and not to that excellencie, which is fashioned for an other. And yet the pretence of these so fine picturers, by pointing out so absolute a president, is, to let us behold thereby, both wherin the best consisteth: what colours it is best knowen by: what a state it keepeth: and also by what ready meane, we may best approche neare it, bycause dispaire to obtaine the verie best it selfe, discourageth all hope. For that missinge any one of these so fined circunstances, as our frailtie will faile either in all, or in most, then we marre the whole moulde. Howbeit we are much bounde to the excellent wittes of those divine writers, who by their singular knowledge, approching neare to the truest, and best, could most truly, and best discern, what constitution they were of: and being of a good civill inclination, thought it their parte, to communicate that with their posteritie, which they from so nighe, had so narrowly decifred, as available to others; for this onely cause, if there ensewed no more of it, that in despaire of hitting the highest, yet by seeing where it lodged, with verie great praise, they might draw neare unto it. For as it is but for paragons to mount quite above all, so is it worthy praise to rest in some degree, which declareth a pearcher, though abilitie restraine will, that it cannot aspire wherunto it would.

But to returne from this so exquisite, to our ordinarie traine, I perswade my selfe, that all my countreymen wishe themselves as wise, and as well learned, as those absolute parentes are surmised to be, though they be content with so much of both, or rather with so litle, as God doth allot them: and that they will have their children nursed as well as they can, without question where, or quarrelling by whom: so as they may have that well brought up by nurture, which they love so well, bequeathed them by nature. And that till the infant can governe himselfe, they will seeke to save it from all such perilles, as may seeme to harme it any kinde of way, or by companie or by occasion: and that with such warinesse, as ordinarie circunspection may, or can worke, in considerate and carefull parentes. And finally that for his well schooling, they that cannot, will [17] wish it, they that can, will have it, with small charge if they may, if they may not with some coste, and very carefully commend the silly poore boy at his first entry, to his maisters charge, not omitting even how much his mother makes of him, if she come not her selfe and do her owne commendacions. So that for these antecedents, as they in precisenes do passe us, so we in possibility go farre beyond them. For our hope is at ankar, and rides in assuraunce, their wishe wandereth still, not like to win the rode. These and such like circunstances they handle formally as in an absolute picture, I tuche but by the waye, as being quite of an other perswasion, nothing given to the unpossible, where possibilitie must take place, though the unpossible *Idaea*, offer great force to fansie. Wherfore I will now take my leave of them, and retourne to my question, when children be to be set to learning. A thing in reason very worthy to be wayed, and in perfourmaunce, very like to prove good, both for health of the bodie, and helpe of the minde, and so much the rather to be well entreated, bycause it is the very first principle, which enterteneth our traine. My countrey parentes then, being so naturall to their children, both for care before schoole, and for choice in schooling, I will commend to their charge, all that, which is to be considered in their first infancie, and tendrest spring, before they be thought fit, to be set to learning, which they will diligently looke to, I am very well assured. Bycause every thing drawes liking, while it is pretie and young, and specially our owne which hath nature to sollicite, and needeth no exhorting, to have it well cherished, where there is no daunger, but in to much dalying, neither yet any feare, but in to fond cokkering.

Lettes.

But in very good earnest, when shall our boye be set to schoole? In all considerations, wherin upon the resolution, something must be executed, and done, this thing is necessarily to be first enquired, whether all, or most, or any of all the circunstances, which be incident to the execution, be in, or without the parties power, which is to execute, so as he may either proceede at his owne libertie, if nothing withstand him, or may not proceede, if he be thwarted by circunstance. For otherwise the liberty to passe on, or the restraint, to staie, being not agreed [18] upon, he that directs by rule may be chekt by arrest. And where he biddes on thus, circunstance maye replie, Ifayth sir no. Wherfore I leave those parentes to their owne discretion, in whom will seekes libertie, to do as she would, and circunstance commandes her, to do as she may. The parent would have his child begin to learne at such a time: circunstance sayes, no. He would have him learne with such a man: some cause contrarieth. In such a place, in such a sorte: his power is to poore, to compasse that he coveteth. Be not all these lettes, and what so ever is so laid, to stop will of his will, where neither counsell can give precept, nor the parent can execute, being so strongly overcharged? It is even like, as if one should saye, the freeman and the bond, be not both in one case. Preceptes be for freemen, which maie do as ye bid them, but circunstance bindes, and wilbe obeyed. Wherfore I must once for all, warne those parentes, which may not do as they would, upon these same lettes which I have recited, or any other like, that they take their oportunitie, when so ever it is offered, bycause occasion is verie bald behind, and seldome comes the better. And seeing circunstance is their bridle, when they feele the raine loose, course it on a maine, and take the benefit of time, the oportunitie of place, the commoditie of the teacher, the equitie of the maner, and what so ever condition else, wherin the freedom of circunstance doth seeme to befreind them. For saving with such a note as this is, I cannot direct them, which can give no counsell, but where *necessitie* is in ward, and *libertie* keepes the keyes.

Libertie.

But if the parent want nothing necessary, for his childes bringing up, neither a place, both convenient for receit, and commodious for distaunce, wherin to have him taught: nor a teacher, sufficient for cunning, and considerate, for either curtesie, or correction, who can traine him up well: nor fit companions, as so fit a place, and so good a maister may picke out of choice, which will throng unto him: And if the child also himselfe, have a witte apte to conceive, what shalbe put unto him: and a body able to beare the travell, which belonges unto learning: me thinke it were then best, that he began to be doing, when he maie well perceive, without travelling his [19] braine, thorough the hardnes of the thing, and neede not be toiled to the wearines of his bodie, thorough the wise handling, of his advised maister. For being in the schoole, he may do somwhat very well, though not very much, wheras roming about, he might hap to do ill, and that very much.

Variety of wittes.

At what yeares I cannot say, bycause ripenes in children, is not tyed to one time, no more then all corne is ripe for one reaping, though mostwhat about one. Some be hastinges and will on, some be hardinges, and draw backe: some be willing when their parentes will: some but willing, when they will them selves, as either will to do well, upon cherishing wisely, or pleasure to play still, upon cokkering fondly, hath possessed their mindes.

But he that deserveth to be a parent, must dispose himselfe to be also a judge, in all these cases: and who is so ill freinded, as he hath not one, with whom to conferre, to learne by advise, the towardnes and time of his young sonnes schooling, if he be not able to looke into it himselfe? They that limitte the beginning to learne by some certaine yeares, have an eye to that knowledge, which it were pitie were loste, say they, and may easely be gayned in those young yeares. I agree with them, that it were great pitie, to lease any thing, that neede not be loste, without great negligence, and may be well gotten, with very small diligence, not endammaging the child. But more pitie it were, for so petie a game, to forgoe a greater, to winne an houre in the morning, and lease the whole daie after: as those people most commonly do, which start out of their beds to early, before they be well awaked: or knowe what it is a clocke: and be drousie when they are up, for want of their sleepe.

If the childe have a weake bodie, though never so strong a witte, let him grow on the longer, till the strength of his bodie, do aunswere to his witte. For experience hath taught me, and calleth reason to record, that a sharp young witte hastened on to wounder at, for the quiknesse of his edge, hath therby most commonly bene hastened to his grave, thorough the weaknesse of body: to the greife of the freindes, whose delite is cut of, and some wite of their witte, for overhasting their child: Nay, what if it hath pleased God to lend him longer [20] life? he never sinketh deepe, but fleeteth still above, with some quicknesse of conceit, continuing that wonder, which he wanne in his childhood: never burdened with much to ballase his head: but still aunswering at reboundes, the fairest crop of so hasty an harvest. Sometime his witte will grow worse, the wonder will vanishe, the bodie will prove feeble, and soone after perishe.

But now if he live, with all these infirmities, of decaying witte, decreasing wonder, puling bodie, he lives with small comfort, in such a world of weaknesse, which usually commeth of to much moisture, the corrupter of such carcasses, the most vile, and violent massacrer, of the most, and best studentes, generally for want of travell, saving onely to their braine, which the more it is occupyed, the sorer it stilleth, and the sorer it stilleth, the sooner it killeth, the moe the more pitie. Wherefore I could wishe the wittier childe, the lesse upon the spurre, and either the longer kept from learning, for turning his edge, as a to sharp knife: or the sklenderer kept at it, for feare of surfait, in one hungring to have it. Yet must not this quickling be suffered to do nothing at all, for feare he grow reasty, if that nothing be dumpishe, and heavie: or passe beyond reclaime, if it be dissolute, and wanton.

The meane conceiver, in some strength of bodie, is the best continuer, and as he serves all places best, in his height of learning, so in all respectes, ye may venture on his schooling, when it shall please you, with but ordinarie regard.

A dull witte in a strong body, if ye like to have it learne, as by learning ye finde it: so till some degree, it may well learne, for necessarie service in the rest of his life: and may be hastened on boldly. For the bodie can beare labour, it is so well boaned, and the witte will not cloye, it so hardly receiveth. The sharpenesse of witte, the maister will sound by memorie, and number: the strength of the bodie, the mother will marke, by complaint, and cause.

A weake witte and as weake a bodie, is much to be moaned, for the great infirmity, and can hardly be helpt, bycause nature is to weake: and therfore it must be thought on, as in a case of despaire, againe against hope: if any thing be goten, [21] a greife to the freindes, which cannot amend it: small joye to him selfe, which cannot avoide it.

A strong witte, in as strong a bodie, is worthy the wishing, of the parentes to bring foorth, of the teacher to bring up. For as it is a thing of it selfe not ordinarie, so where it lighteth, it gives us the gaze, and bides all beginninges, but that which is to soone, bycause God hath provided that strength in nature, wherby he entendes no exception in nurture, for that which is in nature. Such spirites there be, and such bodies they have, if they will, and may so keepe them, with orderly regard, which is extreme hard unto them. For that oftimes they will not do so, but distemper their bodies with disordinate doinges, when pleasures have possessed them, and rashenesse is their ruler. Oftimes they maie not, thorough varietie and weight of important affaires, which commaundeth them too farre in some kinde of calling. But where so ever they light, or what so ever waye they take, they shewe what they be, and alwaye prove either the verie best, or the most beastly. For there can scantly be any meane in those constitutions, which are so notably framed, and so rarely endued. And therefore those parentes which have such children must take great heede of them, as the tippes of evill, if they chuse that waye, or the toppes of good, if they minde that is best. For the middle and most moderate wittes, which commonly supplie eche corner in eche countrey, and serve most assaies, some ordinary meane will serve to order them: but where extraordinarie pointes begin to appeare, there common order is not commonly enough.

This is my opinion concerning the time, when the child shall begin to learne: which I do restraine to the strength of witte and hardnes of body: the one for to receive learning the other not to refuse labour: and therfore I conclude thus that the parent himselfe ought in reason to be more then halfe a judge of the entrie to schooling, as being best acquainted with the particular circunstance of his owne child. Yet I do not allow him to be an absolute judge, without some counsell, unlesse he be a very rare father, and well able to be both a rule to himselfe, and a paterne to others. Bycause mostwhere men [22] be most blinded: where they should see best, I meane in their owne: such a tyrant is affection, when she hath wonne the field, under the conducte of nature, and so imperious is nature, when she is disposed to make affection her deputie.

Exercises. But now for so much as in setting our child to schoole, we consider the strength of his bodie, no lesse then we do the quicknesse of his witte, it should seeme that our traine ought to be double, and to be applyed to both the partes, that the body may aswell be preserved in his best, as the minde instructed in that, which is his best, that the one may still be able to aunswere the other well, in all their common executions. As for the training up of the minde, the waye is well beaten, bycause it is generally entreated on in every booke, and beareth the honour and title of learning.

But for the bettering of the body, is there not any meane to maintaine it in health, and cheifly in the student, whose trade treads it downe? Yes surely, A very naturall and a healthfull course there is to be kept in exercise, wherby all the naturall functions of the body be excellently furthered, and the body made fit for all his best functions. And therfore parentes and maisters ought to take such a waie, even from the beginning, as the childes diet, neither stuffe the bodye, nor choke the conceit, which it lightly doeth, when it is to much crammed. That his garmentes which oftimes burden the bodie with weight, sometimes weaken it with warmth, neither faint it with heat, nor freese it with cold. That the exercise of the body still accompanie and assist the exercise of the minde, to make a dry, strong, hard, and therfore a long lasting body: and by the favour therof to have an active, sharp, wise and therwith all a well learned soule. If long life be the childes blessing for honoring his parentes, why should not the parentes then, which looke for that honour, all that in them lyeth, forsee in youth that their children may have some hope of that benefit, to ensue in their age, which cannot take effect, unlesse the thing be begon in their youth? Which if it be not by times looked unto, they afterwardes become uncapable of long life, and so not to enjoye the reward of their honour, for any thing that their parentes helpe to it, though God will be true, and perfourme that [23] he promiseth, how so ever men hault in doing of their duetie.

And yet tempting is pernicious, where the meane to hit right, is laid so manifest: and the childes honour to his parentes beginnes at obedience in his infancie, which they ought to reward, with good qualities for honour, and may worke them like waxe, bycause they do obey. This negligence of the parentes for not doing that, which in power they might, and in duetie they ought, gives contempt in the children some colour of justice, to make their requitall with dishonour in their age, were it not that the Christian religion doth forbid revenge: which in presidentes of prophanisme we finde allowed, where both curtesie to such parentes, as failed in education of their children is countercharged by lawe: and dissolute parentes by entreating ill, are well entertained of their neglected children: the unfortunate children much moaned for their chaunce, that they came to so ill an ende: and the undiscrete parentes more rated for their charge, which they looked so ill to, wherby themselves did seeme to have forced such an ende.

The minde wilbe stirring, bycause it stirres the body, and some good meane will make it to furnish very well, so the choice be well made, wherin: the order well laid, wherby: and both well kept, wherwith: it shalbe thought best trained. The body which lodgeth a restlesse minde by his owne reste is betrayed to the common murtherers of a multitude of scholers, which be unholesome and superfluous humors, needelesse and noysom excrementes, ill to feele within, good to send abroad.

Neither is it enough to saye, that children wilbe stirring alwaie of themselves, and that therefore they neede not any so great a care, for exercising their bodies. For if by causing them learne so and sitting still in schooles, we did not force them from their ingenerate heat, and naturall stirring, to an unnaturall stilnesse, then their owne stirring without restraint, might seeme to serve their tourne, without more adoe. But stilnesse more then ordinarie, must have stirring more then ordinarie: and the still breding of ill humours, which stuffe up the body for want of stirring, must be so handled, as it want no stilling to send them away. Wherfore as stilnesse hath her direction by order in schooles, so must stirring be directed by well appointed [24] exercise. And as quiet sitting helpes ill humors to breede, and burden the bodie: so must much stirring make a waie to discharge the one, and to disburden the other. Both which helpes, as I most earnestly require at the parent, and maisters hand: so I meane my selfe to handle them both, to the helping of both.

In the meane while, for the entring time thus much. The witte must be first wayed, how it can conceive, and then the bodie considered, how it can beare labour: and the consorte of their strength advisedly maintained. They have both their peculiar functions, which by mediocrities are cherished, by extremities perished, hast doing most harme, even to the most, and lingring not but some, sometimes to the best. And yet haste is most harmefull, where so ever, it setts foote, as we that teache alwaie finde, and they that learne, sometimes feele. For the poore children when they perceive their owne weaknesse, whereof most commonly they maye thanke haste, they both faint, and feare, and very hardly get forward: and we that teach do meet with to much toile, when poore young babes be committed to our charge, before they be ripe. Whom if we beat we do the children wrong in those tender yeares to plant any hatred, when love should take roote, and learning grow by liking.

And yet oftimes severitie is to sowre, while the maister beateth the parentes folly, and the childes infirmitie, with his owne furie. All which extremities some litle discretion would easely remove, by conference before, to forecast what would follow, and by following good counsell, when it is given before. Which will then prove so, when the parent will do nothing in placing or displacing of his childe, without former advise, and communicating with the maister: and the maister likewise without respecting his owne gaine, will plainely and simply shew the parent or freind, what upon good consideration he thinketh to be best. Wherein there wilbe no error if the parent be wise, and the maister be honest.

Chapter 5.

What thinges they be, wherin children are to be trained, eare they passe to the Grammar. That parentes, and maisters ought [25] *to examine the naturall abilities in their children, wherby they become either fit, or unfit, to this, or that kinde of life. The three naturall powers in children,* Witte *to conceive by,* Memorie *to retaine by,* Discretion *to discerne by. That the training up to good manners, and nurture, doth not belong to the teacher alone, though most to him, next after the parent, whose charge that is most, bycause his commaundement is greatest, over his owne child, and beyond appeale. Of* Reading, Writing, Drawing, Musick *by voice, and instrument: and that they be the principall principles, to traine up the minde in. A generall aunswere to all objections, which arise against any, or all of these.*

Now that I have shewed mine opinion concerning the time, when it were best to set the child to schoole, the next two questions seeme to be, what he shall learne and how he shalbe exercised, when he is at schoole. For seeing he is compound of a soule and a bodie: the soule to conceive and comprehend, what is best for it selfe, and the bodie to: The bodie to waite, and attend the commaundement and necessities of the soule: he must be so trained, as neither for qualifying of the minde, nor for enabling of the bodie, there be any such defecte, as just blame therfore may be laide upon them, which in nature be most willing, and in reason thought most skilfull, to prevente such defaultes. For there be both in the body, and the soule of man certaine ingenerate abilities, which the wisedom of parentes, and reason of teachers, perceiving in their infancie, and by good direction avancing them further during those young yeares, cause them prove in their ripenesse very good and profitable, both to the parties which have them, and to their countries, which use them. Which naturall abilities, if they be not perceived, by whom they should: do condemne all such, either of ignoraunce, if they could not judge, or of negligence, if they would not seeke, what were in children, by nature emplanted, for nurture to enlarge. And if they be perceived, and either missorted in place, or ill applyed in choice, as in difference of judgementes, there be many thinges practised, which were better unproved, to the losse of good time, and let of better stuffe, they do bewray that such teachers, [26] and trainers, be they parentes, be they maisters, either have no sound skill, if it come of infirmitie, or but raw heades, if it spring of fansie. If they know the inclination, and do not further it rightely, it is impietie to the youth, more then sacrilege to the state, which by their fault be not suffered to enjoy those excellent benefits, which the most munificent God, by his no niggardishe nature, provided for them both. If they found them, and followed them, but not so fully, as they were to receive: if for want wherwith, it deserves pardon, if for want of will, exceeding blame: and cryeth for correction of the state by them hindred, and small thankes of the parties, no more furthered.

Wherfore as good parentes, and maisters ought to finde out, by those naturall principles, wherunto the younglings may best be framed, so ought they to follow it, until it be complete, and not to staie, without cause beyond staie, before it come to ripenesse, which ripenesse, while they be in learning, must be measured by their ablenes to receive that, which must follow their forebuilding: but when they are thought sufficiently well learned, and to meddle with the state, then their ripenesse is to be measured, by use to themselves, and service to their countrey, in peace, as best and most naturall, in warre, as worse, and most unnaturall, and yet the ordinarie ende of a disordered peace. For when the thinges, which be learned do cleave so fast in memorie, as neither discontinuaunce can deface them, nor forgetfulnesse abolishe them: then is abilitie upon ascent, and when ascent is in the highest, and the countrey commaundes service, then studie must be left, and the countrey must be served.

Seeing therfore in appointing the matter, wherin this traine must be employed, there is regard to be had first to the soule, as in nature more absolute, and in value more precious: and then to the bodie, as the instrument and meane, wherby the soule sheweth what is best to be done in necessity of fine force, in choice of best shew: I will remitte the bodie to his owne roome, which is peculiarly in exercises, saving where I cannot meane the soule, without mention of the bodie, and in this place I wil entreat of the soule alone, how it must be qualified. [27] And yet meane I not to make any anatomie, or resolution of the soule his partes and properties, a discourse, not belonging to this so low a purpose, but onely to pick out some natural inclinations in the soule, which as they seeme to crave helpe of education, and nurture, so by education, and nurture, they do prove very profitable, both in private and publicke. To the which effect, in the litle young soules, first we finde, a capacity to perceive that which is taught them, and to imitate the foregoer. That witte to learne, as it is led, and to follow as it is foregone, would be well applyed, by proprietie in matter, first offered them to learne: by considerate ascent in order, encreasing by degrees: by wary handling of them, to draw them onward with courage. We finde also in them, as a quickenes to take, so a fastnesse to retaine: therfore their memorie would streight waye be furnished, with the verie best, seeing it is a treasurie: exercised with the most, seeing it is of receite: never suffered to be idle, seeing it spoiles so soone. For in defaulte of the better, the worse will take chaire, and bid it selfe welcome: and if idlenesse enter, it will exclude all earnest, and call in her kinsfolkes, toyes and triffles, easie for remembraunce, heavy for repentaunce.

We finde in them further an ability to discern, what is good, and what is ill, which ought foorthwith to be made acquainted with the best, by obedience and order, and dissuaded from the worse, by misliking and frowne. These three thinges, witte to take, memorie to kepe, discretion to discern, and moe if ye seeke, though but braunches to these, which I chuse for my purpose, shall ye finde pearing out of the litle young soules: when you may see what is in them, and not they themselves. Whose abilitie to encrease in time, and infirmitie to crawle at that time is commended to them, which first begot them, or best can frame them. Now these naturall towardnesses being once espied, in what degree they rise, bycause there is ods in children by nature, as in parentes by purchace, they must be followed with diligence, encreased by order, encouraged by comfort, till they come to their proofe. Which proofe travell in time will perfourme, hast knittes up to soone, and unperfit, slownesse to late, and to weake.

But for the best waie of their good speede, that witte maie [28] conceive and learne well, memorie retaine and hold fast, discretion chuse and discerne best, the cheife and chariest point is, so to plie them all, as they may proceede voluntarily, and not with violence, that will may be a good boye, ready to do well, and lothe to do ill, never fearing the rod, which he will not deserve. For wheresoever will in effecting, doth joyne with abilitie to conceive, and memorie to retaine, there industrie will finde frute, yea in the frowne of fortune. By discretion to cause them take to that, which is best, and to forsake that, which is worst, in common dealinges is common to all men, that have interest in children, parentes by nature, maisters by charge, neighbours of curtesie, all men of all humanitie: whom either private care by custome, or publike cure by commaundement of magistrate and lawe, doth compell in conscience to helpe their well doing, and to fray them from ill, wheresoever they meete them,

The rule of discretion.

or when so ever they see them do that, which is naught. And therfore that duetie to helpe them in this kinde for their manners, is incident to maisters but among others, though somwhat more then some others, as to whom it is most seemely, bycause of their authoritie, and most proper, bycause of their charge, whom knowledge best enfourmeth to embrew them with the best: and power best assisteth, to cause them embrace the best: even perforce at the first, till acquaintaunce in time breede liking of it selfe.

But this mannering of them is not for teachers alone, because they communicate therin, as I have said already, both with naturall parentes, to whom that point appertaineth nearest, as of most authoritie with them, and with all honest persons, which seing a child doing evill, are bid in conscience, to terrifie and check him as the quality of the childes offence, and the circunstance of their owne person doth seeme best to require.

Wherfore reserving for the teacher so much as is for his office, to enstruct the child what is best for him in matter of manners, and to see to it, so much as in him lyeth: to set good orders in his government, to see them alwaye well, and one waye still executed and perfourmed, I referre the rest to those, whom either any vertuous consideration of them selves, or any particular duetie, enjoyned by lawe, doth charge with the rest, either [29] by private discipline at home, or by publicke ordinaunce abroade, to see youth well brought up that waye: to learne to discern that which is well from ill, good from bad, religious from prophane, honest from dishonest, commendable from blameworthy, seemely from unseemely, that they may honour God, serve their countrey, comfort their freindes, and aide one an other, as good countreymen are bound to do. But how to handle their conceit in taking, and their memorie, in holding, bycause that appertaineth to teachers wholly: (for all that the parentes and freindes, wilbe medlers somtime, to further their young impes:) I will deale in that, and shew wherin children ought to be trained, till they be found fit for Grammer: wherin neverthelesse, both the matters, which they learne: and the manners, which they are made to, serve for ground to vertue, and encrease of discretion.

As I might verie well be esteemed inconsiderate, if I should force any farre fet divises into these my principles, which neither my countrey knew, nor her custome cared for, so dealing but with those, and resting content with those, which my countrey hath severed to her private use, and her custome is acquainted with of long continuaunce, I maye hope for consent, where my countrey commendeth, and looke for successe, where custome leades my hand, and feare no note of noveltie, where nothing is but auncient.

Reading.

Amongst these my countreys most familiar principles, *reading* offereth her selfe first in the entrie, chosen upon good ground continued upon great proofe, enrowled among the best, and the verie formost of the best, by her owne effectes, as verie many so verie profitable. For whether you marke the nature of the thing, while it is in getting, or the goodnesse therof when it is gotten, it must needs be the first, and the most frutefull principle, in training of the minde. For the letter is the first and simplest impression in the trade of teaching, and nothing before it. The knitting and jointing wherof groweth on verie infinitely, as it appeareth most plainely by daily spelling, and continuall reading, till partely by use, and partely by argument, the child get the habit, and cunning to read well, which being once goten, what a cluster of commodities doth [30] it bring with all? what so ever any other, for either profit or pleasure, of force or freewill, hath published to the world, by penne or printe, for any ende, or to any use, it is by reading all made to serve us: in religion to love and feare God, in lawe to obey and please men: in skill to entertaine knowledge, in will to expell ignorance, to do all in all, as having by it all helpes to do all thinges well. Wherefore I make *reading*, my first and fairest principle of all other, as being simply the first in substaunce, and leaning to none, but leading all other, and growing after so great, as it raungeth over all, being somwhat without other, other nothing without it: and a thing of such moment, as it is vainely begon, if it be not soundly goten, and being once sound it selfe: it delivereth the next maister from manifest toile, and the child himselfe from marvellous trouble, from feare where he failes not, from staggering, where he stops not, with comfort where he knowes, with courage, where he dare, a securitie to the parent, a safty to eche partie. I wishe the childe to have his reading thus perfect, and ready, in both the English and the Latin tongue verie long before he dreame of his Grammar.

The reading of English first.

Of the which two, at whether it were better to begin, by some accident of late it did seeme somwhat doubtfull: but by nature of the tongues, the verdit is given up. For while our religion was restrained to the Latin, it was either the onely, or the onelyest principle in learning, to learne to read Latin: as most appropriate to that effect, which the Church then esteemed on most.

But now that we are returned home to our English abce, as most naturall to our soile, and most proper to our faith, the restraint being repealed, and we restored to libertie, we are to be directed by nature, and propertie, to read that first, which we speake first, and to care for that most, which we ever use most: bycause we neede it most: and to begin our first learning there, where we have most helpes, to learne it best, by familiaritie of our ordinarie language, by understanding all usuall argumentes, by continuall company of our owne countreymen, all about us speaking English, and none uttering any wordes but those, which we our selves are well acquainted with, both [31] in our learning and living.

There be two speciall, whether ye will call them rules, or notes, to be observed in teaching, wherof the first is: That thinges be so taught, as that which goeth before, may induce that, which followeth by naturall consequence of the thing it selfe, not by erronious missorting of the deceived chuser, who like unto an unskilfull hoste oftimes misplaceth even the best of his guestes, by not knowing their degrees.

The second is, that those thinges be put unto children, which being confessed to be most necessarie, and most proper to be learned in those yeares, have lest sense, to their feeling, and most labour, without fainting. For can any growne man so moile him selfe, without to much cumber, with either the principles of Grammar, or cunning without booke, as a child will, the ones memorie being empty, the other being distracte with diversitie of thoughtes? *Reason* directes yeares, and *roate* rules in youth, *reason* calls in sense and feeling of paine, *roate* runnes on apase and mindeth nothing else but either play in the ende, or a litle praise for a greate deale of paines. Now praise never wearies, nor paine ever but wearies, and play pleaseth children with any, yea the greatest iniquitie of circunstance, whether the weather lowre, or the maister frowne, so he will give them leave to go. Though the Latin tounge be already discharged of all superfluities, exempt from custome, to chaunge it, and laid up for knowledge, to cherish it: and of long time hath bene smoothed both to the eye, and to the eare: yet in course of teaching it doth not naturally draw on the English, which yet remaineth in her lees unrackt and not fined, though it grow on verie faire. Our spelling is harder, our pronouncing harsher, our syllabe hath commonly as many letters, as the whole Latin word hath. So that both consequence, and hardnesse preferre the English. Even here must memorie begin her first traine, and store her selfe with such stuffe, as shall laie the best foundation to religion and obedience, which beginning in these yeares, will crepe on very strongly, and no lesse soundly: so that the child cannot but prove very good in age, which was so consideratly entred in his youth. What the thinges shall be, wherin both reading must travell, and memorie must make [32] choice, I will shew in mine Elementarie wherin the whole education before Grammer shalbe comprised.

Writing.

Next to reading followeth *writing*, in some reasonable distance after, bycause it requireth some strength of the hand, which is not so soone staied nor so stiffe to write, as the tongue is stirring and redy to read. And though writing in order of traine do succede reading, yet in nature and time it must needes be elder. For the penne or some other penlike instrument did carve and counterfeat the letter or some letterlike devise first rawly and rudely, neither all at once: then finely and fully, when all was at once, and therby did let the eye beholde that in charact, which the voice delivered to the eare in sounde, which being so set downe to utter the power and knitting of the articulate voice, and afterward observed to expresse them in deede, caused writing be much used as interpreter to the minde, and reading be embrased as expounder to the penne, and expressing that in force, which the penne set downe in fourme. Wherby it must needes follow, that raw and rude charactes, were the primitive writing, which being expressed what they did signifie brought forth reading: and that experience upon triall of their vertues made so much of them both, as she recommended them to profit, to have them appointed for principles in the training up of youth. So that reading being but the expresser of the writen charactes must needes acknowledge and confesse her puniship to writing, of whom she tooke both her being and her beginning.

To limite any one cause how writing began, or to runne over the inventours of thinges to finde out who devised it first, were to gesse at some uncertaine, though probable conjecture, without any assuraunce, to build on, as the thing it selfe is of small importaunce, for any to tarie on. It is more then likely, wherof so ever the first charact

came, that necessitie caught hold of it, to serve her owne tourne, and so enlarged it still, till it came to that perfection which we see it now in. I will neither paint out reading with such ornamentes, as it needes not, neither praise writing with such argumentes, as it craves not. For it is praise enough to a good thing to be confessed good, and what so ever is said more, is doubtfully to ground that, [33] which is determinatly graunted, and to seeke for defence when the forte is surrendred. After that reading was reduced into forme, and brought to her best, she fined her foundresse, and is therfore above all praise, bycause she makes the eye, the paragon sense, by benefit of that object. And writing it selfe hath profited so much, since it hath bene perfited, as it now proves the proppe to remembraunce, the executour of most affaires, the deliverer of secretes, the messager of meaninges, the enheritance of posteritie, whereby they receive whatsoever is left them, in lawe to live by, in letters to learne, in evidence to enjoye. To come by this thing so much commended, so, as it may bring foorth all her effectes redily, and roundly, these notes must be kept. That the maister learne himselfe and teach his scholer a faire letter and a fast, for plainesse and speede: That the matter of his example be pithie, and proper, to enrich the memorie with profitable provision: and that the learning to write be not left of, untill it be verie perfit: bycause writing being ones perfectly goten doth make a wonderful riddance in the rest of our learning. For the master may be bould to charge his child with writing of his geare, when he findes him able, to dispatch that with ease, what so ever is enjoyned him. Neither shall that child ever complaine of dif-
1. ficultie after, which can read and write perfectly before. For first he hath purchased those two excellent faire winges, which will cause him towre up to the top of all learning, as *Plato* in the like case of
7. De Rep. knowledge, termeth *Arithmetick* and *Geometrie* his two wings wherwith to flie up to heaven, from whence he doth fetch the true direc-
2. tion of his imprisoned ignorant. Secondly he hath declared eare he came to that cunning, that his wit would serve him, to proceede on further, as his winges will helpe him, to flie on faster. For in deede during the time, of writing and reading, his witte will bewraie it selfe, whether it may venture further upon greater learning, or were best to stay at some smaller skil, upon defect in nature. But if the child can not do that redily, which he hath rather looked on, then learned, before he remove from his Elementarie, while his maister

conceives quickly, and he perceives slowly, there is verie much matter offered unto passion, wheron to worke. Which commonly [34] brusteth out into much beating, to the dulling of the childe, and discouraging of the maister: and bycause of the to timely onset, to litle is done in to long a time, and the schoole is made a torture, which as it bringes forth delite in the ende, when learning is helde fast, so should it passe on verie pleasantly by the waye, while it is in learning: And generally this I do thinke of perfiting, and making up, as children go on: (seing the argument it selfe doth draw my penne so forcibly forward,) that it must needes be most perfectly good. For what if oportunitie either to go any further at all, or at least to go so on, as their friendes did set them in, be suddenly cut of, either by losse of freindes, or lacke in freindes, or some other misfortune? were it not good that they had so much perfectly, as they are practised in? which being unperfectly had, will either stand them in very small steede, on in none at all. To write and read wel which may be jointly gotten is a prety stocke for a poore boye to begin the world with all.

Writing the English hand first.

The same reasons which moved me to have the child read English before Latin, do move me also, to wishe him to write English before Latin, as a thing of more hardnesse, and redier in use to aunswere all occasions. Thus farre I do thinke that all my countreymen will joyne with me, and allow their children the use, of their letter and penne. For those that can write and read may not gainsaie, least I aske of them why they learned themselves? If they that cannot, do mislike that they have not, I will aske of them, why they wishe so oft for them?

Drawing.

Some controversie before the thing be consideratly thought on, but none after, may arise about this next, which is to draw with penne or pencill, a cosen germain to faire writing, and of the selfe same charge. For penne and penknife, incke and paper, compasse and ruler, a deske and a dustboxe will set them both up, and in these young yeares, while the finger is flexible, and the hand fit for frame, it will be fashioned easely. And commonly they that have any naturall towardnesse to write well, have aknacke of drawing to, and declare some evident conceit in nature bending that waye. And as judgement by understanding is a rule to the minde to discern what is honest, seemly, and sutable in matters of the minde, and such argumentes as fall [35] within compasse of generall reason exempt from sense: so this qualitie by drawing with penne or pencill, is an assured rule for the sense to judge by, of the proportion and seemelines of all aspectable thinges. As he that knoweth best, how to kepe that himselfe, which is comely in fashion, can also best judge, when comelinesse of fashion is kept by any other. And why is it not good to have every parte of the body: and every power of the soule to be fined to his best? And seing that must be looked unto long afore, which must serve us best alwaye after, why ought we not to ground that thoroughly in youth, which must requite us againe with grace in our age? If I or any else should seeme to contemne that principle, which brought forth *Apelles*, and that so knowen a crew of excellent painters, so many in number, so marveilous in cunning, so many statuaries, so many architectes: nay whose use all modelling, all mathematikes, all manuaries do finde and confesse to be so notorious and so needefull: both I and that any else might well be supposed to see very litle, not seing the use of that, which is laboured for sight, and most delitefull to see. Neither is the devise mine, as if it were, repentance hath repulse. For what so ever I do allow in others, which for the devise do deserve wel, I deserved not ill, in mine opinion, if I were my selfe the first deviser therof. That great philosopher *Aristotle* in the eight booke and third chapter of his Politikes, and not there onely, as not he alone, joyneth writing and reading, which he compriseth under this worde, *γϱαμματιϰὴ*, with drawing by penne or pencill, which I translate his *γϱαφιϰὴ*, both the two of one parentage and petigree, as thinges peculiarly chosen to bring up youth, both for quantitie in profit, and for qualitie in use. There he sayeth, that as writing and reading do minister much helpe to trafficque, to householdrie, to learning, and all publicke dealinges: so drawing by penne or pencill, is verie requisite to make a man able to judge, what that is which he byeth of artificers and craftes men, for substaunce, forme, and fashion, durable and handsome or no: and such other necessarie services, besides the delitefull and pleasant.

For the setting of colours I do not much stand in, howbeit if any dexterity that waye do draw the child on, it is an honest [36] mans living and I dare not condemne that famous fellowship: which is so renowned for handling the pencill. A large field is here offered to praise the praiseworthy, and to paint them out well, which painted all thinges so well, as the world still wondereth at the hearing of their workes. But the praise of painting is no part of my purpose at this time, but the appointing of it among the training principles, being so aunciently allowed, so necessarie in so many thinges, so great a ground to so gallant a misterie, as that profession is, wherof *Apelles* was: and last of all, so neare a cosen to the fairest writing, whose cradlefellow it is.

Musicke maketh up the summe, and is devided into two partes, the voice and the instrument, wherof the voice resembleth reading: as yealding that to the eare, which it seeth with the eye: and the instrument writing, by counterfeting the voice, both the two in this age best to be begon, while both the voice and the jointe be pliable to the traine. The voice craveth lesse cost to execute her part, being content with so much onely, as writing, and drawing did provide for their furniture, when they began their houshold. The instrumente seemeth to be more costly, and claimes both more care in keping, and more charge in compassing. For the pleasauntnesse of *Musick* there is no man that doth doubt, bycause it seemeth in some degree to be a medicine from heaven, against our sorowes upon earth. Some men thinke it to be too too sweete, and that it may be either quite forborne, or not so much followed. For mine owne parte I dare not dispraise it, which hath so great defendours, and deserveth so well, and I must needes allow it, which place it among those, that I do esteeme the cheife principles, for training up of youth, not of mine owne head alone, but by the advise of all antiquitie, all learned philosophie, all skilfull training, which make *Musick* still one of the principles, when they handle the question, what thinges be best, to bring youth first up in. If I had sought occasion of raunging discours which I still avoide, but where the opening of some point, doth lighten the thing, and may delite the reader, whom flatte and stearne setting downe, by waye of *aphorisme,* would soone weary (though many not of the meanest would allow of that kinde [37] exceeding well:) I might have found out many digressions long agoe, or if I had taken holde of that which hath bene offered, I have mette with many such, since I began first to write: but of all, in all sortes I do not finde any, wherin speeche might so spreede all the sailes, which she hath, and the penne might use, all the pencilling, which she can: as in painting out the praise and ornamentes of *Musick.* The matter is so ample, the ground so large, the reasons so many, which sound to her renowne: the thing

Musick.

it selfe so auncient, and so honorable, so generall, and so privat, so in Churches, and so without, so in all ages, and in all places, both highely preferred, and richely rewarded: the princesse of delites, and the delite of princes: such a pacifier in passion, such a maistres to the minde, so excellent in so many, so esteemed by so many, as even multitude makes me wonder, and with all to staie my hand, for feare that I shall not easely get thence, if I enter once in. I will not therfore digresse: bycause there is better stuffe in place, and more fit for my purpose, then the praise of *Musick* is. The Philosophers, and Physicians, do allow the straining, and recoyling of the voice in children, yea though they crie, and baule, beside their singing, and showting: by the waie of exercise to stretche, and kepe open the hollow passages, and inward pipes of the tender bulke, whereby *Musick* will prove a double principle both for the soule, by the name of learning, and for the body, by the waye of exercise, as hereafter shall appeare.

But for the whole matter of *Musick*, this shalbe enough for me to say at this time, that our countrey doth allow it: that it is verie comfortable to the wearyed minde: a preparative to perswasion: that he must needes have a head out of proportion, which cannot perceive: or doth not delite in the proportions of number, which speake him so faire: that it is best learned in childehood, when it can do least harme, and may best be had: that if the constitution of man both for bodie and soule, had not some naturall, and nighe affinitie with the concordances of *Musick*, the force of the one, would not so soone stirre up, the cosen motion in the other. It is wonderfull that is writen, and strange that we see, what is wrought therby in nature of *Physick*, for the remedying of some desperate diseases. [38]

Miscontentment.

And yet there groweth some miscontentement with it, though it be never so good, and that not only in personages of whom I make small account, but in some verie good, honest, and well disposed natures, though to stearnly bent, which neverthelesse, for al their stearnnes, wil resigne over their sentence, and alter their opinion, sometimes of themselves upon deeper meditation, what the thing in it selfe is, sometime by inducement, when they fal in with other which are better resolved: but most cheifly then, when *Musick* it selfe consideratly applyed, hath for a while obtained the favorable use of their listning eares. The science it selfe hath naturally a verie forcible strength to trie and to tuche the inclination of the minde, to this or that affection, thorough the propertie of number, wheron it consisteth, which made the *Pythagorian*, and not him alone to plat the soule out so much upon number. It is also very pleasant for the harmonie and concent, wherby the hearer discovers his disposition, and lettes pleasure playe upon the bitte, and dalye with the bridle, as delite will not be drowned, nor driven to hidebare. For which cause *Musick* moveth great misliking to some men that waye, as to great a provoker to vaine delites, still laying baite, to draw on pleasure: still opening the minde, to the entrie of lightnesse. And in matters of religion also, to some it seemes offensive, bycause it carieth awaye the eare, with the sweetnesse of the melodie, and bewitcheth the minde with a *Syrenes* sounde, pulling it from that delite, wherin of duetie it ought to dwell, unto harmonicall fantasies, and withdrawing it, from the best meditations, and most vertuous thoughtes to forreine conceites, and wandring devises. For one aunswere to all, if abuse of a thing, which may be well used, and had her first being to be well used, be a sufficient condemnation to the thing that is abused, let glotonie forbid meat, distempering drinke, pride apparell, heresie religion, adulterie mariage, and why not, what not? Nay which of all our principles shall stand, if the persons blame, shal blemish the thing? We read foolish bookes, wherat to laugh, nay wherein we learne that, which we might and ought forbeare: we write strange thinges, to serve our owne fansie, if we sway but a litle to any lewde folly: we paint and draw pictures, not to be set in Churches, but such as private houses [39] hide with curtaines, not to save the colours, but to cover their owners, whose lightnesse is discovered, by such lascivious objectes. Shall reading therfore be reft from religion? shall private, and publike affaires, lease the benefit of writing? shall sense forgoe his forsight, and the beautifier of his object? Change thou thy direction, the thinges will follow thee more swifte to the good, then the other to the bad, being capable of both, as thinges of use be, and yet bending to the better. Mans faulte makes the thing seeme filthie. Applie thou it to the best, the choice is before thee. It is the ill in thee, which seemeth to corrupte the good in the thing, which good, though it be defaced by thy ill, yet shineth it so cleare, as it bewraieth the naturall beautie, even thorough the cloude of thy greatest disgracing. *Musick* will not harme thee, if thy behaviour be good, and thy conceit honest, it will not miscary thee, if thy eares can carie it, and sorte it as it should be. Appoint thou it

Aunswere.

well, it will serve thee to good purpose: if either thy manners be naught, or thy judgement corrupt, it is not *Musick* alone which thou doest abuse, neither cannest thou avoide that blame, which is in thy person, by casting it on *Musick*, which thou hast abused and not she thee. And why should those people, which can use it rightly, forgoe their owne good, or have it with embasing to pleasure some pevishe, which will not yet be pleased? or seeke to heale sores, which will festure still, and never skinne, though ye plaster them daily, to your owne displeasure. But am I not to tedious? This therfore shall suffise now, that children are to be trained up in the Elementarie schoole, for the helping forward of the abilities of the minde, in these fower things, as commaunded us by choice and commended by custome. *Reading*, to receive that which is bequeathed us by other, and to serve our memorie with that which is best for us. *Writing* to do the like thereby for others, which other have done for us, by writing those thinges which we daily use: but most of al to do most for our selves: *Drawing* to be a directour to sense, a delite to sight, and an ornament to his objectes. *Musick* by the instrument, besides the skill which must still encrease, in forme of exercise to get the use of our small joyntes, before they be knitte, to have them the nimbler, [40] and to put Musicianes in minde, that they be no brawlers, least by some swash of a sword, they chaunce to lease a jointe, an irrecoverable jewell unadvisedly cast away. *Musick* by the voice, besides her cunning also, by the waye of *Phisick*, to sprede the voice instrumentes within the bodie, while they be yet but young. As both the kindes of *Musick* for much profit, and more pleasure, which is not voide of profit in her continuing kinde. All foure for such uses as be infinite in number, as they know best, which have most knowledge and the parentes must learne, to lead their children to them: and the children must beleve, to winne their parentes choice, which may be in all, if they themselves liste, if they liste not, in no more then they like, their restraining conceite neither bridling, nor abbridging any other mans entent, which seeketh after more. And though all young ones be not thus farre trained, yet we may perceive, that all these be used, in particular proofes, and not to be refused in generall trade, where all turnes be served, by setting foorth of all thinges that be generally in use, though not generally used. Thus much of these thinges at this time, which I do meane by Gods grace to handle in their owne Elementarie, as precisely and yet, as properly, as ever I can.

Chapter 6.

Of exercises and training the body. How necessarie a thing exercise is. What health is, and how it is maintained: what sicknesse is, how it commeth, and how it is prevented. What a parte exercise playeth in the maintenaunce of health. Of the student and his health. That all exercises though they stirre some one parte most, yet helpe the whole bodie.

The soule and bodie being coparteners in good and ill, in sweete and sowre, in mirth and mourning, and having generally a common sympathie, and a mutuall feeling in all passions: how can they be, or rather why should they be severed in traine? the one made stronge, and well qualified, the other left feeble, and a praye to infirmitie? will ye have the minde to obtaine those thinges, which be most proper unto her, and most profitable unto you, when they be obtained? Then must ye [41] also have a speciall care, that the bodie be well appointed, for feare it shrink, while ye be either in course to get them, or in case to use them. For as the powers of the soule come to no proofe, or to verie small, if they be not fostered by their naturall traine, but wither and dye, like corne not reaped, but suffered to rotte by negligence of the owner, or by contention in chalenge: even so, nay much more, the bodie being of it selfe lumpishe and earthy, must needes either dye in drowsinesse, or live in loosenesse, if it be not stirred and trained diligently to the best. And though the soule, as the fountaine of life, and the quickner of the body, may and will beare it out for some while, thorough valiauntnesse of courage: yet weaknesse will not be alwayes dissembled, but in the ende will and must bewraie her owne want, even then peraventure, when it were most pittie. Many notable personages for stomacke and courage, many excellent men for learning and skill, in most and best professions have then left their lives, thorough the plaine weaknesse, of their contemned bodies, when they put their countries in most apparent and gladsome hope of rare and excellent effectes, the one of valiantnesse and manhood, the other of knowledge and skill. Seing therfore there is a good in them both, which by diligent endevour may be avaunced to that, for which it was ordained, and by negligent oversight, doeth either decaye quite, or proves not so well, as otherwayes it might, I maye not slightly passe over the bodies good, being both so neare, and so necessarie a neighbour unto the soule: considering I have bestowed so much paines already, and must bestow much more, in the service of the soule: nay rather considering I deale with the bodie but once, and that onely here, wheras I entreat of the soule, and the furniture therof in what so ever I shall medle with, in my whole course hereafter. If common sense did not teach us the necessitie of this point, and extreme feeblenes did not force men to confesse, how great feates they could do, and how active they would prove, if their weake limmes and failing joyntes, would aunswere the lusty courage, and brave swinge of their fierie and fresh spirites: I would take paines to perswade them by argumentes, both of proofe in experience, and of reason in nature, that as it is easie, so it were needefull [42] to helpe the body by some traine, not left at randon to libertie, but brought in to forme of ordinarie discipline, generally in all men, bycause all men neede helpe, for necessarie health, and ready execution of their naturall actions: but particularly for those men, whose life is in leasure, whose braynes be most busied, and their wittes most wearied, in which kinde studentes be no one small part, but the greatest of all, which so use their mindes as if they cared not for their bodies, and yet so neede their bodies, as without the strength and soundnesse wherof, they be good for nothing, but to moane themselves, and to make other marvell, why they take no more heede, how to do that long, which they do so well, being a thing within compasse of their owne care, and knowledge. For who is so grosse, as he will denie that exercise doth good, and that so great, as is without comparison, seing olde *Asclepiades* is by *Galene* confuted, and stawled for an asse: as *Erasistratus* also his dissembling freind? or who is so sore tied either to studie, or to stocks, as he cannot stirre himselfe if he will, or ought not if he may? But the matter being confessed, even by the most idle, and unweildy to be healthfull and good, I shall neede no more reason, to procure assent, and allowaunce for exercise. My whole travell therfore must be to finde out, and set foorth, what shalbe requisite to the perfourmaunce of this point, concerning the traine and exercising of the body, that it may prove healthy, and live long: and be ready to assist, all the actions of the minde.

Wherein therfore consisteth the health of the bodie, and how is it to be maintained untill such time, as nature shall dismantle, and pull it downe her self? To aunswere this question, and withall to declare, how great an officer to health exercise is: I will first shew, wherin health doth consiste, and how diseases do come: then how health is maintained, and disease avoided: Last of all how great a parte is appointed for exercise to plaie in the perfourmaunce therof, bycause I saye, and not I alone, but *Galen* also that great Physician, neither *Galen* onely, though sufficient alone, but all that ever lived, and were cheife of that liverie, that who so can applie the minde well with learning, and the bodie with exercise, shall make both a wise minde, and a healthfull bodie in their best kinde. [43] Wherefore seing I have set downe wherein the traine of the minde doth consist, so much as the Elementarie course doth admit, and must perfourme, and so farre as these my Positions require at this time, whose profession is not to tary, though it tuche them: I wil now handle that other part of exercise, wherwith the bodie is either to be kept in health, or to be helpt to health: and that not onely in the Elementarie, to whom this treatise should seeme to aunswere, but also in the generall student during his whole life: which must alwaye rule himselfe by those circunstances, which direct the application of exercise, according to time, age, & c. and shalbe handled herafter.

1.

2. 3.

1. De sani. tuen.

What is health and sicknesse.

There be in the bodie of man, the force of foure elementes, fire and aire, water and earth, and the pith of their primitive, and principall qualities, heat and couldnesse, moysture and drynesse, which the Physicians call the similarie partes, of the similitude and likenesse that they have, not the one to the other, but the partes of eche to their owne whole, bycause everie least part, or degree of these great ones, beare the name of the whole, as everie part or parcell of fier, is called fier, no lesse then the whole fier, of water, water, of aier, aier, of earth, earth, and everie degree of heat, is heat, of cold, is cold, of moysture, is moysture, of drynesse, is drynesse, though greater and smaller, lesse and more, be epithetes unto them, as either their quantitie, or qualitie doth sprede or close.

There be also in the same bodie certaine instrumentall partes, compounded and consisting in substance of the similarie, which the bodie doth use in the executing of the naturall functions, and workinges therof. Now when these similarie partes be so tempered, and disposed, as no one doth excede any other in proportion to overrule, but all be as one in consent to preserve: and the instrumentall partes also be so correspondent one to an other, in composition and greatnesse, in number and measure, as nature thorough the temperature of the first, may absolutely use the perfectnesse of the last, to execute and perfourme without let or stoppe, what appertaineth to the maintenaunce of her selfe: it is called health, and the contrarie, disease, both in the whole bodie, and in every part therof. In the whole bodie by distemperature of the whole, in some part, by [44] composition, out of place, and disjoynted, by greatnes, being to bigge or to small: by measure, being misshapen and fashionles: by number, being to many and needlesse: or to few, and failing. This health whether it be in the middle degre, wherin all executions be complete without any sensible let: and no infirmitie appeareth, that the bodie feeles with any plaine offence: Or if it be in the perfectest degree, which is so seldom, as never any saw, bycause of great frailty, and britleness in our nature: it never continueth in one estate, but altereth still, and runnes to ruyne, without both speedy and daily, nay without hourely reparation.

The causes which alter, and chaunge it so, be somtime from within the bodie, and were borne with it: sometime from without, and yet not without daunger. From within, the verie propertie and pithe of our originall substance, and matter whence we grew, altereth us first, which as it beginneth, and groweth in moysture, so it endeth, and stayeth in drynesse, and in the ende decayeth the bodie with to much drynesse, which extreame though naturall withering, we call olde age, which though it come by course, and commaundement of nature, yet beareth it the name, and title of disease, bycause it decayeth the bodie, and delivereth it to death. From within also, the continuall rebating, and falling awaye of somwhat from the bodie, occasioneth much chaunge, nay that is most cause of greatest chaunge, and killeth incontinent by meere defect, if it be not supplyed.

To these two causes of inward alteration, there aunswere two other forreine causes, both unholesome, and perillous, the aire, which environneth us, and violence, which is offered us. The former of the two, decaing our health with to much heat, cold, drynesse, and moysture of it selfe: or by noysomnesse of the soile, and corruption in circunstance. The second, by strong hand brusing, or breaking, wounding or wiping awaie, of some one part of the bodie, or els killing the whole consort of the bodie with the soule, and taking away life from it. These foure overthrowes of our bodies and health, olde age, waste, aire, and violence, finde by helpe of nature, and arte, certaine oppositions, which either divert them quite, if they maye be [45] avoided, or kepe them of longer, if they maye be differred, or mittigate their malice, when it is perceived. For forreine violence, foresight will looke to, where casualtie commaundes not, and cannot be foreseene. For infection by the aire, that it do not corrupte and marre so much as it would, wisedome will provide, and defende the bodie from the injuries, and wronges therof. That olde age grow not on to fast, circunspectnes in diet, consideration in clothes, diligence in well doing, wil easely provide, both for the minde not to enfect, first it selfe and then the bodie: and for the bodie not to enforce the minde, by too impotent desires. That waste weare not, meat takes in chardge, to supplie that is drye, and decayeth: drinke promiseth to restore moysture, when it doth diminishe: the breath it selfe, and arteriall pulse, looke to heating and cooling. And *Physick* in generall professing foresight to prevent evills, and offering redresse, when they have done harme, so not incurable, doth direct both those and all other meanes. Now in all these helpes, and most beneficiall aides of our afflicted nature, which deviseth all meanes to save her selfe harmelesse, and deliteth therin, when she is discharged of infirmities, to much stuffes and stiffles, to litle straites and pines, both undoe the naturall. To much meat cloyes, to litle faintes, both perishe the principall. To much liquour drownes, to litle dryes, both corrupt the carcasse. Heat burnes, cold chilles, in excesse both to much, in defect both to litle, and both causes to decaie. Mediocritie preserveth not onely in these but in whatsoever els.

But now what place hath exercise here? to helpe nature by motion in all these her workinges, and wayes for health: to encrease and encourage the naturall heat, that it maye digest quickly and expell strongly: to fashion and frame all the partes of the bodie to their naturall and best haviour: to helpe to rid needelesse, and superfluous humours: reffuse and rejected excrementes, which nature leaves for naught, when she hath sufficiently fed, and wisheth rather they were seene abrode, then felt within. And be not these great benefites? to defend the body by defeating diseases? to stay the minde, by strengthening of her meane? to assist nature being both daily, and [46] daungerously, assailed both within and without? to helpe

Exercise.

life to continue long? to force death, to kepe farre a loufe?

Now as all constitutions be not of one and the same mould, and as all partes be not moved alike, with any one thing: so the exercises must alter, and be appropriate to each: that both the constitution may be continued in her best kinde, and all the partes preserved to their best use, which exercises being compared among themselves one to an other, be more or lesse, but being applyed to the partie
kepe alwayes in a meane, when they meane to do good. Concerning
1. students, for whose health my care is greatest, the lesse they eate,
the lesse they neede to voide: and therfore small diet in them, best
preventeth all superfluities, which they cannot avoide, if their diet
2. be great, and their exercise small. Their exercise must also be very
moderate, and not alter to much, for feare of to great distempera-
3. ture in that, which must continue moderate: and with all it should
be ordinarie, that the habit may be holesome, and sudden chaunge give no cause of greater inconvenience. Wherfore to avoide distemperature the enemie to health, and so consequently to life, and to maintaine the naturall constitution so, as it may serve to the best, wherin her duetie lyeth, and live to the longest, that in nature it can, besides the diet, which must be small, as nature is a pickler, and requires but small pittaunce: besides clothing which should be thin even from the first swadling to harden, and thick the flesh: I do take this traine by exercise, which I wishe to be joyned with learning, to be a marveilous furtherer.

But for diet to avoide inward daungers, and clothing to avert outward injuries, and all such preventions, as are not proper to teachers, though in communitie more proper then to any common man: I set them over to parentes, and other well willers, which will see to them, that they faile not in those thinges: and if they do, will fly to Physicians, by their helpe to salve that, which themselves may forsee. For exercises I will deale, which to commend more then they will commend them selves, when I shall shew both what they be, and the particular profites of every one of them, which I chuse from the rest, were me thinke verie needlesse, and cheifly to me, which seeme sufficiently [47] to praise them, in that I do place them among principles of prerogative. But as in the soule I did picke out certaine pointes, wherunto I applyed the training principles: so likewise in the bodie, may I not also sever some certaine partes, wherunto my preceptes must principally be conformed? that shall not neede. For as in the soule the frute of traine doth better and make complete even that which I tuched not, and so consequently the whole soule: so in the bodie, those exercises which seeme to be appointed for some speciall partes, bycause they stirre those partes most, do qualifie the whole bodie, and make it most active. Wherefore as there I did promise not to anatomise the soule, as neither dealing with Divines nor Philosophers: so do I not here make profession to shew the anatomie of the bodie, as medling neither with Physicians nor Surgeans, otherwise then any of them foure can helpe me in exercise. To the which effect, and ende, I will onely cull out from whence I can, such speciall notes, as both Philosophers, and Phisicians do know to be most true, and both the learned, and unlearned, will confesse to be for them: and such also, as the training maisters may easely both helpe, and encrease in their owne triall. For both reason, and rule, do alwaye commaunde, that the maister be by, when exercise is used, thorough whose overlooking the circunstance is kept, which helpeth to health, and the contrarie shunned, which in exercise doth harme. In the elder yeares, reason at the elbow must serve the student, as in these younger, the maisters presence helpes to direct the child.

But to joyne close with our traine. What partes be they in our bodie, upon whom exercise is to shew this great effecte? or what be the powers therof, which must still be stirred, so to stay, and establish the perpetuitie of health, not in themselves alone, but in the whole bodie, by them? Where joyntes be to bend, where stringes to tye, where synewes to stirre, where streatchers to straine, there must needes be motion: or els stifnesse will follow, and unweildynesse withall: where there be conduites to convey the blood, which warmeth, canales to carie the spirite, which quickneth, pipes to bestow the aire, which cooleth, passage to dismisse execrements which easeth, there must needes be spreding, to kepe the currant large, and [48] eche waie open, for feare of obstructions, and sudden fainting. Where to much must needes marre, there must be forcing out, where to litle must nedes lame, there must be letting in: where thickning threates harme, there thinning fines the substance: where thinning is to much, there thickning must do much, and to knit up all in short, all those offices, wherunto our bodie serveth naturally, either for inward bestowing of nurriture, and maintenaunce of life: or for outward motion, and executions of use, must be chearished and nusled so, as that they do by nature well, and truely, they may do by traine, both long, and strongly. I shall not neede to name the partes, all in one ruk, as of set purpose, which be knowen by their effectes: and the exercises also themselves will shew for whom they serve. But for example first in the partes let us see, whether we can discern them by their working, and properties, that therby the exercise may be pickte, which is most proper to helpe such effectes.

1. Who doth not streight waye conceive, that the lunges or lightes be ment, when he heareth of an inward part, which provideth winde for the harte, to allay his heat, and to minister some clammy matter unto it, whence he may take aire, most fit for his functions, and not at the sudden be forced to use any forreine?

2. Or who doth not by and by see, that the harte is implyed, when he heareth of an other inward part, which is the spring, and fountaine, of the vitall spirite and facultie, the seat and sender out of naturall heat, the occasion and cause of the arteriall pulse, which by one arterie, and way, receiveth cooling from the lunges, by an other, sendeth the vitall spirite, the hote, and hurling blood, thorough out the whole bodie?

3. Or who is so grosse, as not to gesse at the liver, when he heareth of an other inward part, which is the cheife instrument of nurriture, the workhouse of thicke and grosse blood: that feedeth the life and soule: when it desireth meat, and drinke, and what is els necessarie: which conveieth blood thorough the veines to nurrish all partes of the bodie, with the naturall spirit in it, if there be any, verie darke and heavie?

4. Nay hath he any braine, which seeth not the braine plainly laid before him, when he heareth a part of mans bodie named, [49] which breedeth a sowlish, and life spirite, as most pure, so most precious, and rather a qualitie then a bodie, and useth it partly to further the working of that princely, and principall part of mans soule, wherby he understandeth and reasoneth: partly to helpe the instrumentes of sense, and motion, by meane of the sineues, never suffering them to lacke spirite: which is the cheife and capitall cause, why these instrumentes do their dueties well? And so forth in all the partes aswell without, as within sight, whose properties when one heareth and finding that they be helped by such a motion he can forthwith say, that such an exercise is good for such a part:

He can tel what the parte is.

1. Now againe for exercises. Who hearing that moderate running

doth warme the whole body, strengthneth the naturall motions, provoketh appetite, helpeth against distilling of humours and catarres, and driveth them some other waie:

Or that daunsing beside the warmth, driveth awaye numnesse, 2.
and certaine palsies, comforteth the stomacke, being cumbred with
weaknes of digestion, and confluence of raw humours, strengtheneth weake hippes, fainting legges, freatishing feete:

Or that ryding also is healthfull for the hippes and stomacke: that 3.
it cleareth the instrumentes of all the senses, that it thickneth thinne
shankes: that it stayeth loose bellies:

Or that loud speaking streatcheth the bulke, exerciseth the vocalle 4.
instrumentes, practiseth the lungues, openeth the bodie, and all the
passages therof:

Or that loud reading scoureth all the veines, stirreth the spirites 5.
thorough out all the entraulles, encreaseth heat, suttileth the blood,
openeth the arteries, suffereth not superfluous humours to grow
grosse and thicke: who, say I, hearing but of these alone in taste for
all, or of all together by these alone, doth not both see the partes,
which are preserved, the exercise which preserveth, and the matter
wherin?

Wherfore seing exercise is such a thing, that so much enableth the bodie, whom the soule hath for companion in all exploites, a comfort being lightsome, a care being lothesom, a courage being healthy, a clog being heavie, I will, bycause I must, if I meane to do well, plat forth the whole place of exercising the bodie, at ones for all ages. [50]

Chapter 7.

The braunching, order, and methode, kept in this discours of exercises.

Bycause the speciall marke wherat I shoote, is to bring the minde forward to his best, by those meanes which I take to be best, wherin I must of force continue verie long, as in my principall and cheife subjecte, and in no place saving this, entreat of the bodie, but onely how to apply that to it, which I pitche downe here: I thinke it good therefore in this place to perfit, and handle at full the whole title of

exercises with all the circunstances belonging therunto, so sufficiently and fully, as my simple skill can aspire unto: and as the present occasion of a position or passage useth to require, leaving that
which I do not medle with, to those that shall professe the thing,
ether for their owne, or for their childrens health, wherin I will kepe
1. this methode and manner of proceeding. First I wil note somewhat,
2. generally concerning all exercises. Secondly I will chuse out some
especiall exercises, which upon good consideration I do take to be
3. most proper, and propitious to schooles, and scholers. Thirdly I will
applye the circunstances, required in exercise to everie of them, so
neare as I can, that there be no error committed in the executing. For
the better the thing is, if it hit right, the more dangerous it proveth,
4. if it misse of that right. Last of all I will shew the training maister,
how to furnish himselfe thoroughly, in this professed exercising:
bycause he must both applie the minde with learning, and the bodie
with moving, at diverse times, refreshing himselfe, with varietie
and chaunge.

But in handling of these foure pointes, I meane to rippe up no idle question: I terme that idle, where health is the ende, and the question no helpe to it, but cause to discours, and delaye of precept. Such questions be these: who first found out the arte of exercise called *Gymnastice*, or whether it belong to the Physician or no: being a preservative to health: or who first devised the particular exercises: or who were most famous for the executing therof, and a number of such like discoursory argumentes, which learned men having leasure at will, as a [51] schoolemaister hath not, and willing to wade farre, as my selfe could wish, have mined out of the bowelles of antiquitie, and entraules of authoritie, sometimes sadly, and saing in deede much, upon evident and apparent testimonies, sometimes simply, and surmising but some such thing, by very light and slight conjectures: oftimes supported by bare guesse, at some silly word, or some more naked warrant. Wherfore to the matter.

Chapter 8.

Of exercise in generall and what it is. And that it is Athleticall *for games,* Martiall *for the fielde,* Physicall *for health,* praeparative *before,* postparative *after the standing exercise: some within dores, for foule whether, some without for faire.*

The division of exercises.

All exercises were first devised, and so in deede served, either for games and pastime, for warre and service, or for suretie of health and length of life, though somtime all the three endes did concurre in one, sometimes they could not. For why might not an healthfull, and a sound body, both serve in the fielde for a soldiar, and in the sand for a wrastler? But we seldom reade, that the *athleticall* constitution whose ende was gaming, whose exercise was pastime, whose diet was unmeasurable for any man to use, did either deliver the world an healthfull body, being strained beyond measure, or a courageous soldiar, being unweildly to fight, as one compounded and made of fat and fog, brawnie and burdenous.

Athleticall.

The *athleticall* and gaming exercises, were in generall assemblies, to winne some wager, to beare awaie the prise, to be wondered at of the world, or to set foorth the solemnities of their festivall service, and ceremonies in the honour of their idoles: or in publike spectacle to adourne and set foorth, the triumphant and victorious shewes, the sumptuous and costly devises of their princes and states. Wherin we reade, that particular men have shewed such effectes of strength, and sturring, by the helpe of exercise, and traine, as nature her selfe could never attaine unto, though she furthered the feat, and got her selfe the worst, both by empairing of health, and hastning on of death, thorough straining to much. It is more then marveilous [52] to thinke on, and yet we finde it of verie good recorde, what and how incredible weight, both of living creatures, and massier mettal, one mans force hath bene noted to have borne, by being only used to that burthen. Would any man beleve it, if it were not of good writen credit, that one *Milo* so strutted himselfe, so pitcht his feet, so peysed his bodie, as he remained unremoveable from his place, being haled at and pulde by a number of people. *Activitie* hath wrought wonders, *swiftnesse* incredible thinges, and what propertie what not? where nature and ambition were backt with exercise and good will, to do but one thing well.

Martiall.

For the use of warre, and defence, it is more then evident, that exercise beares the bell: Can one have a bodie to abide cold, not to melte with heat, not to starve for hunger, not to dye for thirst, not to shrinke at any hardnesse, almost beyond nature, and above common reache, if he never have it trained? will nimblenesse of limmes awaie with all labour, surpasse all difficulties, of never so divers, and dangerous groundes, pursue enemies to vanquish, reskue freinds to save, retire from danger without harme, thrust it selfe into daunger without daunger, where no traine before made acquaintaunce with travell? Wherupon called the *Romaines* their whole armie *Exercitus*, but bycause it consisted of a valiant number of exercised and trained men? which were not to seeke at a sudden, bycause they had used armes before? how could common weales where the territory was but small, and the enhabitantes few, have still delivered themselves from mightier assailantes, then they seemed defendantes? or in continuall threates, of jeleous neighbours, how could they still have kept their owne, if that small territorie, had not bene thoroughly employed, and that petie paucitie gallantly trained? wherby it was able for hardnesse and sufferance to abide what not? for activitie and manhood, to have mastered whom not? or at the least had good meanes, not to receive any foile, where onely the huger number, and the untrained multitude, were to trie the masterie in fielde against them?

Physicall.

For health it is most manifest that exercise is a mighty great mistresse, whether it be to confirme that which we have by [53] nature, or to procure that which we have not by nature: or to recover that by industrie, and diligence, which we have almost lost, by misfortune and negligence. The exercises which do serve to this healthy end, do best serve for this my purpose, and though an healthfull body be most apt and active, both for gaming to get wagers, and for warring to winne victories, yet in my exercises, I neither meane to dally with the gamester, nor to fight with the warrier, but to marke which way I may best save studentes, who haue most neede of it: being still assailed by those enemies of health, which waxe more eager and hoat, the more weake and cold that exercise is.

What is exercise.

This exercise of ours by forme of definition, is said to be a vehement, and a voluntarie stirring of ones body, which altereth the breathing, whose ende is to maintaine health, and to bring the bodie to a verie good habit. Doth not exercise at this her first entry offer to performe so much as I did undertake for her? health of the body, and an healthy habit of all the limmes: which two effectes, bycause they be good, who doth not desire them? and being got by exercise, why is it not in price? and being reducible to order, why should it not be in traine? They that write of exercise, make three degrees in it, wherof they call the first a preparative, in Greek *παρασκευαστικόν*, the next simply by the name of exercise *γυμνὰσιον* the third a postparative, in Greek *ἀποθεραπευτικὸν*. The preparative served, not to passe rudely, and roughly into the maine exercise, without qualifying the bodie by degrees before, bycause sudden alteration workes ill disposition. The postparative or apotherapeutike followeth the maine exercise, to reduce the body by gentle degrees, to the same quietnesse in constitution, wherin it was, before it was so moved. Which two pointes bycause they rest most in the maisters consideration, which is to oversee the traine, I commit them to his care: so to applie his cunning as he shall see cause in exercising his charge. And yet herein I entend to helpe him, when I shall handle the circunstances which direct exercises.

1. *παρασκευαστικόν.*
2. *γυμνὰσιον.*
3. *ἀποθεραπευτικὸν.*

The third degree, which is enclosed betwene these two, is that same exercise, which I praise so much, and upon whom the other two waite, wherof, as writers make to many, and to [54] finely minced distinctions, so I make account but of one at this time, wherof I do make two braunches, or spieces, the one to be used within dores, and the other abroade, that whether the weather be faire or fowle, the exercise in some kinde may never faile.

γυμνὰσιον.

Chapter 9.

Of the particular exercises. Why I do appoint so manie, and how to judge of them, or to devise the like.

I will not here runne thorough all the kindes of exercises that be named either by *Galene* or any other writer, wherof many be discontinued, many be yet in use, but out of the whole heape I have pickt out these for within dores, *lowd speaking, singing, lowd reading, talking, laughing, weaping, holding the breath, daunsing, wrastling, fensing, and scourging the Top*. And these for without dores, *walking, running, leaping, swimming, riding, hunting, shooting, and playing at the ball*. Wherof though the very most be used oftimes, not in nature of exercises, but either of pleasure, or necessitie, yet they be all such, as will serve well that waie, and be so made account of among the best writers, that deale in this kinde: and for that some of them maye be said to be most proper to men, and farre above boyes plaie: you must remember, that I deale for all studentes, and not for children alone, to whom it is in choice, besides all these to devise other for their good, as circunstance shal lead them. There may also be reasons, to perswade some men to mislike of, I do not thinke all, but I suppose some, of these thinges, which I do appoint, as both commendable and profitable exercises, with whom I will not here strive, but desire them to judge of me, without prejudice, and to stay their sentence, untill they see in what sorte I allow them. For knowing the cause of offence, I might seeme very simple, if I should simply allow that, which is disallowed upon reason, and not misliked without manifest shew of probable cause: and so to reserve the thing, as I did not remove the blame. They must also thinke that nothing is abused, but that both may and ought to be well used, which well, they must use, and refuse the ill: seing where misuse draweth blame, there right use deserveth praise. [55]

Therfore I wishe those that be of yeares, and abilitie to guide themselves to call circunstance to counsell, and consideration to advise. For as consideration shapeth the circunstance, so circunstance is a thing, which maketh all that is done, either to please or displease: to be sent awaie with a cutting checke: or to be bid tarie, with a cheary contenaunce. As for the child in whom wisdom wanteth, to way with discretion, what it is that he doeth, the maister alone must supplie all wantes, or beare all blames, though it be but a simple recompence, to blame wante of consideration, when harme is received. Some man may also say, what needes so many, and mislike the multitude. Of many to chuse some, is usuall in all choice, and where store is, why should choice be stinted? he may lessen the number, that alloweth but of one, and I have pickt out the likest, to satisfie all in diversities of liking, who so shall like any of these, may use them with me, or upon the like ground, may devise himselfe other. In handling of eche of these, I will first shew for what partes, to what end, and in what manner, they be profitable and holesome being moderatly used: then for whom, and with what daunger, they be strained to the contrarie.

Chapter 10.

Of lowd speaking. How necessarie, and how proper an exercise it is for a scholler.

The exercise of the voice which in Latin they name *vociferatio*, in Greek *ἀναφώνησις*, as them *φωνασκόι*, which were the training maisters, in English maye be tearmed lowd speaking, of the height: for though it use all the degrees, which be in the voice, yet is it most properly to take his name, of the lowdest and shrillest, as the most audible in sound, and therfore fittest to give the name, as all thinges els receive theirs, of some one qualitie of most especiall note. The auncient Physicians entertaine it among exercises, bycause it stirreth the bulke, and all those instrumentes, which serve for the deliverie of voice, and utterance of speeche: bycause it aideth, dilateth, and comforteth the lunges in his windworke, it encreaseth, cleanseth, strengtheneth, and fineth the naturall heat: it maketh [56] the sound and soveraigne partes of the bodie strong and pure: and not lightly to be assailed by any disease: it mendeth the colour, and cheareth the countenaunce. Now that it hath these properties they do prove by naturall argumentes. That it practiseth and stirreth the inward partes, and vocall instrumentes, no man may denie, which will confesse, that the mouth alone, is the onely port and passage for speeche. That it encreaseth the naturall heat, the breath it selfe doth most evidently declare, bycause it is always exceeding warme, when one exerciseth the voice, it is so thronged and crusshed with taking in and letting out. That it cleanseth and cleareth, there be two causes to prove: the one is, bycause it maketh the flesh more fine and thinne, and smoother to the hand, not onely thorough stretching and straining the skinne, but by removing excrementes, which naturally thicken and make rugged. The other is, for that by moving the vocall instrumentes the inward moysture consumeth and wasteth, as it doeth appeare by that thicke and grosse vapour, which proceedeth out of his mouth that speaketh alowd, and other congealed excrementes resting of olde in other passages, which this exercise expelled from the inward partes. That it both fines and strengthens the naturall heat, hereby it is more then plaine. For that the inward vesselles and pipes be scoured thereby, and sundry superfluities expelled both at the nose, and mouth, which as they darkened, weakned, and thickned the naturall heat, when they were within the bodie: so being dismissed themselves, they leave it pure, fine, and strong, whereby the partes being sound and cleare more strength groweth on to healthward, and lesse to disease. Herupon it falleth out, that this exercise of the voice, must needes be a singular helpe for them, which have their inwarde partes troubled with moysture, and be of cold constitution, as also for such, as be troubled with weaknesse, or pewkishnesse of stomacke, with vomiting, or bytter rifting, with hardnesse of digestion, with lothing of their meat, with feeding that feedes not, with faintnesse, with naughty constitution, that corrupteth the blood, with dropsies, with painfull fetching their breath, or but then easely, when they sit upright, with consumptions, with any long disease, in the breast or midrife, [57] with apostemes which are broken within the bulke, with quartane agues, with fleame, and also for all those, which be on the mending hand, after sicknesse: for those that are troubled with the scurfe, or Egyptian lepre, called *Elephantiasis*, or whose bellies be so weake, as they cannot avoide, but watry and thin excrementes, for the hikup, for the voice, and her instrumentes, whether naturally resolved, or casually empaired.

Now as this exercise advisedly, and orderly used, is verie good for those effectes in these partes, so rashly and rudely ventured upon, it is not without daunger of doing harme, and cheifly to those which never used it before: it filleth the head and makes it heavie, it dulleth the instrumentes of the senses, which are in the head. It hurtes the voice, and breakes the smaller veines, and is verie unwholesome for such, as are subject to the falling sicknesse, bycause it shaketh the troubled partes too sore: it is daungerous when one is troubled with ill, and corrupt humours, or when the stomacke is cumbred, with great and evident crudities, and rawnes, bycause thorough much chafing of the breath, and the breath instrumentes, it disperseth, and scattereth corrupt humours, thorough out the whole bodie. And as the gentle exercising of the voice, with oft enterlacing of grave soundes, is wholesome, so to much shrilnesse straynes the head, causeth the temples pante, the braines to beate, the eyes to swell, the eares to tingle. Further it is verie unwholesom after meat, bycause the breath being chafed partly by reason of late eating, partly by lowdnesse of the voice as it passeth thorough, gawlleth the throte, and so corrupteth the voice. It is also enemie to repletion, to wearinesse, to sensualitie: for that in those people, which are subject to those infirmities, the great and forcible straining of the voice, doth oftimes cause ruptures and convulsions, so that the commodities, and incommodities of the exercise do warne the training maister to use it wisely and with great discretion. The use of it for the motion is this, that I have said, but for the helpe of learning, it is to some other verie good and great purpose, to pronounce without booke, with that kinde of action which the verie propertie of the subject requireth, orations and other declamatory argumentes, either made by the pronouncer him selfe, or [58] borowed of some other, but cheifly the hoatest *Philippik*, *Catilinarie*, and *Verrine* argumentes, and the rest of that race, either out of many Greeke oratours, or our one and onely Latin *Tullie*, and whether ye list to prose alone, or to be bold with Poetes, and use their meeter. *Coelius Aurelianus* an auncient Romane Physician, though borne at *Sicca* in *Aphricke* speaking of this exercise useth these wordes. They did utter their beginninges or prohemes with a gentle and a moderate voice, their narrations, and reasoning discourses with more straining, and louder: their perorations, and closinges, with a discent, and fall of the voice. And is not that to my saying?

Libro 1. *χρονίων*. cap. 5. de furore.

The manner of this exercise, which *Antyllus* a verie olde Physician doth shew in *Oribasius*, that wrate his bookes unto *Julian* the apostate, whose Physician he was, agreeth also with mine opinion. For having appointed certaine preparatives for nimbling, and spreding the vocall powers, he sayth, that such, as exercised the voice, did first begin lowe, and moderatly, then went on to further strayning, of their speeche: sometimes drawing it out, with as stayed, and grave soundes, as was possible, sometimes bringing it backe, to the sharpest and shrillest, that they could, afterward not tarying long in that shrill sound, they retired backe againe, slacking the straine of their voice, till they fell into that low, and moderate tenour, wherwith they first began. Which wordes do not onely shew, that it was thus used, but also how the voice is to be used, in this exercise generally. But upon what matter, and argument was all this paines bestowed? Those which were unlearned said such things as they could remember, which were to be spoken aloud, and admitted any change of voice in the uttering, now harshe and hard, now smoothe

Lib. 6. cap. 8. De sani. tuen.

and sweete. Those that were bookish recited either *Iambike* verses or *Elegies*, or such other numbers, which with their currant carie the memorie on, but all without booke, as farre surmounting any kinde of reading. I have dwelt the longer in this exercise, bycause it is both the first in rancke, and the best meane to make good pronouncing of any thing, in any auditorie, and therfore an exercise not impertinent to scholers. [59]

Chapter 11.

Of loude singing, and in what degree it commeth to be one of the exercises.

It were to much to wishe, that *Musick* were the most healthy exercise, as it is the most pleasaunt profession, bycause either to much delite would drowne men in it alone, or to much cloying would cause it be quite contemned. Wherfore as it may not diminish other of their due, by occupying to much roome, so by change after other, and distance in it selfe, it continueth in her owne credit. For both varietie refresheth, and distance reneweth, where still the same dulles, and continuance wearies. As *Musick* is compounde of number, melodie, and harmonie, it hath nothing to do with *gymnastick* and *exercise*, but serveth in that sense either for delite and pleasure, and exerciseth desire: or in some respectes concerneth the manering and training up of youth in matter of knowledge, as I said before. Wherunto I was induced not onely by argument, and nature of the thing, but by great authorities of *Plato*, and *Philo*, of *Aristotle* and *Galene*, and whom not? out of all antiquitie, which both allow of the thing in nature, and admit it in pollicie, into the best common weales, as a great worker of much good. But for as much as *singing* useth the voice for her meane, and the voice instrumentes for her utteraunce, and medleth with all sortes, and degrees in sounde base, meane, and triple, which in deliverie do labour, and travell the pipes, it is received among exercises of health, though it be not so forcible, nor can pearce so farre, as loude speaking doth, which doth not much care for any fine concent, so it utter strongly, and straine within compasse: wheras Musick to the contrary standes not much upon straining or fullnesse of the voice, so it be delicate and fine in

Pla. 2. 3. 4. de Repub.

Phil. *Περὶ τῆς εἰς τὰ προπαιδεὺματα συνόδου.*

Aristot. 8. polit.

Galen. 1. De sanit. tuen.

concent. And yet in *Aristotles* opinion, it both exerciseth, and pre- [19. part. probl. 38.] serveth the naturall strength bycause it standeth upon an ordinate, and degreed motion of the voice. We finde in our owne experience, that it sturreth the voice, spreadeth the instrumentes therof, and craveth a cleare passage, as it also lightneth the laborer, and encreaseth his courage, in carying of burdens. It was used in the olde time Physicklike, to stay [60] mourning and greife, for the losse of deare freindes, or desired thinges. In curing diseases, which rise upon some distemperature of the minde, the temperature of time judicially applyed, hath bene found both a straunge and a strong remedie. Alwaye provided, that whether ye say loud, or sing loud, ye neither say to long, nor sing to much, for feare of a worse turne, if any entraill teare, with to much straining, as some times hath proved to true, for the afflicted partie. But to make an ende of *Musick* at this time, though it be neither so strong, nor so stirring an exercise, yet it hath made a great purchace, that it is allowed for one, and therby esteemed a double principle, of more value, where her force is more, in matters of the minde, of very good worth, though of much lesse worke in the health of the bodie. Which seeing it is an exercise within dore, it gaineth with the place a good footing to grow fairer: for whether ye allow it for a cunning exercise, or an exercised cunning, it exerciseth cunning, and encreaseth by exercise.

Chapter 12.

Of loude and soft reading.

Reading is a thing so familiarly knowne, as there needeth no great proofe, that it exerciseth the voice, and therwith all the health, wherof the Physicians admit two kindes, into the raunge of exercises, which be furtherers to health. The one quicke, cleare, and straining, the other quiet, caulme, and staing. The cleare and straining kinde [1.] of *reading*, bycause it stirreth the breath, not sleightly nor superficially, but sheweth what it can do, in the verie fountaine and depth of all the entrailles, it encreaseth the naturall heat, maketh the blood suttle and fine, purgeth all the veines, openeth all the arteries, suffereth not superfluous humours to thicken, neither to congeale and

freese to a dreggie residence within any of those places, which do either receive and lodge, or distribute and dispose, the meat and Lib. 1. c. 2. nurriture. Wherupon *Cornelius Celsus* an eloquent Romain Physician accounteth it one of the finest and fairest exercises. To prove Libro 1. χρονίων. cap. 1. that it is holesome for the head, what more credible witnesses neede we, then *Coelius Aurelianus*, a diligent [61] Physician, and *Annaeus* Lib. 11. Epist. 97. *Seneca* a deepe Philosopher? *Coelius* holdeth this kinde of *reading* to be verie soveraine not onely in headaches, but also in frensies and troubled mindes. *Seneca* used it to stay the rewme, and distillation from the head, which troubled him sore, as a man being both of eager conceit, and earnest studie. Where by the waye, *Coelius* giveth this note, whether ye meane to reskew the pacient, from the headache, or the frantike from madnesse, by this exercise of *reading*, that the matter which is read, be pleasaunt and plaine, and nothing hard to understand, to cause the witte to muse. For that such objectes do no lesse trouble the weake braine, then sore shaking or hard jogging doth the wearied body. Moreover cleare *reading* and loude, doth refreshe not onely the inward partes of the breast, but the stomack also: and comforteth it in feeblenesse, bycause therby phlegmatike excrementes, are without paine both thinned and consumed: wherupon it is held to be verie holesome, to mend a feeble voice, to helpe the colicke, occasioned by cold humours, and to check some consumptions. And to that ende the younger *Plinie* writeth, that his uncle did use it. When I have said it is also good for Lib. de re med. the drie cowghe, I neede not say any more good of it here. *Avicen* the Arabian and princely Physician speaking herof, sayth that in the beginning, this *reading* must be soft and caulme, then mount by degrees, and when the voice seemeth to be in his strength, growing, and long, that then it is hie time, to staie for that time, nor to straine till ye sticke, but to leave with some list, and abilitie to do more. The
2. quiet and staid kinde of *reading*, saving that the working is weaker, doth the best that it can, about all this that is said: and in one pointe it hath obtained a prerogative above the loude, that it is admitted and allowed streight after meat, when the other is licensed and allowed to depart. The maister may so use these two exercises of *reading* and *speaking* as besides the health of the bodie, wherunto they are deputed, they may prove excellent and great deliverers of cunning, and well beseeme the schoole: as to much in either doth trouble the scholer to much, which yet boyes would defend, by the

countenaunce of a commended exercise, were it not, that in boyes exercises, I do require the maisters presence, who will [62] refourme that exercise against their will to his owne discretion. Thus much concerning this exercise, wherby the training maister may perceive, both what the learned have thought of it, and how much the learners are like to gaine by it.

Chapter 13.

Of much talking and silence.

Talking in Latin *Sermo*, as it is accounted an exercise for succouring some partes, so both for eagernesse, and heat, in the nature of speeche, though not of passion, it comes farre behinde others, and is therfore regestred among the meane, and weake exercises. It is thought verie fit for such, as be drousely given: which have their senses daunted, either thorough dreaming melancholie, or dulling phleame. For such kinde of people by talking be cleared, their mindes awaked, their senses freed from the burden of their bodies. That *talking* spendes phleame there is no plainer proofe, then that they which talke much spit stil, which as it commeth partly from the head, partly from the stomacke, partly from the chest: so it declareth, that those partes delite in speeche, and receive comfort from speeche, which makes roome for health, where reume kept residence. But as in these cases, it is counted healthfull: so hath it a force to fill the head, with somwhat more then dinne, and to make it dumpishe. And therefore in aches, and distemperatures of the head, clattering is commended to the cloakbag by Physick. It is also a poyson to the pained eyes: ill for them that voide bloode either at the nose or from the bulke. Wherupon in any such bleading silence is enjoyned. And as silence is a meane both to stay bleading, and to slake thirst, so talking dryes the toungue and provockes thirst, openeth the passage, and promoteth bleading. In so much as *Pline* writeth, that one *Mecenas Messius*, a noble Romain, betooke him selfe to voluntarie silence, the space of three yeares, to staie the casting of blood, which he fell into by reason of some straine. To be short, as silence remedyeth the cough and hikup: so talking pulleth downe, and paines the patient, when agues grow upward, and be

Lib. 27. cap. 6.

in the encrease. Hereupon I conclude, [63] that talking hath great meane either to make or marre, not onely for the subject, wheron the toungue walketh, but also for the object, wherin health resteth.

Chapter 14.

Of laughing, and weeping. And whether children be to be forced toward vertue and learning.

If *laughing* had no more wherfore to be enrouled in the catalogue of exercises, then *weeping* hath, they might both be crossed out. And yet as they be passions, that tende in some pointes, to the purging of some partes, so some may thinke it, a verie strange conceit, to laugh for exercise, or to weepe for wantonnesse. For as laugh one may, with an hartie good will, so weepe none can, but against their wil, to whom it is allotted in the nature of an exercise, and not quite questuarie, as to those wailing women, which wepte for the deade, whom they knew not alive. There be manie and very easie, and much desired meanes, to make one laugh though they have small cause, and lesse devotion to be mery at all, but to make one weepe, is stil againe the haire. For ill newes or matter to weepe for, neither children, nor olde folkes, will thanke you at all. If you meane to make them weepe for joye, or crye for kindenesse, that is an other matter. If the maister should beate his boye, and bring no cause why, but that he sought to have him weepe, so to exercise him to health, and to ridde him of some humours, which made him to moist, the boye would beshrew him, and thinke his maister beate him so, to exercise himselfe, though at the verie conceit of his maisters mad reason, he might brust out in *laughing* streight after his stripes, and so become a patrone to the contrary exercise: a great deale more gracious and more desired in nature, whose enemie greife is, and *weeping* also: as a plaine argument of an unpleasaunt guest. Howbeit seing they be both set downe, by the name of pettie, and pretie exercises, let them have that is given them, seeing they are thought to stirre, and cleare some partes: *laughing* more and better: *weeping* lesse and worse. And therfore the more children laugh for exercise, the more lightsome they be, the more [64] they weepe if it be not in jeast, so much the worse in very good earnest. For I can hardly beleve that much *laughter* can avoide a foole, if it be not for exercise, which is also somwhat rare: or that but a foole can weepe for exercise, which deserves the bat, to make him weepe in earnest.

But for *laughing* in the nature of an exercise and that healthful, can there be any better argument, to prove that it warmeth, then the rednesse of the face, and flush of highe colour, when one laugheth from the hart, and smiles not from the teethe? or that it stirreth the hart, and the adjacent partes, then the tickling and panting of those partes themselves? which both beare witnesse, that there is some quicke heat, that so moveth the blood. Therfore it must needs be good for them to use *laughing*, which have cold heades, and cold chestes, which are troubled with melancholie, which are light headed by reason of some cold distemperature of the braine, which thorough sadnesse, and sorrow, are subjecte to agues, which have new dined, or supped: which are troubled with the head ache: for that a cold distemperature being the occasion of the infirmitie, *laughing* must needes helpe them, which moveth much aire in the breast, and sendeth the warmer spirites outward. This kinde of helpe wil be of much more efficacie, if the parties which desire it, can suffer themselves to be tickled under the armepittes, for in those partes there is great store of small veines, and litle arteries, which being tickled so, become warme themselves, and from thence disperse heat thorough out the whole bodie. But as moderate *laughing* is holesome, and maketh no too great chaunge, so to much is daungerous, and altereth to sore. For besides the immoderate powring, and pressing out of the spirites: besides to much moving and heating, it oftimes causeth extreame resolution and faintnesse, bycause the vitall strength and naturall heat drive to much outward. Wherupon they that laugh, do sweat so sore, and have so great a colour, by the ascending of the blood. And as the naturall heat, and fire it selfe do still covet upward, as to their naturall place, so must it needes be, that the lower roomes lie open, and emptie in their absence, wherby whether soever motion be marred, the naturall heat dyeth, and the vitall force faileth. Besides this, no [65] man will denie, but that this kinde of *laughing*, doth both much offende the head, and the bulke, as oftimes therewith both the papbones be loosed, and the backe it selfe perished. Nay what say ye to them that have dyed *laughing*? where gladnesse of the minde to much enforcing the bodie, hath bereft it of life.

Weeping.

For *weeping* in the nature of an exercise, there is not much to be said, but that is accompanied with crying, sobbing, groning and teares, wherby the head, and other partes are rid of some needlesse humour: though the disquieting do much more harme, then the purging can do good, and the humour were a great deale better avoided some other waye. Wherof some children seeme to be exceeding full, when feare of beating makes them straine their pipes. *Aristotle* must beare both most blame for this exercise, if it displease any, and most praise, if it profit any, who in the last chapter of the seventh booke of his politikes writeth thus of it, and for it. That they do not well which take order, that children straine not themselves, with crying and weeping, bycause that is a meane to their growing, in the nature of an exercise. And that as holding the breath doth make one stronger to labour: so crying and weeping in children, do worke the same or the like effectes. And yet me thinke it should be no exercise, by the verie definition. For if it were vehement, yet is it not voluntarie, and though it did alter the breath, yet it bettereth not the bodie, howsoever it serve the soule.

7. Polit. cap. ult.

But seeing the *gymnastikes* have it, let us lend it them for their pleasure, though we like it not for our owne. It is generally banished by all Physicians as being the mother to manie infirmities, both in the eyes and other partes: neither if it could be avoided in schooles were it worthy the looking on: being the heavy signe of torture and trouble. And though it somtime ease the greived minde to shedde a few teares, as some for extreme anguish cannot let fall one, yet children would be lesse greived if they might shedde none, as some hold it a signe of a verie shrewd boye, when he deserves stripes, not to shew one trikle. Some Physicians thinke by waye of a conserve to the minde, that it ought to be used in schooles sometimes, though not voluntarie, yet in forme of an exercise to warme shrewd [66] boyes, and to expell the contagious humours of negligence, and wantonnesse, the two springes of many streaming evilles: as playing would be daily, at some certaine houres, then to use these exercises, when bookes be out of season.

Lib. 2. παιδ.

The greatest patron of weeping that I finde, leaving *Heraclitus* to his contemplation of miseries, is a soure centurion in *Xenophon,* which sat at the table with *Cyrus* in his pavilion. He commmendeth weeping, wherto he had no great devotion, to discountenaunce *laughing* which he saw allowed, and his reason is: bycause *awe, feare, correction, punishements*, which commonly have *weeping*, either companion, or consequent, be used in pollicy, to kepe good orders in state, and good manners in stay, wheras *laughing* is never, but upon some foolish ground. And yet both *laughing* for exercise may be for a good objecte, and occasion to make laughter, may well deserve praise, when the minde being wearied either about great affaires that are alreadie past, or about preventing of some anguish which is to ensue, doth call *laughing* to helpe, to ease the one, and to avert the other. And this kinde of *weeping*, which the soldiar settes out so, concerneth no exercise, though it commonly follow all unpleasaunt exercises, where the partie had rather be idle with pleasure, then so occupyed to his paine: but it tendeth to the impression, or continuing of vertue in the minde: which should be so much the worse, bycause that waye it seemeth unwilling, where feare is the forcer, and not free will. Which free will is the principall standard to know vertue by, which is voluntary, and not violent: as it is not the best meane, to bring boyes neither to learning, nor to vertue.

Socrates in *Plato* thinketh, that an absolute witte in the best sorted kinde, and above all common sorte, for civill societie, ought not to be forced, as in deede what needes he, being such a paragon? and that free will in such a one so sifted is the right receit of voluntarie traine. But we neither have such common weales, as *Socrates* sets forth, nor such people to plant in them, as *Socrates* had, which he made with a wishe: nor any but subjecte to great infirmities, though some more, some lesse, by corruption in nature, which runneth headlong to unhappinesse, and needeth no beating for not being nought. [67] And therfore we must content our selves with that which we have, and in our countrey which is not so absolute, in our children which be no *Socraticall* saintes, in our learning which will not prove voluntarie, if the child playe voluntarie we must use correction and awe, though more in some, then some, bycause in illnesse there be steps, as in excellencie oddes. Wherof there is no better argument then that which this verie place offereth, not for the soldiars saying, which so commendeth awe, bycause his authoritie is to campishe, though he that brought him in, and platted the best prince were himselfe no foole: but for mine owne collection. For if one neede not to beat children to have them do ill, wherunto they are prone, we must needes then beat them for not doing wel, where

7. De Rep.

nature is corrupt. Onelesse we meete with one, that will runne as swift uphill against nature, to do that which is good, as we all runne downe bancke, with the swinge of nature, to do that which is ill. Which when I finde, I will honour him, as I do none, though I do oft beare with some, in whome there appeareth but some shew of such a one. If under doing well, ye comprehend not learning, ye must needes comprise vertue, and make her meane violence, against all both heavenly *Divinitie*, and earthly *Philosophie*, with whom all vertues be voluntarie, when reason is in ruffe: but not in children even for compassing of the best effectes, whom custome and traine must now and then force foreward, to be ready for reason, when she maketh her entrie, which requireth some yeares. For howsoever *religion, wisedome, duetie*, and reasonable *consideration* do worke in riper age, sure if awe be absent, in the younger years, it will not be well. And who can tell, what even he that under lawe is most obsequious and civill, would of him selfe prove, if lawe, which emportes awe, would leave him at libertie?

Chapter 15.

Of holding the breath.

Though all men can tell, what a singular benefit breathing is, wherunder the use of our life is comprehended: yet they can best tell, which have it most at commaundement. For as [68] they live with others, in societie of common dealinges, so they can execute any thing by the bodie, farre better then others, whether it be politike in the towne, or warlike in the fielde. And all exercises have this ende, most peculiar and proper, by helping the naturall heat, to digest the good nurriture, and to avoide the offall, thorough out the whole bodie. Which what is it els, but to set the breathing at most libertie, being best discharged of impediment and let? And as the libertie of breathing maketh the soldiar to abide in fight long, the runner to continue his race long, the daunser to endure his labour long, and so forth in the rest, which must either have breath at their will, or els shrinke in the midest: so the restraint and binding of the breath, even where it is most at will, (for else it could not abide the restraint,) hath his commoditie, by waye of exercise to assist our health.

Now in breathing there be three thinges to be considered, the taking in, the letting out, and the holding in of the breath, wherof everie one hath his private office to great effect, in the upholding of
health, and maintaining of life. For when we take in our breath, by 1.
the working of the lungues thorough such passages, as be appointed for the use of breathing, we conveigh and fetch in aire into the
roomy and large places of the bulke, to coole the harte and fine the
spirites. When we let out our breath by those same passages, by 2.
which we tooke it in, we discharge the hart of a certaine smoky substance engendred in it, which is conveyed thence, thorough the
same hollow, and roomie places of the bulke. When we hold and 3.
kepe in our breath which is of judgement, and not of such neede as the other two, and done upon cause to helpe nature therby: we must neither fetch aire inward, nor sende those smokie excrementes outwarde, bycause the belly and breast muscles and such fleshy partes as be about the ribbes being violently and vehemently strained and stretched, do for the time as it were mure up, and stop the passage. This keeping in of the breath, by reason of the straine offered to those partes, and heating of the bowells, is therfore heeld for one of the vehement exercises, as it is also a postparative, called before apotherapeutike, bycause after maine stirringes it helpeth to expell those [69] residences, which lynger within the bodie as being lothe to depart: and furthereth those, that are in good waye, and make hast to be gone. They that used this exercise by waye of traine to health, did it in two sortes: for either they strayted onely those muskles, which appertaine to the breast and bulke, and let those be at libertie which belong to the midrife and belly, that the excrementes might have the readier waye downward, being once forced on: or they strayned both all the partes, and all their muscles at one time, that the bowelles also which are beneth the midrife might enjoye the benefit of the exercise, and be as ready to discharge, as the other to drive downe. But for the better and more daungerlesse performing therof, they were wont to swadle the chest, the ribbes, and the belly. Bycause the holding of ones breath unadvisedly and with to much strayning causeth ruptures and divers other infirmities in the interiour vesselles of the bodie. Their meaning was hereby, sometime to strengthen the inward and naturall heat being encreased by exercise: sometime to helpe the breathing partes:

sometime to discharge the breast and bellie of needlesse burden. For the breath being so violently strayted, when it findeth issue forceth his owne passage, and caryeth with him some finish and thinne excrement, either driving it before, if it lye in his waye, or drawing it with him, if he catch it by the waye. Being of it selfe such a strainer, and expeller, it is good for to open the pipes, to fine the skinne, to drive out moysture from under the skinne: to warme, to strengthen and to scoure the spirituall and breathing partes, to make the places of receit more roomy, to encrease strength in labour, to helpe the eare in listening, to remove coldnes or inflations from the entrailles, to stay the hikup and the cowgh: which commeth of some cold distemperature in the windepipes, to remedie the colick, the weaknesse of stomacke, the want or difficultie of breath. So that all those ought to esteeme of it, which have their breathing and spirituall partes either cold or weake, or cloyed with excrementes, or whose bodies can either with much adoe or with none at all expell and ridde superfluous humours, or that be cumbred with much gaping and yawning, with resolution or weaknesse of the toungue, or any vocalle instrument. If it were [70] to be perceived by no waye els, verie children let us see, that holding of the breath doth stirre and strengthen that power in us, wherwith we expell superfluities. For let them staye their breath either laughing long, or weeping fiercely, or upon some such other occasion, and they will either presently or verie shortly after, disburden themselves one waie or other, by ordure, urine, or some other matter at the nose and eares. Now as this exercise is healthfull to manie in good order: so contrariewise to some in disorder it is verie daungerous, bycause oftimes while the breath is to forcibly stopt, the arteries in the jawes, and baulles of the eyes swell so, as they will never come in temper againe. It filleth the head also with a grosse and stuffing humour, as maie easely be seene by the swelling of the vaines and arteries in the neck, by the puffing about the eyes, by the rednesse of the face, and by the strutting of the whole head, all which be manifest signes of repletion. It is daungerous for those which be subject to the falling sicknesse, bycause it encreaseth the disease by that recourse, which the blood hath up into the head: as also to them which spit or cast up blood, for that both the sound and whole inward vesselles do burst with stretching, if they be but weake: or being broken once before, and healed againe, they will then breake out againe, by reason of heat which is encreased in the hollow of the breast, and the overstraining of the said vesselles withall. Moreover such as from their birth have small entraulles and thinne, or the rim of their bellie tender and weake: or that be troubled with renting and ruptures must in no case minde this exercise, bycause it straineth those partes to sore, and lightly teareth them, as it proveth oftimes to pitifull true in young children, which by holding their breath to long, either weeping or otherwise, oftimes breake either the rim of their belly, or the call of their cods, wherby the bowelles and guttes falling downward, they become miserably tormented with incurable ruptures and burstinges: If trumpetters, and those that play upon winde instruments were asked the question, whether they feele not the effect herof somtime, they would shake the head, and so sooth the demaunde, though they said no more. They do write of *Milo* the *Crotoniate*, a great champion in those athleticall [71] exercises, that he used to binde his forehead, his breast, and his ribbes with verie strong tapes, and would never let his breath goe, till the vaines were swelled so full, as they burst the tapes. But this fellow had no fellow in any of those pastimes. It was he that bare the bull upon his shoulder in the *Olympian* assemblie by using to cary him of a litle young calfe. So great thinges be easely compassed, if they be set in hand with, when they be but litle, or medled with, by litle and litle. The best waye to avoide perill in this exercise is to beginne gently, and so to grow on by degrees, and to leave be times before extremitie bidde hoe, and while ye be yet able to do more, neither to force nature to the furthest.

Hier. Mercu. lib. 3. cap. 6.

Chapter 16.

Of daunsing, why it is blamed, and how delivered from blame.

Daunsing of it selfe declareth mine allowance, in that I name it among the good and healthfull exercises: which I must needes cleare from some offensive notes, wherwith it is charged by some sterne people: least if I do not so, it both continue it selfe in blame still, and draw me thither also with it, for allowing of a thing, that is disliked, and by me not delivered from just cause of misliking, which by my choice do seeme to defend it. And yet I meane not here to rippe up, what reading hath taught me of it, though it seeme to have served for great uses in olde time, both athleticall for spectacle and shew: militare for armour and enemie: and Physicall for health and welfare: so many and so notable writers, make so much and so oftimes mention therof in all these three kindes. Some dedicate whole volumes to this argument onely, some enterlace their bravest discourses with the particularities therof, and those no meane ones. And in deede a man, that never red much, and doth but marke the thing cursorily, would scant beleve, that it were either of such antiquitie, or of such account, or so generally entreated of by learned men, all those their writinges stil sounding to the praise and advancement therof: howsoever in our dayes either we embase it in opinion: or it selfe hath given cause of just embasement, by some peoples misuse. Many [72] sortes of it I do reade of, but most discontinued, or rather quite decayed, that onely is reserved, which beareth oftimes blame, machance being corrupted by the kinde of *Musick,* as the olde complaint was: machance bycause it is used but for pleasure and delite onely, and beareth no pretense or stile of exercise, directly tending to health, which is our peoples moane now in our dayes. For where honest and profitable reasons be not in the first front, to commend a thing, but onely pleasaunt and deliteful causes, which content not precise surveiours, there groweth misliking, the partie that exerciseth, not pretending the best, which is in the thing, and the partie that accuseth, marking nothing else but that, which maye move offence.

The sad and sober commodities, which be reaped by *daunsing* in respect of the motion applyed to health be these, by heating and warming, it driveth awaie stifnes from the joyntes, and some palsilike trembling from the legges and thighes, whom it stirreth most, it is a present remedie to succour the stomacke against weaknesse of digestion, and rawnesse of humours: it so strengtheneth and confirmeth aching hippes, thinne shankes, feeble feete, as nothing more: in delivering the kidneys or bladder from the stone, it is beyond comparison good: but now such as have weake braines, swimming heades, weeping eyes, simple and sory sight, must take heede of it, and have an eye to their health, for feare they be disie when they daunce, and trip in their turning, or rather shrinke downe right when they should cinquopasse. Such as have weake kidneys and overheated, may displease them selves, if it please them to daunce, and encrease their diseases, by encreasing their heat.

The *daunsing* in armour, called by the Greekes πυῤῥιχὴ, as it is of more motion in exercise, so it worketh more nimblenesse in executing, when ye deale in the field with your enemies. These be the frutes which are reaped by *daunsing* well and orderly used, for the benefit of health, and the contrary displeasures, which are caught by it, thorough inconsiderate applying of it, by the partie which is not made for it. The blame that daunsing beareth. The blames which it beareth be these. 1. That it revelleth out of time, wherewith Physick is offended: 2. That it serveth delite to much, whereat [73] good manners repine. For these two faultes there is but one generall aunswere: that daunsing is healthfull, though the daunsers use it not healthfully, as other things of greater countenaunce be verie good, though the professours do not so, as their professions do enjoine them. 1. For the first in particular, the rule of health condemnes not daunsing, but the mistyming of it: that it is used after meat, when rest is most holesome: with full stomacke, when digestion should have all the helpe of naturall heat: that to please the beholders, such as use daunsing do displease them selves. And sure if *daunsing* be an exercise, as both all antiquitie doth commend it for, and I my selfe do allow of it by that name: it would by rule of Physick go before meat, and not be used but long after, as a preparative against a new meale: and a disburdener of superfluities, against a surcharge of new diet: Howbeit there be in it some more violent measures then some: and in beginning with the most staydest and most almanlike, and so marching on, till the springing galliard and quicker measures take place, choice in everie one, upon knowledge of his owne bodie, and his emptinesse or saturitie maye helpe health, though the custome of eche countrey commaunde not onely health, though to her harme, but even the verie science which professeth the preservation of health, if desire egge delite, to shew it selfe in place. 2. Whereupon the second blame of *daunsing*, doth especially builde, and take her hold.

To keepe thinges in order, there is in the soule of man but one, though a verie honorable meane, which is the direction of reason: to bring things out of order there be two, the one strongheaded, which is the commaundement of courage, the other many headed, which is the enticement of desires. Now *daunsing* hath properties to serve eche of these, *exercise* for health, which *reason* ratifieth, *armour* for agilitie, which *courage* commendeth, *liking* for allowance, which *desire* doth delite in. But bycause it yeildeth most to delite, and in most varietie of pleasures, desire ministreth most matter to blame, *daunsing* by pleasing desire to much, hath pleased reason to litle, and when reason objecteth inconveniences, it turneth the deafe side, and followeth her owne swinge. For when the tailour hath braved, [74] where nature hath beawtified: when amiablenesse of person hath procured agilitie by cunning, what gallant youthes in whom there is any courage, can abide not to come to shew, having such qualities so worthy the beholding? here will courage shew her selfe, though repentance be her port, here will desire throng in prease, though it praise not in parting. All this doth confesse that *daunsing* is become servant to desire, though not *daunsing* alone: and yet companions in blame be no dischargers of fault. What then? for the generall, seing thinges which man useth, cannot be quite free from misuse, it is halfe a vertue to winne so much, as there be as litle misuse, as may be: and to charge the partie that deserves blame, with hinderance of health, with corruption of manners, with ill losse of good time: which if he care not for, the precept may passe, though he passe not for it. But howsoever *daunsing* be or be thought to be, seing it is held for an exercise, we must thinke there is some great good in it, though we protecte not the ill, if any come by it. Which good we must seeke to get, and praie those maisters, which fashion it with *order* in time, with *reason* in gesture, with *proportion* in number, with *harmonie* in *Musick*, to appoint it so, as it may be thought both seemely and sober, and so best beseeme such persons, as professe sobrietie: and that with all, it may be so full of nimblenesse and activitie, as it may prove an exercise of health, being used in wholesome times, and not seeking to supplant rest, as the rule of health at this daie complaineth. And generally of all ages, me thinke it beseemeth children best, to enable, and nimble their jointes therby, and to stay their overmuch deliting therin in further yeares. The very definition of it declareth, what it was then, when it was right, and what it is now, when it seemes to be wronge, if right in such thinges be not creature to use, and maye change with time, without challenge for the change. They define *daunsing* to be a certaine cunning to resemble the manners, affections, and doinges of men and women, by motions and gestures of the bodie, artificially devised in number and proportion. This was to them a kinde of deliverie, to utter their mindes, by signes and resemblances, of that which came nearest to the thing, and was most intelligible to the lookers on. But [75] now with us, there is nothing left to the daunser ordinarily, but the bare motion, without that kinde of hand cunning (for so I terme their *χειρονομία*) bycause the skill seemed then to rest most in the use of the upper partes, and gesturing by the hand. The credit of our *daunsing* now is to represent the Musick right, and to cause the bodye in his kinde of action to resemble and counterfet that lively, which the instrument in his kinde of composition delivereth delicately: and with such a grace to use the legges and feete, as the olde daunsers used their armes and handes. And as in the olde time both men, wymen and children did use *daunsing* to helpe and preserve their health, to purchace good haviour and bearing of their bodies: so in these our dayes, being used in time, by order, and with measure, it will worke the same effectes of health, haviour and strength, and may well avoide the opinion of either lewdnesse, or lightnesse. Thus much for *daunsing*, as the motion is for health, and the meaning for good.

Chapter 17.

Of wrastling.

For wrastling as it is olde and was accounted cunning sometimes, so now both by Physicians in arte, and by our countreymen in use, it seemeth not to be much set by, being contemned by the most, and cared for but by the meanest. Yet the auncient *Palestra* a terme knowen to the learned, and joined with letters, and Musick, to prove the good bringing up of youth as a most certaine argument of abilitie well qualified, fetcht that name of the Greeke *πάλη*, which we in English terme wrastling, and was alwaye of good note, as wrastling it selfe in games gat victories, in warre tried forces, in health helpt haviour, in the bodye wrought strength, and made it better breathed. *Clemens Alexandrinus* which lived at *Rome* in *Galenes* time in the third booke of his Paedagogue, or training maister, in the title of exercise, rejecting most kindes of wrastling yet reserveth one, as verie well beseeming a civill trained man, whom both seemelinesse

παιδαγ. 3. De exercitiis.

for grace, and profitablenesse for good health, do seeme to recommende. Then an exercise it is, [76] and healthfully it may be used: if discretion overlooke it, our countrey will allow it. Let us therefore use it so, as *Clement* of *Alexandria* commendes it for, and make choice in our market. Wherfore not to deale with the catching pancraticall kinde of wrastling, which used all kindes of hould, to cast and overcome his adversarie, nor any other of that sort, which continuance hath rejected, and custome refused, I have picked out two, which be both civill for use, and in the using upright without any great stouping, the one more vehement, the other more remisse. The
1. vehement upright wrastling chafeth the outward partes of the bodie most, it warmeth, strengthneth, and encreaseth the fleshe, though it thinne and drie withall. It taketh awaie fatnesse, puffes, and swellinges: it makes the breath firme and strong, the bodie sound and brawnie, it tightes the sinews, and backes all the naturall operations. If they that wrastle do breath betwene whiles, it provoketh sweat, bycause the humours, which were gathered together by rest, are egde out by exercise. If they go on still without intermission, it dryeth up the bodie in such sort as the sonne doth. It is good for the head ache, it sharpneth the senses, it is enemie to melancholie, it whetteth the stomacke being troubled with any cold distemperature. And bycause the attemptes to get vantage in wrastling be very eager and earnest wherwith the whole bodie is warmed and set in a heat, it must of force be good for the bellie, being anoyed and cumbred with any kinde of cold. Now contrarie it is daungerous to be delt with in agues, as to vehement and conspiring with the quiverer, in naturall moysture as to filling, where it spreadeth. For the necke and jawes perillous whom it harmes by rowgh handling, and strangleth by much overstraining. For the breast and bulke not of the best, as either bursting some conduit, or stopping some windcourse. Weake kidneis, and wearie loynes maye be but lookers vpon wrastlers. They that be gawled or byled within, may neither runne nor wrastle, for eagering the inward, being in way to amendement, or in will to prove worse. If weake legges become wrastlers, of their
2. owne perill be it, for they do it without warrant. The remisse kinde of upright wrastling, as it is a more gentle exercise, so it breadeth much flesh, and is therfore verie commodious [77] for such as be upon the recoverie after sicknesse, as a kinde of motion, which with

out any danger, bringeth strength and stowtnesse. It is freind to the head, bettereth the bulke, and strengtheneth the sinewes. Thus much for wrastling, wherin as in all other exercises, the training maister must be both cunning to judge of the thing: and himselfe present to prevent harme, when the exercise is in hand.

Chapter 18.

Of fensing, or the use of the weapon.

The use of the weapon is allowed for an exercise, and may stand us at this daie now living, and our posteritie in great stede, as wel as it did those which went before us. Who used it *warlike* for valiauntnesse in armes, and activitie in the field, *gamelike* to winne garlandes and prices, and to please the people in solemne meetinges: Physicklike to purchace therby a good haviour of body and continuance of health. Herof they made three kindes, one to fight against an adversarie in deede, an other against a stake or piller as a counterfet adversarie, the third against any thing in imagination, but nothing in sight, which they called *σχιομαχία*, a fight against a shadow. All these were practised either in armes, or unarmed. The armed fensing is to vehement for our trade, let them trie it, that entend to be warriers, which shall finde it their freinde, if they meane to follow the fielde, where, as in all other thinges use worketh maisterie. But we scholers minde peace, as our muses professe that they will not medle, nor have to do with *Mars*. All these sortes of fensing were used in the olde time, and none of them is now to be refused, seing the same effectes remaine, both for the health of our bodies, and the helpe of our countries. That kinde of fensing or rather that misuse of the weapon, which the *Romane* swordplayers used, to slash one an other yea even till they slew, the people and princes to looking on, and deliting in the butcherie, I must needes condemne, as an evident argument of most cruell immanitie, and beyond all barbarous, in cold blood, to be so bloodie. For their allegation, to harten their people against the enemie, and not to feare woundes: no [78] not death it selfe in the verie deadly fight, that caryeth small countenaunce, where the *Athenian* comes in, which in

Solon apud Lucianum in *ἀναγάρσει*.

cokfights and quailefightes, did so harten their people: bycause those birdes will fight till they fall: without either embrewing their youth with blood, or acquainting their citisens eyes with such sanguinarie spectacles.

Lib. 28. cap. 1. & lib. 36. cap. ult. A thing complained on in the time when it was used, even by them which behelde it, as *Plinie* doth note: and by the *Christianes*
Epist. Lib. 2. which abhorred it, as *Cypriane* cryeth out of it in moe places then one. But for the credit and countenaunce of the exercise, that was
Plato in Lachete then used, and is now to be continued, *Plato*, a man whose authoritie is sacred among Philosophers and studentes, in his dialogue surnamed *Laches*, where he handleth the argument of fortitude and valiantnesse, encourageth young men to learne the use of their weapon: as being an exercise which needeth not to make curtsie to go with the very best and bravest in his parish: either for travelling or strengthening the bodie, besides the cunning of it selfe. The prof-
1. ites which health receives by all these three kindes be these. He that exerciseth him selfe either against an adversarie, or against a post or pillar as deputie to his adversarie heateth himselfe thoroughly, maketh way for execrementes, provoketh sweat, abateth the abundance of flesh, strengtheneth his armes and shoulders, exerciseth
2. his legges and feet marveilously. He that fighteth against a stake stirreth the bodie, plucketh the flesh downe, and straynes the juyce awaye, a peculiar freind to the armes and handes: It refresheth the wearied sense, it setleth the roming humours, it redresseth the fainting and trembling of the sinewes, it delivereth the breast from his ordinarie diseases: it is good for the kidneyes: and the great gutte called *κῶλον*, it furthereth such cariage as must be conveighed
3. downward. The same effects hath the fight against the shadow or the shadowish nothing, but that it is a litle more valiant to light upon somwhat then to fight against nothing. But of all these three, the exercise against an adversarie is both most healthfull, and most naturall to aunswere all assaies: and specially to canvase out a coward, that will neither defend his freinde, nor offend his foe: the cheife frute that should follow fensing. This is the [79] opinion of the best writers concerning fensing, or skill how to handle the weapon: no worse in it selfe, though it be sometimes not worthily used, as it is no lesse profitable, then hath bene said afore: though it shake and shiver weake heades, swimming braynes, and ill kidneys. The mo

reasons any man can bring of him selfe for any of these exercises, the more he fortifieth my choice, which point them but out slightly.

Chapter 19.

Of the Top and scourge.

He that will deny the Top to be an exercise, indifferently capable of all distinctions in stirring, the verie boyes will beate him, and scourge him to, if they light on him about lent, when Tops be in time, as everie exercise hath his season, both in daie and yeare, after the constitution of bodies, and quantities in measure. Of this kinde of Top, that we use now a dayes, both for young and olde people, to warme them in cold weather, I finde nothing in writing, bycause having no yron ringes, nor pinnes, it can neither be the Greek κρῖκος, nor τρόχος, though the running about be bold to borrow the last name *trochus*. For they whirled about, and along, with a marveilous great, though a pretie noyse, and were pastimes for men even in the midst of sommer, when our Tops be bestowed, and laid up against the spring. It resembleth the Latin *Turbo* most, and the Greeke βέμβιξ. The place of *Virgil* in the 7. of his *Aeneis*, where he compareth *Amata* the Queene in her furie to this *Turbo* which the boyes scourged about the wide haule: declareth both what *Turbo* is, and whose play it was, and that it best resembleth our Top. Of βέμβιξ there was an old Greek *Epigram*, which maketh it either the like or the same with our Top.

Οἵ δ' ἄρ' ὑπὸ σκυτάλῃσι θοὰς βέμβικας ἔχοντες,
Ἔστρεφον εὐρείῃ παῖδες ἐνί τριόδῳ.

Which is to say, that children when they had their whirling gigges under the devotion of their scourges, caused them to troule about the broad streates. The harme this exercise may bring must be to the head and eyes, thorough stouping to much forward, or to the backe and shoulders by bending to much [80] downwardes, otherwise it warmeth the bodie, and worketh all the effectes, which those exercises do that either by moving the legges or armes most, and with all the whole bodie in degree, enlarge and stirre the naturall heat either to provoke appetite, or to expell superfluities. The more roome the Top hath to spinne in, the better for the legges and feete, the bigger it is, the better for the armes and handes. The uprighter one scourgeth, the better for all partes, whom neither bending doth crushe, nor moysture corrupt. It were to be wished, that it were whipt with both the handes, in play to traine both the armes, seing use makes the difference, and no infirmitie in nature. As both *Plato* wishing the same professeth it to be most true and our experience teacheth us, both in left handed people, which use but the left, and in double right handed which use both the handes a like, and beare the name of the right hand as the more common in use. But bycause the place of *Plato* concerning the left hande is verie pithie to this purpose though I use not to avouch much in the Greeke toungue, yet me thinke I maye not overpasse it. In the seventh booke of his lawes, allowing the indifferent use of our feete and legges, he complayneth of to much partialitie used towardes the armes and handes, in these wordes, *τά γε περὶ πόδας τὲ καὶ τὰ κάτω τῶν μελῶν οὐδὲν διαφέροντα πρὸς τούς πόνους φαίνεται. Τὰ δὲ κατὰ χεῖρας ἀνοίᾳ τροφῶν καὶ μητέρων οἷον χωλοὶ γεγόναμεν ἕκαστοι. Τῆς φύσεως γὰρ ἑκατέρων τῶν μελῶν σχεδὸν ἰσοῤῥοπούσης, αὐτοὶ διὰ τὰ ἤθη διάφορα αὐτὰ πεποιήκαμεν οὐκ ὀρθῶς χρὼμενοι*, etc. For the performance of any kinde of labour there is no difference, sayeth he, in the legges, and lower partes. But for our armes, thorough ignoraunt nurses and mothers, we be every one of us halfe lamed. For wheras naturally both the armes be almost of equall strength, thorough our owne default we make the difference. And so he passeth on still proving the unnaturall handling of the left hande, when it is left weaker then the right hande is.

Plato.

These be the exercises which I terme within dores, bycause they may be practised at home under covert, when we cannot go abroad for the weather: though all maye be used abroad, if the roome and the weather do serve abroad. Wherein I take [81] it, that I have kept *Galenes* rule in chusing these exercises, and that they be all both pleasant, profitable and parable, the perfect circumstances of all good and generall exercises, not to be costly to compasse, nor unpleasant to loth them, nor unprofitable to leave them. Those that require more libertie of roome, to raunge at will, or to forrage in the

Lib. de parua pila.

field, be these, which I noted before, *walking, running, leaping, swimming, riding, hunting, shooting,* and *playing at the ball.*

Chapter 20.

Of walking.

Among those exercises which be used abroade, what one deserveth to be set before walking, in the order and place of traine? what one have theÿ more neede to know, which minde, the preservation and continuaunce of health? what one is there, which is more practised of all men, and at all times, then walking is? I dare saye that there is none, whether young or olde, whether man or woman, but accounteth it not onely the most excellent exercise, but almost alone worthy to beare the name of an exercise. When the weather suffereth, how emptie are the townes and streates, how full be the fieldes and medowes, of all kindes of folke? which by flocking so abroad, protest themselves to be favourers of that they do, and delite in for their health. If ye consider but the use of our legges, how necessarie they be for the performaunce of all our doings, *nature* her selfe seemeth to have appointed *walking*, as the most naturall traine, that can be, to make them discharge their duetie well. And sure if there be any exercise, which generally can preserve health, which can remedie weaknesse, which can purchace good haviour, considering it is so generall, and neither excludeth person nor age, certainly that is *walking*. Hereupon Physicians when they entreat of this argument, use alwaye to give it, the place of preferment and birthright in this kinde. The auncient Princes, and common weales so highly esteemed of it, as in the places appointed for exercise, whether within their great buildinges, or without, they seemed to minde no one thing more: and still provided walking roomes, [82] to serve for all seasons and times of the yeare, some covert and close, some uncovert and open, some secret and hidden. The reason why they thus regarded *walking*, was great, for as it seemeth to be, so it is in verie deede wholly consecrate to the use of health.

Is it ever red that the athlets or gamesters used walking for an exercise: either in sportes, or in theaters, or in the solemnising of

3. De Rep.

Lib. 1. cap. 9. & penul.

their sacred ceremonies, wherunto they served? did either *Plato* handling this argument, or any good writer else saye that walking was any waye to traine up soldiars withall? Onely *Vegetius* sayeth in his discourse of warfare, that it were good for soldiars to accustome themselves to walke quickly and proportionately, for their better breathing: and *Augustus Cesar*, and *Adrian* the Emperours, did ordeine by constitution, that soldiars both horsemen and footemen should monthly be led abroad to walke and that not only in the plaine fieldes, but in all kindes of soile, to be able by that acquaintaunce with groundes, to make difficultie at none. So that *walking* seemeth to be onely institute both by nature and custome for the use of health: and that in the traine of health, no one thing deserveth better place then it doth: bycause no other thing besides health layth claime unto it.

The use of slow walking after exercise.

Herof there be two kindes, the one used after vehement exercises, the other, which beareth the name of the exercise it selfe. Concerning the former of the two, I have but thus much to saye: bycause the latter is my peculiar subject. That it commeth in place, when other exercises are dismissed, and finished, after purgations ministred by counsell of Physick, after great vomiting: that it is good to refresh the wearied minde: to alter and bring in order the spirites: to loose that which is strayted, to scoure the chest: to make one fetch his breath at ease: to strengthen the instrumentes of the senses, to confirme the stomacke, to cleare and fine the bodie: and not to suffer it after travaile to melt or decaie, but to purge and cleanse it: and that, which is of most account, to dissolve and bannish awaye all affections that procure any feeling of weariesomnes, or disturbaunce to the bodie.

The three principall kindes of walking.

The second kinde of *walking* hath three sortes under him. [83] Wherof the first beareth his name of the kinde of motion, how: The second of the place, where: The third of the time, when the walking is used. Which three also have particular braunches under eche of them, as hereafter shall appeare.

Walking which is named after the time of moving.

Walkinges which take their names of the motion how, be either swift or slow, vehement or gentle, much or litle, moderate, or sore, long and outright, or short and turning: now bearing upon the whole feete, now upon the toes, now upon the heeles.

Moderate walking.

Of all these diversities in *walking* the moderate is most profitable, which alone of all, that I rekened, hath no point either of to much, or of to litle, and yet it is both much, and strayning, which be the two properties of an healthfull walke. It is good for the head, the eyes, the throte, the chest, when they be out of frame: so the partie spit not blood. For distilling from the head, for difficultie of breath, for a moyste and pained stomacke, wherin the nurriture either groweth bitter or corrupteth: for the jaundise, costifnesse, fleeting of the meat in the stomacke, stopping of the urine, ache of the hippes, and generally for all such, as either neede to provoke any superfluitie from the upper partes downward, or to send that packing, which is already in waye to depart. Now to the contrarie it is naught for agues, bycause it encreaseth heat, and so consequently the disease: for the falling evill, for hauking up of blood: and in the time when one is making water.

Swift and quick walking.

Swift *walking* doth heat sore and abateth the flesh, wherupon to ease the colicke, and to take awaie grossenesse, it is accounted a verie good meane.

Slow walking.

Slow *walking* hath the same effectes, that the apotherapeutike hath. And therfore it is good for sickly weake olde men, and those which delite in, or neede walking after meate, to setle it better in the bottome of their stomacke: or that be newly awaked from sleepe, or that prepare themselves to some greater exercise, or that feele any ache in any part, or that have drie bodies. When one hath the head ache it is good to walke first slowly, and after a while a litle faster, and stronger, strutting out the legges. Slow *walking* is also good against the falling sicknesse: bycause without any shaking to the head, it [84] fetcheth the humours downward, where it thinneth and disperseth them, and warmes the whole bodie, without endammaging it. Finally in quartane agues, when the fit is past, in leprosies, for tetters, ringewormes, cankars, and to procure easie fetching of ones breath, it is verie soveraine.

Vehement and to sore.

Vehement or to sore and to eager *walking*, is best for cold folkes, and therfore good to drive away trembling or quaking, it encreaseth puffing and blowing, and yet dissolveth, and disperseth winde. But it is ill for weake heades and feete, and such as are in daunger of the gout. For both the gout and the hippe ache do oftimes come of to much and to sore walking. As to the contrarie gentle walking upon soft straw, or grasse, or upon even ground is good for any gout or inward exulceration, before meat, but not after. For wearinesse is their principall enemie: which heateth and enflameth their jointes to sore: and thereby causeth them to draw stil more matter from the partes further of, to feede their continuall fluxe.

Much and oft.

Much and oft *walking* is good for them that have a distempered bulk or head: that perceive small nurriture in their lower partes, that in their exercises neede more vehement stirring.

Litle and seldome.

Litle *walking* is good for them, that use no bathing or washing after exercise, which must needes walke after meate, to send it downe, to the bottom of their stomacke, and for those which finde some heavinesse in their bodies.

Long and outright.

Long and outright *walking* is nothing so troublesome as the short, that maketh many turnes. It is good for the head, and yet it sucketh up humours, and dryeth to fast.

Long and quicke.

Long and quicke *walking* is good to staye the hikup or yeaxing.

Short and soone *turning* wearyeth sooner: and troubleth the head sorer.

Circular or *walking* round about maketh one disie, and hurteth the eyes.

In *walking* to strout the legges, and beare upon the heeles, is verie good for an ill head, a moyst bulke, a strayned bellie, and for such of the lower partes, as prosper not, yea, though the partie feede well: and generally for all those, in whome superfluities steeme upward. [85]

To beare upon the toes hath bene proved good for ill eyes, and to staye loose bellies.

Bearing upon the whole feete is alwaye incident to some of the other kindes, and therefore joyneth with eche of them in effectes.

Walking which is named after the place.

Walking which taketh the name after the place, is either on hilles and high groundes, or in valleies and lowe groundes: againe the lowe ground is, either even, or uneven: either under covert, or abroad: in the sunne, or in the shade. When one walketh up against the hill, the bodie is marveilously wearied, bycause all the sway and poize of it presseth downe those partes, which are first moved. And for all that such motions be heavie and slow, yet they cause one sweat sooner and sorer, and staye the breath more, then the *walking* downhill doeth: bycause heavie thinges bearing naturally downward, are forced upward against nature. Wherupon heat which beareth the bodie up, as in comming downe it travelleth not of his owne nature, so preasing upward it is burthened with the bodie, whereby it both encreaseth it selfe, provoketh sweat, and stayeth the breath. This kinde of walke afore meate is good for the bulke, which hath not his breath at commandement. *Demosthenes* strengthened his voice by it, pronouncing his orations alowd, as he walked up against the hill, whereby he gat the benefit of breathing, to deliver his long periodes, without paine to himselfe, or breach to his sentence. The knees are most toiled in this kinde of walking, being forced backward contrarie to their nature, and therfore to their griefe.

Plut. in Demost.

Walking downhill draweth superfluity from the head more then the other doeth: but withall it is enemy to feeble thighes, bycause they both move the legges, and support all the whole weight of the bodie above. The change and varietie of the motion causeth that kinde of walking to be best liked, which is sometime uphill, sometime downhill.

Walking downhill.

When ye walke upon even or uneven ground, ye walke either in medowes or grassie places, or in rowgh and brambly, or in sandie and soft. If ye walke in a medow, it is without all contradiction most for pleasure, bycause nothing there anoyeth, nothing offendeth the sense, and the head is fed both with varietie [86] of sweet odours, and with the moysture of such humour, as the medow yeeldeth.

Rough, brambly, and bushy groundes stuffe the head.

Sandie, and cheifly if it be any thing deepe, bycause the walking in it stirreth sore, confirmeth and strengtheneth all the partes of the bodie: and fetcheth superfluities mightily downward. This was one of *Augustus Caesars* remedies, as *Suetonius* writeth, to helpe his haulting and weake legges. For to cleare the upper partes of that which cloyeth them, there is nothing better then to travell in deepe sande.

Walking upon sande.

In Augusti vita. cap. 80.

Walking in a close gallerie is not so good, bycause the ayre there is not so fresh, free, and open, but pent, close and grosse: and therfore stuffeth the bodie, onelesse the gallerie be in the uppermost buildinges of the house, where neither any vapour from the ground can come: and the ayre that commeth is pure and cleare.

Walking in a close gallerie.

The close *walkes*, which were called *cryptoporticus* were not of choice but of necessitie, when extremitie of weather would not let them walke abroad.

Walking in an open place, and cheifly greene, is much better and more wholesome, then under any covert. First of all for the eyes, bycause a fine and subtile ayre comming from the greene to the

Walking in an open place.

bodie, which is more penetrable bycause of stirring, scoureth awaye all grosse humours from the eyes, and so leaveth the sight fine and cleare. Further, bycause the bodie in walking waxeth hoat, the aire sucketh humours out of it, and disperseth what soever is in it more then it can well beare.

Now in *walking* abroad there is consideration to be had to the soile. For *walking* by the sea side ye thinne and drie up grosse humours, by rivers and standing waters ye moyst. Howbeit both these two last be naught, and specially standing waters. Walking not neare any water, as it is not so good as the walke by the sea, so it is much better, then walking neare any other water. Walking in the dew moystes, and harmes.

It is good to walke where birdes haunt.

If ye *walke* in a place where birdes haunt, it is of great efficacie to cleare by the breath, and to disburden the bodie so, as if ye did walke in some higher ground. If there be no winde where ye walke, it cleareth by breath: it disperseth excrements, [87] it slakes and nippes not, and is good for colicks that come of a cold cause. If there be winde, the *Northern* causeth coughing, hurtes the bulke, and yet confirmes the strength, soundes the senses, and strengthens the weake stomacke. The *Southwinde* filles the head, dulles the instrumentes of sense, yet it looseth the bellie, and is good to dissolve. The *Westwinde* passeth all the rest, both for mildenesse, and wholesomnesse. The *Eastwinde* is hurtefull and nippes.

It is better to walke in the shade then in the sunne.

It is better *walking* in the shade then in the sunne: as it is naught for the headache to walke either in the cold or in the heat. And yet it is beter to walke in the sunne, then to stand in it, and better to walke fast, then slowly. Of all shades, those be the best which be under walles or in herboures. It is verie daungerous *walking* neare unto dewye trees, for feare of infection by the sappie dew: bycause dew in generall is not so wholesome, it abateth the flesh, as wymen that gather it up with wooll or linnen clothes for some purposes do continually trye. Now if the dew come of any unwholesome matter, what may it prove to? The best *walking* in shadowes simply is under myrtle and baye trees, or among quicke and sweet smelling herbes, as wilde basell, penyroyall, thyme, and mynt, which if they be wild and of their owne growing be better to wholesome the soile, then any that be set by hande: but if the better cannot be, the meaner must serve. Againe in this kinde of *walke* the faire and cleare aire lighteneth, scoureth, fineth, procureth good breathing, and easie mov-

Daungerous walking under dewy trees.

What effecte the faire and cleare aire hath.

ing. Darke and cloudie aire heavyeth, scoureth not by breath, and stuffeth the head.

Walking which taketh his name after the time.

Walking which is termed after the time, is either in winter or summer: in the morning or in the evening, before meat or after. The most of these differencies will appeare then playnest, when the time for all exercises is generally appointed, in consideration of circunstance, as shall be declared under the title of time. In the meane while *walking* whether in the morning or evening, ought still to go before meat.

The good of the morning walk.

The *morning walke* looseth the belly, dispatcheth sluggishnes, which comes by sleep, thinneth the spirits, encreaseth heat, and provoketh appetite. It is good for moyst constitutions, it nimbleth and quickneth the head, and all the partes in it. [88]

The good and ill of the evening walk.

The *evening walke* is a preparative to sleepe, it disperseth inflations, and yet it is ill for a weake head. Walking after meat is not good but only for such as are used unto it. Yet even they maye not use it to much. It is good also for them, which otherwise cannot cause their meat go downe to the bottome of their stomacke.

And thus much for *walking*, both regarding the manner of the motion, the place where, and the time when. Which circunstances though they be many and divers: yet to purchase the commodities, which walking is confessed to be very full of, they must needes be cared for: considering our whole life is so delt with, as if we hastened on death, against the which, this exercise may be rightly termed an antidote, or counterreceit.

Chapter 21.

Of Running.

The manifest services which we receive by our legges and feete, in *warre* for glorie, to pursue or save, in *game* for pleasure to winne and weare, in *Physick* for health to preserve and heale, do give parentes to understand, that they do suffer their children to be more then halfe maymed, if they traine them not up in their youth to the use and exercise therof. To polishe out this point with those effectuall reasons, which avaunce and set forth nature, when she sayeth in plaine termes, that she meanes to do good: or with those argumentes, wherwith the best authors do amplifie such places, when they finde nature so freindly and forward, (as the anatomistes which survey the workmanship of our bodie, and histories, which note the effectes of swiftnesse, do wonder at nature, and with exercise to helpe her, for that which they see) were to me nothing needefull, considering my ende is not the praise, but the practise of that which is praiseworthy: neither to tell you, what *Alexander* the *Macedonian,* nor what *Papyrius* the *Romain* did by swift foote, nor that *Homere* gave *Achilles* his epithete of his footmanship, but to tell you that *running* is an exercise for health, which if reason cannot winne, wherof every one can judge, sure historie will not, where the authors credit [89] may be called in question as to much favoring the partie whom he praiseth, wherefore I will leave of all manner of by ornamentes, wherwith such as be in love with running do use, to set it forth, and directly fall to the severall kindes there of which differ one from an other, both in the moving it selfe, and also in the manner of the moving, wherupon the effectes, which follow must needes prove divers according to that diversitie. Running of it selfe is helde by the Physicians generally to be a swift exercise, which needeth neither much strength, nor great violence, and in what sorte so ever it is used, it is ill for agues.

1. The first kinde of *running* which beareth his name of the verie motion vehement swift, and withall outright, hindereth health, rather then helpeth it: and if it helpe it any waye, it is in that it abateth the fleshinesse, and corpulence of the body: which if it chaunce to be moyst, swift running will empty it of humours, and stay it also quickly. It hath bene found so wholesome in some diseases of the splene or mylt, as *Aetius* a learned Physician writeth, that he knew some which by walking and running onely, were delivered from all greife and peine there. But it is verie unwhole-
5. part. probl. 9. some for such as have ill heades. Wherupon *Aristotle* in his Problemes asking the question why running which is thought to drive all excrementes downward, if it be vehement and swift should be offensive to the head, not in men and wymen alone, but also in beastes, aunswereth thus: that the swift motion, bycause it strayneth the strength, and stayeth the breath, heates the head with all, and swelles the veines therein: so that they draw unto them forreine meane as cold or heat: and besides that, it enforceth what so

ever is in the breast to ascend upwarde, whereby the head cannot chuse but ake, which is the cause, that swift running is naught for the falling evill. *Galene* thinketh so basely of this kinde of running, as he termeth it, a thing both an enemie to health, to great a thinner of the whole bodie, and such a one, as hath no manner of manly exercise in it. Besides this, it putteth him which runneth so vehemently in daunger of some great convulsion, if he fortune to encounter any violent stop by the way. De parua pila lib.

The second kinde of *running*, which taketh his name of the gentle 2.
and moderate moving, warmes the bodie very well, [90] strengthens the naturall actions, provokes appetite, helpes and turnes rewmes, and catarres, some other waye. And therfore it is commended for a remedie against the swiming of the head, against the drie cough, if ye holde your breath withall, against exulcerations in the inner side of the jawes, and the distorsion or writhing of the mouth, which the Greekes call *κυνικὸν σπάσμα*. For though at the first it seeme to provoke defluxions and distilling of humours, yet within a small time it stayeth them: and therfore it is thought to be good for those, which are pained with the *Ischiatica*, which have much a do to stirre their legges at the first, but after that they have runne a while, they be so nimble and quicke, as if they had never felt any paine in those partes. It strengtheneth the stomacke mightely, and delivereth the bellie from winde, and cold passions: whereby it is thought, and that not without great cause to be verie good for the colike and dropsie: it delayeth the swelling of the milt. For the gnawing of the guttes, and some diseases of the kidneis it is exceeding good, so the kidneies be not either presently, or have not bene of late, subject to some exulceration. To saye that it is wholesome for the legges and feete, were to make a doubt, where none can be, considering *running* is their proper and peculiar action. This exercise for all that it is such a freind to health: yet bringes with it some inconveniences: for it is verie laborious: it cooleth the flesh and furthereth not the feeding. And as naturally of it selfe, it breadeth no great harme, so if it meete with an ill head, or a weake bulke, or burning and hoat urine, it helpes to draw on divers diseases. He that hath any rupture in the twiste, or els where, must forbeare running, as those also, which have infected livers or gauled kidneies. If the chafed deare could speake, he would desire the hunter to give him leave to pisse, when he pursueth him sorest, and that for but so litle

respite, he would shew him a great deale more pastime: but the hunter which knoweth well that the skalding urine will not let him runne long, wil not lend him that leasure: bycause he careth more for the frute of his owne praie, then the effect of the deares prayer. All the other kindes of *running* which follow, take their names of the manner of their moving, wherof the first is the long outright running, which if it continue [91] on gently though long, it warmeth the flesh, and makes it plumpe, and is verie good, for great feeders, though it make the bodie slow and grosse. *Running* streight backward, and withall not hastily, is good for the head, the eyes, the streatchers, the stomacke and the loynes. *Running* round about, thinnes the flesh and streaches it, but cheifly the belly, and bycause of the quicke motion, it gathereth moysture quickly. And therfore *Hippocrates* wisheth them to use it, which dreame of blacke starres, as the fore warning of some forreine disease. It troubleth the head and makes it dizie: it marreth both the bulke and the legges, and therefore would be left. He that runnes uphill straynes him selfe sore, and doth neither his bulke nor his legges any great good. He that runnes downhill makes his head giddy, shakes all within him, and tries the weaknesse, or strength of his hippes. He that runneth in his clothes sweateth sore, and warmes his flesh more: and therefore it is good for them, that have the head ache to runne so: and those that have somewhat to do, to fetch their breath. He that runneth out of his clothes single or naked, sweateth much, which is much more healthfull how litle so ever it be, then much more, with the clothes on. *Hyppocrates* likes running generally more in winter then sommer. *Oribasius* in both, yea though sommer be in his prime and cheife heat. The resolution is, when most sweating is best, which *Aristotle* sayeth is in sommer.

Lib. de insomniis languentium.

3. Lib. de Diaeta.

2. part. proble. 21. 33. 42.

Chapter 22.

Of Leaping.

Leaping should seeme to be somewhat naturall, and chearfull, bycause at any pleasant or joyefull newes, not onely the hart will leape for joye, but also the body it selfe will spring lively, to declare his consent, with the delited minde, and that not in young folkes alone, but also in the elder, whom we commonly say that no ground can hold: so that leaping seemes to stand the body in such a steade for uttering of joy, as the tongue serves the minde to deliver her delite by speche with laughter. The cattell and brute beastes bewraie their contentment, and well liking, by the selfe same meanes, leaping and galloping [92] of them selves in their pasture when they be lustily disposed and in good health. Though in training of the bodie by waye of exercise, there be not so much regard had to the mirth of the minde, as to the motion of the bodie: and yet being an exercise it may not be unpleasant. In which kinde it is noted to be vehement, wherein both strength is used to make the body spring, and swiftnesse to make it nimble: being naturally an interrupted race, as running is a continued leape. It served the olde world in *game* for braverie, and shew of activitie: in *warfare* to skip over diches and hard passages, in *Physicke* for an exercise of health, whereby it became more stately and imperiall, bycause the first famous Romain Emperor *Augustus Caesar*, being troubled with the *Ischiatica* and stone in his bladder, and also having some weaknesse in his left legge and feet, used this running leape, or leaping race to helpe himselfe thereby. There be divers kindes of leaping wherof I will tuch the most likely.

Suetonius in Augusto cap. 83.

Leaping and springing without intermission is good to encrease 1. the naturall heat, to helpe digestion, to dispatche raw humours, though afterward it anoie the head and brest, bycause it shaketh the head verie vehemently: and by reason of much bending and so pressing the backe, it oftimes breaketh some canall in the breast or lungues. To *leape* running is good for such diseases of the head, as 2. have troubled it long. It helpeth the bulke, bycause it useth no violent bending, nor pressing of the bodie, it fetcheth downe such needeles fumes, as otherwise would have ben aspiring upward: it chearisheth weake legges: which prosper not by nurriture, thorough some trembling and benummed flesh. *Leaping* as we do com- 3. monly call it and use it, doth drive idle superfluities downward thoroghly, but bycause it shaketh the bulke to sore, both by to violent moving and to forcible strayning, it is not good for it: though it shew a verie deliver and an active bodie: both to stirre and to do any thing else. It driveth also the stone from the kidneies into the bladder: yet it hurteth the knees by reason of violent and continuall bending them. The *Lacedemonian* wymen, whose picture *Callimachus* the painter, for his foolish curiosity named κακοχειρότεχνος, as [34. Lib. cap. 8.] *Plinie* reporteth, used to leape so, as their heeles did hitte their hippes, which manner of leaping doth [93] both purge and drie. But me thinke I here some gentlewymen saye, fye upon them *Rigs*. Not so. The lawes and custome of their countrey did allow, nay did commaunde them to runne, to leape, to wrastle, and to do all such exercises, both as well, as men, and also with men. Their reason was. They did thinke the childe lame of the one side, whose mother was delicate, daintie, tender, never stirring, never exercising, not withstanding, the father were never so naturally strong, never so artificially trained. And to prevent that infirmitie in their owne youth, [4. de Rep.] they exercised their wymen also, no lesse then their men. As *Plato* wisheth his people in his common weale, which he patterneth for the best. *Skipping* againe the banck, as it helpeth the hippes, so it hurteth the breast: and the same downhill, cleareth the head from superfluities, which it fetcheth downward: It strengtheneth the legges, but it shaketh the bowelles to sore, which is very dangerous, for ruptures any where: for the crooked swelling veines in the legge: for all gouttes: for all those, in whom the humours upon any small occasion will fall downe to the feete: and cause them to swell. Further [Gal. 6. epi. commen. 3. aph. 2.] in cases where it were good to let blood or to purge, if either yeares or some other impediment wil admit neither, to avoide superfluous humours, *leaping* will supply the roome. As it is verie ill for those which pisse blood: or be in a flixe: or have weake or overheated kidneies: or that have at that time, or not long before had, some gaule or exulceration in the kidneies. And yet though the kidneies be sound, leaping will sometime loose a veine. Eche kinde of *leaping* is better accomplished by holding of some weight in the hand for steddinesse, then with the hand emptie and without his ballace.

Chapter 23.

Of Swimming.

In the old time, when they would point at a fellow, in whom there was nothing to be made account of, they were wont to saye, he neither knoweth letter on the booke, nor yet how to *swimme*: wherby it appeareath that *swimming*, was both in great use, and of great price in those daies, which either first brought [94] forth by word or afterward maintained it, seing he was helde for no bodie that could not, or but for a dastard which would not learne the sleight to *swimme*. The traine came bycause it was then best to learne, when the jointes were most pliable, and yet strong withall. The ende was either to save themselves in fightes by sea, or in flightes by lande, where they were to passe rivers, or to assaile enemies by water, or for other such services: as what if *Leander* say it serves for love, and bring both *Hero* to witnesse, which was partaker of the evill, and *Musaeus* the Poete, which described their misfortune? Which considerations may recommende *swimming* to us also: who may stand in neede of it, upon the same causes, and in the like eventes that they did. But bycause it is so necessarie, it would not be uncurteously entertained, and therefore regard must be had in what water ye swimme, for if ye swimme in springes which are naturally hoat, it is stuffing, and yet good for the palsie: so he that swimmeth do use bladders, to ease him selfe withall, and lighten his labour. To *swimme* in marsh waters, and pooles, infecteth both the head and all the residue of the bodie, bycause rotten, and corrupt vapours, enter the pores of the bodie, together with the moysture. It is reasonable good *swimming* in lakes and standing meres, which the larger they be and the clearer, the more commodious and wholesome to swimme in. But no kinde of fresh water is so good to swimme in, as the running river is, cheifly for them, which be in health, to whom besides many other commodities, it serveth for a preparative to sleepe. Yet it is not good abiding long in any fresh water, for feare of perishing the sinues both with cold and moysture, whose issues be the crampe, and the swimmers daunger. But nothing at all, be it never so good for health, be it never so defensible to save, can be gotten without perill in proving. And why should *swimming* dreame of securitie, and never thinke to drowne? Doth it not deale with water, where there is no warrant, but wisedome to forsee? pointe the place, pointe the fight, pointe the daunger and a pointe for daunger: but where you cannot appointe the particularitie, ye cannot warrant the perill. *Cocles*, scaped, it was in a small river, and reskue at hand. *Scoeva* the centurion scaped, he was neare both shippe [95] and shoar. Nay *Caesar* himselfe saved him selfe from drowning, and helde his lettres up drie in the one hand. A signe of courage and cunning, as that

Liuius. C. Caes. Appian.

man had enough: but his shippes were at hand, and it is not writen, that either he swamme alone, or any long waye. But of all daungers to drowne, there is least in the sea, where the swimming is best: for the salt water as it is thicker then the fresh, so it beareth up the bodie better, that it may fleet with lesse labour. The *swimming* in salt water is very good to remove the headache, to open the stuffed nosethrilles, and therby to helpe the smelling. It is a good remedie for dropsies, scabbes and scurfes, small pockes, leprosies, falling awaye of either legge, or any other parte: for such as prosper not so, as they would, though they eate as they wishe, for ill stomackes, livers, miltes, and corrupt constitutions. Yet all *swimming* must needes be ill for the head, considering the continuall exhalation, which ascendeth still from the water into the head. *Swimming* in hoat waters softeneth that which is hardened, warmeth that which is cooled, nimbleth the jointes which are benummed, thinneth the skinne, which is thickned, and yet it troubleth the head, weakneth the bodie, disperseth humours, but dissolveth them not. *Swimming* in cold water doth strengthen the naturall heat, bycause it beates it in: it maketh verie good and quick digestion: it breaketh superfluous humours, it warmeth the inward partes, yet long tarying in it hurtes the sineues, and takes awaye the hearing. Thus much concerning *swimming*, which can neither do children harme in learning, if the maister be wise, nor the common weale but good, being once learned, if either private daunger or publike attempt do bid them aventure. For he that oweth a life to his countrey, if he die on lande, he doeth his duetie, and if he drowne in water, his duetie is not drowned.

Chapter 24.

Of Riding.

If any wilbe so wilfull as to denie *Riding* to be an exercise and that a great one, and fittest also for greatest personages, set him either upon a trotting jade to jounse him thoroughly [96] or upon a lame hakney to make him exercise his feete, when his courser failes him. In all times, in all countries, among all degrees of people, it hath ever bene taken, for a great, a worthy, and a gentlemanly exercise.

Though *Aristophanes* his testimonie, were naught against honest *Socrates*, yet it is good to prove, that riding was a gentlemanly traine, even among the principles of education in Athens. And *Virgile* in the legacie sent to *Latinus*, describeth the same traine in the Romain children, which, sayeth he, exercised themselves on horsebacke before the towne. And *Horace* accuseth the young gentleman in his time as not able to hange on a horse. But to deale with stories either Greeke, or Latin, for the Romain, or other nations exercise in riding in a matter of such store, were more then needeles. The *Romains* had their whole citie divided into partialities, by reason of the foure factions of those exercising horsemen. Who of the foure colours, which they used, Russet, White, Greene, and Blew, were named *Russati, Albati, Prasini, Veneti*. For the warres how great a traine riding is, I would no countrey had tried, nor had cause to complaine, nor the subdued people to be sorofull, though the conquerour do vant himselfe, of his valiantnesse on horsebacke. For health it must needes be of some great moment, or els why do the Physicians seeme to make so much of it? They saye that generally it encreaseth naturall heat, and that it purgeth superfluities, as that to the contrarie it is naught for any sicke bodie, or that hath taken Physicke hard before, or that is troubled with infection or inflammation of the kidneies. They use to devide it into five kindes, *Slow, quicke, trotting, ambling,* and *posting*.

Gal. 7. meth. Pli. epist. 9. lib. 6. Martial. lib. 11. Juvenal.

1. Of *Slow riding* they write that it wearieth the grines very sore, that it hurteth the buttokes, and legges, by hanging downe to long, and that yet it heateth not much: that it hindreth getting of children, and breadeth aches and lamenesse.

2. Of *quicke riding* they saye, that of all exercises it shaketh the bodie most, and that yet it is good for the head ache, comming of a cold cause: for the falling evill: for deafnesse, for the stomack, for yeaxing or hikup, for clearing and quickning the instrumentes of sense: for dropsies: for thickning of thinne shankes: which was found true in *Germanicus Caesar* nephew to [97] *Tiberius* the Emperour, which so helped his spindle shankes. Againe quick riding is naught for the bulke: for a weake bladder, which must forebeare all exercises, when it hath any exulceration: for the *Ischiatica*, bycause the hippes are to much heated and weakned, by the vehementnesse of the motion. Wherupon the humours, which are styrred rest there: and either breede new or augment olde aches.

Suetonius.

3. Of *trotting*, it is said even as we see, that it shaketh the bodie to violently, that it causeth and encreaseth marveilous aches, that it offendes the head, the necke, the shoulders, the hippes, and disquieteth all the entrailes beyond all measure. And though it may somewhat helpe the digestion of meate, and raw humours, loose the belly, provoke urine, drive the stone or gravell from the kidneyes downward, yet it is better forborne for greater evilles, then borne with for some sorie small good.

4. *Ambling* as it exerciseth least, so it anoyeth least, and yet loseth it the bellie.

5. As for *posting*, though it comes last in reading, it will be first in riding, though for making such hast, it harme eche part of the bodie, and specially the bulke, the lungues, the bowells generally, the kidneyes: as what doth it not allway anoy, and oftimes either breake or put out of joynt by falles or straines? It warmes and paires the body to sore, and therfore abateth grossenes, though a grosse man be ill either to ride post himselfe, or for a jade to beare. It infecteth the head, it dulleth the senses, and especially the sight: even til it make his eyes that posteth to run with water, not to remember the death of his friendes, but to thinke how sore his saddle shakes him, and the ayer bites him.

Chapter 25.

Of Hunting.

Hunting is a copious argument, for a poeticall humour, to discours of, whether in verse, with *Homer*, or in prose, with *Heliodorus*. *Dian* would be alleged, as so avoyding *Cupide*. *Hippolytus*, would be used in commendation of continence, and what would not poetrie bring in to avaunce it, whose musicke being solitarie and woddishe, must needes be, nay is very well [98] acquainted with the chace. If poets should faint, and the *Persians* would fight, both for riding and hunting: so that if patrocinie were in question, we neede not to enquire, they would offer them selves, from all countries, and of all languages. But we need not either for praise, or for profe, to use forraine advocats. For hunting hath alway caried a great credit, both for exercising the bodie, and deliting the mynde, as it semes to be verie naturall, because it seeketh to maister, and to take beastes, and byrdes, which are naturally appointed for mans use, and therefore though they be taken and killed, there is no wrong done them. The courteous *Xenophon* as delited himselfe therein, and all the auncient writers, as subscribing to a truth, commend it marveilously, and chiefly, for a proper elementarie to warlike uses, and *Mars* his schoole, whether for valiauntnes or for pollicy, because the resemblaunces of the chiefe warlike executions do fall out in hunting, as the qualitie or courage of the game offereth cause, either to use force and manhoode, or to flie to devise and sutteltie.

lib. de Venat. 1. παιδ.

The *Romain Emperours* did exhibit publike hunting unto the whole people in way of pastime and pleasure. The *Physicians* make much of it: as being an exercise, which containeth under it most of the other stirring exercises, for they that hunt, walke, runne, leape, shout, hallow, ride, and what may they not do, having the whole country for roome, and the whole day for time, to do in what they list? And though *Galene* do restraine it to men of great abilitie, as if hunting were not for every man to use, which is one of the markes, whereby to know the best exercises, that they be parable, and purchaceable even to meane purses: yet we see it in common to most, where restraint by law doth not forbid it. Neither is the charge in respect of the exercise, but in respect of the game, whereon the exercise is employed. To hunt a hare, and course a hart, to chase a bucke, and chafe a bore is not all one, neither for provision, nor for perill though the exercise have small oddes, which being compounded of those exercises that I named, must nedes have the same effectes, that those exercises have besides his owne. To warme the bodie very well, to disperse superfluites, to abate flesh, to lessen overflowing moysture, to make one sleepe soundly, to [99] digest meat, and raw humors, to quicken both the sight and the hearing, to keepe of old age, and finally to make the body most healthfull, and the health most lasting.

De parua pila lib.

Rases a notable Arabicke Physician, writeth that in a great plague there remained almost none alive in a certaine towne, save hunters only, which escaped by reason of their preserving exercise. And *Mithridates* that famous king used hunting so much for his healthes sake, as in seven yeares space, it is written that he never came within house, neither in citie nor countrie. And yet hunting is not good for the head, when it is used with vehemence, as no other vehement exercise is.

3. Commen. 13. tract. cap. 3.

There be but two kindes of *Hunting* to my purpose, the one on horsebacke, the other on foote.

1. They that *Hunt* on horsebake, for so much as they sometime gallop, sometime ride fast, sometime hallow, sometime be stil, and varie so in most actions, seeme to travel every part of their body, and therefore it is thought, that thereby the brest, the stomacke, the entrailes, the backe and legges be strengthened: but it is ill for them, which are troubled with any paine in their head, and daungerous for feare of breaking some veine in the breast: for the stone in the kidneyes, for those that be of hoate constitution of body: for weake bellicawles, and for feare of ruptures, because such thinges fall out oftentimes in hunting on horsebacke: not without losse sometime of life.

2. *Hunting* on foote, hath all the commodities, and incommodities to, that hunting on horsebacke hath, saving the daunger whereunto it is not so much subjecte. And yet the travell of the bodie is more, the body hoater, the legges and feete more strengthened, the appetite to meat more, to make children lesse. Neither of them is good but for strong and healthful bodies, neither can hunting be but harmefull unto them, which use it unadvisedly, without consideration how they runne, by way of pleasure and ordinarie exercise, or at the suddaine of a head, for by tarying abroade all day, and feeding so uncertainely, and so unseasonably, there come sundrie inconveniences.

But of all *Hunting* that is still best, wherein we exercise our selves and our owne bodies most, not our hauks or howndes, because exercises be meanes to make men healthfull, and other [100] thinges be meanes to bring that meane about. Such a kinde of hunting was it which *Chiron, Machaon, Podalyrius, Aesculapius,* the parentes and patrones of physike did use, whose delite therein, is our warrant in choyce, because they being so great physicians, as physicke went then in *Platoes* opinion, did trie that in their owne persons, which they delivered to posteritie for the same use.

Chapter 26.

Of Shooting.

The physicians seeme to commend shooting for the use of health sufficiently, in that they make *Apollo* and *Aesculapius* the presidentes and protectors of *Archerie*, which both be the greatest gods, and chiefest patrones of ther owne profession. And that it is a thing to be beloved, and liked, what argument is there that can be alleadged of comparable force to that of *Cupide* himselfe, which in the matter of love, doth bend with his bow, and enamour with his arrow? But in sadnes to say enough of this exercise in few wordes, which no wordes can praise enough for the commodities which it bringeth to the health of the body: as it hath bene used by divers nations, in diverse sortes, both on horsebacke and on foote, both for peace and warre, for healthfull exercise and pleasant pastime: so none either now doth use it, or heretofore hath used it, more to health, and bettering of the body then our owne countrimen do. As if it were a thing somewhat naturall to *Ilandes*, bycause they of *Crete* and *Cyprus* in olde stories, they of the *Indian* Ilandes in new stories are noted also for neare *Shooting*, strong *Darting*, and streight *Slinging*, whereof the *Balear Ilandes* seeme to take their name. Nay by all auncient monumentes *Shooting* should seeme to be both the eldest, and the usuallest defence in fighting a farre of, which though it have now, and tofore have had great place in the fielde for warfare: yet hath it a great deale better place in our fields for wellfare: and therefore the more, because it consisteth both of the best exercises, and the best effectes of the best exercises. For he that shooteth in the free and open fields may chuse, whether betweene his markes he will runne or walke, daunce or leape, hallow or sing or do somewhat [101] els, which belongeth to the other, either vehement or gentle exercises. And whereas *hunting* on foote is so much praised, what moving of the body hath the foote *hunter* in hilles and dales, which the roving *Archer* hath not in varietie of growndes? Is his naturall heate more stirred then the *Archers* is? Is his appetite better then the Archers is though the proverbe helpe the hungrie *hunter*? Nay in both these the *Archer* hath the vantage. For both his howers be much better to eate, and all his moving is more at his choice: because the *hunter* must follow his game of necessitie, the *Archer* neede not but at his owne leasure. For his pastime wil tary stil, till he come to it, the hunters game is glad to get from him. In fine what good is there in any particular exercise, either to helpe natural heat, or to cleare the body, or to provoke appetite, or to fine the senses, or to strengthen the sinewes, or to better all partes, which is not altogither in this one exercise? Onely regard to use it in a meane doth warrant the *archer* from daunger to himselfe: and an eye to looke about, doth defende the passager from perill by him. I could here speake much, if it were not to much, to say even so much in such a thing, being so faire a pastime, so pleasant to al people, so profitable to most, so familiar to our country, so every where in eye, so knowne a defence, such a meane to offende, as there is no man but knoweth it to be a preservative to health, and therefore well to be numbred among the trayning exercises. And chiefly as it is used in this Iland, wherein the roving must nedes be the best and most healthful, both for varieties of motion in diversities of soile, and by using all *archery*, in exercising one kinde. For in roving, you may use either the butte, or the pricke by the way for your marke, as your pleasure shalbe. This exercise do I like best generally of any rownde stirring without the dores, upon the causes before alleadged, which if I did not, that worthy man our late and learned countrieman maister *Askam* would be halfe angrie with me, though he were of a milde disposition, who both for trayning the *Archer* to his bow, and the scholler to his booke, hath shewed him selfe a cunning *Archer*, and a skilfull maister.

In the middest of so many earnest matters, I may be allowed to entermingle one, which hath a relice of mirth, for in praysing of [102] *Archerie*, as a principall exercise, to the preserving of health, how can I but prayse them, who professe it throughly, and maintaine it nobly, the friendly and franke fellowship of prince *Arthurs* knightes in and about the citie of *London*, which of late yeares have so revived the exercise, so countenaunced the artificers, so enflamed emulation, as in themselves for frindly meting, in workemen for good gayning, in companies for earnest comparing, it is almost growne to an orderly discipline, to cherishe loving society, to enrich labouring povertie, to maintaine honest activity, which their so encouraging the under travellours, and so encreasing the healthfull traine, if I had sacred to silence, would not my good freind in the citie maister *Hewgh Offly*, and the same my noble fellow in that order Syr *Launcelot*, at our next meeting, have given me a sowre nodde, being the chiefe furtherer of the fact, which I commend, and the famosest knight, of the fellowship, which I am of? Nay would not even prince *Arthur* himselfe maister *Thomas Smith*, and the whole table, of those wel known knights, and most active *Archers* have layd in their chaleng against their fellow knight, if speaking of their pastime I should have spared their names? whereunto I am easily led, bycause the exercise deserving such praise, they that love so praiseworthie a thing neither can of them selves, neither ought at my hand to be hudled up in silence.

Chapter 27.

Of the Ball.

The play at the *Ball* seemeth compound, bycause it may be used, both within dores, and without. Wherof good writers have delivered us thus much: that in the olde time there were divers kindes of *balles* and divers kindes of exercise therewith, according to the divers use of the *ball* either small or great: both amongst the *Romaines* and *Greekes*, whose names I use so much, bycause they were best acquainted both with the thinges, and with the right use therof. *Galene* in his first booke of maintaining health, speaking of the *Germains*, who used then to dippe their new borne children into extreme cold water over head and eares, to trie their courage and to harden their [103] skinne, sayeth that he wrate those lessons of health and exercise, no more to the *Dutch* and such rude people as we also were then, then to beares, boares and lyons: but to *Greekes* and such people, as though barbarous in nature, yet by traine and learning, were become greekish as we now are, and the *Romains* then were. So that our examples be fetcht from these two nations, which either used the thinges most, and handled them best: or else enriched their owne tongues with all that was best, and when they had so done set them over unto us. But of all their exercises with the *Ball*, we have not any so farre as I can gesse, by their notes, though we retaine the name: and, yet our playing with the *Ball* worketh the same effectes, which theirs did, as it appeareth by their descriptions. Wherfore seeing they be so farre different from ours, and almost worne out of knowledge even to curious conjectures, which seeke to sift them out, I will neither trouble my selfe with studying to set downe their names: nor my reader with reading to gesse what they were, and how they were used.

Three kindes shall content me, which our time knoweth, wherein all the properties of their *balles*, and all the effectes of their exercises, be most evidently seene. The *hand ball*, the *footeball*, the *armeball*.

1. The litle *hand ball* whether it be of some softer stuffe, and used by the hand alone, or of some harder, and used with the rackette, whether by tennice play with an other, or against a wall alone, to exercise the bodie with both the handes, in everie kinde of motion, that concerneth any, or all the other exercises, is generally noted, to be one of the best exercises and the greatest preservations of health. In so much as *Galene* bestoweth an whole treatise upon the use and praise of it, wherin he compareth it with other exercises, and preferreth it before all, for parabilitie, to be all mens game: for profitablenesse, to do all men good: for pleasauntnesse, to quicke all mens spirites, and in short knits up the some of his conclusion thus. That the use of the litle *ball* doth plant in the minde *courage*, in the bodie *health*, in all the limmes a trim and wel proportionate *constitution*: so it be moderately and advisedly executed. Playing at the *ball* in generall is a strong exercise, and maketh the bodie very nimble, [104] and strengtheneth all the vitall actions. The litle *handball* is counted to be a swift exercise, without violence, and therefore the rakketters in tennyse play, if they use it in that kinde, which is thought to be most healthfull, must shew them selves nymble without strayning, and yet it falleth out most commonly contrarie, while desire to wynne some wager makes the winners loose a benefit, which they wish for more, and would gladly get to better their health by. This playing abateth grossenes, and corpulence, as al other of the same sort do: it maketh the flesh sownd and soft, it is very good for the armes, the greene and growing ribbes, the back, and by reason the legges are mightely stirred therby, it is a great furtherer to strength, it quickneth the eyes by looking now hither, now thither, now up, now downe, it helpeth the ridgebone, by stowping, bending and coursing about: it is verie good for bellies and stomakes, that be troubled with winde or any paine which proceedeth from colde. Now to the contrary it is not good for ill and bleare eyes, raw stomakes, undigested meat, which have more neede of rest then stirring, and for such as will soone be turnesicke,

which the oft turning about of the head and eyes cannot but cause. The playing at tennyse is more coastly and straining to aunswere an adversary, but the playing against the wall is as healthfull, and the more ready, bycause it needeth no adversary, and yet practiseth every kinde of motion, every joynt of the body, and all without danger. Children use this ball diversly, and every way healthfully, in regard of the exercise: if accidentarie faultes fall out among children, in the use of the play, the parties must beare the blame and not the play.

The second kinde I make the *Footeball* play, which could not pos- 2.
sibly have growne to this greatnes, that it is now at, nor have bene so much used, as it is in all places, if it had not had great helpes, both to health and strength, and to me the abuse of it is a sufficient argument, that it hath a right use: which being revoked to his primative will both helpe, strength, and comfort nature: though as it is now commonly used, with thronging of a rude multitude, with bursting of shinnes, and breaking of legges, it be neither civil, neither worthy the name of any traine to health. Wherin any man may evidently see the use of the trayning [105] maister. For if one stand by, which can judge of the play, and is judge over the parties, and hath authoritie to commaunde in the place, all those inconveniences have bene, I know, and wilbe I am sure very lightly redressed, nay they will never entermedle in the matter, neither shall there be complaint, where there is no cause. Some smaller number with such overlooking, sorted into sides and standings, not meeting with their bodies so boisterously to trie their strength: nor shouldring or shuffing one an other so barbarously, and using to walke after, may use *footeball* for as much good to the body, by the chiefe use of the legges, as the *Armeball*, for the same, by the use of the armes. And being so used, the *Footeball* strengtheneth and brawneth the whole body, and by provoking superfluities downeward, it dischargeth the head, and upper partes, it is good for the bowells, and to drive downe the stone and gravell from both the bladder and kidneies. It helpeth weake hammes, by much moving, beginning at a meane, and simple shankes by thickening of the flesh, no lesse then riding doth. Yet rash running and to much force oftentimes breaketh some inward conduit, and bringeth ruptures.

The third kind I call the *Armeball*, which was invented in the 3.

kingdom of *Naples*, not many yeares agoe, and answereth most of the olde games, with the great ball, which is executed with the armes most, as the other was with the feete, and be both very great helpers unto health. The arme in this is fensed with a wodden brace, as the shin in the other with some other thing for meeting with a shrew. The *armeball* encreaseth the naturall heate, maketh way for superfluities, causeth sound sleepe, digesteth meate wel, and dispatcheth raw humors, though it stuffe the head, as all vehement exercises do. It exerciseth the armes and backe chiefly, and next to them the legges, and therfore it must needs be good for such, as desire to have those partes strong and perfit, to digest their meate at will, to distribute profitable juice to the whole body, and to avoide needelesse matter, as well by sweate, as by any other kinde of secret evacuation. And yet it is very ill for a naughtie backe, for hoat kidneyes, for sharp urine, and generally for any that is troubled with infirmities and diseases in those parts which are strained with stirring.

Thus much concerning the particular exercises, which I [106] have pickt out from the rest, as most reducible to our time and countrie, wherein I have not followed the ordinarie division, which the training maisters and Physicians do use, but I devised such a one, as I tooke to be fittest for myne owne purpose regarding our soyle and our seasons. Neither have I rekened up the other antique exercises, but have let them rest with their friends and favorers, which be long ago at rest. For the tumbling *Cybistike*, the thumping *Pugillate*, the buffeting *Cestus*, the wrastling *Pancrace*, the quayting *Discus*, the barlike *Halteres*, the swinging *Petawre*, and such old memorandums, they are to auncient and to farre worne from the use of our youth: the considering whereof may rather stirre conjecture, then staie assurance, what they were, when they were. And of these which I have named, many be farre beyond boyes plaie, for whom alone I do not deale, but for all studentes in generall, neither yet do I exclude either any age, or any person, if I may profit any else beside studentes and scholers. Neither do I tie the trayne to these exercises alone, but alway to some, though not alway to one kinde. The cause and consideration must leade all, which may bring forth the like, and why not the better upon due and wel observed circunstance? For though the general cause do direct much, yet the particular circunstance directeth more, being it self enformed in the generall judgement. The most of these notes, which I have alleaged, were given in *Italie*, *Greece* and *Spaine*, and that climate farre distant, and much differing from our degree. Wherefore our traine upon consideration of the degrees in soyle, in temperature, in constitution, and such like, must appropriate it selfe where the difference is apparent. Therefore both to use these exercises which I have named, to the best, and to devise other by comparison and circumstance, as cause shal offer, I will runne thorough those particularities, which either make by right, or marre by wrong applying, both all that I have said, or that can be devised in this kinde, to preserve health.

Chapter 28.

Of the circumstances which are to be considered in exercise.

There be six circumstances, which leade and direct all exercises, and are carefully to be considered of, by the trayning [107] maister. For either the missing or mistaking of any one of them, may do harme to more then one, and the using of them with circumspection and warynes, doth procure that good to health, which this whole discourse hitherto hath promised.

The sixe circumstances be these, the *nature* of the exercise which ye entend to use: the *person* and *body* which is to be exercised, the *place* wherin, the *time* when, the *quantitie* how much, the *maner* how, whereof I do meane to give some particular advertisements so as I do finde the learned physicianes, and wise health maisters to have handled them in their writings, yet by the way least any man either dispaire of the good, and therefore spare the proving, because the forme of exercise doth seeme so intricate, and there with all to much: or if he be entred in triall, and thinke he shall faile, if he misse in some litle, bycause the charge is given so precisely, to keepe al that is enjoyned: I wish him not to thinke either the errour unpardonable, to regard, or the thing unavailable to health, if either all, or any one of these circumstaunces be not absolutely hyt. For as a perfit healthfull body is not to be found by enquirie, which is not to be hoped for in nature, bycause in so continuall a chaunge such a perfitnes cannot chaunce, our bodyes being subject to so many imperfections: so is it no wonder for men to do what they may, and to wish for the best, though still beyond their reach. If any can come neare them, he breakes no right of use, though he misse the rule of art, which alwaye enjoyneth in the precisest sort, but yet resteth content with that which falleth within compasse of ordynarie circumstance. The reason is, *art* weyeth the matter abstracte, and free from circumstaunce, and therefore having the whole object at commaundement, she may set downe her precept, according to that perfitnes, which she doth conceive: but the execution being chekt with a number of accidentarie occurrences, which *art* cannot comprehend, as being to infinite to collect, must have one eye to her precept, and an other to hir power, and aske consideration counsell, how to performe that with a number of lettes, and thwartings which, art did prescribe, either without any, or at the left, with not so many. [108]

Chapter 29.

The nature and qualitie of the exercise.

The *nature* of the exercise which we use, either to recover health and strength, if they be feebled: or to preserve them, that they feeble not, as it is verie forcible to worke this healthfull effect: so it deserveth verie circumspect consideration, in applying and fitting it to the effect: that the exercise in his degree of motion may aunswere the partie in his kinde of constitution: least by jarring that way too farre, they fall into a greater discord. *Galene* examining the thinges, which do please the displeased infantes, findes out that all their naturall unquietnesse is appeased by three naturall meanes, which the nurse useth, the *pappe* to feede, the *voice* to fill, the *arme* to move. Wherupon he concludeth that *meat* to nourish, *Musicke* to delite, *motion* to exercise be most naturall, which being so, then for the preservation of nature, she must needes have her owne motion, which agreeth best with her owne disposition. For as some exercises go before the maine to prepare the bodie, and some follow to retourne it by degrees into his former state and temper: so some be verie vehement, strong, and strainable: other verie gentle, curteous,

1. Sanit. tuen.

and remisse: which must have echone their application, according unto the qualitie, and state of the bodie, wherunto they are to be applyed. They be also as far distinct and different, as particular circunstance can worke alteration in any respect, as their particular titles before did shew, in their particular braunching and division. And yet therein they swarve not from the generalitie of Physicke, which leaning upon some unfallible groundes, yet lighteth still upon some fallible eventes, which make the whole profession to seeme conjecturall, though in the best and surest kinde of conjecture, if the professour have studied to sufficiencie and observed so long, till discretion have saide, the thing is thus. I will not therfore spend any more labour, about a matter of so great confusion, but as they shall fall out, so will I apply them, that by their proper use, their propertie maye appeare. [109]

Chapter 30.

Of the bodies which are to be exercised.

In the bodie which is to take good of exercise, there be three pointes
to be considered: for either it is *sickly* having his operations tainted 1.
and weake: or it is *healthy* and without any extraordinarie and sen- 2.
sible taint: or it is *valetudinarie*, neither pure sicke nor perfit whole. 3.

To speake first of the weake and sickish bodie, it is to be noted, as hath bene already in parte marked before, that sicknesse assaileth us three wayes: By distemperature, when either the whole bodie, or some parte therof is anoyed with unproportionate heat, cold, drynesse, or moysture: or by misfashioning, when either the whole bodie, or some parte therof, wanteth his due forme, his jumpe quantitie, his just number, his naturall seat: or by division, when any part of the bodie being naturally united upon some weaknesse is dissolved and sundred. And as diseases come by one, or all these three wayes, so health doth defend it selfe by the contrarie, good temperature, good forme, good uniting of partes. It is graunted by the best though contraried by some of the soryest Physicians, that sicke bodies may be put to exercise: so it be well considered before, what kinde of weaknesse the body is in: and what kinde of helpe may be hoped for by the exercise. As for example in sicknesse which commeth by distemperature: if a bodie be distempered with to much heat, it may not be put to any great or earnest exercise, for over heating. If it be to drie and withered, it must forbeare much exercise for feare of overdrying. If it be to hoat and dry both, or to hoat and to moyste both, it must quite abandon exercise, as in the first kinde enflaming, in the second choking. If it be cold and drie it must either never be exercised or verie gently. If it be cold or moyst, then exercise can do it no harme. If it be cold and moyst, it maye boldly abide exercise: which variety commeth upon the effectes, that are wrought by exercises, either in augmenting heat, and stirring humours, or avoiding superfluities. Wherupon the generall conclusion is: that no distempered bodie may use, any great or vehement exercise though some there [110] be, which may venture up on some meane and gentle kinde of stirring, whether the infirmitie concerne the whole bodie, or be so in some parte, as it shake not the whole. If the infirmitie in *fashion* be casuall and come by late misfortune, (for in this kinde naturall weaknesse is ever excepted) exercise maye do good, bycause it will make that streight, which was croked, that smooth, which was rugged, lay that which was swollen, raise that which was layd, emptie that which was full, fill that which was emptie, open that which was close and shut: and so forth, still working the contrarie to the defect, and thereby the amendment. If the fault be in *quantitie*, great and swift exercises will abate, and pull downe the flesh, small and slow will fat and thicken it. If the fault be in *number*, exercise helpeth, as vehement moving driveth the stone and gravell from the straite passages of the kidneyes to the broader, and from thence downe into the bladder. If the fault be in *seat*, no exercise is good, bycause till the part be restored to his place and site, there is no moving to be used, nor yet long after, for feare of displacing it againe. If the fault come by *disunion*, *exulceration*, or *gaule*, the disuniting of the nobler partes, as the braine, the stomacke, the liver, and such other, specially if it be joyned with any ague excludeth all exercises. The baser partes refuse not meane stirring, as the skinne being devided and disunited with scabbes, which come of salt and sharp humours, by motion is freed and delivered of them. This consideration is to be had in the exercising of sicke bodies, whether the sicknesse come by distemperature of humours, by deformitie in composition, or by disunion of partes.

Valetudinarie.

Concerning *valetudinarie* bodies, which be neither alwaye sicke, nor ever whole, and such as be upon recoverie after sicknesse, and aged men, whom yeares make weake and sickish, thus I read: that exercise is verie necessarie for the two first, to strengthen their limmes, to dispatche superfluities, to stirre heat, to restore the bodie to his best habite, alwaye provided that the exercise rise from some mediocritie and slownes by degrees to that height, which the parties may well abide. For to earnest and rash exercise will empaire their health more. Olde men, as by want of naturall heat, they grow full of superfluities, [111] so they must have some pleasant and gentle kinde of exercise, both to stirre the heat, and to ridde awaye those needlesse necessities, which of force inferre sicknes, if they be not enforced awaye. And as they be naturally drie, so they must use no exercise, which dryeth to much. Wherein these foure circunstances are to be considered. 1. First their strength, which being not great, requireth but quiet and gentle exercises. For though *Prodicus* the warie Philosopher in *Plato, Antiochus* the healthy Physician in *Galene, Spurina* the considerate counsellour in *Plinie*, could do straunge thinges in their olde age, by good forsight in their former yeares, yet they be no generall presidentes. 2. Secondly the forme of their bodies. For as good constitutions, can do that meanly and pretily well in their olde age, which they did strongly and stowtly in their youth, so the weake and misfashioned are unfit for exercise. For loude speaking will hurt to narrow bulkes, and any walking fainteth weake legges, and so forth in all imperfections of the like sorte. 3. Thirdly how they have bene used: bycause they will better awaie with their acquainted exercises, then with other, wherunto they have never bene used, the vehemencie and courage of their yong dayes onely excepted. 4. Fourthly what infirmities they be subject unto, as if their heades will soone be giddy, or their eyes sore, or if they be in daunger of sudden falling, then they must avoide all exercises which be offensive to the head. And this rule is generally to be observed in all bodies, that the partes pacient maye not be pressed to sore.

Healthy bodyes.

As for healthy and strong bodies, they are to be esteemed not by absolute perfitnesse in measure and rule, which will not be found, but by performing all naturall functions, without any greife or

painfull let: wherof in some places there is good plentie. For as generally in so many wayes to weaknesse, our bodies never continuyng any one minute in the same state, perfit health in the absolutest degree is not to be hoped for: so in the second degree of perfection, where no sensible let is, no felt feeblenesse, but all ordinaries excellent, though no excellent extraordinarie, there be many bodies to be found healthfull, lustie, and lasting verie long: as the soile wherin they brede and be is of healthfulnesse, and wholesomnesse. Such a
2. De tu. vali. praise [112] doth *Galene* give to his owne, and *Hipocrates* his country: Nay that is the common proofe, where small diet, and much labour accompanieth necessitie in state, and good constitution in body. Now these healthfull bodyes, as they dayly feede, and digest well, so to avoide superfluities, which come thereby, bycause no meat is so meete with the body, as it turneth all into nurriture, they must of necessitie pray ayde of exercise, which must be neither to violent, nor to immoderate, but sutable to their constitution, as in the private description the particuler exercise bewrayeth it selfe, and generally the generall reason suffiseth such a trayner, as can use the consideration of circumstance wisely. In exercising of healthy bod-
1. ies, there be five speciall thinges to be observed. The first is how they have bene used, for looke wherewith they have bene most acquainted, and therein, or in the like they will best continew, and with most
2. ease. The second is what age they be of, for old men must have gentle exercises, children somewhat more stirring, yong men more then they, and yet but in a meane, bycause they are subject to more harme by violence then either children or old men, for that having strong and drie bodyes, thicke and stiffe flesh, fast cleaving to the bone, and the skinne stretched accordingly, they are in great daunger of strong convulsions, and divers ruptures, both of flesh
3. and veines, through extremities of exercise. The third is the state of their body, because fat and grosse men, may abyde much more
4. exercise, then leane may and so in other. The fourth is their kinde of living, for he that eateth much, and sleepeth much, must either exercise much or live but a while. And to the contrary, the spare feeder
5. or great waker, needeth not any such kinde of physicke. The fift is the temperature of their bodyes, for small exercise satisfieth drie or hoat bodyes, in any degree of eager heat. Againe colde bodyes may away with both vehement and very much, for moyst bodyes to

avoide superfluities, exercise and labour is very good, so the bodies be not hoat withall, the humor very much and very soone turned into vapour, and that also neare to the lungues for feare of choking after much stirring. Hoat and dry admit no exercise, hoat and moyst, cold and dry admit some litle. But of all constitutions none is more helpt by exercise [113] then the colde and moyst: because heat and clearing, the two effectes of exercise have their owne subject whereon to worke, which must be weyed in complexions, and states of the body.

Chapter 31.

Of the exercising places.

That the place, wherein any thing is done, is of great force to the well or ill performing therof, and specially in natural executions, there can be no better profe, then that we se, not onely plantes and trees, not onely brute beastes and cattell, but also even the bodies and myndes of men to be altered and chaunged, with the varietie and alteration of the place and soyle, so that for the better exercising of the bodies to the preserving or recovering of health, it is verie materiall to limit some certainety concerning the place. Wherin not to dwell long at this time, bycause in the common place both for learning and exercising togither, I shall have occasion to say more of this matter: these foure qualities are to be observed in the place. First the 1.
place where ye exercise, must have his ground flowred so, as it be not offensive to the body, as in wrastling not hard to fall on, in daunsing soft, and not slipperie. How angrie would a boie be to be driven to scourge his *top* in sand, gravel, or deepe rushes? and so forth in the rest: as is most fit for the body exercised, with lest daunger and best dispatch. The second, that the place be either free from any 2.
wind at all, or if it be not possible to avoide some, that it be not subject to any sharpe and byting winde: which may do the body some wrong, being open, and therefore ready to receive forreine harme by the ayer. Thirdly that the place be open, and not close nor cov- 3.
ered, to have the best and purest ayre at will, whereby the body becommeth more quicke and lively, and after voyding noysom

superfluities, may prove lightsome by the very ayer and soyle. 4. Fourthly that there be no contagious nor noysome stenche neare the place of exercise, for feare of infecting that by new corruption, which was lately cleared by healthful motion. Generally if the place cannot be so fit and favourable to exercise, as wish would [114] it were, yet wisedom may win thus much, that he may be as well appointed, to prevent the ill of every both season and circumstance, as possibility can commonly performe. When great conquests had made states almost, nay in deede to wealthie, and libertie of soyle given them place to chuse, they builded to this end mervelous and sumptuous monuments, which time and warres have wasted, but we which must doe as we may, must be content with that, which our power can compasse, and if the worst fall, thinke that he which placed us in the world, hath appointed the world for us for an exercising place, not onely for the body against infections, but also for the mynde against affections, which being herselfe well trayned, doth make the bodie yeelde, to the bent of her choice.

Chapter 32.

Of the exercising time.

Time is devided into *accidentarie* and *naturall*, and *naturall* againe into *generall* and *particular*. The *naturall time* generally construed is ment by the spring, the summer, the harvest and the wynter: particularly by the howers of the day and night. The *accidentarie time* chaungeth his name still, sometime faire, sometime foule, sometime hoat, sometime colde and so forth. Of this *accidentary time* this rule is given, that in exercise we chuse, as neare as we can, faire weather, cleare and lightsome to confirme the spirites, which naturally rejoyce in light, and are refreshed thereby: not cloudy, darke and thicke, wherein grosse humours make the bodie dull and heavie: againe when there is either no great, or no verie noysome winde to pearce the open pored body, nor to much forreine heat to enflame the naturall: nor to much cold to stiffen it to sore.

2. Part. proble. 21. 33. 42. For the *naturall* time generally taken, *Aristotle* would have the

bodie most exercised in sommer, bycause the naturall heat being then least, and the bodie therefore most burdened with superfluities, then exercise most helpes: both to encrease the inward heat, and to send out those outward dettes. *Hippocrates* againe giving 2. De tuen. vali.
three principall rules to be kept in exercise, to avoide wearinesse, to walke in the morning, maketh this the [115] third to use both more and longer exercise in the winter and cold weather, and most of his favorites hold that opinion. The reason is, bycause in sommer the heat of the time dryeth the bodie enough, so that it needeth no exercise to wither it to much, where the aire it selfe doth drie it enough. *Galene* a man of great authoritie in his profession, pronounceth thus 3. De diaeta.
in generall, that as temperate bodies are to be exercised in a temperate season which he countes to be the spring: so cold bodies are in hoat weather: hoat in cold, moyst in drie, drie in moyst: meaning thereby that whensoever the bodie seemeth to yeeld towardes any distemperature, then the contrarie both time and place must be fled to for succour. Of these opinions iudgement is to chuse, which it best liketh. Me thinke upon divers considerations, they maye all stand well without any repugnance, seing neither *Hippocrates* nor *Galene*, deny exercise in sommer simply, and *Aristotle* doth shew what it worketh in sommer.

For the *naturall time* particularly taken, thus much is said, that it is unwholesome to exercise after meat, bycause it hindereth digestion by dispersing the heat, which should be assembled wholly to further and helpe digestion. And yet both *Aristotle*, and *Avicene*, allow some gentle walking after meat, to cause it so much the sooner setle downe in the stomacke, specially if one meane to sleepe shortly after. But for exercise before meate, that is excedingly and generally commended, bycause it maketh the naturall heat strong against digesting time, and driving away unprofitable humours, disperseth the better and more wholesome, thorough out the whole bodie, wheras after meate it filleth it with rawnesse, and want of digestion: bycause moving marres concoction, and lets the boyling of the stomacke. Now in this place there be three thinges to be considered.

First that none venture upon any exercise, before the bodie be 1.
purged naturally, by the nose, the mouth, the belly, the bladder, bycause the contrarie disperseth that into the bodie, which should

be dismissed and sent awaie: nor before the overnightes diet be thoroughly digested, for feare of to much superfluitie, besides crudity and cholere. Belching and urine be argumentes of perfit or unperfit digestion. The whiter urine [116] the worse and weaker digestion, the yealower, the better.

2. The second consideration is, that no exercise be medled withall the stomacke being verie emptie, and wearie hungrie, least raven- 2. Aph. 16. ing cause overreaching, and *Hippocrates* condemne you, for linking labour with hunger, a thing by him in his *aphorismes* forbid.

The third consideration is not to eate streight after the exercise, before the bodie be reasonably setled. Yet corpulent carcases, which labour to be lightened of their cariage, be allowed their vittail, though they be puffing hoat. The cause why this distance betwene moving and meate is enjoyned, is this, for that the bodie is still a clearing, while it is yet hoat: and the excrementes be but fleeting: so that neither the partie can yet be hungrie, nor the heat entend digestion. Wherupon they counsell him that is yet hoat after exercise, neither to wash himselfe in cold water: nor to drinke wine, nor cold water. Bycause washing will hurt the open body, wine will streight waye steeme up into the head, cold water will offend the belly and lyver, yea sometime gaule the sinewes, nay sometime call for death.

Houres. What *houres* of the daie were best for exercise, the auncient *Physicians* for their soile, in their time, and to their reason, appointed it thus. In the spring about noone, for the temperatenesse of the aire: in sommer in the *morning*, to prevent the heat of the daie: in harvest and winter towardes night: bycause the *morninges* be cold, the dayes short, and to be employed otherwise: and the meat before that time will lightly be well digested. But now in our time, the diet being so farre altered, and never a circumstance the same, no time is fitter for exercise then the *morninge* somewhat before meate: though we entreat the *Muses* not to wonder and muse at it, that we be so boulde with our and their common friend, I meane the *morning*, seeing we seeke to have learning and health joyned together. Which falling both most fit in the *morning*, doth lend us an argument to prove that they were ill sundred, whom the samenes of time so uniteth together. In the *morning* the bodie is light, being delivered of excrementes, strong after sleepe, free from common lettes and without any perill of indigestion, all which fall out [117] quite contrarie in the *evening*.

If any writer allow any other houre after meate, it is in some extremitie of sicknesse, not in respect of exercise: as when the weather is most lowring, and children most heavie and dumpish, why is not then the fittest time to play, by chearing the minde, to lighthen the bodie?

Chapter 33.

Of the quantitie that is to be kept in exercise.

All they which use exercises use them either not so much as they
should, and that doeth small good, or more then they should, and
that doeth much harme, or so as they should, and that doeth much-
good. Wherupon he that hath skill to crie ho, when he is at the
height of his exercise, wherwith nature feeleth her selfe to be best
content, knoweth best wherein the best measure consisteth. But
how may one know the verie pitche in exercise, and when it were
best for one to crie ho? principally by these two generall limittes.
Wherof the first is, when a *vapour* mingled with sweat is sensibly 1.
perceived to proceede from the bodie: when the *vaines* begin to
swell, and the *breathing* to alter. For wheras the ende of exercise is to
strengthen the bodie, and to encrease the naturall heat, whereby the
wholesome juyce is digested, and distributed to the nurriture of the
other partes: and unprofitable residences discharged: if the excercise come not to these degrees of *sweat*, *swelling*, and *breathing*, it is
to weake to worke those effectes, which it doth undertake. The sec- 2.
ond generall limit is, to continue the *exercise* so long, as the *face* and
bodie shall have a fresh colour, the *motion* shalbe quicke and in proportion, and no *wearynesse* worth the speaking shalbe felt. For if the
colour begin to faint, or the bodie to be gaunt, or *wearynesse* to wring,
or the *motion* to shrinke, or the sweat to alter in *qualitie* from hoat to
cold, in *quantitie* from more to lesse, which should naturally
encrease with the exercise, then crie ho, for feare of thinning the
bodye to much, of consuming the good and ill juyces together, of
weakning the naturall heat, of destroying in steade of strengthning:
bycause these be evident shewes, that the bodie wasteth, cooleth
and dryeth more then it should. [118]

Now as these be generall staies not to proceede further, but to rest when we are well: so there be other more particuler, wherein there is regard to be had, to the *strength* or *weakenes* of the partie, to the *age*, to the *time* of the yeare, to the *temperature* of the body, to the *kinde* of life. For in all these measure is a mery meane, and immoderatenes a remeadilesse harme.

They that be of good *strength* may continue longer in exercise, then any other, without some great occasion to the contrary: though they faint, and feele some litle *lassitude* and *wearines*, bycause they will quickly recover themselves. Those that be but *weake* must exercise but a while, bycause any small taint in them, is long and hard to be recovered, and therefore their limit is to be warme, and to be ware of sweating.

2. As touching the difference in age. Olde men, yea though they use the same exercises, wherewith they were acquainted when they were yong, yet must leave ear they either sweat or begin to be wearie, bycause they are drye and wythered. Men of middle *age* must of necessitie keepe the meane lymit, bycause too much offendes them, to litle doth them litle good, both hinder the state of their bodies. *Youth* from seven till one and twenty, will abyde much exercising, very well: wherefore they are allowed without daunger to be hoat and chafe, to puffe and blow, to sweat, to be wearie also to some degree of *lassitude*: for being full of excrementes by reason of ther reacheles diet, they finde great ease in labour and sweat: and being strong withall, a litle *wearines* makes them litle worse. And yet there must be great eye had to them, that they keepe within compasse, and so much the more, the lesse they be above seven yeare old. For too much exercise in those yeares marres their growing, and alters the constitution of their bodies to the worse.

3. For the *time* of the yeare. In *Winter* the exercise may be great, till the body be hotte: but yet sweat not, lest the cold do harme. In the *Spring* more even till it sweat, in the *Harvest* lesse, in the *Sommer* least: because the ayre which environeth the body, doth then of it selfe so wearie and weaken it, as it needeth neither sweating, nor heating, nor wearying with exercise, wherein *Hippocrates* and his *Phisicke* will prevaile against [119] *Aristotle* and his *Philosophie*.

4. For the temperature of the body: Moyst *bodies* may abide much exercise, by much stirring to drie up much moisture, so that they

may sweat, and yet they must take heede of wearynes. Dry *bodies* may very ill away with any exercise, and if with any, it must be such as will neither cause heat nor sweat. Could *bodies* may move till they be throughly warme. Hoat *bodies* must be deintily delt withall. For *heat, sweat,* and great chaunge of their breathing be enemies to their complexion. Hoat and dry for feare of encreasing their qualities to much must be content with either no exercise at all, or with verie litle. Cold and dry may abyde stirring in respect of their coldnes, till they be warme: but for feare of overdrying they must not venture upon sweat. Hoat and moyst must use moderate exercise, bycause to litle dyminisheth not their superfluous moysture: to much melteth to fast, and warmth to much. Whereupon daungerous flixes ensue: so that they must needes avoid great alteration of breath, and to much warmeth. Cold and moyst may exercise them selves till they blow, till they be hoat, and till they sweat. To be short, of any constitution this may best abide exercise, to emptie it of needelesse humors, to stirre the natural heat, and to procure perfit digestion. *Sickemen* may not dreame of any definite *quantitie* in their exercises, bycause according to the variety of their infirmities, both their exercises, and the quantities thereof must be proportionally applyed: so that there can be no certaine rule set for them.

Such as be newly recovered from sicknes, or that be on the mending hand, bycause their strength is feeble, their heat weake, their lymes dryed up, must content themselves with small and competent exercise, for feare of no small inconvenience. Their limit therfore must be to stirre, but not to change breath, to warme, but not to heat, to labour, but not to be wearie: yet as their health growes, their exercise may encrease.

5. For the kinde of life. Such as live moderately and with great continencie, though they be not full of superfluities, and therfore neede not exercise much: yet they must not abandon it quite, least their bodies for want therof, becomming unweildie, lease both the benefit of naturall heat, and good constitution, [120] and avoid not such residence, as of force breedes in them, and in the ende will cause some sicknes crepe on, which comes without warning, bycause *Jupiter*, as both *Hesiode* sayeth, and *Plutarch* subscribeth, hath cut her toungue out, least she tell, when she comes, for that he would have her come stealing, eare she be perceived, as *Galene* also maketh the

litle unperceived, or for the smallnesse contemned to be mother to all illes both of bodie and soule. *Incontinence* breedes much matter for exercise: and therefore requireth much, cheifly to procure sound sleepe, the captaine cause of good digestion. Such as have not used exercises before, and be novices in the trade, must first be purged, then by *meane* and *moderate* ascents, day by day be well applyed, till they come to that degree, wherein those are, which have bene acquainted therewith before. But in all those *degrees* and *mediocrities*, *immoderate* exercise must alway be eschewed, as a very capitall enemie to health causing *children* not to prosper nor grow: *lustie* men to fall into unequall distemperatures, and oftimes agues: *oldmen* to become dry and overwearied. To conclude who is it, to whom it doth not some harme, and from whom it keepeth not some great good. These be the tokens, whereby immoderate exercises be discerned, if ye feele your joyntes to be very hoat: if you perceive your body to be dry and unequall: if in your travell you feele some pricking in your flesh, as if it were of some angrie push: if after sweating your colour become pale: if you finde your selfe faint and wearie more then ordinary, which wearines, fayntnesse and pricking, occupy the credit of a great circumstance in physicke, of *Galene*, and greeke physicianes called *κόπος* of the *latines* and our *Linacer lassitudines*, and come upon dissolution and thinning of grosse humours, being to many at that time to cleare the body of, and pricking as they passe like some angrie bile within the body, whereby the body is both forced to make an end of exercise, and withall is verie wearysome, and stif oftymes after.

4. De tuenda sanita.

Chapter 34.

Of the maner of exercising.

Galene in the second booke of his preservative to health knitteth up three great thinges in verie few wordes, that [121] who so can handle the exercises in due *maner*, with the *apotherapeutike*, or governing the body after exercise, and his *frictions* to rubbe it and chafe it as it should be, is an absolute trayner in his kinde. Wherein we may see the use of *chafing*, and rubbing the body both to be verie auncient, and very healthfull, to warme the outward partes, to open the passages for superfluitie, and to make one active and chearie to deale with any thing afterward. It hath his place every day at tymes, every yeare in seasons, altering upon circumstance, but still both needefull and healthfull, and clearith where it chafeth. For the *apotherapeutike* much hath bene saide already: wherefore this place must serve peculiarly for the *maner* of exercising.

They of old time to whom these rules were first given having all thinges at their will, and sparing for no cost, neither straited for want of time, which they disposed as they listed, and to whom the traine bycause of their libertie and leasure was properly bequeathed, did use many circumstances both ear they entred into their exercise, and when they were in it, and also after that they had ended it, ear they went to meat. Which their curious course, I will briefly runne through, onely to let them see it, which can do no more but see it, bycause the circumstances of our time will skant suffer any to assay it. After that they felt their former meat fully digested, and had at leysure performed what belonged to the purging of their bodies, they disrobed themselves, and were chafed with a gentle kinde of rubber, till that the freshnes of their colour, and agilytie of their joyntes seemed to call for exercise. Then were they oynted with sweete oyle so neatly and with such cunning, as it might sooke into their bodies, and search everie joynt. That being done if they ment to wrastle, they threw dust upon the oyntment: if not, they went to the exercise, which they had most fansie unto, which being ended they rested a while, then with certaine scrapers called *Strigiles*, they had all their filth scrapte of their bodies: afterward they were chafed and rubbed againe, then oynted also againe, either in the *Sunne* or by the *fire*. Then to the *bath*, last of all apparelling them-selves they fell to their meat. And this was not one or two, nor men of might alone, but every one and of every sort, nay, shall I say it? [122] even of every sex. A long and a laboriouse travell, and an argument of much ease, and to much adoe in that, which should be more common.

But in these our dayes, considering we neither have such places wherin, nor the persons by whose helpe, nor the leasure by whose sufferance we maye entend so delicate a tendring of our selves, and yet for all that may not neglect so great a misterie for our owne health, as exercise is, though we cannot reatch to the olde, which perhaps we neede not, smaller provision and simpler fourniture, will serve our turne, and worke the same effectes, nay may fortune better, by helpe of some circunstance peculiar to our selves. Therefore for our *maner* and *order* of exercise, these few and easie considerations may seeme to be sufficient: To *cleare* our bodies from superfluities echewaye, to *combe* our heades, to *wash* our handes and face, to *apparell* our selves for the purpose, to *begin* our exercise first slowly, and so grow on quicker, to *rebate* softly, and by gentle degrees, to *change* our sweatie clothes, to *walke* a litle after, last of all our bodies being setled, to *go* to our meate. This is that which I promised to note concerning the six circunstances of exercise.

Chapter 35.

An advertisement to the training maister. Why both the teaching of the minde, and the training of the bodie be assigned to the same maister. The inconveniences which ensue, where the bodie and soule be made particular subjectes to severall professions. That who so will execute anything well, must of force be fully resolved of the excellency of his owne subject. Out of what kinde of writers the exercising maister may store himselfe with cunning. That the first groundes would be laid by the cunningest workeman. That private discretion in any executor is of more efficacie then his skill.

I have already spoken of the parties, which are to be exercised, and what they are to observe: nowe must I saye somwhat of him, and to him, which is to direct the exercise, and how he may procure sufficient knowledge, wherby to do it exceeding well. And yet the trainers person is but a parcell of [123] that person, whom I do charge with the whole. For I do assigne both the framing of the minde, and the training of the bodie to one mans charge, whose sufficiencie may verie well satisfie both, being so neare companions in linke, and not to be uncoupled in learning. The causes why I medle in this place with the training maister, or rather the training parte of the common maister, be these: first I did promise in my methode of exercises so to do: secondly the late discours of exercise will somwhat lighten this matter, and whatsoever shall be said here, may easely be revived there, where I deale with the generall maister. Beside this, exercise being so great a braunche of education as the sole traine of the whole bodie, maye well commaunde such a particular labour, though in deede I sever not the persons, where I joine the properties. For in appointing severall executions, where the knowledge is united, and the successe followeth by the continuall comparing of the partes, how they both maye, or how they both do best proceede in their best way, how can that man judge wel of the soule, whose travell consisteth in the bodie alone? or how shall he perceive what is the bodies best, which having the soule onely committed to his care, posteth over the bodie as to an other mans reckening? In these cases both *fantsie* workes *affection*, and *affection* overweyneth, either best liking where it fantsieth most, or most following, where it affecteth best, as it doth appeare in *Divines*, who punish the bodie, to have the soule better, and in *Physicians*, who looke a side at the soule, bycause the bodie is there best. Where by the way I observe, the different effectes which these two subjectes, being severed in charge, do offer unto their professours. For the health of the soule is the *Divines* best, both for his honest delite, that it doth so well, and for his best ease, that himselfe faires so well. For an honest, vertuous, godly and well disposed soule, doth highly esteeme and honorably thinke of the professour of divinitie, and teacher of his religion, bycause vertuous dealinges, godly meditations, heavenly thoughtes, which the one importeth, be the others portion, and the best food, to a well affected minde: Wherupon in such a healthy disposition of a well both informed and reformed soule, the *Divine* can neither lacke honor for his person, [124] nor substance for his purse.

Now to the contrarie the health of the bodie, which is the *Physicians* subject, is generally his worst, though it be the ende of his profession, which though he be glad of his owne good nature, as he is a man, or of his good conscience, as he is a Christian, that the bodie doth wel, yet his chymny doth not smoke where no pacient smartes. For the healthfull bodie commonly careth not for the *Physician*, it is neede that makes him sought. And as the *Philosopher* sayeth, if all men were freindes, then justice should not neede, bycause no wrong would be offered: so if all bodies were whole that no distemperature enforced: or if the *Divine* were well and duetifully heard, that no intemperance distempered, *Physick* should have small place: Now the contrary dealinges, bycause the divine is not heard, and distemperature not avoided, do enforce *Physick*, for the healing parte of it, as the mother of the professours gaine: where as the preserving part neither will be kept by the one, neither enricheth the other. In these two professions we do generally see, what the severing of such neare neighbours doth bring to passe, like two tenantes in one house belonging to severall lordes. And yet the affections of the one so tuch the other, as they cause sometimes, both the *Divine* to thinke of the body, for the better support of the soule: and the *Physician* to thinke of the soule to helpe him in his cure with comfort and courage. The severing of those two, sometime shew us verie pitifull conclusions, when the *Divine* dilivers the desperate sicke soule, over to the secular magistrate, and a forcible death by waye of punishement: and the *Physician* delivereth the desperate sicke bodie, to the *Divines* care, and a forced ende by extremitie of disease. I dare not saye that these professions might joyne in one person, and yet *Galene* examining the force which a good or ill soule hath to imprint the like affections in the bodie, would not have the *Physician* to tarie for the *Phylosopher* but to play the parte himselfe. Where to much distraction is, and subalterne professions be made severall heads, there the professions make the most of their subjectes, and the subjectes receive least good, though they parte from most. And severall professing makes the severall trades to swell beyond proportion, everie one [125] seeking to make the most of his owne, nay rather vanting his owne, as simply the highest, though it creepe very low. And therefore in this my traine I couch both the partes under one maisters care. For while the bodie is committed to one, and the soule commended to an other, it falleth out most times, that the poore bodie is miserably neglected, while nothing is cared for but onely the soule, as it proveth true in very *zealous* Divines: and that the soule it selfe is but sillyly looked to, while the bodie is in price, and to much borne with, as is generally seene: and that in this conflicte the diligent scholer in great strength of soule, beares mostwhat about him, but a feeble, weake, and a sickish bodie. Wherefore

1. De san. tu.

to have the care equally distributed which is due to both the partes, I make him but one, which dealeth with both. For I finde no such difficultie, but that either for the cunning he may compasse it: or for the travell he maye beare it, having all circunstances free by succession in houres. Moreover as the temperature of the soule smelleth of the temperature of the bodie, so the soule being well affected, will draw on the bodie to her bent. For will a modest and a moderate soule but cause the body obey the rule of her temperance? or if the soule it selfe be reclaymed from follie, doth it not constraine the bodie forth with to follow? So that it were to much to sunder them in charge, whose dispositions be so joyned, and the skill of such facilitie, as may easely be attained, and so much the sooner, bycause it is the preserving parte, which requireth most care in the partie, and but small in the trainer, as the healinge parte of Physicke requireth most cunning in the professour, and some obedience in the patient.

I do make great account of the parties skill, that is to execute matters which besides diligence require skill: for if he be skilfull himselfe, it almost needes not to give precept. If he be not, it altogither bootes not. If he be skillfull he will execute well, bycause he can helpe the thing, which he must execute if particuler occurrence pray aide at the sudden: if he want skill he will lightly mangle that, which is wel set downe, if he be a medler. Wherefore seing I wish the executors cunning, and yet must be content to take him as I finde him: I [126] will do my best both to instruct infirmitie, and to content cunning. I must therefore have him to thinke, that there be two properties which he must take to be of most efficacie to make a cunning executor. The one is to be ravished with the excellencie and worthynes of the thing which he is to execute. The other is, if he may very easily attaine unto some singuler knowledge in so noble a subject, which both concur in this present execution.

1. The liking of the executors subject.

For graunting the soule simply the preheminence both in substance of being, and in traine to be bettered, can there be any other single subject, (which I say in respect of a communitie directed by divine and humaine law, that is compound, and the principall subject of any mans dealing,) can there be any single subject I say of greater nobilitie, and more worthy to be in love with, either by the partie, that is to finde it, or by him that is to frame it, then healthfullnes of body? which so toucheth the soule as it shakes it withall, if it selfe be not sownd?

What a treasure health is, they that have it do finde, though they feele it not till it faile, when want bewrayes what a jewell they have lost, and their cost discovers how they mynde the recoverie. The ende of our being here is to serve God and our country, in obedience to persons, and perfourmance of duties: If that may be done with health of bodie, it is effectuall and pithie: if not, then with sorow we must shift the soner, and let other succede, with no more assurance of life, then we had made us, without this healthful misterie: in perpetuall change to let the world see, that multitude doth supply with number the defect of a great deale better, but to sone decaying paucity.

To live and that long of whom is it not longed for, as Gods blessing if he know God: as the benefit of nature, if he be but a naturall man.

The state of our bodie, when we are in good health, so lively and lusty, so comfortable and cleare, so quicke and chearie, in part and in hole, doth it not paint us, and point us the valew of so preciouse a jewell, as health is to be esteemed?

The pitifull grones, the lamentable shrikes, the lothsome lookes, the image of death, nay of a pyning death, yea in hope of recovery: the rufull heavines, the wringing handes, the wayling [127] friendes, all blacke before blacke, when health is in despaire, do they not crie and tell us, what a goodly thing health is, themselves being so griesly?

So many monuments left by learned men, so much sumptuousnes of the mightiest princes, so many inventions of the noblest wittes bestowed upon exercises to maintaine this diamond, are they not sufficient to enflame the executour, being a partaker him selfe, and a distributer to others, that the subject wherein he dealeth is both massie, most worth, and most mervelous? let him thinke it to be so, bycause he seeth it is so, and upon that presumption proceede to his so healthfull, and so honorable an execution. In whom his owne judgement is of speciall force to further his good speede. For being well resolved in the excellencie of his owne subject he will both himselfe execute the better, and perswade other sooner to embrace that with zeale, which he professeth with judgement. If you will have me weepe for you, saith the *Poet*, then weepe you first: he shall hardly perswade an other to like of that, which is his owne choice, who shall himselfe not seeme to set by it, where himselfe hath set his choise.

2. How to become a skilfull exercising maister.

The knowledge wherewith, and how to deale therein is so much the easier, bycause it is so generall, and so many wayes to be wonne. I will not seeme to raise up the memorie which can never dye, given to this traine by all both old and new histories: which prayse those vertues and valiances, which they found, but had never had matter to praise, nor vertues to finde, if exercises had not made the personages praiseworthy, whereby they did such thinges, and of so great admiration, as had bene unpossible to any not so trained as they were. What *Philosopher* describeth the fairest forme of the worthiest common weale, either by patterne of one person, as allowing that state best, where one steares all: or by some greater multitude, as preferring that government, where many make much stirre: but he doth alwaye, when he dealeth with the youth, and first trayning of that state, not onely make mention, but a most speciall matter of exercise for health?

Who is it in any language that handleth the *Paedagogicall* argument, how to bring up youth, but he is arrested there, [128] where exercise is enfraunchised? As for the *Physicians*, it is a principall parcell of their fairest patrimonie, bycause it is naturally subject, and so learnedly proved to be by *Galene* in his booke intitled *Thrasybulus*, to that parte of their profession which seeketh to preserve health, and not to tarie till it come to ruine, with their gaine to repare it, though it still remaine ruinous and rotten, which is so repared. Therefore whensoever the maintenance of health, is the inscription of the booke, this title of exercise hath some evidence to shew. Further in the discours of *Exercises* we finde eche where the names of diet, of *waking*, of *sleeping*, of *moving*, of *resting*, of *distemperature*, of *temperature*, of *humours*, of *elementes*, of *places*, of *times*, of *partes* of the *bodie*, of the *uses* therof, of *frictions* and *chafings*, of *lassitude* and *wearinesse*, and a number such, which when the training maister meeteth with among the *Physicians*, or naturall *Philosophers*, what els say they unto him, but that where ye finde us before the dore, ye may be bold to come in? As for naturall *Philosophy* the ground mistresse to *Physik* it must needes be the foundacion to this whole traine. Hence the causes be fet, which prove eche thing either good or bad, either noysome or needefull to health. All naturall *problemataries, dipnosophistes, symposiakes, antiquaries, warmaisters,* and such as deale with any particular occurence of exercise, if ye appose them well: you shall finde them your freindes. This terme *Gymnastice,* which emplyeth in name, and professeth in deede, the arte of exercise, is the verie seat, wheron the trainer must builde. And therefore all either whole bookes, or particular discourses in any writer by the waie, concerning this argument, do will him to rest there. In which kinde, for the professed argument of the whole booke, I know not any comparable to *Hieronymus Mercurialis,* a verie learned *Italian Physician* now in our time, which hath taken great paines to sift out of all writers, what so ever concerneth the whole *Gymnasticall* and exercising argument, whose advice in this question I have my selfe much used, where he did fit my purpose.

By these reasons I do see, and by some proofe I have found, that the waye to be skilfull in the preseruative part of *Physick* and so consequently in exercises, as the greatest member therof, [129] is very ready and direct, bycause it is so plaine, so large, and with all so pleasant: as it is also most honorable, bycause it seekes to save us from that, which desireth our spoile. And therefore this execution requireth a liberall courage, where the gaine is not great, but the disposition much praised. The repairers get the pence, the preservers reason faire. And as the effect commendes the knowledge: so being of it selfe thus necessarie for all, a student may with great credit travell in the cunning, if it were for no more but to helpe his owne health, and upon better affection, or some gainfull offer to empart it with other. For to helpe himselfe he is bound in *nature,* and will do it in deede: to do good to all if he may, he is bound by *dutie,* and so sure he ought. But to helpe as many as he may, and himselfe to, what *nature* can but love? what *dutie* can but like? chiefly where the thing which he must do, may be done with ease, and the good which he shall do, shall gaine him praise, besides the surplus of profit. Some will say perhaps to traine up children, what needes so much cunning: or in so petie a matter what needes so much labour? Though I entreat of it here, where it first beginnes, yet it stretcheth unto all, both ages and persons: neither is the matter so meane, which is the readiest meane to so great a good, but if it were meane, the meanest matter requireth not the meanest maister, to have it well done: and the first groundworke would be layd by the best workeman. For who can better teach to reade, then he which for skill can commaund the language? And what had more neede to be exactly done then that principle, which either marreth the whole sequele, with insufficiencie, or maketh all sound, being it selfe well layd? The thing you will graunt to be of such efficacie, such an executor you despaire of: such a man may be had, nay a number of such may be had, if recompence be provided to answere such sufficiencie. The common not opinion but error is, he hath cunning enough for such a small trifle. It is not that small which he hath, that can do the thing well, but your skill is small, to thinke that any small skill, can do any thing well. He must know a great deale more then he doth, which must do that well, which he doth: bycause *store* is the deliverer of the best effectes, *neede* [130] which sheweth all at once, is but a sorie steward, and must put in band, that he hath some credit, though verie smal substance.

For the skill of the trayner I take it to be verie evident, both whence it may be had, and how plentiful a store house he hath for his provision. Thence he may have the generall groundes, and causes of his cunning.

3. Discretion in the trayner.

But there is a third thing yet besides these two, which is proper to his owne person, which if he have not, his cunning is worth nought. For though he see and embrace the the worthines of his subject, though he have gathered in his whole harvest from out of all writers, yet if he want *discretion* how to apply it according unto that, which is most fit to the verie meanest not bowghes and branches, but even the twigges and sprigges of the petiest circumstances, he is no skillfull trayner: but so much the more daungerous, the more helpe of learning he hath, which will bolden him to much. Therefore of these two other pointes, the one being throughly resolved on, the other perfitly obtained, and all the contemplative reasons well understoode, he must bend his wittes to wey the particularities, whereby both the generall conclusions be brought to be profitable, and his owne judgement to be thought discrete. The want of this is the cause of such a number of discoursers, which swarm ech where, and both like their owne choice, and can say pretily well to the generall position, which is not denyed to any toward youthe, but they shew themselves altogither lame in the particuler applying, which is a thing that attendeth onely upon experience and yeares. The having of it will provide us notable store of excellent executours, to all their profites, upon whom they shall execute. *Aristotle* the great *philosopher* in all his *morall* discourses tieth all those vertues which make mens maners praiseworthie, and be subject to circumstances, to the rule of foresight and *discretion*, whose commendation he placeth in skill of speciallities to direct mens doinges. Therefore it is no dishonour to the trayner, to be reclaymed unto *discretion*, which hath all those so many and so manerly vertues to attend upon her traine. Is not death commendable, and ascribed to valiancie, when it is voluntary, for the common good, by reason of the circumstance? and [131] the saving of life is it not basely thought of, when it had bene better spent, considering the circumstance? Which circumstance is the line to live by, the guide to all our doinges, the tuchestone to try a contemplative creature from an active courage.

In the course of training, a thousand difficulties not possible to be forseene by the generall direction, will offer themselves, and appose the maister, and at the sudden must be salved. What will the trainer do? runne to his booke? nay to his braines. He must remember his rule, that indivisibles and circunstances be beyond the reach of *arte*: and are committed to the *Artificer* whose *discretion* must helpe, where *arte* is to weake: though she give him great light, by fitting this to that, when he hath found wherfore. *Arte* setteth downe the exercise and all the knowen circunstances. The person bringes with it some difficultie in execution, where is the succour? *Arte* will not relent, she can not make curtsie, her knees be groune stiffe, and her jointes fast knit, and yet curtsie there must be. The *Artificer* must make it, and assist his ladie, which if she had not had a man to be her meane, she her selfe would have done all, and trusting to man whom she hath made her meane, why should she be deceyved, and her clyentes be abused, where she commendes them of trust? Children that come to schoole dwel not in one house, not in the same streate, nay not in the same towne, they cannot lightly come at one houre, they be not of one age, nor fit for one exercise, and yet they must have some. The *arte* knoweth my child no more then my neighbours, but the trainer must, and stay those uncertainties upon the arrest of *discretion*: being enstructed afore hand in the generall skill though bound but of voluntarie: as the like cause shall lead the like case.

The rule is, no noysome savour neare the newly exercised: how shall the poore boye do, that is to go home thorough stinking streates, and filthy lanes.

The rule is, change apparell after sweat: what if he have none other? or not there where he sweateth? Here must the trainers *discretion* shew it selfe, either to chuse exercises that be not subject to any such extremities, or to use them with the [132] fewest. But I am to long, neither neede I to doubt of mens *discretion,* though I say thus much of it, which many have and moe wishe for, I shall have occasion to supplie the rest in the generall teacher.

Thus have I runne thorough the whole argument of exercises, and shewed not onely what I thinke of them in generall, but also what be the cheife particulars, and the circunstances belonging thereunto: and according to my promise I have delt with the training maister, and overtreated him to thinke honorably of his profession, to gather knowledge where it is abundantly to be got: and last of all to joine *discretion* as a third companion to his owne admiration and sufficiency.

Chapter 36.

That both young boyes, and young maidens are to be put to learne. Whether all boyes be to be set to schoole. That to many learned be to burdenous: to few to bare: wittes well sorted civill, missorted seditious. That all may learne to write and read without daunger. The good of choice, and ill of confusion. The children which are set to learne, having either riche or poore freindes: what order and choice is to be used in admitting either of them to learne. Of the time to chuse.

Now that the thinges be appointed, wherwith the minde must be first furnished, to make it learned, and the bodie best exercised, to keepe it healthfull, we are next to consider of those persons, which are to be instructed in this furniture, and to be preserved by this exercise: which I take to be children of both sortes, *male* and *female*, young *boyes* and young *maidens*, which though I admit here generally, without difference of sex, yet I restraine particularly upon difference in cause, as herafter shall appeare. But young *maidens* must give me leave to speake of *boyes* first: bycause naturally the *male* is more worthy, and politikely he is more employed, and therfore that side claimeth this learned education, as first framed for their use, and most properly belonging to their kinde: though of curtsie and kindnesse they be content to lend their *female* in youth, the use of their traine in part, upon whom in age they bestow [133] both themselves, and all the frute of their whole traine.

It might seeme sufficient for the determining of this case, to say onely thus much: that they must needes be *boyes* which are to be trained in this sorte, as I have declared, bycause the bringing up of young *maidens* in any kynd of learning, is but an accessory by the waye. But for so much as there be many considerations in the persons, both of *boyes* and *maidens* worthy the deciding, I meane to entreat of them both somwhat largely: and as neare as I can, to resolve both my selfe and my reader in some pointes of controversie and necessitie, or rather in some pointes of apparent necessities, being out of all controversie. For the *male* side, that doubt is long ago out of doubt, that they be to be set to schoole, to qualifie themselves, to learne how to be religious and loving, how to governe and obey, how to fore cast and prevent, how to defende and assaile, and in short, how to performe that excellently by labour, wherunto they are borne but rudely by nature. For the very excellency of executions and effectes where by we do so great things, as we wonder at our selves in all histories and recordes of time, (which be but stages for people to gase on, and one to marvell at an others doings) testifieth and confirmeth that it were great pitie, that such towardnesse should be drowned in us for lacke of education, which never comes to proofe, but where education is the meane. That we can prove learned, the effect doth shew, but that not unlesse we learne, the defect declares. That our bodies can do great thinges, healthfull strength is witnesse to it selfe: but where weaknesse is, what doinges there be, verie want will pronounce. But now in the way of this so commended a traine, there be two great doubtes which
1. crosse me. The first is, whether all children be to be set to schoole,

without restraint to diminish the number. The second is, how to 2. worke restraint, if it be thought needefull. Touching the first question, whether all children be to be set to schoole or no, without repressing the infinitie of multitude, it is a matter of great weight, and not only in knowledge to be resolved upon, but also in deede so to be executed, as the resolution shall probably give sentence. For the bodie of a common weale in proportion is like unto a naturall bodie. In a naturall bodie, if any [134] one parte be to great, or to small, besides the eye sore it is mother to some evill by the verie misfourming, wherupon great distemperature must needes follow in time, and disquiet the whole bodie. And in a bodie politike if the like proportion be not kept in all partes, the like disturbance will crepe thorough out all partes. Some by to much will seeke to bite to sore, some by to litle will be trode on to much: as both will distemper: which if it fortune not to kill in the ende, yet it will disquiet where it greives, and hast forward the ende. But though the pestering of number do overlaie the most professions and partes of any common weale, and harme there where it doth so overcharge, yet I will not medle with any, but this of learning and the learner, which I have chosen to be my peculiar subject. Wherof I saye thus, that to many learned be to burdenous, that to few be to bare, that wittes well sorted be most civill, that the same misplaced be most unquiet and seditious.

To many burdens any state to farre: for want of provision. For the 1. To many learned. rowmes which are to be supplyed by learning being within number, if they that are to supply them, grow on beyound number, how can yt be but too great a burden for any state to beare? To have so many gaping for preferment, as no goulfe hath stoore enough to suffise, and to let them rome helpeles, whom nothing else can helpe, how can it be but that such shifters must needes shake the verie strongest piller in that state where they live, and loyter without living? which needeles superfluitie fleeting without seat, what ill can it but breede? A dangerous residence it is at hoome, still seeking shiftes to live as they may, though with enemitie to order, which neede cannot see. A perilous searcher it is abroode, to seeke to fish in a troubled water, if any cause promote their quarrell, bycause the cleare is not for them, which they have sounded allready. Sure *neede* is an imperious mistres to force conclusions, whether shee build upon *fantsie* and *desire,* which is a *maniheaded neede,* even before *neede,* and mostwhat without *neede*: or upon meere *lacke* and *want* in deede, which though it have but one head, yet that one is exceeding strong, importunate, and furiouse. And shee hath at hand to salve her mischiefes, a ready and an ordinarie excuse, wherewith she will [135] seeme to crave pardon for all that is done by needy men, as there unto enforced by her inevitable violence. A violent remeady, which doth not heale infections, but will alleage cause, where to have mischiefes excused and foregiven.

Wherfore if these mens misdemeanour come of their owne ill, which provision cannot prevent, bycause in best provision ill will be ill, so farre as it dare shew, where wealth workes wantonnes, it deserves correction and punishment. If it come of necessitie, for want of foresight in publike government, to helpe the common, from common blame, and to provide for the private: it would be amended and not suffered to runne, till the harme being received and felt, cause the question be moved, whether such a mischiefe proceede from private insolence, or publike negligence. For as the private is to pay, if it do not performe, when the publike hath provided: so the publike must pardon, if for insufficient foresight, the private prove dissolute, and lend the state a blow. But for my number I neede not to dwell any longer in to many, for troubling all with to many wordes, seeing all wise men see, and all learned men say, that it is most necessary to disburden a common weale of unnecessary number, and multitude in generall, which in some countries they compassed by brothelry, and common stewes, to let the yong spring: in some by exposition and spoile of enfantes, both contrary to nature, and contermaunded by religion: but according to their pollicie and commaunded by their countries. In particuler disposing of them that lived, they cast their account, and as the proportion of their states did suffer: so did they allote them with choice, and constrained them to obey. If such regard for multitude be to be had in any one braunche of the common weale, it is most needefull in schollers. For they professe learning, that is to say the soule of a state: and it is to perilous to have the soule of a state to be troubled with their soules, that is necessary *learning* with unnecessary *learners,* or the publike body with their private, which is the common *wealth* with their private want. For in all proportion, to much is to bad, and to much out of all proportion, and to have to much even of the soule, is not the soundest, where her offices be appointed and lymited in certaine. [136] *Superfluitie* and *residence* bring sickenes to the body, and must not to much then infect the soule sore, being in a *simpathie* with the body? Scholers by reason of their conceit which learning inflameth, as no meane authority saith, become to imperiall to rest upon a litle: and by their kinde of life which is allway idle they prove to disdainefull to deale with labour, unlesse neede make them trot, or the *Turkish captivitie* catch them, the greatest foe that can fall upon idle people, where labour is looked for, and they not used to it. *Contentment* in *aspiring*, which is hard to such wittes, and *patience* in *paines* which they never learned, be the two cognisances, whereby to discerne a civill wit, and fit to enjoye the benefit of his countrie. Now of all overflush in number, is not that most dangerous, which in conceit is loftie, and in life loytering, as the unbestowed scoller by profession is?

S. Paul.

2. To few learned.

To few be to bare and naked: bycause necessities must be supplyed, and that by the fittest. For whereas the defect of the fit enforceth supplement of the lookers on, though not the most likely, but whosoever they be, without further respect, then that they stand by, bycause neede bides no choyce where there is no *pluralitie*, and yet biddes *pluralitie* make choyce: there the unsufficient service of necessarie services breedes much miscontentment, and more shaking to any state. And that chiefly in such pointes, as the state embraseth, and the feeble minister doth nothing but deface. So that the defeat of the generall purpose must be most imputed to the bare defect of insufficient persons. For as to many bringes surfettes, so to few breedes consumptions.

3. Wittes wel sorted.

Wittes well sorted be most civill: This I say bycause to avoyd excessive number, choice is one principall helpe: for in admitting to uses onely such as be fit, and seeme to be made for them, pares of the unfit, and lesseneth the number, which yet would be lookt unto, even at the verie first. For even he that is thought most unfit, and is so in deede, yet will grieve at repulse, unles ye repell him by prevention, ear he come to the sense and judgement to discerne what a heavie thing a flat repulse is. Which *miscontentment* if it range in a number, cannot be without daunger to the common body. As to the contrarie [137] such wittes as be placed where the place needes them more then they the place, do performe with sufficiencie, and proceede with *contentment* of the state that enstawled them. The chiefe signes of *civilitie* be *quietnesse, concord, agrement, fellowship* and *friendship*, which *likenesse* doth lincke, *unliknesse*, undoeth: *fitnesse* maketh fast, *unfitnesse* doth loose: *proprietie* beares up, *improprietie* pulleth downe: *right matching* makes, *mismatching* marres. How then can civill societie be preserved, where wittes of unfit humours for service, are in places of service, by appointment, either unadvisedly made, or advisedly marred. Is there any picture so ill favoured, being compound of incompatible natures, as an execution is, being committed to a contrarie constitution? If fire be to enflame, and cause thinges burne, where water should coole, and be meane to quench, is the place not in danger? If that wit fall to preach, which were fitter for the plough, and he to clime a pulpit, which is made to scale a walle, is not a good *carter* ill lost, and a good *souldier* ill placed? If he will needes lawe it, which careth for no lawe, and professe *justice* that professeth no *right*, hath not *right* an ill *carver*, and *justice* a worse *maister*? If he will deale with *physicke* whose braines can not beare the infinite circumstances which belong thereunto, whether to maintaine health, or to restore it: doth he any thing else, but seeke to hasten death, for helping the disease? to make way to murther, in steede of amendement? to be a *butchars prentice* for a *maister* in *physike*? And so is it in all kindes of life, in all trades of living, where fitnes and right placing of wittes doth worke agreement and ease, unfitnes and misplacing have the contrary companions, disagreement and disease.

4. Wittes misplaced.

Againe wittes misplaced most unquiet and seditious: as any thinge else strayned against nature: light thinges prease upward, and will ye force *Fire* downe? Heavie thinges beare downeward: and will ye have *Leade* to leape up? An imperiall witte for want of education and abilitie, being placed in a meane calling will trouble the whole companie, if he have not his will, as winde in the stomacke: and if he have his will, then shall ye see what his naturall did shoote at. He that beareth a tankarde by meanesse of degree, and was borne for a [138] cokhorse by sharpenes of witte, will keepe a canvase at the Conduites, tyll he be Maister of his companie. Such a sturring thing it is to have wittes misplaced, and their degrees mislotted by the iniquitie of *Fortune*, which the equitie of *nature* did seeme to meane unto them.

Plato in his wished common weale, and his defining of naturall dignities, appointeth his degrees and honors, where *nature* deserveth by *abilitie* and *worth*, not where *fortune* freindeth by *byrth* and *boldnes*, though where both do joyne *singularitie* in *nature*, and successe in *fortune*, there be some rare jewell. Hereupon I conclude, that as it is necessary to prevent to great a number for the *quantitie* thereof: so it is more then necessarie, to provide in the necessarie number for the *qualitie* thereof. Wherein *restraint* it selfe will do much good for the one, and *choice* in restraint will do more for the other. Sure all children may not be set to schole, nay not though private circumstance say yea. And therefore scholes may not be set up for all, though great good will finde never so many founders, both for the place wherein to learne, and for the number also which is for to learne: that the state may be served with sufficiencie enough, and not be pestered with more then enough. And yet by the way for writing and reading so they rested there, what if everie one had them, for *religion* sake, and their necessarie *affaires*? Besides that in the long time of their whole youth, if they minded no more, these two were easely learned, at their leasure times by extraordinary meanes, if the ordinarie be daintie and no schoole nigh. Everie parish hath a minister, if none else in the parish, which can helpe writing and reading.

Of riche and poore children.

Some doubt may rise here betwene the *riche* and *poore*, whether all *riche* and none *poore*, or but some in both maye and ought to be set to learning. For all in both that is decided alreadie, No: bycause the whole question concerneth these two kindes, as the whole common weale standeth upon these two kindes. If all *riche* be excluded, *abilitie* will snuffe, if all *poore* be restrained, then will *towardnesse* repine. If *abilitie* set out some *riche* by private purses for private preferment: *towardnesse* will commende some *poore* to publike provision for publike [139] service: so that if neither publike in the *poore*, nor private in the *riche* do marre their owne market, me thinke that were best, nay that will be best, being ruled by their wittes to conceive learning, and their disposition to prove vertuous. But how may the publike in the *poore*, and the private in the *riche*, make their owne market in the education of those whom they preferre to learning? I will tell ye how. The *riche* not to have to much, the *poore* not to lacke to much, the one by overplus breadeth a loose and dissolute braine: the other by under minus a base and servile conceit. For he that never needeth by supplie of freindes, never strayneth his wittes to be freind to himselfe, but commonly proves retchelesse till the blacke oxe tread upon his toes, and neede make him trie what mettle he is made of. And he that still needeth for want of freindes being still in pinche holdes that for his heaven, which riddes him from neede, and serves that Saint, which serves his turne best, even *Neptune* in shipwracke. Wherby he maketh the right of his judgement become bond for wealth: and the sight of his witte blinde for desire, such slaverie workes want, unlesse Gods grace prove the staye, which is no line to common direction, though it be our onely hope, by waye of refuge. Now then if the wealthy parentes of their private patrimonie, and publike patrones of their supererogatorie wealth, will but drive to a meane in both these two mains, neither shall wealth make the one to wanton, nor want make the other to servile: neither the one to leape to fast, for feare he loose some time, nor the other to hast to fast, for feare he misse some living. Sure to provide for poore scholers but a poore patche of a leane living, or but some meane halfe, is more then halfe a maime, the desire to supplie that which wanteth, distracting the studie more by many partes, then that petie helpe, which they have can possibly further it: bycause the charge to maintaine a scholer is great, the time to prove well learned, long, and when ripenesse is ready, there would be staye to chuse and time to take advice, where neede turnes the deafe eare. The paterne of to prodigall wealth oftimes causeth the toward student to overshoote himselfe by corrupt imitation, as braverie and libertie be great allurers, where studie and staye pretend restraint. [140] And therfore neither must to much be butte to allurementes, nor to litle a burden to judgement: the one the meane to lewdnesse the other a maime to libertie. The midle sorte of parentes which neither welter in to much wealth, nor wrastle with to much want, seemeth fittest of all, if the childrens capacitie be aunswerable to their parentes state and qualitie: which must be the levell for the fattest to fall downe to, and the leanest to leape up to, to bring forth that student, which must serve his countrey best. *Religion* and *learning* will frame them in judgement, when *wealth* and *abilitie* have set them once on foote.

The choosing time.

For the choice of wittes definitely, till they come to the time, or verie neare to it, when they are themselves naturally and for ripenesse of yeares to chuse their owne kinde of life, how so ever circunstance free, or binde their choice, I cannot say much, though I do see what other have said in that behalfe. A quicke witte will take soone, a staid memorie will hold fast, a dull head may prove somwhat, a meane witte offers faire, *praise* bewrayeth some courage, *awe* some, in eche kinde there is likelyhood , and yet error in eche. For as there be faire blossomes, so there be nipping frostes. And till the daunger of revolt be past, the quicke must be helde in hope, the dull without dispaire, the meane the meetest, if the sequele do aunswere. I can limit no one thing, though I see great shewes, where there is such uncertaine motion, both in soule and body, as there is in children. The maisters *discretion* in time and upon triall, may see and say much, and in a number there will some leaders appeare of themselves, as some speciall deare in the whole heard. Where great appearance is, there one may prophecie, and yet the lying spirite may sit in his lippes. For God hath reserved his calling and discovering houres, as all other future eventes to his owne peculiar and private knowledge: probabilities be our guides, and our conjectures be great, though not without exception. What kinde of witte I like best for my countrey, as most proper to be the instrument for learning, it shall appeare herafter. But for the first question of the two, it seemeth to me verie plaine that all children be not to be set to schoole, but onely such as for naturall wittes, and sufficient maintenance, either of their naturall parentes, or civill patrones, shall be honestly [141] and wel supported in their study, till the common weale minding to use their service, appoint their provision, not in hast for *neede*, but at leasure with *choice*.

Chapter 37.

The meanes to restraine the overflowing multitude of scholers. The cause why everie one desireth to have his childe learned, and yet must yelde over his owne desire to the disposition of his countrie. That necessitie and choyce be the best restrayners. That necessitie restrayneth by lacke and lawe. Why it may be admitted, that all may write and read that can, but no further. What is to be thought of the speaking and understanding of Latine, and in what degree of learning that is. That considering our time and the state of religion in our time, lawe must needes helpe this restraint: with the answere to such objections as are made to the contrary. That in choice of wittes, which must deale with learning, that wit is fittest for our state, which answereth best the monarchie, and how such a wit is to be knowne. That choice is to helpe in scholing, in admission into colledges in proceeding to degrees, in preferring to livinges, where the right and wrong of all the foure pointes be handled at full.

In the last title we have concluded, that there must be a *restraint*, and that all may not passe on to learning, which throng thitherward, bycause of the inconveniences, which may ensue, by want of preferment for such a multitude, and by defeating other trades of their necessarie travellours. Our next labour therefore must be, how to handle this *restraint*, that the tide overflow not the common, with to great a spring of bookish people, if ye crie come who will, or ring out all in. Everie one desireth to have his childe learned: the reason is, for that how hardly soever either *fortune* frowne, or *casualtie* chastice, yet *learning* hath some strength to shore up the person, bycause it is incorporate in the person, till the soule dislodge, neither lyeth it so open for mischaunce to mangle, in any degree, as forren and fortunes *patrimonie* doth. But though everie parent be thus affected toward his owne child, as nature leades him to wish his owne best, yet for all that [142] everie parent must beare in memorie that he is more bound to his country, then to his child, as his child must renounce him in countermatch with his countrie. And that country which claymeth this prerogative of the father above the child, and of the child above the father, as it maintained the father eare he was a father, and will maintaine the child, when he is without a father: so generally it provideth for all, as it doth require a dutie above all. And therefore parentes in disposing of their children may upon good warrant surrender their interest to the generall consideration of their common countrie, and thinke that it is not best to have their children bookish, notwithstanding their owne desire, be it never so earnestly bent: if their countrie say either they shall serve in this trade, without the booke: or if shee say I may not allow any more booke men without my to much trouble. I pray thee good parent have pacience, and appoint some other course for thy childe, there be many good meanes to live by, besides the booke, and I wilbe thy childes friend, if thou wilt fit in some order for me. This verie consideration of the countrie, uttered with so milde a speach, spoken by her that is able to performe it, may move the reasonable parent, to yealde to her desire as best, as she can tell the headstrong in plaine termes, that he shall yeelde perforce, if he will not by entreatie. For private affection though supported by reason of strength whatsoever, must either voluntarily bend, or forcibly breake, when the common good yeeldeth to the contrary side.

Seeing therefore the disposition of wittes according to the proportion of ech state is resigned over to the countrie: and she sayth all may not be set to schole, bycause ech trade must be furnished, to performe all duties belonging to all parts: it falleth out in this case of *restraint* which bridles desire, that two speciall groundes are to be considered, which strip away excessive number, *necessitie* and *choice*, the one perforce, the other by your leave.

Necessity.

As for *necessitie*, when the parent is over charged with defect in circumstance, though desire carie him on, it then restraineth most, and lesseneth this number when desire would encrease it, and straines to the contrary. You would have your [143] childe learned, but your purse will not streatch, your remedy is pacience, devise some other way, wherein your abilitie will serve. You are not able to spare him from your elbow, for your neede, and learning must have leysure: a scholers booke must be his onely busines, without forreine lettes, you may be bold of your owne: let booking alone, for such as can entend it, from being called away by domesticall affaires, and necessarie busines. For the scholers name will not be a cypherlike subject, as he is termed of leasure, so must he have it. And they that cannot spare their children so, must forebare their scholing, by the olde *Persian* ordinance, bycause leasure is the foregoer to liberall profession: *necessitie* compelleth and bastardeth the conceit, a venym to learning, whom freedom should direct. You

Xenop. 1. κυρ. παιδ.

have no schole neare you, and you cannot pay for teaching further of, let your owne trade content you: keepe your childe at home. Your childe is weake tymbred, let scholing alone, make play his physician and health his midle end. Which way soever *neede* drives you perforce, that way must ye trot, if he will not amble, and bid Will thinke that well. He that governeth all seeth what is your best, your selfe may be missled either by *ignorance* in *choice*, or *affection* in blood. In these and the like cases *lacke* is the leader, which way soever she straineth. Whereby if the restrained childe cannot get the skil to write and read: I lament that lacke, bycause I have allowed him somuch before, upon some reasonable perswasion even for necessary dealings. For these two pointes concerne every man neare, bycause they submit themselves to everie mans service: yea in his basest busines and secretest affaires. I dare not venture to allow so many the latin tungue nor any other language, unlesse it be in cases, where their trades be knowne, and those toungues be founde to be necessarie for them. For all the feare is, though it be more then feare, where it still falleth out so, least having such benefits of schole, they will not be content with the state which is for them, but bycause they have some petie smak of their booke, they will thinke any state be it never so high to be low ynough for them. Which petie bookemen do not consider, that both clounes in the countrie, and artificers in townes be allowed latin in well governed [144] states, which yet rest in their calling, without *pride* or *ambition*, for that small knowledge, whereby they be better able to furnish out their trades, without further aspiring. Neither measure they the meaner qualities, as the thinges be in nature, but as themselves be in conceit: neither can they consider that at this daye it is not the toungue, but the treasure of learning and knowledge, which is laid up in the toungue whereunto they never came, which giveth the toungue credit, and the speaker authoritie. For want of this right judgement there ensueth in them a miscontentment of minde, not liking their owne state, and a cumbersome conceit, still aspiring higher, that disquieteth the whole state. Wherefore *necessitie* is a good meane to prevent this in many, which would if they could, now may not, bycause they cannot.

Lawe. The second point of *necessitie* I do assigne to *lawe* and *ordinaunce* upon consideration to cut of this flocking multitude, which will needes to schoole. Whereupon two great goods must needes ensue.

Contentment of minde in the partie restrained, when he shall perceive publike provision to be the checke to his fantsie: and timely *preventing*, eare conceit take roote, and thinke it selfe wronged. Bycause it is much better to nip misorder in the verie ground, that it may not take hold, then when it is growen up, then to hacke it downe. He that never conceived great thinges maye be helde there with ease, but being once entred in the waye to mount, and then throwne backward, he will be in some greife and seeke how to returne gaule, whence he received greife, if he chaunce to prove pevish, as repulse in great hope is a perillous grater. Yet in both these cases of necessarie *restraint*, I could wish provision were had to some singular wittes, found worthy the avauncement: either by private patronage, or publike: and yet againe if they passe on, and bewtifie some other trade: that also is verie good, seeing they serve their countrey, whersoever they be loated, and in those also whom libertie of circunstance doth set to schoole *povertie* will appeare, and *towardnesse* call for helpe: and yet the number will neverthelesse prove still with the most.

It is no objection to alleadge against such a lawful restraint, the abilitie of good wittes, and great learning in men, that either [145] now be, or heretofore have bene, which we might have lackt if so strait a *lawe* had bene then: or that it were pitie by severitie of an unkinde *lawe* to hynder that excellencie, which God commonly gives to the poorer sort. To the first I aunswere, besides that, which even *lawe* to that ende will aunswere for it selfe. As in time to come we know not, who shall serve the state, if the *lawe* be made straite, and yet we know well, that he which defendes states will provide sufficient persons, by whom they shalbe served: so in time past or present, if these were not, or those had not bene, whom we now see or of whom we have heard, God would have raised up other, whose benefites in serving governmentes may not be restrained to any degree of men, as they be men, but to the appointment of a civill societie, which hath direction over men: as a thing which God doth most cherish, both in respect of this Church which is of number, and in regard of societie it selfe, which is the naturall ende of mans being here, and not to live alone. And I warrant you whensoever such an orderly *restraint* shalbe put in practise that there wilbe as good foresight had to have necessarie functions served, as there will be regard to draine away the unnecessarie overflow. A thing not new

1. Two objections against restraint by lawe.

2.

faingled, but ever in use, where the common weales, had an eye to distribute their multitude to the best and easiest proportion of their owne state: which otherwise improportionate would breade an *aposteme*. And therefore if the generall judgement appoint it so, it is best to yeelde. And private opinion in politike cases will prove an errour, if the generall liking contrarie it flat. I do not now meane, where the generall is blinded by common errour, but where private conceit can take no exception saving that, which he bredeth from out of his owne braine. If the state of my countrey take order, that my child shall not go to schoole, sure I will obay, and provide some other course, though I like learning exceeding well, and be verie farre in love with it, besides the affection to my child, bycause the squaring with the generall, is to farre out of square for any particular. And I pray you may it not be, that for want of such an ordinance we mist better wittes, then those were, or are, which we either had or have, though we thinke very well of both the sortes, whether [146] now living with us, or tofore parted from us? And doth not *negligence* for want of looking to, overthrow as gaie and gallant heades, as *diligence* by doing even her verie best, hath ever brought to light? Advised and considerate planting is like enough to receive verie good encrease, and eventes in such cases, by authoritie and testimonie of two the greatest oratours in both the best tongues, be but foolish maisters, and febler argumentes.

As for pytying the poore, it is no pitie, not to wish a begger to become a prince, though ye allow him a pennie, and pitie his needefull want. Is he poore? provide for him, that he may live by trade, but let him not loyter. Is he wittie? why? be artificers fooles? and do not all trades occupie wit? sometimes to much, and thereby both straine their owne heades to the worse, and prove to suttle for a great deale their betters. Is he verie likely to prove singuler in learning? I do not reject him, for whom I provide a publike helpe in common patronage. But he doth not well to oppose his owne particular, against the publike good, let his countrie thinke of him enough, and not he of him selfe to much. If *nobilitie* and *gentlemen* would fall to diligence, and recover the execution of learning, where were this objection? The greatest assurers of it affirme, that learning was wont to be proper to *nobilitie*, and that through their negligence it is left for a pray to the meaner sort, and a bootie to corruption, where the professours neede offereth wrongfull violence to the liberalitie of the thing. Do they not therein confesse, where the right of the thing lyeth and themselves to be usurpers, if they should enter upon their owne, whose the interest is, and whom in so many discourses of nobilitie, they themselves blame so much for their so great negligence? They must needes here yeelde without law to their owne confession. But we see God hath shewed himselfe mervelous munificent and beneficiall this way to the poorer sort. I graunt, yet that proves not, but that he bestowed as great giftes of them which shewed not. And that as *diligence* in the one did shew that they had, to the glorie of the giver, and their owne praise: so *negligence* in the other, did suppresse that they had to their owne shame, who neither honoured the giver, [147] nor honested themselves, nor profited their countrie. So that here not the *gift*, but the *shew* is brought in allegation. And why not the greater *talent* hid seeing it is no noveltie? But the other shew. Nomore then that they have. And the other shew not. No argument that they have not. Take order then, that they shew, which have and hide, and then make comparisons. Be great giftes tied to the meane, or banished from the mighty? be there not as good wittes in wealth, though oftimes choked with *dissolutenes* and *negligence*, as there be in povertie appearing thorough *paines* and *diligence*? Nay be there not as untoward *poorelinges*, as there be wanton *wealthlinges*? I know yes, and when untowardnes and an ill inclynation hittes in a base condition, it proves more vile. So that this thing turnes about to my other conclusion, that neither povertie is to be pitied more then the countrey, if pitie must needes take place: neither riches more to be esteemed then the common weale, if wealth must needes be wayed: but that the value in wittes must be heelde of most worth, which hath her haven already appointed, where to harbour her selfe, in maintenaunce to studie, either by private helpe, if the parents be wealthy, or by publike ayde, if povertie praie for it.

Certainly there is great reason (if even the terme, great, be not to small, when the thing is more then needfull, and the time to prevent it, is almost runne to farre) why order should be taken, to restraine the number, that will needes to the booke. For while the Church was an harbour for all men to ride in, which knew any letter, there needed no *restraint*, the livinges there were infinite and capable of that number, the more drew that waye, and found releife that way, the better for that state, which encroached still on, and by clasping all persons, would have graspid all livinges. The *state* is now altered, that *bookmaintenance* maimed, the *preferment* that waye hath turned a new leafe. And will ye let the *fry* encrease, where the *feeding* failes? Will ye have the *multitude* waxe, where the *maintenance* waines? Sure I conceive of it thus, that there is as great difference in ground, betwene the suffring all to booke it in these dayes, and the like libertie to the same number, in the ruffe of the papacy amongst us: as there is betwene the two religions, [148] the one expelled and the other retained, in the grounds of their kinde. The expelled religion was supported by multitude, and the moe had interest, the moe stood for it: the retained must pitch the defence of her truth, in some paucity of choice: seeing the livinges are shred, which should serve the great number. So that our time, of necessitie must restraine: if not: what you breede and feede not, the adversarie part will allure by living, and arme by corrupting, against their unwise countrey, which either bestowed them not at first, or despised them at last. Where your thankes shalbe lost, which brought up, and forsooke, their desert shall sinke deepe, which fed the forsaken. And is it not meere folly by *sufferance* to encrease your enemies force, which you might by *ordinance* supplant at ease? it is the booke, which bredes us enemies, and causeth corruption to creepe, where cunning never came. The enemy state cared not so much for many well learned, as for the multitude though unlearned, which backt much bould ignorance, with a gaie surface of some small learning: our state then must reject the multitude, and rempare with the cunning. Our owne time is our surest touch, and our owne trouble our rightest triall, if wisedome in time do not prevent it, folly in triall will surely repent. It is to no purpose to alledge, when people see, that there is no preferment to be had for all learners, that then the number will decay, and abate of it selfe without any *lawe*: onelesse ye can worke so, as no moe may hope, though but one can hit: or els, if ye can appoint us, how long the controversie for *religion* is like to endure. For while hope is indifferent, eche one will croud: and while *religion* is in brake, eche one under hand, will furnish where he favoreth. The adversarie of our religion, as in deede he needed none, so dreamed he not of any defense, while he was rockt in ease, and his state unassailed by any *miscontentment*: but now that he is skirmished with so much, and so sore gauled, he is driven to studie, and seeketh by new coined distinctions to recover, that credite and reputation which he lost by intruding: wherin as he dealeth more cunningly with the person of his adversarie, so he bewrayeth still the great avantage, which his adversaries cause hath wonne over his. For in disputing, good *Logicians* know that it is an evident shift, to [149] avoide manifest foile, when the disputer in dispaire of his cause, is forced to bend against his adversaries person. And therefore provision must be, to defend by a learned *paucitie*, where the *flocking number* by reason of ingenerate wantes, will prove but a scare crow, and by apparent defection doth encrease the embush, which lyeth still in waite, to intercept our possession. Thus much of *Necessitie*, which stayeth the multitude of learners either by *defect* in *circunstance*, or by *law* in *ordinance*, when the parties be letted, either by *lack* that they can not, or by *law* that they may not, lay claime to the booke.

Choice.

Now are we come to a larger compasse, where libertie gives leave to learne if he can, where forraine circumstances be free, and no let for any to be learned but either his wit, if he be dull, or his will, if he be stubburne. In this kinde, *choise* is a great prince, which by great reason and good advice, abbridgeth that which is to much, and culs owt the best. Which choice, as it begins at the entrie of the elementarie schole, so it proceedeth on, till the last preferment be bestowed, which either the state hath in store for any person, or any person can deserve, for service in the state. And therefore as it keepeth in an ordinate course, so it may full well be orderly handled, and by convenient degrees.

What wit is fittest for learning in a monarchie.

But bycause the *choice* is to be made by the wit, and the wit is to be applied to the frame and state of the countrie, where it continueth: I will first seeke out, what kinde of wit is even from the infancie to be thought most fit, to serve for this state in the learned kinde. Which if it be to stirring, troubleth, if it be well staied, setleth the countrie where it lyveth, so farre as it dealeth. And yet oftymes that wit maketh least shew at the first, to be so plyable, which at the last doth best agree with the pollicy. And therfore it is then to be taken, when it beginnes first to shew, that it will prove such: wherefore precise rejecting of any wit, which is in way to go onward, before due ripenes, as it is harmefull to the partie rejected, so it bewraieth some rashnes in him that rejecteth: bycause the varietie is exceeding great, though the conjectures be as great, and the most likelyhood must needes leade, where certaintie is denied. But to the wittes:

wherein as lacke and law do guide necessitie [150] so the qualitie of the witte, conformable to the state directeth *choice*.

There be three kindes of government most noted among all writ-
1. ers, whereof the first is called a *monarchie*, bycause one prince
beareth the sway, by whose circumspection the common good is
2. shielded, and the common harme shouldred: the second an *oli-*
3. *garchie*: where some few beare all the swinge: the third a *democratie*,
where every one of the people hath his interest in the direction, and his voice in elections. Now all these three be best maintained by those kindes of wit, which are most proper for that kinde of government, wherein they live. But bycause the government of our countrie is a *monarchie*: I will in *choise* seeke out that kinde of wit, which best agreeth with the *monarchie*, neither will I touch the other two, unles I fortune to trip upon them by chaunce. And for as much as I have made the yong child my first subject, I will continue therein still: bycause that which beginneth to shew it selfe neare upon infancie, will so commonly continue, though alteration creepe in sometime. But lightly these wittes alter not, bycause the tokens be so fast and firme in nature, and tend to so certaine and so resolute a judgement.

A wit for learning in a monarchie.

That child therefore is like to prove in further yeares, the fittest subject for learning in a *monarchie*, which in his tender age sheweth himselfe obedient to scholeorders, and eitheir will not lightly offend, or if he do, will take his punishment gently: without either much repyning, or great stomaking. In behaviour towardes his companions he is gentle and curteous, not wrangling, not quarelling, not complaining, but will put to his helping hand, and use all perswasions, rather then to have either his maister disquieted, or his fellowes punished. And therefore he either receiveth like curtesie againe of his scholefellowes: or who so sheweth him any discurtesie, must abyde both chalenge and combate with all the rest.

If he have any excellent towardnes by nature, as commonly such wittes have, whereby he passeth the residue in learning, it will shew it selfe so orderly, and with such modestie, as it shall soone appeare, to have no loftines of minde, no aspiring ambition, no odiouse comparisons joyned withall. [151]

At home he will be so obsequious to parentes, so curteous among servauntes, so dutiefull toward all, with whom he hath to deale: as there will be contention, who may praise him most behinde his backe, who may cherish him most before his face: with prayer that he may go on, with feare of too hastie death, in so od a towardnes of wit and demeanour. These thinges will not lightly make any evident shew, til the child be either in the *grammer schole*, by orderly ascent, and not by two forewardly hast, or upon his passage from the perfited *elementarie*, bycause his yeares by that time, and his contynuance under government, will somwhat discover his inclination. Before that time we pardon many thinges, and use pointes of ambition and courage, to enflame the litle ones onward, which we cut of afterward, for making them to malapart, as in their apparell frise is successour to silke. When of them selves without any either great feare, or much hartening, they begin to make some muster and shew of their learning to this more then that, then is conjecture on foote to finde, what they willbe most likely to prove.

But now to examine these signes more nearely and narowly, which I noted to be in the child that is like to prove so fit a subject for a *monarchie*, in matters of learning: Is not obedience the best sacrifice, that he can offer up to his prince and governour, being directed and ruled by his countrie lawes? And in the principles of government, is not his maister his *monarche*? and the scholelawes his countrey lawes? wherunto if he submit himselfe both orderly in *perfourmance*, and patiently in *penaunce*, doth he not shew a mynde already armed, not to start from his dutie? and so much the more, bycause his obedience to his maister is more voluntarie, then that to his prince, which is meere necessarie. For in perswasions of children, which the parentes will give eare to: in desire to chaunge, where their wills be chekt: in multitude of teachers, who thrive by such chaunges: all meanes be good, where there is such plentie, to offer such parentes as be tikelish, and such scholers as be shifting, removing from maisters and renouncing of obedience. The child hath many shadowes to shift in upon any pretence, and as many baites, to winne his parentes beleefe, and specially if [152] he stand in feare of beating. Whereas neither he, ne yet his parentes, can forsake their prince, upon any colour without forfaiting more then a quarters scholehire. And therfore in so many meanes to change, and some perhaps offered, bycause who will not very willingly deale with such a witte, where his travell will make shew, that child which notwithstanding all these entisementes, will continue both on, and one, and digest dyscurtesies, though his mayster sometyme

chaunce to prove churlish, is the peculiar and proper witte, which I
commende for obedience, and that is like to prove both honestly
2. learned, and earnestly beloved. In his owne demeanour towardes
his fellowes and freindes, and all sortes of people generally, either
at home, or abroade, either in schoole, or elsewhere and in their love
and liking of him againe, doth he not shew forth an evident socia-
bilitie and liklyhood, that he will be very well to be lived withall?
and prove a very curteous man, which is so loving, and so beloved
3. while he is yet a boye? In letting nature shew her owne excellencie
without unsweetning it with his owne sawcinesse, doth he not
argue that he hath stuffe towards preferment, without any sparke
of ambition to move further flame? or to prease to fast forwarde?
which shall never neede: bycause all men that know him, will either
willingly helpe to preferre him, if their voice be in it: or will rejoyce
at his preferment, if they be but beholders. For who will not be glad
to see vertue, which he loveth, avaunced to rewarde? or what can
envie do, in so plausible a case, but set forth the partie, by declaring
his desert, in that she is there? There be many consequentes, which
hange upon these, as neither vertue nor vice be single where they
be, but are alwaie accompanied with the whole troupe of the like
retinue. And one convenience graunted draweth on a number of the
like kinde, as well as one inconvenience draweth on his like traine.

But these be the maine as I conceive at the first blush: obedience to superiours and superioritie, freindlynesse and fellowship toward companions, and equalles: substance to deserve well and winne it, desire to avoide ill and flie it. What duetie either towardes God or man, either in publike or private societie, in any either hie or low kinde of life is there, wherunto [153] God hath not seemed in nature to have framed and fashioned this so toward a youth? and therefore to have appointed him for the use of learning to be ruled by his betters, and to rule his inferiours, nothing offensive nor unpleasant to any? Many such wittes there be, and at them must choice first begin. And as those be the best, and first to be chosen, in whom there is so rare metall, so the second or third after these be unworthy the refusall, in whom the same qualities do appeare, though not in the same, but in some meaner degree. For wheras great ill is oft in place, and proves the generall foe to that which would be better, there meane good, if it may have place, will be generall freind to preferre the better: as even this second mediocritie, if it may be had, as choice will finde it out, will prove verie freindly to set forward all good. Now these properties and signes appeare in some, verie soone, in some verie late, yea oftimes when they are least looked for: as either judgement in yeares, or experience in dealinges do frame the parties.

The plat for the *monarchicall* learner being alwaye reseant in the chusers head, concerning the propertie of his witte: and appearance towardes proofe: the rest is to be bestowed upon the consideration of learning, and towardnesse in children generally (wherof these wittes be still both the first and best frutes) where to stay, or how farre to proceede in the ascent of learning. Whether he be riche or poore, that makes no matter, and is already decided, whether he be quicke or slow, therein is somwhat, and requireth good regard.

Schoole choice.

Wherfore when sufficient abilitie in circunstances bids open the schoole dore, the admission and continuance be generall, till upon some proofe the maister, whom I make the first chuser of the finest, and the first clipper of the refuse, begin to finde and be able to discerne, where abilitie is to go on forward, and where naturall weaknesse biddes remove by times. For if negligence worke weaknesse, that is an other disease, and requires an other medecine, to heale it withall. Now when the maister hath spied the strength or infirmitie in nature, as by lightsomnesse or heavinesse in learning, by easinesse or hardnesse in retaining, by comparing of contrarie or the like wittes, he shall easely sound both, then as his delite wilbe to have the [154] toward continue, so must his desire be, how to procure the diverting and removing of the duller and lesse toward, to some other course, more agreeing with their naturall, then learning is: wherin they are like to go forward verie litle, though their fortune be to go to schoole very long: but here two considerations are to be had: neither to soone to seeke their diverting, till some good ripenesse in time, though with some great paines to the teacher in the meane time, wish them to be weined from booking: neither yet before their bodies be of strength to abide the paines of some more laborious prenticeship. For it may so prove, that those wittes, which at the first were found to be exceeding hard and blunt, may soften, and prove sharp in time and shew a finer edge, though that be not to be made a generall caution, to cover dullardes with all. For the naturall dulnesse will disclose it selfe generally in all pointes, that concerne memorie and conceit: that dulnesse which will once breake out sharp, will shew it selfe by glaunces, as a clowdy day useth, which will prove faire, when all shrews have dined. Wherefore peremptorie judgement to soone, may prove perillous to some: and againe he that is fit for nothing else, for the tendernesse of his bodie, may abide in the schoole a litle while longer, where though he do but litle good, yet he may be sure to take litle harme.

Moreover if the parentes abilitie be such, as he may, and his desire such, as he will maintaine his child at schoole, till he grow to some yeares, though he grow to small learning, the maister must have pacience, and measure his paines by the parentes purse, where he knowes there is plentie, and not by the childes profit, which he seeth will be small. Wherein yet he must impart his opinion continually with the parent both for his duetie sake, and for avoiding of displeasure. But in the meaner sorte the case altereth, for that as a good witte in a poore child, deserves direct punishment, if by negligence he forslow the obtaining of learning, which is the patrimonie to wittie povertie: so a dull witte in that degree would not be dalyed with all to long, but be furthered to some trade, which is the fairest portion to the slow witted poore. Now bycause the maister to whose judgement I commend the choice, is no absolute [155] potentate in our common weale, to dispose of wittes, and to sorte mens children, as he liketh best, but in nature of a counsellour, to joine with the parent, if he will be advised: therfore to have this thing perfectly accomplished, I wish the parentes and maisters to be freindly acquainted, and domestically familiar. And though some parentes neede no counsell, as some maisters can give but litle, yet the wise parent will heare, and can judge: and the skilfull maister can judge, and should be heard. Where neither of these be, neither skill in the teacher to tell it, nor will in the parente to heare it, and lesse affection to follow it, the poore child is wrung to the worse in the meane while, and the parent receives small comfort in conclusion.

This course for the maister to keepe in judging of his scholer, and the parent to follow in bestowing of his child, according to his wit, continueth so long as the child shalbe either under maistership in schole, or tutorship in colledge. During the which time, a great number may be verie wisely and fitly bestowed, unlearned trades sufficiently appointed, the proceding in letters reserved to them, to whom for wit and judgement they seeme naturally vowed: and finally the whole common weale in every braunch well furnished with number, and the number it selfe discharged of to much. Bycause this tyme under the maisters goverment, is the time wherin youth is to be bestowed by forraine direction: for afterward in a more daungerous age, and a more jeoperdouse time, they grow on to their owne choice, and these unfitnesses in nature, or frailtes in maners, being not foreseene to, may cause the friendes forthinke it, and the parties sore rue it. And though the maister shall not allway have his counsell followed in this case, yet if he do signifie his opinion to the parent, his dutie is discharged, and that which I require is orderly performed. For if the parent shew himselfe unwilling to be directed that way, which the maister shall allow, upon great ground, and be blynded by affection, measuring his childes wit to learning, by his doing of some errand, or by telling of some tale, or by marking of some pretie toy, as such argumentes there be used, which yet be no argumentes of a towarde learner, but of a no foolish observer: in this case though the maister to his owne gaine [156] draw on under his hand a desparate wit, the fault is his that would not see, if he that saw did honestly tell it. Whereby it still proveth true, that parentes and maisters should be familiarly lynked in amitie, and contynual conference, for their common care, and that the one should have a good affiance of judgement in the thing, and of goodwill towards himselfe, reposed in the other. Which will prove so, when the maister is chosen with judgement, and continued with conference, and not bycause my neighbours children go to schole with you, you shall have myne to. A common commendation among common coursiters, which post about still to survey all scholes, and never staie in one: and reape as much learning, as the rowling stone doth gather mosse.

But concerning scholes, and such particularities, as belong thereunto I will then deale, when I shall take in hand the peculiar argumentes, of schooles and schooling, both for the elementarie and the gramarian. Wherein we are no lesse troubled with number and confusion in our petie kingdomes, then the verie common weale is molested with the same in greater yeares, and larger scope.

But bycause it were not orderly delt, to rip the faultes, and not to heale them, I wil post all these points over to their owne treatises, in my particuler discourses hereafter, where I will presently helpe, whatsoever I shall blame. The other meanes wherby choice lesseneth number, be admissions into colleges, prefermentes to degrees, advauncement unto livings, wherein the common weale receiveth the greater blow, the nearer these thinges be to publike execution, and therefore the playner dealing to prevent mischiefe before it infect, is the more praiseworthy.

Admission into colleges.

As concerning *colleges* I do not thinke the livinges in them to be peculiar, or of purpose ment to the poorer sort onely, whose want that small helpe could never suffice, though there be some prerogative reserved unto them, in consideration of some great towardnes, which might otherwise be trod down, and that way is held up: but that they be simply preferments for learning, and avauncementes to vertue, as wel in the wealthy for reward of well doing, as in the poorer for necessarie [157] support. And therefore as I give *admission* scope to chuse of both the sortes, so I do restraine it to honest and civill towardnes. For if favour and friendship not for these furnitures, but for private respectes, carie away elections though with some enterlarding of towardnes and learning, and some few to give countenaunce to some equitie of choice, and theerby to maintaine the credit of such places, surely the scholers and heades which devised the sleight, and conceived they were not seene, shall repent without recoverie, and finde themselves bound, and their colleges bowelled, when they shal fele themselves overruled by their owne devise: bycause such as come in so, will communicate the like with others, and never care for the common, which were helpt by the private. For where favour bringes in almost in despite of order, there must favour be returned with mervelous disorder, and yet I do not mislike favour, which helpeth desert, which otherwise might be foiled, if favour friended not. But when the ground wherupon favour buildes is not so commendable, *founders* be discouraged, common *provision* supplanted, *learning* set over to *loytering*, *braverie* made enheritour to *bookes*. Stirringe wittes have their will for the time, and repentance at leasure. The fault hereof commeth from scholers themselves, which first make way to sinister meanes, and afterward blame, and verie meane which they used themselves. For finding some ease at first in working their owne will, either more cunningly to hide some indirect dealing, or more subtilly to supplant some contrary faction: or in deede desiring rather by commaundement to force, and so to seeme somebodie, then of dutie to entreat, and so seeme abject to honestie: they stumble at the last upon the blocke of bondage, being bridled of their owne will, even when they are in ruffe, by the selfe same meanes, which brought them unto it, and thought so to staule them, as themselves would commaund where they caused the speed. These fellowes be like to *Horaces* horse, which to overcome the stag, used man for his meane once, and his maister alway: neither refusing the saddle on his ridg, to be rid on, nether the bit in his mouth, to be bridled by. A brave victory so dearely bought, to the victours bondage, and perpetuall slaverie. Whereas if learning and those [158] conditions which I did lymit to a civill wit in this state, were the end in elections, the unfit should be set over to some other course, in convenient time: the fittest should be chosen, the founders mynde fulfilled: some perjurie for non perfourmaunce of statutes avoided: new *patrones* procured, *religion* avaunced, good studentes encouraged, and favour upon extreame and importunate sute disfranchised: which never will oppose it selfe to so honest considerations, so constantly kept: neither ever doth intrude, without some such sollicitours, as should be sorie for it, and use no meane to have it, which oftimes use this meane, to do il by warrant, as if they were forced to that, which in deede they ment before, and sought favour but for a shadow to hide their devise. Now if you that are to chuse, yeeld so much to your selves, and your owne conceit to bring your devises to passe, though ye wring by the waie, and your state in the ende, why should you not in good truth relent, and give place your selves being in places, to your betters and bidders, which gaive you the roome, and yet would have left all to you, if you would have left any place to reason: or have bene led by right, as ye leaned all to the wronge? you had your will by them, and why not they have theirs of you? requitall among equalles is of common curtesie, recompence in inequalities is enforced of necessitie.

If any metall be to massie, and way downe the ballance, or if any metallish meane, where money will scale, do enter that forte, where is small resistance, that is solde, which ought not, the enheritaunce of vertue: that is bought, which should not, the livelihood of learning: that is betrayed, which neither should for feare, nor ought for freindship, the treasure of the state, and provision of the countrey. And if there be neede, which enforceth such dealing, yet deale, where it is due, and let neede be remedyed, with her owne provision, not by unhonest intrusion. I do not blame any one, bycause my selfe know none, and I thinke well of most, bycause I know some

sincere. But some thing there is that feedeth the generall complaint, and some contentious factions there be, that bring catchers into colleges. For both these two inconveniences, worse then mischeifes as our common law termeth them, I have nothing to say more [159] then to renue the memorie of two accidentes, which happened to the *Romain* common weale, and may be understood by scholers,
1. Offic. 2.
that will marke and applie them. The first is, that in *Tullie*, when *Pontius* the *Samnite* wished that he either had not bene borne untill, or but then borne, when the *Romains* would have received giftes and rewardes. Why? what if? I would not have suffred them to have reigned one day longer, by selling their libertie, they should have become bond. The fellow said much, and that state felt more, when they fell to fingering.

2. The main rot of the Romaine empire.

The second is this, not noted in any one, but observed by all, that marke and write of the declining and ruine of the *Romain Empire*. The principall cause among many, to raze that state, which did rise in the blood of other nations and fell in their owne, was, when their generalls used the helpe of forreine and barbarous fellowes, late foes, new freindes, to overthrow the contrarie factions in their civill warres, both before and in their Emperours time, and let them both smell and taste of the *Romish* wealth and fatnesse of *Italie*. Wherwith the horesons being ravished, ever as they went home sent more of their countreymen to serve in seditious or necessarie defenses: till at the last their whole nations overflew that florishing towne, and that fertile countrey. Wherby that great abundance, that unspeakeable wealth, those inestimable riches, which the whether conquering or ravening *Romaines* had gathered together in so many hundred yeares, from so many severall countries, in a verie small time, became a bootie to that barbarous offall of all kinde of people, which never had any, till they became lordes, both of the *Romain* substance and the soile of *Italie*. A glasse for those to gase on, which will rather stirre to fall, then be still to stand. If ye shew a child an apple, he will crye for it, but if you make a mightier then your selfe privie to your pleasures, if he be desirous to have, and speede not, he will make you crye for it.

But now as favour founded not upon desert, but upon some fetch, is foe to all choice, enforcing for the favorite, so free admissions into colledges, by but mildely and honestly replying: upon favour may helpe it in sufficiency, and lighten the booke of some needlesse burthen, which hurtes not onely in the admission, [160] but also by sending abroade such broad dealers, which corrupt where they go, and poison more incurably, bycause of their meane, which is mothered upon learning, which the cunninger it is, the craftyer meane it is: and of the more credit it is, the more conveiance it hath to corrupt with good colour, though it be to bad, when it is bewrayed. If hope were cut of to speede by disorder, such wittes would streight waye sorte themselves to order, as they be not the most blockheades, which offer violence to order: wherin I must needes say somwhat in plaine truth, and plausible to.

The abusing of great personages.

Those great personages, which be so tempted by the importunity of such petie companions, as seeke them for protection, to force good and godly statutes, are litle bound to them. For what do they? Their owne obscuritie comes in no daunger, as being but underlinges, neither much seene, nor a whit cared for, though they cause the mischeife: but they force good, and well given dispositions, excellent and noble natures, by false and coloured informations, to serve their owne turnes, and to beguile their great freindes: they bring them in hatred of all those, which builde upon the good zeale of vertuous founders. Which thing reacheth so farre, and to so many, as either the possibilitie to enjoye their benefit doth, or the praise of their doing, to procure the like: or the protection of posteritie, which cannot but lament the great misuse, and foull overthrow of their ancestours good and most godly meaning. They cast all men in feare of them to be likewise forced in their best interest, as a principle to tyrannie, and make them be odious to all, whom they would seeme to honour above all. The worst kinde of *caterpillours*, in *countenaunce* fine and neate, in *speeche* delicate and divine, in *pretence* holy and heavenly, in *meaning* verie furies, and divells: to themselves scraping howsoever they cover: to nobilitie and countenaunce, whatsoever shew they make, the verie seminarie of most daungerous dishonour, and therfore worthy to be thrust out, bycause they thirst so much. For if love and honour be the treasures of nobility, the contrarie meane howsoever it be coloured deserves coudgelling out, when it croutcheth most. It is no dishonour to nobilitie, not to have their will, but it is their greatest disgrace to yeilde to that, by unreasonable [161] desire, which they ought not to will, and so make a divorse betwene honestie and honour, which is unseemely, seeing honestie, how basely soever some ruffians regard it, is the verie mother to honour of greatest moment, and in the best kinde. That such honorable natures yeelde to such importunate promoters, halfe against their will, bycause otherwise they cannot be rid of them: their owne and honorable contentment doth oftimes prove, when they have bene answered truely and duetifully, by such either companies, or particulars, as have preferred plaine trueth, before painted colours, whereby noble dispositions do well declare to the world, how unwilling they be to force order by favour, if they be enfourmed of the truth: which will alway prove the enfourmers warrant, and foile such fetchers, when it comes to the hearing. And as the learned *Quintilian* sayth, that in a grammarian it is vertue not to seeme to know all: so sayth pollicy that in the verie highest, it is not good to do all, that authoritie and interest in the extremitie of right maie do, with some warrant to it selfe, though with small liking, where it goeth. Mine antecedent is of mine owne profession, which beareth blame of to much boldnesse, and hath bene thought to presumptuous for knowledg, as *Rhemmius Palaemon* one of our coate, was wount to brag, that learning began to live, and should die with him: My consequent concerneth my countrey, and good will to nobilitie, which as in degree it can do most, so were it great pitie that it should be used, but to worke the best. My chalenge is to those infamous meanes, which dishonour their honorable patrones, defeat honest men of best education, disturbe the state even while they live, poison the posteritie by their president, even when they are dead.

Quintilian.

Palaemon.

Now if *choice* had taken place in the beginning, such impudent wittes had wonne no place, and noble patrones had shaked of such sutes. For as deepe waters do seeme not to runne bycause of their stillnesse: so true vertue and honest learning will tary their calling, and not stirre to soone, to set forth their stuffe, though they be the deepest and most worthy the place. I must crave pardon: a well affected maister speaketh for all poore and toward scholers, well nusled in learning, well given in living, and ill thwarted in livinges, by such visardes of counterfect [162] countenaunces, which one may more then halfe gesse, what they will receive, when none seeth but the offerer: which dare themselves offer such dishonorable requestes to those personages, at whose countenaunces, they ought in conscience to tremble, if that impudencie, which first hath rejected God secretly, and all goodnesse openly, had not tyrannised them to much, so vilely to abuse, where they ought to honour. The consideration of the good, the canvasing for the ill, hath caryed me from colledges, though not from colleginers, where for necessarie roomes there must be boursares, and why not of the learned sorte? Which the more towarde they be, the more trusty they will prove, and cheifly to that colledge, which avaunced them for value. Never wonder if he do sacrifice to the purse, which was admitted either for it, or by it. And yet there is some wrong, to fill private purses for entring, and to punish the common, when they be entred. If they could use it so, as to still it from those, which strayned it from them, when they were to enter, the cunning were great, and the deceit not amisse, where craft is allowed to deceive the deceiver. But the common wrings, for the private wrong, and there the injury is.

2. Preferment to degrees.

Preferment to degrees in schole may, nay in deede ought to be a mightie stripper of insufficiencie, bycause that way, the whole countrie is made either a lamentable spoile to bould ignorance, or a laudable soyle to sober knowledge. When a scholer is allowed by authoritie of the universitie, to professe that qualitie, whereof he beares the title, and is sent abroad with the warrant of his commencement, and want of his cunning, who made either favour and friendship, either countenaunce or canvase, or some other sleight the meane to enstawle him, what must our common countrie then say, when she heareth the bragge of the universities title sound in her eares, and findes not the benefit of the universitie learning to serve her in neede? Shee must needes think that the unlearned and ignorant creature is free from blame, bycause he sought to countenaunce himselfe, as the customarie led him: but she must needes thinke her selfe not onely not bound to the universitie, but shamefully abused, nay most unnaturally offered to the spoile of ignorance and insufficiencie by the universitie, to whom committing her [163] sight shee is dealt with so blindly, in whom reposing her trust, she is betrayed so untruely. For what is it to say in common collection, when the universitie preferreth any, to degree: but as if she should protect thus much. Before God and my countrie, to whom I owe my selfe and my service, whereof the one I cannot deceive, the other I ought not, I do knowe this man, whom I now prefer to this degree, in this facultie, in the sufficiencie of abilitie, which his title pretendeth, not perfunctorilie taken knowledge of, but thoroughly examined by me, to be well able to execute in the common weale of my countrie, that qualitie in art and profession, which his degree endoweth him with: and that my countrie may rest upon my credit in securitie for his sufficiencie: and betrust her selfe unto him upon my warrant, which I do seale with the publike acknowledging of him to be such a one, as his title emporteth, being consideratly and advisedly bestowed upon him by me, as I will answere almightie God in judgement, and my countrie in my conscience and upon my credit. Now what if he be not such a one? where then is your advisednesse? where then is your credit? where then is then your conscience? nay where then is your God whom ye called to witnesse? What if the universitie knew before, that he neither was such a one, neither like ever to prove any such? let him that weyeth this, if it be to light, reject it as counterfect. Let the earnest professours of the truest religion in the universities at this day call their consciences to counsell, and redresse the defect, for their owne credit, and the good of their countrie. If it shall please the universities, to preferre these considerations of countrie and conscience, before any private persuasion (which if it were roundly repelled a while, would never be so impudent, as so to intrude it selfe) the matter were ended, and despaire that way would leave rowme to learning: and send such fellowes to those faculties, which were fitter for them: and not suffer them under the titles of learning, to supplant the learned, and forstaull away their livinges: to the discouraging of the right student in deede, and the defeating of the state. For if ye rip the cause why they seeke to set foorth them selves, with such forraine feathers, being unlikely to looke on, in their owne coloures, if the eye might behold that which the [164] minde conceiveth, ye shall finde that their desire to gaine under honorable titles, is the verie grounde whereupon they goe: which they seeke by indirect wayes, bycause they feele them selves to be of no direct worth. But what fooles be good scholers in deede, to lende such dawes their dignities, under that borowed habit, to rob them of preheminence, and to seeme to be *eagles*, where they be but *bussardes*? Nay do they not discredit the universitie more? as if they there were either so simple, as they could not descrie a *calfe*, or so easie to be entreated, as when they had discried it, they would sweare by perswasion, that the *calfe* were a *camell*? good my maisters make not all priestes that stand upon the bridge as the *Poope* passeth. For then the cobler as one consecrated, bycause his person was in compasse, and his showes within hearing, will sure be a priest, and set nothing by his naule, and as good as you and as fit for a benefice, as those that came to take orders in deede, and deserved them in doing. Looke to it betimes and lende not your garmentes to set forth *bastardt* and bold suters, for feare your selves be excluded, when ye entend to sue, both your labour and your love being lost, through your owne follie.

To seeme is not so much in weight as to be, but in paines it is much more. To counterfeat vertue, and to avoide spying, requireth a long labour, and dayly new devises: to be vertuouse in deede, and learned in deede, craves labour at the first, and lendes leysure in the end, borne out by it selfe, never needing any vele. And therefore great warines must be used to discerne and shake of the counterfeat: smaller consideration will soone finde, and sooner content sufficient stuffe. Let deepe dissembling and dubling *hypocrisie* leape the ladder, and honest *learning* be beholder the while. In these pointes to have worthinesse preferred, and to have choice to seeke, and save it, if a teacher deale thus earnestly, as me thinke I do now, he may deserve pardon as I hope I shall have, considering his end, to him selfe ward is delite, to his charge is their profit: to his countrie is sound stuffe sent from him. And can he be but grieved to see the effect so disorderly defeated, wherunto with infinite toile, with incomparable care, with incredible paines, he did so orderly proceed? I take it very tollerable for any, that hath charge of number [165] and multitude to be carefull for their good, not only in private government, but also in publike protection, so farre, as either the honestie of the cause, or the dutie to magistrate, will maintaine his attempt. As truely in learning and learned executions me thinke it concerneth all men to be very carefull, bycause the thing tucheth themselves so neare in age, and theirs so much in youth.

3. Advauncement to livinges.

For the third part which consisteth in *avauncement* to livinges, as it is commonly handled by the highest in state, and eldest in yeares, which have best skill to judge, and least neede to be misled: so it needes least precept: bycause the misse there is mostwhat without amendes, being made by great warrant: and the hitting right is the blessed *fortune* of ech kinde of state, when value is in place, whence there is no appeale, but pleasure in the perfit: pitie in imperfection: the common good either caried to ruine by intrusion of insufficiencie, or strongly supported by sufficient staie. *Repulse* here is a miserable stripp, that insufficiencie should be suffered to growe up so high, and not be hewed downe before. And some great injurie is offered to the bestowers of prefermentes, that they are made objectes to the danger of insufficient boldnes, which ought to be cut of by sufficient modestie, who pretendeth the claime to be her owne of dutie, and to whom the patrones, would rediliest yeild, if they could discerne, and were not abused by the worthy themselves, which lend the unworthy the worth of their countenance to deceive the disposers, and to beguile their owne selves. But blind bayard, if he have any burden that is worth the taking downe, and bestowing somwhere else, wilbe farre bolder then a better horse, and so farre from shame, as he will not shrinke to offer himselfe to the richest sadle, being in deede no better then a blinde jade and seeking to occupie the stawle where *Bucephalus* the brave horse of duety ought to stand. And in this case of preferrement, store is lightely the greatest enemie to the best choice, bycause in number no condition wilbe offered, which will not be admitted, though some do refuse. The preventing of all or most of these inconveniences, I do take to be in the right sorting of wittes at the first, when learning shall be left to them alone, whom nature doth allow by evident signes, and such sent awaye to some other trades, as are made to that ende. Wherby [166] the sorters are to have thankes in the ende of both the parties, which finding themselves fitted in the best kinde of their naturall calling, must of necessitie honour them, which used such foresight in their first bestowing.

Thus much have I marked in clipping of, of that multitude which oppresseth learning with too too many, as too too many wheresoever they be, overcharge the soile in all professions. For the matter wheron to live justly and truly being within compasse, and the men which must live upon it, being still without ende, must not desire of maintenaunce specially if it be joyned with a porte, wring a number to the wall, to get wheron to live? I neede pinch no particular where the generall is so sore gauled. Marke but those professions and occupations, which be most cloyed up with number, whether they be bookish or not, and waye the poorer sort, wheron at the last the pinching doth light, though it passe many handes before, if to great a multitude making to great a state do not prove a shrew, then am I deceyved: so that it were good there were stripping used, and that be time in yonger yeares. For youth being let go forward upon hope, and chekt with dispaire while it rometh without purveyaunce, makes marveilous a doe before it will die. And if no miserable shift will serve at home, verie defection to the foe, and common enemie will send them abrode, to seeke for that, which in such a case they are sure to finde. Wherefore as countenaunce in the overflowing number, which findeth place in a state doth infect extremely, by seeking out unlawfull and corrosive maintenaunce: so roming in the unbestowed offaull, which findes no place in a state, doth festure fellonly, by seeking to shake it, with most rebellious enterprises.

Chapter 38.

That young maidens are to be set to learning, which is proved, by the custome of our countrey, by our duetie towardes them, by their naturall abilities, and by the worthy effectes of such as have bene well trained. The ende wherunto their education serveth, which is the cause why and how much they learne. Which of them are to learne, when they are to begin to learne. What and how much they may learne. Of whom and where they ought to be taught. [167]

The necessitie of this title.

When I did appoint the persons, which were to receive the benefit of education: I did not exclude young *maidens*, and therefore seing I made them one braunche of my division, I must of force say somwhat more of them. A thing perhaps which some will thinke might wel enough have bene past over with silence, as not belonging to my purpose, which professe the education of boyes, and the generall traine in that kinde. But seeing I begin so low as the first *Elementarie*, wherin we see that young *maidens* be ordinarily trained, how could I seeme not to see them, being so apparently taught?

The proofes why they are to learne.

And to prove that they are to be trained, I finde foure speciall reasons, wherof any one, much more all may perswade any their most adversarie, much more me, which am for them with toothe and naile. The first is the *manner* and *custome* of my countrey, which 1.
allowing them to learne, wil be lothe to be contraried by any of her countreymen. The second is the *duetie*, which we owe unto them, 2.
whereby we are charged in conscience, not to leave them lame, in

3. that which is for them. The third is their owne *towardnesse*, which
God by nature would never have given them, to remaine idle, or to
4. small purpose. The fourth is the excellent *effectes* in that sex, when they have had the helpe of good bringing up: which commendeth the cause of such excellencie, and wisheth us to cherishe that tree, whose frute is both so pleasaunt in taste, and so profitable in triall. What can be said more? our *countrey* doth allow it, our *duetie* doth enforce it, their *aptnesse* calls for it, their *excellencie* commandes it: and dare private *conceit*, once seeme to withstand where so great, and so rare circunstances do so earnestly commende.

The custome of our countrey.

But for the better understanding of these foure reasons, I will examine everie of them, somwhat nearer, as inducers to the truth, ear I deale with the traine. For the first: If I should seeme to enforce any noveltie, I might seeme ridiculous, and never se that thing take place, which I tender so much: but considering, the *custome* of my countrie hath delivered me of that care, which hath made the *maidens* traine her owne approved travell, what absurditie am I in, to say that is true, which my countrie dare avow, and daily doth trie? I set not yong *maidens* [168] to publike grammer scholes, a thing not used in my countrie, I send them not to the universities, having no president thereof in my countrie, I allow them learning with distinction in degrees, with difference of their calling, with respect to their endes, wherefore they learne, wherein my countrie confirmeth my opinion. We see yong *maidens* be taught to read and write, and can do both with praise: we heare them sing and playe: and both passing well, we know that they learne the best, and finest of our learned languages, to the admiration of all men. For the daiely spoken toungues and of best reputation in our time, who so shall denie that they may not compare even with our kinde in the best degree, they will claime no other combate, then to talke with him in that verie tongue, who shall seeke to taint them for it. These things our country doth stand to, these qualities their parentes procure them, as either oportunitie of circunstance will serve, or their owne power wil extend unto, or their daughters towardnesse doth offer hope, to be preferred by, for singularitie of endowment, either in mariage, or some other meane. Nay do we not see in our country, some of that sex so excellently well trained, and so rarely qualified, either for the toungues themselves, or for the matter in the toungues: as they may be opposed by way of comparison, if not preferred as beyond comparison, even to the best *Romaine* or *Greekish paragonnes* be they never so much praised: to the *Germaine* or *French* gentlewymen, by late writers so wel liked: to the *Italian* ladies who dare write themselves, and deserve fame for so doing? whose excellencie is so geason, as they be rather wonders to gaze at, then presidentes to follow. And is that to be called in question, which we both dayly see in many, and wonder at in some? I dare be bould therefore to admit yong *maidens* to learne, seeing my countrie gives me leave, and her *custome* standes for me.

Duetie.

For the second point. The duetie which we owe them doth straitly commaund us to see them well brought up. For what be young *maidens* in respect of our sex? Are they not the seminary of our succession? the naturall frye, from whence we are to chuse our naturall, next, and most necessarie freindes? The very selfe same creatures, which were made for our comfort, [169] the onely good to garnish our alonenesse, the nearest companions in our weale or wo? the peculiar and priviest partakers in all our fortunes? borne for us to life, bound to us till death? And can we in conscience but carefully thinke of them, which are so many wayes linked unto us? Is it either nothing, or but some small thing, to have our childrens mothers well furnished in minde, well strengthened in bodie? which desire by them to maintaine our succession? or is it not their good to be so well garnished, which good being defeated in them by our indiligence, of whom they are to have it, doth it not charge us with breache of duetie, bycause they have it not? They are committed and commended unto us, as pupilles unto tutours, as bodies unto heades, nay as bodies unto soules: so that if we tender not their education duetifully, they maye urge that against us, if at any time either by their owne right, or by our default, they winne the upper roome and make us stand bare head, or be bolder with us to.

They that write of the use of our bodies, do greatly blame such parentes, as suffer not their children to use the left hand, as well as the right, bycause therby they weaken their strength and the use of their limmes: and can we be without blame, who seeke not to strengthen that, which was once taken from us, and yet taryeth with us, as a part of us still: knowing it to be the weaker? Or is there any better meane to strengthen their minde, then that knowledge of God, of religion, of civil, of domesticall dueties, which we have by our traine, and ought not to denie them, being comprised in bookes, and is to be compassed in youth?

That some exercise of bodie ought to be used, some ordinarie stirring ought to be enjoyned, some provision for private and peculiar trainers ought to be made: not onely the ladies of *Lacedaemon* will sweare, but all the world will sooth, if they do but wey, that it is to much to weaken our owne selves by not strengthning their side. That cunning poet for judgement in matter, and great philosopher for secrecie in nature, our well knowen *Virgill*, saw in a goodly horse that was offered unto *Augustus Caesar* an infirmitie unperceaved by either looker on or any of his stable, which came as he said by some weaknes in [170] the damme, and was confessed to be true. *Galene* and the whole familie of Physicians ripping up our infirmities, which be not to be avoided, placeth the seminarie and originall, engraffed in nature, as our greatest and nearest foes. And therfore to be prevented by the parentes, thorough considerate traine, the best and fairest meane, to better weake nature: so that of *duety* they are to be cared for. And what care in *duetie* is greater, then this in traine?

3. Naturall Towardnesse.

Their *naturall towardnesse* which was my third reason doth most manifestly call upon us, to see them well brought up. If nature have given them abilities to prove excellent in their kinde, and yet thereby in no point to let their most laudable dueties in mariage and matche, but rather to bewtifie them, with most singular ornamentes, are not we to be condemned of extreme unnaturallnes, if we gay not that by discipline, which is given them by *nature*? That naturally they are so richely endowed, all *Philosophie* is full, no *Divinitie* denyes. *Plato* and his *Academikes* say, that all vertues be indifferent, nay all one in man and woman: saving that they be more strong and more durable in men, weaker and more variable in wymen. *Xeno* and his *Stoikes* though they esteeme the ods betwene man and woman naturally to be as great as the difference, betwene an heavenly and an earthly creature, which *Plato* did not, making them both of one mould, yet they graunt them equalitie and samenesse in vertue, though they deliver the strength and constancie over unto men, as properly belonging unto that side. *Aristotle* and his *Peripatetikes* confessing them both to be of one kinde, though to different uses in nature, according to those differences in *condition*, appointeth them differences in *vertue*, and yet wherin they agree: alloateth them the same. When they have concluded thus of their

Proclus upon Platoes common weale, and Theodorus Asinaeus upon the question, whether men and wymen have all vertues common.

naturall abilities, and so absolutely entitled them unto all vertues, they rest not there, but proceede on further to their education in this sorte. That as naturally every one hath some good assigned him, wherunto he is to aspire, and not to cease untill he have obtained it, onlesse he will by his owne negligence reject that benefit, which the munificence of *nature* hath liberally bestowed on him: so there is a certaine meane, wherby to winne that perfitly, which [171] *nature* of her selfe doth wish us franckly. This meane they call *education*, whereby the naturall inclinations be gently caryed on, if they will curteously follow, or otherwise be hastened, if they must needes be forced, untill they arive at that same best, which *nature* bendeth unto with full saile, in those fairer, which follow the traine willingly, in those meaner, which must be bet unto it. And yet even there where it is sorest laboured, it worketh some effecte unworthy of repentaunce, and is better forced on in youth, then forgon in age: rather in children with feare, then not in men with greife. Now as the inclinations be common to both the kindes, so they devide the meane of education indifferently betwene both. Which being thus, as both the truth tells the ignorant, and reading shewes the learned, we do wel then perceave by *naturall men*, and *Philosophicall reasons*, that young *maidens* deserve the traine: bycause they have that treasure, which belongeth unto it, bestowed on them by *nature*, to be bettered in them by *nurture*. Neither doth *religion* contrarie religious *nature*. For the *Lorde* of *nature*, which created that motion to continue the consequence of all living creatures, by succession to the like, by education to the best, appointing either kinde the limittes of their duetie, and requiring of either the perfourmaunce therof, alloweth all such ordinarie and orderly meanes, as by his direction in his word may bring them both from his appointment to their perfourmance, from the first starting place, to the outmost gole: that is unto that good, which he hath assigned them, by such wayes as he hath willed them: so that both by *nature* the most obedient servant, and by the *Lorde* of *nature* our most bountifull *God*, we have it in commandement not onely to traine up our owne sex, but also our female, seeing he hath to require an account for naturall talentes of both the parties, us for directing them: them for perfourmance of our direction.

4. Excellent effectes.

The excellent effectes of those women, which have bene verie well trained, do well declare, that they deserve the best training:

which reason was my last in order, but not my least in force, to prove their more then common excellencie. This is a point of such galancie, if my purpose were to praise them, as it is but to give precept, how to make them praiseworthie, as I [172] might soner weary my selfe with reckening up of writers, and calling worthy wymen to be witnesses in their owne cause then worthely to expresse their weight and worth, bycause I beleeve that to be most true, which is cronicled of them. I will not medle with any moe writers to whom wymen are most bound, for best speaking of them, and most spreading of their vertues, then with one onely man a single witnes in person, but above all singularitie in profe: the learned and honest *Plutarch*, whose name emporteth a princis treasure, whose writings witnes an unwearied travel, whose plaine truth was never tainted. Would he so learned, so honest, so true, so sterne, have become such a trumpet for their fame, to triumph by, so have gratified that sex, whom he stood not in awe of: so have beutified their doings, whom he might not have medled with, so have avaunced their honour, to hasard his owne sex, by setting them so hie, if he had not resolutely knowne the truth of his subject? he durst be so bould with his owne Emperour the good *Trajan*, to fore his scholer, in his epistle to him before his booke of governing the comon weale, as to say and call his booke to witnes thereof, that if he went to governe, and overthrew the state, he did it not by the authoritie of *Plutarch*, as disavowing his scholer, if he departed from his lessons. And would that courage have bene forced to frame a false argument? or is so great a truth not to have so great a credit? howsoever some of the lighter heades have lewdly belyed them, or vainly accused them: yet the verie best and gravest writers thinke worthely of them, and make report of them with honour. *Ariosto* and *Boccacio* will be loth to be tearmed light being so great doctours in their divinitie, yet they be somwhat over heavie to wymen, without any great weight as in generall the *Italian* writers be, which in the middest of their loving levities still glaunce at their lightnes, and that so beyound all manhoode, as they feele their owne fault, and dispaire of reconcilement, though they crie still for pardon. As those men know well, which will rather mervell, that I have red those bookes, then mistrust my report, which they know to be true. In all good and generally authorised histories, and in many particuler discourses, it is most evident, that not onely private and [173] particular wymen, being very well trained, but also great princesses and gallant troupes of the same sex have shewed fourth in them selves mervelous effectes of vertue and valure. And good reason why. For where naturally they have to shew, if education procure shew, is it a thing to be wondered at? Or is their singularitie lesse in nature, bycause wymen be lesse accustomed to shew it, and not so commonly employed, as we men be? Yet whensoever they be, by their dealinges they shew us that they have no dead flesh nor any base mettle. Well, I will knit up this conclusion and burne day light no longer, to prove that carefully, which all men may see clearely, and ther adversaries grieve at, bycause it confutes their follie, which upon some private errour of their owne, to seeme fautles in wordes, where they be faithles in deedes, blame silly wymen as being the onely cause why they went awrie.

That yong *maidens* can learne, nature doth give them, and that they have learned, our experience doth teach us, with what care to themselves, them selves can best witnes, with what comfort to us, what forraine example can more assure the world, then our diamond at home? our most deare soveraine lady and princesse, by nature a woman, by vertue a worthy, not one of the nyne, but the tenth above the nyne, to perfit in her person that absolute number, which is no fitter to comprehend all absolutnes in Arithmetike, then she is knowne to containe al perfections in nature, all degrees in valure, and to become a president to those nyne worthy men, as *Apollo* is accounted to the nyne famouse wymen, she to vertues and vertuous men, he to muses, and learned wymen: thereby to prove *Plutarches* conclusion true, that oppositions of vertues by way of comparison is their chiefe commendation. Is *Anacreon* a good poet, what say you to *Sappho*? Is *Bacis* a good prophet, what say you to *Sibill*? was *Sesostris* a famouse prince, what say you to *Semiramis*? was *Servius* a noble king, what say you to *Tanaquill*? was *Brutus* a stowt man, what say you to *Porcia*? Thus reasoneth *Plutarch*, and so do I, is it honorable for *Apollo* a man to have the presidencie over nyne wymen, the resemblers of learning? then more honorable it is for our most worthy *Princesse*, to have the presidencie over nyne men, the paragons of vertue: [174] and yet to be so familiarly acquainted with the nyne *muses*, as they are in strife who may love her best, for being best learned? for whose excellent knowledge and learning, we have most cause to rejoyce, who tast of the frute: and

Philo Judaeus in his discours of the ten commandementes rips out the perfitnes of that number.

Plutarch in his booke of wymens vertues.

posteritie to praise, which shall maintaine her memorie: though I wish their memorie abridged, to have our tast enlarged: our proving lengthened, to have their praising shortened: to be glad that we have her, not to greve, that we had her: as that omnipotent god, which gave her unto us, when we had more neede of such a prince, then shee of such a people, will preserve her for us, I do nothing dout, that we both may serve him, she as our carefull soveraine, to set forth his glory, we as her faithfull subjectes to submit our selves to it.

If no storie did tell it, if no state did allow it, if no example did confirme it, that yong *maidens* deserve the trayning, this our owne myrour, the majestie of her sex, doth prove it in her owne person, and commendes it to our reason. We have besides her highnes as undershining starres, many singuler ladies and gentlewymen so skilfull in all cunning, of the most laudable, and loveworthy qualities of learning, as they may well be alleaged for a president to prayse, not for a patern to prove like by: though hope have a head, and nature be no nigard, if education do her dutie, and will seeke to resemble even where presidentes be passing, both hope to attaine to, and possibilitie to seeme to. Wherefore by these profes, I take it to be very cleare, that I am not farre overshot, in admitting them to traine, being so traineable by nature, and so notable by effectes.

But now having graunted them the benefit and society of our education, we must assigne the end, wherfore their traine shall serve, whereby we may apply it the better. Our owne traine is without restraint for either matter or maner, bycause our employment is so generall in all thinges: theirs is within limit, and so must their traine be. If a yong *maiden* be to be trained in respect of mariage, obedience to her head, and the qualities which looke that way, must needes be her best way: if in regard of necessitie to learne how to live, artificiall traine must furnish out her trade: if in respect of ornament to beawtifie her birth, and to honour her place, rareties in that kinde and seemely for that [175] kinde do best beseeme such: if for government, not denyed them by God, and devised them by men, the greatnes of their calling doth call for great giftes, and generall excellencies for generall occurrences. Wherefore having these different endes allwayes in eye, we may point them their traine in different degrees. But some *Timon* will say, what should wymen do with learning? Such a churlish carper will never picke out the best,

The ende of learning in yong maides.

but be alway ready to blame the worst. If all men used all pointes of learning well, we had some reason to alleadge against wymen, but seeing misuse is common to both the kinds, why blame we their infirmitie, whence we free not our selves? Some wymen abuse writing to that end, some reading to this, some all that they learne any waye, to some other ill some waye. And I praie you what do we? I do not excuse ill: but barre them from accusing, which be as bad themselves: unlesse they will first condemne themselves, and so proceede in their plea with more discretion after a repentant discoverie. But they will not deale thus, they will rather retire for shame, and prove to be nonsuite, then confesse themselves faulty, and blush for their blaming. Wherfore as the communitie of vertues, argueth the communitie of vices naturally in both: so let us in that point enterchaunge forgivenesse, and in hope of the vertues direct to the best, not for feare of the vices, make an open gap for them. Wherefore in directing of that traine, which I do assigne unto young maidens, I will follow this methode, and shew which of them be to learne, and when, what and how much, where and of whom.

Which and when.

As concerning those which are to be trained, and when they are to begin their traine, this is my opinion. The same restraint in cases of necessitie, where they conveniently cannot, and the same freedom in cases of libertie, when they commodiously may, being reserved to parentes in their daughters, which I allowed them in their sonnes, and the same regarde to the weaknesse and strength of their witts and bodies, the same care for their womanly exercises, for helpe of their health, and strength of their limmes, being remitted to their considerations, which I assigned them in their sonnes, I do thinke the same time fit for both, not determinable by yeares, but by ripenesse [176] of witte, to conceive without tiring, and strength of bodie to travell without wearying. For though the girles seeme commonly to have a quicker ripening in witte, then boyes have, for all that seeming, yet it is not so. Their naturall weaknesse which cannot holde long, delivers very soone, and yet there be as prating boyes, as there be pratling wenches. Besides, their braines be not so much charged, neither with weight nor with multitude of matters, as boyes heades be, and therefore like empty caske they make the greater noise. As those men which seeme to be very quicke witted by some sudden pretie aunswere, or some sharp replie, be not alwaye most burthened, neither with lettes, nor learning, but out of small store, they offer us still the floore, and holde most of the mother. Which sharpnesse of witte though it be within them, as it bewraeth it selfe: yet it might dwell within them a great while, without bewraying of it selfe, it studie kept them still, or great doinges did dull them: as slight dealinges and imperious, do commonly maintaine that kinde of courage. Boyes have it alwaye, but oftimes hide it, bycause their stuffe admitteth time: wenches have it alwaye, and alwaye bewray it, bycause their timber abides no tarying. And seeing it is in both, it deserves care in both, neither to timely to stirre them, nor let them loyter to long. As for bodies the *maidens* be more weake, most commonly even by nature, as of a moonish influence, and all our whole kinde is weake of the mother side, which when she was first made, even then weakned the mans side. Therefore great regard must be had to them, no lesse, nay rather more then to boyes in that time. For in proces of time, if they be of worth themselves, they may so matche, as the parent may take more pleasure in his sonnes by law, then in his heires by nature. They are to be the principall pillers in the upholding of housholdes, and so they are likely to prove, if they prove well in training. The dearest comfort that man can have, if they encline to good: the nearest corrosive if they tread awry. And therfore charilie to be cared for, bearing a jewell of such worth, in a vessel of such weaknesse. Thus much for there persons whom I turne over to the parentes abilitie for charge: to their owne capacitie for conceit: in eche degree some, from the lowest [177] in menaltie, to the highest in mistriship.

The time hath tied it selfe to strength in both partes, for the bodie to travell, for the soule to conceive. The exercises pray in no case to be forgot as a preservative to the body, and a conserve for the soule.

What. For the matter what they shall learne, thus I thinke, following the custome of my countrie, which in that that is usuall doth lead me on boldly, and in that also which is most rare, doth shew me my path, to be already troden. So that I shall not neede to erre, if I marke but my guide wel. Where rare excellencies in some wymen, do but shew us some one or two parentes good successe, in their daughters learning, there is neither president to be fetcht, nor precept to be framed. For preceptes be to conduct the common, but these singularities be above the common, presidentes be for hope, those pictures passe beyond al hope. And yet they serve for profe to proceede by in way of argument, that wymen can learne if they will, and may learne what they list, when they bend their wittes to it. To learne to read is very common, where convenientnes doth serve, and *writing* is not refused, where oportunitie will yeild it.

Reading if for nothing else it were, as for many thinges else it is, verie needefull for religion, to read that which they must know, and ought to performe, if they have not whom to heare, in that matter which they read: or if their memorie be not stedfast, by reading to revive it. If they heare first and after read of the selfe same argument, reading confirmes their memorie. Here I may not omit many and great contentmentes, many and sound comfortes, many and manifoulde delites, which those wymen that have skill and time to reade, without hindering their houswifery, do continually receive by reading of some comfortable and wise discourses, penned either in forme of historie, or for direction to live by. Reading.

As for *writing*, though it be discommended for some private cariages, wherein we men also, no lesse then wymen, beare oftentimes blame, if that were a sufficient exception why we should not learne to write, it hath his commoditie where it filleth in match, and helpes to enrich the goodmans mercerie. Many good occasions are oftentimes offered, where it were [178] better for them to have the use of their pen, for the good that comes by it, then to wish they had it, when the default is felt: and for feare of evill, which cannot be avoided in some, to avert that good, which may be commodious to many. Writing.

Musicke is much used, where it is to be had, to the parentes delite, while the daughters be yong, more then to their owne, which commonly proveth true, when the yong wenches become yong wives. For then lightly forgetting *Musicke* when they learne to be mothers, they give it in manifest evidence, that in their learning of it, they did more seeke to please their parentes, then to pleasure them selves. But howsoever it is, seeing the thing is not rejected, if with the learning of it once, it may be retained still (as by order it may) it is ill let go, which is got with great paines, and bought with some cost. The learninge to sing and plaie by the booke, a matter soone had, when *Musike* is first minded, which still preserve the cunning, though discontinuance disturbe. And seeing it is but litle which they learne, and the time as litle wherein they learne, bycause they haste still on toward husbandes, it were expedient, that they learned perfitly, and that with the losse of their pennie, they lost not their pennieworth Musike.

also, besides the losse of their time, which is the greatest losse of all. I medle not with *nedles*, nor yet with *houswiferie*, though I thinke it, and know it, to be a principall commendation in a woman: to be able to governe and direct her houshold, to looke to her house and familie, to provide and keepe necessaries, though the goodman pay, to know the force of her kitchin, for sicknes and health, in her selfe and her charge: bycause I deale onely with such thinges as be incident to their learning. Which seeing the custome of my country doth permit, I may not mislike, nay I may wish it with warrant, the thing being good and well beseeming their sex. This is the most, so farre as I remember, which they commonly use in youth, and participate with us in. If any parent do privately traine up his children of either sex in any other private fantsie of his owne, I cannot commend it, bycause I do not know it, and if it fortune to die within his private walles, I cannot give it life by publike rehearsall. The common and most knowne is that, which I have saide. [179]

How much.

The next pointe *how much*, is a question of more enquirie, and therefore requireth advised handling. To appoint besides these thinges, which are already spoken of, how much further any *maide* maye proceede in matter of learning and traine, is a matter of some moment, and concerneth no meane ones. And yet some petie lowlinges, do sometimes seeke to resemble, where they have small reason, and will needes seeme like, where their petieship cannot light, using shew for a shadow, where they have no fitter shift. And therfore in so doing, they passe beyond the boundes both of their birth, and their best beseeming. Which then discovereth a verie meere follie, when a meane parent traineth up his daughter hie in those properties, which I shall streight waye speake of, and she matcheth lowe, but within her owne compasse. For in such a case those overraught qualities for the toyousnesse therof being misplaced in her, do cause the young woman rather to be toyed withall, as by them giving signe of some idle conceit otherwise, then to be thought verie well of, as one wisely brought up. There is a comlynesse in eche kinde, and a decentnesse in degree, which is best observed, when eche one provides according to his power, without overreaching. If some odde property do worke preferrement beyond proportion, it commonly stayes there, and who so shootes at the like, in hope to hit, may sooner misse: bycause the wayes to misse be so many, and to hit is but one, and wounders which be but onse seene, be no examples to resemble. Every *maide* maye not hope to speede, as she would wishe, bycause some one hath sped better then she could wishe.

Where the question is *how much* a woman ought to learne, the aunswere may be, so much as shall be needefull. If that also come in doubt, the returne may be, either so much as her parentes conceive of her in hope, if her parentage be meane, or provide for her in state, if her birth beare a saile. For if the parentes be of calling, and in great account, and the daughters capable of some singular qualities, many commendable effects may be wrought therby, and the young maidens being well trained are verie soone commended to right honorable matches, whom they may well beseeme, and aunswere much better, [180] their qualities in state having good correspondence, with their matches of state, and their wisedoms also putting to helping hand, for the procuring of their common good. Not here to note, what frute the common weale may reape, by such witts so worthily advaunced, besides their owne private. If the parentes be meane, and the *maidens* in their training shew forth at the verie first some singular rarenesse like to ensue, if they florish but their naturall, there hope maye grow great, that some great matche may as well like of a young maiden excellently qualified, as most do delite in brute or brutish thinges for some straunge qualitie, either in nature to embrase, or in art to marvell. And yet this hope may faile. For neither have great personages alwaye that judgement, nor young *maidens* alwaye that fortune, though the *maidens* remaine the gainers, for they have the qualities to comfort their mediocrity, and those great ones want judgement to set forth their nobilitie.

This *how much* consisteth either in perfiting of those forenamed foure, *reading* well, *writing* faire, *singing* sweete, *playing* fine, beyond all cry and above all comparison, that pure excellencie in things but ordinarie may cause extraordinarie liking: or else in skill of languages annexed to these foure, that moe good giftes may worke more wonder. For meane is a maime where excellencie is the marvell. To hope for hie mariages, is good meat, but not for mowers, to have leasure to take delite in these gentlewomanly qualities, is no worke for who will: Nay to be a paragon among princes, to use such singularities, for the singular good of the general state, and the wonder of her person, were a wish in dispaire, were not true proofe the just warrant, that such a thing may be wished, bycause in our time we have found it, even then, when we did wish it most, and in the ende more marvellous, then at first we durst have wished. The eventes in these wymen which we see in our dayes, to have bene brought up in learning, do rule this conclusion. That such personages as be borne to be princes, or matches to great peeres, or to furnish out such traines, for some peculiar ornamentes to their place and calling, are to receive this kinde of education in the highest degree, that is convenient for their kinde. But princely *maidens* above all: bycause [181] occasion of their height standes in neede of such giftes, both to honour themselves, and to discharge the duetie, which the countries committed to their hands, do daily call for, and besides what matche is more honorable, then when desert for rare qualities, doth joine it selfe, with highenesse in degree? I feare no workmanship in wymen to give them *Geometrie* and her sister sciences: to make them *Mathematicalls*, though I meane them *Musicke*: nor yet barres to plead at, to leave them the lawes: nor urinalls to looke on, to lend them some Physicke, though the skil of herbes have bene the studie of nobilitie, by the *Persian* storie, and much commended in wymen: nor pulpittes to preach in, to utter their *Divinitie*: though by learning of some language, they can talke of the lining: and for direction of their life, they must be afforded some, though not as preachers and leaders: yet as honest perfourmers, and vertuous livers. *Philosophie* would furnish their generall discourses, if their leasure could entend it: but the knowledge of some toungues, either of substaunce in respect of deeper learning, or account for the present time may verie well be wisht them: and those faculties also, which do belong to the furniture of speache, may be verie well allowed them, bycause toungues be most proper, where they do naturally arme. If I should allow them the *pencill* to draw, as the penne to write, and thereby entitle them to all my Elementarie principles, I might have reason for me. For it neither requireth any great labour to fraye young maidens from it, and it would helpe their nedle, to beautifie their workes: and it is maintainable by very good examples even of their owne kinde. *Timarete* the vertuous, daughter to *Mycon*: *Irene* the curteous, daughter to *Cratinus*: *Aristarete* the absolute, daughter to *Nearchus*: *Lala* the eloquent, and ever maide of *Cyzicus*: *Martia* the couragious, daughter to *Varro* the best learned and most loved of any *Romain*, and many mo besides, did so use the *pencill*, as their fame therefore is so much

Plin. lib. 35. cap. 11.

the fairer, bycause the fact in that sex is so seldome and rare.

And is not a young gentlewoman, thinke you, thoroughly furnished, which can reade plainly and distinctly, write faire and swiftly, sing cleare and sweetely, play wel and finely, understand and speake the learned languages, and those toungues also which [182] the time most embraseth, with some *Logicall* helpe to chop, and some *Rhetoricke* to brave. Besides the matter which is gathered, while these toungues be either learned, or lookt on, as wordes must have seates, no lesse then rayment bodies. Were it any argument of an unfurnished maiden, besides these qualities to draw cleane in good proportion, and with good symmetrie? Now if she be an honest woman, and a good housewife to, were she not worth the wishing, and worthy the shryning? and yet such there be, and such we know. Or is it likely that her children shalbe eare a whit the worse brought up, if she be a *Laelia*, an *Hortensia*, or a *Cornelia*, which were so endued and noted for so doing? It is writen of *Eurydice* the *Epirote*, that after she began to have children, she sought to have learning, to bring them up skilfully, whom she brought forth naturally. Which thing she perfourmed in deede, a most carefull mother, and a most skilfull mistresse. For which her well doing, she hath wonne the reward, to be enrowled among the most rare matrones.

Plut. περὶ παιδ. ἀγωγ.

Now there is nothing left to ende this treatise of young *maidens*, but where and under whom, they are to learne, which question will be sufficiently resolved, upon consideration of the time how long they are to learne, which time is commonly till they be about thirtene or fouretene yeares old, wherein as the matter, which they must deale with all, cannot be very much in so litle time, so the perfitting thereof requireth much travel, though their time be so litle, and there would be some shew afterward, wherein their trayning did availe them. They that may continue some long time at learning, thorough the state and abilitie of their parentes have also their time and place sutably appointed, by the foresight of their parentes. So that the time resting in private forecast, I can not reduce it to generall precept, but onely thus farre, that in perfitnes it may shew, how well it was employed.

Where and when.

The places wherein they learne be either *publike*, if they go forth to the *Elementarie* schole, or *private* if they be taught at home. The teacher either of their owne sex, or of ours.

The places.

For *publike* places, bycause in that kinde there is no publike provision, but such as the professours of their training do make [183] of them selves, I can say little, but leave them to that and to their parentes circumspection, which both in their being abroad, during their minority, and in bringing them up at home after their minoritie, I know will be very diligent to have all thinges well. For their teachers, their owne sex were fittest in some respectes, but ours frame them best, and with good regard to some circumstances will bring them up excellently well, specially if their parentes be either of learning to judge, or of authoritie to commaund, or of both, to do both, as experience hath taught us in those, which have proved so well. The greater borne Ladyes and gentlewymen, as they are to enjoy the benefit of this education most, so they have best meanes to prosecute it best, being neither restrained in wealth, but to have the best teachers, and greatest helpes: neither abbridged in time, but to ply all at full. And thus I take my leave of yong maidens and gentlewymen, to whom I wish as well, as I have saide well of them.

Chapter 39.

Of the traning up of yong gentlemen. Of private and publike education, with their generall goods and illes. That there is no better way for gentlemen to be trained by in any respect then the common is being well appointed. Of richmens children which be no gentlemen. Of nobilitie in generall. Of gentlemanlie exercises. What it is to be a nobleman, or a gentleman. That infirmities in noble houses be not to be triumphed over. The causes and groundes of nobilitie. Why so many desire to be gentlemen. That gentlemen ought to professe learning and liberall sciences for many good and honorable effectes. Of travelling into forraine countries: with all the braunches allowance and disallowance thereof: and that it were to be wished, that gentlemen would professe, to make sciences liberall in use, which are liberall in name. Of the trayning up of a yong Prince.

In the last title I did declare at large, how yong maidens in ech degree were to be avaunced in learning, which me thought was verie incident to my purpose, bycause they be counterbraunches [184] to us in the kinde of mortall and reasonable creatures, and also for that in ech degree of life, they be still our mates, and sometime our mistresses, through the benefit of law, and honorablenes of birth. Now considering they joyne allway with us in number and nearenes, and sometime exceede us in dignitie and calling: as they communicate with us in all qualities, and all honours even up to the scepter, so why ought they not in any wise but be made communicantes with us in education and traine, to performe that part well, which they are to play, for either equalitie with us, or soveraintie above us? Here now ensueth another title of mervelous importaunce, for the kinde of people, whereof I am to entreat: bycause their state is still in the superlative, and the greatest executions be theirs by degree, though sometime they leese them by their owne default, and set them over to such, as nature maketh noble by ingenerate vertues. I meane the trayning up of yong *gentlemen* in every degree and to what so ever ascent, bycause even the crowne and kingdome is their height, though it come to the female, when their side faileth. For *gentlemen* will commonly be exempt from the common, as in title, so also in traine, refrayning the publike, though they hold of the male, and preferring the private, to be liker to maidens, whose education is most private, bycause of their kinde, and therefore not misliked: whereas yong gentlemen should be publike, bycause of their use. And for not being such, they beare some blame, as therein contrarying both all the best ordered common weales, and all the most excellent and the learnedest writers, which bring up even the best princes allway with great company.

But seeing they wilbe private, and I take upon me not to leap over any, which light within my compasse, and chiefly yong gentlemen, whose ordinarie greatnes is to governe our state, and to be publike pillers for the prince to leane on, and the people to staie by: their private choice commaundes me a private consideration, which in yong gentlewymen needed not any handling, bycause it beseemeth them to be taught in private: in *gentlemen* it needeth, the case being doutfull, whether private trayning be their best or no. And though this [185] argument succede yong maidens in order of methode, I hope yong gentlemen will not be offended neither with me for the placing, seeing the other sex is in possession of prerogative, nor with them for being so placed, which have wone the best place.

Of private education.

This question for the bringing up of yong gentlemen offereth the deciding of an other ordinarie controversie, betwene *publike* education and *private*, which verie name in nature is enemy to publike, as inclosure is to common, and swelling to much overlayeth the common, not onely in *education*, where it both corrupteth by planting a to private habit, and is corrupted it selfe by a degenerate forme, but also in most thinges else. Yet do I not deny both personall properties and private realities, which law doth allow in private possessions, even there, where friendship makes thinges to be most common by participation. I will therefore speake a litle of this private traine, before I passe to the *education* of *gentlemen*. What doe these two wordes import, *private education*? *Private* is that, which hath respect in all circumstances to some one of choice: as *publike* in all circumstances regardeth every one alike. *Education* is the bringing up of one, not to live alone, but amongest others, (bycause companie is our naturall cognisaunce) whereby he shall be best able to execute those doings in life, which the state of his calling shall employ him unto, whether *publike* abrode, or *private* at home, according unto the direction of his countrie whereunto he is borne, and oweth his whole service. All the functions here be publike and regard every one, even where the thinges do seeme to be most private, bycause the maine direction remaineth in the publike, and the private must be squared, as it will best joyne with that: and yet we restraine *education* to *private*, all whose circumstaunces be singular to one. As if he that were brought up alone, should also ever live alone, as if one should say, I will have you to deale with all, but never to see all: your end shalbe *publike* your meane shalbe *private*, that is to say, such a meane as hath no minde to bring you to that end, which you seeme to pretend: Bycause naturally *private* is sworne enemy to *publike* in all eventes, as it doth appeare when private gaine undoeth the common, though *publike* still pretend friendship to [186] all that is *private* in distributive effects, as it is plainely seene when the *publike* care doth helpe ech private, and by cherishing the singuler maintaineth the generall, whereas the private letteth the publike drowne, so it selfe may flete above. For in deed they march mostwhat from severall groundes to severall issues by most severall and least sutable meanes, the one in nature a rowmy *pallace* full of most varietie to content the minde, the other a close *prison*, tedious to be tied to, where the sense is shakled: the one in her kinde, a *libertie*, a broade *feild*, an open *aire*, the other in the contrarie kinde, a *pinfold*,

Private.

Education.

a *cage*, a *cloister*: Neither do I take these tearmes to make a fit division, where the end is still *common* and the abuse *private*. For how can *education* be *private*? it abuseth the name as it abuseth the thing. If they will say *education* is either good or ill, and use the naturall name, then methinke the disembling which is shadowed in the tearme *private* would soone appeare: though there can be no worse name then *private*, saving where the publike doth appoint it, which in education it will not, thereby to foster her owne foe: though in possessions it do, to have subsidies to sustaine, and paimentes to maintaine her great common charge.

And though in communities of kinde which naturally is devided into spieces, *nature* engraffe *private* differences for distinction sake, as *reason* in man to part him from a beast, yet that difference remaineth one still, bycause there is none better: which countenaunce of best cannot here be pretended, bycause in *education private* is the worst. This *private* renting in sunder of persons, for a pretended best *education*, which must passe on togither after *education* is verie daungerous in all daies, for many *private* pushes, while every parent can serve his owne humour, be it never so distempered: by the secrecie of his owne house, not to be discovered: by the choyce of his teacher, which will be ready to follow, if he forgoe not in folley: by the obedience of his child, which must learne as he is led, or else be beaten for not learning: which must obey as he is bid, or els lease his parent blessing. In *publicke* schooles this swarving in affection from the *publicke* choice in no case can be. The master is in eye, what he saith is in eare: the doctrine is examined: the childe is not alone, and there must he learne that which is laid unto him [187] in the hearing of all and censure of all. Whatsoever inconveniences do grow in *common* schooles, (as where the dealers be men, how can there be but maimes?) yet the *private* is much worse, and hatcheth moe odde ills. Naturally it is not built upon unitie, brad by disunion, to seeme to see more then the common man doth, to seeme to prevent that by *private* wit, which the common doth incurre by unadvised follie: to seeme to gaine more in secrecie, then the common gives in civilitie. By cloistering from the common it will seeme to keepe a countenaunce farre above the common, even from the first cradle. Wherby it becomes the *puffer* up to *pride* in the recluse, and the *direction* to *disdaine*, by dreaming still of bettership: the enemie to unitie, betwene the unequall: the overwayning of ones selfe, not compared with others, the disjointing of agreement, where the higher contemneth his inferiour with skorne, and the lower doth stomacke his superiour with spite: the one gathering snuffe, the other grudge.

This kinde of traine which soweth the corne of dissension by difference, where the harvest of consent is the harbour of common love, the indissoluble chaine of countriemens comfort, may very well be bettered, and much better be forborne, bycause by the waye it tempereth still the poyson of a creeping spite. And certainly the nature of the thing doth tend this way, though chaunging bytimes to better choice, or the common check, which will not be controwled, do many and often times interrupt the course. And though the child in proces prove better, and shew himselfe curteous, contrarie to my note, and the verie nature of private education, thanke naturall goodnesse or experience seene abroad, not the kinde of education, which in her owne sternnesse alloweth no such curtesie, though the childe see it in his parentes, and finde it in his bookes. And somtimes also it maketh him to shepish bashfull, when he comes to the light: as being unacquainted with resort: though generally he be somwhat to childish bold, by noting nothing, but that which he breedes of himselfe in his solitarie traine, where he is best himselfe, and hath none to controwle him, no not his maister himselfe, but under confession, how so ever the title of maister do pretend authoritie and the name of scholer, [188] make shew of obedience in private cloistring. I neede not saie all, but in this short manner, I seeke to give occasion for them to see all, which desire to sift more, both for the matter of their learning, and the manner of their living.

Do ye know what it is for one to be acquainted with all children in his childhood, which must live with them being men in his manhood? Is the common bringing up being well appointed good for the common man, and not for him of more height? and doth not that deserve to be liked on in private, which is thoroughly tryed being showed forth in common, and sifted by the seeing? which without any great alteration, for the matter of traine will be very well content to be pent up within private dores, though it mislike the cloistring, in privating the person. Sure that common which is well cast, must needes helpe the private, as one of her partes and feede one child very well being a generall mother to all: but private be it never so well cast in the sternnesse of his kinde, still drawes from the publike. I count not that private which is executed at home for a publike use, in respect of the place, for so all doinges be private, but that which will be at home, as better so. And why? for the private parties good. But it should seeme generally that the question is not so much for the manner of education, nor for the matter, wherin, but for the place, where, as if that, which is good for all in common, should not be good for some but in private. I must speake it under pardon. The effect commendes the common: for that the common education in the middest of common mediocritie bringeth up such wittes to such excellencie, as serve in all degrees, yea even next to the hyest, wheras private education in the middest of most wealth, if it maintaine it selfe with any more then bare mediocritie both of learning and judgement, when it is at the hyest, let him that hath shewed more, give charge to the chalenge. And yet some one young mans odnesse, though it be odde in deed, overthroweth not the question. And oftimes the report of that odnesse which we see not in effect, but heare of in speeche, falles out very lame, if the reporters judgement be advisedly considered, though for the authoritie and countenaunce of the man, skill give place to boldnesse, and silence to [189] civilitie: which otherwise would replie against it. There is no comparison betwene the two kindes, set affection apart. If the private pupill chaunce to come to speake, it falleth out mostwhat dreamingly, bycause privitie in traine is a punishment to the toungue: and in teaching of a language to exclude companions of speeche, is to seeke to quenche thrist, and yet to close the mouth so, as no moysture can get in. If he come to write, it is leane, and nothing but skinne, and commonly bewrayes great paines in the maister, which brought forth even so much, being quite reft of all helping circunstance, to ease his great labour, by his pupilles conference, with more companie. Which is but a small benefit to the child, that might have had much more if his course had bene chaunged. He can but utter that, which he heares, and he heares none but one, which one though he know all, yet can utter but litle, bycause what one auditorie is two or three boyes for a learned man to provoke him to utteraunce? If he travelled to utter, and one of judgement should stand behinde a covert to heare him, methinke he should heare a straunge orator straining his pipes, to perswade straung people, and the boye if he were alone, fast a sleepe, or if he had a fellow, playing under the bourd, with his hand or feete, having one eye upon his talking maister, and the other eye on his playing mate. If the nyne *Muses* and *Apollo* their president were painted upon the wall, he might talke to them without either laughing or lowring, they would serve him for places of memorie, or for hieroglyphicall partitions. If he that is taught alone misse, as he must often, having either none, or verie small companie to helpe his memorie, which multitude serves for in common scholes, where the hearing of many confirmes the sitter by, shall he runne to his maister? if he do that boldly, it will breede contempt in the ende: if he do it with feare, it will dull him for not daring. And though it be verie good for the child, not to be afrayd to aske counsell of his maister in that, where he doubteth, yet if he finde easie entertainment he will doubt still, rather then do his diligence, not to have cause to doubt. If the private scholer prove cunninger afterward, then I conceive he can be by private education, there was some forreine helpe which avaunced him abroad, [190] it was not his traine within being tyed to the stake, which offereth that violence to my assertion.

Why is private teaching so much used?

But what leades the private, and why is it so much used? there must needes be some reason, which alieneth the particular parente from the publike discipline, which I do graunt to very great ones, bycause the further they rise from the multitude in number, and above them in degree, the more private they grow as in person, so in traine: and the prince himselfe being one and singular must needes embrace the private discipline, wherin he sheweth great value in his person, if by private meanes, he mount above the publike. And yet if even the greatest, could have his traine so cast, as he might have the companie of a good choice number, wherein to see all differences of wittes, how to discerne of all, which must deale with all, were it any sacrilege?

But for the gentleman generally, which flyeth not so high, but fluttereth some litle above the ordinarie common, why doth he make his choice rather to be like them above, which still grow privater, then to like of them below, which can grow no lower, and yet be supporters, to stay up the whole, and liker to himselfe, then he is to the highest? To have his child learne better maners, and more vertuous conditions? As bad at home as abroad, and brought into schooles, not bred there. To avoide confusion and multitude? His child shall marke more, and so prove the wiser: the multitude of examples being the meanes to discretion. Nay in a number, though he finde some lewd, whom to flie, he shall spie many toward, whom to follow: and withall in schooles he shall perceave that vice is punished, and vertue praised, which where it is not, there is daunger to good manners, but not in schooles, where it is very diligently observed, bycause in publike view, necessitie is the spurre. To keepe him in health by biding at home for feare of infection abroad? Death is within dores, and dainties at home have destroyed more children then daunger abroad. Doth affection worke stay, and can ye not parte from your childes presence? That is to fond. And any cause else admittes controwlement, saving onely state in princes children, and princelike personages, which are to farre above the common: by reason [191] of great circunstance. And yet their circunstance were better, if they saw the common, over whom they command, and with due circumspectnesse could avoid all daungers, wherunto the greatest be commonly subject, by great desires, not in themselves to have, but in others that hope, which make the greatnesse of their gaine their colour against justice, where they injurie most. It is enough that is ment, though I say no more: besides that by a *Persian* principle, the seldome seing in princes, workes admiration the more, when they are to be seene.

Send your private Maister with your child to the common schoole.

Use common scholes to the best, joyne a tutor to your childe, let *Quintilian* be your guide, all thinges will be well done, where such care is at hand, and that is much better done, which is done before witnes to encourage the childe. *Comparisons* inspire vertues, *hearing* spreads learning: one is none and if he do something at home, what would he do with company? It is never settled, that wanteth an adversarie, to quicken the spirites, to stirre courage, to finde out affections.

For the maisters valew, which is content to be cloistered, I will say nothing, entertainement makes digressions even to that, which we like not. But if it would please the private parent, to send his sonne with his private maister to a common schoole, that might do all parties verie much good. For the schole being well ordered, and appointed for matter and maner to learne, where number is pretended to cumber the maister, and to mince his labour so, as ech one can have but some litle, though his voice be like the *Sunne*, which at one time with one light shineth upon all: yet the private scholer, by the helpe of his private maister in the common place hath his full applying, and the whole *Sunne,* if no lesse will content him. The common maister thereby will be carefull to have the best: the private teacher will be curiouse to come but to the very best: wherby both the private and publike scholers shall be sure to receive the best. And if the publike maister be chosen accordingly, as allowance will allure even the principall best, private cunning will not disdaine to be one degree beneth, where he knoweth himselfe bettered. And thereby disagreement betwene the two teachers willbe quite excluded which onely might be the meane to marre both my meaning and [192] *Quintilianes* counsell. Sure my resolution is, which if it winne no liking abroade may returne againe homeward, and be wellcome to his maister, that that which must be continued and exercised in publike, the residue of ones life, were best to be learned in publike, from the beginning of ones life. And if ye will needes be private, make your private publike, and drawe as many to your private maister, for your private sonnes sake, seeing you are able to provide rowme, bycause that will prove to be best for your child, as shalbe able to keepe some forme of our multitude, that he may have one companie before him to follow and learne of, an other beneth to teach and vaunt over, the third of his owne standing, with whom to strive for praise of forwardnes. Whereby it falleth out still, that that private is best, which consisteth of some chosen number for a private ende: and that multitude best, where choice restraines number, for the publike service: for in deede the common scholes be as much overcharged with too many, as any private is with to few. Which how it may either be helpt, or in that confusion be better handled, I will hereafter in my private executions declare, seeing I have noted the defect.

To knit up this question therefore of private and publike *education,* I do take publike to be simply the better: as being more upon the stage, where faultes be more seene, and so sooner amended, as being the best meane both for vertue and learning, which follow in such sort, as they be first planted. What *vertue* is private? *wisedome* to forsee, what is good for a desert? *courage* to defend, where there is no assailant? *temperance* to be modest, where none is to chaleng? *Justice* to do right, where none is to demaunde it? what *learning* is for alonnesse? did it not come from collection in publike dealinges, and can it shew her force in private affaires, which seeme affraid of the publike? Compare the best in both the kinds, there the ods wil appeare. If ye compare a private scholer, of a very fine capacity, and worthy the open field, so well trayned by a diligent and a discreat maister as that traine will yeald: with a blockhead brought up under a publike teacher, not of the best sort, or if in comparison ye match a toward private teacher with a weake publike maister, ye say somwhat to the persons but smallie to the thing, which in *equalitie* [193] shewes the difference, in *inequaltie* deceives the doubter, and then most, when to augment his owne liking, he wil make the conference odde, to seeme to avaunce errour, where the truth is against him. And to saye all in one, the publike pestring with any reasonable consideration, though it be not the best, yet in good sooth, it farre exceedeth the private alonenesse, though sometime a diligent private teacher shew some great effect of his maine endevour.

That the circunstance is one in gentlemen and common mens children.

But to the education of *gentlemen* and *gentlemanly* fellowes. What time shal I appoint them to begin to learne? Their witts be as the common, their bodies oftimes worse. The same circunstance, the same consideration for time must direct all degrees. What thing shall they learne? I know none other, neither can I appoint better, then that which I did appoint for all. The common and private concurre herin. Neither shall the private scholer go any faster on, nay perhaps not so fast, for all the helpe of his whole maister, then our boyes shall, with the bare helpe, that is in number and multitude, every boye being either a maister for his fellow to learne by, or an example to set him on, to better him if he be negligent, to be like him, if he be diligent.

Onely this, young *gentlemen* must have some choice of peculiar matter, still appropriat unto them, bycause they be to governe under their prince in principall places: those vertues and vertuous lessons must be still layd before them, which do appertaine to governement, to direct others well, and belong to obedience, to guide themselves wisely. For being in good place, and having good to leese, it will prove their ill, by undiscrete attemptes to become prayes to distresse. And yet for all this, the generall matter of duetie being commonly taught, eche one may applie the generall to his owne private, without drawing any private argument into a schoole, for the privitie not to be communicate but with those of the same calling: considering the property of that argument falleth as oft to the good of the common, whom vertue avaunceth, as the *gentlemens* credit, whom negligence abaseth. What exercises shall they have? The verie same. What maisters? The same. What circunstance else? All one and the same: but that for their place [194] and time, their choice makes them private, though nothing the better for want of good fellowship. And if they prove so well trained, as the generall plat for all infancie doth promise, and so well exercised, as the thing is well ment them, they shall have no cause, much to complaine of the publike, nor any matter at all why to covet to be private. For it is no meane stuffe, which is provided even for the meanest to be stored with.

These thinges gentlemen have, and are much bound to God for them, which may make them prove excellent, if they use them well: *great abilitie* to go thorough withall, where the poorer must give over, eare he come to the ende: *great leasure* to use libertie, where the meaner must labour: *all oportunities* at will, where the common is restrained: so that singularitie in them if it be missed, discommendes them, bycause they have such meanes and yet misse: if it hit in the meaner, it makes their account more, bycause their meane was small, but their diligence exceeding. Whereby negligence in gentlemen is ever more blamed, bycause of great helpes, which helpe nothing: diligence in the meaner is alway more praised, bycause of great wantes, which hinder nothing: and those prefermentes, which by degree are due unto gentlemen, thorough their negligence being by them forsaken, are bestowed upon the meaner, whose diligent endevour made meane to enjoy them.

1. Riche men no gentlemen.

As for *riche* men which being no *gentlemen*, but growing to wealth by what meanes soever, will counterfeat *gentlemen* in the education of their children, as if money made equalitie, and the purse were the preferrer, and no further regard: which contemne the common from whence they came, which cloister up their youth, as boding further state: they be in the same case for *abilitie*, though farre behinde for *gentilitie*. But as they came from the common, so they might with more commendacion, continue their children in that kinde, which brought up the parentes and made them so wealthy, and not to impatronise themselves unto a degree to farre beyond the dounghill. For of all the meanes to make a gentleman, it is the most vile, to be made for money. Bycause all other meanes beare some signe of vertue, this onely meane is to bad a meane, either to matche with great birth, or to mate great worth. For the most [195] parte it is miserably scraped to the murthering of many a poore magot, while lively cheese is lusty cheare, to spare expenses, that *Jacke* maye be a gentleman. If sparing were the worst, though in the worst degree, that were not the worst, nay it hath shew of witte: The rest which I tuch not, be so shamefull and so knowen to be such, and deserve so great hatred as nothing more. Besides the insolencie of the people, triumphing over them in their cuppes, by whom they buy their drinke: which shiftes be shamefull to the world and hatefull to heaven: and too too filthy to be honored upon earth with either armes by harold, or honour by any. He that will read but *Aristophanes* his blinde *Plutus* the God of richesse, and marke the old fellowes fashions shall see his humour naturally, as that poete was not the worst resembler though he were not the best man.

For to become a *gentleman* is to beare the cognisance of vertue, wherto honour is companion: the vilest divises be the readiest meanes to become most wealthy, and ought not to looke honour in the face, bycause it joynes not with justice, which greate wealth by the Greeke verse, *οὐδεὶς ἐπλούτησε ταχέως, δίκαιος ὤν*, is noted to refuse, and commonly dare not name the meane right, whereby it groweth great. And though witte be pretended to have made their way, it is not denied but that witte may serve even to the worst effectes, and to wring many a thousand to make one a gentleman. It is not witte, that carieth the praise, but the matter, wheron, and the manner how it is, or hath bene ill or well employed. Witte bestowed upon the common good with wise demeanour, deserveth well: the same holy given to fill a private purse, by any meane, so it be secrete: by any misdemeanour, so it be not seene: deserveth no prais for that which is seen, but is to be suspected, for that which is not seene. These people by their generall trades, will make thousandes poore: and for giving one penie to any one poore of those many thousandes will be counted charitable. They will give a scholer some petie poore exhibition to seeme to be religious, and under a sclender veale of counterfeat liberalitie, hide the spoile of the ransaked povertie. And though they do not professe the impovershing of purpose, yet their kinde of dealing doth pierce as it passeth: and a thousand pound gaines [196] bowelles twentie thousand persons. Of these kinde of folkes I entend not to speake, bycause their state is both casuall, and belongeth to the common: and their gentilitie bastardise: and yet while I frame a gentleman, if any of them take the benefit of my advice, gentle men must beare with me, if my preceptes be usurped on, where their state is intruded on.

My purpose is to employ my paines upon such as are *gentlemen* in deede, and in right judgement of their unbewitched countrie do serve in best place: neither will I rip up what some write of nobilitie in generall, whether by birth or by discent: nor what other write of true nobilitie, as disclayming in that which vertue avaunceth not: nor what other write of learned nobilitie, as accounting that simply the best, where vertue and learning do beawtifie the subject. One might talke beyond enough, and write beyond measure, that would examine what such a one saith of nobilitie in greeke, such a one in latin, such in other severall toungues, bycause the argument is so large, the use of nobilitie streaching so farre, and so brave a subject cannot chuse but minister passing brave discourses. There be so many vertues to commend it, all the brymmer in sight the clearer their subject is: so many vices to assaile it whose disfiguring is foulest, where it falleth in the face, and must needes be sene.

All these offered occasions, to enlarge and amplyfie this so honorable an argument, I meane to forbeare, and give onely this note unto yong gentlemen: That if their calling had not bene of very great worth in deede, as it is of most shew in place, it could never have wone so many learned workes, it could never have perced so many excellent wittes, to rejoyce with it in good, to mourne with it in ill, and to make the meditation of nobilitie, to be matter for them to marvell. And that therfore it doth stand *nobilitie* upon, to maintaine that glorie in their families with prayse, which learned men in so many languages, do charge them with in precept. My friend to be carefull, that I keepe all well, and my selfe to be carelesse and consume all ill? an honest friend and an honorable care. But what am I? my auncestours to avaunce my howse to honour, my selfe to spoile it, and bring it to decaye? The avauncement vertuous, the advauncer commendable. But what am I? a *gentleman* in [197] birth and nothing else but braverie. A sory shew which shameth, where it shapeth. It is value that gives name and note to *nobilitie,* it is vertue must endow it, or vice will undoe it. The more high the more heynouse, if it fortune to faile: the more bruted the more brutish if it fatall under fame. Which seeing it is so, as I wish the race well, so I wish their traine were good, and if it were possible even better then the common, but that cannot be. For the common well appointed is simply the best, and even fittest for them, bycause they may have it full, where the meaner have it maimed. Their sufficiencie is so able to wyn it with perfection, for leasure at will, for labour at ease, for want the least, for wealth the most, in all thinges absolute, in nothing unperfit, if they faile not themselves.

But bycause I meane briefly to runne through this title of nobilitie, which concerneth the worthiest part of our state and country, whatsoever cavelling the enemies of *nobility* pretend, whose good education must be applied according unto their degrees and endes, to the commoditie and honour of our state and countrie: Before that I do meddle with their traine, and shew what is most for them, and best liked in them, I will examine those pointes which by good education be best got, and being once got do beawtifie them most, which two considerations be not impertinent to my purpose, bycause I tender their education, to have them prove best.

The method of the discourse that foloweth.

My first note in nature of methode must needes be, what it is to be a *gentleman* or a *nobleman,* and what force the termes of *nobilitie* or *gentrie* do infer to be in the persons, to whom they are proper. Then what be the groundes and causes of *gentrie* and *nobilitie*: both the efficient which make them, and the finall why they serve, wherein the rightnes of their being consisteth, and why there is such thronging of all people that way.

Of gentlemanly exercise.

But ear I begine to deale with any of these pointes, once for all I must recommend unto them exercise of the bodie, and chiefly such as besides their health shall best serve their calling, and place in their countrie. Whereof I have saide, methinke, sufficiently before. And as those qualities, which I have set out for the generall traine in their perfection being best compassed [198] by them, may verie well beseeme a gentlemanly minde: so may the exercises without all exception: either to make an healthfull bodie, seeing our mould is all one: or to prepare them for service, wherein their use is more. Is it not for a *gentleman* to use the chase and hunt? doth their place reprove them if they have skill to daunce? Is the skill in sitting of an horse no honour at home, no helpe abroad? Is the use of their weapon with choice, for their calling, any blemish unto them? For all these and what else beside, there is furniture for them, if they do but looke backe: and the rather for them, bycause in deede those great exercises be most proper to such persons, and not for the meaner. Wherefore I remit them to that place.

What is it to be a nobleman or a gentleman?

What is it to be a *nobleman* or a *gentleman*? and what force do those termes of *nobilitie* and *gentilitie* infer to be in those persons, whereunto they are proper? All the people which be in our countrie be either *gentlemen* or of the *commonalty*. The common is devided into *marchauntes* and *manuaries* generally, what partition soever is the subdivident. *Marchandize* containeth under it all those which live any way by buying or selling: *Manuarie* those whose handyworke is their ware, and labour their living. Their distinction is by wealth: for some of them be called rich men, which have enough and more, some poore men, which have no more then enough: some beggers which have lesse then enough: There be also three kindes in *gentilitie*, the *gentlemen*, which be the *creame* of the common: the *noblemen*, which be the *flowre* of *gentilitie*, and the *prince* which is the *primate* and *pearle* of *nobilitie*. Their difference is in *authoritie*, the *prince* most, the *nobleman* next, the *gentleman* under both. And as in the baser degree, the *begger* is beneth all for want of both abilitie to do with, and vertue to deserve with: so the *prince* being opposite to him, as the meere best, to the pure worst, is of most abilitie to do good, and of most vertue to deserve best. The limiting of either sort to their owne lystes, will bewray either an usurping intruder upon superioritie, or a base degenerat to inferioritie, either being ravished with the others dealinges, and neither deserving the degree that he is in. To be vertuous or vicious to be rich or poore, be no peculiar badges to either sort, but common to both, for [199] both a gentleman, and a common man may be vertuous or vicious, both of them may be either rich or poore: landed or unlanded, which is either the having or wanting of the most statarie substance: Examples neede not in familiar knowledge. And as the gentleman in any degree must have forreine abilitie for the better executing of his lawfull authoritie: so there be some vertues which seeme to be wedded properly to that side: As great wisedom in great affaires: great valiancy in great attemptes: great justice in great executions and all thinges excellent, in a great and excellent degree of people. The same vertues but in a meaner degree in respect of the subject, whereon they be employed: in respect of the persons, which are to employ: in respect of circumstance, wherefore they are employed: and all thinges meaner be reserved for the common: of whom I will speake no more now, bycause this title is not for them, though they become the keepers of vertues and learning, when nobilitie becomes degenerate. Hereby it is evident that the tearme of nobilitie amongest us, is restrained to one order, which I named the flowre of gentilitie: and that the gentlemen be in degree next unto them. Whereof where either beginneth, none can dout, which can call him a nobleman that is above a knight. So that whosoever shall use the terme of gentilitie, speaking of the whole order opposite to the common, doth use the ground whence all the rest doth spring, bycause a gentleman in nature of his degree is before a nobleman, though not in the height: as nobilitie employeth the flowre of the gentlemen, which name is taken of the primacie and excellencie of the oddes, and where it is used in discourse it comprehendeth all above the common. When the *Romaine* speaketh of the gentleman in generall, nobilitie is his terme, being in that state opposite to the common, wherein they acknowledged no prince, when that opposition was made. For *generosus* which is our common tearme signifieth the inward valure, not the outward note, and reacheth to any active living creature though without reason, wherein there doth appeare any praisworthy valiance or courage in that kinde more then ordinarie, as in *Alexanders* horse and *Porus* his dog. Therefore whether I use the terme of nobilitie hereafter or of gentilitie, [200] the matter is all one, both the names signifying the whole order, though not of one ground, *nobilitie* being the flower and *gentilitie* the roote. The account wherof how great it is, we may very well perceave by that opinion, which the nobilitie it selfe hath usually of it. For *truth* being the private protest of a gentleman, *honour*, of a noble man, *fayth* of a Prince, yet generally they do all joine in this, *As they be true gentlemen.* Such a reputacion hath the name reserved even from his originall.

Now then nobilitie emplying the outward note of inward value, and gentilitie signifying the inward value of the outward note, it is verie easie to determine, what it is to be a *nobleman,* in excellencie of vertue shewed, and what it is to be a *gentleman* to have excellent vertue to shew. Whereby it appeareth that vertue is the ground to that whole race, by whether name so ever ye call it, *wisedome* in *pollicie, valiance* in *execution, justice* in *deciding, modestie* in *demeanour.* There shall not neede any allegations of the contraries, to grace out these vertues, which be well content with their owne gaines and desire not to glister by comparison with vices, though different colours in contarietie do commend, and thinges contrarie be knowne in the same moment. For if true nobilitie have vertue for her ground, he that knoweth vice, can tell what it bringes forth.

Whether *nobilitie* come by discent or desert it maketh no matter, he that giveth the first fame to his familie, or he that deserveth such honour, or he that enlargeth his parentage by noble meanes, is the man whom I meane. He that continueth it in discent from his auncestrie by desert in his owne person hath much to thanke God for, and doth well deserve double honour among men, as bearing the true coate of right and best nobilitie, where desert for vertue is quartered with discent in blood, seeing aunciencie of linage, and derivation of nobilitie is in such credit among us and alwaye hath bene.

Of infirmities in nobility by discent.

And as it is most honorable in deede thus to aunswere auncestry in all laudable vertues, and noble qualities of a well affected minde: so the defect in sufficiencie where some of a noble succession have not the same successe in pointes of praise and worthinesse, either naturally by simplenesse, or casually, by fortune: though it be to be moaned in respect of their place, [201] yet it is to be excused in respect of the person. Bycause the person is, as his parentes begate him, who had not at commaundement the discent of their vertues, which made them noble, as they had the begetting of a child to enherite their landes. For if they had, their nobilitie had continued on the nobler side. But vertues and worthinesse be not tyed to the person, they be Gods meere and voluntarie giftes to bestow there, wheras he entendes that nobilitie shall either rise or continue, and not to bestow, where he meanes to abase, and bring a linage lowe. Wherefore to blame such wantes, and raile upon nobilitie as to much degenerate, is to intrude upon providence. Where we cannot make our selves, and may clearly see, that he which maketh, hath some misterie in hande, where he setts such markes.

To exhort young men to those qualities, which do make noble and gentlemen, is to have them so excellently qualified, as they maye honest their countrey, and honour themselves. To encourage noble young gentlemen to maintaine the honour of their houses, is to wish them to apply such vertues, as both make base houses bigge in any degree, and tofore did make their families renowmed in theirs. If abilitie will attaine, and idlenesse do neglecte, the ignominie is theirs: if want of abilitie appeare to be so great, as no endevour can prevaile, God hath set his seale and men must cease to muse, where the infirmitie is evident, and thinke that every beginning is to have an ende. Hereby I take it to be very plaine both what the termes of noble and gentle do meane, and what they infer to be in those parties to whom they are proper. For as *gentility* argueth a courteous, civill, well disposed, sociable constitution of minde in a superiour degree: so doth *nobilitie* import all these, and much more in an higher estate nothing bastarded by great authoritie. And do not these singularities deserve helpe by good and vertuous education?

The causes and groundes of nobilitie.

What be the groundes and causes of *nobilitie*, both the *efficient* which make it, and the *finall* for whom it serves? Concerning the *efficient*. Though the cheife and soveraigne Prince, of whom for his education I will saye somwhat herafter, be the best and fairest blossom of *nobilitie*, yet I will not medle any further with the meane to attaine unto the dignitie of the [202] crowne, then that it is either come by, by conquest, which in meaner people is called purchace, and hangeth altogether of the conquerours disposition: or else by discent, which in other conveyances continueth the same name, and in that highnesse continueth the same lawes, or altereth with consent. Neither will I speake of such, as the Prince upon some private affection doth extraordinarily prefer. *Alexander* may avaunce *Hephestio* for great good liking, *Assuerus Hester*, for great good love, *Ptolome Galetes* for secret vertue. And upon whom soever the Prince doth bestow any extraordinarie preferment, it is to be thought that there is in them some great singularity, wherewith their princes, which can judge be so extraordinarily moved. Neither will I say any more then I have said of *nobilitie* by discent, which enjoyeth the benefite of the predecessours vertue, if it have no private stuffe: but if it have, it doth double and treble the honour and praise of auncestrie.

Plutarch. Alexand.

Hester lib.

Aelianus ποικίλ. 2.

But concerning other causes, that come by authoritie, which make noble and gentlemen under their Prince, who be therefore avaunced by their Prince, bycause they do assist him in necessarie functions of his government, they be either single or compound, and depend either holy of learning: or but only for the groundes of their execution. Excellent *wisedome* which is the meane to avaunce grave and politike counsellours, is but a single cause of preferment: likewise *valiancie* of *courage* which is the meane to make a noble and a warrious captaine is but a single cause of avauncement: but where *wisedome* for counsell, doth concurre with *valiancie* of *courage* in the same man, the cause is compound and the deserte doubled. The meanes of preferment, which depend upon learning for the ground of their execution be either *Martiall* for warre and defence abroad, or *politike*, for peace and tranquillitie at home. For the man of warre will seeme to hange most of his owne courage and experience, which without any learning or reading at all hath oftimes brought forth excellent leaders, but with those helpes to, most rare and famous generalles, as the reason is great, why he should prove an excellent man that waye with the assistance of learning which without all learning [203] could attaine unto so much. *Sylla* the cruell in deede, though surnamed the fortunate of such, as he favored, was a noble generall without any learning. But *Caesar* which wondred at him for it, as a thing scant possible to do any great matter without good learning, himselfe with the helpe of learning, did farre exceede him.

Plut. Sylla.

Caesar.

Such as use the penne most in helping for their parte, the direction of publike government, or execute offices of either necessarie service for the state, or justiciarie, for the common peace and quietnesse, without profession of further learning, though they have their cheife instrument of credit from the booke, yet they are not meere dettours to the booke, bycause private *industrie*, considerate *experience*, and stayed *advisement* seeme to chalendge some interest, in their praiseworthie dealing. The other which depend wholy upon learning be most incident to my purpose, and best beseeme the place, where the question is, how gentlemen must be trained to have them learned.

A politike counsellour.

The highest degree wherunto learned valure doth prefer, is a wise *counsellour*, whose learning is learned pollicie: not as pollicie is commonly restrayned, and opposed to plainnesse, but as we terme it in learning and philosophie, the generall skill to judge either of all, or of most thinges rightly, and to marshall them to their places, and strait them by circunstance, as shall best beseeme the present government, with least disturbaunce, and most contentment to the setled state, of what sorte soever the thinges be, divine or humaine, publike or private, professions of minde, or occupations of hande. This man for religion is a *Divine*, and well able to judge of the generalities, and application of *Divinitie*, for governement, a *lawyer*, as one that first setts *lawes*, and knowes best how to have them kept: generally for all thinges, he is simply the soundest, whether he be choosen of the Ecclesiasticall or Temporall, out of whatsoever degree, or whatsoever profession: so able as I say, and so sufficient in all pointes. And though the particular professour know more then he in every particular, which his leasure will not suffer him to runne thorough, like the particular student: yet of himselfe he will enquire so consideratly, and so [204] methodically of the particuler professour, as he will enter into the very depth of the knowledge, which the other hath, and when he hath done so, handle it better, and more for the common good, then the private professour can, for all his cunning in all his particuler: Nay he will direct him in the use, which enformed him in the skill. Of all them that depend wholy upon learning, I take this kinde of man worthyest to be preferred, and most worthily preferred for his learned judgement, the first and chiefe naturally in *divinitie* among *divines* though he do not preach: in *law* among *lawyers* though he do not pleade: and so throughout in all other thinges that require any publike direction.

2. The divine.

Of the secondary and particuler professions, the worthynes of the subject, and the authoritie of the argument preferreth the *divines*. For they dealing carefully with the charge of soules, the principall part of our composition, and the fairest matter that is dealt in, beside the soule of a civill societie which is compounded of infinite particular soules: and being the ministers and trumpettes of the allmightie God, avancing vertue, and suppressing vice, denouncing death and pronouncing life, which be both most sure, and that everlastingly to ensue according to demeanour: do well deserve to be honoured of men, with the simple benefit of their temporall estimation, as what they can do, where they cannot do enough. For what reward for vertue is an olyve braunch, though it signifie the rewarders good will, confessing the thing to be farre above any mortall reward? which estimation yet is not to be desired of them, though it be deserved by them. For humilitie of minde in avauncing the *divine* draweth him still backeward, as officious thankefullnes in the profited hearer doth worthely and well push him still on forward. And as the temporall braunche of the common weale being so many in number hath distinction in degrees, for the better methode in government, which function doth honour the executours: so likewise with proportionate estimation for the parties executours, the church consisting of many, and having charge over all hath her distinction in dignities and degrees to stay that state the better, which would soone be shaken, if there [205] were no such stay: the argument of religion being used mostwhat contemplative, and in nature of opinion, and therefore a verie large field to bring forth matter of controversies, specially in yong men, whose naturall is not staied, though their resolution seeme to be, and their zeale carie them on, to the profit of their hearer, their owne commendation, and the honour of him, whose messengers they are. Howbeit in the middle of all these contradictions, the particuler execution to beleeve this, and to do that, according to ones calling, which is but one in all, to beleeve truely, and to do honestly, by that same one, doth check the diversities of all difference in saying. Which great difference in saying, and diversities in opinion, the church may most thanke the *Grecian* for, who joyning with religion after divorce with philosophie, was as bold to be factious in the one, as he had bene in the other, and could not rest in one, still devided into numbers, as it still appeareth in the ecclesiasticall historie where factious heresies assaile the firme catholike. Neither doth this difference in publike degrees empaire that opinion, that all be but ministers, and in that point equal any more, then that both the prince and the plowman be one, in respect of their humanitie, and first creation. And yet the prince is a thought above him for all he be his brother in respect of old *Adam*. The matter of both these two, the wise *counseller*, and the grave *divines* honour is best proved to be in the worthynes of their owne persons, which is the true ensigne of right *nobilitie*, bycause both their places and lyvinges, in respect of their degree depart and die with them (though their honorable memorie remaine after) and be not transported to their heires, as the inheritaunce of blood, but to their successours, as the reward of vertue. If it so chaunce that the same person for worthynes be successour both in place, and patrimonie, it is most honorable to himselfe, and most comfortable to his friends, and rejoyced at of all men.

3. The lawyer. The peace, and quietnes of civill societie, by composing, and taking up of quarelles, and by directing justice, makes the *lawyer* next, whose publike honour dyeth also with him: and declareth the substaunce of his worthines, though his private [206] name remaine, and his children enjoy the benefit of his getting. As why may not the *divines* to, enjoy that, which their parentes have honestly saved, if they have any surplus, whereon to save, for necessarie reliefe of their necessarie charge in succession? Which among the Jewes was of such countenaunce, as *Josephus*, vaunteth himselfe of his nobilitie that way. And. But it were to large a roming place, to runne over the port that the churchmen have

kept, not among christians and Jewes onely.

4. The Physician.

The *Physician* is next, and his circumstaunce like, and so furth in learning, where the preferment dying with the partie, and transposed to other, not by line in nature but by choice in valure, is the evidentest argument, that those thinges be most worthiely tearmed the best matter of honour, which die with the partie, and yet make him live through honorable remembraunce, though he have no successour but the common weale, which is generally surest, bycause private succession in blood is oftimes some blemish. And yet succession in state, is not allway so steddie, but that the old house may have a very odde maister. These do I take to be the truest, and most worthy causes of nobilitie, lymited not by wealth, but by worth, which accompany the party, and expire with his breath. For sure that which one leaveth behinde him besides an honorable remembraunce of his owne worthynes, cannot noble him while he hath it, nor his, when he leaves it, bycause it bettereth not the owner, but oftimes makes him worse, though it be a necessary stay for that person which is of good worthynes to shew his worth the better. Therefore when wealth is made the way to *gentilitie*: or if it be exceeding great, the gap to *nobilitie*, it is like to some universitie men, which for favour or feasting lend their schole degrees to doltes to intercept those livinges by borowed titles which them selves should have for learning, and might have without let, if they hindered not them selves. But both gentlemen and scholers be well enough served, for overshooting them selves so farre: *nobilitie* being empaired in note, though encreased in number by such intruders, and learning empoverished in purses, though replenished in putfurthes by [207] such interceptours.

Why so many desire to be gentlemen.

Yet it is no mervell if the base covet his best, as his perfection in nature, and his honour in opinion: no more then that the *asse* doth desire the *lions* skin, to be thought though but a while, very terrible to behold. But counterfeat mettall for all his best shew will never be so naturall, as that is, which it doth counterfeat: neither will naturall mettalles ever enterchaunge natures, though the finest be severed, and the *Alcumist* do his best: And for all the *lions* skin, sure the *asse* is an *asse* as his owne eares will bewray him, if ye fortune to see them: or your eares will discerne him, if you fortune to heare him: he will bray so like a beast. I can say no better, though this may seeme bitter, where I see *nobilitie* betraid to donghillrie, and learning to doultrie. You *gentlemen* must beare with me, for I wish you your owne: you scholers must pardon me, I pity your abuse. Your *apes* do you harme, and scratch you by the face, for all the friendship they finde, which if they found not, they might tarie *apes* still. Their suttletie supplantes you, and your simplenes lettes them see, what fellowes you are. Call vertue to aide, and put slaverie in pinfold, let learning leade you, and send loselles to labour, more fit for the shovell then to shuffle up your cardes. Thus much for the causes which make *nobilitie,* whose leader is learning, and honour is vertue, not to use more discourse to prove by particular, where the matter is so plaine, as either vertue will admit praise, or historie bring proofe.

For the finall cause it is most evident, that if some sufficiencie this way be the meane to *nobilitie,* the effect of such sufficiencie doth crowne the man, and accomplish the matter. But wherefore is all this? to shew how necessarie a thing it is to have yong gentlemen well brought up. For if these causes do make the meane man noble, what will they do in him, whose honour is augmented with perpetuall encrease, if with his *nobilitie* in blood he do joyne in match the worthines of his owne person? Wherefore the necessitie of the traine appearing to be so great, I will handle that as well as I can in generall precept, for this present place, as having to deale with such personages, whose *wisedom* is their weight, *learning* their [208] line, *justice* their ballance, *armour* their honour, and all *vertues* in all kindes their best furniture in all executions, and their greatest ornamentes in the eies of all men, all this tending directly to the common good.

The gentlemens train.

As concerning the traine it selfe, wherof I said somwhat before, I know none better then the common well appointed, which the common man doth learne for necessitie at first, and avauncement after: the greater personage ought to learne for his credit, and honour, besides necessarie uses. For which be gentlemanly qualities, if these be not, to *reade,* to *write,* to *draw,* to *sing,* to *play,* to have *language,* to have *learning,* to have *health,* and *activitie,* nay even to professe *Divinitie, Lawe, Physicke,* and any trade else commendable for cunning? Which as gentlemen maye get with most leasure, and best furniture, so maye they execute them without any corruption, where they neede not to crave. And be not sciences liberall in terme, that waye to be recovered from illiberalitie in trade, and can those great livinges be better employed, then in sparing the pillage of the poore people? which are to sore gleaned: by the needie and never contented professours? which making their ende as to do good, and their entent but to gaine, do pluk the poore shrewdly, while they covet that they have not, by a meane that they should not. Bicause though the professours neede do seeke such a supplie, yet the thing which they professe protesteth the contrarie: and prayes for ability in the professour to deale franckely himselfe in the freedome of his cunning, and not to straine her for neede. Doth *Divinitie* teache to scrape, or *Lawe* to scratche, or any other *learning*, whose epithet is liberall? *Divines* do use it, *lawyers* do use it, *learned men* do use it. But their profession is free and liberall, though the execution be servile and corrupt, and cryeth for helpe of *nobilitie* to raunsome it from necessity, which hath emprisoned it so, by the negligence of *nobilitie* who thinke any thing farre more seemly to bestow their time and wealth on, then professions of learning. But if it would please toward young gentlemen to be so wel affected towards their naturall countrey, or to suffer her to overtreat them so farre, as to shoulder out corruption, by professing themselves, who neede not to be covetuous for want of any thing, which [209] have all thinges at will, how blessed were our state, nay how fortunate were even the gentlemen them selves? They may spare number enough that way, besides such furniture, as they do affoord unto the court, to all *martiall* and *militare* affaires, to all *justiciarie* functions by reason of their multitude, which groweth on dayly to farre and to fast, and lessen the middle commoner to much: whose bignes is the best meane, if *Aristotle* say true, as his reason seemes great, for peace and quietnes in any publicke estate, to desire the rich gentlemen, which have most, and the poore meany, which have least, to holde their handes, and put up their weapons, when they would be seditious, as the two extremities in a publicke body. If the couragious gentlemen tooke them selves to armes, and mynded more exercise: if the quieter tooke bookes, and fell unto learning, calling home to them againe by their laudable diligence all those faculties, which they have so long delivered over, for prayes to the poorer, thorough their to great negligence, were not the returne to be received with sacrifice? and would not the other aswell provide for them selves by other trades wherwith to live? Whereby the honestie of that subject, wherein they should travell, would in the meane while, deliver the honest gentlemen from such faultes, as they be now subject unto, while intending so good, they avoided so evill. This were better then braverie, and more triumphant then travelling, to remaine at home with their prince, not to rome abroad with the pilgrime, to see farre in other countries, and be starke blinde in their owne.

Travelling beyond sea.

For what is it to travell, seeing that word hath so sodainly crossed me? I will not here make any *Epitome* of other mens travell, which have set downe whole treaties against this travelling in diverse languages: neither will I amplyfie the thing with any earnest aggravations, which though they may be true, and so may somewhat taint the unadvised travellour, yet they be not worthy the rehearsall here. For what reason carieth it, to finde fault with the forraine, and to foster the fault at home? or for particular misdemener, to condemne some whole nations? or for some error in some few to wish a general restraint? and by to sharp blaming to bitterly to eager not the [210] meanest wittes: as commonly dawes be not most desirous to travell. It is lightly the quintessence which will be a ranging. Silence in thinges peradventure blameworthy, and friendly entertainement where there is no sting, by curtesie wil call, and by liking will winne such dispositions sooner to come to the lure where we would wish to have them, then any either launsing, their woundes by to bytter speches, or aliening their hartes by too much harping on one string: chieflie considering that travell and going abroad for knowledge in learning, and skill in language have for their protection much antiquitie, long time, and great number, though still chekt as either needeles or harmfull: and oftimes countermaunded, not onely by private mens argumentes, but by publike constitutions, of the best common weales, which were very unwilling to have their people to wander.

But what is this travelling? I meane it not in marchauntes, whom necessitie for their owne trade, and oftentimes neede for our use, enforceth to travell, and tarie long from home. Neither yet in souldiers, whom peace at home sendes abroad for skill, in forraine warres to learne how to fend at home, when peace is displeased: which yet both have their owne, and overgreat inconveniences, to the wringing of their countrie. For marchauntes by forcing their naturall soile beyond her proportion to some gainefull commoditie verie utterable abroade, do breede gaules at home, and by bringing in also beyond proportion to serve pleasure and feede fantsie, prove great undoers to a great number, which can neither temper their tast, nor refraine the fashion.

The souldier likewise, which is trained in hoat blood abroad will hardly be but troublesome in cold blood at home: unlesse he be such a one as followed the warres for conscience to his countrie, and of judgement to learne skil, and not upon bare courage, or hardines of nature, or sinisterly to supply some other want. I meane not any of these, ne yet such travellers as *Solon*, to prevent a mischiefe in mutabilitie of his countrie mens mindes, whom he had tyed to his lawes, not revocable till his returne, when acquaintaunce for that time had wone allowance for ever: neither as *Pythagoras*, or *Plato* were, who sought cunning [211] where it was, to bring it where it was not. For *Platoes* journy into *Sicile* proceeded not of his minde to travell, but upon hope to do some good on *Dionisius* the tyrant, who did send for him by *Diones* meane. We neede not to travell in their kinde for learning. We have in that kind thankes be to God for the pen and print, as much at this day as any countrie needes to have: nay even as full if we will follow it well, as any antiquitie it selfe ever had. And yong gentlemen with that wealth, or their parentes in that wealth, might procure, and maintaine so excellent maisters and joine unto them so choise companions, and furnish them out with such libraries, being able to beare the charge, as they might learne all the best farre better at home in their standing studies, then they ever shall in their stirring residence, yea though the desire of learning were the cause of their travell. Which rule serveth even in the meaner personages, which love to looke abroade, and alleadge learning for their shew, which might be better had at home, with their good diligence, and confirmeth it selfe by sufficient persons, which never crossed the sea. Let them favour their owne fantsies never so much, and defende that stoutly, which they have begone youthfully: yet the thing will prove in the end as I have said. And if there be defect, we should devise, as those philosopher travellours did, to helpe it here at hoome in our owne countrie, that we be not allway borowers, where it is but of wantonnesse, bycause we are unwilling to straine out our owne, which of it selfe is able enough to breede, and needeth no more helpes then the generall studie, if it be studied in deede, and not be dalyed with for shew, as I wish it were not, and not I alone. Here lyeth a padde to be pitied though not to be published, they that may amend the thing are in conscience to thinke of it. But what is travell, as it is to be constrewed in this place, where it interrupteth traine, and bringes it in question, whether yong gentlemen, while they use travelling, do use that, which is best both for their countrie, and themselves. What is it to travell? It is to see countries abroad, to marke their singularities, to learne their languages, to returne from thence better able to serve their owne countrie here with such fourniture, as they provided, [212] and such wisedom, as they gathered by observing things there.

Sure a good countenaunce to helpe travelling withall, and to hide her skars, which in some may prove so in deede. But those some be not any generall patternes: in whom, some excellencie in nature, and vertuousnesse in disposition doth turne that to profit and good, which the thing of it selfe doth assure to be dangerous: bycause it may prove to be both perillous and pernicious in those and to those, which for heat are impetuous, for yeares to foreward, for wealth to rachelesse: and proceeding from them may be contagious to others, as cankers will creepe, and the ill taches of every countrey do more easely allure, and obteine quicker cariage to enlarge them selves, then the good and vertuous do. But while they travell thus, as sure me thinke I see, it is but of some errour caryed with the streame, which enwraps them so (onelesse some miscontentment at home in busie and displeased humours, use the colour of language and learning, to absent themselves the better from that, against the which they have conceyved some stomacke) what might they have gained at home in the meane while? sounder learning, the same language, besides the love and liking of their owne countrey soile which breed them, and beares them: by familiaritie, and continuance at home encreased, by discontinuance, and strangenesse mightely empared: while enamouring and liking of forreine warres doth cause lothing, and misliking of that they finde at home. Whereby our countrey receiveth a great blow, thorough alienation of their fantsies, by whom she should be governed, which will rather deale in nothing, then not force in the forreine.

What is the very naturall end, of being borne a countryman of such a countrey? To serve and save the countrey. What? with forreine fashions? They wil not fit. For every countrey setts downe her owne due by her owne lawes, and ordinaunces appropriate to her selfe, and her private circunstance upon information given by continuers at home, and carefull countreymen.

The verie division of lawes, into naturall, nationall, and civill emport a distinction in applying, though the reason runne thorough, and continue generally one. That which is very excellent good abroad, and were to be wished in our countrey [213] upon circunstance which either will not admit it, or not but so troublesomly, as will not quite the coast, nor agree with the state, is and must be forborne here, though it leave a miscontentment in the travellours heade, who likes the thing most, and thinkes light of the circunstance, which he sayth will yelde to it, though experience say no: and in some but petie toyes do shew him, how leaning to the forreine hath misfashioned our owne home. I do not deny but travelling is good, if it hap to hit right, but I think the same travel, with minde to do good, as it alwaye pretendeth, might helpe much more, being bestowed well at home. He that rometh abroade hath no such line to lead him, as the taryer at home hath, onlesse his conceit, yeares, and experience be of better stay, then theirs is, which be causes of this question, and bring travelling in doubt. For the ground of his vyage being private, though taken to the best, is unfreindly to our common. It is like to an idle, lasie, young *gentlewoman*, which hath a very faire heire of her owne, and for idlenesse, bycause she wil not looke to it, combe it, pick it, wash it, makes it a cluster of knottes, and a feltryd borough for white footed beastes: and therfore must needes have an unnaturall perug, to set forth her favour, where her owne had bene best, if it had bene best applied. Is not he worse then mad, that hath an excellent piece of ground, made for fertilitie, and suffereth it to be overgrowen with wedes, while he wandreth abroade, and beholdes with delite, the good housbandes, and housbandrie in other men and other soiles? The president of a copie makes a child resemble wel, and a certaine pitch to deale within a mans owne countrey in such a kinde of life, to his and her avauncement, is the surest, and soundest direction to any young gentleman: first to learne by, and then to live by: and to levell all that waye without any forreine longing.

If he take pleasure in travelling, and no care in expending, both the expense will bring repentaunce, when reason shall reclame, if ever she do, (as in some desperate cases, fantsie is froward, and wil bide no fronting:) and the pleasure bringes some greife, when the gentleman which in youth so much pleased himselfe, in his age shall not be able to pleasure his countrey, whom he cared for so litle, while he so counted of the forreine. [214] Forreine matters fit us not, and though our backes, yet not our braines, if we be not sicke there. Forreine thinges be for us in some cases, but we were better to call home one forreine maister to us, then they should cause us to be forreine scholers, to such a forraging maister, as a whole forreine countrey is, to learne so by travelling, and not by teaching.

Our *ladies* at home can do all this, and that with commendacion of the verie travelled gentlemen: bycause it is not that, which they have seene, that makes them of worth, but that which they have brought home in language and learning, which they do finde here at their retourne. Our *ladie mistresse,* whom I must needes remember, when excellencies will have hearing, a *woman,* a *gentlewoman,* a *ladye,* a *Princesse,* in the middest of many other businesses, in that infirmitie of sexe, and sundrie impedimentes to a free minde, such as learning requireth, can do all these thinges to the wonder of all hearers, which I say young *gentlemen* may learne better at home, as her *Majestie* did, and compare themselves with the best, when they have learned so much, as her *Majestie* hath by domesticall discipline. It may be said that her *Majestie* is not to be used for a president, which of a princely courage would not be overthrowne with any difficulty in learning that, which might avaunce her person beyond all praise, and profit her state beyond expectation. But yet withall it may be said, why may not young gentlemen, which can alledge no let to the contrarie, obtaine so much with more libertie, which her highenesse gat with so litle? It is wealth at will which egges them on to wander, and it is the same, which causeth them continue in the same humour, though they heare it misliked. If they went abroad as *Embassadours,* that their Princes authoritie might make their entrie to great knowledge in greatest dealinges: or if they were excellent knowen learned men, that all cunning would crepe to them, and honour them with intelligence, and notes of importance: or if they went in the traine of the one, or in the tuition of the other, where authoritie and awe might enforce their benefit, and save them from harme, I would not mislike it, to breede up such fellowes, as might follow them in service: but for any other of the particular endes, which be better had at [215] home, I cast of comparisons. Good, plaine, and well meaning young *gentlemen* in purse strong, in yeares weake, to travell at a venture in places of danger to bodie, to life, to living, though our owne countrey be also subject to all the same perills, but not so farre from succour and reskue, drive me to such a traunse, as I know not what to saye. Commende them I cannot bycause of my countrey: offend them I dare not, bycause of them selves, which may by discretion in themselves, and wisedome of their freindes provide well for themselves, as I do confesse, though I feare nothing so much, as the overliking of forreine, and so consequently some underliking at home, which will never let them staye. Olde lawes in some countries enacted the contrarie, and sillie *Socrates* in *Plato* being offered to be helpt out of prison, as unjustely condemned by the furie of the people, and persuasion of his unfreindes: would not go out of his countrey to save his owne life, as resolved to die by commandment of that lawe, thorough whose provision he had lived at home so long. Divisions for religion, and quarrells of state may worke that which is not well for generall quiet, by being hartned abroade with the sight, and hearing of that, which some could be content to see, and heare at home.

Plato 12. de leg.

Plato in his twelfth booke of lawes, seemeth to rule the case of travelling, which moveth this controversie. Where he alloweth both the sending out of his countrymen, into forreine landes, and the receiving of forreine people into his countrey. For to medle neither with forreine actions, nor forreine agentes might savour of disdaine, and to suffer good home orders to be corrupted by our forreine travellers, or their forreine trafficquers might smell of small discretion. Wherfore both to build upon discretion to prevent harme at home, and to banish disdaine to be thought well on abroad: he taketh this order both for such as shall travell abroad into forreine countries from his, and for such as shall repare, from forreine countries unto his. For his owne travellers he enacteth first. That none under fourtie yeares in any case travell abroad. Then restraining still all private occasions, for the which he will not dispense with his lawe, neither graunt any travelling at all: he alloweth the state in publike to send abroad, embassadours, messagers, observers, [216] for so I turne *Plato* his *θεωρούς*.

Such as are sent abroad to warre for the countrie, though foorth of the countrie, he holdes for no travellers, as being still of, and in the state: the cause of their absence continuing their presence, and the place of their abyding, not altering the nature of their being. And the like rekening he maketh of those solemne embassadors, which they sent to communicate in sacrifice with their neighbours, at *Delphi*, to *Apollo*, in *Olympus*, to *Jupiter*, at *Nemea* to *Hercules*, in *Isthmos* to *Neptune*: where he appointed the pacificque, and friendly Embassages to be furnished out of the most, the best, and bravest citisens, which with their port, their presence, their magnificence, might honest, and honour their countrie most: as to the contrary he requireth in his martiall lieuetenant, which in the camp, and fielde shall represent the state of his country, credit, estimation, honour, purchased before by vertue and valure. His observer, whom he alloweth to go abroad to see fashions: he will have not to be above threescore, nor under fiftie yeares old, and such a one, as shall be of good credit in his countrie, for great dealinges, both in warre and peace. For the occasion of his travell pretending to see the manners of men abroad, to marke what is well and them that are good, which be most times there, where the place is least likely: and not to be marred by that which is ill, and them that are naught, which be there oftest, where good orders be rifest: to correct his countrie lawes by the better forreine: or to confirme them by the worse: how can he judge of any of these thinges, which hath not dealt in great affaires, and shewed himselfe there to be a man of judgement? or how is he able to avoide the evill, and cleave to the good, whom yeares have not stayed and given reason the raine, to bridle all desires, that might turne him awry? Such a man, of such a credit, of so many yeares, but no man yonger doth *Plato* send abroad, to learne in forreine countries, and to see forreine fashions, so many of those ten yeares betwene fiftie and sixtie, as shall please him selfe best. But what must this travellour do at his returne? There is a counsell appointed of the gravest divines for religion, of ten justices for law, of the new and old overseers for education, whereof ech one taketh [217] with him one younger man, above thirtie and under fourtie. This counsell hath commission to deale in matters of lawe, either to make new, or to mend the olde: to consider of education, and learning, what is good and quickneth, what is ill and darckeneth. And what the elder men determine that the yonger must execute. If any of these young men behave himselfe not well, the elder that brought him into the parlament, beareth blame of the whole house: those that behave themselves well, are made honorable presidentes to their countrey to behold: as they are most dishonored if they prove worse then other. Where by the waye I note these three thinges. First

the care they had to education, and learning even in their cheife par- 1.
lament. Secondly the reason they had to traine, and use young men 2.
in their parlament. Thirdly their three speciall pointes of governe- 3.
ment, according to the three kindes of persons, which were present
in the parlament, *religion, lawe, education.* How to traine before *lawe,*
how to rule by *lawe,* how to temper both traine, and *lawe* by *divini-*
tie, and *religion.*

Before this counsell, the observer presenteth himselfe at his returning home, and there declareth, what he hath either learned of them abroad, or devised by their doinges, for the helpe of his countrey lawes, of his countrey education, of his countries provision. And if he seemed neither better nor worse, neither cunninger, nor ignoranter, at his returne home, then he was at his departure from home: he was commended for his good will, and no more was said to him. If he seemed better and more skilfull, he was not only honored by the present parlament, while he lived, but by the whole countrey after his death. If he seemed to returne worse, he was commaunded to use companie, neither with young, nor olde, as one like to corrupt under colour of wisedom. And if he obayed that order, he might live still, howbeit but a private life. If he did not obay, he was put to death. As he was also if he were found to be busie headed, and innovating any thing after the forreine concerning either *lawe, living,* or *education.* Beholde the patterne of a travellour, rewarded for his well, punished for his ill: neither ill requited, where he meant but well.

Then for reparers from forreine countries into his, whom he [218]
will have well entertained in any case, he appointeth foure kindes.
The first wherof be *merchantes,* whose mercates, havens, and lodg- 1.
ing, he assigneth to be without the citie but very neare to it: and certain officers to see, that they innovate nothing in the state, that they
do, and receave right, that they have all thinges necessarie, but without overplus.

The second kinde of straungers he appointeth to be such as arrive 2.
for *religion,* for *philosophie,* for *learning* sake, whom he willeth the
Divines, and church *treasurers,* to entertaine, to lodge, to care for, as
the presidentes of true hospitalitie for straungers. That when they
shall have taryed some convenient time, when they shall have
seene, and heard, what they will desire to see or heare: they may
depart without either doing, or suffering any injurie or wrong. And

that during their abode for any plea under fiftie drammes, the *Divines* shalbe judges betwene them, and the other partie: if it be above that summe, that then the maior of the citie shall determine the matter.

3. The third sorte were *Embassadours*, sent from forreine Princes, and states, upon publike affaires. Their entertainment he commendeth to the common purse, their lodging to some generall, some coronell, or some captaine onely. The care of them was committed to the hie *treasurer*, and their host, where they lodged.

4. The fourth kinde was such *observers* from some other place, as his countrey did send abroad before, about fiftie yeares old, pretending a desire to see some good thing among them, or to saye some good thing unto them. This kinde of man he excludeth from none, as being comparable with the best, bycause of his person so advisedly choosen. Who so was wise, wealthy, learned, valiant, might entertaine, and entreat him. When he minded to depart after he had seene, and observed all thinges at full, he was sent away honorablely, with great presentes, and rewardes. Thus thinketh *Plato* both of comers in, and goers out of one countrey into another. But you will say this was a devise of *Plato* in his lawes, as other be in his common weale. Yet it is a wisemans devise, that findes the harme, and would avoide it, and in this our case is well worthy the weying. But as *Plato* neede not to blush for the devise, which is grounded [219] upon incorruption, wherunto we say that travelling is a foe: so if such a lawe were in very deede, politikly planted in any common weale, as it is naturally engraffed in any honest witte: there would be exception notwithstanding against it. In all this *Platonicall* provision, we may easely observe, that his cheife care is by travelling, either to amend the countrey, or not to marre it: and that the forreine usually is a steppemother to a strange countrey. Therefore as young gentlemen maye travell, both for their pleasure, to see forreine countries, and for their profit, to returne wise home: so their owne countrey desires them, to minde that profit in deede, and not to marre it with to much pleasure, which is the cause why that all ages have misliked *travelling*, as the occasion of corruption in most, and thinke it better forborne for hindring of so many, then to be allowed, for the good of some few, which is hasarded at the first, and uncertaine to prove well. The reason of all this is, both for the forreine evill, which may corrupt, and for the very good, which will not fit,

be it never so fit their, from whence it is fetcht.

But to my purpose, and the training at home for home. I remit this travelling abroad to their consideration, which use it, which I dare not quite mislike, bycause I see very many honest people, which have travelled, and the argument of misliking receiveth instance, that the thing may be well used, even bycause some do misuse it, wherunto all other indifferences else be also subject. Nay I dare scant but thinke well of it, bycause my Prince doth allow it, thorough whose licence their travelling is warranted. I say but thus much generally though some traveller do some good to his countrey, even by the frute of his travell, and most in best places: that yet the statarie countrieman doth a great deale more. The reason why is this. The continuall residenciarie at home hath his eye still bent upon some one thing: where he meanes to light, and makes the direct and naturall meane unto it: which though the travellers do alledge to be their minde to, yet their meane is not so fit, as that is, which ordinarily, and orderly is made for the thing. Neither is this allegation generall. For we see the course which the most do use after their returne, to bewraie a passage for pleasure, [220] rather then any sound, and advised enterprise. And therefore I do wish the domesticall traine to be well travelled to better us with our owne, and that we did not so much trie how forraine effects do make us out of fashion, though they feede our fantsies, and that it would please well disposed yong gentlemen to sort them selves betimes to some kinde of learning to make them in deede liberall, their abilitie being throughly fensed, against feare of corruption, to serve their country honorably that way which doth so honour them.

For as all will be lawyers, or in houses of law, and court, to some private end: so what if some of choice became both divines, and physicianes, and so furth in other learned sciences, as I said before? If there be any gentleman in our countrie so qualified at this daie in any kind of learning, is he not therefore praysed, esteemed, and honoured of all others, and above all others of his calling, and somewhat higher to which are not comparably qualyfied? Whence I gather this argument: That the worthynes of the thing is confessed by the honour given unto it, and that such as desire honour ought to seeke for such worthinesse, as enforceth the assured confession of the best deserved honour. And I pray you be not these faculties for their subject to be reverenced, as they are? and for their effectes to be esteemed of speciall account? which have bene allway the very groundes of the best, and most beneficiall nobilitie? I do not hold *Tamerlane*, or any barbarous, and bloody invasions to be meanes to true nobilitie, which come for scourges: but such as be pacifike most, and warlike but upon defense, if the country be assailed: or to offend, if reveng be to be made, and former wrong to be awraked. Neither take I wealth to be any worthy cause to renowme the owner, unlesse it be both got by laudable meanes, and likewise be employed upon commendable works: neither any qualitie or gift, which beawtifieth the body unlesse vertue do commende it, as serviceable to good use, neither yet any endewement of the minde, but onely such as keepe residence in reason, having authoritie in hand, and direction to rule, by the philosophers termed *το ἡγεμονικὸν*. [Philo.] Wherein those qualities do claime a tenure, which I have assigned as foundations to honour, and notes of nobilitie, [221] worthy the esteeming, and of inestimable worth. Who dare abase divinitie for the thing it selfe? or who is so impudent, as not to confesse that profession honorable which hath God himselfe to father, and friend, our most loving, and mercifull maker: the devill himselfe to enemie and foe, our most suttle, and despitefull marrer, the doctrine of life, the daunter of death? Some scruple there is now, which was not sometime when the allurement was larger, the living fatter, and the countenaunce greater: but the matter is now better, though the man be brought both to more basenes in opinion, and barenesse in provision, and will honour a good gentleman, which will seeke honour by it, and ought so to do. [Plut. in Caes.] The time was when the great *Cesar*, at his going furth from his house in his sute for the great pontificate sayd to his mother, that she should either see her sonne at his returne the great bishop, or else no body. Such a step was that state to his whole preferment after. [Ad 1. Nicoclem.] *Isocrates* in his oration, where he frameth a prince, joyneth priesthood with the prince, as two thinges of like care, requiring like sufficiencie in persons, like skill in well handling, which two sayth he, every one thinkes, he can cunningly weild, but hardly anie one can handle them well.

If gentlemen wil not travel and professe *physicke*, let them feele the price of ignorance, and punish their carcasses besides the consumption of their cofers, as all learning being refused by them hath no other way to reveng her selfe, then only to leave them to ignorance, which will still attend to flatter and fawne there where small stuffing is, and that which is most miserable, bycause themselves see it not, will cause them selves to be their owne *Gnatoes*, a most unproper part, to be seene upon a stage, when the same person plaieth *Thraso*, and answereth himselfe, as if he were two. Were it not most honorable for them to see these effectes in their owne persons? *singuler knowledge* where studie is for knowledge and knowledge for no neede? *liberall execution*, where desire to do good, and good for gramercie be the true ends of most honour? where the promises from heaven, the princes upon earth, the perpetuall prayer, and neverdying prayse of the profited people will remember, and require that honorable labour, so honestly employed, that fortunate [222] revenew so blessedly bestowed, not for private pleasure, but for common profit?

Albeit there is one note here necessarily to be observed in yong *gentlemen* that it were a great deale better that they had no learning at all and knew their owne ignorance, then any litle smattering, unperfit in his kinde, and fleeting in their heades. For their knowne ignorance doth but harme them selves, where other that be cunning may supply their rowmes: but their unripe learning though pretie in the degree, and very like to have proved good, if it had taryed the pulling, and hung the full harvest, doth keepe such a rumbling in their heades, as it will not suffer them to rest, such a wonder it is to see the quickesilver. For the greatnes of their place emboldeneth the rash unripenes of their studie, in what degree so ever it be, whether not in digesting that which they have read, or not in reading sufficiently, or in chusing of absurdities to seeme to be able to defende where their state makes them spared, and meaner mens regard doth procure them reverence, though their rashnes be seene, or in not resting upon any one thing, but desultorie over all. A matter that may seeme to be somewhat in scholes, even amongest good scholers: and very much in that state, where least learning is commonly best liked, though best learning be most advaunced, when it joynes with birth in sowndnes, and admiration. As the contrary troubleth all the world, with most perverse opinions, beginning at the insufficient, though stout *gentleman*, and so marching forward still among such, as make more account of the person whence the ground comes, then of the reason which the thing carieth. Wherefore to conclude, I wish yong *gentlemen* to be better then the common in the best kinde of learning, as their meane to come to it, is every way better. I wish them in exercise, and the frutes thereof to be their defendours, bycause they are able to beare out the charge, whereunder the common of necessitie must shrinke: That both those wayes they may helpe their countrie in all needes, and themselves, to all honour.

The Princes traine.

The *prince* and *soveraigne* being the tippe of *nobilitie*: and growing in person most private for traine, though in office most publike for rule, doth claime of me that private note, [223] which I promised before. The greatest prince in that he is a childe, is, as other children be, for soule sometimes fine, sometimes grosse: for body, sometimes strong, sometimes weake: of mould sometime faire, sometime meane: so that for the time to beginne to learne, and the matter which to learne, and all other circumstances, wherein he communicateth with his subjectes, he is no lesse subject, then his subjectes be. For exercise to health, the same: to honour, much above: as he is best able to beare it, where coast is the burden, and honour the ease. We must take him as God sendes him, bycause we cannot chuse, as we could wish: as he must make the best of his people, though his people be not the best. Our dutie is to obey him, and to pray for him: his care willbe to rule over us, and to provide for us, the most in safetie the least in perill. Which seeing we finde it prove true in the female, why should we mistrust to find it in the male? If the prince his naturall constitution be but feeble, and weake, yet good traine as it helpeth forwardnes, so it strengthneth infirmitie: and is some restraint even to the worst given, if it be well applyed, and against the libertie of high calling oppose the infamie of ill doing. Which made even *Nero* stay the five first yeares of his government, and to seeme incomparable good. When the yong princes elementarie is past, and greater reading comes on, such matter must be pikt, as may plant humilitie in such height, and sufficiencie in such neede, that curtesie be the meane to winne, as abilitie to wonder. Continuall dealing with forraine *Embassadoures*, and conferring at home with his owne counsellours require both tongues to speake with, and stuffe to speake of.

And wheras he governeth his state by his two armes, the *Ecclesiasticke*, to keepe, and cleare religion, which is the maine piller to voluntarie obedience: and the *Politike*, to preserve, and maintaine the civill government, which doth bridle will, and enforceth contentment: if he lacke knowledge to handle both his armes, or want good advice to assist them in their dealing, is he not more then lame? and doth not the helpe hereof consist in learning? Martiall skill is needfull: But it would be to defend, bycause a sturring *Prince* still redye to assaile, is a plague to his people, and a punishment to him selfe, and in his most [224] gaine, doth but get that, which either he or his must one daye loose againe, if the losse rest there, and pull not more with it. But religious skill is farre more massive: bycause religion as it is most necessarie for all, so to a *Prince* it is more then most of all, who fearing no man, as above mans reache, and commanding over all as under his commission, if he feare not God his verie next both auditour, and judge, in whose hand is his hart? and what a feare must men be in for feare of most ill, when the Prince feares not him, who can do him most good? Almighty God be thanked, who hath at this daye lent us such a *Princesse*, as in deede feareth him, that we neede not feare her which deserving to be loved desires not to be feared. I wish this education to be liked of the *Prince*, to pull the people onward, by example that they like of, though they cannot aspire to: as I pray God long preserve her, whose good education doth teach us, what education can do, wherby neither this lande shal ever repent, that education of it selfe did so much good in her: and I have good cause to rejoice that this my labour concerning education comes abroad in her time.

Chapter 40.

Of the generall place, and time of education. Publike places, Elementarie, Grammaticall, Collegiate. Of bourding of children abroad from their parentes houses, and whether that be best. The use and commoditie of a large, and well situate training place. Observations to be kept in the generall time.

These two circunstances for the generall place, and the generall time, concerne both the exercise of the bodie, and the training of the minde jointly, bycause they both are to be put in execution in the same place, and at the same time, though not at the same howres. For the particular times, and places I will deale in myne other treatises, where I will accomodate the particular circumstance to the particular argument. Private places, where every parent hath his children taught within his doares have but small interest in this place: bycause such a parent, as he may take or leave of the generall traine, what it shall please him, his owne liking being the measure to [225] leade him: so for exercise, or any other thing he is the appointer of his owne circumstance, and his house is his castle.

Division of publike places.

Publike places be either elementarie, grammaticall, or collegiate.

Collegiate.

For the collegiate places, whether they be in the universities, or without, they be lightly well situate, and for both the traines resonably well builded, specially such as have a cloysture or galerie for exercise in foule weather, and the open fieldes at hand for the faire. If there be any fault in that kinde, it may be set downe, in hope sooner to have it amended in new erections, when such founders shalbe found: then to be redressed in those which be erected already: bicause these buildinges be restrained to the soile, where on they stand. Yet wish for the better may take place, when the want is found, though the effect do follow a long while after, if it ever do at all.

Elementarie.

The elementarie places admit no great counsell, bycause such as enter the yong ones, do provide the rowmes of them selves, and the litle people be not as yet capable of any great exercise: so that there is no more to be said herein but this, that the Elementarie teachers provide their rowmes as large as they may, and that the parentes domesticall care supply: where the maisters provision is not sufficient. For as the collegiate yeares must direct themselves most, bycause they are after a certaine degree set over to their owne government: so the elementarie, bycause of their weakenes and youth must be joyntly helpt betwene the maister and the parent, this point for the petie ones being altogither private, and upon private charge, as the other collegiate is altogither publicke and upon publicke erection though alway proceeding from some privat meane. But if any well disposed wealthie man for the honour that he beareth to the murthered infantes, (as all our erections have some respect that way,) would beginne some building even for the litle yong ons, which were no encrease to schooles, but an helpe to the elementarie degree, all they would pray for him, and he himselfe should be much bound to the memorie of the yong infantes, which put him in remembraunce of so vertuous an act. And rich men which have much more then necessary enough, though none of them thinke he have simply enough, would be stirred forward by all good and earnest people, which [226] favour the publicke weale, whose foundation is laide in these petie infantes, to spend the supererogation of their wealth that waie, where it will do most good to other, and least harme to themselves.

The places where the the toungues be taught, by order and art of grammer, require more observation, bycause the yeares that be or at the least ought to be emploied that way be fittest, both for the fashioning of the body, and for framing of the minde: most subject to the maisters direction, and consist of a compound care, publicke erection, which provideth them places wherein to learne: and private maintenaunce which furnisheth out the rest. The scholers either come daily from their fathers houses to schoole, or be bourded at their charges somewhere verie nigh to the schoole.

3. Grammaticall.

Where there riseth a question whether it be better for the childe to boord abroad with his maister, or some where else: or to come from home daily to schoole. If the place where the parentes dwell, be neare to the schoole, that the nighnes of his maisters house can be no great vantage: or but so farre of, as the very walke may be for the boyes health: and the parent himselfe be carefull and wise withall, to be as good a furtherer in the training, as he is a father to the being of his owne chield: certainely the parentes house is much better, if for nothing else, yet bycause the parent may more easily at all times entend the goodnes of his owne, being but one or few, then the maister can, at such extraordinarie times as the bourding with him, doth seeme to begge his diligence, being both tired before, and distracted among many. Further, all the considerations which do perswade men rather to have their children taught at home, then among the multitude abroad, for the bettering of their behaviour, do speake for their bourding at home, if the parentes will consider the thing well: Bycause the parent may both see to the entertainement of his childe, when he is from schoole, and withall examine, what good he doth at schoole. For undoutedly the maisters be wearied with travelling all the day, so that the private help within their houses, can be but litle, without both overtyring the maister, and shortening his life, and the dulling of the childe, if he still pore [227] upon his booke. Times of recreation must be had, and are as requisite to doe thinges well any long time, as studying is necessarie to

Of bourding abroad.

do any thing well at any time. For can any man but thinke it a great deale more, then a sufficient time for the maister to teach, and the scholer to learne dayly from six in the morning till eleven, and from one in the afternoone till wellnigh six at night, if these houres be well applied? nay if they were a great deale fewer? And may not the residew be well enough bestowed upon solace and recreation in some chaunge to the more pleasant for either partie? In the maisters house, I graunt children may keepe schoolehowers better, and be lesse subject to loytering and trewantrie. The maisters care in his generall teaching may eye them nearer, bycause they be in his so neare tuition, and in place of his owne children, being committed unto his private care by their owne parentes and friendes, he may more easily dispence with their howers, if they fortune to minde many elementarie pointes at one time: and sooner finde out their inclination, then in the generall multitude. And if any particular preferment be incident to his house, without the common wearying both of the scholer and maister, some thing may be done. There be also many private considerations, which some parentes follow in the displacing of their children from their owne houses, which I remit to their thoughtes, as I reserve some to myne owne. If the maister do entend onely such scholers as he bourdeth, and have both in himselfe abilitie to performe, what is needefull for the best traine: and have such a convenient number as will rise to some hight in the traine, I know none better, so the place where he dwelleth, and teacheth do answere in convenientnes, and situation and some circumstances, else. But while he careth to have his bourders learne, sure some slow paying parentes will keepe him leane, if he looke not well to it, and his gaine will go backeward, besides the continuall miscontentmentes. At home spoiles, soilthes, twentie things, are nothing in the parentes homely eye, which selfe same be death abroad, where the parent hath another eye: and yet the things misliked not avoidable even at home. But what if sickenes, nay what if death come in deede, then all things be constrewed to the worst, as if death did not know [228] where the parent dwells. And though the maister doe that which the civill law requireth in deposing, and use not onely so much diligence to preserve, but much more then in his owne, yet all that is nothing. Wherefore as parentes must beware of boording out for their owne good: so maisters must be warie of admitting any for their owne harme. And sure to set downe my resolution, me thinke it enough for the maister to take upon him the traine alone, being so great both for exercise and learning, as I wish him well considered, that can do both well. If parentes dwell not neare the schoole, let some neighbours be hostes, which may and will entend it, and deliver the maister of the parentes care, whom even they will favour more, if they find profit by his schooling. They be distinct offices, to be a parent and a maister, and the difficulties in training do eager sore enough, though the same man be troubled with no more. Boording, that is the undertaking of both a fathers and a maisters charge requireth many circumstances of convenientnes in place, of provision for necessities, of trustie and diligent servauntes, and a number moe: besides indifferencie in the parent to be armed against accidentes, where there is no evident default, and to content truely where there is great desert: as the maister is to give a great account of two severall cures, a personage for his teaching, and a vicarage for his boording. The maisters charge is great of it selfe, but this composition of a duble office is a mervelous matter. If the maister minde his boorders eitheer only or most, where his charge is over moe, where then is his dutie? if not, what gaine have those boorders, by their maisters private? If he teach but boorders let him looke to himselfe, for his charge will prove chargeable moe wayes then one: and those that be best able to put forth to boord, are alway most strait in making all audittes, and to amplifie offences before they be proved, without eitheir conference or contentment. I wish parentes therefore to be warie, ear they set over their owne person for more then the training: and the maisters to be as warie for feare of had I wist. But to the grammer schooles. As the elementaries of force must be neare unto their parentes bycause of their youth, and therefore are not to be denied the middle of cities and townes: so [229] I could wish that grammer schooles, were planted in the skirtes and suburbes of townes, neare to the fieldes, where partely by enclosure of some private ground, for the closer exercises both in covert and open: partely for the benefit of the open fieldes for exercises of more raunge, there might not be much want of roome, if there were any at all. To have a faire schoole house above with freedome of aire for the toungues, and an other beneth for other pointes of learning, and perfiting or continuyng the Elementarie entrances, which will hardly be kept, if they be posted over to private practising at home: to have the maister and his familie though of some good number conveniently well lodged: to have a pretie close adjoyning to the schoole walled round about, and one quarter if no more covered above cloisture like, for the childrens exercise in the rainie weather, as it will require a good minde and no meane purse: so it needs neither the conference of a countrey, as *Lacedemon* did in *Athenaeus*, and *Plato*, as *Athens* did in *Pausanias*, *Suidas* and *Philostratus*, as *Corinth* did in *Diogenes Laertius*: nor yet the revenue of a Romain Emperour, whose buildinges in this kinde, were most sumptuous and magnificent, as *Adrian* the Emperours *Athenaeum*, *Hermaeum* and *Panathaenaicum* at *Tibur*, and *Neroes Thermae* at *Rome*, which in one building furnished out both learning and exercise as it appeareth by the discriptions of their places called, *Gymnasia*, *xysta*, and *Palaestrae*.

There is wealth enough in private possession, if there were will enough to publike education. And yet we have no great cause to complaine for number of schooles and founders. For during the time of her *Majesties* most fortunate raigne already, there hath bene mo schooles erected, then all the rest be, that were before her time in the whole Realme. My meaning is not to have so many, but better appointed both for the maisters entertainment, and the commoditie of the places. Small helpe will make most of our roomes serve, and small studie with great good will and honest salarie to maintaine a sufficient man, will make our teachers able both to enstructe well and to exercise better. The places of learning and exercise, ought to be joint tenementes, and neare neighbours capable of number, which must be limited by the neede of the countrey, [230] where the schoole standeth, and the maisters maintenaunce which way it must rise. For if it rise by the number, better for him few and choice, so they consider his paines accordingly. And sure experience hath taught me, that where the maister is left to the uncertaintie of his stipende to encrease or decrease with his diligence, that there he will do best, and the children profit most, allway provided that he deale with no more, then he can bring up under him selfe, and hasard not his owne credit, nor his childrens profit upon any absolute underteacher. Whose use is not, as we now practise it in schooles, where indeede ushers be maisters of them selves, but to assist the maister in the easier pointes of his charge, which ought to have all under his owne teaching, for the cheife pointes, and the same under the ushers, for more usuall and easie, as in the teaching of the Latin toungue, I will declare more at large. Where the very practise wil confirme my wordes, and prove them to be true.

Againe, it is halfe a wonder ever to bring forth a good scholer in the hart of a great towne: where there be chaunge of schooles, and many straunge circunstances to procure chaunge, as it shall please the child. Who notwithstanding he have his will followed in the chaunge, yet seldome winneth very much by the chaunge: though the second maister oftimes make shew of the formers ground worke, which is made but light of, bycause it kepeth lowe.

If the maisters stipend do rise by foundacion, and standing payment, yet the place may not be overcharged with number: nor the maister with care to provide things needfull any other wayes then onely by his trade. For what reason is it to have a mans whole labour, and to alow him living stant sufficient for a quarter? or what pollicie is it, to have him that should teache well, to be enforced for neede, to medle with some trade, quite different from the schoole. In this pointe the *Pope*, and Canon lawe weare merveilous freindly to maisters, and helped them still with some Ecclesiasticall maintenaunce, as it appeareth in *Gregories Decretales*, the fifth title of the fifth booke, *De Magistris*. And the Glose ripping further then the text, is yet more freindly. And our owne countrey also, in benefit of priviledge, by the common lawe at this day, doth not frowne upon us, and [231] for certaine immunities, letteth us enjoye that benefit, which the *Canonist* meant us. And the good Emperour *Frederick* did further by his freindly and favorable constitution, which he caused to be placed in the fourth booke of *Justinians* new Codex, the thirtenth title, *Ne filius, pro patre*, where the Glosse, making an anatomie of the Emperours meaning, and desirous to do us good, helpeth us particularly and properly to.

Among many causes which make schooles so unsufficiently appointed, I know not any, nay is there any? that so weakneth the profession as the very nakednesse of allowance doth. The good that commeth from and by schooles is great and infinite: the qualities required in the teacher many and resolute: the charges which his freindes have bene at in his bringing up much and heavy: and in the way of preferment, will ye wish any of any worth to set downe his staffe at some petie portion, which even they that praise it, would not be content to have their owne sit downe with, though the founder follow his president, and the time have bene, when with the Church helpe some litle would have served? but the case now is quite altered. In these our dayes eche man will enhaunce in his owne, without reason or remorse: but in professions of greatest neede and most account, they will yeelde no more allowance, then the auncient rent, where all thinges be improved. Yet oftimes they meete with bookmen in some kinds, which wil bite them coursdly. But those bookmen be neither Elementarie teachers, nor yet Grammarians. Our calling creepes low and hath paine for companion, stil thrust to the wall, though stil confessed good: Our comfort perforce is in the generall conclusion, that those thinges be good thinges, which want no praising, though they go a cold, for want of happing. For our schoole places, which I do know, the most are either commodiously situate already, or being in the hart of townes might easely be chopt for some field situation, farre from disturbaunce, and neare to all necessaries. It were no small part of a great and good erection, even to translate roumes to more convenient places, either by exchaunge or by new purchace: and I do thinke that licences to that ende, will be more easely graunted then to build moe schooles. The inconveniences which I my selfe have felt that [232] waye, both for mine owne, and for my scholers health, and the checking of that, which of long I have wished for: I meane some traine in exercise, do cause me so much to commend field roome. Though I my selfe be not the worst appointed within a citie for roome, thorough the great good will towardes the furtherance of learning, and the great cost, in the purchasing, and apparelling the roome to that use, done by the worshipfull companie of the *marchaunttailours* in London. In whose schoole I have bene both the first, and onely maister sence the erection, and their have continued now twenty yeares.

Probitas laudatur et alget.

If ye consider, what is to be done in these roomes which I require, ye shall better judge what roomes will serve. In the schoole the toungues be taught, and the Elementarie traine continued at times therunto appointed, for those, two roomes will serve. An upper, with some convenient discharging the place from noysome ayre, which the verie children cause: and from to great noise if the place be vawted under, or enclosed with other building: and an other beneath likewise appointed, to serve for what else is to be done. They that will have their children learne all that I have assigned them upon good warrant of the best writers, and most commendable custome, if their capacities be according, may have their turne served so: and those that will not, need not, but the oportunity of the place, and the commoditie of such trainers, wherof a smal time wil bring forth a great meany, will draw many on, and procure good exhibitours to have the thing go forward. I could wish we had fewer schooles, so they were more sufficient, and that upon consideration of the most convenient seates for the countries, and shires, there were many put together to make some few good. *Insufficiencie* by distraction dismembers, and weakens: *sufficiencie* by uniting strengthens, and doth much good. To conclude I wishe the roome commodious for situacion, which in training up of youth hath bene an olde care, as it appeareth by *Xenophon* in the schooling of *Cyrus* and the *Persian* order: large to holde, and convenient to holde handsomely. For as *reading*, and thinges of that motion do require small elbow roome: so *writing*, and her appendentes may not be straited. *Musicke* will cumber if it be confounded. Where *writing* wilbe allowed, [233] there *drawing* will not be driven out. But exercise must have scope. And such kinde of roomes, if the multitude be not to bigge, or the waye to schoole not to farre for the infant, with some litle distinctions, and parting of places, will serve conveniently both for the *Elementarie*, and the *Grammarian*, and so much the better.

The time.

For the time there is but litle to be said at this time: bycause in the Elementarie and so onward, I meane by the grace of God to apply all circunstances so neare, and so precisely to schoole uses, as the maister shalbe able streight way to execute: if he do but follow that which shalbe set before him, for *matter* wherin: for *manner* how: for *time* when to do eche thing best. For the generall exercising time. These two groundes of *Hippocrates*, must be still kept in remembraunce, to use no exercise when ye be very hungrie: neither yet to eate before ye have used some exercise.

For the generall learning times: to begin, the strength of body, and conceit of minde were made the generall meanes: to continue, perfectnesse, and use were appointed the limittes: for the midle houres this I thinke, that it were not good, to go to your booke streight after ye rise, but to give some time to the clearing of your body. As also studie after meate, and fast before ye sleepe beareth great blame for great harmes to health, and to much shortning of life. From seven of the cloke, though ye rise sooner, (as the *lambe* and the *larke* be the proverbiale leaders, when to rise and when to go to bead) till tenne before noone, and from two till almost five in the after noone, be the best and fittest houres, and enough for children wherin to learne. The morening houres will best serve for the memorie and conceiving: the after noone for repetitions, and stuffe for memorie to worke on. The reasons be the freenesse, or fulnesse of the head. The other times before meat be for exercises, as hath bene fully handled hertofore. The houres before learning, and after meate, are to be bestowed, upon either neating of the bodie, or solacing of the minde, without to much motion: wherin as I said before the greatest part, and the best to be plaid consisteth usually in the trainers discretion, to apply thinges according to the circunstances of person, place, and time. To conclude [234] we must be content with those places, which be already founded, and use those houres which be already pointed to the best that we can, and yet prepare our selves towardes the better, when soever it shall please God to send them. And by perswasion some maisters maye well enough bring wise parentes to yeelde unto this note, and to give it the triall. In the meane time some excellent man having the commoditie of a well situate house, and being able to commaund his owne circunstance, neither depending of other mens helpe, wherof he cannot judge, and so that way leasing some authoritie in direction, may put many excellent conclusions in triall.

Chapter 41.

Of teachers and trainers in generall, and that they be either Elementarie, Grammaticall, or Academicall. Of the Elementarie teachers abilitie, and entertainement. Of the Grammer maisters abilitie and his entertainement. A meane to have both excellent teachers, and cunning professors in all kindes of learning, by the division of colleges according to professions: by sorting like yeares into the same roumes: by bettering the studentes allowance and living: by providing and maintaining notable well learned readers. That for bringing learning forward in his right and best course, there would be seven ordinarie ascending colleges for Toungues, for Mathematikes, for Philosophie, for Teachers, for Physicians, for Lawyers, for Divines, and that the generall studie of Lawe would be but one studie: Every of these pointes with his particular proofes, sufficient for a position. Of the admission of teachers.

Although I devided the traine of education into two partes, the one for learning to enrich the minde: the other for exercise to enable the body: yet I reserved the execution of both to one and the same maister: bycause neither the knowledge of both is so excessive great, but it may easely be come by: neither the execution so troublesome, but that one man may see to it: neither do the subjectes by nature receive partition seeing the soule and body joyne so freindly in lincke, and the one must needes serve the others turne: and he that seeth [235] the necessitie of both, can best discerne what is best for both. As concerning the trainers abilitie, whereby he is made sufficient to medle with exercises, I have already in my conceit sufficiently enstructed him, both for the exercises themselves, and for the manner of handling them according to the rules and considerations of *Physick*, and *Gymnastick*, besides some advertisements given peculiarly to his owne person: wherin I dwelt the longer, and delt the larger, bycause I ment not to medle with that argument any more then once, and for that point so to satisfie the trainer, wheresoever he dwelt, or of what abilitie soever he were, as if he listed he might rest upon my rules being painfully gathered from the best in that kinde. If he were desierous to make further search, and had oportunity of time, and store of bookes: I gave him some light where to bestow his studie.

Now am I to deale with the teaching maister, or rather that propertie in the common maister, which concerneth teaching: which is either *Elementarie* and dealeth with the first principles: or *Grammaticall* and entreth to the toungues: or *Academicall*, and becomes a reader, or tutour to youth in the university. Teachers. Elementarie. Grammaticall. Academicall.

For the *tutour* bycause he is in the universitie, where his daily conversation among a number of studentes, and the opinion of learning which the universitie hath of him: wil direct choice and assure desire: I have nothing to saye, but leave the parentes to those helpes, which the place doth promise. 1. Academicall.

For the *Elementarie* bycause good scholers will not abase them- 2. Elementarie.

selves to it, it is left to the meanest, and therfore to the worst. For that the first grounding would be handled by the best, and his reward would be greatest, bycause both his paines and his judgement should be with the greatest. And it would easily allure sufficient men to come downe so lowe, if they might perceave that reward would rise up. No man of judgement will contrarie this pointe, neither can any ignorant be blamed for the contrarie: the one seeth the thing to be but low in order, the other knoweth the ground to be great in laying, not onely for the matter which the child doth learne: which is very small in shew, though great for proces: but also for the manner of handling his witte, to harten him for afterward, [236] which is of great moment.

Of the Elementary teachers entertainment.

But to say somwhat concerning the teachers reward, which is the encouragement to good teaching, what reason is it, though still pretended, and sometimes perfourmed, to encrease wages, as the child waxeth in learning? Is it to cause the maister to take more paines, and upon such promise, to set his pupille more forward? Nay surely that cannot be. The present payment would set that more forward, then the hope in promise, bycause in such varietie and inconstancie of the parentes mindes, what assuraunce is there, that the child shall continue with the same maister: that he maye receive greater allowance with lesse paines, which tooke greater paines, with lesse allowance? Besides this if the reward were good, he would hast to gaine more, which new and fresh repare of scholers would bring, upon report of the furthering his olde, and his diligent travell. What reason caryeth it, when the labour is lesse, then to enlarge the allowance? the latter maister to reape the benefit of the formers labour, bycause the child makes more shew with him? why? It is the foundacion well and soundly laid, which makes all the upper building muster, with countenaunce, and continuaunce. If I were to strike the stocke, as I am but to give counsell, the first paines truely taken, should in good truth be most liberally recompensed: and less allowed still upward, as the paines diminish, and the ease encreaseth. Wherat no maister hath cause to repine, so he maye have his children well grounded in the *Elementarie.* Whose imperfection at this day doth marveilously trouble both maisters and scholers, so that we can hardly do any good, nay scantly tell how to place the too too raw boyes in any certaine forme, with hope to go forward orderly, the ground worke of their entrie being so rotton underneth. Which weaknes if the upper maister do redresse, when the child commeth under his hand, he cannot but deserve triple wages, both for his owne making, and for mending that, which the *Elementarie* either marred with ignoraunce, or made not for haste, which is both the commonest, and the corruptest kinde of marring in my opinion. For the next maisters wages, I do conceive, that the number in ripenesse under him, will requite the *Elementarie* allowance, be it never so [237] great. For the first maister can deale but with a few, the next with moe, and so still upward, as reason groweth on, and receives without forcing. For the inequalitie of children, it were good a whole companie removed still togither, and that there were no admission into schooles, but foure times in the yeare quarterly, that the children of foresight might be matched, and not hurled hand over head into one forme as now we are foreced, not by substaunce, but by similitude and conjecture at the sudden, which thing the conference betwene the maisters in a resolved plat will helpe wonderfully well forward, when the one saith this have I taught, and this can the child do: the other knoweth this ye should teach, and this your childe should do. Thus much for the *elementarie* maister, that he be sufficiently appointed in himselfe for abilitie, and sufficiently provided for, by parentes for maintenaunce. Now whether one man, or moe shalbe able to perfourme all the *elementarie* pointes, at divers houres, or of force there must be more teachers, that shalbe handled in the *elementarie* it selfe hereafter. Once fore all good entertainement by way of reward, will make very able men to leane this way, and one course of training will breed, a mervelous number of sufficient trainers, whose insufficiencie may now be objected, that such cannot presently be had, though in short time they may. And if there must be moe executours, entertainement will worke that to, and convenientnes of rowme will bring all togither.

3. Grammer maisters.

My greatest travell must be about the *grammer* maister, as ech parent ought to be verie circumspect for his owne private that way. For he is to deale with those yeares, whereupon all the residew do build their likelyhoode to prove well or ill. Wherein by reason of the naturall agilitie of the soule and body, being both unsettled, there is most stirre, and least stay: he perfiteth the *Elementarie* in course of learning: he offereth hope or despaire of perfection to the *tutor* and universitie, in their proceeding further. For whom in consideration of sufficient abilitie, and faithfull travell I must still pray for good

The Grammer maisters entertainement and his sufficiencie.

entertainement, which will alway procure most able persons. For it is a great daunting to the best able man, and a great cutting of of his diligent paynes, when he shall finde his whole dayes [238] travell not able to furnish him of necessarie provision: to do good with the best, and to gaine with the basest, nay much lesse then the lowest, who may entend to shift, when he must entend his charge: and enrich him selfe, nay hardly feede himselfe, with a pure, and poore conscience. But ye will perhaps say what shall this man be able to performe, for whom you are so carefull, to have him so well entertained? to whose charge the youth of our country is to be committed? If there were no more said, even this last point were enough to crave enough, for that charge is great: and if he do discharge it well, he must be well able to do it, and ought to be very well requited for doing it so well. Besides his maners and behaviour, which require testimonie and assurance: besides his skill in exercising and trayning of the body, he must be able to teach the three learned toungues, the *latin*, the *greeke*, the *hebrew*, if the place require so much, if not, so much as is required. Wherin assuredly a mediocritie in knowledge, will prove to meane, to emplant, that in another which he hath in himselfe. For he that meaneth to plant but some litle well: must himselfe farre exceede any degree of mediocrite. He must be able to understand his writer, to maister false printes, unskilfull dictionaries, simple conjectures of some smattering writers concerning the matter of his traine, and be so appointed ear he begine to teach, as he may execute readyly, and not make his owne imperfection, to be a torture to his scooler, and a schooling to him selfe. For it is an ill ground to grow up from ignoraunce by teaching, in that place, where no ignorance of matter at least should be, at the very first: though time and experience do polish out the maner. He must have the knowledge of all the best grammers, to give notes by the way still, though he burden not the childes memorie of course, with any more then shalbe set downe. There are required in him besides these, and further pointes of learning to, as I will note hereafter, *hardnes* to take paines: *constancie* to continew and not to shrinke from his trade: *discretion* to judge of circumstances: *lightsomnes* to delite in the successe of his labour: *hartines* to encourage a toward youth: *regard* to thinke ech childe an *Alexander*: *courteous lowlines* in himselfe, as if he were the meanest, though he were knowne to be [239] the best. For the verie least thing in learning, will not be well done, but onely by him, which knoweth the most, and doth that which he doth with pleasure and ease, by reason of his former store. These qualities deserve much, and in our scooles they be not generally found, bycause the rewardes for labour there be so base and simple, yet the most neare is best in choice, and many there be which would come neare, if entertainement were answerable. Let the parentes, and founders provide for the one: and certainely they shall finde no default in the other.

A meane to have excellent teachers, and professours generally.

There were a way in the nature of a seminarie for excellent maisters in my conceit, if reward were abroad, and such an order might be had within the universitie: which I must touch with licence and for touching crave pardon, if it be not well thought of, as I know it will seeme straunge at the first, bycause of some difficultie in perfourming the devise. And yet there had never bene any alteration to the better, if the name of alteration had bene the object to repulse. This my note but by the way, though it presently parhapes doe make some men muse, yet hereafter upon better consideration, it may prove verie familiar to some good fantasies, and be exceeding well liked of, both by my maisters of the universities them selves, and by their maisters abroad. Whereby not onely schoolemaisters, but all other professours also shalbe made excellently able to performe that in the common weale which she looketh for at their handes, when they come from the universitie. But by the way I protest simply, that I do not tender this wish, as having any great cause to mislike the currant, which the universities be now in: but graunting thinges there to be well done already, I offer no discourtesie in wishing that good to be a great deale better. My conceit

The foure particuler meanes.

resteth in these foure pointes: what if the colleges were devided by 1.
professions and faculties? what if they of the like yeares, and the like 2.
profession, were all bestowed in one house? what if the livings by 3.
uniting were made better, and the colleges not so many: though
farre greater? what if in every house there were great pensions, and 4.
allowances for continuall and most learned readers: which woud end their lives there? what harme could our countrie receive thereby? [240] nay, what good were not in great forwardnes to be done, if this thing were done? And may not the state of the realme do this by authoritie, which gave authoritie to founders to do the other, with reservation of prerogative to alter upon cause? or is not this question as worthy the debating to mend the universities, and to

plant sownd learning: as to devise the taking away landes from colleges, and put the studentes to pension, bycause they cannot use them without jarring among themselves? Were there any way better to cut away all the misliking, wherewith the universities be now charged, and to bring in a new face of thinges both rarer and fayrer?

In the first erection of schooles and colleges, *privat zeale* enflamed good founders: in altering to the better, *publicke consideration* may cause a commoner good, and yet keepe the good founders meaning, who would very gladly embrace any avauncement to the better in any their buildinges. The nature of time is upon sting of necessitie, to enfourme what were best: and the dutie of *pollicie* is, advisedly to consider, how to bring that about which time doth advertise. And if time do his dutie to tell, can *pollicie* avoide blame in sparing to trie? And why should not *publike consideration* be as carefull to thinke of altering to fortifie the state now, as *private zeale* was hoat then to strengthen that which was then in liking?

But I will open these foure interrogations better, that the considerations which leade me, may winne others unto me, or at the least let them see, that it is no meere noveltie which moveth me thus farre.

Of the division of colleges.

Touching the *division* of *colleges* by professions and faculties, I alleege no president from other nations, though I could do diverse, begining even at *Lycaeum, Stoa, Academia* themselves, and so downeward, and in other nations east and southeast ascending upwarde, where studentes cloystured them selves together, as their choice in learning lay: but private examples in their applying to our country may be controuled by generall exception. If there were one college, where nothing should be professed, but languages onely, (as there be some people which will proceede no further) to serve the realme abroad, and studies in the universitie, in that point excellently and absolutelie, [241] were it not convenient? nay were it not most profitable? That being the ende of their profession, and nothing dealt withall there but that, would not sufficiencie be discried by witnes of a number? and would not dayly conference and continuall applying in the same thing procure sufficiencie? Wheras now every one dealing with every thing confusedly none can assuredly say, thus much can such a one do in any one thing, but either upon conjecture which oftentimes deceiveth even him that affirmes: or else upon curtesie which as oft beguiles even him that

The college of toungues.

beleveth. These reasons hold not in this point for toungues onely: but in all other distributions, where the like matter, and the like men be likewise to be matched. For where all *exercises*, all *conferences*, all both private, and publike *colloquies*, be of the same argument, bycause the soile bringeth foorth no other stuffe, there must needes follow great perfection. When toungues, and learning be so severed, it will soone appeare, what ods there is betwene one that can but speake, and him that can do more, whereas now some few finish wordes, will beare away the glorie from knowledge, without consideration, that the gate is without the towne as dismantling bewraies, though it be the entrie into it.

The colledge for the mathematikes.

If an other colledge were for the *Mathematicall* sciences I dare say it were good, I will not say it were best, for that some good wittes, and in some thinges not unseene, not knowing the force of these faculties bycause they never thought them worthey their studie as being without preferment, and within contempt, do use to abase them, and to mocke at mathematicall heades, bycause in deede the studie thereof requireth attentivenes, and such a minde, as will not be soone caried to any publike shew, before his full ripenes, but will rest in solitarie contemplation, till he finde himselfe flidge. Now this their meditation if they be studentes in deede: or the shadow of meditation, if they be but counterfettes, do these men plaie with all, and mocke such mathematicall heades, to solace themselves with.

Plato 7. de rep.

Wherein they have some reason to mocke at mathematicall heades, as they do tearme them, though they should have greater reason, why to cherish, and make much of the mathematicall [242] sciences, if they will not discredit *Socrates* his authoritie, and wisedome in *Plato*, which in the same booke avaunceth these sciences above the moone, whence some learned men fetch his opinion, and force his judgement, as the wisest maister against such as allow of correction in schooles: which they would seeme to banishe, till their owne rod beat them. The very end of that booke is the course that is to be kept in learning in the perfitest kinde, which beginneth at the mathematikes, and it dealeth more with the necessitie of them, then with the whole argument besides: as it is no noveltie to heare that *Plato* esteemed of them, who forbad any to enter his *Academie*, which was not a *Geometrician*, whereunder he contained the other, but specially her sister *Arithmetike*.

For the men which professe these sciences, and give cause to their discountenaunce, they be either meere ignorant, and maintaine their credit with the use of some tearmes, propositions, and particularities which be in ordinarie courses that way, and never came nigh the kernell: or having some knowledge in them in deede, rather employe their time, and knowledge aboute the degenerate, and sophisticall partes of them, applyed by vaine heades to meere collusions though they promise great consequences: then to the true use, and avauncement of art. Howbeit in the meane time, though the one disgrace them with contempt, and the other make them contemptible, by both their leaves I do thinke thus of them: but what a poore thing is my thought? yet some thing it is where it shalbe beleeved. In time all learning may be brought into one toungue, and that naturall to the inhabitant, so that schooling for toungues, may prove nedeles, as once they were not needed: but it can never fall out, that artes and sciences in their right nature, shalbe but most necessarie for any common weale, that is not given over unto to to much barbarousnes. We do attribute to much to toungues, which do minde them more then we do matter chiefly in a monarchie: and esteeme it more honorable to speake finely, then to reason wisely: where wordes be but praised for the time, and wisedom winnes at length. For while the *Athenian*, and *Romaine* popular governementes did yeald [243] so much unto eloquence, as one mans perswasion might make the whole assembly to sway with him, it was no mervell if the thing were in price, which commaunded: if wordes were of weight, which did ravish: if force of sentence were in credit, which ruled the fantsie, and bridled the hearer. Then was the toungue imperiall bycause it dealt with the people: now must it obey, bycause it deales with a prince, and be servaunt unto learned matter, acknowledging it to be her liege, and mistresse. All those great observations of eloquence, are either halfe drowned, for want of a democratie: or halfe douted of for discredit of divinitie: which following the substance of matter, commendeth unto us the like in all studies.

For the credit of these *mathematicall* sciences, I must needes use one authoritie of great, and well deserved countenaunce among us, and so much the rather, bycause his judgement is so often, and so plausibly vouched by the curteouse maister *Askam* in his booke, which I wish he had not himselfe, neither any other for him entitled the *scoolemaister*, bycause myselfe dealing in that argument must needes sometime dissent to farre from him, with some hasard of myne owne credit, seeing his is hallowed. The worthy, and well learned gentleman *Sir John Cheeke*, in the middest of all his great learning, his rare eloquence, his sownd judgement, his grave modestie, feared the blame of a *mathematicall* head so litle in himselfe, and thought the profession to be so farre from any such taint, being soundly and sadly studied by others, as he bewraid his great affection towards them most evidently in this his doing. Being himselfe provost of the kings colledge in *Cambridge*, in the time of his most honored prince, and his best hoped pupill, the good *king Edward*, brother to our gracious soveraine *Queene Elizabeth*, he sent downe from the court one maister *Bukley* somtime fellow of the saide colledge, and very well studyed in the *mathematicalls* to reade *Arithmeticke*, and *Geometrie* to the youth of the colledge: and for the better encouraging of them to that studie gave them a number of *Euclides* of his owne coast. Maister *Bukley* had drawne the rules of *Arithmeticke* into verses, and gave the copies abroad to his hearers. My selfe am to honour the memorie of that learned knight, being partaker my selfe [244] of his liberall distribution of those *Euclides*, with whom he joyned *Xenophon*, which booke he wished, and caused to be red in the same house, and gave them to the studentes, to encourage them aswell to the greeke toungue, as he did to the *mathematikes*. He did I take it asmuch for the studentes in S. *Johns* colledge, whose pupill he had once bene, as he did for us of the kinges colledge whose provost he then was. Can he then mislike the *mathematicall* sciences, which will seeme to honour Syr *John Cheeke*, and reverence his judgement? can he but thinke the opinion to proceede from wisedom, which counteth *Socrates* the wisest maister? Nay how dare he take upon him to be a maister, not of art, but of artes (for so is the name,) which hath not studyed them, ear he proceeded? Are not the proceeders to reade in any of those sciences publickely, by the vice chauncelours appointment, after they have commenced? and do they not promise, and professe the things, when they seeke to procure the titles? And with what face dare ignorance open her mouth, or but utter some sounde of words, where she hath professed the weight of matter? So that the very university her selfe doth highly esteeme of them if she could entreat her people to esteeme of their mothers judgement. These sciences bewray them selves in many professions and trades which beare

Sir John Cheeke.

not the titles of learning, whereby it is well seene, that they are no prating, but profitable grounds: not gay to the shew, but good to be shewed, and such meanes of use, as the use of our life were quite maimed without them. Then gather I, if bare experience, and ordinarie imitation do cause so great thinges to be done by the meere shadow, and roat of these sciences, what would judiciall cunning do, being joyned with so well affected experience? Neither is it any objection of account to say, what should marchaunts, carpentars, masons, shippmaisters, maryners, devisours, architectes, and a number such do with latin, and learning? do they not well enough without, to serve the turne in our countrie? If they do well without might they not do better with? And why may not an English carpentar, and his companions speake that toungue to helpe their countrie the more, being gotten in youth, eare they can be set to other labour, which the *Romaine* artificer [245] did naturally use, seing it is more commendable in ours, where labour is the conquerour, then in the Romain where nature was commendour? As if none should have Latin but those which were for further degrees in learning.

The tounges be helpes indifferent to all trades as well as to learning. Neither is the speaking of Latin any necessarie argument of deeper learning, as the Mathematicall sciences be the olde rudimentes of young children, and the certaine directours to all those artificers, which without them go by roate, and with them might shew cunning. I maye not at this time prosecute this position, as to fremd for this place: but after my Elementarie and toungue schoole, I meane to search it to the very bottom, with the whole profession
1. of those faculties, if God send me life, and health. For the while this shall suffise that these sciences, which we terme the Mathematicalles in their effectuall nature, do worke still some good thing, sensible even to the simple, by number, figure, sound, or motion: In the
2. manner of their teaching they do plant in the minde of the learner, an habite inexpugnable by bare probabilities, and not to be brought to beleeve upon light conjectures, in any other knowledge, being still drawne on by unfallible demonstrations: In their similitudinarie
3. applications, they let one see by them in sense the like affection in contemplative, and intelligible thinges, and be the surest groundes to retourne unto in replies and instances, either upon defect in memorie, or in checke of adversarie, contrarie to the common simil-

itudes. For when ye compare the common weale to a ship, and the people to the passagers, the application being under saile, maye be out of sight, when ye seeke for your proofe. But in these sciences the similitudinarie teaching is so certain in applying, and so confirmed by effectes: as here is nothing so farre from sense, and so secret in understanding, but it will make it palpable. They be taken from the sense, and travell the thought, but they resolve the minde. And though such as understand them not, do mislike them, which yet is no reason in them, nor any disgrace to the thing misliked by them, seeing ignoraunce misliketh: yet those that understand them, maye boldly mislike the mislikers, and oppose the whole auncient Philosophie, and all well appointed [246] common weales against such mockmathematicalles, without whose helpe they could not live, nor have houses to hide their heades, though they thanke not their founders.

If *Philosophie* with her three kindes had the third colledge, were it 3. The colledge for Philosophie.
thinke you unproper? Then the naturall might afterward proceede
to *Physick*, whom she fitteth: the Politicke to *Lawe*, whom she
groundeth: the morall to *Divinitie*, whom she helpeth in discourse.
Which three professions *Divinitie, Lawe, Physick* should every one be
endowed with their particular colledges, and livinges. To have the
Physician thus learned, it were nothing to much, considering his 4.
absolutenesse is learning, and his ignoraunce butcherie, if he do but Gal. περὶ ἀρίστης
marke his owne maister *Galene* in his booke of the best profession. αἱρέσεως.
For the *Divine* to tarie time, and to have the handmaiden sciences to 5.
attend upon their mistres profession, were it any hindrance to his
credit, where discretion the daughter of time is his fairest conusance, and if he come without her, what sternesse so ever he pretend in countenance, we will measure the man, though we marke
his sayinges? The *Lawyers* best note in the best judgementes is con- 6.
tentment, not to covet to much, and for that desire not to strive to
gaine to much: not beyond the extremitie of lawe, but farre on this
side the extremitie of right. And can digesting time be but commodious in this case, and contempt of toyes eare he enter into them,
be but mother to contentment? Time to bread sufficiencie, and sufficiencie to bring sound judgement, cut of all matter of blame, and
leave all matter to praise. But in this distribution where is *Logicke*
and *Rethoricke*, some will saye? Where is *Grammer* then will I saye?
A directour to language. And so *Logicke*, for her demonstrative part,

plaieth the *Grammer* to the *Mathematicalles*, and naturall *Philosophie*: for her probabilitie to morall, and politike, and such other as depend not upon necessitie of matter. *Rhetoricke* for puritie without passion doth joyne with the writer in any kinde, for perswasion with passion, with the speaker in all kindes, and yet both the speaker dealeth sometime quietly, and the plaine writer waxeth very hoate.

1. The necessitie of the college for toungues.

Of these colledges, that which is for *toungues* is so necessary as scant any thing more. For the toungues being receites for [247] matter, without the perfect understanding of them, what hope is there to understand matter? and seeing wordes be names of thinges applyed and given according to their properties, how can thinges be properly understood by us, which use the ministrie and service of wordes to know them by, onelesse the force of speeche be thoroughly knowen? And do you not thinke that every profession hath neede to have a title of the signification of wordes, as well as the civill lawyer? I do see in writers, and I do heare in speakers great defectes in the mistaking of meaninges: and evident errours thorough insufficiencie herin. And as *toungues* cannot be better perfitted, then streight after their entrie by the grammer schoole: so they must be more perfitted, then they can be there. And what if some will never proceede any further, but rest in those pleasaunt kinde of writers, which delite most in gaing of their language, as poëtes, histories, discourses, and such, as will be counted generall men?

2. The necessitie of the Mathematicall colledge.

As for the *Mathematicalles*, they had the place before the toungues were taught, which though they be now some necessarie helpes, bycause we use forreine language for conveaunce of knowledge: yet they push us one degree further of from knowledge. That the *Mathematicalles* had the place, and were proposed still to children, he that hath read any thing in Philosophie cannot be ignorant. *Plato* is full of it, and termeth them commonly the *childrens entraunce*, but cheifly in the seventh booke of his common weale. So is his scholer though long after his death *Philo* the *Jewe* (whom even his countrieman *Josephus*, a man somwhat parciall in praising other, yet calleth a singular man for eloquence and wisdome, speaking of his embassage to *Caius* the Emperour) but specially in that treatise, which he maketh of the foretraine, for so I turne *Platoes* *προπαιδεία*, and *Philoes* *προπαίδευμα*. There he deviseth, as he is a perpetuall allegoriser, *Sara* to be the image of *Divinitie*, and *Agar* the figure of all other handmaiden sciences, wherin he wisheth a young man to

Philo. *περὶ τῆς εἰς τὰ προπαιδεύματα συνόδου.*

deale very long, or he venture upon *Sara*, which will not be fertil but in late, and ripe yeares. He construeth both in that place, and in *Moses* his life also, those wordes of the bringing up of *Moses* in all the doctrine of the *Aegyptians*, to be meant in the Mathematicalles, which was the [248] traine of that time, and the brood of that soile, or there about. And to saye the trueth let any man marke the course of all auncient learning, and he shall finde, that it could not be possibly otherwise, but that the *Mathematicall* was their rudiment, though no historie, no describer of common weale, no setter forth of Philosophers life, no Philosopher himselfe had tolde it us? Is not *Aristotles* first booke of all in course of his teaching, his *Organum*, which conteineth his whole *Logicke*? and in his proofes for the piking out of his *syllogismes* doth he not bewraie, wherin he was brought up? I use *Aristotle* alone for example, bycause our studentes be best acquainted with him: whom yet they cannot understand without these helpes, as one *Bravardine* espied well, though not he alone, who tooke the paines to gather out of *Euclide* two bookes purposely for the understanding of *Aristotle*. Can his bookes of Demonstration, the *Analytica posteriora* be understood without this helpe? His whole treatise of Motion wheresoever, commonly fetcht from the verie forme of the thing moved: His confutation of others by the nature of Motion, and site: His *Mathematicall* discriptions in many places: His naturall *Theoremes* echwhere can they be conceived, much lesse understood by any ignorant in this pointe? Wherin *Aristotle* sheweth us his owne education, to whom he commendeth the like, if we like of him, whose liking will not fall, though fooles oftimes shake it. It were to infinite to use proofes in so generall and so knowne a case, which the whole antiquitie still allowed of, and the famous *Athenian* common weale used even then, when she had the great brood of the most excellent persons, for her ordinary traine to her youth as *Socrates* still alledgeth in *Plato*: or rather *Plato* fathering the speach upon *Socrates* sayth so himselfe. *Aristippus* after his shipwrake found releife thorough that train, and encoraged his companions upon sight of Geometricall figures in the sande. He that will judge of these sciences in generall, what degree they have in the course of learning, and wherin they be profitable to all other studies whatsoever, let him read but either *Proclus* his foure bookes upon *Euclides* first in Greeke, or bycause the greeke is ill, and corruptly printed *Io. Barocius*, a young gentleman of *Venice* which hath turned [249] them into Latin, and corrected the copie. Though many have delt in the argument they be but secondarie to *Proclus*. For he handleth every question that either makes for them, or against them cheifly in his first booke. It were to much for me to stand upon enumeration of testimonies in this place, that the auncient schooling did begin at the *Mathematicall* after the first *Elementarie*, while they minded sound learning in deede, and sequestred their thoughtes from other dealinges in the world. He that marketh but the ordinary metaphores in the eloquentest Greeke writers of that time, whence we prescribe, shall easily bewray, where in the auncient discipline travelled. To alledge the *Romain* for learning is to alledge nothing, 6. Aeneid. whose cunning *Virgile* describeth to lye in governement, and conquestes, remitting other faculties to other people. For till the forreine learning in latter yeares, was translated into their toungue, of themselves they had litle. *Rhetoricke, poetrie, historie, civill lawe,* and some petie treatises of *Philosophie*, and *Physicke* were the *Romaines* learning. Some one, or two as *Gallus*, and *Figulus* were noted for the *Mathematicalles*, as many yeares after them *Julius Firmicus*, and some architecture *Mathematicke* in *Vitruvius*. But their owne stories can tell, what an afterdeale in the wynning of *Syracusae Archimedes* by those faculties put *Marcellus* their generall unto, which yet was as carefull to have saved *Archimedes*, if the rashnesse of a rude soldiar had not prevented his proclamation: as *Demetrius* πολιορκητής was to save *Protogenes* at *Rhodes*. After the state was brought to a monarchie, the Greekes overlaid their learning, as it appeareth, from *Dionysius* of *Halycarnassus*, and *Strabo*, which were in *Augustus Caesars* time, downe still in a number of most notable Grecians, which served that state continually both for training up their young Emperours, and for all other kinde of learning: so that the authoritie of the *Mathematicall* must be fetcht from the Grekes, though they themselves borowed the matter of other nations, and were founders onely to language, methode, and those faculties, which serve for the direction of language.

3. The necessitie of the colledge for Philosophie.

For *Philosophie* to have the third place it will be easily obtained, though there be some pretended doubt in the order of the partes for the training. We use to set young ones to the morall [250] and politike first, and reason against *Aristotles* conclusion, that a young stripling is a fit hearer of morall *Philosophie*. But *Aristotle* himselfe being well brought up in the *Mathematicalles* placeth naturall

Philosophie next unto them, as very intelligible unto very young heades, by reason of their necessarie consequence, and *Theoreticall* consideration. Wheras the other partes being subject to particular circunstance in life are to be reserved for elder yeares. For not onely the *Philosophicall* resolution, but also the very religious was in the best, and eldest time to cause youth abide long in study, and to forbeare publike shew, till it were very late. To make *Logicke*, and *Rhetoricke* serve to those uses, and in those places, where I appointed them, was no absurdity. For *Rhetoricke*, there will be small contradiction, though declamations, and such exercises seeme to make some further claime. *Pythagoras* his five yeares silence, hath a meaning that ye heare sufficiently, eare ye speake boldly. And *Socrates* that great maister in *Plato* calleth *Logicke* the ridge, or toppe of the *Mathematicalles*, as then to succeede, when they were gotten: and good reason, why, bycause their methode in teaching, and order in proving did bring forth *Logicke*. As he that will make *Plato* the example to *Aristotles* preceptes shall easily perceave.

4. 5. 6. The necessitie of three colledges peculiar for Divinitie, Law, Physicke.

For *Divinitie*, *Lawe*, and *Physicke* to have their owne colledges, for their full exercises, and better learning, then now thus to have their studentes scattered, it is a thing that implyeth no great repugnaunce with any reason, and is not without president. As for the *Lawe*, if the whole studie were made one and whatsoever appertaineth to that profession, for either Ecclesiasticall, or Temporall use were reduced into one body, had our countrey any cause to complaine? or but great cause to be very glad? wheras now three severall professions in lawe, bewraye a three headed state, one *English* and *French*, an other, Romish Imperiall, the third Romish ecclesiasticall, where meere *English* were simply our best. I shall not neede to say any more herein, but onely give occasion to those which can judge, and helpe it, to thinke of the position: the distraction of temporall, civill, and Canon lawe being in many pointes very offensive to our countrey. [251]

Some difficultie there will be to winne a colledge for such as shall afterward passe to teache in schooles.

7. The seventh colledge for training maisters, and the necessitie therof.

There is no diverting to any profession till the student depart from the colledge of *Philosophie*, thence he that will go to *Divinitie*, to *Lawe*, to *Physicke*, may, yet with great choise, to have the fittest according to the subject. He that will to the schoole is then to divert. In whom I require so much learning to do so much good, as none of

the other three, (honour alway reserved to the worthinesse of the subject which they professe,) can chalenge to himselfe more: either for paines which is great: or for profit which is sure: or for helpe to the professions: which have their passage so much the pleasaunter, the forwarder studentes be sent unto them, and the better subjects be made to obay them: as the scholing traine is the trak to obedience. And why should not these men have both this sufficiencie in learning, and such roome to rest in, thence to be chosen and set forth for the common service? be either children, or schooles so small a portion of our multitude? or is the framing of young mindes, and the training of their bodies so meane a point of cunning? be schoolemaisters in this Realme such a paucitie, as they are not even in good sadnesse to be soundly thought on? If the chancell have a minister, the belfray hath a maister: and where youth is, as it is eachwhere, there must be trainers, or there will be worse. He that will not allow of this carefull provision for such a seminarie of maisters, is most unworthy either to have had a good maister him selfe, or herafter to have a good one for his. Why should not teachers be well provided for, to continue their whole life in the schoole, as *Divines, Lawyers, Physicians* do in their severall professions? Thereby judgement, cunning, and discretion will grow in them: and maisters would prove olde men, and such as *Xenophon* setteth over children in the schooling of *Cyrus*. Wheras now, the schoole being used but for a shift, afterward to passe thence to the other professions, though it send out very sufficient men to them, it selfe remaineth too too naked, considering the necessitie of the thing. I conclude therfore that this
1. trade requireth a particular college, for these foure causes. First for
the subject being the meane to make or mar the whole [252] frye of
2. our state. Secondly for the number, whether of them that are to
3. learne, or of them that are to teache. Thirdly for the necessitie of the
4. profession which maye not be spared. Fourthly for the matter of
their studie which is comparable to the greatest professions, for language, for judgement, for skil how to traine, for varietie in all pointes of learning, wherin the framing of the minde, and the exercising of the bodie craveth exquisite consideration, beside the staidnes of the person.

These seven colledges being so set up, and bearing the names of the thinges which they professe, for *Toungues*, for *Mathematickes*, for *Philosophie*, for *Traine*, for *Physicke*, for *Lawe*, for *Divinitie* were there any great absurditie committed either in the thing if it were so, or in me for wishing it so? If it had bene thus appointed at the first, as it might, if the whole building had bene made at once, which is scant possible where thinges grow by degrees, and buildinges by patches: it would have bene liked very well, and the Universities in their commencementes, and publike actes would have commended their pollicy, and wisedome, which first did appoint it. And maye not that be now toucht without blame, which if it had bene then done, had deserved great honour, and when soever it shall be done will deserve everlasting memorie? and maye now be well done, seeing we have all thinges needful for the well doing redie: And why should it seeme straunge to wish such an alteration, seeing greater chaunges have bene both wished, and wrought within this our time? Sad, and lingring thoughts, which measure common weales as buildinges grounded upon some rocke of marble, finde many, and sober difficulties: resolute mindes make no bones: there is stuffe enough, the places be ready, the landes be neither to be begd, ne yet to be purchased, they be got, and given already: they maye be easily brought into order, seeing our time is the time of reformation. Before my wish be condemned, I desire my reader to consider it well, and marke if it maye take place, and whether it maye not with great facilitie.

2. The second meane, to sorte like yeares into the same roomes.

For sorting like yeares into one roome, which was my second interrogatorie, it is no new device, nor mine: All good common weales not fained by fantsie, but being in deede such, [253] have used it both for likenes of education in like yeares, and for trying out where most excellencie lodged, to bestow prefermentes upon apparant desert, besides that it is most fit, and emulation to the better doth best beseeme like yeares. The greeke poet saith, that God draweth allway the like to the like, and therefore men may well follow the president.

3. The third meane to better the studentes maintenaunce.

For uniting of colledges, enlarging of the united, and bettering studentes livinges, I dare say none of them wilbe against me, which for a better living will chaung his colledge. Neither will he thinke it any great losse to leave his old poore place, for a fatter rowme, which for such a one will abandon the universitie and all. Sure the livings in colledges be now to to leane, and of necessitie force good wittes to fly ear they be well feathered. More sufficiencie of living will yeald more convenient time and furniture to studie, which two be the onely meanes to procure more sufficiencie in learning, more ripenes in judgement, more stay in maners. The necessitie of studentes may thus be supplyed of their owne, and they not forced by accepting of exhibition at some handes to admit some bondage under hand. Restraint will ridde needelesse number: sufficient livinges will maintaine, and make the nedefull number sufficiently well learned. I neede not staie any longer here. For methinke all those good studentes joyne with me in this fourme of the universitie, whom want, and barenes of living will not suffer to tarie long enough there, and better it were for our countrie to have some smaller meanie wel trayned, and sufficiently provided, then a loose number, and an unlearned multitude. And there were two questions more worthy the resolution, then all *Iohannes Picus* the erle of *Mirandula* his nine hundred propounded at *Rome*: the one whether it were agreable to the nature of learning being liberall in condition to be *elemosinarie* in maintenaunce: the other whether it were for a common weale to have the conceit bound to respectes, bycause of private exhibition, which ought to direct simply, without respect, saving to the state alone. For sure where learning growes up by props, it leaseth her propertie: where the stocke of it selfe will beare up the bowes, there it must be best, if choice be made leader, and fit wittes bestowed on bookes. [254] My three forraine pointes for the furtheraunce of learning be, *choice* for wittes, *time* for furniture, *maintenaunce* for direction: what shalbe peculiar to the partie, himselfe must tender, as therein being detter to *God*, and his countrie. *Diligence* to apply his wit, *continuaunce* to store his time, *discretion* to set furth his maintenaunce, are required at his handes.

4. The fourth meane for readers.

For *readers* of yeares, of sufficiencie, of continuance, methinke I durst enter into some combat that it were beyonde all crie profitable, and necessarie, to have whom to follow, and of whom to learne how to direct our studies, for *yeares* auncient fathers: for *sufficiencie* most able to enstruct: for *continuance* cunning to discerne persons, and circumstaunces: for *advise* skillfull to rule rash heades, which runne on to fast, being armed with some private opinion of their owne petie learning. What was *Plato* to the *Academikes*? *Aristotle* to the *Peripatetikes*? *Xeno* to the *Stoiks*? *Epicure* to the *Epecurians*? *Aristippus* to the *Anicerian* and *Cyrenaike*? and other such fathers to the famulies of their professions, but *readers*? It is a mervell to thinke on, how longe those fellowes continued in their profession as *Diogenes*

Laertius doth note. It should seeme that *Plato* taught above fiftie yeares, reckening the time that he left *Speusippus* his deputie during his travell into *Aegypt* and that way: whereby both himselfe proved an excellent maister, and his hearers proved most excellent scholers. They that have bene acquainted with cunning *readers* any where will subscribe to this I know.

Private studie tied to one booke led by one braine: not alway the best (as what counsellour is commonly worse to ones selfe, then himselfe?) so proceeding as the first impression leads, be it what it can be, cannot compare for judiciall learning with the benefit of hearing one, nay of repeating to one upon interrogatories after reading, to trie his judgement, his keeping, and remembrance: which one hath red, and digested all the best bookes, or at the least all the best bookes in that kinde, whereof he maketh profession: which hath a judgement settled and resolute by the helpe of all those good braines: which hath dealte with thousandes of the pregnantest wittes, whom experience hath taught stay, whom the common weale [255] by sufferance commendes as sufficient. He that is not acquainted with such an excellent reader or teacher (for both the names import one thing) and that with repetition, but pleaseth himselfe with his owne private studie, as he taketh more paines undoutedly, so getteth he lesse gaine I dare assure him, having in one lecture the benefit of his *readers* universall studie, and that so fitted to his hand, as he may streight way use it, without further thinking on: whereas when he hath beaten his owne braines privatly about a litle, for want of time to digest, being to forward to put foorth, he uttereth that which he must either amend upon better advice, or quite revoke when he findes he is over shot. Wherfore such *readers*, or rather such *nurses* to studie, must needes be maintained with great allowance, to make their heaven there, where ye meane to use them. Whose service, for the benefit that comes from them will save their whole hier in very bookes, which the student shall not so much neede, when his *reader* is his librarie: neither must they be soules, as we tearme them, though of great reading, neither is it enough to have read much, but they must be of great government withall, which are to bring up such a frie of governers. And therefore that great sufficiencie doth still call for great recompence to be tyed to a stake for it all ones life time.

That this wish is most profitable to the universitie, and hurthfull no not to any particular.

But now I pray you by this wish of mine be the universities in common sence any whit endammaged? if they were, so the harme were but some litle and the good exceeding great, the dammage might be consumed by the greatnes of the good. I finde not any harme offered them, they lease no landes, studentes be not put to pensions, they that be thought fit, finde better and fuller maintenaunce, better meane is made to prove learned, by such excellent *readers*, which the cunninger they be, the more affable they be, and thereby the fitter to satisfie any studentes dout in that which they professe. And where yong men may staie untill they be singular, and have good meanes to make them singular, is not the thing to be wished, and he that wisheth it, not to be thought to wish the *universitie* harme, where it is universally holpen? If this transposing of houses to this use were commaunded by authoritie, and by [256] some helpe of wealthy patrones for the common goods sake, were happily accomplished, the *universitie* should lease nothing, though they break up for a time, and the studentes gave place, to masons, and carpenters, nay though the whole revenew of all the colledges were for that time bestowed upon the alteration. And yet all that trouble should not neede, if the first were first begune, and so particularly in order, neither should any student now well placed complaine of the chaunge if he would set himselfe to any certaine profession. This is but my conceit which the effect will confirme, and wise considerations will finde, that it carieth a good ground: besides that it is all ready in verie neare possibilitie, without any great charge, and with verie great good, as also certainetie, and greatnes of annuitie would streight way raise up *readers*, and afterward continew them. How good, and how easie a thing this were, the attempt by so many particular *readers* would shew, which being themselves excellently well learned in those argumentes, that I do appoint to colledges, and professing them in convenient houses of their owne, would undoutedly drawe as many into their private hostelles, as there be now studentes in publicke colledges. All this my wish offereth greater difficulty, in the maner, how to worke it: then dout of profit, in the thing, if we had it. Howbeit harder thinges have bene easily accomplished, but any more profitable was never compassed: neither doth it repent me to wish that, which I would rejoyce to see. If the hindring lie in cost, it is somwhat, and yet but small, considering what is ready: if in good will: that is all, and yet but ill, considering what it hindereth. For no learning is so well got, where her helping meanes be severed, as where all be united, which those colledges would cause: a thing neither of novelty, as of an old ground and elswhere practised: neither injuriouse, to any offering profit to all. I do finde my selfe so armed in the point, as if there were any hope in the thing to be effected, I could answeare any objection of difficultie, which might arise against it, either from without the *universitie*, or from within, either for any communitie, or for any private, that it would be best for all, neither any breach of good now well laied, nor any hindraunce to any, which findes himselfe at ease, as the present is now appointed. [257] But will ye have everie one rise through all these degrees of learning, ear he become a professour? yea surely I. But who moveth the question? either he that cannot judge, who is therefore to be pardoned: or he that would be doing, who is therefore to be blamed: or he that doth not way it, which would be desired to do: or he whom neede hasteneth, whose case is to be pitied. And yet of all these foure, only he, that desireth to shew him selfe ripe in his owne, though raw in other mens opinion, will contrarie the conclusion: for ignoraunce, will yeeld upon better instruction: just consideration, wil relent after waing: good wittes oppressed with want, and yet waing the truth, will wish for more wealth to tarie their full time, and the cariage of their cunning: but the hastie heades, to whom any delaie is present death, which will be doing, eare they can do well, but in their owne conceites they will stand against it, and scrape all defences, though while they do scrape, they descrie them selves to be extreme ignorant. For if sufficiencie be the onely meane to perfit the professour, and to profit the publike, insufficiencie overthrowes both. And as he that meaneth to turne before, may lymit his ascent: so he that will be perfit in the end and last profession ought at the least to have the contemplative knowledge of all that goeth before, though he practise but at pleasure. The generall gaine thereby is this that while the studentes youth is wedded to honest, and learned meditation, the heat of that stirring age is cooled which might harme in publicke, and set all on fire: ripe judgement is got, to stay, not to stirre: and all ambitiouse passions mervellously daunted through resolutenes of judgement. It is no reason, where see ye the like? but it is a great reason, the like is worth seeing, and who so comes neare, is still better liked, then he that dowteth of it. The want of triall, is some shift for a time, but the triall that hath bene, may lead us to the like, and procure good allowance. And sure till the yong professours be made to tarie longer, and studie sounder, neither shall learning have credit, nor our countrie be but sicke. It is not my complaint, though I joyne with the complainantes. If ye meane to take learning before you, you will never move the question. It is not he that hath, and knoweth, which moveth [258] the question, but he that knoweth not and should. What should a *divine* do with the *mathematikes*? why was *Moises* trained in all the *Aegyptians* learning? Nay in one reason for all, why will ye condemne in *divinitie*, or execute in *law*, the sciences which ye know not, but finde the name condemned? and I pray you with what warrant? what if that be not the name? or what if the thing be not such? a condemnation without evidence where the judge presumeth, and knoweth not the skill, which he saith is naught. The *Physician* should have all, and if he have not, he is most to be blamed, bycause the parents of his profession durst not professe without them, and make them under meanes. To be short I wish they had them, which mislike that they have not, and give ignorance the raigne. For if they had them, we should heare no speach, but praise and proufe, admiration and honour.

But to turne to my byace againe which was the mother, and matter to my wish, this colledge for teachers, might proove an excellent nurserie for good schoolemaisters, and upon good testimonie being knowne to so many before, which would upon their owne knowledge assure him, whom they would send abroad. In the meane time till this come to passe, the best that we can have, is best worthy the having, and if we provide well for good teachers, that provision will provide us good teachers.

The admission of teachers.

There remaineth now one consideration in the admitting not of these, whom I admit without any exception, for all sufficiencie in religion, in learning, in discretion, in behaviour: but of such as we daily use, and must use, till circumstances be bettered which are in compasse of many exceptions. The admitter or chuser considering what the place requireth must exact that cunning, which the place calleth for: the partie himselfe must bring testimonie of his owne behaviour, if he be altogither unknowen: and the admission would be lymited to such a schoole in such a degree of learning, as he is found to be fit for. For many upon admission and licence to teach in generall, overreach to farre, and marre to much, being unsufficient at randon, though serving well for certaine by way of restraint. Thus much for the trainer, which I know will better my patterne [259] if preferment better him: with whom I shall have occasion to deale againe in my grammer schoole: where I will note unto him what my opinion is in the particularities of teaching.

Chapter 42.

How long the childe is to continue in the elementarie ear he passe to the toungues, and grammer. The incurable infirmities which posting hast worketh in the whole course of studie. How necessarie a thing sufficient time is for a scholer.

Hastie preasing onward is the greatest enemie, which any thing can have whose best is to ripe at leasure. For if ripenes be the vertue, before it is greene, after it is rotten: and yet the excesse is the lesse harme: bycause it may joyne, and be compounded with the vertue, and be called rotten ripe: and at the least be cast away, without any more losse, then of the thing it selfe, as it appeareth in frutes. The defect to plucke before ripenes, breedes ill in the partie which tasteth therof, and causeth the thing after a bite or two to be cast away to: unlesse it be in longing wymen, whose distemperate delite upon a cause not common, doth give us to judge, that too timely taking, is but for some disordered humours. This plucking before ripenes in my position tendeth to this ende. I have appointed in my elementarie traine *reading, writing, drawing, singing, playing*: now if either all these be unperfitly gotten, where all be attempted, or some, where some: when the childe is removed to the grammer schoole, what an error is committed? The thinges being not perfit, to serve the consequence, either die quite if they be not sevearly called on: or come forward with paine, where the furtherance is in feare. How many small infantes have we set to *grammer*, which can scarecely reade? how many to learne *latin*, which never wrate letter? And yet though some litle one could doe much better then all his fellowes, it were no harme for him to be captaine a good while in his *elementarie* schoole, rather then to be a meane souldier in a captaine schoole. The displeasoures be beyond all proportion pernicious, beyond all multitude many, which this posting pulles [260] after it. And if moning could amend them, I would not onely mone them, that they be so many, but also mourne for them, that they be so helpeles. It is a world to see the weakenes of children, and the fondnes of friendes in that behalfe. It is to much, that may be understood, where so much is said: the fault is generall, and the onely cause, which both makes children loth to learne, and the maisters seeme to be tormenters in their teaching. For the maister hasting on to the effect of his profession, and the scholer drawing backe, as not able to beare the burden: there riseth a conflict in the maister, with passion, if it conquere him: against passion if he conquere it. If the maister be verie sharp witted in delivering, and the boy slowheaded in receiving, then the passion will lightly conquer. Which it cannot doe, where wisedome and consideration in the maister be armed aforehand with pacience, or where experience and wearines of extremitie have wrought a calmenes. And as in the maister passion breedes heat, so in the childe infirmitie breedes feare, and so much the more, if he finde his maister somwhat to fierce. Whereupon neither the one nor the other can do much good at all, and all through this hastie imperfection being the matter of heat in the one, and of feare in the other. Whereof if the boy were not in daunger how peart would he be, and what a pleasure would the maister take in such a perfit perteling? but when the childe is so weake, as both he himselfe feeles it in his learning, and the maister findes it in his teaching, tell the parent so he will not beleeve it. So blynde is affection in the parent which cannot see: and in stoore of teachers, he shall finde some, which will undertake, and condemne the misliker. Whereby chaunge feedes his humor for the time, and repentance his follie long after, when the default proves uncurable, and the first maister is admitted among the prophetes. Such a thing it is to prevent illes in time, and when warning is given not to mocke the intelligence, nor to blame the watchman.

If the imperfections which come more of haste then of ignoraunce from the Elementary schoole would take up their *Inne* there, and raunge no further, the moane were not so much, bycause [261] there were some meane to redresse: but now as one billow driveth on an other: so hast beginning there makes the other successions in learning trowle on too too headlong. Be young children set to soone to their *Grammer* onely? be none sent to the *Universitie*, which when they come thence some yeares after, might well with good gaine returne to the *Grammer* schoole againe? I will not saye that they were not ready when they went, but peradventure they were ready, and forgat that they were so. Do not some good honest wittes in the middest of their studie finde the festering of haste, and wishe though in vaine that they had bene more advised in their passage? and if they recover that which they misse and wish for, do they not finde the learned conclusion trew: that such thinges be extreme painful to setled memories, which were very pleasaunt passages to the youngest boyes? He that beginnes his *Grammer* in any language, when he is a *Graduate*, may perhaps wish for some way without *Grammer*, and covet a *Compendium*. The *Universities* can best judge of the infirmities in our *Grammer* schooles, when they finde the want in those yonglinges, whom they have from us, but not sent by us: we our selves see them, but we cannot salve them. Private affection overrules all reason: straungenesse betwene the parent and maister cuttes of conference in the removing: and in some places multitude of schooles marres the whole market: where store is the sore, and oportunitie to alter an allurement to the worse. So that by degrees the *Elementarie* feebleth the *Grammarian*: and the *Grammarian* transporteth his weaknesse from his schoolemaister to his *Universitie tutour*. Such a matter it is to stay hast at the first, which distempereth till the last. I would not have the *Universities*, but to thinke freindly of me, bycause though I finde fault, I seeke it not: neither blase I it with discredit to them, but wish it healed with the profit of my countrey, as I well know the most, and best of them there do.

Doth not want of sufficient time (I meane not for taking degrees, bycause that time may be complete from the proceeders first arivall into the *Universitie*) but for want of age and yeares: and therwithall for the want of that, which yeares do bring, oftimes send abroad youthes, whose degrees deserve place, [262] but their depth deserves none? That prentice is to hastely out of his yeares, which being at one and twentie free from his maister, is eare foure and twentie free from his thrift both reft of goodnesse, and left goodlesse. If men abroad had not a sensible judgement in yeares, that young ware cannot be but greene, how sprooting faire so ever it doth shew: youth might deceive them with titles, as it deceives it selfe with opinions. *Yeares* without *stuffe* maye beguile before *triall: yeares* with *stuffe* will abide the *stampe*: *Stuffe* without *yeares* is wounderous for a while, but it is subjecte to quicke withering, and to fade of wonder. Neither *stuffe* nor *yeares*, is extreme pitifull, and the very ground of my complaint, bycause neither few yeares can provide great *stuffe*, yea to the best witte: nor many yeares to any witte, without great studie, which is a death there, where the defecte is great. How fortuneth it then, that either freindes be so foolish, or studentes so unstayed, to haste so with so much waste? The causes be: *impacience*, which can abide no tarying, where a restlesse conceit is full frawght: *libertie*, to live as he listeth, bycause he listeth not to live as he should: *braverie*, to seeme to be some body, and to cary a countenaunce: *hope* of preferment, to desire dignities before abilitie to discharge. In the meane while: the *common weale* becomes private: the *generall* weapeth, while the *particular* winneth: and yet the winning is no soundnesse, but shew. What notable men have dealt with, and against the forestaulling of sound time in professions? Among many if onely *Vives* the learned *Spaniard*, were called to be witnesse, he would crave pardon for his owne person, as not able to come for the goute, but he would substitute for his deputie his whole twentie bookes of disciplines, wherin he entreateth, how they come to spoile, and how they may be recovered. Lacke of time not onely in his opinion, but also in whose not? bringes lacke of learning, which is a sore lacke, where it ought not to be lacking. The cankar that consumeth all, and causeth all this evill is haste, an *unadvised, rashe, hedlong counsellour*, and then most pernicious when it hath either some apparence in reason that the child is ripe: or the hartning of some maister, which either is disposed to follow where he seeth replying past cure: or that cannot discern colours, bycause [263] he is that in his degree, which the childe is in his: both unripe: the one to teach, the other to remove.

But what if hope of exhibition make an Universitie man straine? and either perswade abilitie, or promise to supplie, where abilitie wantes? Nay what if exhibitours of some litle, seeke recompence to soone, and halfe force some poore scholer to toile with imperfection?

When the unripe boye findeth any such meane to go to the Universitie, the maister shall never know, till he be booted, if he do know then: for feare of stopping his journey by contrarie counsell: that is by reason to stay him, which runnes to his owne harme.

Time of it selfe, as it is the noblest circunstance wherwith we have to deale: so it hath a bredth in it selfe capeable of to much, to litle, and enough.

To much *time* is seldome found fault with justly, though some time pretended, bycause it is seldome taryed for in this kinde wherwith I deale.

To litle *time* is that wheron I complaine, and so much the more harmefull, bycause hast to attaine unto the desired ende makes it seeme no fault till the blow be given.

Time enough is that meane which perfiteth all, the *Elementarie* in his kinde, the *Grammarian* in his, the *Graduate* in his, and so profiteth the *common weale* by perfiting all: the *prerogative* to thought: the *mother* to truth: the *tuchestone* to ripenesse: the *enemy* to errour: mans only stay, and helpe to advice.

For the Grammarians *time*, though it be not within this argument, as many other thinges which the affinitie drew in, yet thus much may I say. That his perfitnesse hath a pitche, and his yeares yeilde his good, as it shall appeare in his owne place, whose time must needes be limited, bycause he is so placed after the *Elementarie*, and before the *Universitie*, as the well appointing of his *time* shall disapoint neither of them. For the *times*, and yeares of studie before degrees in the Universitie, *Plato* himselfe in his exquisite *republike* cannot, nor doth not appoint them better then they be there already, if the *Grammar*, and *Elementarie* haste marred not, and made them that come to soone seeke also to proceede to soone, yet even so fulfilling [264] statutes, which appoint the continuing yeares, though smallie for their benefit, which are not appointed in yeares, and lesse then not appointed in substaunce. The distances betwene degrees orderly employed, and the midle learninges being caryed before them, as it is imported by their stiles: might worke in the most very reasonable knowledge, for methode and ground in habite, though not for particulars, which be alwayes endlesse, still without art, though most within experience, for their most needfull number. Now if that helpe of readers, which I wished for, were put in execution, me thinke, the world should see, a marveilous number of excellent professours in every degree. I am to long in talking of to litle: but the times hanging one upon another have led me thus onward: wherfore it is now time for me to determine that time, which I do take to be enough for the *Elementarie*. When the child can read so readily, and roundly, as the lenght of his lesson shal nothing trouble him for his reading: when he can write so faire and so fast, as no kinde of exercise shalbe tedious unto him for the writing: when his penne or pencill shall delite him with bragge: when his *Musicke* both for voice, and hand is so farre forward, as a litle voluntarie will both maintaine, and encrease it: all which thinges the second maister must have an eye unto: then hath the *Elementarie* had time enough. If the parent account not of all, yet perfitnesse in his choice must be his cheife account. The childes ordinarie exercises, will continue his writing, and reading, himselfe will alwaye be drawing, bycause it deliteth his eye, and busieth not his braine. But for *Musicke*, the maister and the parentes delite must further it. For that in those yeares, children be Musicall rather for other then for them selves. Once in, this is a certaine ground, and most infallible, that in tarying long, and perfiting well, there is no losse of time, specially seeing those qualities even alone, be a pretie furniture of houshold if they be well gotten. The hasting on to fast to see the frute too soone, when circunstances perswade tarying, is to winne an houre in the morning, and to lease the daye after. Thus much concerning the *Elementarie* time, determinable not by yeares, but by sufficiencie. If yeares could be limittes to knowledge, as they be very good leaders, [265] the rule were more certaine: but where witte goeth not by yeares, nor learning without, sufficiencie is the surest bounder, to set out, wherin enough is. Howbeit in the *Elementarie,* and so forth I will limit the time somwhat nearer, with all the considerations, both for varietie of the matters which are to be learned, and the men which are to teach, and such thinges as seeme not so proper to be set downe here.

Chapter 43.

How to cut of most inconveniences wherwith schooles and scholers, maisters and parentes be in our schooling now most troubled. Wherof there be two meanes, uniformitie in teaching and publishing of schoole orders. That uniformitie in teaching hath for companions dispatch in learning, and sparing of expenses. Of the abbridging of the number of bookes. Of curtesie and correction. Of schoole faultes. Of friendlinesse betwene parentes and maisters.

A great learned man in our dayes thought so much of the troublesome and toilsome life, which we teachers lead, as he wrate a pretie booke of the miseries of maisters. We are to thanke him for his good will: but when any kinde of life be it high, be it low, is not troubled with his proportion to our portion, we will yeild to misery. Our life is very painfull in deede, and what if beyond comparison painfull? Much a do we have, and what if none more? Yet sure many as much, though they deale not with so many, and moe more miserable, bycause they better not so many. But I will neither rip up those thinges, which seeme most restlesse in us, though the argument offer spreding: neither will I medle with any other trade, no lesse troublesome then teaching, by comparing to seeme to lessen: bycause comparisons in miseries be uncomfortable to both, though some ease to either. To what purpose should I shew, why the maister blames this, the parent that, the child nothing more then the rod, though he will not but deserve it? Such a disease we have to repine at the paine, and not to waye the offence, which deserveth the paine. Why beat ye him sayeth one? Why offended he sayeth none? so hard a thing it is to finde [266] defense for right, so easie a thing it is to finde qualifying for wrong. Therefore to omit these unpleasaunt rippinges, I will deale with the remedies how to cut of the most of those, which he calles miseries, I terme *inconveniences*, wherwith the trade of teaching at this day seemeth to have a great conflict. Which counsell though it be first laid for the youngest scholers, yet may it well be translated further, and beseeme both the biggest, and best, in any learned course. P. Melancthon.

These remedies I take to be two: The one *uniformitie* in *teaching*, which draweth after it, *dispatch* in *learning*, and *sparing* of *expenses* about to great a number of bookes. 1.

The other is *publike schoole lawes*, set downe, and seen, which bring with them for companions *agreement* of parents and teachers, *continuance* of scholers, *conference* to amend, *comfort* to freindes, and *commoditie* to the common countrey. 2.

For *uniformitie* in *teaching* how many gaules that will heale, wherwith schooles be now greived, it will then best appeare, when it Uniformitie in teaching.

shalbe shewed, what good it will worke, and how necessarie a thing it is, to have all schooles reduced unto it. That there is to much variety in teaching, and therfore to much ill teaching (bycause in the midst of many bypathes, there is but one right waye) he were senseles, that sees not: if he either have taught, or have bene taught himselfe. Which whence it springeth, diversities of judgement bewraie, that men have gotten by better or worse training up in youth: by lesse or more travell in studie: by longer or shorter continuance at their booke: by liking or misliking some trade in teaching: by accommodating themselves to the parentes choice: and many wayes moe, which either brede varietie, or else be bred by varietie. But of all varieties there is none vayner, then when ignoraunce sweares that that is an *aphorisme*, the contrarie wherof sound knowledge hath set downe for a sure *oracle*. Now in this confusion of varieties what hinderance hath *youth*? what discredite receive *schooles*? what inequalities be the *Universities* molested with? what toile is it to *Tutours*? how small riddaunce to *readers*? when diversities of groundworke do hinder their building, and the scholers weakenesse discrieth his maister? And yet oftimes the weake maister bringes up a strong scholer, by [267] some accident not ordinarie, and the cunninger man by some ordinarie let makes small shew of his great labour. Do not the learners also themselves commonly when they come to yeares and misse that commoditie, which ther maisters could not give them, being very weake themselves, then blame their fortune and feele the want of foresight? For if varietie had bene wipte awaye by uniformitie, even the weakest maister might have done very well if he had had but a meane head to follow direction being set downe to his hand.

This pointe is so plaine as many of the best learned, and of the best teachers also oftimes complaine of it, and wish the redresse, though they still draw backe, and spare their owne paines for any thing they publish: perhaps not having the oportunitie and leasure which so great an enterprise craveth: perhaps being induced by hope that some other will start up, and publish the amendment. Whereby all the youth of this whole Realme shall seeme to have bene brought up in one schoole, and under one maister, both for the matter and manner of traine, though they differ in their owne invention which is private and severall to every one by nature, though generall and one to every one by art. Which thing must needes turne to the profit of the *learner*, whose *straying* shalbe straited, that he cannot go amisse: to the ease of the *teacher* whose *labour* shalbe lightened, by the easinesse of his curraunt: to the honour of the *countrey*, which thereby shall have great store of sufficient stuffe: and the immortall *renown* of that carefull *Prince* which procured such a good. Which benefit say I must proceede from some *uniforme* kinde of teaching set downe by authoritie, that one waye to supplie all wantes, and no one to disdaine, where obedience is enjoyned. And wheras *difference* in judgement worketh *varietie*: *consent* in knowledge will plant *uniformitie*. Which consent, as it must be enforced by authoritie, so must it proceede from some likenesse of abilitie in teachers, namely in that thing wherof they are teachers: though both in executing the same, and for some other qualities they may differ much.

Now the onely waye to worke this likenesse or rather samenesse in abilitie, where otherwise the oddes is so odde, were to set downe in some certain plat, the best that may seeme to be, [268] if that which is best in deede may not be had, as why not? both what and how to teach, with all the particular circunstances, so farre forth as they ordinarily do fall within common compasse, and may best beseeme the best ordered schooles, which both the meane teacher may wel attaine unto, and the cunning maister may rest content with, and so they both in that pointe prove equall, while the meaner mounting upword with fethers made for him, and the cunninger comming downward at the shew of the lure, they both meete in the midde waye, and flying forward like freindes, pay their price with their pastime, and mend their faire with their praye, no dishonour offered him, whom mo qualities do commend: and a great helpe to him that cannot swimme without. In whom diligence borne up, will worke no lesse wonder, nay may fortune more, then greater learning in the other, whom either over weyning may make insolent, or loytring negligent. And sure as I may be deceived herein, so have I some reason very favorable to my seeming, that it were more fitting for the common profit, to provide a certaine direction to helpe the meane teacher, which will continue in the trade without either any or very late changing of his course, and so a long time do much good, then to leave it at randon to the libertie of the more learned, who commonly use teaching, but to shift with for a time, and be but pilgrimes in the profession, still minding to remove to some other kinde of life, either of more ease, which allureth soone, or of more gaine which enforceth sore. So that in the meane time the scholers cannot profit much, while the maisters deale like straungers, which entending one day to returne to their countrey, as nature calleth homeward, though profit bid tary, cannot have that zealous care, which the naturall countrieman, and continuall travellour of nature hath, and of duetie sheweth. And though conscience cause some odde honest man to worke well, and discharge his duetie in that rowling residence: yet neither be priviledges generall, nor lawes levelled after some few, and that foolish fellow, was fretished for cold, which followed the fond *swallow*, that flew out to timely, and to farre before her fellowes. An order must be generall to the liking of the better, who should alwaye wishe it, and the leading of the [269] weaker, who shall alway neede it.

If when this order for matter and manner of teaching shalbe set downe, the executor prove negligent, and prolong the effect, or else quite defeat it, by ill handling of that, which was well ment, the surveiors and patrones of schooles must overlooke such teachers, of themselves if they can, if not, they may call for the assistaunce of *learning*, which for cunning can, and of curtesie will seeke to further such a thing. Our preceptes be generall, the particular must perfourme, and amend his owne accident. I have but sleightly noted the surface of *uniformitie* in teaching, and the disjoynting of skill by misordered varietie, and yet who is so blinde as he may not thereby discerne, that the one strips away the evilles which the other bringes in, and thereby cuttes of many encombraunces from schooles?

Dispatch in learning.

Now *uniformitie* in *teaching* once obtained, doth not *dispatch* in *learning* incontinently follow? which consisteth in choice of the best and fittest authours at the first, and continuaunce in the same: in the best exercises and most proper to the childes ascent in learning: and generally in the maisters orderly proceeding, and methode in teaching: whereby the child shall not learne any thing, which he must or ought to forget, upon his maisters better advise: nor leave any needefull thing unlearned till his maister grow to better advise. The maister himselfe shall not neede to chaunge his course, as he chaungeth his skill, now coursing on to fast by to much rashnes: now retiring to late by to louse repentaunce: finally neither the maister nor the scholer shall busie themselves to long about a litle, and never the better, nor hast to fast on, and never a whit the further. The best course being hit on at the first, as appointment may procure it, one thing helpeth an other forward naturally, without forcing: that which is first taught maketh way for that which must follow next, and continuall use will let nothing be forgot, which is once well got, and the rising up by degrees in learning will succede in proportion, without losse of time or let of labour, either by lingring to long, or by posting to fast, which cannot now possibly be brought about, while thinges be left to the teachers discretion, whereof, [270] as the most be not alway the best, so even the verie best cannot alway hit those thinges, which in deede are best, while the *customarie education* is helde for a sanctuarie: *alteration* to the better is esteemed an heresie: *allowance* is measured by private liking: *unthankefulnes* is made harbour to desert: and the very *bookes* which we use be not appropriate to our use. I touch no mo stoppes then may easily be removed, if *authoritie* take the matter in hand. Private lettes must have private lessons, and personall circumstance shall have rowme to pleade in, at an other time.

These enormities then shew them selves, when children do chaunge both schooles and maisters: where alteration hindereth beyond all crie, the new maister either thinking it some discredit to himselfe to beginne where the old left, or misliking the choice which the former hath made, or in deede by dispraysing him to seeke to grace himselfe: or the order of his schoole not admitting the succession, as in deede they be all diverse. Sometimes the boy being ungrounded, by his maisters ignorance if he could not, by his negligence if he did not the thing which he could, will not bende to be bettered, but must keepe the same countenaunce which he himselfe conceiveth of himselfe. And this commonly falles out so, when the parentes be pevish, and thinke their child disgraced if he be once set backward (for so the tearme is) whereas in verie deede he is bidde but to looke backe, to see that which he never saw, and ought to have seene verie substantially. Which disorder proceeding from the parentes overruleth us all, causing great weakenes, and much mismatching in the fourmes of our schooles: so that we either cannot, or may not finde fault even to amend it, whereas the order being one, and planted by authoritie, though the childe use to chaunge often, yet his profiting is soone perceived: and the parentes also wilbe well contented, when they suspect no partialitie by private passion, and see indifferencie in publicke provision. Such be the frutes which *varietie* bringes foorth, *perillous* in great affaires, still gathering strength by traine in those petie principles: wheras to the contrarie *uniformitie* is full of contentment. Nothing continueth one in our schooles but the common grammer set furth by authoritie, [271] which confirmeth mine opinion both by pollicie in the first setting out, and by profit in the long continuing, wherein we all agree perforce as in a case of higher countenaunce, and already ruled. Which booke whether it may stand still with some amendement, or of necessitie must be cast some other way, for better method, it shall then be seene when comparisons come in season, that the alteration may shew, whether there were cause to chaunge, or some injurie offered to chaunge without cause. For both that booke, and all the like, which serve for direction and method must be fashioned to the matter which they seeme to direct by rule and precept, being not of themselves, but made to serve others. This we have by it, that *uniformitie* out of al controversie is best, but whether it selfe be best, that is yet in controversie.

Sparing of expences.

For *sparing* of *expenses*, the second commoditie which *uniformitie* bringes with her, this is my opinion: while it is left to the teachers libertie to make his owne choice, both for the booke which he will teach and the order how, betweene the varietie of judgementes, and inequalitie of learning in teachers, which by order must be made one, by consent never will, the parentes purses are pretily pulled, and poore men verie sore pinched both with chaunge of bookes, the maister oft repealing his former choice: and also with number, while every booke is commended to the buyer, which either maketh a faire shew to be profitable: or otherwise is sollicited to the sale, as in our dayes necessitie must sell, where such an overflush of bookes growes chargeable to the printer. For the old periode is returned, that *Juvenall* found in his time, learned and unlearned must needes write, he is marde that comes lag. Nay ordinarily some few leaves be occupied in the best chosen, and biggest booke, besides the oft leasing and much spoiling of them sachels and all, to their gaines it may be said that sell them, though to the parentes losse that buy them, and those of the meaner sort, whose children maintaine schooles most, and swarme thickest in all places and professions, which thing might be farre better used, if the best onely were bought, and with the losse of his bookes the childe lost no more. All which inconveniences may easily be remeadied, and with small adoe. [272] For whatsoever is needefull to be used in schooles, may be verie well comprised in a small compasse, and have all his helpes with him being gathered into some one pretie volume compounded of the marrow of many: neither will the charge be great, the ware being small, and our profession is not to perfit, but to enter. Neither yet hereby is any injurie done to good writers, whose bookes may verie well tarie for the ripenes of the reader, and that place which is dew to them, in the ordinarie ascent of learning and studie, being no intruders into rowmes to meane for them, and content to take that place whereunto they are marshalled by their value, and degree: to their praise which made them, when the student can judge: to the studentes profit, when he can understand: and the fast retaining of them, when order maintanes memorie.

In our *grammer* schooles we professe the toungues nay rather the entraunce of toungues. Everie profession that is penned in any toungue ministreth to her student those wordes that be proper to her owne subject. Which wordes be then best gotten when they follow the matter, as they will do most willingly in the peculiar studie of the same profession. If a *grammarian* therefore be entred to *write, speake,* and *understande* pretily in some well chosen argument best to follow for aptnes ech way, though he neither know all, nor most wordes in any toungue, which is reserved to further studie: yet our schooles be discharged of their dewtie, in doing but so much. They that assigne *grammer* maisters wherein to travell, appoint them *histories,* and *poetes,* though they make some choice of men, and some distinction of matter in regard of vertuous maners and purenes of stile. In our schooles what time will serve us to runne over all these? nay to deale but with some few of them throughly? how then? Is not some litle well pickt, and printed alone the praise of our profession and the parentes ease? And be not the maine bookes to be consigned over to the right place in their owne calling? Some vaines be rapt, and will needes prove *poetes,* leave them the art of *poetrie,* and the whole bookes and argumentes of *poetes.* Some will commend to memorie, and posteritie such actes and monumentes, as be worthy the remembrance: Let them have the rules, whereby [273] the penning of *histories* is directed to write thereby with order: and the matter of *histories* to furnish out their stile. If men of more studie and greater learning have leysure and list to reade, they may use *histories* for pleasure, as being but an after meates studie: neither tyring the braine, nor tediouse any way: as they be not generally to build on for judgement: bycause ignorance of their circumstances make some difficultie in applying, and great daunger in proving. They may also runne over *poetes*, when they are disposed to laugh, and to behold what bravery *enthousiasme* inspireth. For when the *poetes* write sadly and soberly, without counterfeating though they write in verse, yet they be no *poetes* in that kinde of their writing: but where they cover a truth with a fabulous veele, and resemble with alteration. We are therefore to cull out some of the best, and fittest for our introductorie, and to send away the rest to their owne place, in the peculiar professions, and that not in *poetes* and *histories* alone, but also in all other bookes whatsoever, which be at this day admitted into our schooles. The *poetes* wordes be verie good, and most significant, as it appeareth by *Platoes* whole penning, whose eloquence is thought fit for sainctes, if any heavenly creature had a longing to speake *greeke*. And in the latin they have the same grace, in his judgement, which best understoode what wordes were best, as being himselfe the best, and eloquentest oratour, speaking of them in that booke, wherein he both sheweth his eloquence most, and useth the personages of the most eloquent oratours, to deliver his minde. The quantitie of *syllabes* is to be learned of them, to avoid mistiming, as the wise writer *Horace* pointeth the poet therfore first to frame the tender mouth of the yong learner.

De oratore.

Moreover some verie excellent places most eloquently, and forcibly penned for the polishing of good manners, and inducement unto vertue may be pickt out of some of them, and none more then *Horace*. We may therefore either use them, with that choice: or helpe the point our selves if we thinke it good, and can pen a verse that may deserve remembraunce. Such an helpe did *Apollinarius* offer unto his time, as *Sozomenus*, and *Socrates* the scholer, report in their ecclesiasticall histories. [274] For *Julian* the renegate spiting at the great learning of *Basill, Gregorie, Apollinarie*, and many moe, which lived in that time, which time was such a breeder of learned men, as in *Christian* matters and *religion* we reade none like, by decree excluded the *christian* mens children from the use of prophane learning wherin the christian divines were so cunning as they stopt both his, and his favorites mouthes with their owne learning, they passed them all so farre. Then *Apollinarius* conveighed into verses of all sortes, after the imitation of all the best prophane poetes divine and holy argumentes gathered out of scripture whereby he met with *Julianes* edict, and furnished out his owne profession, with matter and argument of their owne. Now in misliking of profane arguments some such helpe may be had and appropriate to our youth. But there must be heede taken, that we plant not any poeticall furie in the childes habit. For that rapt inclination is to ranging of it selfe, though it be not helpt forward, where it is, and would not in any case be forced where it is not. For other writers, *number* and *choice* of wordes, *smoothnes* and *proprietie* of composition with the *honestie* of the argument must be most regarded. *Quintilianes* rule is very true and the verie best, and alway to be observed, in chusing of writers for children to learne, to picke out such as will feede the wit with fairest stuffe, and fine the toungue with nearest speach. So that neither slight, and unproper matters, though eloquentlie set foorth, neither weightie and wise being rudely delivered be to be offered to children, but where the honestie and familiaritie of the argument is honored and apparelled with the finesse and fitnes of speach. Which thing if it be lookt unto in planting *uniformitie*, and pointing out fit bookes, besides many and infinite commodities which will grow thereby to the whole realme, assuredly the multitude of many needelesse volumes, will be diminished and cut of. So that *uniformitie* in schooling may seeme very profitable seeing it will supplant so great defectes, as the likelyhood gives, and plant the redresse, which in nature it importeth: besides that which the common weale doth gaine by acquainting yong wittes even from their cradeles, both to embrace and apply orderly *uniformnes*, which in thinges subject to sense is delitefull [275] to behold: in comprehensions of the minde is comfortable to thinke on: in executions and effects is the staie whereon we stand, and the steddiest recourse to correct errors by. I am led by these reasons and many the like, to thinke that either nothing in deede, or very litle in shew, can justly be alleaged to the contrary but that such an order must needes be verie profitable, to give schooles a purgation to voide them of some great inconveniences: as I take the thing also to be verie compassable, if authoritie shall like of it, without which an opinion is but shewed, and dieth without effect.

I entend my selfe by the grace of God to bestow some paines therein, if I may perceive any hope to encourage my travell. If any other will deale I am ready to staie, and behold his successe: if none other will, then must I be borne with, which in so necessarie a case do offer to my countrie all my duetifull service. Wherein if any upon some repining humor shall seeme to stomake me, bycause being one perhaps meaner then he is himselfe, I do thus boldly avaunce my doinges to the stage, and view of my countrie: yet till he step foorth and shew us his cunning he hath no wrong offred him, if another do speake while he wilbe silent. And whosoever shall deale in generall argumentes, must be content to put up those generall pinches, which repining people do use them most, when they are best used, and esteeme it some benefit, when doing well he heareth ill: and thinke that he hath gotten a great victorie if he please the best, and profit the most, as he may profit all and yet displease many: either through *ignorance* bycause they cannot discerne: or through *willfulnes* being wedded to prejudice: or ells through *disdaine* bycause it spiteth some, to see other above spite. A disease proper to basest dispositions, and of meanest desert, to pinch the heele where they pricke at the head.

But such as meane to do well, howsoever their power perfourme, so the height of their argument overtop not their power to farre, and discover great want of discretion in medling with a matter to much surmounting their abilitie, they may comfort and encourage themselves with that meaning, if their doing do answere it in any resonable proportion, and [276] thinke it a thing, (as it is in deede) naturally, and daily accompanying all potentates either in person, or propertie, and therefore no disgrace to any meaner creature to wrastle with repyning and sowre spirites even verie then, when they worke them most good, which are readyest to repine. If the doinges be massive they will beare a knocke: if they be but slender, and will streight way bruse, beware the warranting. As in this my labour I dare warrant nothing, but the warines of good will, which even ill wil shall see: if it have any sight to see that is right, as commonly that way it is starke blinde, and somuch the more incurablely, bycause the blindnes comes either of unwillingnes to see, or of an infected sight, that will misconsture and deprave the object. I crave the gentle and friendly construction of such as be learned, or that love learning, and yet I neede not crave it, bycause learning that is sound in deede and needes no bolstering, and all her lovers and favorers, be verie liberall of friendly construction, and nothing partiall to speake the best, even where it is not craved. I must pray, if prayer will procure it, the gentle and curteouse toleration of such, as shall mislike. For as I will not willingly do that, which may deserve misliking: so if I once know wherein, I will satisfie throughly. And therefore in one word, I must pray my loving countriemen, and friendly readers, this to thinke of me, that either I shall hit, as my hope is, and then they shall enjoy it: or if I misse, I will amend, and my selfe shall not repent it.

2. Schoole orders publicke.

The second remedie to helpe schoole *inconveniences* was to set downe the schoole *ordinaunces* betwene the maister, and his scholers in a publicke place, where they may easily be seene and red: and to leave as litle uncertaine or untoucht, which the parent ought to know, and whereupon misliking may arise, as is possible. For if at the first entry the parent condiscend, to those orders, which he seeth, so that he cannot afterward plead eitheir ignorance, or disallowing, he is not to take offence, if his childe be forced unto them, when he will not follow, according to that fourme, which he himselfe did confirme by his owne consent. And yet when all is done the glosse will wring the text. Wherefore the *maner* of teaching, the ascent in fourmes, the *times* of admission, the *prevention* to have fourmes equall, [277] the *bookes* for learning, and all those thinges, which be incident unto that *uniformitie*, wherof I spake, being already knowen to be ratified by authoritie, as I trust it shalbe: or if not, yet the same order in the same degrees being set downe, which the maister privately according to his owne skill entendes to kepe: it shalbe very good to take away matter of jarre betwene the parentes and the maister, in the same table publickly to be seene, and shewed to the parentes, when they bring their child first to schoole, besides all that, which I have generally touched to set downe also in plaine and flat termes, what *houres* he will kepe, bycause there is 1. great consideration in that, what to have fixed and perpetuall, and wherein to give place to particular occasions, as there be very many, why all children cannot kepe all *houres*, though the schoole *houres* must still be certaine: and discretion must be the determiner. Againe what *occasions* he will use to let them go to play, which be now very 2. many, and very needefull, while ordinary exercises be not as ordinarily admitted, as ordinarie schooling, is ordinarily allowed: and such other thinges as the schoole shall seeme necessarily to require. 3. For a certaintie resolveth, and preventes douting.

Of curtesie and correction.

But he must cheifly touch what *punishment* he will use, and how much, for every kinde of fault, that shall seeme punishable by the *rod*. For the *rod* may no more be spared in schooles, then the *sworde* may in the *Princes* hand. By the *rod* I mean *correction*, and *awe*: if that sceptre be thought to fearfull for boyes, which our time devised not, but received it from auncientie, I will not strive with any man for it, so he leave us some meane which in a multitude maye worke obedience. For the private, what soever parentes say, my ladie *birchely* will be a gest at home, or else parentes shall not have their willes. And if in men great misses deserve and receive great punishment, sure children may not escape in some qualitie of punishment, which in quantitie of unhappinesse will match some men. And if parentes were as carefull to examine the causes of beating, as they are nothing curious to be offended without cause for beating, themselves might gaine a great deale more to their childrens good: and their children lease nothing, by their parentes assurance. But commonly in such cases rashnesse hath [278] her recompence, the errour being then spied, when the harme is incurable, and repentance without redresse. Terme it as ye list, beate not you saye for learning but for lewdnesse. Sure to beate him for learning which is willing enough to learne, when his witte will not serve, were more then frantike: and under the name of not learning to hide and shrowd all faultes and offenses, were more then foolish: and what would that childe be without beating, which with it can hardly be reclaimed? in whom onely lewdnesse is the let, and capacitie is at will? The ende of our schooles is learning: if it faile by negligence, punish negligence: if by other voluntarie default, punish the default. Spare learning: so that still the refuge must be to the maisters discretion: both for manners, and for learning, whom I would wish to set downe as much in certaintie as he can, at the beginning, and to leave as litle as he may to the childes report, who will alway leane and sway to much to his owne side, and beare away the bell, even against the best maister, cheifly if his mother be either his counsellour, or his attourney: or the father unconstant, and without judgement.

The maister therfore must have in his table a *catalogue* of schoole faultes, beginning at the commandementes, for *swearing*, for *disobedience*, for *lying*, for *false* witnesse, for picking, and so thorough out: then to the meaner heresies, *trewantry*, *absence*, *tardies*, and so forth. 1. παιδ. Such a thing *Xenophon* seemes to meane in rekening up the faultes, which the *Persian* used to punish, though he limit not the penaltie, what, nor how much. Which in all these I wish our maister to set downe with the number of stripes also, immutable though not many. Wherin the maister is to take good heed, that the fault may be confessed, if it may be, without force, and the boye convicted by verdit of his fellowes, and that very evidently. For otherwise children will wrangle amaine, and affection at home hath credulitie beyond crye, which makes the boye dare, what reason dare not. If any of their fellowes be appointed monitours, (as such helpes of Lieutenauncie must be had, where the maister cannot alwaye be present himselfe) and take them napping, they wil pretend spite, or some private displeasure in most manifest knaverie. And if ye correcte, as your Lieutenant must [279] have credit, if you meane to keepe state, that must go home to prove beating without cause. If the maister differre execution, that delaie will enstruct them to devise some starting hole, and that also if it be not heard in schoole wilbe heard at home.

To tell tales out of schoole, is now as commonly used to the worst, as in the old world it was high treason to do it at all. There be as many prety *stratagemes* and devises, which boyes will use to save themselves, and as pleasaunt to heare as any *apopthegme* in either *Plutarch, Aelianus,* or *Erasmus.* The maister therefore must be very circumspecte, and leave no shew, or countenaunce of impunitie deserved, where desert biddes pay. It were some losse of time in learning, to spend any in beating, if it did not seeme a gaine that soundeth towardes good, and seekes amendement of manners. It is passing hard, to reclaime a boye, in whom long impunitie hath graffed a carelesse securitie, or rather some deepe insolencie: and yet freindes will have it so, and beating may not be for discouraging the boye, though repentaunce be in rearward. It is also not good after any correction to let children grate somwhat to long of their late greife, for feare of to great stomaking, onlesse the parentes be wise and stedfast, with whom if a cunning, and a discrete maister joyne, that childe is most fortunate which hath such parentes, and that scholer most happie which hath light on such a maister. But certainly it is most true, let plausibilitie in speach use all her excusing and blanching colours that she can, that the round maister, which can use the rod discretely, though he displease some, which thinke all punishment undiscrete, if it tuch their owne, doth perfourme his duetie best, and still shall bring up the best scholers: As no maister

" of any stuffe shall do but well, where the parentes like that at home,
" which the maister doth at schoole: and if they do mislike any thing,
" will rather impart their greife and displeasure with the maister pri-
" vately, to amend it, then moane their child openly, to marre that
" way more then they shall make any way. The same faultes must be
" faultes at home, which be faultes at schoole, and receive the like
" reward in both the places, to worke the childes good by both
" meanes, correction as the cause shall offer, commendacion as neede
" shall require. [280]

They that write most for gentlenesse in traine reserve place for the rod, and we that use the terme of severitie recommend curtesie to the maisters discretion. Here is the oddes: they will seeme to be curteous in termes, and yet the force of the matter makes them confesse the neede of the rod: we use sharp termes, and yet yeilde to curtesie more, then even the verie patrones of curtesie do, for all their curifavour.

Wherin we have more reason to harp on the harder stringe for the trueth of the matter, then they to touch but the softer, so to please the person: seeing they conspire with us in the last conclusion, that both correction and curtesie be referred to discretion. Curtesie goeth before, and ought to guide the discourse, when reason is obeyed which is very seldome: but the corruptnesse in nature, the penalties in lawe, courage to enflame, desire to entice, and so many evilles assailing one good do enforce me to build my discourse upon feare, and leave curtesie to consideration: as the bare one reason of reason obeyed, a thing still wished, but seldome wel willed, doth cause some curteous conceit, not much acquainted with the kinde of government, upon some plausible liking, to make curtesie the outside, and keepe canvase for the lyning: but ever still for the last staffe to make discretion the refuge. Wherin we agree, though I privately chide him, and saye why dissemble ye? Under hand he aunswereth me, I lend the world some wordes, but I will witnesse with you, I do not speake against discrete correction, but against hastinesse, and crueltie. Sir I know none, that will either set correction or curtesie at to much libertie, but with distinction, upon whom they be both to be exercised: neither yet any, that will praise cruelty: and all those, that write of this argument, whether Philosophers or others allow of punishment, though they differ in the kinde.

7. De rep. Plato.

And it is said in the best common weale, not that no punishment is to be used, but that such an excellent naturall witte, as is made out of the finest mould would not be enforced, bycause in deede it needes not: neither will I offer feare, where I finde such a one: neither but in such a common weale shall I finde such a one. And yet in our corrupt states we light sometime upon one, that were worthy to be a dweller in a farre better. [281] And I will rather venture upon the note of a sharp maister to make a boye learne that, which may afterward do him service, yea though he be unwilling for the time, and very negligent: then that he shall lacke the thing, which maye do him service, when age commeth on, bycause I would not make him learne, for the vaine shadow of a curteous maister. It is slavish sayeth *Socrates* to be bet. It is slavish then to deserve beating sayeth the same *Socrates*. If *Socrates* his free nature be not found, sure *Socrates* his slavish courage must be cudgelled, even by *Socrates* his owne confession. For neither is punishment denied for slaves, neither curtesie for free natures. This by the waye, neither *Socrates* nor *Plato* be so directly carefull in that place, for a good maister in this kinde, as the place required, though they point the learner. And in deed where they had *Censores* to oversee the generall traine, both for one age and other, there needed no great precept this waye. If parentes might not do this, neither children attempt that, then were maisters disburdened: If all thinges were set in stay by publike provision, private care were then mightily discharged. But *Socrates* findes a good scholer which in naturall relation inferreth a good maister. And yet *Philippe* of *Macedonie*, had a thousand considerations in his person, moe then that he was *Alexanders* father, and it is not enough to name the man, onelesse ye do note the cause why with all, and in what respect ye name him. A wise maister, which must be a speciall caveat in provision, wil helpe all, either by preventing that faultes be not committed, or by well using, when soever they fall out, and without exception must have both correction and curtesie, committed unto him beyond any appeal. *Xenophon* maketh Cyrus be beaten of his maister, even where he makes him the paterne of the best Prince, as *Tullie* sayeth, and mindes not the trueth of the storie, but the perfitnesse of his devise, being him selfe very milde as it appeareth still in his *journey* from *Assyria* after the death of *Cyrus* the younger. For a *soule* there could not be one less *servile* then he, which was pictured out beyond exception: for *impunitie*, there could not be more hope, then in a Prince enheritour,

1. παιδ.

1. Ad Quintum Frat.

ἀνάβασις.

and that is more, set forth for a *paterne* to Princes. And yet this Princes child in the absolutenesse [282] of devise, was beaten by his devise, which could not devise any good traine exempt from beating beinge yet the second ornament of *Socrates* his schoole.

The case was thus, and a matter of the *Persian* learning. A long boye had a short coate, and a short boye had a long one: The long boye tooke away the short boyes coate, and gave him his: both were fit: But yet there arose a question about it. *Cyrus* was made judge, as justice was the *Persian* grammer. He gave sentence, that either should have that which fitted him. His maister bette him for his sentence: bycause the question was not of fitnesse, but of right, wherein eche should have his owne. His not learning, and errour by ignorance, was the fault, wherfore he was punished. And who soever shall marke the thing well, shall finde, that not learning, where there is witte to learne, buildeth upon *idlenesse*, unwilling to take paines, upon *presumption* that he shall carie it awaye free, and in the ende, upon *contempt* of them, from whom he learned to contemne, where he should have reverenced. Slight considerations make no artificiall anatomies, and therfore will smart, bycause they spie not the subtilities of creeping diseases. It is easie for negligence in scholers, to pretend crueltie in maisters, where favour beyond rime, lendes credit beyond reason. But in such choice of maisters where crueltie maye easily be avoided, nay in such helpe by Magistrate, where it may be suppressed: and in such wealth of parentes which may change where they like not, if I should here a young gentleman say he was driven from schoole, he should not drive me from mine opinion, but that there was follie in the parentes, and he had his will to much followed, if his parentes had the training of him, or that his gardian gave to much to his owne gaine, and to litle to his wardes good, if he were not himselfe some hard head besides, and set light by learning, as a bootie but for beggers. For gentlenesse and curtesie towarde children, I do thinke it more needefull then beating, and ever to be wished, bycause it implyeth a good nature in the child, which is any parentes comfort, any maisters delite. And is the *nurse* to liberall wittes, the maisters *encouragement*, the childes *ease*, the parentes *contentment*, the *bannishment* of bondage, the *triumph* over torture, [283] and an *allurement* to many good attemptes in all kinde of schooles.

But where be these wittes, which will not deserve, and that very much? and where much deserving is, who is so shamles as to deny correction, which by example doth good, and helpes not the partie offender alone. Give me meane dispositions to deserve, they shall never complaine of much beating: but of none I dare not say, bycause insolent rechelessenes will grow on in the very best, and best given natures, where impunitie profers pardon, eare the fault be committed. My selfe have had thousandes under my hand, whom I never bet, neither they ever much needed: but if the rod had not bene in sight, and assured them of punishment if they had swarved to much, they would have deserved: And yet I found that I had done better in the next to the best, to have used more correction, and lesse curtesie, after carelessenesse had goten head. Wherfore I must needes say, that in any multitude the rod must needes rule: and in the least paucitie it must be seene, how soever it sound. Neither needeth a good boye to be afraid, seeing his fellow offender beaten, any more then an honest man, though he stand by the gallowes, at the execution of a fellon. This point for punishment must the maister set downe roundly, and so as he meaneth in deede to deale, bycause the pretence is generally, not so much for beating, as for to sore beating, which being in sight, the conclusion is soone made, and he that will prevent that sore, may see that set downe, which is thought sufficient. Wherunto if the parent submit himselfe in consent, and his childe in obedience the bargain is thorough, if not there is no harme done.

If the schoole rest upon the maister alone, thus must he do if he meane to do well, and to continue freindship where he meanes to do good. If it be some free foundacion, the founders must joyne with the maister, if they meane that the frute of their cost shalbe commodious to their cuntrey. Leave nothing to had I wist where ye may aunswere ye wist it. When any extraordinary fault breaketh out, as *Solon* said of parricide, that he thought there was none such in nature, conference with the parent, and evident proofe before punishment, will satisfie all [284] parties. And ever the maister must have a fatherly affection, even to the unhappyest boye, and thinke the schoole to be a place of amendment, and therfore subject to misses.

The maisters yeares, and alonenesse.

For the maisters yeares, I leave that to the admitters, as I do his alonenesse. Sufficiency of living wil make mariage most fit, where affection to their owne, worketh fatherlynesse to others: and insufficiencie of living will make a sole man remove sooner, bycause his cariage is small. Most yeares should be most fit to governe, both for constantnesse to be an ancker for levitie to ride at, which is naturally in youth: and for discretion and learning, which yeares should bring with them. But bycause there be errours I leave this to discretion. The admitters to schooles have a great charge, and ought to prove as curious as the very best Godfathers, whose charge yet is farre greater, then the account of it is made, among common persons. These thinges do I take to be very necessarie meanes, to helpe many displeasures wherwith schooling is anoyed, and to plant pleasure in their place. And yet when all is done the poore teacher must be subject to as much, as the sunne is, to shine over all, and yet see much more then he can amend: as the divine is, which for all his preaching, cannot have his auditorie perfit: as the Prince is, who neither for reward nor penalty can have generall obedience. The teachers life is painfull, and therfore would be pityed: it is evidently profitable, and therfore would be cherished: it wrastles with unthankfullnesse above all measure, and therefore would be comforted, with all encouragement. One displeased parent will do more harme upon a head, if he take a pyrre at some toy, never conferring with any, but with his owne cholere: then a thousand of the thankfullest will ever do good, though it be never so well deserved. Such small recompence hath so great paines, the very acquaintance dying when the child departes, though with confessed deserte, and manifest profit: Such extreme dealing will furie enforce, where there is no fault, but that conceit surmiseth, unwilling to examine the truth of the cause, and lother to reclame, as unwilling to be seene so overshot by affection. This very point wherby parentes hurte themselves in deede, and hinder their owne, though they discourage teachers, would be looked unto by [285] some publike ordinaunce, that both the maisters might be driven to do well, if the fault rest in them: and the parentes to deale well, if the blame rest there: considering the publike is harmed, where the private is uncharmed, to ende it in meter as my president is.

But in the beginning of this argument I did protest against *Philip Melanchthons* miseries, and therefore I will go no further, seeing what calling is it, which hath not his cumbat against such discurtesies? The proverbe were untrue, if a man should not be as well a wolfe to man, as he is tearmed a God, and did not more harme, in unkyndenesse, then good in curtesie: so marvelosly fraught with ill and good both, as *Plinie*, cannot judge whether nature be to a man, a better mother, or a bitterer stepdame. But patience must comfort where extremitie discourageth: and a resolute minde is a rempare to it selfe, upon whom as *Horace* saith, though the whole world should fall, it might well crush him perforce, but not quash him for feare.

Chapter 44.

That Conference betwene those which have interest in children: Certainetie of direction in places where children use most: and Constancie in well keeping that, which is certainely appointed, be the most profitable circumstances both for vertuous manering and cunning schooling.

Of all the meanes which pollicie and consideration have devised to further the good training up of children, either to have them well learned, or vertueously manered, I see none comparable to these three pointes: *conference* betwene those persons, which have interest in children, to see them well brought up: *certainetie* in those thinges, wherein children are to travell, for their good bringing up: *constancie* in perfourming that, which by *conference* betweene the persons is set *certaine* in the thinges: that there be either no change at all after a sound limitation: or at least verie litle, save where discretion in execution, is to yeald unto circumstaunce. Therfore I entend to utter some part of mine opinion concerning these three things: [286] *conference* to breede the best: *certainetie* to plant the best: *constancie* to continue the best: and first of *conference*. Which I find to be of foure cooplementes: *parentes* and *neighbours*: *teachers* and *neighbours*: *parentes* and *teachers*: *teachers* and *teachers*: whereof everie one offereth much matter for the furthering of both learning and good maners in children. Under the name of *neighbours* I comprehend all forraine persons, whom either commendable dewtie by countrie law: or honest care of common curtesie doth give charge unto, to helpe the bettering of children, and to fraie them from evill.

1. Conference betwene parentes and neighbours.

Now if parentes in pointes of counsell use to conferre with such, they may learne by some others experience: how to deale in their owne. And as this point is naturally provided to assist infirmitie, which craves helpe of others, where it standes in dout: so there is a naturall injunction wherby all men are charged to bestow their good and faithfull counsell, where it is required, doing thereby great good to the parties, and no harme to themselves, unlesse it be to be rekened a harme, to gaine the opinion of wisedom, the estimation of honestie, and the note of humanitie, and a well given disposition. This consideration resteth most in the partie mover, which is to receive advise, when himselfe shall require it. The next is an evident signe of an excellent inclination, which of it selfe will doe good, even bycause the thing is good, though he be not conferred with. For if such persons will conferre with parentes, when they spy any thing that is not well in their children is it not honorable in them to deale so honestly? is it not wisdome in parentes to constrew it most friendly? is it not happie for those children which have such carefull forraine helpers abroad, such considerate naturall hearers at home? A simple meaning in both the parties, the *neighbour* to tell friendly, the *parent* to take kindely, and to execute wisely will do marvelous much good. And what is this else but to love thy neighbour as thy selfe, when thou mindest his childe good, as thou doest thine owne? And what is it else but to thinke of thy neighbour, as thou wouldest be thought on thy selfe, when thou beleevest him in thine, as thou wouldest be beleeved in his? A true president of naturall *humanitie,* a religious patterne of honest *neighbourhoode,* [287] which in no other thing can declare more good will, in no other thing can do one more good, then in respect to his children, whether ye consider the childrens person, or the thing which is wished them. For in deede what be children in respect of their persons? be they not the effects of Gods perfourmaunce in blessing? of his commaundement in encrease? be they not the assurance of a state which shall continew by succession, and not dy in one brood? be they not the parentes naturall purtracte? their comfort in hope, their care in provision? for whom they get all, for whom they feare nought? And can he which desireth the good of this so great a blessing from heaven, so great a staie for the countrie, so great a comfort to parentes, devise how to pleasure them more in any other thing? for to wish children to be honest, vertuous, and well learned, is to wish that to prove perfitly good, which standeth in a mammering, to prove good or bad. And can this so great a good wish but proceede from a passing honest disposition, and most worthy the embrasing? Nay most happy is that state, where youth hath such a staie, in such libertie, as it is, not to helpe unlesse one list. Hereupon I conclude that *conference* betwene *parentes* and others, whether by way of asking counsell, or by advertisemente to check faultes, is very profitable for the weale of the litle ones.

2. Conference betwene teachers and neighbours.

This *conference* may fall betwene the *neighbour* and the *teacher*. Wherein the *teacher* must be verie warie bycause he hath to deale with the informer for credit: with his scholer for amendment: with the parent for liking. When the parent dealeth with his owne childe, either of his owne knowledge, or by credited report, his doome is death or life, the child hath no appeale, but either must amend, or feele the like smart. At the *teachers* dealing, upon any advertisement, there may and wilbe taken many pretie exceptions. Why did you beleeve? why should he medle? why dealt you in this sort? And whatsoever quarell miscontentment can devise, being incensed with furie: or some extreme heat, as angrie nature is an eager monster. And in deede some overthwart conceit may move the complainant, whatsoever the pretence be. Againe some wise man, may light upon so convenient a maister, as he may prove a better meane [288] to redresse, then the parent will be, in whom blinde nature will neither see the childes fault, nor the friendes faith. But how soever it be, the maister must be warie, where his commission is not absolute. But in the wise handling of this civill *conference* the childe shall gaine much towardes his well doing, when wheresoever he shall be, or whatsoever he shall do, he shall both finde it true, and feele it so, that either his parent or his maister, or both together see him, if any other bodie see him.

3. Conference betwene parentes and teachers.

The next *conference* is betweene *parentes* and *maisters*, whereof though I have saide much, yet can I never say to much, the point is so needefull: bycause their friendly and faithfull communicating workes perpetuall obedience in the childe, contempt of evill, and desire to do well: seeing both they travell to make one good. There is nothing so great an enemie to this so great a good as credulitie is in parentes, not able to withstand the childes eloquence, when shed of teares, and some childish passion do plead against punishment for assured misdemeanour. But though for the time such parentes seeme to wynne, bycause they have their will: yet in the conclusion, they want their will, when they wish it were not so. Before change either of place, to proceede onward to further learning: or of maisters, when the old is misliked, and a new sought for, then this *conference* is a mervelous helpe. For in change of place, it growndes upon knowledge, and growes by advice: in change of maisters, it is mistresse to warines not to lease by the change. For can the new maister understand and judge of the childes fault in so small a time, as the old maister may amend it if he be conferred with? You are offended with the former maister, have ye conferred with him? have ye opened unto him your owne griefe, your childes defect, his owne default? are ye resolved that the fault is in the maister? may not your sonne forge? or may he not halt, to procure alteration upon some private pevishnes? *Cyrus* as *Zenophon* writeth surprised the king of *Armenia* being tributarie to the *Median* but minding to revolt, when the *Assyrians* armie should enter into *Media*. And yet though he found him in manifest blame, he left him his state, as the best steward for the *Medians* use, considering the partie pardoned is bound by defect, he that shall be chosen, will [289] thanke his owne merit, not the chusers munificence. Such consideration had *Cyrus*, and such *conference* with him, whom he knew to be a foe, before he surprised him, and yet found the frute of his considerate *conference* and his determination upon his *conference*, to be exceding good and gainefull for himselfe after, and his friendes for the time. A number of ills be avoided, and a number of goodes obtained by this same *conference* betwene *parentes* and *maisters*. If the *maister* be wise and advisedly chosen though he chaunce to misse, he knowes to amend: if he neither be such a one, nor so consideratly chosen, yet *conference* will discover him, and shew hope her listes, and what she may trust to. But not to dwel any longer in this point, wherein elsewhere I have not bene parciall, I must needes say thus much of it at once for all, that no one meane either publike or private makes so much for the good bringing up of children, as this *conference* doth.

παιδ. 3.

4. Conference betwene teachers.

The last *conference* I appoint to be betwene those of the same professions, whereby the generall traine is generally furthered. For whersoever any subject is to be dealt in by many, is not the dealers *conference* the meane to perfit dealing? and to have that subject absolutely well done, which it selfe is subject to so many doers? Is either the patient any worse if the *Physitians* conferre, or their facultie baser by their being togither? is not the case still clearer, where there is *conference* in law? is not the church the purer where *confer-*

ence is in proufe? and doth not the contrarie in all do much harme in all? And do ye thinke that conference among teachers would not do much good in the traine? or is the thing either for moment so meane, or for number so naked, as it may not seeme worthy to be considered upon? Or can there any one, or but some few, be he or they never so cunning, discerne so exactly, as a number can in common *conference*? do not common companies which professe no learning, both allow it, and prove it, and finde it to be profitable? where it is used among teachers for the common good, it profiteth generally by sending abroad some common direction. In places where many schooles be within small compasse, it is very needefull to worke present good, and to helpe one another, where all may have enough to bestow their [290] labour on.

But this *conference*, and that not in *teachers* alone must be builded upon the *honest care* of the *publike good*, without *respect* of *private gaine*: without *sting* of *emulation*: without *gaule* of *disdaine*: which be and have bene great enemies to conference: great hinderers to good schooling: nay extreame ruiners in cases above schooling, and yet for the footing of that, which must after prove fairest, good schooling is no small onset. I neede not to rip up the position to them, that be learned, which know what a mischeife the misse of *conference* is, where it ought to be of force, and is shouldered out by distempered fansie. He that can judge, knoweth the force of this argument, which followeth where many illes seeke to choke one good, which themselves were displaced, if that good tooke place: that good must needes be a great one, and worthy the wishing, that it may procure passage. Of *conference* I must needes say this, that it is the cognisance of humanitie, and that of the best humanitie, being used for the best causes that concerne humanitie, and all humaine societie. I dare enter no deeper in this so great a good: but certainely in matters of learning there would be more *conference*, even of verie conscience. And if that honest desire might bring downe great hart, the honorable effect would bring up great good, in all trades beyond crie, in our traine beyond credit. In matters of engrosing, and *monopolies*, in matters of forestauling and intercepting there is dealing by *conference* among the dealers, which we all crie out of, bycause it makes us crie, in our purses. And yet we are slow to trie that in the good, which proves so strong in the ill, and was first pointed for good. I use no authorities to prove in these cases, where reason her selfe is in place, and standeth not in neede of alleaging of names, bycause she may well spare her owne retinew, where her hoste himselfe doth tender his owne service.

2. Certaintie.

The next point after *conference* is the chiefe and best ofspring of all wise *conferences, certainetie* in direction, which in al thinges commendes it selfe, but in bringing up of children it doth surpasse commendation both for their manners and their learning. This same so much praised *certainetie* concerneth the [291] limiting of thinges, what to do and what to learne, how to do and how to learne, where, when, and so forth to do that, which fineth the behaviour, and to learne that which advaunceth knowledge. For children being of themselves meere ignorant must have *certainetie* to direct them: and trainers being not dailie to devise, are at once to set downe certaine, both what themselves will require at the childrens hand for the generall order: and what the children must looke for at their handes for generall perfourmance. This *certainetie* must specially be set sure, and no lesse soundly kept, in *schooles* for *learning*, in private *houses* for *behaviour*, in *churches* for *religion*, bycause those three places, be the greatest aboades, that children have.

1. Certainetie in schooles.

Concerning *certainetie* in schoole pointes, and the benefit thereof, I have delt verie largely in the last title: so that I shall not neede to use any more spreading in that point, saving onely that I do continue in the same opinion: as the thing it selfe continueth in it selfe most assuraunce of best successe, when the childe knoweth his *certainetie* in all limitable circumstances, whether he be at schoole himselfe to provide that must be done: or if he be not there, yet to know in abscence, what is done there of course. So that where ignorance of orders cannot be pretended, there good orders must needes be observed, which ordenarily bringe foorth a well ordered effect. The best and most heavenly thinges be both most certaine, and most constantly certaine, and the wisest men the certainest to builde on, in the middest of our uncertaineties. So that *certainetie* must needes be a great levell, which procureth such liking in those thinges where it lighteth. In *schooling* it assureth the parentes, what is promised there, and how like to be perfourmed, by sight of the method and orders set downe: it directeth the children as by a troden path, how to come thither, as their journey lieth: it disburdeneth the maisters heade, when that is in writing, which he was in waying, and when experience by oft trying hath made the habit able to march on of it selfe without any renewing: whereunto mutabilitie is everie day endaungered.

2. Certainetie in private houses.

The second point of *certainetie* entereth into families and private *houses*, which in part I then touched, when I wished the parentes so to deale at *home*, as there might be a *conformitie* betwene [292] *schoole* and *home*. This point will prevent two great inconveniences even at the first, besides the generale sequele of good discipline at home. For neither shall schooles have cause to complaine of private corruption from home, that it infecteth them, when nothing is at home done or seene, but that which is seemely: neither shall the schooles lightly send any misdemeanour home, when the childe is assured to be sharpely chekt, for his ill doing, if it appeare within doares. This is that point which all writers that deale with the *oeconomie* of househoIdes, and pollicie of states do so much respect, bycause the fine blossomes of well trained families, do assure us of the swetest flowres in training up of states, for that the buddes of private discipline be the beauties of pollicie. I shall not neede to say, what a good state that familie is in, where all thinges be most certainely set, and most constantly kept, which do belong to the good example of the *heades*, the good following of the *feete*, the good discipline of the whole *house*. Though some not so resolute wittes, or gredier humours will neither harken to this rule, nether keepe it in their owne, bycause the distemperature is both blinde, and deafe, where the minde is distempered, and violently given over either to extreame desire of gaine, or to some other infirmitie which cannot stoup to staid order: yet those *families* which keepe it, finde the profitablenesse of it. There children so well ordered by *certaineties* at *home*: when to rise: when to go to bed: when and how to pray evening and morning: when and how to visit their parentes ear they goe to bed, after they rise, ear they goe abroad, when they returne home, at tables about meat, at meeting in dutie with officious and decent speches of course, well framed, and deulie called for, cannot but prove verie orderly and good. He that in his infancie is thus brought up, will make his owne proufe his fairest president, and what housholde knoweth not this is extreame farre of from any good president. Obedience towardes the prince and lawes is assuredly grounded, when private houses be so well ordered: small preaching will serve there, where private training settes thinges so forward. Being therefore so great a good, it is much to be thought on, and more to be called for. [293]

3. Certaintie in Churches.

Now can *certaintie* being so great a bewtifier both to publik *schooles*, and private houses, be but very necessary to enter the Church with children upon *holydaies*? to have all the young ones of the Parish, by order of the Parish set in some one place of the Church? with some good over looking, that they be all there, and none suffred to raunge abroad about the streates, upon any pretence? that they may be in eye of parentes and parishioners? that they may be attentive to the Divine service, and betime learne to reverence that, wherby they must after live? I do but set downe the consideration, which they will execute, who shall allow of it, and devise it best, upon sight of the circunstance. How other men will thinke herof I know not, but sure me thinkes, both publikly and privately, that *certaintie* in *direction* where it may be well compassed, is a merveilous profitable kinde of regiment, and best beseeming children, about whose bettering my travell is employed. In the very executing it sheweth present pleasure, and afterward many singular profites: and is in very deede the right meane to direct in *uncertainties*, as a stayed yearde to measure flexible stuffe. *Bladders* and *bullrushes* helpe *swimming*: the *nurses* hand the *infantes going*: the *teachers line* the *scholers writing*, the *Musicians tune*, his *learners timing*: what to do? by following *certaintie* at first to direct *libertie* at last. And he that is acquainted with *certaintie* of *discipline* in his young yeares will thinke himselfe in exile, if he finde it not in age, and by plaine comparisons, will reclaime misorders, which he likes not, to such orders as he sees not. Who so markes and moanes the varietie in *schooling*, the disorder in *families*, the dissolutenesse in *Church*, will thinke I saye somwhat.

3. Constancie.

The third part of my division was *constancie*. For what availeth it to *conferre* about the best, and to set it in *certaine*, where *mutabilitie* of mindes upon every infirmitie either of judgement, or other circunstance, is seeking to retire, and to leave that rouling, which was so well rewled. In this point of *constancie* there be but two considerations to be had, the one of knowledge in the thing, the other of discretion in the use. For he that is resolved in the goodnesse and pith of the thing, will never revolt, but like a valiant general building upon his owne knowledge, [294] is certaine to conquere, what difficultie so ever would seeme to dasle his eyes, or to dash his conceit. It is weake *ignorance* that yeildes still, as being never well setled: it is *pusillanimitie* that faintes still, not believing where he sees not. Assured *knowledge* will resemble the great *Emperour* of all, which is still the same and never changeth, which set a lawe, that yet remaines in force even from the first, among all his best and most obedient thinges. The *sunnes* course is *certaine*, and *constantly* kept. The *moone* hath her moving without *alteration*, and that so *certaine*, as how many yeares be their eclypses foretold? A good thing such as wise *conference* is most like to bring forth, would be *certainly* knowen, and being so knowen would be *constantly* kept. The fairest *bud* will bring forth no frute, if it fall in the prime, but being well fostered by seasonable weather, it will surely prove well. The greatest thinges have a feeble footing, though their perfitnesse be strong, but if their meane be not *constant*, that first feeblenesse will never recover that last strength. I medle not with change of states, nor yet with any braunches, whose particular change, quite altereth the surface, of any best setled state, but with the training of children, and the change therin: which being once certaine would in no case be altered before the state it selfe upon some generall change do command alteration, wherunto all our schooling must be still applyed, to plant that in young ones, which must please in old ones. As now our teaching consisteth in toungues, if some other thing one daye seeme fitter for the state, that fitter must be fitted, and fetcht in with procession. But yet in changes this rule would be kept, to alter by degrees, and not to rush downe at once. Howbeit the nature of men is such, as they will sooner gather a number of illes at once to corrupt: then pare any one ill by litle and litle with minde to amend.

Concerning *discretion*: there is a circunstance to be observed in thinges, which is committed alwaye to the executours person, and hath respect to his judgement, which I call no change, bycause in the first setting downe that was also setled, as a most certaine point to rule accidentarie *uncertainties*, which be no changes, bycause they were foreseene. Such a supplie hath justice in positive lawes by equitie in consideration, as a [295] good chauncellour to soften to hard constructions. That is one reason why the *monarchie* is helde for the best kinde of government, bycause the rigour and severitie of lawe, is qualified by the princesse mercie, without breche of lawe, which left that prerogative to the princesse person. The conspiracie which *Brutus* his owne children made against their father for the returne of *Tarquinius* even that cruell Prince, leanes upon this ground, as *Dionysius* of *Halicarnassus*, *Livie*, and others do note. So that *discretion* to alter upon cause in some uncertaine circunstance, nay to alter circunstance upon some certaine cause, is no enemie to *certaintie*. When thinges are growen to extremities then change proves needefull to reduce againe to the principle. For at the first planting, every thing is either perfitest, as in the matter of creation: or the best ground for perfitnesse to build on, as in truth of religion: though posteritie for a time upon cause maye encrease, but to much putting to burdeneth to much, and in the ende procures most violent shaking of, both in religious and politike usurpations.

But this argument is to high for a schoole position, wherefore I will knit up in few wordes: that as *conference* is most needefull, so *certaintie* is most sure, and *constancie* the best keeper: that it is no change, which *discretion* useth in doing but her duetie: but that altereth the maine. Which in matters engraffed in generall conceites would worke alteration by slow degrees, if foresight might rule: but in extremities of palpable abuse it hurleth downe headlong, yea though he smart for the time whom the change doth most helpe. But in our schoole pointes the case falleth lighter, where whatsoever matter shalbe offered to the first education, *conference* will helpe it, *certaintie* will staye it, *constancie* will assure it. Thus much concerning the generall positions wherin if I have either not handled, or not sufficiently handled any particular point, it is reserved to the particular treatise hereafter, where it will be bestowed a great deale better, considering the present execution must follow the particular.

Chapter 45.

The peroration, wherin the summe of the whole booke is recapitulated and proofes used, that this enterprise was first to be [296] *begon by Positions, and these be the most proper to this purpose. A request concerning the well taking of that which is so well ment.*

Thus bold have I bene, with you (my good and curteous countriemen) and troubled your time with a number of wordes of what force I know not, to what ende I know. For my ende is, to shew mine opinion how the great varietie in teaching, which is now generally used, maye be reduced to some uniformnesse, and the cause why I have used so long a preface, as this whole booke, is, for that such as deale in the like arguments do likewise determine before, what they thinke concerning such generall accidentes, which are to be rid out of the waye at once, and not alwaye to be left running about to trouble the house, when more important matters shall come to handling. Wherin I have uttered my conceit, liking well of that which we have, though oftimes I wishe for that which we have not, as much better in mine opinion, then that which we have, and so much the rather to be wished, bycause the way to winne it is of it selfe so plaine and ready. I have uttered my sentence for these pointes thus, wherin if my cunning have deceived me, my good will must warrant me: and I have uttered it in plaine wordes, which kinde of utterance in this teaching kinde, as it is best to be understood, so it letteth every one see, that if I have missed, they may wel moane me, which meaning all so much good have unhappily missed in so good a purpose. Upon the stearnesse of resolute and reasonable perswasions, I might have set downe my Positions aphorismelike, and left both the commenting, and the commending of them to triall and time: but neither deserve I so much credit, as that my bare word may stand for a warrant: neither thought I it good with precisenesse to aliene, where I might winne with discourse. Wherupon I have writen in every one of these argumentes enough I thinke for any reader, whom reason will content: to much I feare for so evident a matter, as these Positions be, not assailable, I suppose, by any substantiall contradiction. For I have grounded them upon reading, and some reasonable experience: I have applied them to the use, and custome of my [297] countrey, no where enforcing her to any forreine, or straunge devise. Moreover I have conferred them with common sense wherin long teaching hath not left me quite senselesse. And besides these, some reason doth lead me very probable to my selfe, in mine owne collection, what to others I know not, to whom I have delivered it, but I must rest upon their judgement. Hereof I am certaine that my countrey is already very well acquainted with them, bycause I did but marke where upon particular neede, she her selfe hath made her owne choice, and by embrasing much to satisfie her owne use, hath recommended the residue unto my care, to be brought by direction under some fourme of statarie discipline. Now then can I but thinke that my countreymen will joyne with me in consent, with whom my countrey doth communicate such favour? Seeing her favour is for their furtheraunce, and my labour is to bring them to that, which she doth most allow.

The examining of all the contentes of this booke.

And what conclusion have I set downe wherin they maye not very well agree with me, either for the first impression which set me on worke, or for the proofe, which confirmeth the impression? My first meaning was to procure a generall good, so farre as my abilitie would reach, I do not saye that such a conceit, deserveth no discourtesie for the very motion, how soever the effect do aunswere in rate: but this I may well thinke, that my countrymen ought of common courtesie to countenaunce an affection so well quallified, till the event either shrine it with praise, or shoulder it with repulse. I do not herein take upon me dictatorlike to pronounce peremptorily, but in waye of counsell, as one of that robe, to shew that, which long teaching hath taught me to saye, by reading somwhat, and observing more. And I must pray my good countreymen so to construe my meaning, for being these many yeares by some my freindes provoked to publish something, and never hitherto daring to venture upon the print, I might seeme to have let the raine of all modesty runne to lowse, if at my first onset I should seeme like a *Caesar* to offerre to make lawes. Howbeit in very deede my yeares growing downward, and some mine observations seeming to some folkes to crave some ütteraunce, upon shew to do some good: I thought rather to hasard my [298] selfe in hope of some mens favour, then to burie my conceit with most mens wonder. But before I do passe to mine Elementarie, which I meane to publish next after this booke, I must for mine owne contentation examine what I have done in this, to see whether I have hit right, or writen any thing that
1. may call repentaunce. Was I not to cut this course, and to begin at
2. Positions? And are not these the cheife and onely groundes in this
3. argument? And in speking of these have I in any point passed
beyond my best beseeming? For the first. Whether I ought to begin
1. at Positions, or no, that is not in doubte now I hope, bycause I made
that pointe very plaine in the beginning of my booke: but whether I have done well to dwell so long in them, that may seeme to deserve some excuse, if I mislike it myselfe: or else some cause, to satisfie other.

If I had had to do with either *Romain*, or *Grecian*, in their owne language, where these thinges be familiarly knowen, I would not have taryed in them any long while, but dealing with my countrymen in my countrey toungue, in an argument not so familiar to my countrey, and yet desiring to become familiar unto her: I thought it good rather to saye more then enough, to leave some chippinges: then by saying to litle, to cause a new cruste, where none should be: and to referre the rest of my suppressed meaning to my learneddest reader, to whose use as I needed not to write, so in deede I do not, though I wish him well, and pray the like againe. They that frame happy men, absolute oratours, perfit wisedome, paragonne Princes, faulteless states, as they have their subject at commaundement, which they breede in the commentarie of their owne braines: so their circunstances being without errour, where their maine is without match, neede very few wordes, as being in daunger of very few faultes. But I deale with a subject, which is subject to all uncertainties: with circunstances, which are checkt with many objections, lying open, to much disturbance, cavilled at by every occasion: where one sillie errour, is of strength enough, to overthrow a mans whole labour. I thought it good therefore to declare at large, what my meaning was, to satisfie therby even the meanest understandinges, that waye to procure mine opinion the freer passage, when it should passe [299] by none, which understood it not. I could not but begin with them, bycause herafter I shall have so many occasions to make mention of them, to directe the traine by them, to referre my selfe unto them, which if they had not bene handled here, they might and would have troubled me there. Besides this, I would gladly (if I could obtaine so much at their handes) that all my countrymen did thinke, as I do in these same pointes, that by their consent my good speede might go on, with the readier and rounder currant, so that I cannot conceive, but that I was both to begin my treatise at Positions, as the primitive in such discourses, and to dwell long in them, to satisfie my most readers.

Now whether these be the cheife groundes in preparative to that, 2.
which I entend to deale in, I thinke there is none, but may very easily judge. For what is it wherunto my travell to come hath promised her endevour? to helpe children to be well taught for learning: to tell their maisters, how to exercise them for health: to aide the common course of studie in what I can for the common good. And what accidentes belong unto such an argument, if these which I have quoated out do not? Must there not be a time to begin, to continue, to ende

the course of schoole learning? Then time must needes come in consideration. Must there not be somthing, wherin this time must be bestowed, both to have the minde learned, and the body healthfull? Then the matter of traine, and the kinde of exercises could not have bene passed over. Must there not be some upon whom these things are to be imployed in these times, of both the sexes, and of all degrees? Then the generall schooling of all young ones, and the particular training of young maidens, and bringing up of young gentlemen must needes have their handling. Could these thinges be done with out convenient place? cunning teachers? and good schoole orders? I thinke no. And therefore I picked these out, as the onely circunstances, that were proper to mine argument, and that were to be handled eare I entred my argument, if I had never seene any writer before use the same choice.

3. But how have I delt in them. For the time to begin I have measured it by strength of body and minde that may well awaye with the travell in learning without emparing of the [300] good of either parte. For the continuing time in every degree of studie, I have limited it by sufficiencie and perfitnesse of habit, before the student remove. For the ending time, the bounder of it is abilitie to serve the common countrey, and the private student in every particular calling. In this distinction and sorting of time, I thinke I have so dealt,
2. as no reason will gainsaye me. For pointing so many thinges to be learned in the Elementarie schoole, as I do it upon good warrant, so is no man injuried by it, and every man may be helpt by it. For though neither all men deale with all, nor all men can obtaine all, it is no reason but that those which will and may, shall know what is best to get: and that those which neither will nor can, yet maye see, what they maye and ought to get, if circunstances serve. For the traine is to be framed after the height, which freedome in circunstance maye well attaine unto. A poore mans purse will not stretch so farre: must abilitie therfore be to much restrained? Some mans time will not dispense with all: must therfore the libertie of leasure be forced to the fetter? Some parente makes light of that, which some other esteemeth greatly: must he therefore be disapointed of his liking, which alloweth, to serve his humour, which misliketh? Some maime in some circunstance may be some particular let: must therefore parciality in not pointing the best prove the generall losse?

The best being set downe, without evident dispaire to come by it,

or manifest noveltie to disgrace it, why should it not be sought for
by them, which are willing to have it, and know the meanes how?
It is no noveltie for some to towre above the clowdes though other
in the same flight do but flutter about the ground, and yet with commendation. For where the whole is good, and partible by degrees,
everie ascent hath his praise, though the prerogative be his that
mounteth highest. And therefore my plat is to satisfie those which
will medle with the most, and yet so left at libertie, as it may serve
even them, which seeke but for the least. For the choice of wittes and 3.
restraint of number, not to pesture learning with to great a multitude, no wisedome will blame me. For the helpe and health of body, 4.
that the doinges of the soule may be both strong and long, to joine
ordinarie exercise in forme of traine, [301] who so shall mislike, I
will match him with melancholie, with fleame, with reumes, with
catarres, and all needelesse residences, to see how they will musle
him. The limitation of certaineties in maisters for their securitie, and
parentes for their assurance, if it be well wayed is worth the wishing. For the places and personall circumstances, who so will cavill, 5.
neither deserves such a place to be trained in, nor such a maister to
be trained by, nor such parentes to provide him such a traine. For
the good bringing up of yong gentlemen, he that taketh no care, is 6.
more than a foole considering their place and service in our countrie: and so of all the rest. But did any man thinke that I would not 7.
mention my dealing in trayning up of yong maidens, whether that
be to be admitted in such sort as I have appointed it? That is such a
bulwarke for me, as who so shall seeme to pinch me for dealing liberally with them, had neede to arme himselfe against them. For they
will translate the crime, and becomming parties themselves discharge me from daunger for using them so curteously. Is that point
in suspition of any noveltie or fantasticallnes to have wymen
learned? Then is *nature* fantasticall for giving them abilitie to learne:
custome for putting them to it: *pollicie* for placing them where to use
it: in all ages in all degrees, in all countries, both at home and abroad.
Innovation it is not, for I reade it, I see it, I finde it, it is not my devise.
I put the case, that it were one of my wishes, that wymen might
learne, if they did not. Assuredly the proufe that we see, the profit
that we feele, the comfort that we have, the care that we have not,
the happines we enjoy, the mishap we avoide, the religion we live
by and like, the superstition we fly from and hate, the clemencie we

finde, the cruelitie we feare, by the meere benefit of our learned princesse, whom God hath so rarely endewed and endowed, give me leave to wish that sexe most successe in learning, and her majesties person all successe in living: all the residew, all the best, and her highnes alone all above the best: as wish can aspire, where nothing else can come. In generall I do not remember any thing, that I have dealt in, but it may be very well digested by any stomake, if it be not to farre distempered.

My wishes perhaps may seeme sometimes to be novelties. [302] Novelties perhappes, as all amendementes be to the thing that needeth redresse, but not fantasticall, as having their seat in the cloudes. If no man did ever wish, then were I alone. If my wish were unpossible though it made shew of very great profit, impossibilitie in deede, would desire profit in wish to be content with repulse: but where the thing is both profitable, and possible to, why should not profitable possibilitie have rowme, if wishing may procure it? I wish commodious situation and rowme in places for learning and exercise. Our countrie hath it not echwhere, nay scant any where as yet. Even by wishing that it had, I graunt that it hath not but I would not have wished it, if the meane had bene hard: and the motion naturally goeth before the effect. I wish that the colledges in the universities were devided by professions: I wish grave and learned readers: I wish repetition to the same readers, yea even for the best graduate, that is yet an hearer. I wish neither heresie nor harme, ne yet any thing, but that may very well be wrought, and deserves endlesse wishing till it be brought to an ende. I wish restraint to stop overflush, and such other things whereto I dare stand, and assuredly beleeve, that I wish my countrie very great good, as I hope many wilbe partakers with me in wish, to be partakers of the good. But some wil say what neede you to medle with so much, or so high matters your selfe creeping so low? Syr, I did professe in the beginning under ech title to deale in the generall argument, for all my professing the elementarie example. And by the way I do thinke, that I may deserve some more equitie in construction, bycause I do entend to my great paines to helpe my wish forward, and to travell for the helping, and healthing of all studentes. Wherfore I conclude thus, that seeing my dealing in those positions was occasioned of so good a ground, and hath so passed through them, as I hope it may abide the tuch, I must crave of my good and curteouse countriemen to laie up allouance in hope, and misliking in pardon, till the event dischardge both, and make me bound to all, and some benefited by me.

FINIS.

To the curteous reader.

It is no new thing, to heare of errours in printing, be the print never so good. Wherefore for distinctions either misplaced, or quite left out, and such other faultes, as will not clearelie lame the sense, I must desire my good reader to helpe me and the print either with his pen, or with acknowledging the sense without the pen. But bycause these few oversightes do seeme to alter my meaning and to maime the argument, I have therefore noted them my selfe to have them the better observed.

Facie 9. force her to *it*. for to *that*.
51. *suppected* in some copies. for *supported*.
94. brought foorth *by word*. for *that byword*.
101. and *lear-* countrieman. for *learned*.
127. where one *stirres* all. for *steares* all.
162. chiefly to *the* colledge. for *that* colledge.
192. what vertue is *primate*. for *private*.
221. in marg. Ad 1. *Necocleon*. for Ad *Nicoclem*.
222. whether *not in* digesting. for *in not*.
227. the parents *heavenly* eye. for *homely* in some copies.
229. some *great* number. for some *good*.
230. the fifthe title of the *first* booke. for *fifth* booke.
236. to strike the *stocke*. for the *stroke*.
256. helpe of *the* wealthie patrones. *the* out.
258. and *gave* ignorance the raigne. for *give*.
275. without which *any* opinion. for *an*.

❧ Textual Notes and Variants

All changes are listed here, except end-line hyphenation, the normalization of i/j and u/v, the suppression of long 's,' and the expansion of contractions and abbreviations. Words following the square brackets appear in the original, and are given in their original form (except for long 's'). Press variants (noted by forme) and authorial corrections from the errata list (on page 294) are so indicated parenthetically; all corrections not otherwise identified are my own changes to the text. The numbers that follow these variants, corrections, and emendations are page and line numbers of the 1581 text. Barker PH D, appendix 4, 281–93 lists the variants as they appear in individual copies. In the following g stands for marginal gloss, hl for headline.

1.13 for Thomas Chare.] dvvelling in the blacke Friers by Ludgate (variant * outer) *1r.13

[In 1581 only] EPISTLE. should read EPISTLE *2v.hl

[In 1581 only] THE EPISTLE.] DEDICATORIE (variant * outer) *3r.hl

4.37 labour (if] labour) if (variant * inner) *3v.23

5.27 healthfull] healtfull (variant * outer) *4v.10

5.29–30 Your Majesties most humble and obedient subject *Richard Mulcaster*] Your Maiesties most humble and obedient subiect RICHARD MULCASTER. (variant * outer) *4v.13–14

6.6 Quod,] Quod (MS, letter from Mulcaster to Ortelius, 24 April 1581; see Bibliography part 1) 2*1r.7

7.30 referre:] referre, (MS) 2*1v.7

8.1 ARGUMENTES] ARGVMEMTES 2*2r.1 These 'arguments,' or content summaries, appear on sigs 2*2r–4v of the original and also precede each chapter in the book proper, possibly from the same manuscript. I follow the text of the chapter headings which appear to have been set more carefully. I have however corrected the chapter headings, using 2*2r–4v in several instances: 'circunstance' (for 'circunctance' at 21.13 in this edition/8.4 in 1581), 'dores' (for 'daores' 61.1/51.12), 'exercises. Why' (for 'exercises, why' 63.24/54.8), 'infirmities' (for 'infirmites' 184.24/183.25) 'disallowance' (for 'dissallowance' 184.29/183.30), 'sciences' (for 'scieces' 184.31/183.32), 'children' (for 'childre' 221.26/224.22), 'entertainement' (for 'entertaiment' twice at 230.26–7/234.15–16), 'and' (for 'aud' 230.27/234.16), 'meanes' (for 'meeanes' 258.32/265.11), 'in' (for 'is' 258.34/265.13). For the convenience of the reader, I have added page numbers to the contents of each chapter; these were not supplied in the original.

20.10 Grammarian:] Grammarian: 6.31–2

21.13 *circunstance*] *circunctance* 8.4 (see 2*2r above)

22.13 ende:] ende: 9.3

22.33–4 to that,] to it, (see errata list 294) 9.25

23.11 authoritie] authoirtie 10.4

27.18 *were*] *weere* (variant B inner) 14.28

35.33 be] he 23.36

39.13 discern] dscern 27.25

42.5 proper] propter 30.29

43.15–16 write, as the tongue is stirring and redy to read. And though] write as the tongue is stirring & redy to read. And thogh (variant D outer) 32.5–6

48.10 recoyling] recoylong 37.19

50.36 foorth] foorh 40.17

53.20 time,] time 43.11

53.34 instrumentall] iustrumentall 43.25

56.21 but] hut 46.23

57.32 eche] 4eche (variant; the 4 in the page number slipped down into the first line of the text in some copies) 48.hl–1

59.11 bulke,] bulke 49.23

59.15 thorough out] thorought 49.27 (this could also read simply 'thorough')

60.31 supported] suppected (variant G inner) suspected (another variant; the variant 'supported' is correct on authority of errata list 294) 51.6

60.35 Physicall] Phisicall (variant G inner) 51.10

61.1 dores] daores 51.12 (see 8.1 above)

62.29 nor] not 53.7

63.24 exercises. Why] exercises, why 54.8 (see 8.1 above)

66.34 disperseth] disperpleth (see note in commentary) 57.19–20

69.30 staing.] staing, 60.24

69.23 heat] health (variant H outer) 60.28

70.11 where] Where 61.6

70.14 red] read (variant H outer) 61.9

70.23 younger *Plinie*] young *Plinie* (variant H outer) 61.19

72.22 exercise] excercise 63.24 (see note in commentary)
72.27 a great] agreat 63.29
72.34 lightsome] light some (loose line) 63.36
74.2 sobbing,] sobbing 65.7
75.17 best] beast 66.27
79.15 athleticall] achleticall 70.38
80.33 hippes,] hippes 72.19
81.2 them] then 72.28 (because of the repeated pronoun, 'them' seems much better than 'then', though 'then' could work)
81.18 holesome] wholesome (variant K outer) 73.7
82.11 worthy] worhy 74.4
84.18 egde] eggde (variant K outer) 76.17
84.33 wrastle, for] wrastle. For (variant K outer) 76.34
85.20 warriers, which] warriers. Which (variant K outer) 77.23
86.19 excrementes] execrementes 78.22
88.31 home] whome (variant K outer) 80.36
90.31 third] thrid 83.2 (see note in commentary)
91.4 For] Fot 83.15
93.33 cleare.] cleare, 86.16
94.16 excrements,] excrements 86.38
94.29g trees.] trees 87.15g
95.26 21.] *21.* 88.14
101.2 by that word] by word (errata list 294) 94.1
101.17 palsie:] palsie 94.16
105.16 De parua pila lib.] De pa r pila lib. (variant; type slipped) 98.25–6g
106.28 therein,] thererin, 100.4
106.30 opinion] opininon 100.5
107.31 vantage] vantange 101.8
108.16 learned] lear- (errata list 294) 101.32
109.14 both] boh 102.32
110.31 therby] ther by (line break) 104.11–12
111.10g 2.] (not in 1581)
111.17 legges,] legges. 104.36
111.25 sides] si des (line break) 105.6–7
112.34 Neither] Nether (variant O inner) 106.17
114.8–9 commandement] commaundemet ('e' contraction not marked) 107.29
116.31 *exulceration*] *exulration* 110.19–20
120.5 cannot] connot 113.36
120.7 appointed] aopointed 114.2
122.3 argumentes] argmentes 115.38
124.1 to] ro 118.1

136.32 *frictions*] frictions (variant Q outer) 121.2–3
126.34 *chafing*] chafing (variant Q outer) 121.4
127.16 time] time, (variant Q outer) 121.22
127.27 scrapte] scrapt (variant Q outer) 121.34
127.31 it?] it, (variant Q outer) 121.38
129.27 heavenly] heauently 123.34–5
130.21 1. De san. tu.] (some copies omit) 124.30–1g
130.36 and that] an that (variant Q outer) 125.10
130.38 sickish] sickeish (variant Q outer) 125.12
133.15 steares] styrres (errata list 294) 127.32
133.31 *moving*] moouing (variant Q outer) 128.11
134.2–3 *dipnosophistes, symposiakes*] *dionosophyses, symposiates* (variant Q outer) 128.21–2
134.5 your] yours 128.24
134.12–13 sift out of] sift of out (variant Q outer) 128.32
134.14 argument, whose] argument. Whose (variant Q outer) ment. whose (another variant) 128.34
135.8 executor] excutor 129.30
138.16 considerations] con- considerations 133.6–7
138.27–8 wonder] vonder 133.19
141.29 to avoyd] to a- to auoyd 136.29–30
142.35 will] will 138.1
143.7 it is necessary] it necessary 138.11
144.27 himselfe] kimselfe 139.37
144.30 burden to] burdento 140.2
144.33 fittest] fitteth 140.5
148.8 blood.] blood 143.21
153.16 if he] ifhe 149.12
154.37 parentes, so curteous] parentes, so curteou (variant) parentes, so curteo u (variant: loose line) 151.1
155.3 lightly] lighly 151.7
155.21 submit] su bmit 151.26
165.6 that] the (errata list 303.15) 162.12
165.15g degrees.] degrees 162.22
165.18 universitie] vniuersite 162.25
167.1 within] with in 164.14
167.13 counterfeat:] counterfeat 164.27
168.1 suffered] fuffered 165.17
168.32–3 where the] wherethe 166.12
168.38 deceyved:] deceyued: 166.18
170.9 withstand] withstaud 167.28

170.11 for the] forthe 167.30
170.15g countrey.] ountrey. 167.35–6g
174.26–7 howsoever] howsouer 172.24–5
174.30 beloth] be loth 172.28
174.39 and] [omitted] 173.1 (though it is given in catchword at 172.39)
175.22 comprehend] compre hend 173.23–4
176.18 education] educa tion 174.22–3
176.33 if for] iffor 175.1
177.35 with weight] withweight 176.7
178.21 therfore] ther fore 176.34–5
179.24 if for] iffor 177.21
180.17 How much.] Howmuch 179.1
181.31 extraordinarie] exaraordinarie 180.20
183.2 thoroughly] thorougly 181.35
183.12 housewife] housewise 182.7–8
184.24 infirmities] infirmites 183.25 (see 8.1 above)
184.29 disallowance] dissallowance 183.30 (see 8.1 above)
184.31 sciences] scieces 183.32 (see 8.1 above)
185.34 taught in private] taught in in private 184.36–7
186.15 cognisaunce)] cognisaunce) 185.22
186.26 your end] yo ur end 185.33
187.18 for] for for 186.28–9
188.3 spite:] spite: 187.16
[In 1581 only:] Aa ij (variant Aa outer) AA ij (variant) 187.39
190.24 without] with out 189.24
190.19g private] pri uate 190.3–4g
191.23g Maister] M. (expanded) 191.11
192.10 *Quintilianes*] *Qintilianes* 192.1
192.31 amended] amen ded 192.23
192.33 private] primate (errata list 294) 192.25–6
194.7–8 private. For] priuate, for (variant Bb inner) 194.6
194.30 state:] state, (variant Bb inner) 194.29
194.31 *gentilitie*] gentility (variant Bb inner) 194.30
194.34 beyond] beyong (variant Bb inner) 194.34
195.16 justice which greate] iustice, which greate (variant Bb inner) iustice, where the great (another variant) 195.18–19
195.27 prais for that which is seen, but is to be suspected,] prais, for that which is seen, but is to be suspected, (variant Bb inner) praise, for that which is seene, but is to be suspect, (another variant) 195.30
195.32 veale] vaile (variant Bb inner) 195.35
196.16 needes] needees 196.23

196.22 ill] il (variant Bb outer) 196.30
196.29 auncestours] ancetours 196.36
197.10 traine] trane (variant Bb outer) 197.19
197.16g foloweth] folow eth 197.28–9g
197.22g gentlemanly] gentle manly 197.33–4g
197.23 the bodie] rhe bodie 197.34
197.31 their] the (variant Bb inner) 198.5
198.1 *nobilitie*] *nobilite* (variant Bb inner) 198.14
198.12 of *gentilitie*] of the *gentilitie* (variant Bb inner) 198.26
198.13 *nobilitie*] *nobiltie* 198.27
199.30 shewed] shewed 200.12
203.19 ministers] miniters 204.18–19
203.22 according] ac- according 204.21–2
203.36 distinction] distincton 204.37
203.37 better] bettter 204.38
203.39 to] ro 205.3
206.14 *nobilitie*] *nobilitie* 207.28
207.7 contrarie] conrrarie 208.25
207.24 affaires,] affaires 209.4
208.6g sea.] sea, 209.30g
208.11 travellour] ttauellour 209.33
208.13 misdemener] misdeemener (variant Dd outer) 209.36
209.10 acquaintaunce] acquaintauce 210.37
209.12 where it] where is 211.1
209.14 upon] vp on 211.2
211.7 state, is] state is 213.3
211.27 overgrowen] ouergrower 213.24
213.3 drive] Drive 215.5
213.26 abroad] adroad 215.31
214.8 state of his] state ofhis 216.15
214.18 how] h ow 216.26
214.20 judgement] iudge ment 216.28–9
214.28 of ten] often 216.37
215.13 departure] departnre 217.25
215.21 were] vere 217.33
215.22 either] eithet 217.35
217.1 from whence] fromwhence 219.18
217.26 fensed] fen sed 220.7
217.34 are] are: 220.16
218.21 daunter] danuter 221.6
218.30g Ad Nicoclem.] Ad I. Nicocleon. (errata list 294) 221.17–18g

219.25 not in] in not (errata list 294) 222.16
220.18 of his] ofhis 223.11
220.30 humilitie] humililie 223.24
[In 1581 only:] 224 is incorrectly numbered '214'
221.26 children] childre 224.22 (see 8.1 above)
[In 1581 only:] 226 is incorrectly numbered '1[turned 2]6'
223.28 considerations] considetations 226.28–9
224.22 abilitie] abililie 227.26
224.30 homely] heauenly (errata list 294 and variant Ff inner) 227.34
225.27 of had] ofhad 228.35
226.1 good] great (errata list 294) 229.11
226.25 neighbours] neigbours 229.37
227.15 alow] allow (variant Ff inner) 230.29
227.21 fifth] first (errata list 294) 230.35
230.11 discretion] distretion 233.37
230.26 *entertainement*] *entertaiment* 234.15 (see 8.1 above)
230.27 *and*] *aud* 234.16
230.27 *entertainement*] *entertaiment* 234.16 (see 8.1 above)
232.31 stroke] stocke (errata list 294) 236.21
234.1g entertainement] enter tainement 237.36–7g
234.22 false] falfe 238.21
234.38 though] thoug 238.38
235.12g generally.] generally 239.15g
236.33 but that] butthat 241.3
237.13g mathematikes.] mathe matikes 241.24–5g
237.26 mathematicall] mathe- ticall 241.38–242.1
237.31 in schooles:] inschooles: 242.5
238.4 deede] deeede 242.20
239.2 credit] ceedit 243.20
239.4 eloquence,] eloquence 243.23
239.11 *Elizabeth*] *Elizaheth* 243.30
239.12 *Bukley*] *Bnkley* 243.31
239.16 *Bukley*] *Bnkley* 243.36
239.24 colledge] colldege 244.6
240.2 to the] tothe 244.25
240.4 experience] exeperience 244.27
240.11 without] with out 244.34–5
242.7g necessitie] neces sitie 246.36–7g
242.24g necessitie] neces sitie 247.18–19g
243.14 brought] brough 248.10
243.19 *posteriora*] *prosteriora* (variant Hh outer) 248.16

243.35 generall] gene- nerall (variant Hh outer) 248.33–4
244.17 *Figulus*] *Figulns* 249.18
244.19 *Vitruvius.*] *Vitruuius* 249.20
244.26 *Augustus*] *Angustus* (variant Ii outer) 249.28
244.34g necessitie] neces sitie 249.35–6g
245.18g 4.5.6.] 3.4.5. (incorrect numeration of the points; I here omit '6.' from 245.33g [215.1g in 1581])
248.24 direction:] direction: 254.2
248.29g readers.] rea ders 254.11–12g
248.39 in] in in 254.19–20
250.4 landes,] landes 255.28
250.14 wealthy] the wealthy (errata list 294) 256.1
250.3 goods] good 256.1
250.17 revenew] re uenew 256.4
251.7 *universitie,* or from within, either] *vniuertie,* or from within, eitther (variant Ii outer) 256.35
251.12 But] but 257.3
252.13 The] T*he* 258.9
252.17 give] gave (errata list 294) 258.13
252.28g admission] admis sion 258.25–6g
252.36 such a] sucha 258.34
258.32 *meanes*] *meeanes* 265.11 (see 8.1 above)
258.34 *in*] *is* 265.13 (see 8.1 above)
261.20 beseeme] be seeme 268.4
262.7 discharge] dischage 268.33
[In 1581 only:] 269 incorrectly numbered '[turned 2]69'
262.39 never a] nener a 269.29–30
263.6 without] with out 269.35–6
263.12 *allowance*] *allowancc* 270.4
264.38 bookes] kookes 271.37
265.33 will] wlll 272.36
265.34 monumentes] monumen[turned t]es 272.37
266.5 *enthusiasme*] *enthousiame* (variant Mm outer) 273.10
266.35 children] Children 274.5
266.38 verses] ver ses 274.8–9
267.35 an opinion] any opinon (errata list 294) 275.9
273.39 *impunitie*] *impuritie* (variant Nn outer) 281.36
276.19 with all] withall (variant Nn outer) 284.26
276.19 encouragement.] encouragement 284.26
277.24 things:] things 285.36
277.28 *parentes* and *teachers*] *parentes* and *tachers* 286.4

278.18 execute] excute 286.32
278.38 which] wich 287.15
279.7g teachers] tea chers 287.27g
279.12 appeale] ap peale 287.29
279.20 maister,] maister., 287.38
279.29g Conference] Conferene 288.9g
281.32g 4.] [one copy omits] 289.15g
280.39 where] were 289.25
281.14 *conference,*] *conference* (variant Oo inner) 290.2
281.34 *monopolies*] *monopoleis* 290.25
[In 1581 only:] 291.39 Oo ij missigned 'O ij'
[In 1581 only:] 292 incorrectly numbered '291'
283.7 sequele] sequell (variant Oo outer) 292.2
283.12 doares] doores (variant Oo outer) 292.8
284.14 that *certaintie*] that*certaintie* 293.13
286.28 *booke*] *kooke* 295.37
290.16 strength] strenght 299.37
291.1 should] shonld 300.25
[In 1581 only] 302 incorrectly reads '303'
292.17 rowme] rowmeh (second state of variant Pp inner) rowmh (first state of variant) 302.9

LOCATION OF COPIES

Copies seen are starred once; copies machine-collated are starred twice. Fuller descriptions of all but four of these are given in Barker PH D, appendix 1, 225–41. Copies not starred have been described to me by librarians from the respective insitutions. An (a) after a copy indicates it is *STC* 18253a (Vautrollier), of which there are 20 copies; no (a) indicates it is *STC* 18253 (Vautrollier and Chard). There are other copies in private hands.

Ann Arbor, University of Michigan (a)
Boston Public Library *
Cambridge, King's College **
Cambridge, Magdalene College (a) *
Cambridge, Queen's College (a) *
Cambridge, St John's College *
Cambridge University Library *
Cambridge University Library (Peterborough Cathedral) (a) *
Cambridge, Mass, Harvard University (a) *

Chicago, Newberry Library (a) *
Edinburgh, National Library of Scotland (a) *
Greensboro, NC, University of North Carolina
Liverpool University Education Library *
London, British Library (a) *
London, Dulwich College
London, St Paul's School *
London, Sion College *
London, University ['copy 1 of 1st issue'] *
London, University ['copy 2 of 1st issue'] *
London, University ['copy 3 of 2nd issue'] (a) *
New Haven, Yale University (Beinecke) (a) **
New Haven, Yale University (History of Medicine) (a) **
New York, Columbia University *
New York, Pierpont Morgan Library
Oxford, Bodleian Library (a) *
Oxford, St John's College (a) *
Oxford, Wadham College *
San Marino, Huntington Library *
Skipton Public Library (a) *
Stratford-upon-Avon, Shakespeare Birthplace Trust (a)
Urbana, University of Illinois [copy 1]
Urbana, University of Illinois [copy 2] (a)
Washington, DC, Folger Shakespeare Library [18253] **
Washington, DC, Folger Shakespeare Library [18253a 1] (a) **
Washington, DC, Folger Shakespeare Library [18253a 2] (a) **
Washington, DC, Folger Shakespeare Library [18253a 3, incomplete] (a) **
Washington, DC, Library of Congress **
Wellington, NZ, Alexander Turnbull Library (a)
Untraced: Quaritch catalogue of November 1906, item 323, a presentation copy from 'Richard Mulcaster to his Friende Mr. Ferdinando Fildinge.' A Ferdinand Fyldinge in Venn *Athenae Cantabrigienses* part 1, 2:137 matriculated at Gonville in 1555 and may have married Isabel Ashley. Mulcaster's wife was Katherine Ashley and so Ferdinand Fildinge may be a relative by marriage. Dr Arthur Freeman kindly checked and found that Quaritch has no further information on the sale.

❧ Commentary

The notes are keyed to page and line number. The addition 'g' refers to the marginal gloss.

In the earlier version of my work I followed the first edition of the *Oxford English Dictionary*, and for this revision I decided not to adjust the references to the second edition (1989), which, though a masterful work of organization of text, adds hardly a thing to the record for Early Modern English (Brewer 'The Second Edition of the *Oxford English Dictionary*'). *Positions* (in the edition of Quick) was used by the compilers of the first edition of *OED*, and part of my task was to modify the record of that work. The general accuracy of the *OED* is excellent, despite weakness in the area of chronology and occasional misdefinition (all corrections are starred in the index); general problems in dating have been taken up by Bailey ed *Early Modern English* and Schäfer *Documentation in the 'O.E.D.'* In my notes, 'cited' without a date means the passage in *Positions* was cited in the *OED*; 'first cited' means that the passage is the earliest usage cited in the *OED*; 'first citation' with a date gives the earliest *OED* usage; other abbreviations are those standard in the dictionary.

Generally, only the first use of a word in a particular sense is defined in the commentary, but all annotations are indexed. The reader should therefore check the index for words apparently not glossed. Because Mulcaster's wordplay is so relentless, the definitions should be taken only as starting points. Inevitably the commentary will be incomplete: Montaigne, speaking for all readers, finds 'subject for doubt in what the commentary has not deigned to touch on' (*Essais* 3.13).

For fuller citations of publications referred to below, see the bibliography. Translations of standard classical works are taken from the Loeb Classical Library.

1.1 POSITIONS] propositions, assertions, theses (sb 2)

1.2–3 PRIMITIVE] primary (a 3 cited)

1.3 CIRCUMSTANCES] adjuncts of an action – time, place, manner, cause, etc (sb 2). This word is deceptively close to our modern sense of 'prevailing conditions,' but as Mulcaster shows in chapter 3, he is using the term in the fairly technical sense familiar to students of rhetoric.

1.9 *erected*] established, founded (v 9 obs). The building was erected in the modern sense during the reign of Edward III (228.23 note).

3.1ff *TO THE MOST VERTU- / OUS LADIE*] This 'Epistle Dedicatorie' is reprinted in Gebert ed *An Anthology of Elizabethan Dedications and Prefaces* 54–7. In the Appendix to his edition, Quick comments that the tone of the letter 'is not that of a stranger, but rather of an old acquaintance, who is sure of a friendly reception' (303), a pleasant but doubtful conjecture. Mulcaster's court connection was by 1581 limited solely to the dramatic activities of the Merchant Taylors' boys under his direction (Chambers *The Elizabethan Stage* 2:75–6), though later he received gifts from the Queen (see introduction, lxviii). *Positions* is one of seven works known to have been dedicated to Elizabeth in 1581 (Williams *Index of Dedications* 61).

3.5 traine] training, education (sb[1] 4 only citation; the word is found throughout *Positions*)

3.7 enable] strengthen (v 3a citing 231.7)

3.8 countenaunce] patronage, favour (sb 8; here with the extra sense of 'notice')

3.9 credit] reputation, power derived from that reputation (sb 5–6)

3.10–11 common patronage ... conceites] ie, to what extent would the patronage of a lesser knight or city merchant encourage my ideas? ('Conceit' sb 5)

3.13 my first travell] Despite this unequivocal statement, *The Quenes Majesties Passage* of 1559 (*STC* 7590–1) has been ascribed to Mulcaster; see introduction, xl and note 11. If what Mulcaster says here and at 288.18–19 is to be believed, *Positions* is indeed his first printed work. The combined sense in 'travell' of 'labour,' 'voyage,' and 'literary work' is found throughout *Positions*.

3.27 consequence] outcome, with the special sense of the conclusion to a syllogism (sb 3 obs)

4.7 obsequious] dutiful, obedient (a 1)

4.9 title] chapter (sb 2 obs; there is possibly a play on 'tittle' or a jot, a whit). Of the authors who dedicated books to Elizabeth in 1581, only one other went so far as to ask her to read the accompanying work, and did so as diffidently as Mulcaster. Thomas Lupton *A Persuasion from Papestrie* sig a2r says: 'And thoughe there might seeme in mee, too muche boldenesse, to crave of your Majestie, to reade this presently: yet I beseech your Highnesse to view and peruse it at your leysure conveniently.' Of course, for his educational reforms to be put into effect, it was important that Mulcaster have the attention of the Queen. The topos of diffidence may come from Horace *Epistles* 2.1.1–4 where he acknowledges he may be taking Augustus away from matters more important than poetry.

4.10 the paw of a Lion] Tilley L313 'A lion is known by his paw (claw)' (cf Erasmus *Adagia* in LB 2:347D trans CWE 32:200 'Leonem ex unguibus aestimare'). The comparison of Mulcaster's own work with the Queen's majesty ('Lion') is rather daring, though Mulcaster lessens the impact of the statement by his play on 'proverbe' and 'propertie.'

4.15 officious] dutiful (a2 obs first citation 1588)

4.15–16 referendarie] judge, referee in a dispute (sb 1; *OED* cites this under sb 3 'one who ... furnishes news ...; a reporter', but the act of judging is surely implied in the last clause of Mulcaster's sentence.)

4.22 conceit] opinion (sb 4 obs; see 3.11)

4.27 commoditie] benefit (2c obs)

5.8–9 all Grammers into one fourme] Mulcaster refers to what was called 'Lyly's Latin Grammar,' the 'Authorized Grammar,' or the 'Royal Grammar', which had become stabilized by 1549 (*STC* 15611) as [William Lily and John Colet] *A Short Introduction of Grammar*. The small text laid out in English an analysis of the parts of Latin speech, contained a separate Latin grammar, and concluded with several items also in Latin, a poem by Lily (the famous 'Carmen de moribus,' beginning 'Qui mihi discipulus ...'), the Lord's Prayer, the Creed, the Ten Commandments, etc. It was by decrees of Henry VIII, Edward VI, and Elizabeth I the standard introductory text, and was printed in many editions in vast numbers. The work, though often ascribed to Lily alone, was a composite of earlier grammars by Colet, Erasmus, Lily, and other scholars. As the preface of 1549 (reprinted in later editions) indicated, the work was designed specifically to bring greater uniformity into the teaching of grammar in the schools, and thereby to counteract the variety and turnover of both boys and schoolmasters, problems of central importance to all in the teaching profession. The role of the grammar in religious conformity was also important in its adoption. The very complicated story of the text (which in one form or another remained standard until the middle of the nineteenth century through some 350 separate editions) is told by Flynn 'The Grammatical Writings of William Lily, ?1468–?1523,' Baldwin *William Shakspere's Small Latine* 2:690–701, Tuck 'The Latin Grammar Attributed to William Lily,' C.G. Allen 'The Sources of "Lily's Latin Grammar": A Review of the Facts and Some Further Suggestions,' and, for a slightly earlier period, Shaw 'The Earliest Latin Grammars in English.'

5.13 rarely] unusually well (adv 3 first citation 1590)

5.23 petie] insignificant; appropriate to elementary learning (a pun, used often in *Positions*, on 'Petty' a 2 [this passage first cited] and an adjective from 'Petty' B 2 sb)

5.25 do soure even a sweete] Proverbial; Tilley M839 ('Sweet meat will have sour sauce')

6.1ff. *AVTHOR IPSE AD librum suum.*] The usual practice was for an author or publisher to preface a work with the commendatory verses of other writers, or with verses addressed to a patron or patrons. Mulcaster was himself rather skilled at composing Latin verses for the works of others; see introduction, lxvii. In the only poem introducing his *Elementarie*, Mulcaster begins: 'Nae tu parue liber, non debes tristior ire, / Quod frontem decorent carmina nulla tuam' (Little book, you need not go forth sadly because no songs adorn your brow; sig ¶3r; an echo of the opening lines of Ovid's *Tristia*). The poem here is translated as follows:

> *The Author to His Book.* That innate natural desire to be of service dislikes the slothful course of an indolent way of life. Frugal with food, ever hungry, devoted to hard toil, and prodigal of the midnight oil, this desire urges forward the work (undertaken). It brings it forth as soon as it has observed that the work will be able to bear the light, even though, filled with considerable fear, it laments the work's exposure. It grieves that its offspring, which could have remained safely at home, has been sent forth, exposed to a thousand perils. And pale with fear of criticism from an alien judge, it afflicts its own hope (for success) with foreboding. But the work needs the sun to survive, it must go forth, and duty (*iura*) summons that which a concern for the public good has generated. Its welfare must be entrusted to a Fortune guided by provident virtue and the great right hand of the Father. And so to a raging Neptune the learned little skiff commits its sails, the only hope in the midst of the waters. But my hope is greater, for my undertaking is in the hands of the race of the Gods which is present with its unerring divine power in doubtful matters. Go then, little book, you who are to be the first gamble (*tessera*) of your parent, entrust yourself to your fate. And because, wherever you go, you will endure in the midst of your journeys the most unrestrained criticisms of men concerning you, report what each one notes down and finds wanting in you, that I may be more careful in the future. In the meanwhile, humbly beg pardon for both of us, for what will be your error was originally mine. An error will be ascribed to neither of us once I have become aware of it, since a corrected fault will cause no offence. It will be your concern to report the parts which may be erroneous; it will be my task to correct them. For the novelty of this undertaking, unattempted by

> any of our forefathers on this very course on which you are proceeding, threatens us both with many errors and failings. Surely I shall not permit such defects to remain, once I have found them out. The friendly goodwill of my reader is so dear to me that I want those faults deleted which will displease him. (Translated by F.A.C. Mantello)

The poem was appended in autograph to Mulcaster's letter to Abraham Ortelius, 24 April 1581; Mulcaster contracted many of the Latin forms here spelled out by the compositor, but otherwise there are only the two minor differences noted in the apparatus. In the conventional image of the little boat, Mulcaster combines the double meaning of 'literary work' and 'voyage' found in his regular use of the word 'travell' (3.13).

8.1ff THE ARGUMENTES ... TITLE.] By 'title' is here meant 'division or part of a work or subject' (sb 2 citing 227.21; see 4.9). These 'argumentes' appear with some modifications as chapter headings in the body of the work. There are a number of discrepancies in spelling between the two settings (eg, retaining here the original page numbers, 2*2r.24 '*whereby*' for 25.1 '*wherby*'; 2*3r.36 '*master*' for 122.23 '*maister*'; 2*4v.3 '*too*' for 265.11 '*two*'). Substantive differences are, again with original paging, 2*3r.37 '*the*' (122.26 omits); 2*3v.1 '*in*' (122.28 '*of*'); 2*3v.19 '*learne to*' (141.10 omits); 2*4r.28 '*her*' (234.22 '*his*'); 2*4r.37 '*maketh*' (259.8 '*worketh*'). The question here is which setting more accurately represents Mulcaster's manuscript. From the evidence of the omissions, it would appear that the forms in sig 2* are closer, and that possibly the headnotes were set from the preliminaries. The readings of '*his*' for '*her*' and '*worketh*' for '*maketh*' are not easily explained, and show considerable latitude on the part of the compositor(s), if indeed the preliminaries were the basis for the headnotes and not a separate manuscript.

9.23 *whether*] ie, weather (spelling repeated at 61.1). Mulcaster lists 'weather' and 'wheather' in the Generall Table of *Elementarie*, sig 2E3r; the compositor's spellings in the phrase 'whether the weather be faire or fowle' (63.21–2) show a clear difference between the two, and quite likely represent manuscript authority.

15.11 sharp a rehersall] harsh or unpleasant restatement (of the current problems) (sb 1)

15.12g The quotation marks in the margins are used to indicate a parenthetical general observation. Marginal quotation marks are used only three times more in the text, each time differently, at pp 181, 271–2, 281. There are many instances in *Positions* where they could have been used, as almost every page has some tag of sententious wisdom, and it is therefore difficult to understand why they have been used the few times they have. See, for background, G.K. Hunter 'The Marking of *Sententiae*.'

15.13 aggravation] irritation (sb 6 [*OED* supplies no citations]; that there is a physical sense to the word is carried by the medical imagery running through this paragraph – 'healed,' 'gaules,' 'pacient,' etc)

15.18 empeached] hindered ('impeach' v 1–2)

15.19 gaules] irritations ('gall' sb² 2)

15.20 partie pacient] person under cure (that 'partie' is not an adjective is shown by its use at 15.12; for a similar construction, see 'partes pacient' 117.34)

15.22 apayd] satisfied, contented (v 1)

15.24–5 sowreth not the meane] does not make the instrument (of healing) bitter (to the saved man) (sb² 10)

16.1 furthwith] forthwith ('Furth' obs)

16.1 bewraied] revealed, made known (v 4)

16.1 chek] reprimand, censure (sb¹ 4 and 4b)

16.2 I have taught ...] From what he says here, Mulcaster began teaching in 1559, possibly right after he served in the first parliament of Elizabeth's reign. In September 1561 he was officially appointed headmaster of the new school (at 228.29 he says he has taught there 'now twenty yeares'). Where he taught from 1559 to 1561 is not known.

16.10 lettes] hindrances, obstructions (sb¹ 1)

16.21 reaper] This is the first instance of an image which is used throughout. Images of planting and husbandry are commonplace in writings about education; eg, Quintilian 1.3.5; 'On the Education of Children' in Plutarch *Moralia* 2B, 2E, 4C, 8B, 9B; Erasmus *De pueris* in LB 1:491D (CWE 26:300); Elyot *The Boke Named the Governour* 1.4 ed Croft 1:28; Ascham *Toxophilus* in *English Works* ed Wright 58–9; Montaigne *Essais* 1.26 in *Oeuvres complètes* ed Thibaudet and Rat 147.

16.22 allow] approve (of 'my travell') (v¹ 2b; an unusual intransitive use)

16.23 meaning] intention (vbl sb¹ 1)

16.24 naturall English toungue] Cf 288.38ff and *Elementarie* sigs 2F2r, 2G4v (and, for a lengthy defence of English, K3rff and 2H2rff). In a letter 'To all Gentle Men and Yomen of Englande' in his *Toxophilus* (in *English Works* ed Wright xii–xvii), Ascham admits he writes not for the delectation of the learned as much for 'the pleasure or commoditie, of the gentlemen and yeoman of Englande, for whose sake I tooke this matter in hande' (xiv). For an extensive background to Ascham's and Mulcaster's statements, see R.F. Jones *The Triumph of the English Language* especially chapter 2, 'The Language of Popular Instruction' 32–67. Jones describes the deep sense of duty that impelled many scholars to make ancient learning available to their countrymen; there was, however, some resistance to the popularization of learning, above all in the professions (50).

16.37 mostwhat] for the most part ('Most' a C cited)

16.38 no latinistes] Of the fathers of 692 pupils under Mulcaster, only 21 (3 percent) were involved in work requiring some kind of advanced education (church, law, medicine). The great majority of the others were in the cloth trade and the remainder in a vast miscellany of other occupations (introduction, lxv–lxvi).

17.7 Latin] speak or write Latin (v obs 1b 1)

17.11 dedicate] dedicated (pa ppl, an obs form; removal of the last syllable is called apocope)

17.12 the terms of learning] How to use the 'terms of art,' the specialized vocabulary associated with any learned discipline, in order to communicate with an unlearned audience was a problem discussed by a number of authors; see R.F. Jones *Triumph of the English Language* 71ff. It was felt that many of the special terms in the classical languages could not be properly translated into a language as impoverished as English.

17.15 first blush] first glance (sb 2)

17.18 intitled] given a rightful claim ('Entitle' v 4)

17.19 warrant] promise (v 7b obs)

17.21 pith] force (sb 4)

17.25 conceit] notion, idea (1 obs)

17.31 foundation] The image ('plat,' 'ground') is used throughout *Positions;* cf Tilley F619 'Be sure to build on a good foundation.'

17.31 Grammarian] studies in grammar ('Grammarian' is being used here as the substantive form of the adjective, meaning 'of the grammar school or studies'; see also 18.38 and 19.17. The adjective 'Grammarian' is not in *OED;* normally the word was a noun: one versed in the study of grammar, or a pupil in grammar studies.)

17.32–4 Elementarie ... to the Grammar schoole] The division between elementary and grammar school education was not very neatly drawn in Mulcaster's time. The elementary or 'petty' student studied the ABC, basic writing and reading, and learned the Catechism, perhaps in Latin. He might have done this in a special school or in the lowest class in a grammar school. Grammar studies could begin between the ages of six and eight, though usually later; the boy could leave for university or work at about fifteen or sixteen, often a year or two older (Brown *Elizabethan Schooldays* 44–7; Stowe *English Grammar Schools* 127; and see note 31.22–3 below).

17.35 president] precedent (an alternative spelling; it is used in *Elementarie* sig 2C4r)

18.1 methode] Thomas Wilson *The Rule of Reason* (1551) sig E4v defines 'method' as 'The maner of handeling a single Question, and the readie waie howe to teache and sette forth any thyng plainlie, and in order, as it should be, in latine, Methodus.' Method is a principal topic in the history of philosophy; in the Renaissance, a self-conscious concern with method (or 'the maner of proceding' as Mulcaster puts it) is found in any learned and in many a popular treatise. Any 'art' or regular subject of human inquiry was felt to have a content based on a very few premises. If these premises could be articulated they would provide an almost immediate entry into the art. Of course in the hands of certain writers, method was (and remains) a highly complex area of philosophy, concerned with problems of language and epistemology. For others, 'method' became synonymous with 'simplification,' and in an age of popular instruction a philosophically respectable theory of simplification was bound to be quickly embraced and used to its fullest advantage. The many manuals of learning organized around highly schematic structures (eg, Ascham's *Toxophilus*, Dee's Preface to Euclid's *Elements* tr Billingsley) are the response of writers, trained in the method of Aristotle and his sixteenth-century commentators, to the popular need for rapid instruction in the arts. For general background, see Neal W. Gilbert *Renaissance Concepts of Method* and Vasoli *La dialettica e la retorica dell'Umanesimo*. Howell *Logic and Rhetoric in England, 1500–1700* deals with the debate over method as it developed in England. The principal figure in the new method was Pierre de la Ramée or Petrus Ramus (d 1572), whose work Mulcaster does not refer to, though in 1589 Nashe *Works* 1:48 (see my introduction, xliii) associates him with 'Rams horne rules' (for Ramist method, Ong *Ramus, Method, and the Decay of Dialogue*).

Mulcaster's 'method' is less dialectical than rhetorical. He is concerned to establish the 'primitive groundes' (18.10) and 'first principles' that may be agreed on by his reader, but he does not continue with a closely structured dialectic, relying rather on the statement of 'positions,' as a series of persuasions that his recommended changes in education be understood and allowed. Thus, his method is rhetorical and circumstantial, following argument of 'apparence in probable conjecture' (23.30).

18.6 resolutely] positively, definitely (adv 1 obs)

18.6 enureth] comes into operation (v 3)

18.8 empeachment] hindrance ('Impeachment' sb 1)

18.9 compound] settle (v 6)

18.10 Mathematicall] mathematician (sb B 3 obs). Mathematical writings, especially Euclid's *Elements*, provided a schematic method which was adapted for other arts by Renaissance writers; see Neal W. Gilbert *Renaissance Concepts of Method* 81–2. The method of mathematics, which in an important passage much later in *Positions* Mulcaster characterizes as working by 'unfallible demonstrations,' is not applicable to rhetorical method, but is mentioned here only as a forceful parallel.

18.14 confessions] admissions, concessions (sb 3)

18.18 naturall philosopher] ie, in our terms, a scientist
18.20–1 *Aristotle* ... eight whole bookes] ie, the eight books of the *Physics*.
18.23 entreateth of] deals with (v 1)
18.24 the verie divine] As Mulcaster suggests, the problem of method was important to sixteenth-century theologians; Neal W. Gilbert 'Humanism and the Method of Theology' in his *Renaissance Concepts of Method* 107–12.
18.26 professe] lay claim (v 3)
19.5 haste, to post]
19.6 timely] early (a 1)
19.8–9 scouring] rushing (v[1] 1b)
19.12 carie the countenaunce] be the basis of one's reputation ('Countenance' sb 9)
19.13 proyned] ordered ('Prune' v[1] 4, meaning 'To set in order' first citation 1592; cf *Elementarie* sig C3r 'so well proined and so pikked')
19.13 hast is such a foe ...] Proverbial; cf Tilley F409 'As good a foe that hurts not as a friend that helps not' and H198 'The more haste the less speed'; Mulcaster has written his own proverb here, but it has resonances of these two from Tilley.
19.28–9 beside my schoole ... beside my selfe] ie, by digressing he will show himself to be not quite on the topic of education, but not mad or out of his wits either.
19.33–4 thinke their penny good silver] think well of themselves for no good reason (Tilley P194)
19.35 controwler] director, manager ('Controller' 4)
19.37 devise] opinion, notion (sb 4)
19.39 petinesse] triviality, insignificance ('Pettiness' first citation; also with a play on 'petty' as 'having to do with elementary education')
20.2 marchandable] merchantable, saleable ('Merchantable' 1)
20.4 resolve] free from doubt, bring to understand (v 15 obs)
20.5–6 make more deintie] be more loth, be warier ('Dainty' sb 7 obs)
20.10 him] Though this pronoun might suggest that 'Elementarie' means 'elementary master,' it seems from 18.36 that 'Elementarie' is one of the 'two degrees in learning' and that the pronoun 'him' is impersonal. See 17.32–4 note.
20.16 primitively] at first (adv 1 first citation 1607)
20.19 places] separate particular subjects in the argument ('Place' sb 7b obs; cf Greek 'topos' and Latin 'locus')
20.20 positive] absolute, non-comparative ('Positive' a 5 first citation 1606)
21.1 fantasticall] capricious, arbitrary ('Fantastic' a 4b)
21.2–4 it were an argument ... to displace the meane] ie, just as capricious behaviour disgraces the individual (but does not affect our understanding of

man in general) so the impossible (or ideal) argument seems to threaten our understanding of the mean or everyday average. Mulcaster here and in the next few pages rejects the ideal educational schemes of the ancients in favour of a program based on the actual practice of his own 'circumstances' of time, place, manner, etc. The wordplay on 'man'/'mean,' repeated immediately below, is used elsewhere (for instance back at 15.22).

21.16 *authors*] authorities (sb 4, though sense 3 'writer' is included here)

21.27 controwle] direct, hold sway ('Control' v 4 and cf 'controwler' 19.35)

21.28 chek] restraint by controlling power (sb[1] 9)

21.29–30 authour ... alledger] 'Author' here (as at 21.16) means 'authority'; 'alledger' is 'one who cites the authority.'

22.2 toward] apt, willing to learn (a 3 obs)

22.5 affiaunce] assurance ('Affiance' sb 2)

22.7 soothe] confirm ('Sooth' v 4)

22.13 fined] refined ('Fine' v[3] 1; cf 'fining' 22.37)

22.16 wisemen] Often spelled as one word (*OED* 'Wise man'). That an understanding of the contingent and the circumstantial is the basis for wisdom is an unusually secular claim.

22.17 ods] difference ('Odds' sb 2)

22.24 staied] steady, sober ('Staid' a 3 'of the intellect' cf 18.33)

22.25–6 maketh of all nothing, and of nothing all] Despite proverbial ring, not in Tilley or *ODEP*; the figure is antimetabole.

22.29 raunge] classify, arrange ('Range' v[1] 1)

22.37 *Aristotle*] *Topics* 1.7 (103a)

22.37 fining of] clarifying by discussing in detailed points ('Fine' v[3] 1 and 5; cf 'fined' 22.13)

22.10 praise at the parting] ie, praise our advice only after she has used it and has discovered its true worth (Tilley P83 'Praise at parting'; used again at 82.13)

23.14 stay] support, sustain (v[2] 1b)

23.19–20 two sortes of authours] What follows is a differentiation between methods used by logic (which proceeds by 'a necessitie of a demonstrable subject') and by rhetoric (which proceeds not by necessity of conclusion but by the form of the argument). Aristotle *Rhetoric* 1.1.10 (1355a) shows how the syllogism and the enthymeme are the respective bases for the two arts. The enthymeme is a kind of syllogism, but deals with 'probabilities and signs,' not with necessary truths (ibid 1.2.13 [1357a]). Mulcaster explains how circumstance cannot be discussed in terms of strict logic, but only through 'probable conjecture.' In the following paragraph he goes further to include law, medicine, and divinity as essentially 'rhetorical' subjects that are best considered in the light of circumstance.

23.33–4 lawes ... Phisicke ... Divinitie] Law, medicine, and divinity were the three post-graduate faculties, and were commonly referred to together (see *Elementarie* sig E2v, where they are 'the thre professions').

23.38 staie] control, restraint (sb[3] 2 obs)

24.12–13 accident ... substance] non-essential property ... essential property ('Accident' sb 6 and 'Substance' 1–2, two commonly contrasted terms in scholastic philosophy)

24.13 currant] tendency, drift (of opinions) ('Current' sb 6 first citation 1595)

24.21 to the barre] to judgment (cf 'forced to the stage' 26.11)

24.32 threpte upon] ascribed to ('Threap' v 4b)

24.32 Pollicy] government, conduct of public affairs ('Policy' sb[1] 2 obs)

24.34 schoole pointes] points argued in the debates of the public schools of the university ('School-point' obs)

24.34–5 of account] esteemed ('Account' sb 11)

24.39–25.1 *Plato ... Aristotle ... Cicero ... Quintilian*] Four principal sources of ancient educational theory and practice for the Renaissance and referred to throughout *Positions*.

25.7 wringeth the writer, and wreasteth his meaning] twists the writer's intention and overstrains his meaning ('Wring' v 9b and 'Wrest' v 5)

25.16 supposalles] opinions ('Supposal' sb 3)

25.16 fleeter] deserter (of his country's best interests) (sb 1; not necessarily a 'shifty person' as *OED* suggests in a query with this as the only citation)

25.17 pikt] picked (with additional sense of 'culled,' for afterwards the matter grows)

25.23–4 *Nature ... reason ... custome ... experience ... profit*] These are the five main sources of argument used by Mulcaster in *Positions* and *Elementarie*; his use of these topics is especially apparent in the opening chapters of *Elementarie*, in which he offers a defence of his elementary program.

25.27–8 a student ought rather to invest himselfe in the habite of his writer] Mulcaster argues for 'emulation,' not 'imitation': 'The fact that *aemulatio*, instead of *imitatio*, became the battle-cry of the best humanists from Poliziano ... to Erasmus and subsequently throughout the sixteenth century, is today a commonplace,' according to Hans Baron 'The *Querelle* of the Ancients and the Moderns as a Problem for Renaissance Scholarship' 15; on *aemulatio* see G.W. Pigman III 'Versions of Imitation in the Renaissance' 22ff.

25.32 maine] ie, main thing (with aural play on 'name' reversed; see 289.12)

26.2 For with the alledging of authours ...] Mulcaster is very inconsistent in this regard. Chapters 6 through 35 of *Positions*, based to a great extent on Mercuriale's richly annotated *De arte gynmastica*, are full of cited authorities. Chapters 36 through 45 have in comparison relatively few citations.

26.11 forced to the stage] brought into the open (cf 24.21)

26.20–2 If controversie arise ... the man shal not slyp] ie, if an argument in itself is a good one, it will not be laid to rest easily. If the argument depends solely on the arguer, so long as he is strong will he prevail (despite the proverbial style, not in Tilley or *ODEP*).

26.25 *Rhetorick* takes testimonies] For the differences between rhetoric and logic in so far as their respective uses of witnesses are concerned, see Aristotle *Rhetoric* 1.15.13ff (1375b–6a), Quintilian *Institutio oratoria* book 5, and Cicero *Topica* 19.73ff. Mulcaster follows in this classical tradition.

26.30–2 But for so much as *Reason* ... to presence] ie, because Reason is the basis of any honour they gain, writers must try to leave themselves in the background, and should set only Reason herself before the reader ('preferre her to presence' means 'place her in a position of superiority' as in *OED* 'Prefer' v 4 and 'Presence' 2b)

27.4 fansie ... will] ie, truth is distorted when it is acted upon by these human faculties that shape opinion

27.6 opinative] opinionative ('Opinative')

27.10 overtreat them] prevail upon them by entreaty (v)

27.11 in pointes] in (shared) conclusions (sb 29, or perhaps 'matters under discussion' 27)

27.26 leasing] losing, loss ('Leesing' vbl sb[1])

27.30 Such of the auncient writers] The authors of the 'best framed commonweales' would be Plato (*Republic* and *Laws*) and Aristotle (*Politics*). Mulcaster's other main source in this section is Quintilian. The differences between public and private education are not debated in Plato or Aristotle whereas they are in Quintilian (see 28.16 note). Another possible source is the essay (today believed to be of unknown authorship) 'On the Education of Children' in Plutarch's *Moralia*; because this essay is derivative of earlier authors and was itself copied by so many Renaissance authors, it is hard to tell if Mulcaster actually used it.

27.34–28.1 they do fetch ... farre of] ie, they find the basis for their educational program very early in the child's development (The sentence reads, in skeletal form, 'Such of the auncient writers ..., before they call it in question ... they do fetch ...' The clause '[which] they devise' modifies 'kinde.')

28.1–2 what regard is to be had to the infante] For example, Plato *Laws* 7.794A–B; 'On the Education of Children' in Plutarch *Moralia* 3C–F; Quintilian *Institutio oratoria* 1.1.4–5; Elyot *The Boke Named the Governour* 1.4 ed Croft 1:28ff; Lyly *Euphues* in *Works* ed Bond 1:264ff (following the essay in Plutarch).

28.2 moile] distress themselves (v 4c)

28.4 fines] fineness

28.5 controversie about milkes] A very popular topic: Plato *Republic* 5.460C–D;

Aristotle *Politics* 7.15 (1336a); 'On the Education of Children' in Plutarch *Moralia* 3C–D; Elyot *The Boke Named the Governour* 1.4 (ed Croft 1:29); Lyly *Euphues* in *Works* ed Bond 1:264ff (again, following the essay in Plutarch). There was considerable concern about wet-nursing in sixteenth-century England; see Lawrence Stone *Family* 99ff.

28.6 complexion] composition of humours (sb I 1–2 obs). Mulcaster sets forth a summary of the theory of humours and physiology in chapter 6 of *Positions*; see note at 53.22

28.8 choice] preference (sb 7 obs first citation 1601 for 'special value, estimation')

28.8 forreine] not of the household or family ('Foreign' a 2b obs first citation 1604)

28.10 what companie is to be choosen] Again, one of the standard topics: Plato *Laws* 7 passim; Aristotle *Politics* 7.15 (1336a–b); Quintilian *Institutio oratoria* 1.1.8–9; 'On the Education of Children' in Plutarch *Moralia* 3F–4A; Elyot *The Boke Named the Governour* 1.4 ed Croft 1:31; Lyly *Euphues* in *Works* ed Bond 1:267ff (following the essay in Plutarch).

28.13 choice ... choice] special selection ... well chosen, appropriate (sb 1; a 2 first citation 1588; cf also 28.7 note; typical variation of a single word by Mulcaster)

28.14–15 in good sadnes] in earnest (sb 2b)

28.15 exquisite] accurate, carefully adjusted (a 2)

28.16 private, or publike] at home (under a tutor) or in a formal institution (such as a free endowed grammar school) (*OED* 'Public school' 1 differentiates 'private' and 'public' for education; terms are commonly juxtaposed in Latin as well as English; eg, Quintilian 1.Pr.10; not in Tilley or *ODEP*.)

28.16–17 they still preferre the publike] Plato *Republic* 5.462 and *Laws* 7 passim, in favour of public schooling; Aristotle *Politics* 8.1.2 (1337a) ('it is manifest that education also must necessarily be one and the same for all ...'); Quintilian 1.1.1–31 debates the issue at length, and recommends public schooling; 'On the Education of Children' in Plutarch *Moralia* 4A–C prefers a special tutor. Elyot *The Boke Named the Governour* 1.6 (ed Croft 1:35ff) and Ascham *Scholemaster* in *English Works* ed Wright 171 both recommend tutors. For this important issue, there are also Erasmus *De pueris* in LB 1:504A–D trans CWE 26:325f and Vives *On Education* 2.2 (trans Watson 64ff). See also below 185.40.

28.23 appoint the parentes] As do Quintilian 1.1.6–7 and 'On the Education of Children' in Plutarch *Moralia* 5A.

28.25 platte] scheme ('Plat' sb[3] 3–4). The word is used often by Mulcaster, and has the sense of 'program' or 'curriculum' as well as the architectural sense of 'scheme' or 'plan.'

28.29 mediocritie] middle state (sb 1). Used often by Mulcaster as a synonym for 'mean'; at 36.6 it is contrasted with 'extremities.'

28.30–1 not to that excellencie, which is fashioned for an other] Cf Quintilian 1.Pr.19–20. The nature of 'perfection' in teaching is discussed at some length in Ascham's *Toxophilus* in *English Works* ed Wright 55–68. Toxophilus thinks that principles in teaching should be based on an attainable 'mediocritie' rather than on an impossibly difficult perfection. Philologus, on the other hand, explains the importance of 'perfect' models which force the learner to transcend himself (K.J. Wilson 'Ascham's *Toxophilus* and the Rules of Art' has an informed discussion of this issue).

28.32 absolute] perfect, consummate (a 4; see 29.33)

29.4 narrowly] carefully, with close attention (adv 1)

29.9 pearcher] one who aspires ('Percher' sb 1; cf *Elementarie* sig B4v '*Q[u]intilianes* cokking boy stil perching, still aspiring')

29.18–19 nurture ... nature] 'Nature' and 'nurture' were proverbially linked together. See Tilley N47 and N357 and *ODEP* 'Nature passes nurture' and 'Nurture is above (passes) nature.' The terms are found often in education literature, for instance in the title of chapter 16 of Pierre de La Primaudaye's *Académie françoise* (1577) 'De la Nature, et nourriture,' translated into English as 'Of Nature and Education' (trans T.B. [1586] 170), or in Francis Clement *The Petie Schole* 33 'wherin as all children are by nature inwardly fraught (as saith the wise *Solomon*) with folly and ignoraunce: so may they be readily reformed by diligent nourture and erudition, which that wise king termeth the rod of correction.' One of the longest contemporary pieces of English writing on 'nature' and 'nurture' is the debate between Euphues and the old gentleman of Naples, in Lyly *Euphues* in *Works* ed Bond 1:186–94.

29.23 considerate] prudent (a 2 first cited this passage; cf also 150.20)

29.27 silly] helpless, defenceless (a 1b obs first citation 1587)

29.31 our hope is at ankar] Hebrews 6:19, hope is 'an ancre of the soule, both sure and stedfast'; de Tervarent *Attributs et symboles* 27 cites various artistic representations of the anchor as a symbol of hope (the device of the dolphin and anchor is another form of the traditional symbol). Mulcaster may here be making a little nod to Vautrollier, his publisher, whose device and motto 'Anchora spei' are found on the title page.

29.32 rode] place to anchor, sheltered spot near shore ('Road' sb 3)

29.35–6 though the unpossible *Idaea*, offer great force to fansie] Although Mulcaster again rejects the notion of perfection as being too impractical for our daily experience, he does assess its capacity to inspire. An idea, in his psychology, is not experienced by the senses, though it may have a existence in the faculty of phantasy; for these terms, see introduction, xvii–xviii.

30.2 enterteneth] occupies the attention of (v 9 first citation 1598)

30.11–12 fond cokkering] foolish indulging or pampering ('Cocker' v[1]; cf 31.28 'cokkering fondly')

30.22 chekt by arrest] stopped (or possibly 'rebuked') by the judgment (of circumstance) ('Check' v^1 13 or 11; 'Arrest' sb^1 13 obs)

30.30 to stop will of his will] Compare the proverbs 'Will is a good boy when Will is at home' (Tilley W399 and *ODEP*) and 'Will is a good son, and will is a shrewd boy' (*ODEP*). In each case, 'will' is both 'inclination, appetite' and a boy's name. Perhaps here, the first 'will' should read 'Will.' (See also 39.29 and 148.6; the play is found at 16.15ff.)

30.37–8 occasion is verie bald behinde, and seldom comes the better] Tilley T311 'Take time (occasion) by the forlock, for she is bald behind' and B332 'Seldom comes the better' (ie, things rarely get better than they are now). The image of Occasion is found repeatedly in art and literature as well as emblems; for Spenser's Occasion in book 2 of *The Faerie Queene* see Manning and Fowler 'The Iconography of Spenser's Occasion.'

30.39 bridle] Cf Tilley B671 'To give one the bridle (reins)'

31.2 commodity] suitability (sb 1)

31.4–6 For saving with such a note as this is ... *libertie* keepes the keyes.] ie, I may guide only those who are free to follow my advice (In this little allegory, 'necessity' has been locked up and 'liberty' of choice holds the keys.)

31.22–3 ripenes in children, is not tyed to one time] Cf Aristotle *Politics* 7.15 (1336b–7a): 'For those who divide the ages by periods of seven years are generally speaking not wrong, and it is proper to follow the division of nature, for all art and education aim at filling up nature's deficiencies.' Also, Plato *Laws* 7.793Eff and 810A, with strict directions by age. Quintilian does not specify ages, rather developmental stages in book 1 of *Institutio oratoria*. R.L. DeMolen tried to solve the problem of 'Ages of Admission to Educational Institutions in Tudor and Stuart England' 207–19 but was not considered successful by Charlton 'Ages' or Lawrence Stone 'Ages.' Cressy 'School and College Admission Ages,' after an analysis of the debate, concludes that for the early seventeenth century 'the usual age of grammar school admission was 11 or 12 and the normal age for going to university was 17' (177), though he too emphasizes that there is no evidence to see the ages 'tyed to one time.'

31.24–5 hastinges ... hardinges] early ripening fruits (or vegetables) ... slowly developing fruits ('Hasting' a (sb) B1; 'Harding' sb 1). Compare Tilley H203 'He is none of the hastings' and the passage by Ascham *Scholemaster* in *English Works* ed Wright 192 where he compares the choice of scholars to the choice made by children of apples. Quintilian 1.3.3 comments that a 'precocious intellect rarely produces sound fruit [pervenit ad frugem].'

31.29 he that deserveth to be a parent] The responsibility of parents for the education of their children is emphasized in 'On the Education of Children' in Plutarch *Moralia* 4A–5C and 6A–B and by Elyot *The Boke Named the*

Governour 1.6 (ed Croft 1:36–7). For an extended exhortation to parents to care for the religious education of their young, see John Stockwood, *A Sermon Preached at Paules Crosse ... the 24. of August. 1578. Wherin ... is at Large Prooved, that it is the Part of All Those that are Fathers, Householders, and Scholemaisters, to Instruct All Those under their Governement, in the Word and Knowledge of the Lorde*. Such advice follows in the tradition of the early reformers, such as in Bucer's *De regno Christi ad Ed. VI* (1548), for which see Allan H. Gilbert 'Martin Bucer on Education.'

32.1 lease] lose ('Leese' v^1; see above 27.26)

32.11 wite] blame, reproach (sb^2 2)

32.13 fleeteth] floats (v^1 1)

32.15 wanne] won

32.15 ballase] ballast

32.16 aunswering at reboundes] returning in kind ('Rebound' sb 3d)

32.21–2 to much moisture] Moisture is one of the four elements, the imbalance of which in the body can lead to illness. Children are especially susceptible to moisture. For an explanation of the theory of humours, see below 53.22 note.

32.25 stilleth] distilleth ('Still' v^2 1 obs); 'distillation' here refers to the process by which the elemental moisture in the body is condensed into phlegm in the head. Because the body is cold, ie, unexercised, and the brain is hotter, the moisture condenses there. Too much undischarged phlegm can cause illness. See 53.22 note.

32.27 upon the spurre] at full speed (sb^1 2c)

32.28 sklenderer] more slightly ('Slender' a 10; so spelled in *Elementarie* sigs D4v and 2D3v)

32.29–30 quickling] child who learns quickly (not in *OED* under 'Quickling' or '-ling'. Mulcaster favours this diminutive form, rather like the Ciceronian diminutive '-ulus'; see index under '-ling'.)

32.30 reasty] rancid (a obs 1)

32.31 dumpishe] dull, slow-witted (a 1 obs)

32.33 meane conceiver] pupil whose mind apprehends and reasons with moderate speed. Cf Quintilian 1.3.3 (quoted above at note for 31.24–5) and Ascham *Scholemaster* in *English Works* ed Wright 193.

33.4 complaint, and cause] any illness suffered by the child and by the cause of that illness (or, instead of 'illness,' 'utterance of pain'; 'Complaint' sb 1 'utterance of pain' is much older than sb 6 first citation 1705 'bodily ailment')

33.5 moaned] lamented (v 1)

33.13 ordinarie] customary, normal (a 3)

33.13 gives us the gaze] causes us to look (an inverted sense of 'Gaze' sb 3a obs)

33.31 assaies] trials, tests (put against them or their country) (sb 1)

34.3 mostwhere] in most places ('Most' C obs)

34.5 such a tyrant is affection] Although it has been argued that sixteenth-century domestic relations were cooler than our own (according to Lawrence Stone and Ariès and other authorities), there is plenty of evidence to show that many parents were extremely fond of their children and able to show this affection openly (Keith Thomas 'Children'). Mulcaster's many injunctions against parental affection suggest that, in his view, such affection was a regrettable norm. He seems to argue that such affection works against the interests of the school (his recurring theme of the 'private' undermining the 'public').

34.14–15 As for the training up of the minde, the waye is well beaten] The assumption is that the reader could consult many different texts on the training of mind. It is curious that Mulcaster does not recommend any such texts in particular.

34.17 the bettering of the body] Exercise is dealt with at much greater length, below, chapter 6 and following. Here Mulcaster comments on diet and clothing; the latter topic goes unmentioned later on. The main point of his suggestions here is that moderation be followed in clothing the child. It is interesting that he does not warn against undue finery (a commonplace in school statutes and any writing about youth), but holds close to his subject which is the physiological significance of clothing.

34.23 as] so that (adv 21 obs)

34.23 stuffe] clog, choke up (v^1 12, applied in particular to 'bodily humours')

34.24 lightly] commonly, often (adv 6b obs)

34.26 faint] enfeeble, weaken (v 5 cited)

34.28–9 dry, strong, hard] See notes at 32.21–2 and 53.22. Dryness was considered the elemental state towards which children should be directed, in contrast with the moisture which was usually too abundant in their physiological system.

35.4 may worke them like waxe] ie, the parents may form the children easily (the change in number from 'child' to 'children' is found thoughout the paragraph). Like the image of planting, 31.22ff and elsewhere, the proverbial comparison (Tilley W136) of the child's mind to wax or soft clay is commonplace in educational writing: 'Of the Education of Children' in Plutarch *Moralia* 3F; Erasmus *De pueris* in LB 1:494A trans CWE 26:305–6; Ascham *Scholemaster* in *English Works* ed Wright 200; Montaigne *Essais* 1.26 ed Thibaudet and Rat 162 (cites Persius 3.23–5).

35.9 revenge] The contrast between pagan and Christian notions of revenge is found in many other writers; see Campbell 'Theories of Revenge in Renaissance England' and the first chapter of Bowers *Elizabethan Revenge Tragedy 1587–1642*.

35.12 entertained of] discussed on the subject of (v 9 obs)

35.17 stirring] This and the next paragraph contain many figurative plays on 'will' and 'well' and 'stir' and 'still.'

35.20–3 The body which lodgeth ... superfluous humors] ie, the body that contains a restless mind is, at rest, more than ordinarily subject to the influence of 'unholesome and superfluous humors'

35.25 children wilbe stirring] Cf Plato *Laws* 2.653E: 'every young creature is incapable of keeping either its body or its tongue quiet'; also Erasmus *De pueris* in LB 1:512F trans CWE 26:341.

35.28 ingenerate heat] The 'ingenerate heat' or, more commonly below, 'natural heat' is the innate energy of the living being, in humans contained, according the medical authorities, within the heart. According to Hippocratic doctrine, the heart was 'fed' by air (which kept the fire of the heart burning); in Aristotle, the air cools and thus moderates the effects of heat (Hoeniger *Medicine and Shakespeare* 101). Mulcaster here and elsewhere seems to follow a version of the Aristotelian system. (*OED* 'ingenerate' a 1 'inborn, innate' cites this passage, but not as a medical term.)

36.14 Whom if we beat] For similar sentiments, see Quintilian 1.3.13–17; Elyot *The Boke Named the Governour* 1.9 ed Croft 1:50; Ascham *Scholemaster* in *English Works* ed Wright 188, 199. Some teachers were inconsistent in their pleas for the reduction of punishment in the schools. John Stockwood, master of the free school in Tunbridge, in his *Sermon* of 1578, deplores the 'cruell and butcherly beatyng' which takes the pupil to a 'mislike and lothynge of learning' (89). A few words later, however, he enjoins, 'Let the name of God and of his Christe be hearde often in youre scholes: let it be familiar unto your scholers by continuall beating it into theyr heades' (91–2). The ambivalent metaphorical language suggests what may also have been Mulcaster's opinion. See introduction, lxiv–lxv.

37.14–15 qualifying] investing with proper or essential qualities (v 3 citing 138.22)

37.27 they] ie, natural abilities

37.30 unproved] not taken to the test, not performed ('Prove' v B I 1 also ppl a 1)

37.31 let of better stuffe] hindrance of better things ('Let' sb^{1} 1)

37.37 niggardishe] niggardly (a cited)

38.1–2 as they were to receive] ie, as the older persons were (intended by God) to receive these excellent benefits in their children or pupils

38.6 younglings] children (sb 1)

38.7–8 not to staie, without cause beyond staie] ie, not to delay, without a better reason than delay itself ('Stay' v^{1} 2b obs 'pause, break off'; 'Stay' sb^{3} 1 'delay')

38.19–20 then studie must be left, and the countrey must be served] The belief that the end of education is found in action for the state is common to most writers on the subject, either classical or Renaissance. See Aristotle *Politics* 8.1 (1337a); Quintilian 1.Pr.10; 'On the Education of Children' in Plutarch *Moralia* 8A–B; Vives *Of Education* trans Watson 283; Elyot *The Boke Named the Governour* 1.4 ed Croft 1:28. A lively statement on this topic is found in a work published two years earlier than *Positions*. Stephen Gosson writes 'If it be the dutie of every man in a common wealth, one way or other to bestirre his stumpes, I cannot but blame those lither contemplators very much, which sit concluding of Sillogismes in a corner, which in a close study in the University coope themselves by fortie yeres togither studying all thinges, and professe nothing. The Bell is knowen by his sounde, the Byrde by her voyce, the Lyon by his rore, the Tree by the fruite, a man by his woorkes. To continue so long without mooving, to reade so much without teaching, what differeth it from a dumbe Picture, or a deade body: No man is borne to seeke private profite: parte for his countrie, parte for his friendes, parte for himselfe' (*Schoole of Abuse* sig E2r–v).

38.31–2 some natural inclinations in the soule] Here, as in *Elementarie* sigs B4rff, Mulcaster specifies the mental qualities found in the aptest students, namely 'a capacity to perceive that which is taught them, and to imitate the foregoer,' 'a quickness to take, so a fastnesse to retaine,' and 'an ability to discern, what is good, and what is ill.' This passage may be compared with Plato *Republic* 7.535A–6B where Socrates gives the five ideal qualities for the student: keenness and ready powers of acquisition, good memory, love of labour, love of truth, and moral virtue. Quintilian 1.3.1 lists four such natural abilities: power of memory, imitation, an easy absorption of instruction, and a mind that is not too fast or precocious. Ascham, in *Scholemaster* in *English Works* ed Wright 194–7, finds seven 'Trewe notes of a good witte,' six of which are taken from Plato; Ascham's student is 'apte by goodnes of witte, and appliable by readines of will to learning,' 'good of memorie,' 'given to love learning,' has a 'lust to labor, and a will to take paines,' is 'glad to heare and learne of an other,' 'naturallie bold to aske any question, desirous to searche out any doute,' and 'loveth to be praised for well doing.' For the Greek terms and the sources in Plato, see *Schoolmaster* ed Ryan 27 note 29.

38.36 foregoer] example, pattern (sb 2)

39.2 fastnesse] tenacity, retentiveness (sb 4 cited)

39.2–4 memorie ... is a treasurie] The expression is a commonplace. Cf Tilley M870 'Memory is the treasure of the mind' and Sidney *Apology* ed Shepherd 122, and the classical writers Cicero *De oratore* 1.5.18 and Quintilian 11.2.1 (using the word 'thesaurus').

39.4 receite] capacity, size ('Receipt' sb 15)

39.15 pearing] appearing ('Pear' v obs)
39.19 towardnesses] natural aptitudes ('Towardness' 2; cf 22.2)
39.27 chariest] requiring greatest care ('Chary' a 7 obs 1)
39.29 that will may be a good boye] See 30.30 note.
39.32–3 frowne of fortune] reversal of the common proverb 'When Fortune smiles' Tilley F615
39.37 cure] care, heed, concern (sb[1] 1)
39.39 fray] frighten, drive away (v[1] 2a–b obs)
40.2 that duetie to helpe them] Mulcaster emphasizes the responsibility of the schoolmaster in the moral instruction of manners. In English writing this role of the teacher is understood but rarely stressed. An elaborate outline of the master's non-academic responsibilities is, however, given in Thomas Becon *A New Catechisme* in *Worckes* 1:538r and following, especially 541v–2r where of manners it is said 'Let the scholemaster instruct them [his pupils], how they shal behave them selves in the temples: abrode in the stretes: at home in the houses: in theyr playes and pastimes: at the table in dinner or supper: toward their parentes, magistrates, superiors, elders, citesins, scholefelowes, and generally towarde all men and in all thinges.' Erasmus' *De civilitate morum puerilium*, a standard text available also in English, was an outline of proper behaviour.
40.2–3 incident] pertinent (a[1] 3 obs)
40.6 enfourmeth] furnishes, equips ('Inform' v 3–4)
40.6 embrew them with] steep them in ('Imbrue' 4)
40.38 farre fet] far-fetched ('Far-fet' a 2)
41.1–2 severed to] set apart for, segregated for (v 1f, 'in Biblical language')
41.13 For the letter is the first] As in Quintilian 1.1.25–6. Mulcaster begins his outline of the elementary program by discussing letters in the sections on the alphabet in *Elementarie*.
41.15–16 by daily spelling, and continuall reading] The teaching of reading is outlined in Clement's *Petie Schole* 11ff, and is described in some detail in Brinsley's *Ludus Literarius* 12–27. Mulcaster's *Elementarie* is concerned less with reading than with spelling (orthography or 'right writing') as a preparation for reading; the mechanics of the teaching of reading are hardly touched on (see sigs C3r–v and G3v–4v), though presumably they would have been dealt with in some detail later. Cf Quintilian 1.1.25–37.
41.34–6 reading ... before ... Grammar] The statutes of many schools are quite strict that the entering pupil know how to read before beginning studies in grammar. Merchant Taylors' School, for instance, required entrants to 'read perfectly & write competently, or els lett them not be admytted in no wise' (Draper *Four Centuries of Merchant Taylors' School* 246). See also 17.32–4 note.
41.37–8 accident] non-essential property (as at 24.12 note). Mulcaster suggests

that the dominance of Latin in English education was due mainly to the influence of the Roman Catholic church, whose presence in England was an historical aberration. He is not, however, very critical of Roman Catholicism; change in religion he sees as principally *historical* rather than doctrinal (see especially 23.34–6). But he does see the Anglican church as most appropriate for England; at 42.6 he speaks of himself and his readers as 'restored to libertie.'

42.1 onelyest] unique ('Only' a 5 cited)

42.4 abce] alphabet, abc ('ABC' sb 1). The standard beginning text was the *ABC with the Catechism* for which see Baldwin *William Shakspere's Petty School* 121–36 and Anders 'The Elizabethan ABC with the Catechism.'

42.5 proper] The text reads 'propter,' which is a misprint; the same phrase 'most proper' appears at 42.23.

42.7 nature, and propertie] The phrase was part of the Litany in Edwardian and Elizabethan prayerbooks (in a prayer beginning 'O God, whose nature and propertie is, ever to have mercie ...') and would therefore be well known to Mulcaster's readers (*The Prayer-book of Queen Elizabeth 1559* ed Benham 5 and 60 and Cuming *A History of Anglican Liturgy* 92). Considering Mulcaster's argument that the English language is 'most proper to our faith,' a verbal reminiscence from the *Book of Common Prayer* seems appropriate here.

42.26 cumber] trouble, inconvenience (sb 2)

42.29 *Reason* directes yeares, and *roate* rules in youth] Aristotle, *Politics* 8.3 (1338a): 'it is plain that education by habit must come before education by reason.' Quintilian 1.1.19: 'the elements of literary training are solely a question of memory, which not only exists even in small children, but is specially retentive at that age.' Interestingly, in the introduction to [Lily and Colet] *A Shorte Introduction of Grammer* (1549), the pupil is expected to know his work 'not by rote, but by reason' (sig A3r).

42.33–4 play pleaseth children with any, yea the greatest iniquitie of circunstance] ie, play makes children happy even in the worst circumstances

42.35 the Latin tounge] Although Tudor authors wrote a great deal on the nature of the English language, I have not found other sixteenth-century English comments, such as Mulcaster briefly makes here, on the comparative philology of English and Latin. The notion that English is changing, whereas Latin is fixed, is a commonplace; no writers that I have read, however, go on to differentiate between spelling, pronunciation, and 'syllable.' Mulcaster's suggestion that English is intellectually more demanding of the young than Latin is an interesting point. Other authors supported the teaching of English in schools, even in the grammar schools; see Nelson 'The Teaching of English in Tudor Grammar Schools' and Stowe *English Grammar Schools* 104ff.

43.1 unrackt and not fined] undecanted and unpurified ('Rack' v 1 and 'Fine' v3 1; an image of language as a maturing wine)

43.2 syllabe] syllable ('Syllab, Syllabe')

43.4 consequence] sequence, order (ie, of instruction in English before Latin) ('Consequence' sb 2b first citation 1597)

43.13 *writing*] Mulcaster returns to this subject in more detail in *Elementarie* sigs G4v–H1v. The passage on the history of writing (43.17ff) should be compared with his allegory of language in *Elementarie* sigs H4vff. On Elizabethan teaching of handwriting see Brinsley *Ludus Literarius* 27–40 ('How the Master may direct his Schollars to write verie faire, though himselfe be no good Pen-man'), Schulz 'The Teaching of Handwriting in Tudor and Stuart Times' (on the training of scriveners), Heal *The English Writing-masters and Their Copy-Books 1570–1800*, and Baldwin *William Shakspere's Petty School* 159–63. For handwriting instruction as ideological formation, see Goldberg, *Writing Matter*. See also 45.31 note below.

43.33 puniship] inferiority ('Punyship' cited)

44.7–8 to seeke for defence when the forte is surrendred] Not in Tilley or *ODEP*, though it is reminiscent of the analogous Tilley s838 'When the steed is stolen shut the stable door.'

44.8–9 After that reading was reduced . . . she fined her foundresse] ie, once reading was perfected as a skill, it was used to perfect writing

44.10 she makes the eye, the paragon sense] ie, reading makes the eye the paragon sense because reading (by means of the eye) interprets writing. For 'paragon sense' compare Plato *Phaedrus* 250D ('For sight is the sharpest of the physical senses'); Dee Preface to Euclid *Elementes* trans Billingsley sig b1r ('the eye, the light of our body, and his Sense most mighty'); Lomazzo *A Tracte Containing the Artes* trans Haydocke 95 ('the *Eie*, which is the principall sense') – a commonplace in Elizabethan writing.

44.14 they] ie, people generally

44.23 riddance] progress or dispatch in work ('Riddance' 3 first citation)

44.25 geare] matter (sb 11c). The 'geare' the proficient student might be charged with writing is a fair copy which his fellow students would then be asked to follow.

44.29–30 as *Plato* ... termeth *Arithmetick* and *Geometrie*] The gloss gives *Republic* 7. Socrates (immediately after the allegory of the cave, at 7.522Eff) shows how arithmetic and geometry, as well as astronomy and music, are means by which the soul may arrive at a higher knowledge. For this, and the passage immediately preceding, cf also *Laws* 7.810B: 'But superior speed or beauty of handwriting need not be required in the case of those whose progress within the appointed period is too slow.'

45.3 brusteth] bursts ('Brust' v)

45.8 making up] supplying deficiencies, making complete (v 96c)

45.20–1 write English before Latin] ie, to write the English secretary hand before italic script ('Latin' adj 5 means 'roman' as a term in typography; otherwise the *OED* does not give this sense; possibly Mulcaster means 'write English orthography before Latin orthography,' but the gloss specifies 'hand').

45.28g Drawing.] For a brief survey of the elementary program in drawing see *Elementarie* sigs H1v and C3v. There is little contemporary writing on the teaching of drawing in England; according to Richard Haydocke, the art 'never attained to any great perfection amongst us (save in some very feawe of late) yet it is much decayed amongst the ordinarie sorte' (prefatory letter to his translation of Lomazzo *A Tracte Containing the Artes* ¶5r). In his letter to Ortelius, 24 April 1581, Mulcaster writes enthusiastically of the teaching of drawing, asks for information about books, and claims to have read Dürer's *De humani fabrica libri quatuor*, Vitruvius, Pliny (presumably what we would call book 35 of the *Historia naturalis*), Quintilian (probably 1.10.34–49 on geometry), Polydore Vergil (*De rerum inventioribus libri octo* 2.24 'De origine picturae, et quis primum colores inuenerit, aut penicillo pinxerit'), Caelius Rhodoginus (ie, Ricchieri, *Lectionum antiquarum libri triginta*, probably 29.24), and Aelian (*Varia historia*). The list is impressive, and suggests a serious attempt to familiarize himself with some basic sources. See introduction, xxi–xxii.

45.30 pencill] brush, or lead pencil (the *penicillum* was a fine brush and is the more likely sense; the pencil with 'lead' or graphite was, however, known and used by the mid-1560s by Conrad Gesner [Petroski *The Pencil* 36ff]; *OED* for the lead pencil first cites Brinsley 1618)

45.31 For penne and penknife ...] A standard list; cf Clement, *Petie Schole* 52: 'The Writer must provide him these seven: *paper, incke, pen, penknife, ruler, deske,* and *dustbox,* of these the three first are most necessarie, the foure latter very requisite' (Clement goes on to describe the function of each of these items in detail). The pen here is of course the quill or reed, both of which required fairly constant sharpening with the penknife.

45.32 dustbox] container holding the dust (fine sand) shaken over the wet ink to facilitate drying (sb first citation)

45.36–46.3 And as judgement ... all aspectable thinges] ie, what understanding does for judgment in the improvement of mental operations, drawing does for the sense of vision in the observation of physical reality

46.3 aspectable] capable of being seen, visible ('Aspectable' 1 first citation 1614)

46.11 *Apelles*] Apelles, the great painter of classical antiquity (fourth century BC), is commonly referred to by English writers as the most famous artist of the past; see for instance Nashe *Anatomie of Absurditie* in *Works* ed McKerrow 1:21 and 44, and Lyly's *Campaspe* (1584), where Apelles is a character. He and the rest of the 'crew of excellent painters' would have been known to Mulcaster from Pliny *Historia naturalis* 35.31ff. See 45.28g note.

46.13 statuaries] sculptors of statues (sb 1 first citation)

46.14 mathematikes] ('Mathematics' first citation)

46.14 manuaries] handicraft trades ('Manuary' B sb 2; not to be confused with 'those who work with their hands,' for which see 198.6 and note)

46.14–15 notorious] well known (a 1)

46.17 devise] opinion, notion (see 19.37 note; sb 4; 'Device' also has the meaning of 'figure' or 'conceit,' which might possibly apply to the rhetoric of the preceding sentence; 'Device' 10)

46.18 repentance hath repulse] contrition (or sorrow) is refused me ('Repentance'; 'Repulse' sb 2b) The sentence may be paraphrased 'Neither is this opinion mine; if it were, I would not be sorry.'

46.23–4 *γραμματικὴ* ... *γραφικὴ*] writing ... drawing. Aristotle *Politics* 8.2 (1338a): 'reading and writing [*grammata*] are useful for business and for household management and for acquiring learning and for many pursuits of civil life, while drawing [*graphikê*] also seems to be useful in making us better judges of the works of artists'; cf. also 8.2 (1337b): 'reading and writing [*grammatikê*] and drawing [*graphikê*] being taught as being useful for the purposes of life and very serviceable.' Mulcaster cites these arguments from Aristotle in his letter to Ortelius (see 45.28g note).

46.34–6 if any dexterity that waye do draw the child on, it is an honest mans living] In *Elementarie* sig H1v the same point is made. Elyot would disagree; for him, drawing, painting, and carving 'ones beinge attayned, be never moche exercised, after that the tyme cometh concerning businesse of greatter importaunce.' Elyot has no intention of making, as he says 'a prince or noble mannes sonne, a commune painter or kerver' (*The Boke Named the Governour* 1.8 ed Croft 1:48).

47.7 *Musicke*] There are further comments on music in *Elementarie* sigs B1r, C4v, D1r, and H1v–2v. In what follows, Mulcaster enthusiastically supports the teaching of music in schools. Apparently he practised what he preached. Sir James Whitelocke, a former pupil, states that his master's care 'was also to encreas my skill in musique, in whiche I was brought up by dayly exercise in it, as in singing and playing upon instruments' (*Liber Famelicus* ed Bruce 12). Mulcaster's interest is also shown in his poem 'In musicam Thomae Tallisii, et Guilielmi Birdi,' forty-two lines of praise of music, of Queen Elizabeth's skill in music, and of Tallis and Byrd, prefaced to their *Sacrae cantiones* (reprinted in Boyd *Elizabethan Music* 286–9 with translation). Walter Woodfill, in his *Musicians in English Society from Elizabeth to Charles I*, claims that the Elizabethans were not generally well instructed in music, although music was a popular pastime. Mulcaster's vigorous advocacy of musical instruction was unusual, and 'Besides the cathedral and collegiate-church schools, and the Newark song school, only about half a dozen [schools, including Merchant Taylors'] seem to have taught music' (222).

47.9 seeth with the eye] Proverbial; cf Tilley M1322 'Music is the eye of the ear.'

47.18 a medicine from heaven] A commonplace observation, found in Aristotle *Politics* 8.5 (1339b); Dee, Preface to Euclid, *Elementes* trans Billingsley sig b3r; Nashe *Anatomie of Absurditie* in *Works* ed McKerrow 1:30; Gosson *Schoole of Abuse* sig B1r; Lodge [Reply to Gosson's *Schoole of Abuse*] 27–8.

47.19 Some men thinke it to be too too sweete] Elyot warns against an extreme devotion to music: 'It were therfore better that no musike were taughte to a noble man, than, by the exact knowlege therof, he shuld have therin inordinate delite, and by that be illected to wantonnesse, abandonyng gravitie, and the necessary cure and office, in the publike weale, to him committed' (*The Boke Named the Governour* 1.7 ed Croft 1:41). Ascham twice approvingly quotes Galen: 'Muche musike marreth mennes manners' (*Toxophilus* in *English Works* ed Wright 13, and *Scholemaster* in ibid 190). The Puritan attitude towards music (generally hostile, though there are exceptions) is represented in Gosson *The Schoole of Abuse* sig A8v–B3r and Stubbes *The Anatomie of Abuses* sig O3v–6r (the chapter is entitled 'Of Musick in Ailgna [ie, Anglia backwards], and how it allureth to vanitie'). Thomas Lodge, in his [Reply to Gosson's *Schoole of Abuse*] 25–32, offers a defence of music; Lodge had been a pupil of Mulcaster. See also the section 'Music Praised and Blamed' in Hollander *The Untuning of the Sky* 104–22. Aristotle *Politics* 8.4 (1339a)ff argues the praise and blame of music at length; Mulcaster refers to his argument in *Elementarie* sig B1r.

47.24–5 by the advise of all antiquitie] Plato *Republic* 4.424B–E; Aristotle *Politics* 8.4 (1339a)ff (for further Greek sources see Marrou *History of Education in Antiquity* 134–41); Quintilian 1.4.4; Ascham *Toxophilus* in *English Works* ed Wright 12–16 and *Scholemaster* in ibid 190; Elyot *The Boke Named the Governour* 1.7 ed Croft 1:38–43 – all offer extensive parallel advice.

47.30 *aphorisme*] See 287.18 for a similar comment. Mulcaster's 'respect for the aphorism as a repository of intellectual authority' is discussed briefly by Vickers *Francis Bacon and Ranaissance Prose* 62 and 72. See also introduction, lvi note 1. An example of an educational treatise organized by 'aphorisms' is Richard Argentyne's translation of Ulrich Zwingli's *Certeyne Preceptes* (1548); in this work 'aphorisms' are 'brefe sentences ... declaring the absolute meaning of the thing' (sig a5r) and are presented as short paragraphs that set forth a single proposition on education or the behaviour of the young.

47.36 spreede] spread ('Spread' v)

47.37–8 the praise and ornamentes of *Musick*] The praise of music was a standard topic of the Renaissance, as for instance in the Count's speech in

Castiglione *The Book of the Courtier* trans Hoby. The important classical precedent was Plutarch's essay 'On Music' in *Moralia*. An English *Praise of Musicke* appeared five years after *Positions*; the author (perhaps John Case, who also wrote a Latin *Apologia musices* in 1588 [see *STC* under his name, though see Binns *Intellectual Culture* 436–43]) set forth many of the conventional defences of music also used by Mulcaster, both here and in the poem to Tallis and Byrd (see 47.18 note). Background is given in chapters 1 to 3 of Hollander *The Untuning of the Sky*.

48.9 The Philosophers] Here probably Plato *Laws* 7.792A and Aristotle *Politics* 7.17 (1336a); see also the notes for chapters 10, 11, and 12 below.

48.10 recoyling] falling back, returning (to normal) ('Recoil' v[1] 7 first citation 1599)

48.20–1 out of proportion ... proportions] outsized ... harmonies (sb 4b first citation 1710 and 10; with a play on number on the musical and mathematical senses, as 49.1 'the propertie of number')

49.2 *Pythagorian*] Pythagoras, the late sixth-century BC philosopher, and his school were famous in the sixteenth century for their 'subtill conclusions and misteries of Arithmetike Musike and geometrye' (Cooper 'Dictionarium' in *Thesaurus*). For the relation of number and soul, see Heninger *Touches of Sweet Harmony* 71ff.

49.4 concent] harmony, concord of several voices or parts ('Concent' 1 first citation 1589)

49.5 bitte ... bridle] Not in Tilley, though see 30.39ff. The image of the horse as a metaphor for pleasure is found in Shakespeare *Venus and Adonis* lines 259ff and in Marlowe *Hero and Leander* 2.141–5, among other places.

49.6 hidebare] Not in *OED*. Either two words, 'hide bare', as 'seek concealment in shame,' or one word as it is in the text, meaning 'worn down to the hide' (as in 'threadbare'). The former seems a better parallel to 'drowned.'

49.9 lightnesse] lewdness, wantonness (sb[1] 7b obs)

49.9–10 matters of religion] See above, 47.19 note.

49.12 *Syrenes*] The Sirens, in Homer *Odyssey* 12.153–200, were allegorized by classical and Renaissance commentators as representations of pleasure, drawing Odysseus away from the duty of his journey (D.C. Allen *Mysteriously Meant* 93, 96, etc). Mulcaster pushes the allegory: here the Sirens are bad music, contrasted with the good music of duty.

49.25 but such as private houses hide with curtaines] In the galleries of many sixteenth-century English collectors, pictures were often protected by a curtain (*Shakespeare's England* 2:6). That there might be good moral cause for hiding the pictures is an unusual suggestion, though no doubt some of the Italian and French pictures imported into England may have seemed lascivious to some observers.

49.28 reft] taken away ('Reave' v[1] 6)

49.29–30 Shall sense forgoe his forsight, and the beautifier of his object?] ie, shall sense do without drawing, the art which helps sense to see more clearly and which beautifies the objects of sense? (That 'drawing' is being referred to here is apparent from the order of the series beginning at 49.21.)

49.30–2 Change thou thy direction ... bending to the better] ie, whether you are inclined to good or to evil, the arts (of reading, writing, drawing) will be more easily applied to the good; an art is morally neutral, but when it is put into use, it seems to be applied more easily, more appropriately, to good ends than bad. The whole of Quintilian 2.16 is given over to this argument; see also Isocrates *Nicocles* 40ff; Aristotle *Rhetoric* 1.1 (1355b); Sidney *Apology* ed Shepherd 125–6.

49.32–3 Mans faulte makes the thing seeme filthie.] Cf Quintilian 2.17.40 'Quod non artis sed hominis est vitium' ('This is not the fault of the art, but of the man').

49.39 sorte] choose as fitting or suitable; apportion notes and harmonies as one hears them ('Sort' v[1] 14 first citation 1591 and v[1] 1)

50.6–7 have it with embasing to pleasure some pevishe, which will not yet be pleased] ie, have music in a degraded form in order to attempt to please some spiteful persons who still will not be pleased ('Embase' 2; 'Peevish' a 2)

50.22 by some swash of a sword, they chaunce to lease a jointe] The point seems to be that a musician, or anyone trained in an instrument, knows the extreme worth of every one of his fingers and will therefore not hazard them in foolish duelling. (An unusual suggestion; the passage is quoted by Woodfill *Musicians in English Society* 215.)

50.31 liste] choose (v[1] 2b)

50.34 all these] ie, all four subjects of the elementary curriculum (as at 50.27 'All foure')

50.39 as precisely and yet, as properly] as exactly and yet, as excellently ('Properly' 4, which also has another sense 2 of 'exactly')

51.1 Chapter 6.] Chapters 6 through 35 form a single discussion of physical education for the pupil and the scholar. For background and analysis of this part of *Positions*, see introduction, xxiiff.

51.8 soule and bodie] See introduction, xviiff.

51.8–9 sweete and sowre] Proverbial; cf Tilley S1038 'Take (mingle) the sweet with the sour.'

51.16–17 to get them ... to use them] ie, 'those thinges, which be most proper unto [the mind]'

51.20 by contention in chalenge] ie, by the custom of duelling (?)

51.21–2 the bodie ... lumpishe and earthy] A commonplace in Platonic and Neoplatonic philosophy; see for instance Plato *Timaeus* 72Dff, on the physical body.

51.26 dissembled] disguised (v 2 obs)
51.28 stomacke] courage (sb 8a obs)
51.34 them both] ie, body and soul
51.34–52.1 which by ... as otherwayes it might] ie, '[each of] which by diligent endevour may be avaunced to that for which it was ordeined, and [each of which] by negligent oversight doeth either decaye quite, or proves not so well as otherwayes it might'
52.6 furniture] furnishing, preparation (sb 1 obs)
52.11 swinge] impulse (sb[1] 3)
52.15–16 ordinarie] orderly, methodical (a 1 obs)
52.18 in leasure] freely occupied (sb 5 and as at 60.25–6, here with an additional sense of 'physical leisure')
52.20 studentes] Ascham makes a similar point about the physically inactive life of the scholar at the beginning of *Toxophilus* in *English Works* ed Wright 4.
52.23 moane themselves] lament ('Moan' v 1b as reflexive)
52.26 grosse] A play on 'unperceptive' and 'physically lazy, sensual' ('Gross' a 13 and 8c; see 58.20 and note).
52.28–9 *Asclepiades ... Galene ... Erasistratus*] Mulcaster follows the *De sanitate tuenda* of Galen (AD 129?–199) for some of the background to medical theory and for general observations on health. Galen's medical doctrine lies behind all of the recommendations regarding health and exercise in *Positions*, although much of the theory comes to Mulcaster via Mercuriale's *De arte gymnastica*. Erasistratus of Ceos and Asclepiades of Prusa (of the third and first century BC respectively) were opposed to the Hippocratic theory of humours, and for this were attacked by Galen. Both are 'confuted' on the subject of exercise in *De sanitate tuenda* 1.8 trans Green 25: 'Now when we must consider whether any other exercise is essential for the preservation of health, although Asclepiades is opposed and clearly condemns exercises, and though Erasistratus cautiously approves but otherwise agrees with Asclepiades, almost all other physicians approve them not only for satisfaction but for health.'
52.28 stawled for an asse] put into a stall of a stable as an ass (ie, treated like a fool) ('Stall' v[1] 8 fig cited; the ass is the traditional scholastic sign for a non-intelligent being, as in Vives *In pseudodialecticos* ed and trans Fantazzi 30–1 note 7)
52.32 unweildy] feeble, infirm ('Unwieldy' a 1 obs; with additional sense of 'oversized and hence awkward', from 'gross' and 'great' above)
53.2 officer] agent (sb 1 obs)
53.8 liverie] party, group (sb 3b obs; also suggests the sense of 'distinctive formal clothing,' for doctors had a recognizable style of academic dress)
53.9–10 a wise minde, and a healthfull bodie] A commonplace: Galen *De sanitate*

tuenda 1.8 (trans Green 26); also in Juvenal *Satires* 10.356 ('mens sana in corpore sano'); Horace *Odes* 1.31; Seneca *Epistles* 10.4; Plutarch 'Advice about Keeping Well' in *Moralia* 137E, picked up from Plato *Timaeus* 88B.

53.14 profession] stated desire or vow (sb I 1b)

53.22 foure elementes] What follows from here to the end of the chapter is an outline, in conventional terms, of Hippocratic-Galenic medical theory. Mulcaster may have taken the general form of his presentation from *De sanitate tuenda* 1.1–6 where Galen, in defining health, gives a summary of his physiological doctrine. Outlines similar to the one Mulcaster provides are found in many sixteenth-century English (or translated) treatises, for instance in Sir Thomas Elyot *Castel of Helth* (1541) sigs B1rff, Philip Moore *The Hope of Health* (1565) sig A4vff, and [Guy de Chauliac] *Guydos Questions* (1579) sigs B4v–K4r.

For a useful summary of the theory which is behind so much Aristotelian, Galenic, and sixteenth-century medical writing, one may turn to the treatise on *Nature of Man* usually ascribed to Hippocrates (in *Hippocrates* trans Jones 4:1–41). In this short tract, the author begins (as does Mulcaster) with the four elements of Empedoclean philosophy. Fire, air, water, earth are the basic components of all created matter, and are the material representations of the qualities (or ideas) of heat, dryness, moistness, and coldness. A healthy man is formed of a balance of these elements and qualities, which are materially present in the body as four humours, blood (hot and moist), phlegm (cold and moist), yellow bile (or choler, which is hot and dry), and black bile (or melancholy, which is cold and dry). 'The body of man has in itself blood, phlegm, yellow bile and black bile; these make up the nature of his body, and through these he feels pain or enjoys health. Now he enjoys the most perfect health when these elements are duly proportioned to one another in respect of compounding, power and bulk, and when they are perfectly mingled. Pain is felt when one of these elements is in defect or excess, or is isolated in the body without being compounded with all the others. For when an element is isolated and stands by itself, not only must the place which it left become diseased, but the place where it stands in a flood must, because of the excess, cause pain and distress' (trans Jones 4:11–13).

A definition of good health in terms of precise ratios of the humours is impossible to state. That is because the qualities vary according to physical type, to age, to the seasons of the year, and even to the time of day, so that the humoral balance is constantly shifting. Disease, which manifests itself as a severe imbalance, is cured by restoring the balance, by withdrawing the superfluous humour or humours. Cures, therefore, could become exceedingly complex. The maintenance of health was a problem of great intricacy. (A good modern summary of this doctrine is R.E. Siegel *Galen's System of Physiology and Medicine*; also Hoeniger *Medicine and Shakespeare* for sixteenth-century controversies and applications.)

The health of children was a special area of concern for physicians. For England, besides Mulcaster's chapters in *Positions*, there are T. N[ewton]'s translation of G. Grataroltus *A Direction for the Health of Magistrates and Studentes* (1574) and John Jones *The Arte and Science of Preserving Bodie and Soule in Healthe, Wisedome, and Catholike Religion* (1579), especially chapter 36. Children tend to be moist in complexion, and are in danger if this moistness is not expelled as sweat or phlegmatic discharge. The heat of exercise encourages this evacuation. And yet, because children have abundant 'natural heat' (the innate energy of life found within the heart as at 35.28), too much exercise causes a radical imbalance by overincreasing their heat. Some heat is necessary to drive out the moistness of the body lest this moistness be distilled (for instance, as superfluous phlegmatic discharge) in the head, especially because the sedentary classroom life of children does not sufficiently excite this heat. But too much activity would dry out the system altogether – hence Mulcaster's constant warnings for moderation in the exercise of young scholars.

Elementarie sigs D4vff discusses the relation of man's physiology to his psychology; and see also introduction, xxiiff.

53.25 similarie partes] In a chart appended to John Jones *The Bathes of Bathes Ayde* (1572–4), 'temperaments or complexions' are subdivided into 'simple' and 'compound.' These simples (or Latin 'similia') are 'Hot. Cold. Moist. Dry.' The term 'similarie partes' was more often used in anatomy, for which see next note.

53.34 instrumentall partes] Defined by John Banister *The Historie of Man* (1578) fol 1r, quoting Vesalius, as follows: 'All the partes of mans body are either *Similar*, or *Simple* with sence, as are *Ligamentes, Fibres, Membrans, Flesh*, and *Fatte*: or els *Dissimilar*, or *Instrumentall*, as the *Veine, Artery, Sinew, Muscle, Finger*, and other *Organs* of the whole body: which are made so much the more instrumentall, by how much the greater store of *Similar* partes with the instrumentall are compounded.' The chief instrumental parts of the body are the heart, the brain, and the liver (see 58.8 note). It may be that by 'instrumentall partes' Mulcaster is referring to the 'complexions' or ordered state of the humours in the body (a sense which should follow from his apparent definition), but if so, his vocabulary is at variance with contemporary usage.

53.37 tempered] ordered, regulated (v 7 obs)

54.3 temperature] proportioned mixture (sb 2 obs; synonym for 'complexion,' the ordered state of humours in the body)

54.7 distemperature] disordered or distempered condition of the humours ('Distemperature' 2; see preceding note)
54.14 perfectest degree] The concept of 'perfect health' is rejected also by Galen *De sanitate tuenda* 1.5 trans Green 13ff.
54.20 propertie and pith] distinctive quality and essential part ('Property' sb 5b obs; 'Pith' sb 4)
54.23 drynesse] The evolution of the body from a moist youth to a dry old age is discussed in Galen *De sanitate tuenda* 1.2 trans Green 6–7. See also 53.22 note.
54.28 rebating] diminishing, lessening (v^1 7a obs)
54.30 incontinent] immediately (cf 'Incontinently' adv^2)
54.30 defect] deficiency (sb 1 first citation 1589)
54.37 hand brusing] ie, by boxing, wrestling, etc
55.6 casualtie] chance (sb 1 obs)
55.13 waste] ie, the natural wearing away of the body through work, movement, etc
55.16 breath ... arteriall pulse] In the Galenic system, the arterial pulse carries the natural heat transformed as vital spirits through the body; breathing is the manner by which the natural or innate heat is cooled. See notes at 35.28 and 58.8.
55.22 stuffes and stiffles] clogs or chokes up and stifles ('Stuff' v^1 12 obs 'of bodily humours' as also at 34.23)
55.23 straits and pines] keeps ill supplied and exhausts or consumes ('Strait' v obs 8; 'Pine' v 4)
55.24 perishe] destroy (v 3 obs)
55.27 Mediocritie preserveth ...] In *De sanitate tuenda* 1.6 trans Green 20–1, Galen makes this point emphatically. Mediocrity, or the mean, is a central doctrine in both the medical and educational theory of Mulcaster.
55.29 what place hath exercise here?] Cf Galen: 'The uses of exercise, I think, are twofold, one for the evacuation of the excrements, the other for the production of good condition of the firm parts of the body' (*De sanitate tuenda* 2.2 trans Green 54).
55.33 haviour] bearing, behaviour ('Haviour' 2; an aphaeresis)
55.36 stay] support, sustain (v^2 1)
55.37 meane] instrument, agent (ie, the body) (sb^2 10)
56.1 a loufe] aloof
56.2 all constitutions be not of one and the same mould] As argued by Galen *De sanitate tuenda* 2.1 trans Green 51; Mercuriale *De arte* 4.9 (211–12). Mulcaster has already shown that he believes that this is true for students' minds as well as their bodies (eg, 31.22–3: 'ripenes in children, is not tyed to one time').
56.8 in a meane, when they meane to do good] in moderation, when they intend

to do good ('Mean' sb[2] 1b obs; 'Mean' v[1] 1) Cf Galen *De sanitate tuenda* 2.12 trans Green 92: 'Therefore the trainer of the lad under consideration, having a perfect constitution, understands the effects of all exercises, but selects in each kind those which are intermediate between both extremes. For the best condition of the body requires neither fast nor slow exercise, but intermediate and moderate; and in the same way neither vigorous and violent nor sluggish and weak, but again moderation is best: for it is not desired to change but to preserve the perfect constitution of the body.'

56.8–9 Concerning students] Galen does not discuss the health of students specifically, though he does recommend moderate diet and exercise for younger children. For youths of fourteen to twenty-one years both Galen and Aristotle advise strenuous physical activity, a point not raised by Mulcaster, many of whose older students would fall into the lower end of this category (*De sanitate tuenda* 1.12 trans Green 94; Aristotle *Politics* 8.4 [1339a]).

56.11 avoide] void, excrete (v 4b obs; one must 'avoid superfluities' in order to maintain a proper humoral balance)

56.20 pickler] one who eats sparingly (a 1)

56.21 clothing ... thin] Perhaps following Aristotle *Politics* 7.15 (1336a); cf above, 34.25ff.

56.30 salve] heal, remedy (v[1] 2–3)

56.36 prerogative] pre-eminence, superiority (sb 2b obs)

57.18 reason at the elbow] Cf 42.29ff.

57.25 stringes] ligaments ('String' sb 2a 'ligament, tendon, nerve'; Mulcaster seems to have the sense here of ligament only, as it is defined in Banister *Historie of Man* fol 41r 'A Ligament is called of ... the Latins *Vinculum*, which we translate a Bond.' Cf also [Guy de Chauliac] *Guydos Questions* sig D2r: 'strings or lynes' are 'of the nature of sinewes, howbeit they breede of the bones'; and Adrianus Junius *The Nomenclator, or Remembrancer* trans John Higgins (1585) 21: 'Ligamentum ... The ligatures or strings of the bones.')

57.26 synewes] nerves (sb 2 obs)

57.26 streatchers] muscles and tendons (not in *OED*; perhaps these are equivalent to the 'cordes' in [Guy de Chauliac] *Guydos Questions* sig D2v: 'where the cordes without foorth are cut the member leeseth boowing, and when they within foorth are cut the member leeseth the stretching.')

57.27 unweildyness] weakness, infirmity ('Unwieldiness' 2 obs; cf 52.32 and note)

57.28 conduites] natural passages in the body (sb 3a)

57.29 the spirite, which quikneth] 'Spiritus, is an ayrie substance, subtile stirring the powers of the bodie to performe their operation,' according to the appended chart in John Jones *Bathes of Bathes Ayde*.

57.29 pipes] respiratory passages (sb[1] 6; almost always in plural, as at 74.8 and 189.38)
57.33 fainting] growing weak (v 2)
58.1 nusled] nursed, cherished fondly ('Nuzzle' v[2] 4 first cited)
58.3 ruk] multitude, throng ('Ruck' sb[1] 3b first cited)
58.8 lunges] In conventional medical doctrine of the period the lungs (or lights) are not considered to be one of the four principal organs. Elyot, for instance, gives instead 'the stones of generation' (*Castel of Helth* sig D2r; for the same see also Moore *The Hope of Health* sig A7r and [Guy de Chauliac] *Guydos Questions* sigs C3v–4r: 'the heart, the lyver, the braine, and the genitalls, all the other be called unprincipalls' sig C3v). Was it a schoolmaster's sense of delicacy that prompted Mulcaster to substitute lungs for the generative organs? His treatment of the lungs follows the standard physiology. Air is received in the lungs through the mouth and nostrils, and is mixed with blood from the right ventricle of the heart; the cooling mixture passes to the left ventricle where it is transformed by the heart's natural heat to 'vital spirits' and distributed to the rest of the body (Banister *Historie of Man* fol 91r).
58.12 forreine] 'Forreine' air is that which has not been prepared by the lungs, and hence is unusable by the heart (see preceding note).
58.13 the harte] The heart is 'the fountaine of vitall heate, and perfector of vitall spirites, after they are laboured in the lunges' according to Banister *Historie of Man* fol 92r. The heart provides the arterial pulse, but it was not regarded by the early physicians as a pump (as it came to be by William Harvey), but more as a furnace (R.E. Siegel *Galen's System of Physiology and Medicine*, especially 83–7).
58.18 hurling] violently moving (v 1 obs)
58.20 grosse] lacking in delicacy of perception, and physically sensual (a conflation of 'Gross' a 13 with 8c). The liver is the source of natural spirits which are carried from it through the whole body by the venous blood. Natural spirits govern the process of digestion as well as the 'concupiscible faculty' (John Jones *Bathes of Bathes Ayde*, chart; Banister *Historie of Man* fol 75r).
58.27 braine ... braine] intellectual power ... organ in skull (sb 4 fig and 1). For Banister *Historie of Man* fol 6r the brain is 'the habitation of reason'; it is also, according to Jones *Bathes of Bathes Ayde*, chart, the source of animal spirits, which are carried through the body by the 'sinewes' or nerves, and are the vehicles of sense or feeling.
58.29 sowlish] soul-like, of the nature of the soul ('Soulish' 2 first cited)
58.29 life spirite] (This use of 'life' in adjectival relationship to a noun predates any of those in *OED* 'Life' sb especially sense 17.)

58.39 running] This subject is discussed in chapter 21 below.

59.2 helpeth against distilling] The superfluous humours must be expelled from the body while they are in their excremental form, and must not be allowed to rise upwards in the body to the head, where they may accumulate to the great danger of the patient (see 53.22 note).

59.2–3 catarres] catarrh, phlegmatic discharge from the nose and eyes ('Catarrh' sb 1 obs; not to be confused with the modern sense of 'rheum' or 'cold')

59.4 daunsing] Discussed in chapter 16 below.

59.7 freatishing] becoming chilled ('Freatish' v[1] obs first cited)

59.8 ryding] Discussed in chapter 24 below.

59.11 loud speaking] ie, speaking aloud (this subject discussed in chapter 10 below)

59.11 bulke] trunk, thorax (sb[1] 2 obs)

59.14 loud reading] ie, reading out loud (this subject discussed in chapter 12 below)

59.15 suttileth] refines (not in *OED* under 'Subtle' v, but see 'Subtle' a 1 and 2) By being heated as result of the increased action of the heart, the blood becomes finer and moves through the arteries more quickly, and distributes the vital spirits more rapidly throughout the system.

59.17 grosse] dense, thick (a 8a obs).

59.17–18 in taste for all] ie, as a mere selection of all the possible exercises

59.25 plat forth] sketch out a plan of (v[4] 1)

59.30 speciall marke wherat I shoote] This image is common in sixteenth-century writing, and is found often especially in the works of Ascham (see Tilley M667–669 and S388–390 and Greene 'Roger Ascham: The Perfect End of Shooting').

59.35 perfit] bring to completion (v 1)

59.35 title] matter ('Title' sb 2b, with only fourteenth-century citations)

60.3 passage] observation ('Passage' sb 14c first citation 1649)

60.6 methode] See 18.1 and the note on method. In treating of exercise, Mulcaster's schematic or 'branching' division of topics is quite apparent; he begins with division of soul and body, then looks at exercise of the body under three divisions martial, athletical, and gymnastic, and then under gymnastic considers sports indoors and outdoors. Although he relies on his sources for particular definitions, his partition of the argument is strictly his own.

60.12–13 hit ... misse] Proverbial, following from 59.30; Tilley H475 'Hit or miss'

60.20–1 Such questions be these] These and other questions are raised in the opening chapters of Mercuriale's *De arte gymnastica*, Mulcaster's main source for his observations on exercise (see introduction, xxivff). Mercuriale begins with 'De principiis Medicinae' (on the origins of medicine), and in the following chapters touches on the theory of hygiene, definition of gymnastics, classical praises of gymnastics, 'Quo tempore, & quo pacto coeperit gymnastica' (when and how gymnastics began), and spends seven chapters describing the architecture and use of the ancient gymnasia. Mulcaster skips all this material and his detailed reliance on Mercuriale begins only with book 1, chapter 13 (see 60.33 note).

60.25 discoursory] digressive, not directly to the point (see above, line 20 'cause to discours, and delaye of precept,' where 'discourse' seems to mean 'elaborated speech'; *OED* defines 'Discursory' as 'of the nature of "discourse" or reasoning; argumentative' and gives this passage as the earliest citation)

60.28 entraules] inner parts (sb[1] 5b obs first citation 1584)

60.28 sadly] in earnest, gravely ('Sadly' adv 7 obs; cf 28.14–15)

60.30 simply] in a foolish, silly, or stupid manner (adv 5)

60.33 Chapter 8.] This chapter begins with material adapted from Mercuriale, *De arte*, 1.13 'De trium gymnasticae specierum differentiis, bellica, legitima siue medica, & uitiosa seu athletica' (on the differences between the three kinds of gymnastics, the martial, the proper or medical, and the corrupt or athletic); 1.14 'De uitiosa Gymnastica, siue Athletica' (on athletic, or corrupt gymnastics); and 1.15 'De uiuendi Athletarum ratione' (on the athletes' manner of living). Mercuriale's argument here is little more than a string of citations from classical sources (Galen, Aristotle, Plato, Celsus, and others). Athletes are said (69) to be 'somnolentos, segnes, ignauos, desides, uertiginosos ... morbosos' (sluggish, lazy, slothful, indolent, and suffering from dizziness and disease; quoting Plato); their excessive diet causes them to be deformed in shape (73, quoting Aristotle). In his one paragraph on the subject (61.14ff) Mulcaster gives us Mercuriale's conclusion, and spares us the lengthy argument. In the paragraph on martial exercise (61.35ff) Mulcaster follows Mercuriale's authorities (66–7), but gives his argument a political emphasis at the end (62.7ff) which Mercuriale lacks. The end of the chapter is based on *De arte* 2.1, 'Quid sit exercitatio, et quomodo differat a labore & motu' (definition of exercise, and its difference from labour and movement) and 5.2, 'De singularum exercitationis differentiarum effectibus' (on the effects of each of the kinds of exercise), for which see 62.33 note and 63.2–3 note.

61.9 gaming] athletic contest (vbl sb 2 obs first citation 1587)

61.13 fog] flabby waste flesh (sb[2] 1 obs first citation 1586; see also 'Foggy' a 3a)

61.13 burdenous] heavy, ponderous, burdensome (a 1 obs)

61.29 *Milo*] Milo of Croton (fl c 500 BC) was the most celebrated athlete of antiquity. Pausanias *Description of Greece* 6.14.5–9 tells several tales about Milo, including the one given here. Mulcaster may owe his reference to

Mercuriale *De arte* 1.5 (73) or to Galen *De sanitate tuenda* 2.9 trans Green 83. Milo was often used by Renaissance writers to show the grotesque results of extreme physical training; Erasmus, for instance, says 'Our concern is not to train athletes, but philosophers and statesmen; it is enough that they should enjoy good health, which certainly does not need to be accompanied by the physique of a Milo' (*De pueris* in LB 1:503B trans CWE 26:323).

61.30 peysed] balanced ('Peise' v 3 obs)

61.31 haled] hauled, pulled (v[1] 1)

61.36 beares the bell] takes the prize (proverbial; Tilley B275 'He bears away the bell')

62.8 *Exercitus*] This word derivation is not in Mercuriale *De arte* 1.13, and is Mulcaster's own addition.

62.9 seeke] attack (v 6 obs)

62.10 how could common weales] In the following lines, Mulcaster may not be thinking as much about Athens, Sparta, or Rome, as about the precarious military situation of England at this time.

62.33 This exercise of ours by ... definition] The definition follows Mercuriale *De arte* 2.1 (78), in which exercise is 'motus corporis humani uehemens, uoluntarius, cum anhelitu alterato uel sanitatis tuendae, uel habitus boni comparandi gratia factus.'

63.1 in price] in honour or renown (sb 9 obs)

63.2–3 They that write of exercise, make three degrees in it] Cf Mercuriale *De arte* 5.2 (236): 'Tres praecipuas exercitationum differentias ab antiquis Medicis excogitatis fuisse constat, quarum prima exercitium *παρασκευαστικόν*, siue praeparatorium, altera *ἀποθεραπευτικόν*, tertia simpliciter exercitatio nuncupata fuit.' Mercuriale goes on for two pages to define these terms, with elaborate classical citations. Mulcaster jumps from 2.1 to 5.2 (78 to 263) of Mercuriale's text, clearly subordinating it to the train of his own argument.

63.4–5 postparative] having to do with restoring the body after exercise ('Post-' A 1a 1) For the ancients (and hence for Mercuriale) this was an important part of the whole program of physical training. Galen has much to say about the methods of massage which normally followed the workout in the gymnasium (*De sanitate tuenda* 2.2–7 trans Green 53–78). The whole issue of massage is passed over silently by Mulcaster.

63.8 apotherapeutike] having to do with restoring the body after exercise (not in *OED*)

63.19 minced] chopped up ('Minced' ppl a 1b fig first cited)

63.21 whether ... weather] See 9.23 note.

63.26 all the kindes of exercises that be named either by *Galene* or any other writer] Galen *De sanitate tuenda* 2.8–10 trans Green 79ff and Mercuriale *De*

Arte books 2 and 3. Mulcaster omits boxing, pancratic wrestling (a form of boxing combined with wrestling), discus throwing, several forms of ball-play, tumbling, and many other sports. See also 112.25ff and note.

64.16 well] welfare, profit (sb[2] 1, a common sixteenth-century usage)

64.23 checke] rebuke, reproof (sb 4; cf 16.1)

64.31 likest] most suitable ('Like' a 6a obs)

65.1 Chapter 10.] As explained in the introduction, xxivff, in his chapters 10 through 27 on the particular sports, Mulcaster's reliance on Mercuriale's *De arte gymnastica* follows a regular pattern. Mercuriale discusses the historical background and practice of individual sports in books 2 and 3. In books 5 and 6 he again presents the same sports, in the same order, but here analyses their medical benefits in greater detail. Thus 'vociferatio,' the subject of chapter 10, is found in *De arte* 3.7 'De Vociferatione, & risu' (on speaking aloud and laughter) and at 6.5 'De vocis exercitationum facultatibus, & primo de vociferatione & cantu' (of the properties of the exercises of the voice, first of speaking out loud, and of singing). Because of the two-part presentation and unavoidable duplication of some material in Mercuriale, it is often difficult to tell which of the two chapters Mulcaster is following, although in the case of chapter 10 his debt is quite apparent. For some background here, see Finney 'Vocal Exercise in the Sixteenth Century.'

65.4 The exercise ...] From here to 67.5 Mulcaster follows *De arte* 280–3.

65.5 *φωνασκοί*] teachers of declamation and singing (Liddell-Scott *Lexicon*). The role of the *phonascus* in the Roman curriculum is explained by Quintilian 11.3.19.

65.6 of the height] of the highest point or degree (see *OED* 'Height' sb 16 'At ... height' although this phrase not given; perhaps Mulcaster has confused Mercuriale's 'in superioribus,' 'in the preceding remarks')

65.16 windworke] process or function of respiration ('Wind' sb[1] 31; only citation)

65.16 soveraigne] efficacious, potent ('Sovereign' a 3, a special medical sense)

65.24 thronged] compressed violently, squeezed, crushed (v 1 obs)

66.3 thickned the naturall heat] A superfluity of cold and wet excrements, if unexpelled, can cause the natural heat (contained within the heart, and carried throughout the body as vital spirit in arterial blood) to lose its fineness and warmth.

66.10 pewkishnesse] inclination to vomit (*OED* defines this under 'Pukish' a[2] as '[state] of being addicted to vomiting,' which is not quite right; this is the only passage cited. Mercuriale's term [281] is 'stomachicus.')

66.11 rifting] belching (v[2] 2; 'ructans' in Mercuriale)

66.13 naughty] unhealthy (a 6)

66.13 dropsies] diseases in which watery fluids accumulate in the connective tissues of the body (sb 1)

66.16 apostemes which are broken within the bulke] gatherings of purulent matter or large deep-seated abscesses which have broken in the thorax ('Aposteme' sb i obs; Mercuriale's phrase [281] is 'apostemata in thorace rupta')

66.17 quartane agues] fevers characterized by paroxysms every fourth (in moderning reckoning, every third) day ('Quartan' a 1). See Hippocrates *Nature of Man* 15 trans Jones 4:39–41, who describes the four kinds of fevers – 'the continued, the quotidian, the tertian, the quartan' – all usually caused by an excess of bile.

66.17 fleame] phlegm ('Phlegm' A *a*, a common sixteenth-century spelling; cf *Elementarie* sig 2A3v 'fleam')

66.18 on the mending hand] in process of cure (Tilley H93 'To be on the mending hand')

66.19 scurfe] morbid condition of the skin, especially of the head, characterized by flakiness ('Scurf' sb[1] 1 obs; the modern usage applies to the results of the disease, not to the disease itself)

66.19 Egyptian lepre, called *Elephantiasis*] Mercuriale (281) says simply 'in elephanticis.' The ancient physicians of Alexandria referred to nodular leprosy as 'elephantiasis,' but by the sixteenth century leprosy as we know it had been differentiated from elephantiasis, though the latter term was still often used. Thus, William Turner refers to 'the disease nowe called Lepre, but Elephantiasis of olde writers' (*A Booke of the Natures and Properties ... of the Bathes* [1562] fol 9v). For a history of the term there is Koelbing et al *Beiträge zur Geschichte der Lepra.*

66.19–21 whose bellies be so weake, as they cannot avoide, but watry and thin excrementes] Mercuriale's term (281) is simply 'in coeliacis,' referring to coeliac disease, whose symptoms Mulcaster correctly describes.

66.22 resolved] dispersed, dissipated (v 3, a medical term)

66.29 falling sicknesse] epilepsy ('Falling' ppl a 5)

66.32 cumbred] distressed, burdened (v 2 and 4; Mercuriale's term is 'uexetur')

66.32 crudities] undigested food (or humours?) (sb 2; Mercuriale [283] has 'cruditates')

66.32 rawnes] indigestion (sb 3b obs)

66.34 disperseth] Emended on the grounds that 'disperpleth' is not a recognizable word, that the verb is in a parallel sense here to 'scattereth,' and that Mercuriale (283) reads only 'distribuantur.'

66.37 pante] throb ('Pant' v 3; Mercuriale [283] has 'palpitationes')

67.6 commodities and incommodities] advantages and disadvantages ('Commodity' 1 obs; 'Incommodity' 2)

67.7 The use of it ...] From here to 68.7, Mulcaster follows *De arte* 159 ('Modus autem ...') to 159 ('... Plutarchus ... disseruit').

67.13–14 the hoatest *Philippik, Catilinarie*, and *Verrine* argumentes] the passionate denunciations by Cicero of Antony, Catiline, and Verres ('Philippic' a 2b first citation 1614; 'Catilinarie' first citation 1594 under 'Catiline' a; 'Verrine' not in *OED*). The suggestion does not appear in Mercuriale *De arte* 3.7 or 6.5, though there are references to the speaking of Demosthenes. Although Cicero's orations were not taught extensively in the schools (Bolgar 'Classical Reading in Renaissance Schools' 21), his rhetorical style had an important influence on Mulcaster and his contemporaries; see introduction, livff.

67.16 list] incline (v[5] first citation 1626 as a term in sailing; the verb includes the sense of 'wish' as in 'List' v[1] 2)

67.16 *Coelius Aurelianus*] A Numidian doctor of the fifth century AD who translated and who is the sole classical authority for the transmission of two treatises *On Acute Diseases* and *On Chronic Diseases* by Soranos of Ephesos (second century AD). See Caelius Aurelianus *On Acute Diseases and On Chronic Diseases* ed and trans Drabkin. The mistaking of Caelius Aurelianus as the author of the work (which Mulcaster picked up from Mercuriale *De arte* 159) was common in the Renaissance; see Sarton *Appreciation of Ancient and Medieval Science during the Renaissance* 15–16. The reference to *Chronic Diseases* 1.5 ('Mania') is from Mercuriale 164. Note that Mulcaster gives the title of *Chronic Diseases* in Greek in the gloss on this page and also on page 70; the work was known only in a Latin text, and is never referred to in Greek by Mercuriale.

67.19 prohemes] proems

67.23 *Antyllus*] A famous surgeon who flourished at the beginning of the second century AD. His writings on dietetics, general therapeutics, and surgery are known principally from the fragments in Oribasius' *Collectiones medicae*.

67.24 *Oribasius*] Oribasius lived in the fourth century AD, and was personal surgeon to the Roman emperor Julian. His *Collectiones medicae* consisted mainly of excerpts from earlier writers. For Oribasius' reputation in the Renaissance, Sarton *Appreciation* 35–6. Mulcaster got the reference and the material from Mercuriale *De arte* 159, who in turn refers to Oribasius *Collectiones* 6.8 (6.9 in the edition of Daremberg, et al).

67.26 nimbling] making nimble (v 1 obs; see also 82.32 which *OED* cites)

66.29 stayed] sustained (v[1] 16b obs; *OED* suggests that the word has a musical sense, but does not provide citations)

67.30 grave] low in pitch, deep in tone (a[1] 6 first citation 1609)

68.8 Chapter 11.] This chapter is based on Mercuriale *De arte* 3.7 'De Vociferatione, & risu,' which contains a short section on singing; specifically,

68.18–69.3 loosely follows *De arte* 160. Mercuriale also discusses singing in *De arte* 6.5, 'De vocis exercitationum facultatibus, & primo de vociferatione & cantu.' The inclusion of singing as a separate topic of exercise in *Positions* seems entirely appropriate, considering Mulcaster's enthusiastic consideration of the subject in chapter 5.

68.12 profession] activity (not quite 'occupation' in the sense of vocation, as in *OED* 'Profession' III 6a–b)

68.14–15 other ... other] ie, other exercises

68.24–5 *Plato*, and *Philo*, of *Aristotle* and *Galene*] The references are Mulcaster's own, though Plato and Aristotle are mentioned in the passage he is following (see 68.8 note). The gloss for Plato gives *Republic*, books 2, 3, and 4, but Mulcaster may wish to cite specifically 2.376E, where Socrates speaks on gymnastics and music. Philo Judaeus was not even consulted by Mercuriale for *De arte* (see the 'Auctorum nomina' in 1573 ed sig *6r–v); Mulcaster refers to *περὶ τῆς πρὸς τὰ προπαιδεύματα συνόδου* ('De congressu quaerendae eruditionis gratia,' 'On Mating with the Preliminary Studies') 16 (in vol 4 of [*Works*] trans Colson). Aristotle has a lengthy argument over the merits of music in *Politics* 8.5–7 (1339b–40b). Galen *De sanitate tuenda* 1.8 trans Green 26 mentions music as important in forming 'the habit of the mind' (see 124.31 note). These citations are evidence of Mulcaster's independence from Mercuriale's text, and show that he has gone to greater trouble to investigate the background of the academic side of the curriculum.

68.26 in pollicie] prudently, expediently (sb[1] 3 and 4)

68.28 meane] instrument (perhaps with a pun on 'middle or intermediate part in musical composition'; sb[2] 10 and 2; see 68.30)

69.1 *Aristotles* opinion] From Mercuriale *De arte* 160. Aristotle *Problemata* 19.38 (920b): '... we enjoy rhythm because it has recognized and orderly numerical arrangement and carries us along in an orderly fashion; for orderly movement is naturally more akin to us than one without order, so that such rhythm is more in accordance with nature.'

69.7 physicklike] medicinally ('Physic' 6 1)

69.9 temperature] A pun on 'combination of humours in the body,' the more general sense of 'the action or process of tempering or restoring balance,' and the musical term 'to temper,' meaning 'to tune an instrument' ('Temperature' 5 obs and 1 obs; 'Temper' v 15 obs; see also 118.36 note).

69.12 turne] Although the context would suggest a musical sense along with the sense of 'a change for the worse,' the earliest musical usage for 'Turn' in *OED* is 1801 (sb 5).

69.24 Chapter 12.] This chapter is based on the section on reading in *De arte* 6.6 'De lectionis, sermonis, risus, & fletus qualitatibus' (on the properties of reading, speaking, laughter, and weeping). 69.26 to 70.35 follows *De arte*

285–6. Like speaking, reading out loud is logically included here as part of the physical training of the prospective *rhetor*, although Mulcaster dwells on the physical benefits alone of the two activities.

69.30 staing] lingering ('Stay' v[1] 7)

69.33 naturall heat] The phrase appears in all but one of the copies as 'naturall health'; the emendation is based on the single press-variant and on the fact that Mercuriale's term here is 'calor' (*De arte* 285). For a definition, see 35.28.

70.1 freese] congeal (but not with the sense of 'become ice or frost'; the senses of 'Freeze' v 1–7 all refer to temperature; this sense not in *OED*)

70.1 dreggie] impure, polluted (a)

70.2 dispose] distribute (v 4 obs)

70.3 *Cornelius Celsus*] Cornelius Celsus was a Roman encyclopedist of the first century AD. Only his books of medicine survive; the *De medicina* was discovered in 1426 and was the first classical medical text to be printed (1478). Celsus, Galen, and Oribasius are the three principal sources for Roman medical practice (Sarton *Appreciation* 12–14). Celsus recommends 'clara lectio' in *De medicina* 1.2.6, but Mulcaster got the reference from Mercuriale *De arte* 285.

70.6 *Coelius Aurelianus*] From *Chronic Diseases* 1.1.19, via Mercuriale *De arte* 285.

70.7 *Seneca*] *Epistulae morales* 78.5 (and 15.7 on reading); the reference in Mercuriale *De arte* 285, is to 'epis. 97.' which does not correspond to modern numbering of the letters.

70.11 eager conceit] impetuous disposition ('Eager' a 5 obs; 'Conceit' sb 2c)

70.13 frantike] lunatic (sb obs)

70.13 jogging] shaking (v 3 cited)

70.23 *Plinie*] In the letter to Babius Macer (*Epistulae* 3.5) in which he describes the elder Pliny's life and habits, the younger Pliny mentions several times that his uncle enjoyed being read to, but does not say if he made a habit of reading out loud. Mulcaster carries the erroneous reference over from Mercuriale *De arte* 285, which reads, after a description of some of the physical benefits of reading, 'quod cognoscens Plinius maior, dum voce atque stomacho laboraret, in eorum remedium claram lectionem exercuisse, auctor est illius Nepos' (knowing which, Pliny the elder, when he suffered in voice and stomach, practised reading aloud as a remedy for each, according to his nephew).

70.25 cowghe] cough (variant spelling; sb 1 cited)

70.25 *Avicen*] Avicenna (980–1037), the Arabic philosopher, wrote a *Liber canonis* on medicine which was well known in the Renaissance (Sarton *Appreciation* 39–45). His advice on reading may be found, as it is reported here, in the edition of Venice, 1507, fol 57r, and in Gruner *A Treatise* 386–7. Mulcaster picked the reference up from Mercuriale *De arte* 285, but the marginal reference to 'Lib[er]. de re med[icinae].' is his own invention.

70.38–71.1 as to much in either ... a commended exercise] ie, too much reading or speaking harms boys, who none the less defend these activities which they enjoy, by arguing that they are recommended exercises

71.3 against their will] ie, boys want more of the exercise of speaking or reading, the master wants less

71.7 Chapter 13.] This chapter, like the one preceding, is based on *De arte* 6.6, 'De lectionis, sermonis, risus, & fletus qualitatibus,' follows *De arte* 286–7 from 71.9 to 72.3, and omits all learned references except the story from Pliny (71.30 note).

71.10–11 in the nature of speeche, though not of passion] ie, the nature of speech makes it a mean and weak exercise, even though the passion which accompanies speech may make it seem a more extreme form of physical activity than it actually is

71.18 spit] Unclear, both here and in Mercuriale ('sputa ex loquentis ore ... emantia'; 286), whether the action is the habitual spraying of the listener by the overly garrulous, or whether it refers to the regular expectoration used by certain speakers to punctuate their speech.

71.25 clattering is commended to the cloakbag by Physick] rapid noisy chatter is recommended to be stored in a place where it will be silenced, according to received medical doctrine ('Clattering' vbl sb 2; 'Cloakbag' obs 'bag in which to carry a cloak or other clothes,' not in this figurative sense, though see quote under 1579. Cf also Nashe *Anatomie of Absurditie* in *Works* ed McKerrow 1:45: 'A man may baule till his voice be hoarse, exhort with teares till his tongue ake and his eyes be drie, repeate that hee woulde perswade, till his stalenes dooth secretlie call for a Cloake bagge.')

71.30 *Pline*] *Natural History* 28.17.62: 'Maecenas Melissus, we are told, imposed a three-year silence on himself because of spitting of blood after convulsions.' The reference, quoted as is except the spelling 'Messius,' is in Mercuriale *De arte* 286.

71.32–3 casting] spitting up (vbl sb 1)

71.34–5 pulleth downe] lowers or depresses in health ('Pull' v 24d first citation 1586)

72.3 walketh] moves (v^1 3e obs)

72.4 Chapter 14.] After he has touched on the matter of beating, Mulcaster turns to the physiology of laughing and weeping and follows Mercuriale *De arte* 3.7, 'De Vociferatione, & risu' and 6.6, 'De lectionis, sermonis, risus, & fletus qualitatibus' (see notes for 73.4, 73.10, and 74.36). The comments on laughing can be compared with Laurent Joubert's medically based *Traité du ris* (1579; trans de Rocher as *Treatise on Laughter*). Mulcaster returns to the issue of punishment at the end of the chapter.

72.14 questuarie] gainful ('Quaestuary' A adj first citation 1594)

72.14 those wailing women] This may be a specific reference: possibilities in classical literature are *The Trojan Women*, probably that of Seneca, or the death of Dido in Virgil's *Aeneid*. Or perhaps there is a suggestion of a local or foreign custom of mourning.

72.18 againe the haire] against one's natural bent or inclination (Tilley H18 'It goes against the hair')

72.22 exercise] Spelled 'excercise' in the text, which is probably a misprint. The spelling contradicts all others in the book, Mulcaster's own derivation from the Latin (see '*Exercitus*' 62.8), and the spelling in *Elementarie* sig 2A3r 'exercise.'

73.1 much *laughter* can avoide a foole] Cf the proverb 'A fool is ever laughing' (Tilley F462); 'avoide' may have the medical sense, ie much laughter cannot void or expel the superfluous humours of a fool.

73.2 a foole can weepe] Perhaps a suggestion of the proverbial 'The fool's tears are not to be trusted' (Tilley F520).

73.4 But for *laughing* ...] From here to 73.10, the text loosely follows Mercuriale *De arte* 287–8.

73.20 tickled under the armepittes] This unusual suggestion follows Mercuriale *De arte* 287.

73.27 resolution] weakening, slackness (sb 5; the term in Mercuriale [287] is 'resolutio')

73.36 papbones] jawbones (following Mercuriale's term [288] 'laxata ... maxillarum ossa.' *OED* defines, under 'Pap' sb[1] 3, 'a name for each of the pair of ribs beneath the paps [i.e., nipples],' and cites only this passage. 'Papbones' are actually jawbones for eating pap, or very soft food, an ironical coinage by Mulcaster.)

73.38 enforcing] exerting (v 5, but cites only 1490; usually found in this sense as a reflexive verb)

74.8 pipes] voice and respiratory passages (see above 57.29 note)

74.8 *Aristotle*] *Politics* 7.15 (1336a). Quotation and reference from Mercuriale *De arte* 160.

74.22 Physicians] Mercuriale *De arte* 288, cites Galen, Celsus, and others.

74.29 conserve] preservative (sb 1 obs)

74.32 contagious humours of negligence, and wantonnesse] Mulcaster's own ironic medical prescription.

74.36 *Heraclitus*] Heraclitus was traditionally the weeping philosopher, in contrast with Democritus, the laughing philosopher; *Greek Anthology* 9.148; Lucian 'Philosophies for Sale' *Dialogues* 13f; Seneca *Dialogi* 4.10.5 and 9.15.2.

74.37 a soure centurion in *Xenophon*] Mulcaster took the reference from Mercuriale *De arte* 288, but he displays a more detailed knowledge of the story than mere reliance on Mercuriale would suggest. Aglaïtadas' commendation of weeping comes from Xenophon *Cyropaedia* 2.2.11–16.

75.19 *Socrates* in *Plato*] *Republic* 7.536E and ff. The reference is not in Mercuriale and the whole paragraph is Mulcaster's own reflection.

75.22 sifted] separated out (from the other lesser people) (v 1b fig)

75.30 *Socraticall* saintes] Perhaps a reminiscence of Erasmus' famous 'Sancte Socrates, ora pro nobis,' in 'Convivium religiosum' *Colloquia* in ASD 1/3:254; see also Marcel '"Saint" Socrate patron de l'humanisme.' (*OED* a first citation)

75.36 campishe] belonging to, of the nature of, the soldier's camp (a; first citation)

76.3 downe bancke] downhill ('Bank' sb[1] 2a–b; the phrase 'down bank' is not given, but 'up-bank' for 'up-hill' was a recognized northernism in the nineteenth century)

76.3 swinge] influence (sb[1] 1 obs)

76.9 ruffe] pride, elated state (sb[6] 2b cited)

76.18 Chapter 15.] Although breathing exercises are perfectly familiar to practitioners of yoga, elocution, and acting, readers of Mulcaster's time might have been somewhat taken aback by the subject of this chapter. He has based his comments on Mercuriale *De arte* 3.6, 'De Spiritus cohibitione' (on holding the breath) and 6.4, 'De spiritus cohibitionis facultatibus' (on the faculties of holding the breath). See notes for 77.2, 78.5, and 79.14.

76.20 all men can tell, what a singular benefit breathing is] Quoted by Lewis *English Literature in the Sixteenth Century* 348, as an amusing instance of Mulcaster's pedagogical seriousness.

77.2 Now in breathing there be three thinges] From here to 78.5 Mulcaster follows Mercuriale *De arte* 152–3.

77.10–11 smoky substance] The technical term is 'fuligines' (*De arte* 153), and refers to the exhaust of the heart whose operation may be likened to that of a furnace (see 58.13 for Mulcaster's brief description of its operations).

77.18 mure up] block, or wall up (v 2 first citation in the figurative sense)

77.23 residences] sediments, deposits (sb 2 obs)

77.26 strayted] confined ('Strait' v 4)

77.34 they were wont to swadle the chest] There is an illustration on page 155 of the 1573 *De arte* which Mulcaster would have seen if he used the second or later edition of the book (see figure 2); the text also gives a brief verbal description of the practice. The point is to protect the upper body from hernia and other internal trauma.

78.3 finish] fineish, somewhat refined ('Fineish' a first citation 1583)

78.5 Being of it selfe such a strainer] At this point, Mulcaster ceases to rely on *De arte* 3.6 and turns to 6.4, to follow loosely Mercuriale's text on 278–80 from

Figure 2 Mercuriale *De arte gymnastica* (1573) 155

here to 79.26. The order of the matter is broken, however, by an aside on Milo which is borrowed from the earlier chapter in Mercuriale (see 79.14 note).

78.15 cloyed] obstructed (v[1] 6 obs)

78.29 in temper] in proper condition (sb 1 obs)

78.33 strutting] swelling with fullness (vbl sb[1] obs)

79.4 renting] rending, tearing (vbl sb[2] obs)

79.9 call of their cods] membrane (in the area) of their testicles ('Caul' sb[1] 4 obs and see also 106.9; 'Cod' sb[1] 4)

79.14–15 sooth the demaunde] declare the claim to be true (v 2 obs)

79.14 *Milo*] For Milo of Croton, see 61.29 note. Mulcaster's gloss is to *De arte* 3.6 (154), where Mercuriale describes Milo's breathing exercises. 'It was he that bare the bull ...' (Tilley B711), added by Mulcaster, refers to the well-known anecdote in which Milo, by daily lifting up of a young calf, was able to carry it as a bull when the calf became full grown.

79.25 bidde hoe] call one to stop ('Ho' int[2] A obs)

79.27 Chapter 16.] In *De arte* 2.3 Mercuriale, according to classical precedent, divides 'saltatoria' (dancing) into 'cubistica' (tumbling), 'sphaeristica' (ball-playing), and 'orchestica' (to music). Chapters 4, 5, and 6 give the historical background for these divisions. Chapter 7 deals with 'de fine saltationis, & de loco' (on the end and the place of dancing). The medical implications of all forms of dancing are discussed in 5.3, 'De saltatoriae effectibus.'

Mulcaster depends less heavily on Mercuriale in this chapter. Dancing was extraordinarily popular in England at the time, both in village and folk culture and in court and other sophisticated circles. Queen Elizabeth loved dancing, and her enthusiasm was well known (see *Shakespeare's England* 2:437ff). Mulcaster therefore did not feel obliged to explain the history and benefits of dancing as he had for other exercises. He did, however, work to defend dancing against its Puritan critics, who were writing just about the time of *Positions*. Stephen Gosson, in *The Schoole of Abuse* (1579) sig B8v, names dancing as one of 'suche delightes as may win us to pleasure, or rocke us a sleepe,' though elsewhere in the same work he is less harsh on dancing than he is on actors and acting (eg, sigs D3v–4r). John Northbrooke, through his interlocutor Age, rails against dancing for pleasure as 'vaine, foolish, fleshly, filthie, and divelishe,' and goes on to support his claim at great length in a 'Treatise against Dauncing' which concludes *A Treatise Wherein Dicing, Dauncing, Vaine Playes or Enterluds with other Idle Pastimes &c. Commonly Used on the Sabboth Day, are Reproved by the Authoritie of the Word of God and Auntient Writers* (?1577) 113ff (see note for 81.4 below). Northbrooke claims that dancing *per se* is bad, whereas more temperate moralists are inclined to see bad or good in the intentions of the dancers. Mulcaster, like Ascham (*Scholemaster* in *English Works* ed Wright 217), speaks well of dancing as a fit activity for a student, though he does not go so far as Elyot (*The Boke Named the Governour* 1.19–25 ed Croft 1:203–69) who sees dancing to be a guide to the moral virtues.

79.32–3 some sterne people] Referring to critics like Gosson and Northbrooke; see preceding note.

80.4 militare] military, martial (a obs)

80.5 so many and so notable writers] Mercuriale, in *De arte* 2.6 (95ff), cites, among others, Homer, Plato, Quintilian, Xenophon, Pliny the Elder, and Galen.

80.13 embase] lower, degrade (v 2 obs)

80.14 embasement] lowering in dignity (sb 1 obs)

80.17 machance] perhaps ('May' v^1 12 obs cited)

80.20 moane] complaint (sb 1)

80.23 precise surveiours] over-exact, fastidious (even puritanical) examiners ('Precise' a 2; 'Surveyor' 4b fig first citation 1606)

80.27 sad and sober] grave and serious ('Sad' a 4 obs; 'Sober' a 4), ie, as opposed to the lighter and pleasurable benefits of dancing. From here to 81.6, Mulcaster follows Mercuriale *De arte* 240.

80.29–30 palsilike] ('Palsy' sb C c cites only this passage.)

80.32–3 confirmeth] strengthens, makes physically firm (v 10 obs)

80.36 swimming] affected with dizziness (ppl a 5 first citation 1607)

Figure 3 Mercuriale *De arte gymnastica* (1573) 98

80.39 cinquopasse] dance the cinquepace ('Cinquepace' v 1). The cinquepace, or cinq-pas, a five-step part of the lively galliard, is concluded by a vigorous leaping motion (Dolmetsch *Dances of England and France from 1450 to 1600* 102ff).

81.4 *daunsing* in armour] There is an illustrative woodcut in Mercuriale *De arte* 98 of 'Pyrrhichia saltatio,' showing men dressed in armour (see figure 3). This and the quasi-religious 'chorea' are the only two forms of dancing theoretically allowed by the censorious Northbrooke (*A Treatise* 113–14). Although the sword-dance was an ancient Saxon and Scottish custom, there is no mention in the standard histories (for instance, Dolmetsch, *Shakespeare's England*, or Strutt) that dancing in armour was performed at this time, though at a slightly later period armed men appeared in masques (for instance, in Jonson's *Prince Henry's Barriers* and *A Challenge at Tilt*).

81.10 The blames] Mulcaster here concerns himself chiefly with the moral drawbacks of the sport, whereas for other sports he is concerned about physical deficiencies. Mercuriale *De arte* 240 notes that dancing is inappropriate for those suffering from vertigo, epilepsy, coeliac disease, kidney malfunction, or seminal discharge.

81.17 mistyming] (vbl sb 1 a first citation)

81.27 staydest] most dignified ('Staid' a 2; this form not given in *OED*)

81.27 almanlike] like the allemande, a stately dance ('Almain' a and sb 2–3; this form not in *OED*; for a good description of the dance, see Dolmetsch *Dances of England and France* 144ff)

81.28 galliard] quick and lively dance (Dolmetsch *Dances of England and France* 102ff). The 'springing' part of the galliard is at the end of the cinq-pas, which concludes the galliard as a whole (see 80.39 note). It was customary to begin with a slower dance such as a pavanne or allemande and move to a sprightlier dance such as the galliard.

81.29 saturitie] fullness (sb obs)

82.7 braved] adorned, made splendid (v 6 obs first citation 1590). The expression 'the tailour hath braved, where nature hath beawtified' sounds proverbial, but is not in Tilley or *ODEP*.

82.12 repentance be her port] ie, courage will have the demeanour of repentance. Why sorrow or contrition is the outward bearing of the dancer's courage is not clear.

In Shakespeare's *Much Ado about Nothing*, in the masque scene, repentance is referred to in connection with dancing. Beatrice says: 'For hear me, Hero – wooing, wedding, and repenting, is as a Scotch jig, a measure, and a cinque-pace; the first suit is hot and hasty like a Scotch jig, and full as fantastical; the wedding mannerly-modest, as a measure, full of state and ancientry; and then comes Repentance, and with his bad legs falls into the cinque-pace faster and faster, till he sink into his grave' (2.1.65–71). The editor of the text quoted, Dover Wilson, comments 'This is probably a reference to some familiar representation of "Repentance" either in pictures or on the stage of the old moralities,' but gives no evidence for his supposition; other commentators do no better. The 'last parte of daunsinge' is 'Modestie' in Elyot's *The Boke Named the Governour* 1.25 ed Croft 1:267–9.

82.12–13 here will desire throng in prease, though it praise not in parting] here desire of the dancers for their partners will cause them to assemble in a crowd, though that same desire (unsatisfied) will not leave them happy when the dancing is over. This is a difficult passage, because 'prease' is an old spelling for both 'press' (crowd) and 'praise,' and 'praise' is an old spelling for 'press,' so the words are not only homonyms, but interchangeable. 'Praising at parting' is a proverb, Tilley P83 (this passage cited).

82.20–1 which if he care not for it, the precept may passe, though he passe not for it] if he does not care for dancing, the injunction (to cease dancing because of its improper and immoral use) may go unheeded by him, though he care not for the advice. An awkward construction, due to the author's striving for a pun on the word 'passe' as 'pace' or 'dance' ('Pass' v 12 and 23; *OED* does not have 'Pace' to mean 'dance' as either v or sb, though 'Pace' sb 1 is recognized as a movement in dancing).

82.36 creature to use] instrument or servant of habit ('Creature' 5 first citation 1586; 'Use' sb 11)

82.37 They define *daunsing*] The definition follows Mercuriale *De arte* 96, who in turn follows Plato, Aristotle, and Plutarch.

83.4 ordinarily] according to settled method (adv 1 obs)

83.6 *χειρονομία*] elaborate movement of the hands found in classical dancing. As a Greek term and as the Latin 'gesticulatio manuum,' it is described briefly in Mercuriale *De arte* 100 and 240.

83.20 Chapter 17.] This chapter is based on Mercuriale *De arte* 2.8, 'De luctatoria' (on wrestling) and 5.5, 'De luctae commoditatibus, & incommoditatibus' (on the benefits and disadvantages of wrestling). See notes for 83.25, 83.32, and 84.11.

Though wrestling is recommended by Elyot (following Galen) in *The Boke Named the Governour* 1.17 ed Croft 1:173–4 and Ascham *Scholemaster* in *English Works* ed Wright 217, and is quite acceptable to Mulcaster, apparently the sport had fallen off by the late sixteenth century, at least in the London area (Strutt, following John Stow, in *Sports and Pastimes* 70), though it retained its traditional popularity in the countryside (*Shakespeare's England* 2:452ff).

83.25 the auncient *Palestra*] The classical 'palaestra' or area, often covered, for wrestling and other sports (with the gymnasium nearby) is discussed at great length in Mercuriale's *De arte* 1.6; the derivation of the term from the Greek *pale* is found on 102–3. See also note at 226.13.

83.32 *Clemens Alexandrinus*] From Mercuriale *De arte* 105, referring to Clement of Alexandria's treatise *Christ the Educator* (called in Mercuriale simply 'Paedag.'); the context of Clement's recommendations on wrestling may be found in *Christ the Educator* trans Wood 240.

84.5–6 the catching pancraticall kinde of wrastling] the *pancratium*, a combination of boxing and wrestling, or what we might call free-for-all wrestling (a obs first citation). The sport is illustrated in the 1573 *De arte* (106; see figure 4).

84.10 remisse] free from vehemence (a 4)

84.11 vehement upright wrastling] Illustrated in *De arte* (1573) 104. Mulcaster follows *De arte* 244–6 from here to 85.2.

84.18 egde out] forced out ('Edge' v[1] 6 first citation 1677; see also 'Egg' v[1])

84.30–1 windcourse] respiratory passage (not in *OED*; Mercuriale's phrase for 'stopping some windcourse' is 'spiritus interceptionis ex constrictionibus' in *De arte* 245)

84.32 gawled] afflicted with too much gall (see 'Galled' ppl a[1] first citation 1604 with slightly different meaning and 'Galled' ppl a[2], whose meaning of 'irritated' is possibly suggested here too. Mercuriale reads simply 'in ulceribus internis' in *De arte* 245.)

Figure 4. Mercuriale *De arte gymnastica* (1573) 106

84.32 byled] afflicted with too much bile (not in *OED*; see preceding note)

84.33 eagering] irritating ('Eager' v obs 1 in this sense; Mercuriale's verb is 'exasperentur' in *De arte* 245)

84.33–4 in way ... in will] Perhaps an early hint of *ODEP* 'Where there's a *will*, there's a way' (first citation 1640; not in Tilley).

84.37 commodious] beneficial (a 1 obs)

85.6 Chapter 18.] Follows Mercuriale *De arte* 3.4, 'De pugnarum generibus' (on the kinds of combats), and 6.2, 'De pugnarum effectibus' (on the effects of combats). See notes for 85.14, 85.17, 85.26, 86.6, and 86.15.

Fencing grew in popularity as an organized sport in the sixteenth century. In 1545, Ascham noted 'For of fence all mooste in everye towne, there is ... Masters to teache it, wyth his Provostes Vsshers Scholers and other names of arte & Schole' (*Toxophilus* in *English Works* ed Wright 62). By the 1580s the Italian style of rapier-fighting with its elaborate rules was superseding the older fashion of sword and buckler, and in the 1590s treatises illustrating the art began to appear, for instance the *True Arte of Defence* (trans 1594), by Giacomo di Grassi, a fencing master of Modena. Mulcaster, who follows Mercuriale pretty closely in this chapter, makes no mention of contemporary English fencing techniques, though like Elyot (*The Boke Named the Governour* 1.17 ed Croft 1:181) and Ascham (*Scholemaster* in *English Works* ed Wright 217), he approves of armed combat as a suitable sport, so long as it is not taken to excess.

85.12 prices] prizes ('Prices' sb headnote explains this was the common early spelling; cf *Elementarie* sig 2C4r 'price')

85.14 three kindes] The division and brief description follow Mercuriale *De arte* 273.

85.17 *σχιομαχία*] Although Mulcaster follows *De arte* 273, he could have consulted also page 141, which tells how *schiomachia* (ie, *skiomachia*), or 'shadow-fighting,' was 'non solum cum umbra manibus, atque cruribus pugnare, uerum etiam aduersus columnam, & aduersus palum ... aut murum' (not only for fighting against a shadow with the hands and legs, but also against a column, and against a stake ... or wall).

85.26 That kinde of fensing] In his condemnation of ancient gladiatorial combats, Mulcaster follows Mercuriale *De arte* 142–5, and borrows a number of citations (see notes for 85.34, 86.6, 7, and 9).

85.30 immanitie] monstrous cruelty (2 obs)

85.34 the *Athenian*] The reference, from *De arte* 144, is to Lucian's dialogue 'Anacharsis, or Athletics' 37, where Solon explains to Anacharsis a principle of training applied to Athenian youth: 'What would your feelings be if you should see quail-fights and cock-fights here among us, and no little interest taken in them? You would laugh, of course, particularly if you discovered that we do it in compliance with law, and that all those of military age are required to present themselves and watch the birds spar to the uttermost limit of exhaustion. Yet this is not laughable, either: their souls are gradually penetrated by an appetite for dangers, in order that they may not seem baser and more cowardly than the cocks, and may not show the white feather early on account of wounds or weariness or any other hardship' (trans Harmon 4:61–3). The reading *Anagarsei* for *Anacharsei* is Mulcaster's.

86.3–4 sanguinarie] attended by bloodshed (a 1 first citation 1625)

86.6 *Plinie*] *Natural History* 28.2.4 tells how epileptics drink the blood of gladiators as a curative, and 36.69.203 how gladiators become stronger by drinking lye made from ashes, but in neither of the glossed passages does Pliny indicate disapproval of gladiators. Mulcaster picked up the references from *De arte* 143.

86.7 *Cypriane*] In his letter 'To Donatus' 7, St Cyprian is highly critical of the public combats of the gladiators (*Treatises* trans Deferrari et al 12–13). Reference from Mercuriale *De arte* 143. (Other references untraced, though Mulcaster says there are 'moe places then one.')

86.9 *Plato*] The *Laches*, which is principally an analysis of moral and spiritual courage, begins (178–80) with Lysis wondering if 'that art of fighting in armour' is a proper way for a young man to learn fortitude. The reference is in *De arte* 145 and again at 274.

86.15 The profits which health receives] Following Mercuriale *De arte* 273–4, from here to line 38. Mulcaster changes the order of presentation, but the medical information is the same.

86.22 juyce] humours (sb 2)

86.24 roming humours] ie, those humours which move about the body (Mercuriale sees the exercise as serving 'ad humores firmandos' in *De arte* 273)

86.27 *κῶλον*] colon (the Greek form here is a common wrong spelling for *κόλον* [E. Rummel]). Mercuriale (273) gives only 'colo intestino' in Latin and Mulcaster has turned this into Greek.

86.29 shadowish] resembling shadow (a 2 obs first citation 1642)

86.32 assaies] attacks, assaults (sb 15; also has the sense of 'occasions' sb 21–2)

86.31–2 canvase out] shake out, discover (with secondary meaning of 'buffet, thrash'; 'Canvass' v 4 and 2)

86.33 freinde ... foe] 'Friend' and 'foe' were proverbially linked, though Mulcaster does not seem to have any particular proverb in mind; cf Tilley F686 'Better a new friend than an old foe' and F697; also *ODEP* 'Misfortune makes foes of friends' and 'Make not *friend* thy foe.'

87.3 Chapter 19.] Very loosely based on Mercuriale *De arte* 3.8, 'De cricilasia, trocho, petauro, & pilamalleo,' and 6.7, 'De cricilasiae, trochi, & pilamallei qualitatibus.' See notes for 87.18, 22, and 28.

The whipping-top (a top kept in motion by a whip or 'scourge') was a well-known toy of Mulcaster's day, both for children and, less commonly, for adults (*Shakespeare's England* 2:481); other varieties of tops were the peg-top, string-drive top, and the hand-twirled top of bone (Fraser *A History of Toys* 87). Hoops were also popular.

87.7–8 lent, when Tops be in time] March was the traditional time for playing with tops in England (*Shakespeare's England* 2:481; this passage quoted in partial proof).

87.13 *κρῖκος* ... *τρόχος* ... *trochus*] The Greek *krikos* and *trochos* and the Latin *trochus* are forms of the hoop, and were often equipped with rings running loosely about the circumference or pegs inserted in the inner rim in order to make ringing or humming noises (Harris *Sport in Greece and Rome* 133–41). There is a woodcut of *trochos* in the 1573 *De arte* (166).

87.16 bestowed] stowed away, put in storage (v 2)

87.20–2 *Turbo* ... *βέμβιξ*] Both the Latin and the Greek *bembix* mean 'whipping-top.'

87.18 *Virgil*] *Aeneid* 7.378–84, by way of Mercuriale *De arte* 165–6

87.20 haule] hall

87.22 an old Greek *Epigram*] Quoted in Greek with a Latin translation by Mercuriale *De arte* 165. The lines are from Callimachus 'On Pittacus' in *Greek Anthology* 7.89.9–10; the text in a modern edition reads differently:

οἱ δ' ἀρ' ὑπό πληγῇσι θοὰς βέμβικας ἔχοντες
ἔστρεφον εὐρείῃ παῖδες ἐνι τριόδῳ·

and is translated 'The boys at the broad cross-roads were whipping their swift tops' (*The Greek Anthology* trans Paton 2:55).

87.26 gigges] whipping tops (sb[1] 1 obs; see also 'Whirligig' sb 1; *OED* cites this passage under 'Whirling' ppl a)

87.27 devotion] command (sb 6 obs cited)

87.27 troule] roll or spin about ('Troll' v 3 first cited)

87.28 The harme ...] Following Mercuriale *De arte* 289–90, from here to 88.5.

88.8 *Plato*] *Laws* 7.794. The passage is not found in Mercuriale, and shows a special interest of Mulcaster in the subject (perhaps from teaching penmanship to children?). A modern translation of the passage reads: 'but, as a matter of fact, in the case of the feet and the lower limbs there is plainly no difference in working capacity; and it is due to the folly of nurses and mothers that we have all become limping, so to say, in our hands. For in natural ability the two limbs are almost equally balanced; but we ourselves by habitually using them in a wrong way have made them different' (trans Bury 2:25).

88.31 covert] shelter (sb 2)

88.34 *Galenes* rule] In his short treatise, *De parvae pilae exercitatione*, Galen runs through the various qualities of the best form of exercise – that it is easy to engage in, that it exercises all parts of the body equally, and that it does not cause harm. Ball-playing, he goes on to show, is the best balanced of all sports. Mulcaster's use of Galen's 'rule' (actually 'rules') may be second-hand (following one of the many references to the ancient work in *De arte gymnastica*, though none in the context of the two chapters on the *trochus*), or it may be first-hand, as the Latin translation by J. Goupylus, first published in Paris 1543, was available in a number of editions (see Durling 'Chronological Census').

88.35 parable] readily prepared or procured (a obs first cited; see also 110.14)

88.37 loth] be reluctant to do ('Loathe' v 4; less intense than present-day English 'feel disgust for')

89.3 Chapter 20.] This chapter is a summary of Mercuriale *De arte* 5.11, 'De deambulationum qualitatibus,' and 5.12 'Iterum de deambulationum qualitatibus.' See 89.5 note, and also 89.28 note for a digression to 3.2, 'De ambulatione.' Walking was one of the few sports allowed to the undergraduates in English universities; see the passage in Burton, a student of Christ Church (94.17 below).

89.5 among those exercises] From here to 95.18, Mulcaster radically condenses Mercuriale *De arte* 259–68.

89.12 suffereth] allows (v 18b obs). This commment on weather is not in

Mercuriale, and reflects Mulcaster's English experience.

89.28 walking roomes] These are the 'close *walkes*' or '*cryptoportici*' referred to again at 93.29–36. The walking rooms of the ancients are described by Mercuriale *De arte* 134–5; Alexander Severus and Lucullus are examples of 'ancient Princes' who recommended them, Athens and Rome of 'common weales' where they were used.

89.29 covert] roofed over (a 1; no sixteenth-century citation)

89.33 gamesters] players at games, athletes ('Gamester' 1 obs first cited)

90.1 *Plato*] ie, in his discussion of gymnastics in *Republic* 3.403cff

90.3 *Vegetius*] F. Vegetius Renatus (perhaps late fourth century AD), *Epitoma rei militaris* 1.9 as cited in Mercuriale *De arte* 135. *The Foure Bookes of Flavius Vegetius Renatus ... of Martiall Policye* were translated into English by John Sadler, 1572.

90.6 *Augustus Cesar*, and *Adrian*] Again, from Mercuriale, who cites Vegetius *Epitoma rei militaris* 1.27 in *De arte* 135.

90.9 plaine] open, free from obstructions (a^1 3 obs; Mercuriale *De arte* 135 reads simply 'in campis')

90.11 institute] ordained (ppl a obs; see also v 1)

90.22 strayted] constricted, narrowed ('Strait' v obs 3)

90.27 affections] maladies, diseases (sb 10)

90.31 third] Emended from 'thrid,' which is either a misprint or (less likely) an obsolete dialect (Scottish) form of 'third' (see *OED* 'Third' a headnote); *Elementarie* sig 2E1v has 'third.'

90.36–7 now bearing vpon the whole feete, now upon the toes, now upon the heeles] Three different kinds of walking (not just three parts of the single step), as distinguished by Mercuriale *De arte* 259–60.

91.12 falling evill] falling sickness, epilepsy ('evil' a II 7b; no sixteenth-century citation)

91.12 hauking upp] spitting up (v^3 2 first citation; modern sense)

91.13 and in the time when one is making water] This (somewhat unexpected?) prohibition is from Mercuriale *De arte* 261 'mingentibusue aut feminis defluuium patientibus' (in those who urinate, or in women suffering from their periods).

91.14 abateth] diminishes (v^1 9, with no sixteenth-century citations; but see v^1 10 int)

91.24 strutting] protruding, thrusting (v^1 4b first citation 1583; 'Strutting' ppl a 5 has later and slightly different uses)

91.29 tetters] inflamed eruptions of the skin (sb 1)

91.38 exulceration] ulceration, or sore spot affected by ulceration (sb 1–2)

92.2 fluxe] morbid or excessive discharge, ie, from the 'gout or exulceration' (sb I 1)

92.3 distempered] disturbed in humoral balance (ppl a[1] 2 obs first citation 1595; equivalent to 'distemperate')
92.13 yeaxing] hiccuping ('Yexing' vbl sb)
92.18 strout] strut
92.21 steeme] rise as vapour ('Steam' v 3 first citation 1582)
92.31 sway] force, pressure (sb 3 obs)
92.32 poize] weight ('Poise' sb I 1 obs)
93.2 Demosthenes] Plutarch 'Demosthenes' 11.2 in *Lives*; reference, not mentioning the source in Plutarch, from Mercuriale *De arte* 263
93.8 griefe] physical pain or discomfort (sb 6 obs)
93.16 brambly] (a; first citation)
93.25 *Suetonius*] 'Divus Augustus' 80 where Augustus is said to have cured his legs 'remedio harenarum.' That this remedy may have been 'walking in sand' (and not an applied dressing made of sand and reeds) is an interpretation considered likely by Mercuriale *De arte* 264.
93.34 *cryptoporticus*] covered gallery or passage, from Mercuriale *De arte* 265 (cf 89.28 note).
94.4–5 it ... it] ie, the body
94.8 moyst] render (the humours) moist (v 2 obs; *OED* cites 94.12 'moists' for this sense)
94.14 cleare by the breath] ie, clear the body of humours by means of the breath (Mercuriale's phrase in *De arte* 265 is 'ad euocandum per halitum')
94.17 nippes not] is not hurtful (v[1] 6 'to affect injuriously by the cold'; see line 23)
94.17 If there be winde] Mulcaster follows Mercuriale *De arte* 265ff. Cf Burton *Anatomy of Melancholy* 2.2.3 'Ayre Rectified. With a Digression of the Ayre,' an essay on the qualities and commodities of the air and winds of various places. In the next member (or chapter) of his *Anatomy*, 'Exercise Rectified of Body and Minde,' Burton shows that 'to walke amongst Orchards, Gardens, Bowres, Mounts and Arbors, artificiall wildernesses, greene thickets, Arches, Groves, Lawnes, Rivulets, Fountaines, & such like pleasant places ... to disport in some pleasant plaine, parke, run up a steepe hill sometimes, or sit in a shady seat, must needs be a delectable recreation' (ed Kiessling et al 2:72–3).
94.21 dissolve] disperse morbid humours (v 8; obs medical term)
94.28 herboures] arbours, shaded or covered alleys or walks ('Arbour' 5b obs)
94.31–2 do continually trye] ie, try to abate their flesh, lose weight (the suggestion is from Mercuriale *De arte* 267)
94.36 wholesome] make wholesome or salubrious (not in *OED* as a verb)
95.14–15 inflations] flatulences (sb 2)
95.21 purchase the commodities] gain the advantages ('Purchase' v II 4 obs; 'Commodity' 3 obs)

95.23 cared for] taken account of (v 3 has slightly different sense of 'provide for' or 'look after')

95.25 counterreceit] receipt, or drug, used in opposition to a disease; antidote ('Receipt' sb 2 obs and 'Counter-' II 2; this compound not in *OED*)

95.26 Chapter 21.] This chapter follows *De arte* 5.7, 'De cursus natura' (on the nature of running); also discussed by Mercuriale in 2.10, 'De cursu' (on running). Detailed discussion of Mercuriale in this chapter is given in the Introduction.

Running is one of the sports fit 'for a Courtlie Jentleman to use' in Ascham's *Scholemaster* in *English Works* ed Wright 217. Sir Thomas Elyot approved of running as 'bothe a good exercise and a laudable solace' (*The Boke Named the Governour* 1.17 ed Croft 1:174) and it seems likely that Mulcaster read Elyot on the subject (see 96.8 note). Running in sixteenth-century England is touched on briefly in *Shakespeare's England* 2:454, and Strutt *Sports and Pastimes* 65; both suggest it was held in universal esteem, but cite few references. Castiglione *Courtier* 97 approves of running, but only if the young gentleman does not let himself be beaten by men of a lower class.

96.8 *Alexander ... Papyrius ... Achilles*] All three cited together by Elyot *The Boke Named the Governour* 1.17 ed Croft 1:175–6 as examples of great runners of the ancient world: 'The great Alexander beyng a childe, excelled all his companions in rennyng'; 'one of the mooste noble capitaynes of all the Romanes toke his name of rennyng, and was called *Papirius Cursor*, which is in englisshe, Papirius the Renner'; 'and therfore Homere, throughout all his warke, calleth hym swifte foote Achilles.' These classical references are not in Mercuriale, and very likely Mulcaster picked them up from Elyot, although the sources (Plutarch 'Alexander' 5, Livy 9.16, and the *Iliad* passim) are not at all obscure.

96.23 The first kinde of *running*] From here to 98.29, the end of the chapter, the text follows Mercuriale *De arte* 249–53.

96.29 mylt] milt, spleen ('Milt' sb I 1)

96.29 *Aetius*] References from Mercuriale *De arte* 250. Aetius of Amida (in Mesopotamia) lived during the sixth century AD and became court physician to Justinian. His medical collection the *Tetrabiblon* was incompletely printed in Greek and Latin in the sixteenth century (preface by Ricci to Aetios of Amida *The Gynaecology and Obstetrics ... tr. from the Latin Edition of Cornarius, 1542* 1–13).

96.32 *Aristotle*] Reference from Mercuriale *De arte* 250. *Problemata* 5.9 (881b) reads: 'Why does rapid running produce headache both with man and with other animals? And yet, generally speaking, running seems to draw down the waste products, just as walking does.'

96.39 meane] condition, quality (sb² I 1)

97.3 *Galene*] *De parvae pilae exercitatione* [3] ed Kühn 5:906; reference is from *De arte* 249.

97.16 *κυνικὸν σπάσμα*] *kunikon spasma*, literally, 'dog-like convulsion or spasm'; unilateral facial paralysis (Bell's palsy). The term is from Mercuriale *De arte* 250.

97.17 defluxions] flows of humours from one part of the body to another (sb 2 a obs; see also 102.8 note)

97.19 *Ischiatica*] sciatica ('Ischiatica' sb first citation)

97.26 gnawing of the guttes] wrenching pain in the stomach (Mercuriale's expression is 'uiscera torquentur' in *De arte* 250)

97.36 twiste] junction of the thighs, crotch (sb¹ 3 obs)

97.38 chafed] vexed, irritated (v 5; see also 105.23 and note)

98.14 *Hippocrates*] *Regimen* 4.100, from Mercuriale *De arte* 253. Mulcaster's gloss ('Liber de insomniis languentium' or Book on the Sleeplessness of Those Unwell) seems to be his own invention; the section in Hippocrates is 'On Dreams.'

98.24 single] in slight clothing, in garment of single thickness (a 9–10 obs)

98.26–9 *Hyppocrates ... Oribasius ... Aristotle*] These citations on running follow Mercuriale *De arte* 253 closely, with the interesting addition of the marginal gloss lifted from *De arte* 221 (ch 4 'De tempore exercitationibus apto'). The passage in Hippocrates is found in *Regimen* 3.50 ed Jones 4:373ff, Oribasius in 6.22; Aristotle in *Problemata* 2.21, 33, 42.

98.30 Chapter 22.] This chapter follows Mercuriale *De arte* 2.11, 'De saltu' (on leaping) and, at greater length, 5.8, 'Quid praestet saltus' (on the use of leaping).

Leaping is recommended by Ascham (*Scholemaster* in *English Works* ed Wright 217), and was a common sport in the sixteenth century. But it was not a formal skill until the seventeenth century, if Strutt (*Sports and Pastimes* 188) is correct.

99.1–2 no ground can hold] A variation of the proverb 'He thinks that the ground carried him not' (Tilley G466)? Curiously, the earliest use of 'jump for joy' in the *OED* is 1775 ('Jump' v I 1c), though 'leap for joy' (98.34) is found in Luke 6:23 (see 'Leap' v 3 first citation 1611).

99.13 It served the olde world] The ancient authorities (Plato, Aristotle, Galen, Oribasius, et al) for the athletic, martial, and medical uses of 'saltus' are given in Mercuriale *De arte* 117–18.

99.17 Romain Emperor] From here to the end of the chapter, Mulcaster follows Mercuriale *De arte* 254–5. The reference to Suetonius ('Divus Augustus' 83) is taken from *De arte* 254.

99.30 fumes] noxious vapours rising from the stomach to the brain (sb 4 obs)

99.31 chearisheth] is good for ('Cherish' v 5)

99.39 *Lacedemonian* wymen] Callimachus' statue of the 'saltantes Lacaenae' is described in Pliny *Natural History* 34.19.92; reference is made in Mercuriale *De arte* 118 and 254. Why Mulcaster calls Callimachus a painter and his work a picture is not very clear, for both Pliny and Mercuriale call him principally a sculptor and his works statues.

100.1 κακοχειρότεχνος] *kakocheirotechnos;* Mulcaster has turned what Mercuriale calls 'cacirotechnus' [sic] (*De arte* 118) into a Greek form. Modern editions of Pliny read *catatexitechnus,* translated by Rackham in the Loeb edition as 'one who wastes his skill in driblets.'

100.4 *Rigs*] wanton women (sb[4])

100.5 The lawes and custome] Mulcaster's own observations about Spartan women.

100.12 *Plato*] Mulcaster's own reference, which should probably be to *Republic* 5 (452 or 457), as there is nothing like this about the exercise of women in book 4.

100.14 againe the banke] uphill ('Bank' sb[1] 2 obs meant 'hill'; Mercuriale's phrase is 'uersus altum' in *De arte* 255)

100.16 the crooked swelling veines in the legge] Mercuriale *De arte* 255, has 'varicibus,' which Mulcaster translates here by a description (the earliest use of 'varicous' or 'varicose' in *OED* is 1597).

100.21g Gal. 6. epi. commen. 3. aph. 2.] This reference, taken from *De arte* 255, is to part 3 of Galen's *Commentary on Hippocrates' Epidemics Book VI,* aphorism 2 (ed Kühn 17B:7ff).

100.24 flixe] flux (see 92.2 note above)

100.30 ballace] ballast, weight (this non-technical sense is not in *OED* 'Ballast' sb, though it is in v 2)

100.31 Chapter 23.] Based on Mercuriale *De arte* 3.14, 'De natatione' (on swimming) and 6.12, 'De natationis, et piscationis effectibus' (on the effects of swimming and of fishing).

Swimming received its earliest formal treatment as a skill in England in Everard Digby's *De arte natandi* first published in 1587 and translated in abridged form in 1595 (Orme *Early British Swimming* chapter 4; West 'Spenser, Everard Digby, and the Renaissance Art of Swimming'; Strutt *Sports and Pastimes* 74; *Shakespeare's England* 2:458). Swimming is in Ascham's list of approved sports (*Scholemaster* in *English Works* ed Wright 217). Its heartiest recommendation comes from Elyot *The Boke Named the Governour* 1.17 ed Croft 1:176–81, who gives a number of classical examples which may have influenced Mulcaster (see 101.36 through 101.39 and notes).

100.33 In the old time] From here to 101.9, Mulcaster follows *De arte* 182.

100.34–5 he neither knoweth letter on the booke, nor yet how to *swimme*] From Mercuriale *De arte* 182, who is quoting an ancient proverb (cf Erasmus

Adagia in LB 2:156C 'Neque natare, neque literas' trans CWE 31:330–1; not in Tilley or *ODEP*).

101.4 dastard] dullard (sb 1 obs)

101.4 sleight to *swimme*] precise art or method of swimming (sb[1] 4)

101.9 *Leander*] The story of Leander's fatal attempt to swim across the Hellespont to be united with the beautiful priestess Hero was well known in the Renaissance, both from Ovid's *Heroides* (18 and 19) and from Musaeus' *Hero and Leander* (often read in the Latin translation of Marcus Musurus). See MacLure's introduction to Marlowe *Poems* xxv–vi. The reference is Mulcaster's own, and is not in Mercuriale.

101.13–14 But bycause it is so necessarie] Following Mercuriale *De arte* 303–5, from here to 102.21.

101.17 bladders] Animal bladders were prepared and inflated and used as floats (*Shakespeare's England* 2:458 and see also *OED* 'Bladder' sb 3).

101.22 meres] lakes or ponds (sb[1] 2 cited)

101.33 warrant] security (sb[1] 3 obs); ie, there is no security when one is in the water, except for the knowledge of potential danger.

101.35 warrant] keep safe from (v 1 obs)

101.36–8 *Cocles ... Scoeva ... Caesar*] These are not in Mercuriale, and Mulcaster may have picked the references to Cocles and Caesar from Elyot *The Boke Named the Governour* 1.17 ed Croft 1:178–9, where Horatius Cocles' defence of Rome against Porsenna and his subsequent escape in the waters of the Tiber, and Caesar's escape at the battle of Alexandria are both described (ultimately from Livy 2.10.11 and Suetonius 'Divus Julius' 64 or Plutarch 'Julius Caesar' 49 in *Lives*). M. Caesius Scaeva distinguished himself under Caesar at Dyrrhachium (Plutarch 'Julius Caesar' 16 in *Lives* and Lucan 6.140ff); the lesser-known story of his swimming is in Valerius Maximus 3.2.23 (cf Plutarch 'Julius Caesar' 16).

102.6–7 nosethrilles] nostrils (common sixteenth-century spelling; see 'Nose-thirl')

102.8 falling] wasting (not in this sense in *OED*; Mercuriale's term is 'defluxio' [*De arte* 304], which refers to the flowing away of the beneficial humours from the afflicted part; Mulcaster uses 'defluxions' at 97.17)

102.12 exhalation] vapour (here, presumably, of a cold and wet, or phlegmatic, nature; sb 1)

102.25–7 if he die on lande, he doeth his duetie, and if he drowne in water, his duetie is not drowned] ie, if a man dies on the land, he fulfils his obligation to the state, but if he drowns, his obligation to the state is not yet fulfilled (because he should have known how to swim) ('Duty' sb 5c [with sense of military obligation] and 4).

102.28 Chapter 24.] This chapter follows Mercuriale *De arte* 3.9, 'De Equitatione' (of riding) and 6.8, 'De equitationis facultatibus' (on the uses of riding); see 103.18 note.

Although Mulcaster stays pretty close to what Mercuriale has to say, there was quite a range of books available to him on the subject of riding, had he wished to consult them. Blundeville's translation of F. Grisone's *Ordini di cavalcare* appeared in 1566; C. Corte, who worked for the earl of Leicester, wrote *Il cavalerizzo* (1573), summarized in English by Thomas Bedingfield as *The Art of Riding* in 1584. See the bibliography to the article on 'Horsemanship, with Farriery' in *Shakespeare's England* 2:408–27, for more titles. Ascham deplores the declining interest of young gentlemen in riding: 'For, of all outward qualities, to ride faire, is most cumelie for [the young gentleman], most necessarie for his contrey, and the greater he is in blood, the greater is his praise, the more he doth excede all other therein' (*Scholemaster* in *English Works* ed Wright 199). Elyot strongly advises youthful training in riding the 'great horse' as preparation for military service (*The Boke Named the Governour* 1.17 ed Croft 1:181–6).

103.1–2 *Aristophanes ... Socrates*] Possibly a reference to the *Clouds* of Aristophanes, in which Socrates is made to represent the intellectual excesses of the Sophists and is contrasted with the horse-loving Pheidippides, son of the countryman Strepsiades. Mulcaster seems to be saying 'even though the *Clouds* is an inadequate attack on Socrates, it is good evidence that riding was a subject to be learned by gentlemen in Athens.' The reference is not in Mercuriale, who does, however, mention defences of riding by Plato (*Laches*) and Ischomachus and Socrates (in Xenophon's *Oeconomicus*). The references to Aristophanes here and at 195.10 suggest that Mulcaster was familiar with his work.

103.3 *Virgile*] Aeneid 7.162–3: 'ante urbem pueri et primaeuo flore iuuentus / exercentur equis' (before the city, boys and youths in their early bloom exercise on horseback). Mulcaster's own citation.

103.4 legacie] legation, embassy (sb 3 obs)

103.6 *Horace*] *Odes* 3.24.54–5: 'nescit equo rudis / haerere ingenuus puer' (the freeborn lad, unpractised, knows not how to ride his steed). Mulcaster's own citation.

103.9 The *Romains*] The ancient Roman horse-racing teams are described in Mercuriale *De arte* 168, where much of the matter merely glossed here is quoted at length (ie, Galen *De methodo medendi* 7.6 [ed Kühn 10:478]; Pliny the Younger *Letters* 9.6; Martial *Epigrams* 11.33; Juvenal *Satires* 11.197ff). Harris *Sport in Greece and Rome* 193ff describes the ancient horse-racing factions.

103.10 partialities] factions (sb 2b obs)

103.15 sorofull] Perhaps should read 'sorowfull' (as in *Elementarie* sig 2D3v).

103.18 The saye that] From here to 104.21, the end of the chapter, Mulcaster follows *De arte* 292–5, in summary fashion.

103.23 *posting*] fast riding (vbl sb[1] 2 obs first citation 1589 and 'Post' v[1] 2; not to be confused with the present-day sense of rhythmical up and down riding on a trotting horse)

103.24 grines] groin

103.33 *Germanicus Caesar*] As described in Suetonius 'Caligula' 3; Mulcaster follows Mercuriale *De arte* 292.

104.6 gravell] urinary crystals (sb 4)

104.15 paires] impairs, worsens (v[2] 1 obs; an aphaeresis)

104.17 ride post] ride with speed ('Post' adv a obs)

104.22 Chapter 25.] This chapter follows Mercuriale *De arte* 3.15, 'De Venatione' (on hunting) and 6.13, 'De venatione conditionibus' (on the circumstances of hunting).

Most writing on hunting of this period was translated from other languages (*Shakespeare's England* 2:334–50, especially 350). This is surprising, considering the importance of hunting both as sport and as source of food. Even the well-known *Noble Arte of Venerie or Hunting* (1575) of George Tuberville is 'little more than a translation of *La Vénerie de Jacques du Fouilloux*, published in 1561' (334). Elyot has a chapter of the *The Boke Named the Governour* 1.18, on 'The auncient huntyng of Greekes and Romanes' (ed Croft 1:186–203), which he terms a 'laudable exercise' (186). It was one of the most highly esteemed sports for the gentleman and nobleman, though it would have been frowned on as an activity for students, including members of the two universities. Mulcaster is favour of that hunting 'wherein we exercise our selves and our owne bodies most, not our hauks and howndes' (106.23–4).

104.24 humour] disposition (sb 6b first citation 1590)

104.25 *Homer ... Heliodorus*] Both Homer's *Odyssey* and Heliodorus' *Aethiopica* (a long prose romance in Greek of the third century AD) were known to Renaissance readers, the latter as an example of pastoral. But why these authors are cited here for their copious arguments on hunting is unclear; *Odyssey* 19.429–66, has the dramatic story of Odysseus and the wild boar, but not much else, and there are no hunting scenes in the *Aethiopica*, except for the capture of a runaway bull (at 10.28ff).

104.25 *Dian*] A common Renaissance source for Diana as the Roman goddess of hunting was Ovid *Metamorphoses* 3.163 and 3.252; for her virginity see ibid 1.486–7 and 1.694–5. Mulcaster is saying that Diana is a good exemplum to be used in praise of hunting because she avoided Cupid in favour of the chase.

104.26 *Hippolytus*] Hippolytus was the son of Theseus and the Amazonian princess Hippolyta, and was beloved of Phaedra, his stepmother. According to some versions of the tale, he did not return her passion because he was more interested in hunting (hence, as Mulcaster says, an example of 'continence'), so the unhappy Phaedra killed herself. Theseus then erroneously accused his son of involvement with her, and had the young man killed. Hippolytus' interest in hunting is dwelt on in Ovid *Heroides* 4.37ff. Mulcaster owes his reference to Mercuriale *De arte* 307, where Seneca's version of the story is mentioned. Along with Ovid, Mulcaster had probably read Seneca's *Hippolytus* (or *Phaedra*), for it was a popular work (indeed had been translated c 1567).

104.28 woddishe] sylvan, wild, woodish (a 2 obs first citation 1588).

104.30 faint] be afraid, lose courage (v 1)

104.30 *Persians*] The Persian love of hunting would have been known to Mulcaster from Xenophon *Cyropaedia* 1.2.10–11, 1.4.7–8, etc.

104.31 patrocinie] patronage (sb obs); ie, there is no shortage of patrons to defend or praise hunting.

105.1 naturally appointed for man's use] A commonplace: see K. Thomas *Man and the Natural World* 18–21

105.3 *Xenophon*] Mercuriale *De arte* 186 quotes from Xenophon *Cyropaedia* 1.2.10 ('In a word, it is not easy to find any quality required in war that is not required also in the chase'). Mulcaster's gloss 'lib. de Venat.' is to Xenophon's 'On Hunting' referred to at *De arte* 185.

105.10 *Romain Emperours*] Following Mercuriale *De arte* 187, who refers to Suetonius ('Divus Augustus' 43.2).

105.16 *Galene*] From Mercuriale *De arte* 187. In the *De parvae pilae exercitatione* (On the exercise of the little ball) 2, Galen recommends ball-playing as affordable and enjoyable by all, and therefore a more suitable sport than hunting which requires dogs, horses, arms, and nets (ed Kühn 5:900–1).

105.19–20 purchaceable] procurable (a a obs first citation 1611)

105.23 chafe] harass (v 5 'vex, irritate'; Mulcaster uses the verb twice in relationship with hunted animals, here and at 97.38)

105.32 *Rases*] Reference from Mercuriale *De arte* 187 (with correct reference to 30. contract. 13. c. 3). Rhazes or Muhammed ibn Zakariya al-Razi (850–932?) was an Arabic physician. His important medical manual was printed as *Elhavi siue continens* in 1486 and he had a wide reputation in Renaissance medical theory (Sarton *Appreciation* 40).

105.35 *Mithridates*] Anecdote from Mercuriale *De arte* 187. Mithridates VI the Great, King of Pontus in Asia Minor, was the opponent of Rome in the second century BC. His exploits are described in Appian's *Mithridatic Wars* and Plutarch's *Lives*, though this specific episode comes from Justinus'

Epitoma historiarum Philippicarum of Pompeius Trogus 37.2, who explains that Mithridates assumed this outdoor life in order to avoid the plots of his enemies, not for 'his healthes sake.'

105.40 There be but two kindes] From here to 106.22, Mulcaster borrows material from Mercuriale *De arte* 306–8.

106.3 hallow] chase pursue with shouts ()v 2

106.4 travel] cause to work, employ ('Travail' 1 c obs)

106.9 bellicawles] cauls, or membranes, of the belly; omentum ('Caul' sb[1] 4, and see 79.9 note; this form not in *OED*)

106.20 of a head] spontaneously (variant of 'of one's own head'?; 'Head' sb 33 obs)

106.27 *Chiron, Machaon, Podalyrius, Aesculapius*] The names are taken from Mercuriale *De arte* 185. Chiron was the centaur who was learned in medical lore and who educated Achilles, Asclepius, and Jason (Homer *Iliad* 4.219; Xenophon *On Hunting* 1.1–2). Machaon and Podalirius, sons of Aesculapius or Asclepius, the god of healing, were themselves skilled physicians (*Iliad* 2.731–2 and 4.200ff). Chiron, Machaon, and Podalirius are mentioned as hunters by Xenophon *On Hunting* 1.13–14.

106.30 *Platoes* opinion] Probably *Republic* 3.408D: 'Physicians, it is true ... would prove most skilled if, from childhood up, in addition to learning the principles of the art they had familiarized themselves with the greatest possible number of the most sickly bodies, and if they themselves had suffered all diseases and were not of very healthy constitution.'

106.32 Chapter 26.] Mercuriale discusses archery in *De arte* 2.13, 'De Iaculatione' (on throwing) and 5.10, 'De disci, atque iaculationis effectibus' (on the effects of the discus and throwing); except for a few borrowed references, this chapter is Mulcaster's own work. Indeed, this and the next chapter are the two most original on particular sports, suggesting that Mulcaster had a greater familiarity with archery and ball-play than with those sports described earlier in the book.

Traditionally, shooting of the longbow was the premier English sport. But after a modest revival in the reign of Henry VIII, archery underwent a decline, so much so that by 1603 John Stow was to say 'What should I speake of the auncient dayly exercises in the long bow by Citizens of this Citie, now almost cleane left off and forsaken? I overpass it: for by the meane of closing the common grounds, our Archers for want of roome to shoote abroade, creepe into bowling Allies, and ordinarie dicing houses, nearer home, where they have roome enough to hazard their money at unlawful games: and there I leave them to take their pleasures' (Stow *Survey* ed Kingsford 1:104). Even the enactment of statutes for the maintenance of archery (for instance that of March 1572 [Hughes and Larkin no 587]) had little effect, for as Elyot had pointed out as early as 1531, 'yet who effectuelly puttethe his hande to continual execution of the same lawes and provisions [for the maintenance of archery]? or beholdyng them dayly broken, wynketh nat at the offendours?' (*The Boke Named the Governour* 1.27 ed Croft 1:302–3). Still, in the 1580s there was a continuing interest in the sport, as was shown by the activities of the two London companies of archers (see 108.25–6 note).

Sir Nicholas Bacon, in his Regulations for St Alban's School (1570), required of the parents that 'Ye shall allow your child at all times, a bow, three arrows, bowstrings, a shooting glove, and a bracer to exercise shooting' (Carlisle *Concise Description* 1:517), one of the few extant Elizabethan provisions for sport in school. There are essays on archery in Strutt *Sports and Pastimes* 39–58 and *Shakespeare's England* 2:376–88; Parker *Compendium of Works on Archery* is a chronological list of English writings.

106.35 *Apollo* and *Aesculapius*] Apollo and Aesculapius are traditional patrons of archery as well as of medicine. Mercuriale mentions them together at *De arte* 129, 130, and 258.

106.35 presidentes] presiding patrons or deities (sb i b fig first citation c 1611)

107.6 in sadnes] earnestly (see 28.14–15 note)

107.13–14 *Crete* ... *Cyprus* ... *Indian* Ilandes] That archery is natural to islands is not in Mercuriale, and has not been traced, though see next note.

107.16 the *Balear Ilandes* seeme to take their name] The suggestion is that the Balearic Islands owe their name to the Greek *ballô*, to throw, following Mercuriale *De arte* 129, where there is a short passage on the 'Balearica funda' or sling in the preceding chapter 'De disco & halteribus.' Cf also Cooper 'Dictionarium' in *Thesaurus* sv 'Baleares': 'Two ylandes in the Spanyshe sea ... the one called *Maiorica* ... the other, named *Minorica* ... Florus wryteth, that the custome is in those ylandes, that when the chyldren are hungry, their mothers set up their breakefast on the ende of an hyghe beame or pole, so that they can not comme unto it untill they stryke it downe with their slynges: by which practise the people of those countreys becomme very cunnynge in that feate' (the anecdote in Cooper comes from Florus 1.43, in turn from Strabo 3.5.1).

107.19 tofore] previously, before (adv 1 obs)

107.30 the proverbe helpe the hungrie *hunter*] *ODEP* 'Hungry as a hunter, As' (not in Tilley)

107.31 vantage] advantage

108.1 in a meane] moderately

108.3 passager] traveller, wayfarer ('Passenger' 1b)

108.14 rownde] energetic ('Round' a 11)

108.16 *Askam*] Mulcaster's praise for Ascham echoes Ascham's own praise for his early patron Sir Humphrey Wingfield: 'Woulde to god all Englande has used or wolde use to lay the foundacion of youth, after the example of this worshipful man in bringyng up chyldren in the Booke and the Bowe ...' (*Toxophilus* in *English Works* ed Wright 97). Roger Ascham (c 1515–68) was often mentioned by contemporary and later writers as a lover of and authority on archery; see Ryan *Roger Ascham* 56–9. *Toxophilus*, his two-part learned dialogue on that sport, was first published in 1545.

108.22 relice] taste, flavour ('Relish' sb[1] 1b first citation 1592)

108.25 franke] liberal, bounteous (a[2] 2)

108.25–6 prince *Arthurs* knightes] Prince Arthur's Knights were a society of some three hundred prosperous London men who were keen enthusiasts of archery. The group was active in the 1580s, a rival organization to the older Duke of Shoreditch archers, whose splendid gathering in 1583 of three thousand participants is mentioned in Nichols *Progresses ... of Queen Elizabeth* 2:411 and described in detail in W.M.'s *A Remembrance of the Worthy Show and Shooting by the Duke of Shoreditch and his Associates ... 1583* rpt in Roberts *The English Bowman* 253–75 (the original no longer extant; not in *STC*). Mulcaster does not seem to have been a prominent member of Prince Arthur's Knights; his initials do not appear in R. Robinson's book of Arthurian devises, *The Auncient Order, Societie and Unitie Laudable, of Prince Arthure, and his Knightly Armory of the Round Table* (1583). Prince Arthur was a name with special meaning for the Tudors; Henry VIII's first son was of that name, and the finest knight in Spenser's *Faerie Queene* was also a Prince Arthur. A group which called itself by this name and which engaged in the traditional patriotic sport would be seeking the favour of the court. See Millican *Spenser and the Table Round* especially 54–64.

108.32 under travellours] subordinate labourers ('Under-' prefix[1] 6a; 'Travailer')

108.34 maister *Hewgh Offly*] Hugh Offley (d 1594) was a leatherseller who served as sheriff of London in 1588 (Stow, *Survey* ed Kingsford 1:145, 151, and 2:185, 292). Robert Greene dedicated *The Spanish Masquerado* (1589) to him (Millican *Spenser and the Table Round* 175). He is also identified as Sir Lancelot in Richard Robinson's *The Auncient Order* (see Millican 63 and fig). He organized a splendid display of Prince Arthur's Knights in c 1587, for which see the descriptive 'Prolusion of "Prince Arthur, with his Knights of the Round Table"' in Nichols *Progresses ... of Queen Elizabeth* 2:529–30 and also Chambers *Elizabethan Stage* 1:139.

108.38 maister *Thomas Smith*] Thomas Smith or Smythe of Ostenhanger in Kent, a well-to-do London haberdasher and 'Chiefe Customer for her Majestie in the Porte of the London,' who died in 1591. Robinson's *The Auncient Order* is dedicated to him and to the society of archers (*The Auncient Order* sig 3*1r–3r); he is also the dedicatee of Robinson's translation of Leland's *Assertio inclytissimi Arturij Regis Britanniae* (1582) along with Arthur, Lord

Grey, and Sir Henry Sidney (*DNB* under Sir Thomas Smith, 1558?–1625, his son, and Millican *Spenser and the Table Round* 59 and note).

109.6 hudled up] concealed ('Huddle' v 1 obs cited)

109.7 Chapter 27.] Mercuriale discusses ball play in *De arte* 2.4, 'De Sphaeristica' (on ball play), 2.5, 'De Pilae ludo secundum Latinos' (on the game of ball according to the Romans), 5.3, 'De saltatoriae effectibus' (on the effects of leaping), and 5.4, 'De ludorum pilae effectibus' (on the effects of the ball games). He talks about the ancient sports of 'sphaeristica,' 'cubistica,' 'follis,' 'pila trigonalis,' 'pila paganica,' 'harpastum,' and others, none of which really corresponds to Renaissance tennis, football, or 'armeball.' Nevertheless, Mulcaster finds a way to use Mercuriale in this chapter. As he suggests at 109.26–9, he transfers to English sports the curative aspects of Greek ball games and 'pila et malleus' (see 110.28 and 111.38 notes).

'Handball,' consisting of simple games of catch or bouncing a ball against a wall, was a common sport for children in the period. A competitive form known as 'fives' originated in France as jeu-de-paume (*Shakespeare's England* 2:459), and later evolved into tennis. Tennis was highly recommended by educational writers as a sport for gentlemen (Ascham *Scholemaster* in *English Works* ed Wright 217; James I *Instructions* cited in Strutt *Sports and Pastimes* 87), though Elyot decided to 'passe over' tennis in speaking of indoor exercises (*The Boke Named the Governour* 1.16 ed Croft 1:171, but see also 1:292–4). The rules of court tennis are different from those of lawn tennis; the court was enclosed and points were scored by hitting the ball through small openings at opposite ends of the court or by scoring a winning 'chase' in which the player tried to land the ball at a farther point from the net than his opponent had done (see description in Lilly C. Stone 'English Sports and Recreations' 448–9). Most of Mulcaster's students would never have had a chance to play the game as they would not have had access to a court, though by at least 1597 there were public courts in London for rent (Strutt *Sports and Pastimes* 86) and there were courts in Oxford in the 1590s.

Mulcaster's approval of football is unusual. Most writers condemned the sport outright, Elyot for instance saying that the game is 'nothinge but beastly furie and exstreme violence; wherof procedeth hurte, and consequently rancour and malice do remaine with them that be wounded; wherfore it is to be put in perpetuall silence' (*The Boke Named the Governour* 1.27 ed Croft 1:295–6; see also *Shakespeare's England* 2:462–3). In 1584 any minister or deacon at Oxford who went into the field 'to playe at foot-ball' was to be 'forthwith banished the Universitie' (Wood *History and Antiquities* ed Gutch 2:220). The image one has of the game is a free-for-all, with no clearly defined rules; Mulcaster recommends a limited number of players, who are required to play position. His suggestion points the direction the evolution of the game was to take. Discussed in Strutt *Sports and Pastimes* 93–7, Magoun *History of Football* (Mulcaster at 26–8, with debt to Mercuriale acknowledged and an unsupported claim he may have read treatises on *calcio* an organized and aristocratic form of football in Italy), Rowse *The Elizabethan Renaissance: The Life of the Society* 192.

'Armeball' is Mulcaster's name for what was known as 'windball' or 'balloon,' apparently an early form of volleyball or handball. It is described by Gervase Markham in 1615 as 'a strong & moving sport in the open fields, with a great ball of double leather fild with winde, and driven to and fro with the strength of a mans arme arm'd in a bracer of wood' (*Countrey Contentments* 1:109). There is an illustration from Erasmo di Valvasone *La caccia* (c 1602) in Lilly C. Stone 'English Sports' 460. The game is not mentioned by Elyot or Ascham, and may have had greater popularity in the seventeenth century, though Jones in 1572 recommended a similar sport (see Strutt *Sports and Pastimes* 90–1 and *Shakespeare's England* 2:453 and 462).

109.16 *Galene*] *De sanitate tuenda* 1.10 trans Green 32. Not in this context in Mercuriale, and further evidence that Mulcaster read *De sanitate tuenda*.

110.14 parabilitie] quality of being easily procured or got (sb obs first citation 1654; see 'parable' at 88.35 and note)

110.28 This playing abateth grossenes] From here to line 36, following Mercuriale *De arte* 241.

110.33 ridgebone] backbone ('Ridge-bone' cited)

110.38 turnesicke] dizzy (A adj obs)

111.25 standings] positions (this sense not in *OED*; see vbl sb 8–9 for 'position as determined by seniority' or 'status')

111.29 And being so used] Following Mercuriale *De arte* 242 from here to line 33.

111.38 *Armeball*] Mercuriale, speaking of 'pila et malleus' tells that it was 'non multis ab hinc annis in Regno Neapolitano inuentum' (devised not many years ago in the kingdom of Naples), *De arte* 167. Mulcaster has borrowed this bit of history and rather inaccurately applied it to 'armeball.' 'Pila et malleus' corresponds rather to English 'pall-mall' ('in which a boxwood ball was driven through an iron ring suspended at some height above the ground in a long alley' *OED* 'Pall Mall' 2), especially popular in the seventeenth century, and an ancestor of croquet. 'Armeball' is played quite differently (see 109.7 note). Mulcaster goes on to use Mercuriale's description of the medical qualities of 'pila et malleus' (see 112.6 note.)

112.1 answereth] corresponds to (v 28 obs)

112.6 shrew] troublesome or evil thing (sb^2 2 obs)

112.6 The *armeball* encreaseth the naturall heate] From here to 112.17, following Mercuriale *De arte* 290–1.

Figure 5 Mercuriale *De arte gymnastica* (1573) 162

112.15 sharp urine] painful urination ('Urine' sb[1] 2 obs)

112.25–7 the tumbling *Cybistike* ... the swinging *Petawre*] Each of these ancient sports is discussed at length by Mercuriale, and with the exception of the first, is illustrated in the 1573 edition of the *De arte* with a woodcut. 'Cybistike' is the art of tumbling in gymnastics (from *kubistao*), and is found in *De arte* 2.3, 'De saltatoria' and 5.3, 'De saltatoriae effectibus.' 'Pugillate,' 'Cestus,' and 'Pancrace' are all forms of hand-to-hand combat, analysed together in 2.9, 'De pugilatu, & pancratio, & caestibus,' and 5.6 'De pugillatus, pancratii, & caestum facultatibus.' '*Cestus*' is a special form of boxing, in which the contestants' hands are wrapped round with straps of hide studded with metal balls. '*Pancrace*' is the classical 'pancratium,' a free-for-all wrestling less formal and more violent than upright wrestling or 'luctatio' (see 84.5–6 note). The '*discus*' and '*halteres*' refer to the discus or quoit and the dumb-bells of modern as well as ancient games. They are analysed in *De arte* 2.12, 'De disco & halteribus' and 5.9, 'De halterum condicionibus.' The '*Petawre*,' the classical 'petaurum,' is the subject of some confusion in *De arte* 163, where it is described as a form of swing (and is also depicted as such in a woodcut; see figure 5). Actually the 'petaurum' is a spring-board. Reliance on Mercuriale has caused Mulcaster to refer to the 'swinging *Petawre*.'

Despite the italics and the foreignness of these terms, Mulcaster introduces them as English words as their endings prove; even so, none of his usages are listed in *OED* ('Cybistike' not in *OED*; 'Pugillate' first citation 1768; 'Cestus'2 first citation 1734; 'Pancrace' not in *OED* but see 84.5–6 note; 'Discus' 1 first citation 1656; 'Halteres' first citation 1533; 'Petawre' not in *OED*, though see 'Petaurist' first citation 1656).

112.26 quayting] quoiting, hurling ('Quoit' v 2 means 'to throw like a quoit' or discus)

112.28 memorandums] ('Memorandum' sb 4 obs first citation 1592 'reminder')

113.12 Chapter 28.] Chapters 28 through 34 contain material from book 4 of *De arte*, where Mercuriale introduces the specifically medical aspects of gynmastics in a long general analysis. Mulcaster has kept the same order of topics, but has severely condensed his material, having reduced forty-four pages of Latin to sixteen pages of English. In the headings for this and the following chapters, I merely indicate the corresponding chapters in Mercuriale and note any additions made by Mulcaster to his source. Such additions, it should be stressed, are extremely few, these pages being little more than a summary of Mercuriale's main arguments. Mulcaster mostly omits Mercuriale's citations and discussions of ancient opinion.

This chapter follows *De arte*, 4.1 'De ratione agendorum, & de exercitationis usu' (on the manner of proceeding, and of the use of exercise). It is interesting to note how smoothly Mercuriale's 'ratio' or method fits into Mulcaster's larger method declared at the beginning of *Positions*, and it may well be that book 4 of *De arte gymnastica* provided Mulcaster with a method of circumstances to be applied to education. Method was an important part of medical writing and Galen provided one of the most detailed analyses of method for the Renaissance. See next note.

114.4–5 the rule of art] From 114.3 to the end of the chapter is Mulcaster's own observation. The importance of considering 'circumstance' was stressed in chapter 3 above. The difficulty in reconciling art and circumstance in education is analysed in chapter 7 of *Elementarie*, where art is the elementary program and circumstance is 'nature.'

114.16 Chapter 29.] Based very loosely on *De arte* 4.5 'De exercitationum differentijs' (on the kinds of exercise), in which Mercuriale discusses in detail the three stages of exercise (as at line 31), divisions of exercise according to light, location, continuity, intensity, and so on. The reference to Galen may be from Mulcaster's own reading (see 114.24 note).

114.19 feebled] weakened (v 2 obs)

114.24 *Galene*] Not in the corresponding section of Mercuriale. In his *De sanitate tuenda* 1.7 trans Green 24, Galen says: 'And if [infants] chance to be distressed or to cry, the best appeasement of their unhappiness is the nurse's nipple put in their mouth. For these three remedies for the distress of infants have been found by nurses taught by experience, one which we have just mentioned and two others, moderate rocking and a certain modulation of the voice ...' In the next chapter Galen adds that clean diapers will also keep them happy.

114.34 strainable] violent (a obs 2 cited)

114.34 curteous] gentle, benign ('Courteous' a 1e, normally applied to persons)

115.15 Chapter 30.] This chapter follows, in greatly reduced form, *De arte* 4.6, 'De corporum morborum, & sanitatis generibus' (of the kinds of bodily diseases, and health), 4.7, 'An corpora aegra ullo pacto exerceri conueniat' (whether it is proper for diseased bodies to be exercised in any way), 4.8, 'De corporibus valetudinarijs, & senilibus exercendis' (on exercising infirm and aged bodies), and 4.9, 'De corporibus sanis exercendis' (on exercising healthy bodies) (205–15).

115.20 *valetudinarie*] not in robust health (a 1a first cited, though perhaps closer to the Latin sense of unwell)

115.26 jumpe] exact, precise (a obs first cited)

115.32 contraried] contradicted (v obs 2b cited)

116.20 lay] reduce (v^1 4 obs)

116.27 straite] narrow (a 3)

116.29 *seat*] placement in the body (sb 14 and 19)

117.13 inferre] induce, bring upon (v 1 obs)

117.17–19 *Prodicus ... Antiochus ... Spurina*] All three referred to in Mercuriale *De arte* 210. Prodicus is a mistaken reference by Mercuriale to Herodicus, whose long walks are mentioned by Plato in *Phaedrus* 227E and who appears in *Republic* 3.406Aff as the original valetudinarian; see also Aristotle *Rhetoric* 1.5 (1361b). Interestingly, Prodicus is the name of the wary philosopher in *Protagoras* especially 340E and other dialogues (as well as the pseudo-Platonic *Axiochus* 366Bff), and it seems that Mulcaster recognized the name well enough to give him the epithet, but not well enough to see Mercuriale's mistake. Antiochus, an old but active physician, is described in Galen *De sanitate tuenda* 5.4 trans Green 202. Pliny (*Letters* 3.1) sets forth in detail the very full day of Vestricius Spurinna, a spry old Roman.

117.21 presidentes] precedents, exemplars ('Precedent' sb 4 obs)

117.34 pacient] under cure ('Patient' B sb 2 used as a modifier; cf 15.18 'partie pacient')

118.5–6 all ordinaries excellent, though no excellent extraordinarie] ie, all regular operations of the body in excellent form, though none of these excellently working operations exceeds what is usual ('Ordinary' sb 16a)

118.9 *Galene ... Hipocrates*] From Mercuriale *De arte* 212, where only Galen is mentioned. The passage in *De sanitate tuenda* 2.7 trans Green 75 reads 'But of our own country, which has a moderate width, the central portion has the best climate, such as exists in the fatherland of Hippocrates ...' Perhaps Mulcaster started with Mercuriale, then turned to Galen to read the fuller account where he would have found Hippocrates' name.

118.14 meete with] proper for (a 3; the usual phrase, according to the *OED*, was 'meet for, to'; the rhyming pun 'no meat is so meete' is typical.)

118.35 waker] abstainer from sleep (sb[1] 1 obs cited)

118.36 temperature] humoral balance (see notes for 54.3 and 69.9)

118.38 away with] tolerate ('Away' adv 16; the verb was commonly suppressed in this form)

119.10 Chapter 31.] Based on Mercuriale, *De arte*, 4.10 'De locis in quibus exercitationes fieri debent' (of the places in which exercises ought to be done) (215–19).

119.22 foure qualities] Mercuriale *De arte* 216 gives three: that there be 1) an absence of drafts, 2) proper openness and ventilation, and 3) freedom from corrupt air, though on 219 he does mention that the ground be level. Mulcaster's first requirement, that the ground be 'flowred so' is his own invention, as is his accompanying example.

119.23 flowred] floored ('Floor' v; see headnote to sb[1] for this variant spelling)

120.8–18 When great conquests ...] An additional meditative reflection by Mulcaster on some of the edifices described by Mercuriale *De arte* 217–18, and possibly also a rueful comment on the building in which Merchant Taylors' School was housed, erected some two hundred years earlier in the reign of Edward III (on the building, see Draper *Four Centuries* 1–2, and below 228.23ff).

120.19 Chapter 32.] Based on Mercuriale *De arte* 4.11, 'De tempore exercitationibus apto' (on the proper time for exercising) 220–6.

120.23 harvest] autumn (sb 1 obs)

120.34 *Aristotle*] *Problemata* 2.21, 33, 42 (868a, 869b, 870b); reference from Mercuriale *De arte* 221; the same references have been used already at 98.29g.

121.4 *Hippocrates*] *Regimen* 3.68; reference from Mercuriale *De arte* 221.

121.11 *Galene*] *De sanitate tuenda* 2.7 trans Green 75; reference from Mercuriale *De arte* 221.

121.19–20 *Hippocrates ... Galene ... Aristotle*] All three references from Mercuriale *De arte* 221–2. They are to Hippocrates *Regimen* 2.65; Galen *De probis pravisque alimentorum succis liber* 13 (ed Kühn 6:811ff); for Aristotle, see 120.34 note.

121.25 *Aristotle*, and *Avicene*] From Mercuriale *De arte* 223; references to Aristotle *Problemata* 5.28, and 30 (883b and 884a); Avicenna *Liber canonis* (1507) 58v (Gruner *Treatise* 396).

121.33 concoction] digestion (sb 1 obs; 'concoction' could actually refer to any one of the three processes – digestion in the stomach, the transformation of chyme into blood, or the secretion of bodily fluids)

121.33 lets the boyling] prevents the digestion ('Let' v[2] 1; this sense of 'boiling' not in *OED*, but from the context seems to be a synonym for 'concoction')

122.3 cholere] yellow bile (one of the four humours; see 53.22 note and 'Choler' sb[1] 1)

122.5 the yealower, the better] ie, better because the more choler or yellow bile is being passed

122.7–8 ravening cause overreaching] voracious desire (for food) leads to excessive or exaggerated result ('Ravening' vbl sb and 'Raven' v 3; 'Overreaching' vbl sb and 'Overreach' v 9)

122.8 *Hippocrates*] *Aphorisms* 2.16; with reference, from Mercuriale *De arte* 223.

122.11 carcases] bodies (sb 2 obs). The claim that 'corpulent carcases ... be allowed their vittail' is based on the belief that food will pass through their overheated systems undigested if they eat immediately after exercise, and they will therefore lose weight.

122.16 entend] occupy itself with ('Intend' v 12 obs)

122.31 *Muses*] Here, the patron goddesses of learning, who are best attended to in the morning (Mulcaster's own observation).

123.4 lighthen] lighten

123.6 Chapter 33.] Based on Mercuriale *De arte* 4.12, 'Quanta fieri debet exercitatio' (how much exercise ought to be done) (226–31).

123.14 verie] exact, precise (a 5 obs)

123.27 wring] harm, injure (v 5b)

123.28 shrinke] wither or shrivel, through failure of strength (v 1 obs)

123.30 crie ho] call to stop ('ho' int2 obs)

124.5 measure] due proportion (sb 11a obs)

124.18 offendes them] causes them pain (v 6 obs)

124.20 from seven till one and twenty] ie, the period of the second and third climacterics (Mercuriale has 'Pueri a primo usque ad tertium aetatis septenarium' in *De arte* 228)

124.22 chafe] become hot (v 7 obs; cf 97.38)

124.24 reacheles] reckless, imprudent ('Reckless' a 1)

124.35–6 *Hippocrates ... Aristotle*] Following Mercuriale *De arte* 229; references to Hippocrates *Regimen* 3.68; Aristotle *Problemata* 2.21 (868a) and 33 (869b); see notes for 120.34 and 121.4.

125.12 warmth] warmeth (as at line 14)

125.24–5 competent] moderate (3b obs cited)

125.36–7 *Jupiter*, as both *Hesiode* sayeth, and *Plutarch* subscribeth, hath cut her toungue out] Hesiod *Works and Days* 102–4, and quoted in Plutarch *Moralia* 105E ('Of themselves diseases come upon men continually by day and by night, bringing mischief silently; for wise Zeus took away speech from

them'). This reference is Mulcaster's own addition.
125.38 *Galene*] '... the seeds of all diseases are in us. But ... these are so small that they escape our attention' *De sanitate tuenda* 1.5 trans Green 15.
126.4 captaine] principal (a obs cited)
126.11 unequall] of an uneven humoral balance ('Unequal' 3d first citation 1703 'of an uneven condition')
126.17 push] boil or pimple (sb² obs)
126.20–1 *Galene ... Linacer*] The subject of *De sanitate tuenda* 1.5 is *kopos*, translated by Thomas Linacre as 'lassitudo' (as in the edition of Lyons: G. Rovillius, 1548, a typical example of a small copy of the text which could have been available to Mulcaster). Linacre was the famous English humanist scholar and physician who translated several of Galen's works into Latin early in the century. His translation of *De sanitate tuenda* was highly praised by Erasmus (*Opus epistolarum* ed Allen no 862) and Elyot (*The Boke Named the Governour* 1.16 ed Croft 1:171). Maddison et al *Essays on the Life and Work of Thomas Linacre c. 1460–1524*, has an essay by Richard J. Durling on 'Linacre and Medical Humanism' 76–106, a discussion of Linacre as translator of Galen.
126.27 Chapter 34.] Following Mercuriale *De arte* 4.13, 'De modo exercendi' (on the manner of exercising) (231–3)
126.29 *Galene*] The role of the trainer is outlined briefly in *De sanitate tuenda* 2.12 trans Green 92–5.
127.2 chearie] in excellent spirits, lively ('Cheery' a 1 first citation 1611)
127.9 straited] confined (v obs 7)
127.21 oynted] anointed ('Oint' v obs)
127.22 sooke] soak (this spelling not in *OED*)
127.26 *Strigiles*] The strigil was a scraper with which the ancient athlete cleaned off the dust, sweat, and oil which had accumulated on his body during exercise (Harris *Sport in Greece and Rome* 21). There is a woodcut in 1573 *De arte* 18 [=31].
127.35 But in these our dayes] This sentence is Mulcaster's digression from the text of Mercuriale, to which he immediately returns in the next sentence with a summary of the concluding pages of book 4 of *De arte* 232–3.
127.37 tendring] care (v² 3d obs)
128.1 reatch to the olde] ie, achieve the ancient skill in exercise ('Reach' v¹ 17 obs)
128.7 echewaye] in every way (as a single word, not in *OED*; see 'Each' A and B la)
128.13 Chapter 35.] Although the subject of physical education is still being pursued in this chapter, Mulcaster has moved beyond Mercuriale *De arte gymnastica*, in which there is no drawn-out discussion of the role of the training master. While there was at the time instruction in private

households by trainers, there seems to have been no formal curricular instruction in sports, though some school statutes permitted 'shooting in Long bows, *Chess*, running, wrestling, and leaping' (Carlisle *Concise Description* 2:586, quoting the rewritten statues of St Mary Overey, 1614, probably the basis for the similarly worded statutes of the Free Grammar School of Camberwell, 1615, in ibid 2:561). In this chapter, unique in Elizabethan pedagogical writing, Mulcaster stresses that the master have a strong theoretical grounding for training the young in sports and physical exercises.

129.15 posteth over] assigns, hands over the responsibility (v[1] 7a obs)

129.16 *fantsie* workes *affection*] mental faculty by which images are received and generated directs the action of one's disposition or attitude ('Fantasy' sb 1 (see also 7); 'Work' v 20; 'Affection' sb 5)

129.20 there best] ie, their best, the body being the thing physicians are best able to work with. This sense of 'best' is just one of several being played with in this passage.

129.30 best] ie, best effect (from 'effectes' line 21).

129.33 worst] ie, worst effect (again, from 129.21); when the physician is doing his job most effectively, his profession suffers.

129.36 his chymny doth not smoke] ie, his earnings are insufficient to buy fuel for the fireplace (although the phrase sounds proverbial, it is not in Tilley or *ODEP*)

129.38 *Philosopher*] Aristotle *Nicomachean Ethics* 8.1 (1155a): 'if men are friends, there is no need of justice between them.'

130.2–3 no distemperature enforced] no imbalance of humours overcame (the bodies) by violence ('Enforce' v 9 obs)

130.6 avoided] voided (as humoral discharge), or prevented, kept off (two senses: 'Avoid' v 4 obs and 10 obs first citation 1608, respectively)

130.10–11 like two tenantes in one house belonging to severall lordes] Sounds proverbial, but not in Tilley, though cf L445 'many lords many laws.'

130.21 *Galene*] *De sanitate tuenda* 1.8 trans Green 26: 'The habit of mind is impaired by faulty customs in food and drink and exercise and sights and sounds and music. Therefore the hygienist must be skilled in all these, and must not consider that it concerns the philosopher alone to mould the habit of the mind.'

130.24 distraction] division, drawing apart (sb 1 obs first cited from 245.30)

130.24 subalterne] subordinate (a 2b cited)

130.29 vanting] vaunting (variant spelling of 'Vaunt' v 5 first citation 1592)

130.30 couch] place, set (v[1] 14 obs)

130.35 sillyly] poorly, badly ('Sillily' adv 1 first cited)

132.8 effectual] effective (a 2 obs)

132.14 long of] ie, 'long, of'
132.15–16 naturall man] ie, man living in a state of nature, not of grace, and without knowledge of God
132.21 shrikes] shrieks (obsolete spelling; see 'Shrike' sb[1])
132.32 massie] weighty, significant (a 4; in this sense first citation 1588)
133.1 *Poet*] Horace *Ars poetica* 102–3: 'si vis me flere, dolendum est / primum ipsi tibi' (if you would have me weep, you must first feel grief yourself).
133.24 *Galene*] Mulcaster could have learned about *Thrasybulus* (a theoretical treatise by Galen on the curative and conservative ends of medicine) from Mercuriale *De arte* 12, or from Galen *De sanitate tuenda* 1.4. What he says here is no evidence that he read it. See 241.24 note.
133.30 eche where] everywhere ('Each-where' obs)
134.1 fet] fetched
134.2–3 *problemataries, dipnosophistes, symposiakes, antiquaries, warmaisters*] A problematory is one who deals in problems or academic disputations as in Aristotle's *Problemata* ('Problematory' 1). The dipnosophist and symposiac engage in learned discussions at dinners or drinking parties; from the title of Athenaeus' *Deipnosophistae* (*Doctors at Dinner*, a second-century AD Greek encylopedic work in dialogue form; if this popular compilation was not known to him first-hand, Mulcaster could have run across the title in Erasmus' *Adagia*, where it is often referred to) and Plato's *Symposium* ('Dipnosophist' 1 but see also 'Deipnosophist'; 'Symposiac' sb 1, but see also 'Symposiast'). An antiquary is a student of antiquity ('Antiquary' sb 3 first citation 1586) and a war-master is an instructor or one skilled in the art of war (not in *OED*).
134.4 appose] examine, confront with hard questions (v[1] 1 obs)
134.7 seat] basis, foundation (sb 21 an obs fig sense)
134.11 *Hieronymus Mercurialis*] Mulcaster's first acknowledgment that the preceding material on physical education comes from Girolamo Mercuriale's *De arte gymnastica*. On Mercuriale, see introduction, xxivff.
134.23 repairers get the pence] ie, those who look after the body receive the rewards (good health, commendation of others) for doing so. The phrase sounds proverbial, but it is not in Tilley or *ODEP*.
135.5 principle] commencement (sb 1 obs)
135.14 *store*] abundance (of learning and skill) (sb[1] 4 obs)
135.16 in band] in bond, in surety (sb[1] 11 obs)
135.30 bolden] embolden (v)
135.31 resolved on] decided on (v 23c first citation 1585)
136.4 *Aristotle*] In the *Nichomachean Ethics* 6.5 (1139a) and ff, *phronesis* (prudence or practical wisdom), which allows one through experience to understand of the particularities of lived experience, is a principal intellectual virtue.

136.9 reclaymed unto] called back to ('Reclaim' v 2b)
136.11 valiancie] bravery, courage (1)
136.19 salved] remedied (v^1 3) or overcome (v^2 2 obs)
136.21 indivisibles] those things which are inseparable (from the situation at hand) (B sb first citation 1644). In this passage, Mulcaster again stresses the difference between art (theory) and circumstances (practice). Art is seen as inflexible in the face of circumstances, to which she must indeed curtsey. The artificer, that is, the one who practises the art, is free to follow the dictates of art or to drop them and improvise according to the situation. The assumption seems to be that art is somehow outside of the artificer's control, and that art cannot be redefined in the light of experience. Despite Mulcaster's emphasis on the need for good method, here and elsewhere he shows a real distrust of the kind of theory that method generates.
136.27 groune] grown
136.37 stay] bring to a halt (v^1 20)
137.1 bound but of voluntarie] ie, bound to theory only by his will, and therefore not by necessity
137.4–5 stinking streates, and filthy lanes] A reminder that many of Mulcaster's pupils were poor city boys, and that all the inhabitants of the city had to live in an environment which Londoners of today would consider intolerable. This observation, the one above about where the boys lived (136.32–4), and the one following (lines 6–7) about a boy's possible lack of a change of clothing, suggest that Mulcaster has considered the 'circumstances' of the contemporary situation in terms that his readers might instantly comprehend. The problem of the clothes is one of the very few suggestions that Mulcaster might himself have had the boys doing sports in the school.
137.17 overtreated] prevailed upon by entreaty ('Overtreat' v obs)
137.19 admiration] ie, his ability to think honourably of his profession (the first of the three divisions of the end of the chapter; see 131.32g and following; 'Admiration' 3 obs 'the faculty of exciting either wonder or agreeable surprise and approbation')
138.1 children of both sortes] Education of girls is discussed below in chapter 38 (169.10ff).
138.3–4 difference in cause] ie, girls are just as intelligent as boys, but there is no political or social cause that they must be as well educated
138.5–6 naturally the *male* is more worthy] A commonplace of the Renaissance theorists; see Maclean *The Renaissance Notion of Woman*. Mulcaster's thoughts on the subject are expanded in chapter 38 below.
138.22 qualifie themselves] invest themselves with (the following prudential) qualities (v 3 first cited)
138.24 fore cast] forecast (as in *Elementarie* sig 2A4r)

138.24 prevent] act in anticipation (1c obs)

138.38 whether all children be to be set to schoole] The debate over who was to be educated was argued in broader terms by the 1580s than earlier, as the schools expanded to take in a broader cross-section of the population. In what follows, Mulcaster makes a plea for a rational program that considers social, political, and religious aspects of the question. See Introduction. (Background may be found in Simon *Education and Society* chapter 15 'The Triumph of the Vernacular' and Stone 'The Educational Revolution in England.')

139.7–8 like unto a naturall bodie] The commonplace is as old as Plato (*Republic* 5.462D, 464B; *Laws* 12.964E) and is found in sixteenth-century English authors (eg, Starkey *Dialogue* ed Burton 135 'such sores and diseases in our body politic' or Sir Thomas Smith *De Republica Anglorum* [1583] 4). See Barkan *Nature's Work of Art*, especially 61–115; Hale *The Body Politic*; Archambault 'The Analogy of the "Body" in Renaissance Political Literature.' Mulcaster's development of the analogy follows the Galenic medical theory he set forth in chapter 6.

139.16 pestering] overcrowding (from 'Pester' v 2 obs)

139.24 To many] In this and following passages Mulcaster predicts a social phenomenon which actually came to pass. At the beginning of Elizabeth's reign there was a marked need for an educated clergy and an educated laity, who would subscribe to the tenets of the Church of England, and part of the reason for the sudden expansion of the universities was to satisfy this need. But by the 1580s, the universities had already begun to turn out more graduates than could be supported by church livings, and by the end of the century there was a real employment problem for university graduates (what to do on graduation is a major theme in the Parnassus Plays of the 1590s). It has even been argued (Curtis 'The Alienated Intellectuals of Early Stuart England') that the lack of places in society for the university educated led to their becoming a source of social agitation and a contributing factor to the Civil War.

139.27 yt] it (not abbreviated 'that'; the formula is repeated three lines below)

139.28 goulfe] gulf (variant spelling; 'Gulf' sb 4b first cited)

139.29 rome] roam (and perhaps also 'room' – 'to let them room' means 'to prevent them from having places')

139.30 shifters] idle, thriftless fellows, or those who practise petty shifts or tricks (sb 3 obs)

139.31–2 living] livelihood, support (vbl sb 3; not quite 'ecclesiastical living' as might be inferred)

139.32–3 superfluitie ... seat ... residence] These words continue the medical image begun above (at line 7). 'Residence' is a play on 'humoral sediment' and on 'home.'

139.32 fleeting] moving aimlessly about (ppl a 2)

139.34–5 which neede cannot see] ie, their need for a livelihood prevents them from seeing that their 'shiftes to live' cause them to threaten the established social order

139.35–6 fish in a troubled water] Proverbial; Tilley F334 'It is good fishing in troubled waters.'

139.37 cleare] unmuddied, undisturbed water

139.37–8 *neede* is an imperious mistres] Proverbial; cf Tilley N60 'Necessity is the best schoolmistress' and N61 'Necessity is the mother of invention.'

140.1 *maniheaded neede*] Cf Tilley H278 'As many heads as Hydra.'

140.2 mostwhat] for the most part ('Most' a C)

140.4 salve] make good, smooth over (v^1 3 obs)

140.7 A violent remeady] ie, pleading need as an excuse for their violence is in itself a 'violent' or excessive remedy

140.11–12 ill will be ill] proverbial, reminiscent of Tilley I41 'Ill will never speaks well' in sound if not in sense.

140.26–7 to let the yong spring] to prevent the generation of the young, to prevent young persons from being born ('Spring' v^1 10). I have been unable to find any references to control of population by brothelry in classical literature; works like Plutarch's 'The Dialogue on Love' in *Moralia* and the pseudo-Lucianic 'Affairs of the Heart' (*Erotes*) show that for the Greeks homosexuality, not prostitution, was the alternative to regular marital and pre-marital sex.

140.27 exposition and spoile] exposure or abandonment and destruction ('Exposition' 1b first cited; 'Spoil' sb 8 obs cites 224.29) Mulcaster's knowledge of the ancient practice of exposure may be from Plato *Republic* 5.459E–460C, though the practice was carried on through the Middle Ages into the Renaissance, when children were increasingly given to the foundling hospitals (Boswell *The Kindness of Strangers* covers to the end of the thirteenth century, with some later observations).

141.3 in certaine] in definite number ('Certain' sb B II 4 obs)

141.5–6 their conceit which learning inflameth] Paul in 1 Corinthians 8:1: 'Knoweledge puffeth up.'

141.9 the *Turkish captivitie*] 'Turkish captivitie' is Mulcaster's phrase for that loss of freedom which befalls those lazy men who are unable to withstand the great energy and discipline of the Turkish invaders. To Christians, the great advance of the Moslem hordes in the early sixteenth century was evidence of their organization, commitment, and self-discipline, as well their savagery. Chew *The Crescent and the Rose: Islam and England during the Renaissance* especially chapter 3 'The Present Terror of the World' discusses the English idea of the Turkish character during the Tudor and early Stuart period.

141.14 overflush] superfluity (v [sic] first cited from 264.28)
141.19 lookers on] ie, those not trained to serve the state or normally engaged in service to the state
141.22–3 unsufficient service of necessarie services] inadequate performance of necessary offices (sb[1] 6, 4)
141.31 of] off
141.34–5 prevention] ie, stopping (him) from the execution of (his) design (sb 4a obs first citation 1582)
142.10 execution] task (or carrying out of a task) (sb 2b obs)
142.11–12 fire ... water] Fire here, as at line 29, is a sign of ambition (see 142.29 note). Fire and water are linked in many proverbs, eg, Tilley F246 'As contrary as fire and water,' W110 'To mix fire and water,' as well as F253, F254, F285, and W87. See also 156.11–12.
142.13–14 If that wit fall to preach, which were fitter for the plough] The figure of the unlearned preacher was commonly evoked in anti-Puritan literature. For instance, Pasquil in the anti-Martinist tract *Pasquil and Marforius* says that when he arrived in England 'I frequented the Churches of the Pruritane Preachers, that leape into the Pulpet with a Pitchfork, to teach men, before they have either learning, judgment, or wit enough to teach boyes' (in Nashe *Works* ed McKerrow 1:73). For a discussion of a similar phrase spoken by William Tyndale in 1522 or 1523 and its significance for the vernacular translation of the Bible, see Thompson 'Scripture for the Ploughboy and Some Others.'
142.27 misplaced] Following the parallel syntax of the opening sentences of the two previous paragraphs, this might read: 'wittes misplaced be most unquiet ...' The verb 'be' may have been accidentally omitted by the compositor.
142.29–30 *Fire ... Leade*] This passage makes more explicit the image of fire as a sign of ambition (see note for lines 11–12 above). Tilley F256 'Fire descends not' and L134 'As heavy as lead'.
142.33 naturall] innate disposition (sb 10 obs)
142.34 beareth a tankarde] A 'tankard-bearer' was a hired labourer who bore water from the conduits in the City of London to private houses. There was a Brotherhood of St Christopher of the Water-Bearers of London, whose *Rules, Ordinances and Statutes* are dated 20 October 1496, but the company was never very significant (it was not, for instance, one of the sixty London companies at the Mayor's feast in the Guildhall in 1531), and the image of an ambitious man seeking votes to be made Master of this company is intended to be ludicrous ('Tankard-bearer'; Besant *London in the Time of the Tudors* 397; Stow *Survey* ed Kingsford 2:190–2, for a list of the companies in 1531; the character Cob in Jonson's *Every Man in His Humour* is a water-bearer, for whom see [*Works*] ed Herford and Simpson 9:342).

142.35 cokhorse] exalted position, place of ascendancy ('Cock-horse' sb 3 first cited)

142.36 canvase] soliciting of favour ('Canvass' sb 6 first cited 1790)

142.37–8 mislotted] wrongly assigned ('Mis-' prefix[1]; 'Lot' v 4; this form not in *OED*)

143.2 *Plato*] See especially *Republic* 2.375A–376E where Plato outlines the personal qualities necessary in those elected as guardians.

143.21 daintie] scarce (a 2 obs)

143.21–3 Everie parish ... reading.] There is evidence that by the early seventeenth century 'all over the country, sometimes in the tiniest hamlets, educated parsons, curates, or unbeneficed schoolmasters were teaching a handful of boys up to university level' (Lawrence Stone 'Educational Revolution' 46). From what Mulcaster says, this practice was being followed at a slightly earlier period. Francis Clement introduces his *Petie Schole* (9) with a poem to the young pupil, in which he says:

> Come, litle childe, let toyes alone,
> and trifles in the streete:
> Come, get thee to the parish Clarke.
> H'is made a Teacher meete.

143.24 the *riche* and *poore*] Some instances of the problems of the poor in obtaining an education are given in Simon *Education and Society* 370ff, and see also the note above for 138.38. Because of the large number of poor boys allowed a free education at Merchant Taylors' School, Mulcaster had a special interest in this issue ('Statutes' in Draper *Four Centuries* 243).

143.29 *abilitie*] ie, ability to pay, in contrast with 'towardnesse,' which is ability to do the work

143.29 snuffe] express dissatisfaction (v[2] II 7 'To express scorn, disdain, or contempt' obs)

143.33 marre their owne market] Proverbial; *ODEP* 'The Market is marred,' repeated later at 255.17. See the next note.

143.36–7 make their owne market] Proverbial; Tilley M672 'He has made a good market' and note the play at line 33 above.

144.2 under minus] insufficiency (not in *OED*).

144.4 retchelesse] negligent, having no care or consideration for himself ('Reckless' a 1b–c)

144.5 blacke oxe] Proverbial; Tilley O103 'The black ox never trod on his foot' (The black ox was a symbol for 'misfortune, adversity, old age' *ODEP* 64–5; a note on the history of the proverb is given by Archer Taylor 'The Proverb "The Black Ox Has Not Trod on His Foot" in Renaissance Literature,' where

Mulcaster's use of the proverb is classified under the sense of 'He is inexperienced, has not known sorrow or care' [267].)

144.8–9 *Neptune* in shipwracke] Calling upon non-Christian powers in shipwreck is satirized by Erasmus in his 'Naufragium' (*Opera omnia* ASD 1/3:325ff), although there is no reference in the colloquy to a prayer to Neptune. In Horace *Odes* 1.5 the speaker who has been saved from drowning (in love passion for the handsome Pyrrha) makes an offering to the god of the sea.

144.14 supererogatorie] (a first citation 1593)

144.20 maime] grave defect, blemish (sb c obs)

144.25 neede turnes the deafe eare] Proverbial; Tilley E13 'To turn a deaf ear.'

144.27 braverie] ostentation, showiness (sb 3)

144.28 pretend] indicate, signify (v 11 obs)

144.29 butte to] end or object of (sb[4] 4 first citation 1594; with sense too of 'target,' following 'overshoote' at line 27)

144.32 welter] live at ease (with sense of 'wallow'; "Welter' v[1] 2a obs cited)

145.6 prove] prosper, thrive (v 10 obs)

145.9 faire blossomes ... nipping frostes] Proverbial; variation on Tilley F774 'Sharp frosts bite forward springs.'

145.16–17 some speciall deare in the whole heard] Despite its proverbial ring, not in Tilley or *ODEP*. For another deer image, see above at 97.38.

145.18 the lying spirite may sit in his lippes] Cf 1 Kings 22:22: 'the Lorde hath put a lying spirit in the mouth of all these thy prophets.'

145.19–20 God hath reserved his calling and discovering houres] ie, those hours in which God summons the believer and reveals himself ('call' v 6)

146.19 spring] generation (as at 140.27), with play on 'overflow' and 'tide' in the same passage

146.19–20 ring out all in] ie, invite all those who are inclined to join the learned (to 'ring all in' refers to the last peal of bells before the beginning of a church service, as in 'Ring' v[2] 7c; the 'out'/'in' play is a characteristic figure in Mulcaster's prose)

146.20 Everie one desireth to have his childe learned] Cf Ascham: 'Yet all men covet to have their children speake latin: and so do I verie earnestlie too' (*Scholemaster* in *English Works* ed Wright 185).

146.21–2 *casualtie*] chance, accident (sb 1 obs)

146.24–5 forren and fortunes *patrimonie*] ie, inheritance passed on to the child from outside the family or from fortune ... in other words, a patrimony which is not subject to one's own control, the way learning is, and not the easy victim of mischance or fate ('Patrimony' 1c fig first cited from 158.16)

146.29 countermatch] rivalry, competition (sb 3 only citation)

147.5 booke men] scholars ('Bookman' first citation 1583)

147.8 fit in] conform to (v[1] 8 first citation 1611)

147.14 bend, or forcibly breake] Proverbial?; cf Tilley B566 'Better bow than break.'

147.31 booking] studying (not in *OED* in this sense)

147.34 cypherlike] meaningless ('Cipher' 2 fig 'non-entity'; this combined form not in *OED*)

147.36 the olde *Persian* ordinance] Xenophon *Cyropaedia* 1.2.15: 'all the Persians may send their children to the common schools of justice. Still, only those do send them who are in a position to maintain their children without work; and those who are not so situated do not.'

147.37 bastardeth] renders illegitimate, bastardizes (v obs)

148.3 weake tymbred] weakly built, weak-limbed ('Timber' v 1 obs)

148.4 midle end] mean (as in Aristotelian mean? – as such, not in *OED*)

148.5–6 bid Will thinke that well] See notes for 30.30 and 39.29.

148.8 leader] Still continuing with the image of the horse; here 'lacke' is the lead horse who pulls the others in whatever direction she wishes.

148.16–17 toungues ... necessarie] Printing and some areas of trade and finance were the only non-professional occupations in which a knowledge of Latin might have proved more than just superficially useful. Training in other languages was certainly practical for those London merchants involved in overseas trade, and such training was available from private tutors in the city. Some of the instructors composed manuals; the works of Florio (*Firste Fruites*, 1578; *Second Frutes*, 1591) and Holiband (Desainliens) (*The French Schoolemaister*, 1573; *The Frenche Littelton*, [1576]) provide the best examples of this material. Mulcaster wrote an introductory poem ('In τετϱαγλωττίαν doctissimi Claudij Holibandi, alias Desainleins') for Holiband's *Campo di Fior* (1583). Language instruction is discussed in Simon *Education and Society* 386 and Curtis 'Education and Apprenticeship' 71.

148.20 smak] superficial knowledge (sb[1] 3b obs cited)

148.22 clounes] rustics, countrymen (sb 1)

148.33 cumbersome] troublesome, wearisome (a 2 obs; with a secondary sense of 'weighty')

149.10 perillous grater] extremely affecting annoyance ('Perilous' a 2 obs; 'Grater' 3 obs cited)

149.15 loated] distributed, allotted ('Allot' v 1; this spelling not given in *OED* under 'Lot' or 'Loat'; cf 172.39 'alloateth')

150.3 improportionate] disproportionate (a obs first cited)

150.6 contrarie] oppose, strive against ('Contrary' v 1 obs; cf 173.23)

150.13 squaring] dissension, contention (vbl sb 2 obs)

150.13 out of square] out of the normal or proper state or condition (sb 19)

150.20 considerate] well-considered (a 1)

150.21–3 eventes ... be but foolish maisters] ie, the outcome of any project is a poor guide as to how one should proceed at the beginning. A reworking of Tilley E220 'Experience is the mistress of fools,' perhaps from Erasmus *Adagia* in LB 2:38E trans CWE 31:78 'Eventus ... stultorum magister est,' which is from Livy 22.39.10, and in turn from Homer *Iliad* 17.32 ('when it is wrought even a fool getteth understanding'), Achilles speaking to Aeneas. Mulcaster ascribes the saying to 'two of the greatest oratours in both the best tongues,' but I have been unable to find the saying in Demosthenes or Cicero, presumably the 'oratours' of whom he speaks. Demosthenes and Cicero are, however, sources for another classical proverb which runs something like 'we may judge the success of a project only by its outcome,' found in *First Olynthiac* 11 and in *Ad familiares* 1.7.5 ('ex eventu homines de tuo consilio existimaturos'), *Pro Rabirio Postumo* 1, and *Ad Atticum* 9.7a (Balbus and Oppius to Cicero).

150.24–5 a begger ... a prince] Proverbial; cf Tilley K67 'A king or a beggar.'

150.25 allow him a pennie] Not one of the many proverbs on pennies in Tilley.

151.12 honested] conferred honour upon (v obs 1)

151.15 the other ... the other] the one, the other. The rapid pointing of this passage is unusual, but the rhythm is distinctly Mulcaster's, so the periods are left as they are.

151.21–2 *poorelinges* ... *wealthlinges*] children of the poor ... children of the wealthy ('poorling' 1: 'Wealthling' first cited)

151.25–8 neither poverite ... most worth] poverty and wealth are both insignificant when set against the larger need of the country for intelligent men

151.35–6 while the Church was an harbour] Mulcaster suggests that the old Roman Catholic church provided an 'infinite' number of livings (ie, in the monastic and cathedral foundations destroyed by Henry VIII), whereas the new Church of England provides fewer places for the educated clergy. Nevertheless he seems to be aware that the universities were at the time of his writing undergoing a great expansion, and that the unemployment problem he predicts was due as much to the greater number of graduates as to the smaller number of livings (cf 139.24 note).

152.2 *bookmaintenance*] livelihood provided by book-learning (a nonce-word; not in *OED*)

152.2–3 turned a new leafe] Proverbial; Tilley L146 'To turn over a new leaf.'

152.6 booke] apply oneself to the study of a book (this sense not in *OED* 'Book' v; see also 147.31)

152.20 *ordinance*] authoritative governing ('Ordinance' sb 6 obs; or perhaps in a narrower sense 'law')

152.25 rempare] strengthen, fortify (itself) ('Rempare' v obs cited)

152.34 in brake] immovable, indifferent (sb[6] b 'To set one's face in a brake: to assume an immovable expression of countenance' first citation 1607)

153.5 foile] Wrestling term meaning 'the fact of being almost thrown' (sb[2]; the language in the sentence – 'shift', 'bend' – corresponds with this sense).

153.9 scare crow] something not really formidable ('Scarecrow' 2b fig first citation 1589)

153.24 ordinate] orderly, regular (a 2–3 obs)

154.4–7 *monarchie ... oligarchie ... democratie*] This division of government into three types was commonplace. Sir Thomas Smith begins his *De republica Anglorum* (1) with 'They that have written heretofore of Common wealthes, haue brought them into three most simple and speciall kindes or fashions of gouernement. The first where one alone doth governe, is called of the Greekes *Μοναρχία*, the second, where the smaller number, commonly called of them *'Αριστοκρατία*, and the thirde, where the multitude doth rule *Δημοκρατία*.' Similar 'Theories of the Constitution and of Sovereignty' are outlined in part 2 chapter 10 of J.W. Allen *A History of Political Thought in the Sixteenth Century*. Possible Greek sources known to Mulcaster for the three types of government might be Plato *Republic* 1.338D, Aristotle *Rhetoric* 1.8.4 (1365b) (where aristocracy is added to make four) and *Politics*, and the fragmentary essay by Plutarch called 'On Monarchy, Democracy, and Oligarchy' in *Moralia* 826Bff.

154.7 beare all the swinge] maintain full authority, hence, do as they wish ('Swinge' sb[1] 1; Tilley S1045 'To have one's full swing'; *ODEP* 'Swinge')

154.21–2 the fittest subject for learning] The reader may wish to compare the moral qualities of obedience, friendliness, desire to please, and avoidance of bad behaviour with the intellectual qualities of the ideal pupil outlined in chapter 5 above, 38.34ff.

154.25 stomaking] feeling of resentment (vbl sb)

154.35 loftines of minde] intellectual pride or haughtiness ('Loftiness' see 'Lofty' a 2)

154.35–6 odiouse comparisons] cf Tilley C576 'Comparisons are odious'

154.37 obsequious] obedient (a 1)

155.2 od] singular in merit, rare (a 6 obs)

155.5 two] too

155.5 forewardly] eager ('Forwardly' B adj obs first cited)

155.10 frise] heavy woollen cloth ('Frieze' sb[1] 1). In Linthicum *Costume in the Drama of Shakespeare* 75–6 frieze is described as a cloth suitable for military wear, etc, but no mention is made of it as cloth for the dress of young men. The suggestion in this passage is that children were dressed up when very young, but were then clothed in rougher garb when they grew older.

155.25 meere] absolutely, altogether ('Mere' B adv; see 'Merely' adv[2] 2 obs)

155.29 tikelish] unsteady, fickle ('Ticklish' a 4 first citation 1606; this passage cited under sense 3 'easily upset in temper,' but the context suggests that it should be given under sense 4)
155.33 ne] nor ('Ne' conj[1] 1)
155.34 upon any colour] under any pretence (sb 12 b obs)
155.38–9 continue both on, and one] ie, remain constant and singleminded
156.10 unsweetning it with his own sawcinesse] Not proverbial, though there are a number of proverbs with 'sweet' and 'sauce'; eg, Tilley M839 and S97.
156.17 plausible] deserving of applause (a 1 obs)
157.6 reseant] resident ('Resiant' A adj 1b obs first cited)
157.17 clipper of the refuse] one who trims off the unwanted portion ('Clipper'[1] 2 'one who clips coins'; 'Refuse' sb[2] B 1b first citation 1603; continuing the 'rare metall' image at 156.34 and see also 156.35–6, 161.30)
157.22 lightsomnesse] cheerfulness (sb 1 cited)
158.1–2 a clowdy day ... will prove faire, when all shrews have dined] Tilley W218 'It will be fair weather when the shrews have dined.' Shrews were traditionally evil ('Shrew' sb[1] and sb[2]); presumably once they had dined and removed themselves to their dens, the weather would improve. Mulcaster uses a chiasmus: one would normally associate 'naturall dulnesse' with cloudy weather, but here it is made to be like fair weather or sunshine breaking forth on dull and cloudy days.
158.16 forslow] neglect ('Forslow' v 1 obs)
158.25 domestically] ie, well enough to know each other's families (or perhaps 'intimately' from *OED* 'Domestic' a 1b obs first citation 1612)
158.38 vowed] destined ('Vow' v[1] 2 and see 'Avow v[2] obs 2)
159.4 jeoperdouse] perilous, risky ('Jeopardous' a obs 1; spelled 'iepardous' in *Elementarie* sig 2B2v)
159.6 forthinke] regret, repent of ('For think' v obs 4)
159.14 by marking of some pretie toy] Ambivalent sense: either 'by the way the child looks at or observes a plaything' ('Mark' v 14: 'Toy' sb 6 first citation 1586) or 'by the way the parent observes some silly antic or frivolous comment made by the child' ('Toy' sb 2–3).
159.24–5 my neighbours ... myne to.] An observation in direct speech by the parent.
159.26 coursiters] those who wander about (with additional sense of 'tramps, vagabonds,' though not a primary sense in this case; 'Cursitor' obs 3)
159.27–8 as the rowling stone doth gather mosse] A reworking of the proverb Tilley S885 'A rolling stone gathers no moss' and Erasmus *Adagia* in LB 2:821A 'Saxum volutum non obducitur musco.'
160.21 bowelled] disembowelled (ppl a a first citation 1589)
161.4 *Horaces* horse] *Epistles* 1.10.34–41. In order to defeat the stag, his constant

enemy, the horse sought the aid of man, who rode the horse to victory, but afterwards refused to get off. Horace concludes

> sic qui pauperiem veritus potiore metallis
> libertate caret, dominum vehet improbus atque
> serviet aeternum, quia parvo nesciet uti

('So he who through fear of poverty forfeits liberty, which is better than mines of wealth, will in his avarice carry a master, and be a slave forever, not knowing how to live on little.')

161.5 ridg] backbone (sb[1] 1 obs)

161.32–3 that is solde, which ought not, the enheritaunce of vertue] ie, the inheritance of virtue is sold, though it ought not to be (this syntactical inversion is repeated twice more)

162.2 catchers] those who catch (or grasp) at livings

162.3–4 two inconveniences, worse than mischiefes as our common law termeth them] In common law, an 'inconvenience' refers to the injury suffered by the *general public* from the application of a particular law. A 'mischief' is an injury suffered by an *individual* from the application of a law ('Inconvenience' sb 3c obs; 'Mischief' sb 3b obs). Abuses in admissions and appointments to livings are two inconveniences which Mulcaster wishes to see stopped, even though a reform of the current system may well bring about 'mischiefs,' or individual cases of unfair treatment.

In the eyes of the state, a mischief (by which few suffer) is better than an inconvenience (by which many are harmed), although from an individual's point of view a mischief might well be more unfair than an inconvenience. The terms were proverbial; see Tilley M995 'Better once a mischief than always an inconvenience' and I62 'Better an inconvenience than a mischief.' That Mulcaster favours mischiefs over inconveniences is consistent with his belief that the 'public' is more important than the 'private.'

162.8 *Pontius* the *Samnite*] Shortly after his victory over the Roman army at the Caudine Forkes (321 BC), Gaius Pontius the Samnite general was in turn defeated by the Romans. In *De officiis* 2.21.75 Cicero has him say: 'I would that fortune had withheld my appearance until a time when the Romans began to accept bribes, and that I had been born in those days! I should then have suffered them to hold their supremacy no longer.'

162.13 fingering] touching money with unworthy motives (v 2b cited)

162.14 not noted in any one, but observed by all] ie, there is no remembered source for this observation, though it is suggested by all the writers on the subject. An interesting parallel interpretation may be found in the chapter on 'The Fall of the Power, Learning, the Eloquence of the Romaines' in Louis LeRoy *Of the Interchangeable Course, or Variety of Things in the Whole World* (English trans 1594) 81v: 'Which disorders continued till such time, as the

Empire fatally approaching to his end; was abandoned for a pray to the barbarous Nations. For, these Emperours unadvisedly thinking to fortifie themselves by the mercenarie and auxiliarie armes of strangers, whom they sent for to their succour and service; weakning the proper and naturall forces of the Empire, which their auncestours had used in the getting of it: they drew, ere they were ware of it, many of the Northren nations into the countries, lands, and seigniories of their obedience' (French text in *De la vicissitude ou variété des choses en l'univers* [1576] 73v).

162.22 horesons] sons of whores (common term of contempt; 'Whoreson' obs), who are 'ravished' by the wealth of Rome

162.31 glasse for those to gase on] ie, a 'mirror' of history for the reader to contemplate; if you allow people driven by greed near your wealth, as the Romans allowed the barbarian hoards, you may suffer for it.

162.32 if ye shew a child an apple, he will cry for it] Sounds proverbial, but not in Tilley or *ODEP*.

162.36 fetch] contrivance, dodge, trick (sb^1 2)

162.39 lighten the booke] ease the numbers of those enrolled ('Book' sb 9; see citation of 1557 for school admission book)

163.2 broad] unrestrained ('Broad' a 8; other senses include 'open, obvious' or 'unconcerned with strict moral norms,' senses 5 and 11 respectively)

163.6 good colour] seeming virtue (sb 11)

163.27–8 *caterpillours*] greedy parasites (sb 2 fig, a common term of reprobation)

163.30 they] ie, the 'caterpillours' who attempt to gain the protection of the nobility

164.10 fetchers] tricksters (see 162.36 and note; this form not in *OED*)

164.11 *Quintilian*] *Institutio oratoria* 1.8.21: 'Ex quo mihi inter virtutes grammatici habebitur aliqua nescire' (Consequently I shall count it a merit in a teacher of literature that there should be some things which he does not know).

164.15 antecedent] Mulcaster sets up what Quintilian calls a consequential argument ('consequentia, quamvis ex prioribus dent argumentum ad ea quae sequuntur', 'consequential [arguments] ... argue from the past to the future,' *Institutio oratoria* 5.10.76), which is continued at lines 19 ('My consequent') and 22 ('My chalenge').

164.17–18 *Rhemmius Palaemon*] Suetonius *De grammaticis* 23, where Quintus Remmius Palaemon, the notorious Roman grammarian, 'declared that letters were born with him and would die with him' ('secum et natas et morituras litteras iactaret').

164.28–9 deepe waters ... stillnesse] Cf the proverbial 'Water runs smoothest where it is deepest' (Tilley W123).

164.33 nusled] trained, educated ('Nuzzle' v^2 3 obs)

165.3 coleginers] members of colleges ('Collegianer' obs cited)

165.4 boursares] students on scholarships ('Bursar' 2, according to *OED* a Scotch term)

165.10 still] extract, obtain (by distillation) (v 5b from 'Distill')

165.13 wrings] suffers punishment (v 19c)

165.22 enstawle] place in an office or position, install ('Install' v[1] 1b first citation 1647)

165.26–7 countenance] pretend, make a show of (v 2 obs first citation 1590)

165.7 customarie] usual practice (see 'Customary' a 1 first citation 1607 and 'Customary' sb 1b first citation 1796)

165.32–3 common collection] inference by the general public (4 obs)

166.6 advisedly] prudently, cautiously (adv 1–2 obs)

166.9 advisednesse] prudent consideration, caution (sb obs)

166.23 forstaull away] appropriate ('Forstall' v 1b obs first cited)

166.25–6 forraine feathers] Cf Tilley F163 'Fair feathers make fair birds' and F153 'The feather makes not the bird.'

166.27 unlikely] unseemly (a 3b obs)

166.27 if the eye might behold] Not in Tilley or *ODEP*.

166.31 dawes] jackdaws (or fools; 'Daw' sb 2a and c, with reference also to the fable by Aesop about the jay in peacock's feathers)

166.37–8 make not all priestes that stand upon the bridge as the *Poope* passeth] Expression not traced; despite its possible Latin origin (*'Poope'* from 'pontifex' and 'bridge' from 'pons'), it is not in Besso's inclusive *Roma e il Papa nei proverbi e nei modi di dire.*

166.38 cobler] Proverbial; cf Tilley C480 'Let not the cobbler go beyond his last' (Erasmus *Adagia* in LB 2:228A 'Ne sutor ultra crepidam'). Also compare 142.13ff.

167.2 naule] awl (obs; see 'Naulle')

167.4 *bastardt*] Either a misprint or, more likely, a participial adjective ('bastarded'); cf 147.37.

167.6 both your labour and your love being lost] Mulcaster's phrasing, like Shakespeare's title *Love's Labour's Lost*, is a play on certain common proverbial and near-proverbial expressions of the time. Some of these are: 'labour of love' ('Love' sb 8b); 'there's no love lost between them' ('Love' sb 8d); 'labour is light where love doth pay' (*ODEP*); 'lost labour' ('Labour' sb 1b); 'to labour in vain' (Tilley L3); 'you lose your labour' (Tilley L9). Mulcaster's phrase is the only one I have come across that shares all three words with Shakespeare's title.

167.8 To seeme is not so much in weight as to be] Cf Tilley S214 'Be what thou would seem to be' and Xenophon *Cyropaedia* 1.6.22: 'There is no shorter road ... than really to be wise in those things in which you wish to seem to be wise; and when you examine concrete instances, you will realize that what I say is true. For example, if you wish to seem to be a good farmer when you are not, or a good rider, doctor, flute-player, or anything else that you are not, just think how many schemes you must invent to keep up your pretensions' (Cambyses to his son Cyrus).

167.9 counterfeat] This sentence becomes clearer if the punctuation reads 'counterfeat:'

167.15 dubling] evasive ('Doubling' ppl a 3 first cited)

167.15–16 leape the ladder] ascend swiftly in social position ('Ladder' sb 1c fig; 'Leap' v 6 fig; in proverbial usage, a ladder was then, as now, a sign of ambition, as in Tilley L26 'To turn one's back on the ladder by which one rose')

167.20 ward] guardianship, care (of the young) ('Ward' sb[2] 2a–b)

167.37 perfit] perfection ('Perfect' D 1 first citation 1842)

167.38–168.1 *Repulse* here is a miserable stripp] refusal of offices to those overeducated applicants is a poor way to reduce the number of such applicants ('Strip' sb 1, from 'Estrepement,' a legal term meaning the spoil or waste of land or timber)

168.9 blind bayard] Tilley B112 'Who is so bold as blind Bayard?' Bayard was the famous horse of Roland in medieval romance; his name had come to be applied humorously to any horse (sb[1] 2).

168.14 *Bucephalus*] 'An horse, whiche woulde suffre no man to come on his backe but onely great kyng Alexander: who syttyng on him did mervailous battayles, and escaped wonderfull daungers. Finally beyng .xxx. yeres olde, he died, not of any wounde, but onely by extreeme labours and sundry bruises. Over whom Alexander builded the citie called *Bucephala*, after the horses name' (Thomas Cooper 'Dictionarium' sv 'Bucephalus' in *Thesaurus*). Interestingly, the name 'Bucephalus' was used ironically in much the same way as 'Bayard' (*OED* 'Bucephalus' first citation 1601).

168.26 clipping of] paring off, removing (vbl sb[2], for which see 'Clip' v[2] 1: see also 157.17 above)

168.31 porte] retinue of attendants (sb[4] 2b)

168.31–2 wring a number to the wall] ie, force a number to desperate measures to maintain themselves (cf Tilley W15 'To be driven to the wall' and W185 'The weakest goes to the wall')

168.32 pinch] find fault with (v 9b obs)

168.38 stripping] severe pruning (as in 'estrepement,' for which see 167.39–168.1 and note)

169.2 a doe] ado

169.9 fellonly] wickedly, in a 'felon' manner ('Felonly' adv obs cited)

169.10 Chapter 38.] For background on this discussion of the education of women, see introduction, xxxff.

169.26 young *maidens* be ordinarily trained] Girls attended the elementary schools, and occasionally received instruction in the elementary classes of some few grammar schools (a girl stands at the front of the class in the title-page woodcut of a 1610 edition of Alexander Nowell's *Christianae pietatis prima institutio*). They did not, however, customarily study at the grammar schools and never in the higher forms. Only men went to university. Any advanced instruction for women would have come from a private tutor (Gardiner *English Girlhood at School* 182ff, on girls in schools 96, 200).

169.30–1 toothe and naile] Proverbial; Tilley T422 'Tooth and nail.'

170.5 that tree] Cf Tilley T497 'The tree is knowen by the fruite' (Matthew 12:33); the image is returned to at 1745.39 and 181.16.

170.15 tender] cherish, treat with affectionate care (v[2] 3d obs)

170.31 taint them for it] ie, accuse them of being unable to speak as well as men (v A4 obs first citation 1619 'To accuse of a crime or dishonour' as in 'Attaint' v 7)

170.36–7 some of that sex so excellently well trained] Lady Jane Grey and Queen Elizabeth were the most celebrated for their learning, but there were others, for instance the daughters of Sir Anthony Cooke (Mildred, married to William Cecil; Anne, married to Sir Nicholas Bacon, and mother of Francis Bacon; Elizabeth, married to Sir Thomas Hoby and later to John, Lord Russell; and Catherine, married to Henry Killigrew), and the three daughters of Edward Seymour, duke of Somerset. Also very well known for being 'so rarely qualified' were Jane Foxe (later countess of Westmoreland) and Mary Sidney, Sir Philip's sister and later countess of Pembroke. These women followed in the tradition of Margaret (More) Roper, who, because of her father's reputation and Erasmus' personal interest in her education, was often mentioned as a paragon of learning by continental as well as English writers. (See Friedman 'The Influence of Humanism on the Education of Girls and Boys in Tudor England'; 'The Scholars of the Sixteenth Century,' a chapter in Hill *Women in English Life* 1:126–44 [quoting Mulcaster at 142–4 as 'a more liberal view']; Labalme ed *Beyond Their Sex: Learned Women of the European Past*; McMullen 'The Education of English Gentlewomen 1540–1640'; Stopes 'Sixteenth Century Women Students'; and Travitsky 'The New Mother of the English Renaissance.') It is interesting that Mulcaster does not provide a list of names, in spite of the fact that he is determined not to 'alledge authorities.' Such a list of learned women (with many English examples) may be found in works like Lodovico Domenichi's *La Nobilità delle donne* (1549), revised in English by William Barker in 1559 as *The Nobility of Women* 153ff or Thomas Bentley's *The Monument of Matrones* (1582) sig B7r–v.

171.1–3 the best *Romaine* or *Greekish paragonnes* ... the *Germaine* or *French* gentlewymen ... the *Italian* ladies who dare write themselves] For some of the ancient paragons whom Mulcaster has in mind, see below at 175.28ff, 182.34ff, and 183.15 and notes. Some of the women commonly praised as later examples include Hroswitha, Marguerite of Navarre, Louise Labé, Emilia Pia, Isabella d'Este, Vittoria Colonna, and the daughters of Willibald Pirckheimer. Lists of 'foeminae doctae' appear in almost all of the important books on women, such as I. Ravisius Textor's collection of essays *De memorabilibus et claris mulieribus* (1521), especially its 'De illustribus foeminis opusculum, incerto authore' (176vff), Dufour's *Les Vies des femmes celebres* (1504; ed Jeanneau in 1970), or Vives' *De institutione feminae Christianae* (1523; trans Richard Hyrde c 1529). Sir Thomas Elyot's *The Defence of Good Women* (1540) is an English praise of feminine virtue, mostly dwelling on classical examples. Mulcaster seems to have known Boccaccio's *De claris mulieribus* (1473, etc), perhaps the most famous of all of these works – see 174.29–30 and also 182.34–9 and note.

171.4–5 geason] rare, extraordinary (a 3 obs)

171.16 aloneness] state of being alone or unmarried (*OED* 'aloneness' does not have sense of 'celibacy'; cf 275.38)

171.16 weale or wo] Proverbial; cf Tilley w186–9, especially w188 'No weal without woe.'

171.23 garnished] adorned (v 6 obs)

171.24 indiligence] want of application, negligence (sb obs 1)

171.30 bare head] ie, in an attitude of respect

171.31 the use of our bodies] See above, 88.8ff, where Plato is cited.

171.35 that, which was once taken from us] ie, Adam's rib (Genesis 2:21–2; see also below 178.13)

172.4 ladies of *Lacedaemon*] See above 99.39 and note.

172.8 *Virgill*] The story of Virgil's skill as a judge of horses and of his reward of a daily portion of bread by the Emperor Augustus appeared in editions of the *Vita* by Donatus from the fifteenth century onwards, but has no authority in the ancient texts (Comparetti *Vergil in the Middle Ages* trans Benecke 354–5; for a typical example, see the Virgil of Venice: A. Pincius 1536, sig A2r; some further background is given in two letters by A.C. Taylor and M. Gaster respectively on 'Virgil and the Bread' in *Times Literary Supplement*, 28 August and 4 September 1937).

172.11 *Galene*] The sources of the 'inevitable and intrinsic,' or natural, diseases of the body are analysed by Galen in *De sanitate tuenda* 1.2 trans Green 6–8.

172.25 gay] embellish, make gay ('Gay' v obs first cited)

172.27g Proclus upon Platoes common weale, and Theodorus Asinaeus] Proclus, the fifth-century Neoplatonic philosopher, wrote a commentary on Plato's *Republic*, the eighth dissertation of which is 'Of the arguments, in Book 5 of the *Republic*, that attempt to prove that as the virtues of men and women are common, so is their education.' The ninth dissertation is 'On the arguments of Theodorus Asinaeus which tend to establish that virtue is identical in men and women, and an examination of what Socrates said.' Theodorus Asinaeus was an earlier Neoplatonic philosopher whose arguments are frequently referred to in Proclus (see Pauly-Wissowa *Real-Encyclopädie* Reihe 2 [1934] 5/2:1833–8 sv 'Theodoros 35'). Mulcaster's knowledge of Proclus may have been second-hand, but it could have come from an edition of the commentary such as that appended to the Greek edition of Plato's works edited by I. Operinus (Basel: I. Valderus 1534, in which see 2:416–22 for dissertations 8 and 9); for a modern edition see *Commentaire sur la République* trans Festugière (1970). The contemporary debate about the nature of women's virtue, in which ancient philosophers as well as the scholastics were usually cited, is analysed in Maclean *The Renaissance Notion of Woman* 6–27.

173.2 they reste not there, but proceede on further] Continuing with a paraphrase of Proclus' commentary on the *Republic* (dissertation 8.237).

173.13 bet] beaten, driven (v[1] 16)

173.24–5 consequence] succession, course ('Consequence' sb 2b obs first citation 1597)

173.35 talentes] skills, capabilities, invested sums of money (as in the biblical parable, Matthew 25:14–30)

174.3 galancie] delicacy, nicety (sb obs only citation)

174.11–12 *Plutarch*] Plutarch's essay on the 'Bravery of Women' was often cited by Renaissance writers on the praise of women. It was one of the *Moralia* (242Eff), which were often printed, in Greek or Latin editions. 'Mulierum virtutes' was also reprinted separately, for instance in the Latin translation of A. Ranutinus in Textor's *De memorabilibus et claris mulieribus* 3v–14v.

174.21 his epistle to him] The epistle from Plutarch to Trajan is first referred to and quoted in book 5 of John of Salisbury's *Policratus* (late twelfth century), and has no classical authority. The tradition that Plutarch taught Trajan is based on this spurious letter. See Barrow *Plutarch and His Times* 48, and 181–3 for an English translation of the letter.

174.29–30 *Ariosto* and *Boccacio*] Mulcaster's statement that he had read and enjoyed Ariosto and Boccaccio would have struck some of his readers as a daring admission for a schoolmaster (at line 36 he suggests that some of his readers 'will rather mervell'). Roger Ascham's well-known blast against all things Italian was the more typical view of an older generation; even Sir John Harington ten years later took considerable pains in his translation, introduction, and notes to emphasize the moral worth of Ariosto.

Ludovico Ariosto's *Orlando furioso* was known to Elizabethan readers at this time only in Italian or by reputation. The only English version was the tale of Ariodante and Ginevra by Peter Beverly (1565); Harington's translation did not appear until 1591. In 1583, the boys of Merchant Taylors' performed 'A historie of Ariodante and Genevora' before the Queen at Richmond (Feuillerat ed *Documents* 350), and it is possible that Mulcaster himself wrote the play. Perhaps Mulcaster introduced his pupils to Ariosto; both Spenser and Lodge were closely familiar with *Orlando furioso*. For background, see Sammut *La fortuna dell' Ariosto nell'Inghilterra elisabettiana* especially 29ff.

Giovanni Boccaccio wrote *De claris mulieribus* in the 1350s, and the work was available in the sixteenth century in the edition of M. Apiarus (eg, Berne 1539). It had been translated in part by Henry Morley, Lord Parker, but his version remained in manuscript until 1943 (*Forty-Six Lives* ed Wright). For the reputation of *De claris mulieribus* in England, see Wright *Boccaccio in England* 28–36. Mulcaster may have known the *Decameron*, which was not translated entire until 1620 (ibid 113ff).

175.9 burne day light] Proverbial; cf Tilley D123 'You burn daylight' (ie, you waste your energy needlessly).

175.20 worthy] The comparison of Elizabeth as mistress of the Nine Worthies to Apollo as master of the Nine Muses is a nicely worked similitude. (The Nine Worthies are usually listed as Joshua, Hector, David, Alexander, Judas Maccabeus, Julius Caesar, King Arthur, Charlemagne, and Godfrey of Boulogne or Guy of Warwick; the suggestion of course is that Elizabeth has great military prowess. Apollo the 'president' of the Muses is found again at 190.3.)

175.21 that absolute number] In his *Decalogue* 20ff (*Works* 7), Philo analyses the nature of the 'supremely perfect' number ten.

175.23–4 valure] worthiness, merit ('Valure' sb obs 1a, and see 'Valour' I a)

175.28–32 *Anacreon ... Porcia*] The same comparison between men and women is made by Plutarch in 'Bravery of Women' in *Moralia* 243B–C. Anacreon and Sappho are Greek lyric poets; Bacis is the male equivalent of a Sibyl, and is a generic name for a seer of ecstatic religion in antiquity; Sesostris was a king of Egyptian mythology and Semiramis was, according to Greek mythology, the builder of the city of Babylon; Servius, king of Rome in the sixth century BC, in legend was believed to have built the first walls of the city, and Tanaquill, wife of Tarquinius Priscus, an early Roman king, became an active leader during the period of succession following her husband's death (all in *Oxford Classical Dictionary* 2nd ed; Sesostris, Semiramis, and Tanaquill are treated in Thomas Cooper 'Dictionarium' *Thesaurus* [1565]).

175.33 presidencie] direction, leadership ('Presidency' 1 first citation 1591 or 3 first citation 1608)

176.14 undershining] of inferior brightness (ppl a only citation; also, 'shining beneath')

176.17 head] issue, result (sb 31)

176.21 overshot] wide of the mark, in error (v 3b obs)

176.37 point] indicate (v[1] 10, with additional sense of 'appoint,' from 'Point' v[2] 2 obs. Peacham's example of aphaeresis, the 'taking away of a letter, or sillable, from the beginning of a word,' is 'poynted ... appoynted,' in *Garden of Eloquence* [1577] sig E2r; the figure is very common in Mulcaster's writing, and is used by him to emphasize alliteration.)

176.38 *Timon*] 'A man of Athens, notable for his inhumanitee, and hatynge of the company and societie of men' (Thomas Cooper 'Dictionarium' *Thesaurus*), hence, generally, a misanthrope or highly critical person ('Timon' first citation 1588).

177.11 nonsuite] unwilling to pursue their claim (a obs b first citation 1679)

177.34 prating ... pratling] idly chattering ('Prating' ppl a cited and 'Prattling' ppl a were synonymous)

177.36 like empty caske] Proverbial; cf Tilley v36 'Empty vessels sound most.'

177.39–178.2 be not alwaye most burthened, neither with lettes, nor learning, but out of small store, they offer us still the floore, and holde most of the mother] A difficult passage: the sharp-witted young men do not bear within themselves either the self-control (to stop talking) or the knowledge (to talk intelligently), but they keep talking with the little (store) they have, and in so doing they yield up to us the floor, and they imitate most closely the behaviour of the mother. Women are being compared to these chatty males (who may be the equivalent of Osric in *Hamlet*).

178.8 timber] value, worth (sb[1] 4b refers specifically to those growing trees which form part of a freehold inheritance, ie, trees which must not be cut down by the tenant, but which must be allowed to stand and mature as the owner wishes.) The point is that the worth of the girl makes itself known much more early than that of the boy; ie, the true worth of the girl does not have to be waited for.

178.11–12 of a moonish influence] under the influence of the moon ('Moonish' a obs cited; though not suggested by *OED*, an indirect and delicate reference to the menstrual cycle)

178.19–20 dearest ... nearest] A common expression, though not in Tilley or *ODEP*; see *OED* 'Near' adv[2] 13 'near and dear' 1548.

178.20–1 corrosive] severe annoyance ('Corrosive' B sb 3 obs; cf Lyly *Euphues* in *Complete Works* ed Bond 1:241: 'I was halfe perswaded that [women] were made of the perfection of men, & would be comforters, but now I see they have tasted of the infection of the Serpent, and will be corasives.')

178.22 vessel of such weaknesse] Biblical and proverbial; cf Tilley W655 'A woman is the weaker vessel' (1 Peter 3:7)

178.25 menaltie] condition of being menial or a servant ('Menialty' first cited; though see also 'Menalty' where 'mean' refers to the middle class)

178.25 mistriship] status of mistress of household ('Mistress-ship' 1 first cited; a likely Mulcastrian spelling)

179.15–16 private cariages] secret affairs ('Carriage' 16 obs first citation 1609); ie, one must not put one's secret affairs into writing lest they be found out

179.19 goodmans mercerie] goods or merchandise of a man of substance or of a husband ('Goodman' 4, 2b; 'Mercery' 1 does not have this figurative sense)

179.39–180.1 that with the losse of their pennie, they lost not their pennieworth also] ie, that with the loss of their insignificant studies, they don't also lose the little they've learned. Tilley P188–219 has proverbs about pennies, but none corresponds.

180.2 *nedles*] A medieval figurative sense of 'needle' was 'an object of trifling importance or value' ('Needle' sb 1b last citation c 1460), and Mulcaster may be playing with this sense as well as with 'needle' as the sign of the industrious housewife (as for instance in Lyly *Euphues* in *Complete Works* ed Bond 1:319–20, where Livia, a wise lady of the court, writes 'fitter it is with the nedle to practise howe to live, then with the pen to learne how to love'). Note the visual (and perhaps aural?) rhyme of 'medle' and '*nedles*' in the sentence.

180.22 lowlinges] low-born persons (sb only citation)

180.23 petieship] pettiness, littleness (sb only citation)

180.24 shew for a shadow] Cf Tilley S408 'More show than substance,' which may be hinted at here.

180.26 beseeming] appearance (vbl sb 1 obs first citation 1611, from Shakespeare)

180.27 meere] absolute, or extreme ('Mere' a[2] 4)

180.30 toyousnesse] ornamentalness ('Toyous' obs cites only this passage for this word)

181.8 beare a saile] be prosperous ('Sail' sb[1] 3)

181.8 calling] high position (vbl sb 10 obs has only 'position ... rank,' which this use seems to go beyond)

181.17 private] private interest (sb 4 obs; or perhaps an adjective modifying 'weale')

181.19 florish] cause to bloom or thrive ('Flourish' v 5 obs)

181.20 naturall] natural gift or power (sb 4 obs, normally plural)

181.26 mediocrity] middle state or condition (4 obs)

181.29–30 beyond all cry] to a certainty ('Cry' sb 17a obs)

181.34 good meat, but not for mowers] Proverbial; Tilley M832 'No meat for mowers' (ie, food unsuitable for, or unobtainable by, people of low degree); see also *ODEP* 'Meat ...'

181.36 a paragon among princes] A further reference to and praise of Queen Elizabeth (cf 175.15ff).

182.3 eventes in] outcomes of, results (showing) in ('Event' sb 3, and perhaps also 4 'what befalls a person'; cf 150.21 and note)

182.14 workmanship] material craftsmanship, labour in handicrafts (sb 1 obs)

182.16 urinalls] glass vessels used for medical examination of patients' urine (sb 1 obs), a conventional sign of the physician

182.18 by the *Persian* storie] I have found no reference to Persian women studying herbs. Both Strabo *Geography* 15.3.8 and Xenophon *Cyropaedia* 8.8.14 describe the study of herbs as part of the training of the noble soldier. As Mulcaster knew the *Cyropaedia,* he may have had the following passage in mind: 'The boys of that time used also to learn learn the properties of the products of the earth, so as to avail themselves of the useful ones and keep away from those that were harmful.'

182.21 lining] contents, substance (vbl sb[1] 3 fig)

182.32 fraye] frighten (v[1] 2; cf 28.15 and note); ie, the labour involved would not frighten them off from drawing

182.34–7 *Timarete ... Martia*] Pliny *Natural History* 35.40.147. Mulcaster, or an intermediary source, has considerably altered the material in Pliny, which reads: 'Pinxere et mulieres: Timarete, Miconis filia, Dianam, quae in tabula Ephesi est antiquissimae picturae; Irene, Cratini pictoris filia et discipula, puellam, quae est Eleusine, Calypso senem, et praestigiatorem Theodorum, Alcisthenen saltatorem: Aristarete, Nearchi filia et discipula, Aesculapium. Iaia Cyzicena, perpetua virgo, M. Varronis iuventa Romae et penicillo pinxit et cestro in ebore imagines mulierum maxime et Neapoli anum in grandi tabula, suam quoque imaginem ad speculum.' (There have also been women artists – Timarete the daughter of Micon who painted the extremely archaic panel picture of Artemis at Ephesus, Irene daughter and pupil of the painter Cratinus who did the maiden at Eleusis, a Calypso, an Old Man and Theodorus the Juggler, and painted also Alcisthenes the Dancer; Aristarete the daughter and pupil of Nearchus, who painted an Asclepius. When Marcus Varro was a young man, Iaia of Cyzicus, who never married, painted pictures with the brush at Rome (and also drew with the *cestrum* or graver on ivory), chiefly portraits of women as well as a large picture on wood of an Old Woman at Naples, and also a portrait of herself, done with a looking-glass.) The descriptive epithets in Mulcaster's version ('vertuous,' 'curteous,' and so on) seem to be a fanciful addition to the original, and it is difficult to see their appropriateness other than heightening the importance of women generally. That Mulcaster picked up this material second-hand is perhaps indicated by the additional reference to Marcia, daughter of Marcus Terentius Varro the encyclopedist mentioned in Pliny; this reference is from

Boccaccio's *De claris mulieribus* 64 trans Guarino 144–5, where Boccaccio confuses Marcia with Iaia (sometimes spelled Laia or Lala, though incorrectly according to modern editors of Pliny, such as Gerhard Winkler).

183.6 *Logicall* helpe to chop] A catchphrase; Tilley L412 'To chop logic.' By suggesting that women might go on to study rhetoric and even to bandy about the terms and arguments of logic, Mulcaster is going beyond the usual limits set for women's education, as is suggested in Shakespeare, when Old Capulet mocks Juliet with 'How how, how how, chopped logic!' (*Romeo and Juliet* 3.5.149).

183.15 A *Laelia*, an *Hortensia*, or a *Cornelia*] Quintilian 1.1.6: 'Nam Gracchorum eloquentiae multum contulisse accepimus Corneliam matrem, cuius doctissimus sermo in posteros quoque est epistolis traditus: et Laelia C. filia reddidisse in loquendo paternam elegantiam dicitur, et Hortensiae Q. filiae oratio apud Triumviros habita legitur non tantum in sexus honorem.' (We are told that the eloquence of the Gracchi owed much to their mother Cornelia, whose letters even to-day testify to the cultivation of her style. Laelia, the daughter of Gaius Laelius, is said to have reproduced the elegance of her father's language in her own speech, while the oration delivered before the triumvirs by Hortensia, the daughter of Quintus Hortensius, is still read and not merely as a compliment to her sex.) Ascham praises Cornelia as a teacher (*Scholemaster* in *English Works* ed Wright 185).

183.16 *Eurydice* the *Epirote*] 'Of the Education of Children' in Plutarch *Moralia* 14B–C says the parent should emulate 'the example of Eurydice, who, although she was an Illyrian and an utter barbarian, yet late in life took up education in the interest of her children's studies.' Though this passage in the pseudo-Plutarchan essay calls Eurydice an Illyrian and though, in an epigram quoted in the essay, she says she is from Hierapolis (not here a real place, just a 'sacred city'), Mulcaster says she is 'the Epirote.' Epeirus is in northern Greece, lying between the Adriatic and Macedonia. According to Strabo (7.7.8), the Epeirotes mingled with the Illyrians and the Macedonians, but even he is specific that Eurydice, though she lived in the vicinity, was not native. Mulcaster's confusion may come from remembering that Eurydice is mentioned by Strabo in the section that begins with discussion of the Epeirotes.

183.26 about thirtene or fouretene yeares old] Although Mulcaster does not recommend grammar school studies as such for girls, he does suggest that girls spend about the same amount of time, or slightly less, at their education as boys would at grammar school.

184.15 ply all at full] work away at all (the subjects) in full detail ('Ply' v^2 4a; see also 'Apply' v 17)

184.17 Chapter 39]. This is the longest chapter in *Positions*. For a discussion of the background to the education of the gentleman, which this chapter principally treats, see introduction, xxviiiff.

185.1 counterbraunches] constitutent subdivisions, ie, in the category of 'mortal and resonable creatures' ('Counter-' 8 only citation)

185.6 communicate] share (v 5 obs)

185.8 communicantes] sharers (not in *OED* in this sense, though see 'Communicant' sb 3)

185.13 superlative] highest degree, ie, in society (sb B 3 first citation 1583)

185.14 though sometime they leese them] ie, sometimes those born into the nobility fail in their socially appointed tasks, and men of lower degree but of inborn virtue must take it on themselves to perform 'the greatest executions'

185.23 use] (later) employment (in the commonwealth) (sb 87c)

185.30 ordinarie] A play on 'of political jurisdiction' and 'normal, customary' (a 2 and 3a–b).

186.1–2 *publike* education and *private*] For some of the following arguments in favour of public education, Mulcaster is indebted to Quintilian *Institutio oratoria* 1.2.1–31, and even borrows particular images from his source (see notes for 186.17, 188.19, and 191.37). Mulcaster's point of view may be contrasted with those of Vives and Erasmus. Both authors are strongly opposed to the low level of morality and scholarship to be found in the schools of their time (Vives *On Education* trans Watson 66ff; Erasmus *De pueris* in LB 1:504Aff trans CWE 26:325f), though if a good public school were to be found, they would concur with the view of Quintilian. The topic is of great interest to Mulcaster, who was writing against the kind of private tutoring promoted by earlier writers such as Elyot and Ascham; see Introduction.

186.2–3 as inclosure is to common] The seizure of public pastures and arable land by private landowners for personal profit was a social issue of profound concern throughout the sixteenth century (the practice was severely condemned by More in his *Utopia*). Philip Stubbes inveighs against 'landlords' who he says 'inclose commons, moores, heaths, and other common pastures, wher out the poor commonaltie were wont to haue all their forrage and feeding for their cattell, & (which is more) corne for them selves to lyve uppon ... to the great impoverishing and utter beggering of whole townes and parishes' (*Anatomie of Abuses* [1583] sig I8r). An account of the facts and issues regarding Tudor enclosures is given by Thirsk 'Enclosing and Engrossing.'

186.15 cognisaunce] special mark (by which we are recognized) (sb 5)

186.17 whether *publike* abrode, or *private* at home] Quintilian's ideal orator is trained to have a capacity for the administration 'of public and private business' ('publicarum privatarumque rerum') in *Institutio oratoria* 1.Pr.10.

187.4–5 naturall name] ie, the word in its most basic sense, the word 'education' in a sense which corresponds to the true nature of education

187.12 engraffe] engraft, implant ('Engraff,' 'Engraft' 2 fig)

187.13–16 yet that difference ... *private* is the worst] ie, a private *difference* (perhaps in the Latin sense of *differentia*, meaning 'species') can't be brushed aside, as there is no better way to distinguish between individuals. Nevertheless, you can't necessarily go on to say that private education is the best way to differentiate one person from another; on the contrary, it is the worst way (for reasons given above and below) to discern the individuality of men.

187.17 which] who

187.18 pushes] A double sense of 'ambitious efforts to succeed' and 'swellings, pustules' (sb^1 1c first citation 1655; sb^2, this latter sense made emphatic here by 'humour' and 'distempered').

187.29 *common*] public ('Common' a 5–6, and looking back to 'common' against 'inclosure' 186.2–3)

187.32 brad] bred, engendered (spelling variant, not in *OED* under 'Breed')

187.37 *puffer* up to] sweller of, increaser of ('Puffer' in *OED* does not have this sense, but see 'Puff' v 5b obs; also 141.6. and note)

187.38 bettership] superiority (not in *OED* under 'Better' or '-ship')

187.39 overwayning] overweening, excessive self-estimation ('overweening' vbl sb 1; this spelling not given)

188.4 snuffe] contempt (sb^2 1)

188.8 forborne] endured, tolerated ('Forbear' v 1–2 obs)

188.18–19 when he comes to the light] Cf Quintilian 1.2.19: 'Deinde cum proferenda sunt studia, caligat in sole et omnia nova offendit, ut qui solus didicerit quod inter multos faciendum est' (Again when the fruits of his study have to be displayed to the public gaze, our recluse is blinded by the sun's glare, and finds everything new and unfamiliar, for though he has learnt what is required to be done in public, his learning is but the theory of a hermit).

188.19 resort] concourse or assemblage of people (sb 5 obs)

188.23 but under confession] ie, except in public disclosure (as opposed to the private class with his tutor) ('Confession' 1)

188.24 make] ie, 'do make' (parallel to 'do pretend')

188.37 privating] secluding, keeping private ('Private' v 2 obs cited)

189.15 give charge to] attack by contradicting ('Charge' sb 16–17 in figurative sense; this phrase not in *OED*)

189.16 odnesse] quality that sets (the young man) apart ('Oddness' 2 obs first cited)

189.16 odde] unusual, unique (a 6 obs)

189.22 affection] good will, or bias (sb 6 or 8 obs)

189.26 thrist] thirst (common variant spelling; see 'Thirst' sb)

189.34–5 what one auditorie is two or three boyes] Cf Quintilian 1.2.31: 'Et sane concipiat quis mente vel declamantis habitum vel orantis vocem, incessum, pronuntiationem, illum denique animi et corporis motum, sudorem, ut alia praeteream, et fatigationem, audiente uno: nonne quiddam pati furori simile videatur? Non esset in rebus humanis eloquentia, si tantum cum singulis loqueremur' (Imagine the air of a declaimer, or the voice of orator, his gait, his delivery, the movements of this body, the emotions of his mind, and, to go no further, the fatique of his exertions, all for the sake of one listener! Would he not seem little less than a lunatic? No, there would be no such thing as eloquence, if we spoke only with one person at a time). Yet medieval and Renaissance handbooks on letter-writing tended, by their emphasis on private communication, to allow rhetoric a smaller 'auditory.'

189.38 pipes] respiratory passages, or voice (sb[1] 2 cited; see above, 57.29 note)

190.3 If the nyne *Muses* and *Apollo* their president] The use of visual clues as mnemonic devices was explained by Cicero (eg, *De oratore* 2.86–8) and Quintilian (11.2.1–51), and was a commonly accepted (though not necessarily commonly practised) part of the study of rhetoric in the Renaissance. For an English treatment of the subject, see Thomas Wilson *Arte of Rhetorique* ed Mair 212–18. The history of mnemonics is told by Yates *The Art of Memory* and Carruthers *Book of Memory*. Mulcaster's point here is that the boy needs some kind of ordered series of clues for his memory ('places of memorie'), either painted on the wall or seated before him (the seating arrangement, and even the faces of the audience, were considered as valid clues). If there is nothing in front of him to provide such clues, he will have to be running continually to his master for reminders. By 'hieroglyphicall partitions' Mulcaster refers to the use of known series of symbolic images (seven ages of man, four seasons, etc), in order to make easily remembered divisions of a subject.

190.9 sitter by] ie, the student who assumed the master's chair to give a formal oration to the class ('Sitter' 5 [a]; 'a sitter by' was 'one who takes office temporarily'). The 'hearing of many' (ie, a large audience) would encourage him, and would strengthen his resolve to do well.

190.11–14 And though it be verie good ... have cause to doubt.] ie, if the boy is encouraged to come too often to the master with unresolved questions, the boy will never learn how to make up his own mind

190.17–18 being tyed to the stake] ie, it was not his private training being set forth as the final and ineluctable reason for his cunning which seems to contradict my assertion (but rather some other 'forreine helpe' which accounted for his success) ('Tie' v 2, where 'tie to the stake' means 'put in an inescapable position'; see also *ODEP* 'Stake, to be bound to a')

190.20 alieneth] estranges (v 1)

191.2 lewd] ignorant, ill-bred (a 4 obs)

191.6 necessitie is the spurre] Not in Tilley or *ODEP*; cf Tilley N58 'Necessity is a hard weapon.'

191.10 fond] foolish, silly (along with the present-day sense of 'affectionate'; a 2)

191.11 controwlement] censure ('Controlment' 4 obs); ie, the parental affection should be censured

191.11 state] high estate or rank (sb 16b obs)

191.16–17 great desires] ie, great desires on the part of the common to gain the most for itself against the claims of justice

191.19 injurie] inflict damage, injure ('Injury' v obs 3)

191.20 *Persian* principle] Perhaps a reference to Xenophon *Cyropaedia* ('principle,' 'princes'), although not (so far as I can tell) to any particular passage describing the modesty of Cyrus, which is referred to throughout, for instance in the young prince's games, in which 'he did not challenge his mates to those in which he knew he was superior, but he proposed precisely those exercises in which he knew he was not their equal' (1.4.4).

191.23 *Quintilian*] *Institutio oratoria*, 1.2.9: 'Verum in studiis magis vacabit unus uni. Ante omnia nihil prohibet esse illum nescio quem unum etiam cum eo, qui in scholis eruditur.' (I now turn to the objection that one master can give more attention to one pupil. In the first place there is nothing to prevent the principle of 'one teacher, one boy' being combined with school education.)

191.30 which is content to be cloistered] ie, who is happy to remain a private master or tutor

191.37 like the *sunne*] Although the expression sounds proverbial in English (Tilley S985 'The sun shines upon all alike'; cf Matthew 5:45), Mulcaster is following Quintilian 1.2.14: 'Non enim vox illa praeceptoris ut cena minus pluribus sufficit, sed ut sol universis idem lucis calorisque largitur' (The voice of a lecturer is not like a dinner which will only suffice for a limited number; it is like the sun which distributes the same quantity of light and heat to all of us).

192.3 curiouse] careful, attentive (a 1 obs)

192.10 *Quintilianes* counsell] ie, his counsel in favour of public schooling in *Institutio oratoria* 1.2.1–31; see 186.1–2 note.

192.15 make your private publike] The best example of a private household which also served as a school was at Cecil House in London, where Lord Burghley accepted wards of the court into his care; at one time there were as many as twenty wealthy young gentlemen studying there (this 'school' is described in Hurstfield *The Queen's Wards* 255–9). At an earlier period, young men and women were regularly brought up in the households of the nobility; such was the education of Thomas More in the household of Cardinal Morton. During Elizabeth's reign the old custom still prevailed, but boarding schools were found increasingly to be an acceptable substitute (Philip Sidney, for instance, was sent to Shrewsbury). It might be said that certain teachers also made 'their public private' by taking in boarders in their own households.

192.25 overcharged with too many] Mulcaster is writing at one of the peaks of demand for schooling. Shrewsbury grew from 266 boys in 1566 to 360 in 1581 (Oldham *History of Shrewsbury School* 4–17), and at least six other Elizabethan schools are known to have had more than a hundred boys (Berkhamsted, Merchant Taylors', St Paul's, St Alban's, St Savior, Tiverton; see Stowe *English Grammar Schools* 188–9). But what Mulcaster means by 'too many' is not very clear. In 1569 he was criticized by the Court of Merchant Taylors for taking on more than the statutory 250 boys (Draper *Four Centuries of Merchant Taylors' School* 15).

192.27 private executions] ie, those parts of the work ('Execution' 2b obs first cited; see 142.10 and note) in which he examines particular aspects of education. (Although he continues to deal with the issue of overcrowding in general terms, in his treatment of choice, conference, and buildings, he never again picks up the topic in particular terms, either in *Positions* or *Elementarie*.)

192.33 What *vertue* is private?] ie, which of the following virtues can indeed be termed private? (The answer, of course, is none of them.) The compositor's first reading of 'primate' for 'private' is understandable both from handwriting (he miscounted minims) and sense (the list looks as though one might be asked to choose which of the four cardinal virtues is best).

192.34 desert] reward, ie, given by *another person* to the deserving person. The point is that there is no good in having wisdom without using it and being rewarded for it publicly (a classical if not a Christian doctine, and hence in keeping with the four classical virtues being presented).

193.2 open field] public competition ('Open' a 13)

193.6 smallie] not much (adv obs 3)

193.8–9 conference] comparison (ie, between public and private) (sb 3 obs)

193.30–1 obedience, to guide themselues wisely] Here 'obedience' seems from the parallel structure to mean 'self-discipline, command of oneself' (sense not in *OED*), perhaps because the obedient person obeys himself well.

193.36 communicate] shared (ppl a)

194.12 go thorough] execute a design, complete a task in successive stages ('Go' v 63a obs)

194.34 impatronise] promote, advance ('Impatronize' v obs 2 'patronize, favour' first citation 1629)

194.39–195.1 it is miserably scraped ... to spare expense] ie, maggotty ('lively') cheese is bought or sold to spare expenses, so that the merchant's son may have the trappings of a gentleman

195.1–2 *Jacke* maye be gentleman] Proverbial; Tilley J3 'Jack would be a gentleman.'

195.10 *Aristophanes*] Plutus, the god of wealth, insisted on visiting only just, wise, and honest men, and for this he was blinded by Zeus; Aristophanes *Plutus* 87–92. Aristophanes was not studied much in the English schools (he is hardly mentioned by Baldwin in *William Shakspere's Small Latine*, though for a number of Latin editions of Aristophanes in the stock of the Oxford bookseller John Dorne in 1520, see 1:103). Aristophanes was, however, considered a suitable author by Erasmus (LB 1:521D trans CWE 24:669), and *Plutus* was used as a Greek text in the Jesuit program and was the play of Aristophanes most translated into modern languages in the sixteenth century (Bolgar *Classical Heritage* 357, 508–9).

195.17 the Greeke verse] 'no one gets rich quickly if he is honest,' Menander *The Toady* [a fragment] 42 ed Allinson 386–7. Menander's work was known in fragments quoted by other authors. Erasmus comments in *De ratione studii* after praising Aristophanes, Homer, and Euripides, 'For Menander, to whom I would have given even the first place [as poet], is not extant' (in LB 1:521D trans CWE 24:669).

195.21 wring] distress or afflict by oppression ('Wring' v 5c)

195.23–8 Witte bestowed ... not seene.] ie, using craft or mental acuity to achieve some public good deserves applause, but the same craft used to fill a private purse in secret or by criminal methods is morally wrong, even though the wrongness of it is not immediately apparent

195.25 holy] wholly

195.34 of purpose] on purpose, designedly (sb 10 arch)

195.34 pierce] wound deeply (v 5)

195.35 a thousand pound gaines] ie, a thousand pounds' gain

195.37 casuall] uncertain, subject to chance or accident (a 5 obs)

195.38 bastardise] bastardized, degenerate (shortened form of 'Bastardized' ppl a)

196.3 vnbewitched] unenchanted, ie, with clear perception (v)

196.4–5 what some write of nobilitie in generall] The writing on nobility and the gentleman is vast, and is described in general outline in Mason *Gentlefolk in the Making* especially chapter 2 'From *The Governour* of Sir Thomas Eylot to the *Basilikon Doron* of King James I' and Kelso *The Doctrine of the English Gentleman in the Sixteenth Century*, which has a long bibliography. The issues discussed here by Mulcaster are touched on in Elyot's *The Boke Named the Governour*, Lawrence Humphrey's *Nobles* (1563), the anonymous *Institucion of a Gentleman* (1555), and the dramatic dialogue *Gentleness and Nobility*.

196.9 beyond enough] more than is sufficient ('Enough' is used in the modern sense, though the combination with the preposition is unusual; this phrase is not in *OED*)

196.13 minister] furnish (with content) (v 2)

196.14 brymmer] more apparent ('Breme' a obs 2)

196.24 doth stand ... upon] behooves (v 78q obs)

196.26–7 My friend to be carefull, that I keepe all well ...] 'My friend' is the one who praises nobility, and who is careful to define the significance of what it is to be noble. 'I' refers to the noble youth or gentleman who is noble only in birth and finery, but who is not noble in virtuous behaviour.

196.35–6 the more bruted the more brutish if it fatall under fame] The more nobility is talked about, the less noble it becomes if it prove fatal as a result of ill report ('Fatal' as a verb not in *OED*).

198.4 *manuaries*] those who work with their hands ('Manuary' B sb 1 obs first cited; it is defined lines 6–7)

198.5 subdivident] that which subdivides ('Subdivident' only citation)

198.26 statarie] fixed, established ('Statary' a obs first citation)

198.26 Examples neede not] examples are not wanting

199.11 *Romaine*] In his definition of Latin terms, Mulcaster may be forcing the senses a bit. 'Nobilis' sometimes did refer more to social status, and 'generosus' to origins (from 'genus') and inner worth ('generositas'). Nevertheless the distinction is blurred in classical authors, as may be seen in the citations to Thomas Cooper's *Thesaurus*, sv 'Generosus' and 'Nobilis.'

199.37 *Alexanders* horse and *Porus* his dog] For Alexander's horse Bucephalus, see 168.14 and note. Porus was a mighty warrior-king of India who was defeated in battle by Alexander the Great. Porus did not have a pet dog, but an elephant which 'showed remarkable intelligence and solicitude for the king, bravely defending him ... and when it perceived that its master was worn out with a multitude of missiles and wounds, fearing lest he should fall off, it knelt softly on the ground, and with its proboscis gently took each spear and drew it out of his body' (Plutarch 'Alexander' 60 in *Lives* 699). The confusion of an elephant with a dog may be from an intermediary source, or may be due simply to a lapse of memory – in the section of Plutarch immediately following the passage on Porus there is a description of the death of Bucephalus and also of Alexander's pet dog Peritas. Alexander named cities after both animals (61 in *Lives* 699).

199.32–3 vertue is the ground to that whole race] Proverbial?; cf Tilley v85 'Virtue is the true nobility.'

199.36 glister] sparkle, glitter (v 1)

199.37 commend] appear attractive (v 4 obs 'to adorn or grace,' normally transitive)

200.7 coate] ie, of arms (sb 4; note the play 'desert ... is quartered ... with discent')

200.8 aunciencie] ancientness, antiquity ('Anciency' obs; see also 'Ancienty')

200.22 meere] ie, performed (or given) by Himself alone ('Mere' a[2])

201.5 bastarded] lowered, debased (ppl a obs)

201.13 purchace] plunder ('Purchase' sb 1 obs)

201.15 conveyances] ie, in the legal sense, as transfers of property or rights

201.18–20 *Alexander ... Hephestio ... Assuerus Hester ... Ptolome Galetes*] Hephaestion was a friend to Alexander the Great, who advanced him to honours and high rank (Plutarch 'Alexander' passim, especially 72 in *Lives* 704D–E, which describes Alexander's grief at his favourite's death). The story of Esther, who becomes the queen of King Assuerus and who saves her fellow Jews from massacre, is told in the biblical Book of Esther ('Assuerus,' or the Assyrian, is now believed to be Xerxes II). The relationship of Ptolemy to his favourite Galetes (or 'Galestes' in some texts) is described in Aelianus *Varia historia* 1.30 trans Fleming 8r–v.

201.34 *valiancie*] valour (sb)

201.35 warrious] warlike (a obs only citation)

202.7–9 *Sylla ... Caesar*] The cruelty of Lucius Cornelius Sulla (surnamed Felix) was not apparent until he became dictator of Rome (Plutarch 'Sulla' 31–2 in *Lives* 472A–E), when he slaughtered many of his opponents. The comparison of Sulla and Caesar with respect to their learning does not appear in either of Plutarch's lives, though Caesar's education and skill as an orator is referred to in 'Caesar' 3 in *Lives* 708D–E, and his superiority as a warrior to Sulla and several others is analysed in ibid 15 (714E).

202.19 stayed *advisement*] sober or careful reflection or deliberation ('Staid' a 3; 'Advisement' 2 obs)

202.25 pollicie] political cunning (in a negative sense as in 'Policy' sb[1] 3, quoting Shakespeare *1 Henry IV* 1.3.108 'base and rotten policy,' and quite different from the sense which Mulcaster gives in the following lines)

202.29 strait] confine within limits (v obs 7)

204.1 naturall] innate disposition (see 142.33 note)

204.10 the *Grecian*] Not any particular Greek, but Greeks in general, whose many heresies are outlined in the histories of Eusebius, Sozomenus, and others.

204.19 old *Adam*] ie, in respect of the fact that both were born descendants of Adam (cf Tilley A29 'The old Adam')

204.21 ensigne] emblem, badge (sb 3)

204.37 *Josephus*] *Autobiography* 1–2

204.38 And.] This one-word sentence is found in all examined copies of the text. It is aposiopesis, the sudden breaking off in discourse, and is set ironically against the first word of the next sentence, 'But ...'

205.2 so furth] similarly ('Forth' 9b obs)
205.10 state] estate, inheritance
205.10–11 the old house may have a very odde maister] Sounds proverbial, yet not in Tilley, though cf H772 'The house shows the owner' and M729 'One master in a house is enough.' Mulcaster suggests that some family lines produce eccentric heirs, and that it is better that the commonwealth, and not the single heir, inherit the general value and learning of the truly noble and honourable man.
205.20–1 for favour or feasting] as a gift or for personal gain
205.27 putfurthes] those who seek advancement (not in *OED*, though see 'Put' v^1 42d)
205.30–1 the *asse* doth desire the *lions* skin] Proverbial; Tilley A351 'An ass in a lion's skin' (from Aesop).
205.35 severed] separated (v I 1e obs first citation 1626, and see following note)
205.35 *Alcumist*] One of the principal claims of the alchemists was that they could change one metal into another by transferring its essence. Thus, if the essence of gold could be captured and transferred to any other 'natural metal' such as lead, the lead would become gold. By 'the finest be severed,' Mulcaster refers to the severing or removal of the essence of the finest metal, which would then be transferred to the baser one. It is interesting to see his scepticism towards alchemy in the same year that John Dee began his experiments in 'angel-magic.' For an explanation of alchemical refinement see Shumaker *The Occult Sciences in the Renaissance* 170ff and Read *Through Alchemy to Chemistry* chapter 3; for Dee, see French *John Dee* 110.
205.36 the *asse* is an *asse* as his own eares will bewray him] Proverbial; Tilley A355 'An ass is known by his ears.'
205.38 dunghillrie] vile condition or practice ('Dunghill'; this use recorded as a nonce-word; because of the animals here – ass, lion, ape, and, further down, jackdaw – perhaps an echo of Aesop's story of the cock who prided himself as king of the dunghill; cf also 194.35)
206.1 doultrie] stupidity, condition of being a dolt ('Dolt' sb, this use recorded as a nonce-word)
206.3 *apes*] Apes were supposed to be vicious, but the passage does not correspond with any of the ape proverbs in Tilley A262–74. 'Apes' here, of course, are those who ape their betters.
206.7 loselles] good-for-nothings ('Losel' sb)
206.8 shuffle up your cardes] ie, direct your affairs ('Shuffle' v 2)
206.38 in terme] in the very sense of the word (sb 13–14b, normally as 'in terms')
207.24 *justiciarie*] (a 1 first citation)
207.27 *Aristotle*] *Politics*, 4.9 (1295a–1296b), especially 1296a: 'That the middle form of constitution is the best is evident; for it alone is free from faction,

since where the middle class is numerous, factions and party divisions among the citizens are least likely to occur.'

207.29 meany] dependants ('Meinie' obs 2) or host, flock ('Many' B sb 2 obs)

208.6 For what is it to travell] Travel was an essential part of the gentleman's education by the seventeenth century, but at this slightly earlier time it was still a matter for debate. In his *De peregrinatione, et agro Neapolitano libri II* (1574; englished as *The Traveiler*, 1575), Jerome Turler lists seven of the most common objections against travellers, the most pointed being that they bring home little for themselves or for their countrymen (English trans 88–92). Ascham went further, and claimed they brought home dangerous customs (*Scholemaster* in *English Works* ed Wright 222–36). In his suspicion of the benefits of travel, Mulcaster follows Ascham. Most writers were more in favour of travel; they include Haly Heron ('Of Travel' in *The Kayes of Counsaile* [1579] ed Heltzel 63–79) and William Bourne (in his manual *A Booke Called the Treasure for Traveilers* [1578]). Heron and Bourne treat travel as a serious educational activity that must be prepared for, much as in the spirit of Bacon's essay 'Of Travel.' See also *Shakespeare's England* 1:198–223 and Charlton *Education in Renaissance England* 215–26.

208.15 eager] provoke (them not to travel) ('Eager' v obs)

208.16 dawes] The daw (jackdaw) was proverbially stupid, so here 'dawes' are 'persons of low intelligence.' Moreover, jackdaws do not migrate. So Mulcaster is saying that he does not wish to provoke stupid persons (who are quite happy staying at home) into travelling.

208.17 lightly] commonly (as at 34.24; with a play here on 'airily,' to go with 'quintessence')

208.17 quintessence] In the familiar sense of 'highest essence of matter,' here figuratively applied to the best of the gentlemanly class.

208.20 lure] ie, as in hawking, and following from the imagery of birds ('dawes') and air ('lightly,' 'quintessence') above

208.22 aliening] estranging, making hostile ('Alien' v 1)

208.22 too much harping on one string] Proverbial; Tilley S936 'To harp upon one string,' and see also S934–5.

208.38 utterable] saleable ('Utterable' a 1 obs first cited)

209.7 sinisterly] with evil intent ('Sinisterly' adv 4 obs)

209.8 *Solon*] Plutarch 'Solon' 25 in *Lives* 92D. Soon after Solon had enacted his laws, people came to him with questions about the interpretation of these laws; 'wishing to be wholly rid of these perplexities ... he made his ownership of a vessel an excuse for foreign travel, and set sail, after obtaining from the Athenians leave of absence for ten years. In this time he hoped they would be accustomed to his laws.'

209.11 *Pythagoras*] Pythagoras travelled to Egypt in his early years, according to

Diogenes Laertius *Lives* 8.3. Plutarch reports a tradition that Pythagoras also travelled to Italy to teach the Sabine king Numa, but does not have much faith in the story ('Numa' 1 and 8 in *Lives* 60A, 65D).

209.11 *Plato*] Plutarch 'Dion' 11 in *Lives* 962C–D tells how Dion, Plato's friend and disciple, invited the philosopher to Sicily at the behest of Dionysus, the tyrant of Syracuse.

209.15 kinde] manner, way (sb 8)

209.23 standing] fixed, stationary (ie, desk-bound) (ppl a 11)

209.35 straine out] extract by pressure, squeeze out (v^1 9 obs first citation 1709 in figurative sense)

209.38 padde] lurking or hidden danger (sb^1 3 obs, as in the proverb Tilley P9 'There is a pad [toad] in the straw')

210.4–5 What is it to travell?] Cf the definition in Turler *The Traveiler* 5: 'Traveill is nothing else but a painetaking to see and searche forreine landes, not to bee taken in hande by all sorts of persons, or unadvisedly, but such as are meete thereto, eyther to the ende that they may attayne to such artes and knowledge as they are desirous to learne or exercise: or else to see, learne, and diligently to marke suche things in strange Countries, as they shall have neede to use in the common trade of lyfe, wherby they maye profite themselves, their friends, and Countrey if neede require.'

210.17 rachelesse] heedless ('Reckless' 1)

210.18 taches] blemishes, faults (sb^1 2 obs)

210.25 stomacke] ill-feeling, hostility (sb 8c obs)

210.30 warres] wares

211.2 nationall] ie, of the law which regulates public behaviour of the nation as a whole (not quite this in *OED* a 1 first citation 1597), as opposed to the 'natural' law which regulates our innate behaviour as living beings and the 'civil' law which regulates private rights and duties (though see 'Civil' a 2 which seems to overlap with this sense of 'national')

211.7 quite the coast] justify the expense ('Quite' from 'Requite'; 'coast' a variant spelling of 'cost,' for which see the spelling at 239.16)

211.19 vyage] voyage (an early spelling; 'Voyage' sb headnote)

211.23 feltryd] matted, tangled ('Felter' v obs 1; 'Feltered' ppl a cited)

211.23 borough] dwelling place ('Burrow' sb^1, though see other senses: 'heap or mound' [sb^2], 'shelter' [sb^3], or even possibly 'town or large inhabited area' ['Borough' 2 obs]. Because of the spelling none of the senses is entirely separate from the others in *OED*.)

211.23 white footed beastes] ie, lice

211.24 perug] wig ('Peruke' sb 2)

211.25 applied] cared for, attended to (v^1 3 and see 'Apply' v 16 obs)

213.27 resemble] imitate, copy (v^1 3b obs first citation 1613), that is, the precedent of the original (or 'copy') will cause the child to draw well

211.30 pitch] position taken up and maintained, fixed opinion (sb[2] 14 obs fig first citation 1600)

211.38 fronting] defiance, confrontation ('Fronting' vbl sb first citation; 'Front' v[1] 3)

212.2–3 Forreine ... sicke there.] ie, though foreign clothes may suit us, foreign ideas are not right for our minds, unless our minds are sick

212.39 at a venture] at random, by chance (sb 1c; with a play on the modern sense of 'adventure' as 'daring enterprise' or 'hazardous activity')

213.3 traunse] state of extreme apprehension or doubt ('Trance' sb 1 obs)

213.10 sillie] defenceless, or, senseless, foolish (a A 1b obs, or 5)

213.10 *Socrates* in *Plato*] Socrates explains his resolution to remain in prison until his execution, according to Athenian laws, in Plato's *Crito* (51cff).

213.12 unfreindes] enemies (sb 1 cited)

213.18 *Plato*] From here to 216.18, Mulcaster summarizes Plato *Laws* 12.950D–953E.

213.34 θεωρούς] The *theoros* is 'one who travels to see men and things' (Liddell-Scott, *Lexicon*; usually 'envoy, ambassador')

214.1–3 *Delphi* ... *Neptune*] Plato *Laws* 12.950E: 'It is right that embassies should be sent abroad to Apollo at Pytho and to Zeus at Olympia, and to Nemea and the Isthmus, to take part in the sacrifices and games in honour of these gods ...' Delphi, Olympia (not Olympus), Nemea, and Isthmos were the locations of temples to Apollo, Zeus, Herakles, and Poseidon respectively (see Strabo 8.3.30, 8.6.19, 8.6.22, 9.3.2ff).

214.3–4 Embassages] ambassadorships ('Embassages' 3 and 'Ambassages' 3)

214.28 of ten] The original read 'often' and has been corrected to follow the passage in Plato; see 213.18 note.

215.28 mercates] markets

215.36 presidentes] those in charge (sb 2)

216.1 drammes] drachmas (sb[1] 1)

216.8 coronell] colonel

216.29–30 the forreine usually is a steppemother to a strange countrey] ie, foreign things (customs, clothing, etc) usually are not good for the welfare of the country into which these things have been imported (or, at least, not as good as local things)

217.13 residenciarie] dweller, one who is resident ('Residentiary' sb 2 first citation 1615)

217.14–15 makes the ... meane] takes steps, uses efforts ('Mean' sb[2] 10d obs)

218.3 *Tamerlane*] Tamburlaine, the Tartar king Timur Khan (1336–1405), had in the Renaissance an almost proverbial reputation for cruelty. See Hallett Smith 'Tamburlaine and the Renaissance' in 126–31; Una Ellis-Fermor's introduction to Marlowe *Tamburlaine*, especially 17–48; and Battenhouse *Marlowe's 'Tamburlaine'* 129–49. There is approving description of Tamburlaine in LeRoy *Of the Interchangeable Course, or Variety of Things* trans R.A. (1594) 107vff and 119v–120r (97rff and 108v–109r in Paris edition of 1576).

218.6 awraked] avenged ('Awreak' v obs 3)

218.7 renowme] make famous, celebrate ('Renown' v 1 cited)

218.11 endewement] adornment ('Enduement' obs b first citation 1609)

218.13 *το ἡγεμονικὸν*] the authoritative part of the soul (Liddell-Scott *Lexikon*). The term appears in the first paragraph of Philo's 'On Nobility' in *De virtutibus* 187 (ed Colson 8:278–9) and the relevant passage was translated from the Latin of Lawrence Humphrey into English as 'For that, whyche simply good is, consisteth nor in any forrein happe nor ornament or grace of body: no nor in everye parte of the minde. But onelye it, whych is princesse and lady of the rest' ('The Lytle Treatyse of Philo a Jewe, Concernynge Nobilitye' in Humphrey *The Nobles or of Nobilitye* [1563] sig 2A1r).

218.21 daunter] subduer, vanquisher (sb 1 obs; the misprint 'danuter' is a simple transposition)

218.26 *Cesar*] Plutarch 'Caesar' 7 in *Lives* 710D: 'The day for the election came, and as Caesar's mother accompanied him to the door in tears, he kissed her and said: "Mother, to-day thou shalt see thy son either pontifex maximus or an exile [φυγάς]."'

218.27 great pontificate] office of *pontifex maximus*, head of the principal college of priests of ancient Rome ('pontificate' sb a first citation)

218.30 *Isocrates*] *To Nicocles* 6: 'And the cause of this inconsistency and confusion [between the benefits of being king and its dangers] is that men believe that the office of king is, like that of priest, one which any man can fill, whereas it is the most important of human functions and demands the greatest wisdom.'

218.35 travel] study ('Travail' v 2c obs)

219.1 stuffing] gain (a figurative sense of 'Stuffing' vbl sb 2a–b)

219.2–4 *Gnatoes ... Thraso*] Characters from Terence's *Eunuchus*. Thraso is the braggart soldier and Gnato is his follower and flatterer. Cf Humphrey *The Nobles* sig f1r: 'For gaine sometime Gnathos, somtime Thrasoes, Importunately boasting their bravery, as in *the Comicall Poete*,' speaking of counterfeit wealthy noblemen. For the widespread academic knowledge of Terence in England, see Baldwin *Shakspere's Five-Act Structure*, especially chapter 16, and for mention of this passage in *Positions*, ibid 174–6.

219.8 gramercie] thanks, ie, no material gain ('Gramercy' in phr obs 3; cf Tilley G278 'God-have-mercy fills not the physician's purse')

219.21 hung] delayed until ('Hang' v 17 intr, though see note for v 6 'To hang fire'). 'Taryed the pulling, and hung the full harvest' sounds proverbial, especially with the pun on the plant 'tare' in 'tarying,' but it is not in Tilley or *ODEP*.

219.23 quickesilver] ie, the rapid movement of the wandering minds of the ignorant gentlemen

219.29 desultorie] (a 1 first citation)

220.2 charge] burden (sb 8 fig obs)

220.6 The *prince*] The education of the prince was a topic of supreme importance in medieval and Renaissance educational writing. For the sixteenth century, important treatises were Erasmus *Institutio principis Christiani*, the treatises of Vives written for Princess Mary, the work of Antonio de Guevara, put into English by Thomas North as *The Diall of Princes* (1557), and Johann Sturm *De educatione principum*. For the education of Mary, Edward, and Elizabeth, see Baldwin *William Shakspere's Small Latine* 1:185–284. Background to the theoretical writings is given by L.K. Born in chapters 4 and 5 of his introduction to Erasmus *The Education of a Christian Prince*. Mulcaster's observations on this subject are very brief and are presented only as part of his larger argument regarding the education of the gentleman.

220.27 *Nero*] According to Suetonius ('Nero' 9–10) the emperor behaved himself for the beginning of his reign, though he does not specify how long Nero projected this image of 'incomparable good.' Tacitus *Annals* (books 13 and ff) paints a rather different picture; even before he became emperor, Nero was a cruel sensualist.

220.31 curtesie be the meane to winne] ie, courteous (or 'courtly, gentle') behaviour is the means to win the affection of his subjects (the clause is set in parallel to 'humilitie in such height,' a quality taught to the prince so that he does not become too arrogant)

221.3 sturring] unstable, inconstant ('Stirring' ppl a 1b fig; with the sense of 'restless')

221.7 massive] (a 2a first cited)

221.11 in whose hand is his hart?] Not in Tilley or *ODEP*, though 'hand and heart' sounds proverbial.

221.34–222.1 myne other treatises] ie, later parts of the serial work to which *Positions* is an introduction

222.3 doares have] ie, 'doares, have'

222.7 his house is his castle] Proverbial; Tilley M473 'A man's house is his castle.'

222.20 admit no great counsell] ie, require no great deliberation

222.31–2 erection] foundation, establishment of an institution ('Erection' 8a)

222.34 murthered] tortured, ie, because of the discomfort they suffer in old school buildings ('Murder' v 1e)

223.7 The places where the toungues be taught] In what follows, Mulcaster describes the physical location and plan of a grammar school. His ideas are discussed by Seaborne *The English School: Its Architecture and Organization 1370–1870* 22–5 as 'the first more or less systematic treatment of the subject.' Mulcaster's requirements of a two-storey structure, a covered cloister, and master's lodging are reflected in some contemporary architecture. There is no evidence, however, that schools were specially located near open fields (225.30–5) for the purpose of exercise.

223.16–17 better for the childe to boord abroad with his maister] Many schools, especially the older foundations such as Eton (Mulcaster's old school) and Winchester took boarders. Usually, though, masters were prohibited from taking boys as boarders. 'Foreign' boys, ie, those boys from out of town, were usually put up in neighbouring houses (see Brown *Elizabethan Schooldays* 40–52). Mulcaster may himself have run a small boarding school outside of London sometime between 1588 and the 1590s, if evidence brought forward by DeMolen is correct ('Richard Mulcaster' 54–5). DeMolen says that Mulcaster 'was in effect conducting a private elementary school in his own residence' while he was teaching at Merchant Taylors' (39). Mulcaster does say he has elementary teaching being done 'within mine own house' (*Elementarie* sig 2F3v),and in the following discussion (at 224.8, 16, and 19) the 'house' referred to seems to be a private building. The term 'house' can mean 'home or personal abode,' and also 'building' or even 'college' ('House' sb 2 or 4, and see also quote on page 53 of DeMolen's article where the Merchant Taylors refer to themselves as at 'this howse').

223.32–3 entertainement] occupation (sb 7)

224.3 six in the morning] According to the statutes of Merchant Taylors' School (which follow those of St Paul's), 'The children shall come to the schoole in the mornyng at seaven of the clock both winter & somer, & tarry there untill eleaven, and returne againe at one of the clock, and depart at five' (Draper *Four Centuries* 246). Other schools did require attendance from six to eleven and from one to six (see Stowe *English Grammar Schools* 136), some schools varying according to the time of year and the availability of morning and afternoon light. The school day varied from eight to ten hours. Yet Mulcaster recommends just six hours for classroom work, from seven to ten in the morning, and two until five in the afternoon – 'enough for children wherin to learne' (see 229.37–230.2). The rest of the school day would be for exercises, or for 'neating of the bodie, or solacing of the minde, without to much motion' (229.8–9).

224.9 trewantrie] idleness (sb 2 cited; the sense of 'absence from school without leave' is later)

224.29 soilthes] instances of soiling or staining ('Soilth' obs only citation)

224.29 twentie things] ie, a fairish number
224.35 deposing] safe keeping (v 1b trans obs)
225.8 eager] irritate (v obs)
225.22 those] ie, those parents
225.23 strait] severe, stern (a 7 obs)
225.23 audittes] searching examinations (sb 3 fig)
225.25 set over] make over, transfer (v 150c first citation 1594)
225.27 had I wist] had I but known (Tilley H8 'Beware of Had I wist' and H9–10)
225.36 freedome of aire for the toungues] 'Good Studentes' should be 'bestowed in a mild, sweete and softe aier ... for the recreation and pleasure of wittes: the windowes ... ought to have aspect towardes the East and West, for the South resolveth the wit and dulleth it and filles the braine with hurtfull vapour: and the wind of the North (as in winter when it is cold) hindreth the memory, and is hurtfull to the lyver and lightes, because it stirres uppe defluxion,' according to Fenton *A Forme of Christian Pollicie* (1574) sig 2A2r (trans by Fenton from an unidentified French source).
225.38 entrances] initiations into learning ('Entrance' sb 2c obs first citation 1612)
226.2 close] courtyard, quadrangle (sb[1] 3a obs)
226.6–13 *Lacedemon ... Rome*] References to ancient buildings for sport are taken from Mercuriale *De arte gymnastica* 1.6 'De gymnasiis antiquorum' (On the gymnasia of the ancients). Mulcaster has lifted a few of the authorities cited there: on Spartan gymnasia, Athenaeus (*Deipnosophistae* 1.4), Plato (*Laws* Book 1 and *Theaetetus*); on the three gymnasia of Athens, Pausanias the geographer (taken by Mercuriale from the *Lexicon* of 'Suidas') and Philostratus (his life of Herod Atticus). The references to the Athenaeum, Hermaeum, and Panathenaeicum of Hadrian come from Mulcaster's misreading of Mercuriale, who says that Pirro Ligorio (a sixteenth-century writer on Roman antiquities) claimed to have discovered these structures in the vast complex of Hadrian's villa at Tibur (or Tivoli); but, Mercuriale goes on to say, Ligorio was mistaken, for they were not necessarily for sport but for scholarship or even possibly for festival celebrations. (Hadrian did build an Athenaeum in Rome in AD 135, a lecture hall, and he also built the Panhellenion in Athens, location of the ceremonies and contests of the Panhellenic games; perhaps Mulcaster remembered these in his misreading.) The Thermae or baths were built in Rome by Nero in AD 62–4 (Mercuriale cites Martial 7.34 'Who worse than Nero? What better than Nero's baths?').
226.13 *Gymnasia, xysta, Palaestrae*] The terms range in meaning in Latin and Greek: generally the *gymnasium* was a school for physical exercise, most often for wrestling, attached to a sports ground; the *xystum* (or *xystus*) was a covered portico used for athletic exercises ('Xystus' first citation 1664; there is

also a neuter form 'xystum'; described in Vitruvius 5.11); and the *palaestra* was an exercise ground, part of a complex of structures (Vitruvius 5.11; also see above, 83.25).

226.18 mo schooles erected] This statement is a forgivable exaggeration. According to numbers in Stowe *English Grammar Schools* (1908, but so far not yet superseded in any comprehensive way), of the at least 332 schools known to exist in Elizabeth's reign, 148 or more were founded prior to 1558, 115 are first mentioned in 1558–81, and 69 are first mentioned in the period following; in other words, fewer than half (about 44 percent) of the schools at the time of Mulcaster's writing had been founded in the recent past, and many of these schools may have been refoundations of earlier institutions. Nevertheless the activity in education was intense and certainly unprecedented. (The dates are from Stowe, appendices A and B, 156–70, in turn based on Carlisle, and the Schools Inquiry Commission Reports of the nineteenth century; the figures are my totals of the information in Stowe; those schools described only as founded during Elizabeth's reign were divided equally between the periods before 1581 and following; school histories are listed in Wallis *Histories of Old Schools*.)

226.35 absolute underteacher] mere usher ('Absolute' a 6; 'Underteacher' first cited, see 'Under-' 6a). Mulcaster had three ushers, or assistant masters, working under him at Merchant Taylors' School. (They are named at the back of H.B. Wilson *The History of Merchant-Taylors' School* 1177–85.) As he notes in line 36, these ushers tended to work independently of one another.

227.15 stant] barely (not in *OED*; perhaps this is a misprint for 'scant' or 'skant', but the 'st' ligature in the 1581 text would suggest otherwise)

227.20 *Gregories* Decretales] Gregory IX *Decretales* 5.5 (in the edition of Rome 1584) is entitled 'De magistris & ne aliquid exigatur pro licentia docendi (Of teachers, and that nothing be demanded for the licence to teach), and is subtitled 'Ecclesia cathedralis prouidere debet magistro de beneficio, qui clericos eiusdem ecclesiae, & alios gratis doceat' (The congregation of the church ought to provide a benefice for the master to teach freely clerics of the same church and others). This principle, according to the gloss, was supported by the Lateran Council and the Council of Trent.

227.24 immunities] Schoolmasters were exempt from certain forms of taxation (1 Elizabeth c.21.30, quoted in Prothero *Select Statutes* 36). These reliefs, and other unnamed immunities in *Elementarie* sig 2K2r, were apparently threatened in Parliament, but were protected by Sir Walter Mildmay and other members of the Court of Exchequer. (See next note.)

227.27–8 *Justinians* new Codex] *Codicis Dn. Iustiniani ... libri XII* 4.13 (edition of Antwerp 1575, cols 668–71): 'Ne filius pro patre, vel pater pro filio emancipato, vel libertus pro patrono, vel seruus pro domino conueniatur'

(That one may not take an action against the son in place of the father, or against the father in the place of an independent son, or a freedman in place of his patron, or against a servant in the place of a master). The 'Noua constitutio Friderichi,' dated 1158 and appended to the title, applies the same principle, that one may not be sued for the debts of another, to 'omnibus qui causa studiorum peregrinantur scholaribus, et maxime diuinarum atque sacrarum legum professoribus' (all scholars who for the sake of studies travel, above all, professors of divine and holy laws). The gloss enlarges the sense of the law slightly, by stating (in part) 'Imperator primo praecipit quod scholares secure vadant ad loca studiorum, & nullus eis iniurias inferat' (The Emperor first enjoins that scholars may travel safely to their places of study, and that no one may inflict injuries upon them).

227.37–8 set downe his staffe at] be content with ('Staff' sb[1] 5d first citation 1584, and see also Tilley s804 'To set up one's staff,' which has a slightly different sense of 'To abide in a place')

228.2–3 the case now is quite altered] Proverbial; Tilley c111 'The case is altered' (the proverb is the basis for the title of Ben Jonson's play of 1609); also 285.17–18.

228.3 enhaunce in his own] ie raise his prices as he wishes (v 4b obs)

228.6 the auncient rent] ie, in other kinds of work each man is paid whatever he can get, but in teaching the 'rent,' or amount paid remains what it was in former times. Indeed, payments of £10 per annum were common in the fifteenth century (Orme 'Schoolmasters'), as they were still in the late sixteenth century.

228.6 where] ie, in a time when

228.7 bookemen] A rueful comment on those 'bookmen,' or other university-trained professionals, who have no regard for schoolmasters, indeed who 'bite them coursdly,' despite their common investment in book-learning.

228.7 coursdly] with perverse ill-temper, malignantly ('Cursedly' adv 3 obs)

228.10 thrust to the wall] worsted, treated badly ('Wall' sb[1] 14 obs; Tilley w15 'To be driven to the wall' and w185 'The weakest goes to the wall')

228.12–13g Probitas laudatur & alget.] Juvenal 1.74: 'Honesty is praised, and yet it freezes.'

228.12 happing] covering (vbl sb[2] b, from 'Hap' v[2] 'to cover with clothing')

228.15 chopt] exchanged (v[2] 1 obs)

228.17 translate] transfer (v 1)

228.18 licences] Licences were customarily required to be issued to schoolmasters by the local ecclesiastical authority, but such licenses may not be referred to here. Mulcaster may here be using 'licences' instead in the sense of 'leaves, permissions' (sb 1) on the part of the governing bodies of schools to allow these schools to move 'to more convenient places.'

228.23–4 I my selfe be not the worst appointed] The original building of Merchant Taylors' School was part of the Manor of the Rose, built in the reign of Edward III and a former property of the de la Pole family of Suffolk. The school property consisted of 'the west gate-house, a long court or yard, the winding stairs at the south end of the said court, on the east side thereof, leading from the court to the leads over the chapel, as also to two galleries over the south end of the court, the said two galleries, and part of the chapel' (Norman 'Sir John de Pulteney and His Two Residences in London' 269; see also the plan of the district with the school marked on the plate opposite page 257). The property cost £566 13s 4d; new schools cost anywhere from £34 to £600 (Stowe *English Grammar Schools* 138 note 79). Shrewsbury, the only other school of a size comparable to Merchant Taylors' (360 boys in 1581, compared to Merchant Taylors' statutory limit of 250), had no central building, but was run from 'a number of ordinary houses bought and adapted for school use' (Seaborne *The English School* 21).

228.29 twenty yeares] Mulcaster was formally elected headmaster of Merchant Taylors' School on 24 September 1561 (Draper *Four Centuries* 8–9), nineteen years and six months before *Positions* was entered on the Stationers' Register (on 6 March 1581). What he says here suggests the book was written (or at least revised) shortly before publication. It also shows that he had taught for two years before his appointment at the School; see note for 16.2–3, where he says he has taught 'now two and twentie yeares.'

228.36 vawted] vaulted (var sp 'Vault' v[1]; cf *Elementarie*, sig 2D2v 'vawt' and 'vawter'). Sounds from beneath or the adjoining part of the building may have been a problem at the early Merchant Taylors' School.

229.1–2 turne served] needs satisfied ('Turn' sb 30b)

229.4 meany] many (var sp of 'Many' a and sb)

229.5 exhibitours] those who support the exhibition or foundation with money, ie, patrons ('Exhibitor' does not have this sense, but see 'Exhibition' 1–2 and 'Exhibit' v 2b obs first citation 1601)

229.12 *Xenophon*] According to *Cyropaedia* 1.2.4, Persian youths were schooled in a garrison which formed part of a large complex of government offices.

229.15 appendentes] subordinates (eg, drawing, penmanship) ('Appendent' B sb 2 first citation 1587)

229.28 *Hippocrates*] *Aphorisms* 2.16, as above, 122.8 and note.

229.33 use] customary practice (ie, what society and school demand of the pupil, and what the pupil himself can become accustomed to)

229.36 fast] soon (from 'Fast' adv 4 'very near')

229.38 the *lambe* and the *larke* ... when to rise and when to go to bed] Proverbial; Tilley B186 'Go to bed with the lamb and rise with the lark' (it may seem as though they are reversed here, but actually they are arranged in chiasmus).

230.3 morening houres] In a late sixteenth-century grammar school timetable reproduced in Stowe *English Grammar Schools* 186–8, new material was to be presented in the morning, and review, deskwork, and memory work were to done in the afternoon. At Eton in the 1560 timetable new work was presented in mid-morning, and memory work was recited in the afternoon; Baldwin *William Shakspere's Small Latine* 1:353ff. Mulcaster's suggestion seems to be a moderate statement of common practice.

230.8 neating] making neat, cleaning (v obs 1 cited)

230.18 some excellent man] Perhaps Mulcaster himself later tried to put his 'many excellent conclusions in triall' in his schools in the country and at Milk Street; so hypothesizes DeMolen 'Richard Mulcaster' 54–6.

230.21 leasing some authoritie] ie, no longer under the control of 'other men'

230.23 Chapter 41.] On this chapter, see introduction, xxxiiiff.

231.19 advertisements] precepts, instructions (sb 2 obs)

231.32 the *tutor*] On the role of the university tutor, see Charlton *Education* 145ff, Curtis *Oxford and Cambridge* 79–81, and McConica 'The Collegiate Society' in McConica ed *The Collegiate University*, esp 693ff. It seems that some tutors took moral as well as intellectual care of their charges. Nashe's satirical 'Letter of *Harveys* Tutor to his Father, as touching his manners and behavior' in *Have with You to Saffron-Walden* in *Works* ed McKerrow 3:65–9, gives a glimpse, albeit distorted, of a tutor and his undergraduate pupil.

231.37–232.1 the *Elementarie* ... is left to the meanest] Cf Clement *Petie Schole* (1587) 4: 'Children (as we see) almost everie where are first taught either in private by men or women altogeather rude, and utterly ignoraunt of the due composing and just spelling of wordes: or else in common schooles most commonlie by boyes, verie seeldome or never by anie of sufficient skill ...' Baldwin *Petty School* 137–58 gives a full description of the sixteenth-century 'abecedarius.' Quintilian 2.3.1–12 argues for the need to have an excellent rather than a mediocre teacher instruct the very young.

232.6 contrarie] contradict (v obs 2b)

232.10 proces] (future) development (sb 9 first citation 1638)

232.13g entertainment] pay (sb 2b obs). Low pay to teachers was a common complaint, even by masters such as Mulcaster, who ran a big and prosperous city school. See introduction, xxxiv, and the notes for 228.6 and 234.2.

232.24 repare] gathering ('Repair' sb[1] 3 obs)

232.30 muster] show forth, appear (v[1] 1c obs)

232.30 countenaunce] (pleasing) outward aspect, appearance (sb 2 obs)

232.30 continuaunce] durability, permanence (sb 6 obs)

232.31 strike the stroke] have great influence ('Stroke' sb[1] 3d obs)

233.12–13 foure times in the yeare] In the six years 1576–81, boys were admitted in every month of the year except February at Merchant Taylors'; see

Robinson *Register* 1:25–7 (the listing is incomplete, but it is set forth in chronological order).

233.14 hand over head] recklessly (Tilley H70 'Hand over head')

233.15 similitude] ie, apparent similarity between the scholars being accepted into the school and the boys already in a particular form

233.22 whether one man, or moe] In chapter 11 of *Elementarie* Mulcaster gives a survey of his complete elementary program, and concludes that it can be taught by one man, though 'the Elementarie master is not commonlie the cunningest ...' (sig H3r). Though he intends one master to teach writing, reading, drawing, music, and sport (231.8–9), he never deals with this issue directly and in detail.

233.24–5 Once fore all] ie, once and for all (the phrase introduces his main point, reiterated at the end of the paragraph)

234.2 it is a great daunting to the best able man] At Merchant Taylors' Mulcaster was paid the same as his ushers, £10 a year, though his pay for many years was supplemented with another £10 by Richard Hilles, the founder of the school. The high master of St Paul's School received just over £33 a year. Mulcaster's low salary was a cause of continual sparring between him and the court of the Merchant Taylors. Actually, his salary was fairly typical, though for masters of smaller schools.

234.2 of of] ie, off of

234.3g sufficiencie] ability to support himself (sb 1 obs)

234.5 gaine with the basest] ie, earn on a par with the lowest paid, receive the poorest kind of pay

234.14 Besides his maners and behaviour] The statutes of Merchant Taylors' School (following those of St Paul's) required: 'a man in body whole, sober, discreete, honest, verteous, & learned, in good & cleane Latine l.rature, &, also, in Greeke, yf such may be gotten. A wedded man, a single man, or a priest, that hath noe benefice, with cure, office, nor service, that may lett his dew business in the schoole' (Draper *Four Centuries* 241). Mulcaster omits the ecclesiastical requirement for licensing, chiefly that the master 'de religione ... piorum hominum testimonio commendari' (in the matter of religion ... be commended by the witness of holy men) (cited in Wood *The Reformation and English Education* 62). The qualifications of the grammar school master in school statutes are outlined in detail in Stowe *English Grammar Schools* 55ff. Mulcaster's additional requirement of Hebrew may reflect the curriculum at Merchant Taylors' and a few other schools, including Westminster, but it would not normally be insisted on. In spirit what Mulcaster says here follows Quintilian 1.4.2–5 and Erasmus *De ratione studii* in LB 1:522F trans CWE 24:672ff, although Mulcaster does not ask for the kind of encyclopedic knowledge (agriculture, military science, architecture, cooking, etc) which the earlier writers (and Milton later) wished to see in a teacher of literature.

234.15 assurance] declaration from witnesses (sb 3 first citation 1609)

234.22 false] The 1581 text here reads 'falfe': perhaps a bad joke by the compositor at Mulcaster's expense, and easily missed in proof-reading because of the similarity of long 's' and 'f' in this type. That a teacher be able 'to maister false printes' is an important skill at a time when the level of error, even in Latin and Greek, was much higher than would be deemed acceptable today.

234.37 to thinke ech childe an *Alexander*] Quintilian, 1.1.24: 'Fingamus igitur Alexandrum dari nobis impositum gremio, dignum tanta cura infantem (quanquam suus cuique dignus est)' (Let us assume therefore that Alexander has been confided to our charge and that the infant placed in our lap deserves no less attention than he – though for that matter every man's child deserves equal attention).

235.9–10 a seminarie for excellent maisters] In what follows, Mulcaster suggests a complete reform of the university into seven principal colleges or faculties. His plan culminates with the seventh college for the training of teachers, for which see 245.33ff and note. The idea of the seven colleges seems to be Mulcaster's own, though to a certain degree he follows the precedent of the continental universities such as Bologna or Montpellier; an example of a professional school much closer to his experience was of course the Inns of Court, where the academic and moral education of the students was undertaken in the context of a single professional faculty (for the Inns of Court, see 245.21 note).

235.15 object to repulse] ie, reason to reject (the new plan or idea)

235.19–20 maisters of the universities them selves, and by their maisters abroad] The 'maisters of the uniuersities' are the MAS, who still had power to vote in convocation, though the real administrative power was by Mulcaster's time centred in the heads of the colleges and in the office of the vice-chancellor. The 'maisters abroad' are the crown and the privy council. As Curtis notes, with slight exaggeration, 'ultimate control of the universities resided in the Crown. Oxford and Cambridge were, and had been since the Reformation, royal institutions. The monarchs accomplished their purposes both by direct intervention in the affairs of the universities and by the control of appointments and promotions' (*Oxford and Cambridge* 175; he gives examples of how this control worked on 26–8).

236.1–2 taking away landes from colleges] The first Chantries Act (1546) was interpreted by some as an appropriation by the crown of all college properties, but Henry VIII personally assured the colleges that they could maintain their lands as before (Curtis *Oxford and Cambridge* 40). This was the last great threat against the economic independence of the educational foundations, though through the century there was a continuing fear that the attack might be renewed; William Harrison, in 1577, referred to college properties as 'lands some greedie gripers doo gape wide for' (*Description* 88).

236.10 upon] ie, at the time of

236.12 advertise] indicate (v 5)

236.23 *Lycaeum, Stoa, Academia*] The schools of Aristotle and the Peripatetics, Zeno and the Stoics, and Plato and his followers, respectively; see below 248.35ff and note.

236.24 other nations] Many of the universities of southern Europe were organized in clearly divided faculties. Bologna, for instance, was a union of separate faculities of medicine, law, arts, and theology. Montpellier is the best example in France of this kind of university; Paris, by contrast, was more centrally organized and had a system of colleges. Many of the early universities had been formed as guilds of students who gathered together and sought out masters; such foreign groups were often called 'nations,' a sense which Mulcaster seems to be playing with here. See Rashdall *The Universities of Europe in the Middle Ages* ed Powicke and Emden 1:497ff, 2:115ff, and for the 'student-university,' 1:176ff.

237.4 *colloquies*] conversations or debates ('Colloquy' sb 1 first citation)

237.8 finish] ie, finished, polished; or 'fineish'

237.12 *mathematicall* sciences] At the time at which Mulcaster was writing, mathematics were not studied as consistently or in as detailed a way as many other subjects in the universities. Though the Cambridge statutes of 1549 required the first-year undergraduate to hear lectures in mathematics (comprising the cosmography of Mela, Pliny, Strabo, or Ptolemy), the statutes of 1558 replaced mathematics by rhetoric, even though there was a continuing provision for a professor of mathematics; see Ball *A History of the Study of Mathematics at Cambridge* 13–14. The nova statuta 1564/5 of Oxford required post-graduates preparing for the MA to read '*Arithmeticam* vel Boetii vel Tunstalli vel Gemmephrisii ... *Geometriam* vel Euclidis, vel Vitellionis *Perspectiuam* ... *Astronomiam* vel Iohannis de Sacro Bosco vel *Theoricam Planetarum*, vel Ptolomei *Almogestam*, vel quemlibet alium librum Ptolomei' (The Arithmetic either of Boethius, Tunstall, or Gemmephrisus ... either the Geometry of Euclid or the Perspective of Vitellio ... the Astronomy of Johannis de Sacro Bosco, or the Theory of the Planets [ie, of Georg Peurback] or the Almagest of Ptolemy, or any other book of Ptolemy) (Gibson *Statuta antiqua* 378). Feingold *The Mathematicians' Apprenticeship* argues that the subject did remain part of an unstated but reasonably vigorous curriculum, especially for the MA (41). And yet, despite these requirements, it seems that most of the interesting work in mathematics was being done in the city of London after the scholars had left the university. One of Mulcaster's former pupils led the field; in 1588 Thomas Hood was appointed to a lectureship in mathematics at Staplers' Chapel, Leadenhall Street, a lectureship endowed by Thomas Smith, son of the Thomas Smith praised by Mulcaster above, 108.38. See Johnson *Astronomical Thought* 196–205 and also his 'Thomas Hood's Inaugural Address'; for background, Feingold, McLean *Humanism and the Rise of Science* 107–68, and E.G.R. Taylor *The Mathematical Practitioners of Tudor and Stuart England*, especially chapter 2, which outlines the largely practical and non-theoretical studies of mathematics being made in Elizabethan England; the general humanist background is presented in Rose *The Italian Renaissance of Mathematics*.

237.24–5 mocke at mathematicall heades] Despite what Mulcaster says, many Elizabethan writers were favourable to mathematical studies; see Kocher *Science and Religion* 151–3. Nashe in *Pierce Penilesse* (*Works* ed McKerrow 1:172) notes that certain unnamed mathematicians are atheists, but does not pursue the matter. 'Heades' has here the sense of 'persons with a certain (mathematical) disposition' (sb 7a).

237.20 flidge] ready to fly, fledged ('Fledge' a 1 in a figurative sense)

237.27–8 *Socrates ... Plato*] *Republic* 7.522ff

237.29 above the moone] to a great degree, extravagantly ('Moon' sb 3b; cf Tilley M1114 'He casts beyond the moon' meaning 'he indulges in wild conjectures')

237.30 force] reinforce (v^1 13 obs)

237.32 till their owne rod beat them] Cf Tilley S802 'To be beaten with one's own staff,' R153 'He has made a rod (staff) for his own tail (head),' or W26 'Let his own wand ding him.'

237.36 forbad any to enter his *Academie*] One of the best-known anecdotes in the life of Plato, found, for instance, in John Tztetzes, a Byzantine author of the twelfth century: 'Over his front doors Plato wrote: "Let no one unversed in geometry come under my roof"' (*Book of Histories* 8.972–3 trans Thomas *Selections* 1:387). For a brief account, see Riginos *Platonica* 138–40. That the injunction was familiar to English readers is shown by its mention in Recorde *The Pathway to Knowledg, Containing the First Principles of Geometrie* (1551) sig [yogh]2r 'Plato ... wrote this sentence on his schole house dore ... Let no man entre here ... without knowledge in Geometry.'

238.4 nigh the kernell] near to the very essence (of the art) ('Kernel' sb^1 8 fig)

238.7 collusions] tricks or ambiguities in words or meanings (sb 3 obs)

238.12 In time all learning may be brought into one toungue] One should note that Mulcaster states this future hypothesis to support his argument for present change. He is using, in other words, a kind of argument by prediction (called by the rhetoricians diabole): you say something may happen in order to convince your reader that something else you are proposing should happen.

238.17 We do attribute to much to toungues] Mulcaster here gives a curious political interpretation to the traditional debate over *res* and *verba*. In an ancient democracy, the ability to sway others and to engage in debate was, he argues, clearly essential to the proper conduct of government ('Then was the toungue imperiall'). In a monarchy, however, one must obey, not try to convince others against the royal will, and therefore fine eloquence should be eschewed in favour of 'substaunce of matter.' (I do not see how this expressed opinion is consistent with Mulcaster's own high style, except in so far as he may be arguing that his own writing is full of 'substaunce of matter.')

238.19 speake finely, then to reason wisely] An echo of the proverb Tilley S721 'Speak fitly or be silent wisely'?

238.20 for the time] ie, for the time being (sb 40 obs)

238.24 in price] highly esteemed (sb 8 obs)

238.26 bridled] controlled, mastered (v 2)

238.28–9 servaunt unto learned matter] See note for 238.17. Despite his obvious love of rhetorical flourish, Mulcaster here takes an essentially nominalist point of view. (That *res* should have precedence over *verba* is stated most strongly in the writings of Francis Bacon, where the humanist rhetoric was vigorously attacked.)

238.35 countenaunce] repute (sb 9 obs)

238.37 *Askam* in his booke] In his *Scholemaster*, Ascham often refers to 'the cunningest Master, and one of the worthiest Jentlemen that ever England bred, Syr *John Cheke*' (*English Works* ed Wright 268; other references throughout, though see especially Cheke's lesson on Sallust, 297ff). Although Mulcaster seems to have read Ascham's *Scholemaster* with some care, he seldom refers to it in *Positions*.

239.3 *Sir John Cheeke*] Sir John Cheke (1514–57) was Provost of King's College, Cambridge, from 1548 until the accession of Mary in 1553. Although Cheke was a renowned scholar of Greek, his political ambitions kept him away from an academic life at Cambridge for most of his time as Provost, except for brief stays in the summer and fall of 1549 and again in 1552. His interests in mathematics were chiefly in the area of astrology. (E.G.R. Taylor *Mathematical Practitioners* 168; *DNB*; McLean *Humanism and the Rise of Science* 130–1; and Strype *The Life of the Learned Sir John Cheke, Kt.* [1705] 49, 46, and 116 for the dates he was in Cambridge.)

239.12 maister *Bukley*] William Buckley (died c 1572) was, like Mulcaster, a scholar at Eton and King's College, Cambridge, where he graduated BA in 1542 and MA in 1545. He was a fellow of King's from 1540 to 1550. He was made prebend of Lichfield in 1550, but resigned the post soon afterwards. In 1551 he was tutor to the Royal Henchmen (or court pages). His *Arithmetica memorativa, sive compendaria arithmeticae tractatio* was first published in 1567 ('nunc primum in lucem edita' reads the title page of that edition) by Thomas Marsh (*STC* 4009). Later editions appeared as part of John Seton's *Dialectica* (in 1570, 1572, 1574, etc; *STC* 22250.8 and following). I do not know what to make of Mulcaster's claim that he received a copy of this work some time in 1548–50, unless his copy was manuscript, or the poem was part of an early edition now lost and for some reason not given notice by publisher or author in the edition of 1567. *Arithmetica memorativa* is a poem in Latin, just over three hundred lines in length, an instructional guide to various arithmetical operations; sections of the work are headed, for instance, 'De additione,' 'De subtractione,' etc, leading on to more exotic information in the second part, for instance, 'Modus formandi numeros ad auream regulam' (the way to dispose numbers according to the golden rule). Judging from a copy, interleaved and heavily annotated (late sixteenth-century hand), of the 1574 edition in the Folger Library (*STC* 22252), the work may have been of some practical use to the student who wished to master the basics of arithmetic. (*DNB*; Cooper and Cooper *Athenae Cantabrigienses* 1:292; Venn *Alumni Cantabrigienses* 1:248; E.G.R. Taylor *Mathematical Practitioners* 169, which oddly omits reference to the *Arithmetica memorativa*)

239.16–20 *Euclides ... Xenophon*] As his gift from Cheke, Mulcaster probably received one of the many shorter versions of Euclid's *Elements* published before 1549; there is a chronological list in Thomas-Stanford *Early Editions of Euclid's Elements*. A likely text is that of J. Voegelin (eg, Paris: C. Wechel 1534, an octavo of 36 leaves); a full text, such as the folio of Basel: J. Herwagen 1533 (Adams E980), could run to about 200 leaves, and would have been too expensive to hand out in quantity. Without a comprehensive bibliography of Renaissance editions of Xenophon, it is difficult to tell which of the Greek texts may have been given to the undergraduates along with the Euclid. Perhaps they received something like the two-part quarto of the *Cyropaedia* of Paris: C. Wechel 1538–9 (Adams X32). A search of the libraries of King's and St John's revealed no likely texts, certainly none inscribed by Cheke. It is pleasing to suppose that the many references to Xenophon's *Cyropaedia* in *Positions* come from the copy given by Cheke to Mulcaster.

239.31 proceeders] bachelors proceeding to the degree of Master of Arts (for a general note on the university curriculum in mathematics, see 237.12 note)

240.9 devisours] architects (sb c obs cited, with sense of 'planner')

240.16–17 labour is the conquerour] Tilley L5 'Labour overcomes all things' (adapted from Virgil *Georgics* 1.145 'labor omnia uicit').

240.20 indifferent] impartially pertinent (a[1] r 4 obs)

240.22–3 olde rudimentes] ie, anciently devised first principles taught to a beginner. Note the chiasmus, in which there is a contrast between 'olde' and 'young' and a similarity of sense between 'rudimentes' and 'children.'

240.26 to fremd] too foreign ('Fremd' a 1b only citation)

240.30 in their effectual nature] in the way they achieve their ends (a 2 obs and see 'Effective' A 2b obs)

240.35–6 similitudinarie] expressing similitude or comparison (a c first citation). The point is that it is easier to see the relationship between the physical and the mental when one is working with numbers than when one is working with words. Mathematics has greater actuality.

241.1 compare the common weale to a ship] A common similitude, from Plato *Statesman* 302A and *Laws* 7.803A–B; cf Erasmus *De copia* in LB 1:103ff trans CWE 24:641–2, passage beginning 'What a wealth of parallels can be derived from ships and sailing!'

241.2 under saile] ie, under way. Mulcaster has taken a figurative sense from his image, and used it to describe how his image works.

241.13 mockmathematicalles] ie, those who mock mathematicians (see 237.17 'to mocke at mathematicall heades' and 'Mathematical' sb B 3 obs)

241.14 hide their heades] shelter themselves ('Hide' v[1] 1 d; also 'hide in shame')

241.20 *Divinitie, Lawe, Physick*] These higher faculties at Oxford and Cambridge were not administered through the colleges, but through the universities proper. There were no special colleges for divinity, law, or medicine, though a college was proposed for legal studies (see 245.21 note), and certain colleges tended to welcome lawyers (All Souls, Oxford) or physicians (Gonville and Caius, Cambridge). General background on the professional faculties is found in Curtis *Oxford and Cambridge* 149–64.

241.23 absolutenesse] perfection, perfected state (sb 1 obs)

241.24 Galene] *Γαληνοῦ πρὸς Θρασύβουλον περὶ ἀρίστης αἱρέσεως* (Galen's Book to Thrasybulus on the Best Sect) in Kühn ed 1:106–223. Referred to in *De sanitate tuenda* 1.4 trans Green 12). See 133.24 note.

241.25 tarie time] ie, were a clergyman to delay, to spend extra time to master the sciences would be to his credit. Perhaps there is an echo of Tilley T323 'Time and tide tarries for no man.'

241.26–7 discretion the daughter of time] A modified proverb; cf Tilley T580 'Truth is time's daughter' (and see 257.12 and note).

241.27–8 conusance] cognizance, emblematic motto (sb obs 3)

241.33 digesting time] Proverbial?; cf Tilley T326 'Time devours all things.'

241.37–8 where is *Logicke* and *Rethoricke*] Logic and rhetoric, the staple subjects of the undergraduate curriculum of the Elizabethan university, have been left out of Mulcaster's scheme. Here he suggests somewhat elliptically that they will be studied in the colleges of mathematics and philosophy.

242.3 *Rhetoricke*] The following sentence is itself a small rhetorical tour de force, with its strongly balanced construction: 'puritie without passion'/'perswasion with passion,' 'writer'/'speaker,' 'any kinde'/'all kindes,' and with the complicated reversal at the end. The gist of the sentence is rather simple: rhetoric may be used for different emotional effects by writers and speakers.

242.8 receites] places for storage ('Receipt' sb 12 obs)

242.10–11 wordes be names of thinges applyed and given according to their properties] Cf *Elementarie* sig X4v: 'words be voluntarie, and appointed upon cause.'

242.22 gaing] making gay ('Gay' v obs; see 172.25)

242.29 *Plato*] *Republic* 7.522–32, where mathematics is discussed as part of the *προπαιδεία* or 'foretraine.'

242.33 *Josephus*] *Jewish Antiquities* 18.259: 'Philo ... a man held in the highest honour ... and no novice in philosophy' led a delegation to Gaius in Rome, in the winter of AD 38–9 or 39–40 (ed Feldman 9:153 note b).

242.36 *Platoes προπαιδεία*] See above, line 29 note.

242.37 *Philoes προπαίδευμα*] Philo's *Περὶ τῆς εἰς τὰ προπαιδεύματα συνόδου*, *On Mating with the Preliminary Studies* in *Works* 4, is an elaborate allegorization of the biblical story of Genesis 16.1–6, in which Hagar is seen as school-learning with which one must spend many years before coming to Sarah, or true wisdom (usually called *philosophia* in the text, eg at 78–80 or 139ff). Though Moses' learning and interest in numbers are mentioned (at 132 and 89 respectively), there is nothing in the work about his having learned mathematics from the Egyptians; the subject is treated in Philo's *Moses* 1:21–3 in *Works* 6.

243.1 or] ere, before ('Or' adv[1] C 1b)

243.11 *Aristotles* first booke] The following passage is a brief argument that a background in mathematics may assist one to understand the logic of Aristotle. As Mulcaster says, he uses the example of Aristotle because 'our studentes be best acquainted with him.' The study of Aristotle was basic to the curriculum in both universities, though the political and ethical works were perhaps more popular in the 1570s and 1580s than the works in logic and metaphysics (Curtis *Oxford and Cambridge* 119). Nevertheless, scholars would be exposed to all aspects of 'the philosopher's' works. See also next note.

243.16 these helpes] On the extensive use of Aristotle commentaries in the Tudor universities, see McConica 'Humanism and Aristotle in Tudor Oxford.' In 1589 Nashe vigorously condemned the use of helps: 'those yeares which should bee imployed in *Aristotle* are expired in Epitomies' (Preface to Greene's *Menaphon* in Nashe *Works* ed McKerrow 3:318). See also Curtis *Oxford and Cambridge* 100.

243.16 *Bravardine*] Thomas Bradwardine (d 1349), archbishop of Canterbury and Oxford philosopher, wrote a number of works on mathematics including *De arithmetica speculativa*, *De arithmetica practiva*, and *De geometria speculativa*. The last of these, to which Mulcaster probably refers, was published in Paris by Jean Petit in 1511 as *Geometria speculatiua Thomae Brauardini recolligens omnes conclusiones geometricas studentibus artium & philosophiae Aristotelis valde necessarias simul cum quodam tractatu de quadratura circuli nouiter edito* (Speculative geometry of Thomas Bradwardine gathering together all conclusions in geometry most necessary for students of arts and Aristotelian philosophy, along with a certain newly edited tract on the squaring of the circle). The tract is almost exclusively an analysis of the theorems of Euclidean geometry; its application to a study of Aristotle would be apparent only to the philosophically sophisticated. It is not clear, from what he says here, whether Mulcaster possessed that sophistication, indeed whether he had himself actually used the work or merely seen a reference to it or heard about it second-hand. Bradwardine had of course an outstanding reputation as a mathematician and philosopher, but this work is not usually considered part of his commentary work. See Emden *A Biographical Register ... to ... 1500* 1:244–6; Lohr 'Medieval Latin Aristotle Commentaries Authors: Robertus–Wilgelmus' 172–3.

243.31 *Socrates ... Plato*] See above, 242.29 note.

243.32 *Aristippus* after his shipwrake] Described in Vitruvius 6.Pr.

243.37 *Proclus* his foure books upon *Euclides* first] Proclus' *Commentary on the First Book of Euclid's Elements* appeared in an edition prepared by Simon Grynaeus from a single Greek manuscript (Basel 1533), but was entirely re-edited by Francesco Barozzi, who used five additional manuscripts in the preparation of his translation, *Procli Diadochi Lycii philosophi platonici ac mathematici probatissimi in primum Euclidis Elementorum librum commentariorum ... libri IIII. a Francisco Barocio patritio Veneto ... editi* (Padua: G. Perchacinus 1560). Barozzi's Greek text was never printed, but his interpretations of certain passages are still accepted by modern scholars (according to Morrow, translator of Proclus *A Commentary on Euclid's Elements* xliv). Mulcaster's form of the name '*Io. Barocius*' (for Franciscus) shows a slight carelessness. In book 1 (Barozzi's edition) Proclus outlines the arguments for and against the study of mathematics; in book 2, i–xi, he does the same for geometry.

244.12 *Virgile*] the prophecy of Anchises in *Aeneid* 6.851–3

tu regere imperio populos, Romane, memento
(hae tibi erunt artes) pacique imponere morem,
parcere subiectis et debellare superbos.

(Remember thou, O Roman, to rule the nations with thy sway – these shall be thine arts – to crown Peace with Law, to spare the humbled, and to tame in war the proud.)

244.17 *Gallus, & Figulus*] Gaius Sulpicius Gallus is mentioned in Quintilian (1.10.47) and Pliny (*Historia naturalis* 2.9.53) for a lecture on eclipses he gave to the Roman army in 168 BC. In Pliny (2.19.83) his views on astronomy are compared with those of Pythagoras. Publius Nigidius Figulus (d 45 BC) was a contemporary of Varro with whom Aulus Gellius liked to compare him as a scholar and encyclopedist (*Noctes Atticae* 19.14; and, for several fragmentary observations on astronomy, 3.10.2 and 14.1.11). Only fragments of the work of Gallus and Figulus survive, and Mulcaster's knowledge of their names would have impressed even a relatively well read classicist.

244.18 *Julius Firmicus*] Julius Firmicus Maternus (fl AD 334–7) was the author of an astrological treatise, *Matheseos libri VIII*, which appeared in editions in the late fifteenth and early sixteenth centuries (listed in edition of Kroll and Skutsch [1913] 2:xxviiiff).

244.19 *Vitruvius*] Mulcaster refers to books 9 and 10 of the *De architectura* of Vitruvius; the two books deal with the measurement of time and with mechanical contrivances respectively, and contain a considerable number of observations on practical mathematics (see also 243.32).

244.20 *Archimedes*] Archimedes' inventions prevented Marcus Claudius Marcellus' easy capture of Syracuse (212 BC). When Marcellus was in the end victorious, one of his soldiers unknowingly killed Archimedes, who was drawing geometrical figures in the dust. Marcellus was saddened by his death, and provided for his burial. The story is mentioned by Proclus (see 243.37 note) in his *Commentary* 1.13 (41), and is told in full by Livy 24.34 and 25.31.

244.23 *Demetrius*] Demetrius I of Macedonia, surnamed *poliorketes* or 'taker of cities,' had a great respect for the art of Protogenes the painter, whom he protected during the siege of Rhodes (Pliny *Historia naturalis* 35.36.104, and see also Plutarch 'Demetrius' 22 in *Lives* 898).

244.25 overlaid] supplemented or added to significantly ('Overlay' v 2–3 means 'deck all over' or 'cover,' in both senses, excessively)

244.26 *Dionysius* of *Halycarnassus*, and *Strabo*] Dionysius of Halicarnassus (in south-west Asia Minor) was a historian and rhetorician who settled in Rome towards the end of the first century BC. Strabo the geographer, who wrote about the same time, had come to Rome from Amaseia (in Pontus, northern Asia Minor). Dionysius' *Roman Antiquities* first appeared in print in the late fifteenth century, and was re-edited several times in the sixteenth. Strabo's *Geography* also went through several editions in the early and mid sixteenth century.

244.31 borowed the matter of other nations] The Egyptian origins of geometry are stressed by Proclus *Commentary* 2.4 (65).

244.36–7 morall and politike first] Senior grammar school students would be introduced to moral and political philosophy through their reading of Cicero (often *De officiis*) and the historians (Sallust and Caesar were popular); issues in both would be debated in short classroom disputations (see Baldwin *William Shakspere's Small Latine*, especially 2:578–616).

244.37 reason against *Aristotles* conclusion] Modern punctuation would require a comma after 'reason.' Aristotle *Nicomachean Ethics* 1.2 (1095a), argues that youngsters should be kept away from moral philosophy, the study of which should be postponed until later years.

245.2 consequence] logical order (sb 3b)

245.7–8 *Logicke*, and *Rhetoricke*] Cf above, 241.37–8 and following.

245.11 *Pythagoras*] Diogenes Laertius *Lives* 8.10 tells how 'For five whole years [the disciples of Pythagoras] had to keep silence, merely listening to his discourses without seeing him [ie, he lectured at night], until they passed an examination.' The silence of Pythagoras' pupils was commonly referred to in Renaissance literature; there is for instance 'Pithagoras the silencer' in Nashe (*Works* ed McKerrow 3:274).

245.12 *Socrates*] In *Republic* 7.527B and 533B–C, Socrates stresses the importance of geometry in philosophical inquiry.

245.13 ridge] upper part ('Ridge' sb[1] 2; cf 161.5 where it means 'backbone')

245.16–17 *Plato* the example to *Aristotles* preceptes] Although Plato taught Aristotle, he is here made ironically to serve as an example of Aristotle's precepts on the need for training in mathematics and logic for moral philosophy.

245.21 As for the *Lawe*] Studies in common law (*'English & French'*) were flourishing at the Inns of Court, but studies in canon law ('Romish ecclesiasticall') and civil law ('Romish Imperiall') had undergone a serious decline during the century. Canon law studies had been formally abolished from the universities in 1535, but by the Visitation Articles of 1549 were re-established as part of civil law at Oxford. During the early part of Edward's reign there was talk of refounding Clare College as a college of civil law, but it came to nothing, and by the mid-1550s Nicholas Carr wrote 'The civil law is despised and contemned, and even where the study still survives it is pursued for the most part in a corrupt fashion' (cited in Mullinger *University of Cambridge* 2:138). Nevertheless, there was a definite need for the training of civilians (who worked in the various ecclesiastical courts), and with the appointment of Alberico Gentile to the Regius Professorship at Oxford, the subject underwent a small rebirth. (Mallet *History* 2:83 and 117; Mullinger *University of Cambridge* 2:133–8 and 423–5; Curtis *Oxford and Cambridge* 155–61, who describes the course at both universities and shows why civil lawyers continued to be needed; and Prest *The Inns of Court* 115–73.)

245.33–4 such as shall afterward passe to teach in schooles] In late sixteenth-century England, teachers learned their profession by doing it, usually starting during their own grammar school days when, as senior students, they would be called upon to instruct the younger boys. Godshouse (founded 1439) was a late medieval attempt to train grammarians at Cambridge, but the college was refounded in 1506 as Christ's College, and the original purpose laid aside. The last degree in grammar was given at Oxford in 1568 (Mallet *History* 2:132 note 3). During the century there were a few observations on the need for the better training of teachers, but no school or institute as such was founded until the beginning of the nineteenth century. See Charlton 'The Teaching Profession in Sixteenth- and Seventeenth-Century England' 46–7.

246.13–14 If the chancell have a minister, the belfry hath a maister] ie, if an organization has someone in charge of its main purpose, then there will be a ruling hand on its minor (and possibly more prominent or noisy) subsidiary functions. Not in Tilley or *ODEP*.

246.18 his] ie, his own children

246.22 *Xenophon*] *Cyropaedia* 1.2.5

247.4–5 thinges grow by degrees, and buildinges by patches] Not in Tilley or *ODEP*.

247.6 commencementes, and publike actes] ie, in the public ceremonies of the universities, the wisdom of the founders would be celebrated

247.15 some rocke of marble] Proverbial?; cf Tilley R151 'As fixed as a rock.'

247.16 make no bones] Proverbial; Tilley B527 'He made no bones of it.'

247.19 reformation] Various senses: 'rebuilding,' 'social change,' 'religious movement of protestantism' ('Reformation' 2 obs, 3, 3b; all three senses found in usage of the period)

247.29 greeke poet] Homer *Odyssey* 17.218; the phrase 'like will to like' was proverbial in English from Chaucer onwards (*ODEP* and Tilley L286; see also Erasmus *Adagia* in LB 2:78D and 79E trans CWE 31:165–8 ['simile gaudet simili']).

247.34 for a better living will chaung his colledge] Perhaps here is a reason for Mulcaster's switch from King's to Peterhouse during his undergraduate years at Cambridge.

247.37 livings in colledges be now to to leane] University was expensive in the early 1580s. George Peele, who went to Christ Church, Oxford, during the 1570s, is estimated (perhaps somewhat generously) to have spent a total of £90 during his seven years (Horne *The Life and Minor Works of George Peele* 34). Thus, a scholarship like that left by Archdeacon Watts of £5 per annum for a promising boy of Merchant Taylors' would have covered not quite all the costs of a modest undergraduate career (H.B. Wilson *History* 30–2).

Christopher Marlowe, who was at Corpus Christi during the early 1580s, received a shilling a week in term, from a scholarship established in 1575 by Archbishop Parker at £3 6s 8d per student per year; as Marlowe's biographer points out, the range of costs and support was enormous; Bakeless *The Tragicall History of Christopher Marlowe* 1:49–54 and 72–5. See also Mullinger *The University of Cambridge* 2:396ff.

247.38 fly ear they be well feathered] Proverbial; Tilley F164 'He would fain fly but he wants feathers.'

248.8 fourme] order ('Form' sb 8 first citation 1595, with second sense of 'course of exercises or lectures in the university' sb 11c obs; there is a possible third sense of 'reform,' an aphaeresis)

248.11 meanie] group, assembly ('Meinie' 3 obs)

248.13 *Iohannes Picus*] Pico's defence of nine hundred theses had a fabulous ring to it; it is also referred to by Dee, Preface to Euclid, *Elementes* trans Billingsley sig *1r. Giovanni Pico della Mirandola (1463–94) was the great Neoplatonist of fifteenth-century Florence. His theses were published but were never defended, as they were subject to severe papal censure; they have been edited in a modern edition by Bohdan Kieszkowski as *Conclusiones sive theses DCCCC* (1973). For specifically English background, see Parks 'Pico della Mirandola in Tudor Translation' and Weiss 'Pico e l'Inghilterra.'

248.16 *elemosinarie*] ('Eleemosynary' A a 2 first citation 1654)

248.17 respectes] ie, deferential regards for those who, in a system of private charity, are supplying the funds (sb 17a obs first citation 1612)

248.21 bowes] Not clear; the sense permits either 'bows' (ie, of ships being constructed with the support of 'props' and 'stocke') or 'boughs' (as of the tree of learning which 'grows up' supported by 'props' in one case, or supported by its own 'stalk,' or trunk, in the other). Because of the many images of growing, planting, etc, throughout, the second interpretation may be dominant.

248.35–7 *Plato* to the *Academikes* ... *Aristippus* to the *Anicerian* and *Cyrenaike*] For a similar list of the schools of ethical philosophy and their founders, cf Diogenes Laertius *Lives* 1.19. The Annicerian school of philosophy is a branch of the Cyrenaic school of Aristippus, and was founded by Annicerus; Diogenes Laertius 2.85 and 96–7.

249.1–2 *Plato* taught above fiftie yeares] Diogenes Laertius *Lives* 3.6–7. Speusippus was Plato's nephew who succeeded him as head of the Academy (ibid 4.1–5); there is no mention in Diogenes Laertius of Speusippus' serving as his uncle's deputy during the voyage to Egypt, made very early in Plato's career (and there is nothing on this anecdote in Riginos *Platonica*).

249.8 what counsellour] Tilley C703 'He that is his own counselor knows nothing sure but what he has laid out'

249.9 first impression] Cf Tilley I45 'The first impression is hard to cancel.'

249.13 digested] assimilated mentally, classified and reflected upon ('Digest' v 7 and 2–3; there is a sense here of 'made digest of')

249.25 beaten his owne braines] Proverbial; Tilley B602 'To beat one's brains.'

250.4 lease] lose (ie, are deprived of) ('Lease' v[1] obs a 1, in much the same sense as throughout, though here with a confusing play on 'to lease' as 'to rent')

250.4–5 put to pensions] ie, forced to pay fees (a 'pensioner' at Cambridge had no support from his college)

250.12 holpen] helped ('Help' v A 2; this form of the past participle was used into the nineteenth century)

250.19 begune] Mulcaster's spelling in *Elementarie* sig Y4r is 'begon,' and it is unclear why here the compositor would have favoured 'begune' (with contracted 'n') when he could just as easily have spelled 'begun' without the 'e.'

250.31 hostelles] By suggesting that readers set up their 'hostelles' or halls, Mulcaster is recommending a return to the medieval university in which teachers competed for pupils whom they trained for the university examinations. 'A hall came into being when a master leased a building, usually on annual terms, from a townsman, an ecclesiastical corporation, or even a college, and then rented rooms to scholars over whom he may have exercised some measure of discipline' (Curtis *Oxford and Cambridge* 39). There were still a few hostels or halls in the late sixteenth century, but they were now run like colleges, though without formal foundation (ibid 36; see also McConica 'The Rise of the Undergraduate College' in McConica ed *The Collegiate University* 51ff). The kind of extra-statutory instruction Mulcaster mentions here would be familiar to those readers who knew something of university life; teachers of foreign languages and other subjects ran small schools or tutoring services in both Oxford and Cambridge (Curtis 137ff).

251.24 scrape all defences] gather together all arguments (in favour of their point of view) ('Scrape' v 5)

251.36–7 It is no reason, where see ye the like? but it is a great reason, the like is worth seeing] ie, just because one may ask 'Where see ye the like?' is no reason to doubt the value of this educational program. But because this program is worth seeing, there is great reason to strive for it.

252.3–4 It is not my complaint, though I joyne with the complainantes.] ie, though I am not the originator of such a view, I agree with the originators (cf 247.24 'it is no new device, nor mine')

252.7 *Moises*] See above, 242.37ff and note. The spelling is a common variant in English writers.

252.15 the parentes of his profession] Mulcaster has already referred above (241.24ff) to the broad education expected of doctors by Galen.

252.16 under meanes] supporting and basic methods (to the profession) ('Under' may mean also 'inferior, unworthy of consideration' if the sentence reads 'parentes ... durst not ... make them under meanes'; but it seems more likely that the sentence reads 'parentes ... make them under meanes')

252.18 raigne] rein ('gave ignoraunce the raigne' means 'let ignorance have her own way,' as in 'Rein' sb[1] 2b and Tilley B671 'To give one the bridle (reins)'; a further sense is of course 'reign')

252.20–1 mother ... matter] With a pun on Latin *mater* (mother).

252.39 though serving well for certaine by way of restraint] ie, though they do a good job when they are restrained to a specific or 'certain' situation in which their talents are best used

253.8 *posting hast*] In *A Shorte Introduction of Grammar* (1549) reference is also made in the preface 'To the Reader' to 'this postynge haste,' which 'overthroweth and hurteth a greate sorte of wyttes, and casteth them into an amasednesse' (sig A2v). For the sense of 'posting' as 'fast riding' see 103.25 and note; also cf .19.5.

253.11 preasing] pressing (see 82.12 and note)

253.12 ripe] ie, ripen

253.13 before it is greene, after it is rotten] Tilley R133 'Soon ripe soon rotten.' 'After' here means 'afterwards.'

253.19 longing wymen] Pregnant women were thought to be addicted to unripe fruit; in Webster's *The Duchess of Malfi*, Bosola, to test her pregnancy, feeds the Duchess green apricots, 'The first our Spring yeelds,' and comments 'how greedily she eats them!' (2.1.72–3 and 162 in *Complete Works* vol 2).

253.27 consequence] sequence, course (of studies) (sb 2b obs first citation 1597)

253.32 captaine] leading student (sb 10 first citation 1706; see introduction, lxiii, for another sixteenth-century example) as well as figurative sense of 'military leader' (sb 3–4)

254.3 It is a world to see] it is a great thing, a marvel, to see ('World' sb 19c obs; Tilley w878 'It is a world to see')

254.4 fondnes] want of judgment (sb 1)

254.21 peart] lively, receptive (a 6)

254.22 perteling] lively and receptive child (sb obs 1 defines as 'pert or sharp child')

254.24–5 blynde is affection] Proverbial?; Tilley A48 'Affection is blind reason' and also *ODEP* under 'Affection'; neither has sixteenth-century citations (cf also Tilley L506 'Love is blind' and L517 'Love is without reason'; there may be here an echo of S206 'Who so blind as he that will not see?')

254.26–7 the misliker] ie, the master who understands the child's inherent weakness, and who therefore mislikes the parent's blindness

254.27 his] ie, the parent's

254.31 to blame the watchman] Not in Tilley or *ODEP*.

254.35–6 one billow driveth on an other] Cf Tilley M1004 'Mischiefs, like waves, never come alone.'

254.37 trowle] spin like a top (see 87.27)

255.11 *Compendium*] abridgment, epitome (of grammar studies in the language) (sb 1 cites only this passage, and defines as 'A short cut; "the near way"'; perhaps sense 2, given here, is closer to Mulcaster's meaning)

255.14 salve] cure (v^1 2 obs in fig sense)

255.14–15 affection overrules all reason] Cf Tilley L517 'Love is without reason' and see 254.24–5 note above.

255.15 straungenesse] coolness, uncomplying attitude ('Strangeness' 2 obs)

255.16 removing] ie, of the student from the grammar school to the university

255.17 marres the whole market] Proverb; see 143.33 and 37 and notes.

255.17 store] abundance (sb^1 4 obs; Tilley S903 'Store is no sore')

255.23 blase ... it] trumpet it abroad, make it known publicly ('Blaze' v^2 2)

255.31 prentice] The apprentice usually finished his term of service at twenty-four years of age (according to 5 Elizabeth I c 4 sections 19 and 24, as cited by Curtis 'Education and Apprenticeship' 67; for text see Prothero *Select Statutes* 45–54).

255.33 reft] deprived (usually by theft) ('Reave' v^1 2 obs)

255.38 *stampe*] official mark certifying the quality or genuineness of goods (sb^3 12a); young men with substance will survive close scrutiny as to their inner worth

256.5 fortuneth] happens (v 3b)

256.6 haste so with so much waste] Proverbial; Tilley H189 'Haste makes waste.'

256.10 countenaunce] demeanour (of dignity) (sb 1 obs)

256.15 *Vives*] Juan Luis Vives (1492–1540) was one of the great humanist scholars of his day. He was the author of textbooks and works on education, philosophy and theology. Though Spanish, he spent much time in England in the retinue of Katherine of Aragon. One of Vives' most popular works was the *Linguae Latinae exercitatio*, a series of dialogues for schoolboys; in one passage he refers to his gout:

> Magister: Sed quid agit Vives noster?
> Nepotulus: Dicunt eum agere athletam, non tamen athletice.
> Magister: Quid isthuc rei est?
> Nepotulus: Quia luctatur semper, sed parum fortiter.
> Magister: Cum quo?
> Nepotulus: Cum suo morbo articulari.
> Magister: O luctatorem dolosum, qui primum omnium invadit pedes!
> Hipodidascalus: Immo lictorem saevum, qui totum corpus constringit.
> (*Opera* [1782] 1:299)

(M: But what is *our Vives* doing? N: They say he is training as an athlete, not yet by athletics. M: What is the meaning of that? N: He is always wrestling, but not bravely enough. M: With whom? N: With his gout. M: O mournful wrestler, which first of all attacks the feet. H. Nay, rather cruel victor which fetters the whole body [trans Watson 34].)

On Vives' health, see Noreña *Juan Luis Vives* 118–20. Vives' dialogues would have been known to many Elizabethan readers who would have met the work at school (Baldwin *William Shakspere's Small Latine* 1:497 and 724ff); from the off-hand nature of the reference here, it would seem very possible that Mulcaster taught Vives' dialogues at Merchant Taylors' School. Vives' 'twentie bookes of disciplines' are the famous *De disciplinis*, first published in Bruges in 1531, a work of seven books 'De causis corruptarum artium,' (on the causes of the corruption of the arts), five 'De tradendis disciplinis' (on the transmission of the arts), and eight 'De artibus' (on the arts, in this case, mostly on questions of philosophy); for background see Vives *On Education* trans Watson, and Sinz 'The Elaboration of Vives's Treatises on the Arts.'

256.22 cankar] Cf Tilley C56 'The canker soonest eats the fairest rose.'

256.26 replying past cure] ie, the pupil's answers seem to be beyond correction

256.26 cannot discern colours] ie, cannot see things as they are

256.29 exhibition] For this and 'exhibitours,' line 31, see 229.5.

256.35 booted] ie, dressed for his 'journey' to the university. The master won't know if the pupil is ready to go until he's dressed, and then it is too late to prevent him from going (cf Tilley B538 'They that are booted are not always ready'). There is a suggestion in Peacham *Compleat Gentleman* (1622) that one rides to the university (38), and on arrival – 'even with the pulling off your Boots' (39) – one must first look to the choice of one's friends.

257.8 till the blow be given] ie, until the time comes

257.12 *mother* to truth] Cf Tilley T329a 'Time is the father of truth and experience is the mother of things,' and see 241.27 note.

257.25–7 appoint ... appointed ... appointed] set in order by law ... fitted out or equipped ... fitted out or equipped ('Appoint' v 10; 'Appointed' ppl a 3)

257.29 stiles] distinguishing or qualifying titles ('Style' sb 18b)

257.32–3 for their most needfull number] ie, the most necessary number of 'particulars,' or little details of fact and technique, may be grasped by the student in the time normally allotted. To expect him to learn everything is, of course, impossible, even though he may encounter many of these 'endlesse' particulars in the disorganized jumble that experience sets before him. The important thing is that the students have 'method and ground,' or an orderly technique for understanding experience.

258.1 roundly] fluently and rapidly (adv 6–7)

258.4 bragge] show, display (sb^1 3 obs)

258.5–6 voluntarie] short musical piece, perhaps extempore (C sb 2b, a common present-day sense)

258.7 the second maister] the usher or assistant master in charge of the elementary pupils

258.24 bounder] limit, boundary (sb 4 arch)

259.3 A Great learned man] Philipp Melanchthon (1497–1560), the important humanist reformer of early sixteenth-century Germany. His 'De miseriis paedagogorum oratio' written about 1533 is a short declamation (not a 'booke') on problems of teachers and the need for good masters in the schools. Mulcaster shows no familiarity with the work beyond the title, though the text was certainly available; Gabriel Harvey owned a copy of Melanchthon's *Selectarum declamationum ... tomus primus* (Strasbourg 1564; see Stern *Gabriel Harvey* 227); the 'Oratio' is on 522–69 of that edition. A modern text is Melanchthon *Werke* ed Stupperich 3:70–81. Melanchthon was extremely influential as an educator and writer of textbooks; see Manschreck *Melanchthon: The Quiet Reformer* 131–57.

259.6–7 but when any kinde of life be it high, be it low, is not troubled with his proportion to our portion, we will yield to misery] ie, we teachers will admit to having greater misery than other professions only when any other kind of life of whatever degree is not troubled in the same way that teachers' lives (as described by Melanchthon) are troubled. In other words, Melanchthon has spoken truly of the miseries of schoolmasters, but he could have added that all professions have their miseries, and schoolmasters are no different from anyone else.

259.29 *uniformitie*] T.W. Baldwin, in a chapter entitled 'The Movement toward Authorized Uniformity' (*William Shakspere's Small Latine* 1:164–84), shows how standardization had been achieved in the early forms of grammar in instruction by the late 1540s. Yet, despite what he says elsewhere ('the sixteenth century grammar school curriculum was highly organized and had by the middle of the century been standardized into essential uniformity' 1:435), there was not all that much consistency in the quality of teaching or even in the texts used in the senior forms at many schools. Mulcaster's attack on the inconsistencies of the grammar schools seems therefore to be justified. But few readers then or now would agree that 'there is but one right waye' in teaching, or would like to see 'all the youth of this whole Realme' as though 'brought up in one schoole, and under one maister'; Mulcaster seems to have forgotten his earlier words on 'mediocritie, which furnisheth out this world, and ... excellencie, which is fashioned for an other' (28.29–31).

An attempt was made by the Privy Council to provide greater uniformity in the curriculum of grammar schools; in 1582 it prescribed the use of Christopher Ocland's versified history of England, *Anglorum praelia*, which history, according to the title page of the book 'Nobilissimi Regiae Maiestatis consilarij in omnibus huius regni Scholis praelegenda pueris praescripserunt' (the counsellors of the Queen's noble majesty, ie, privy councillors, have commanded to be read by youths in all the schools of this kingdom). Considering his enthusiasm for the Queen and for state-directed education, it comes as no surprise to find that Mulcaster wrote a dedicatory poem to the second part of this work, *Εἰρηναρχία sive Elizabetha* sig $3r. See Simon *Education and Society* 324.

260.4 one right waye] Cf Tilley W148 'There is no one way but one' (where 'way' means 'method' or 'fashion').

260.13 *aphorisme*] received truth (sb 2 first citation 1590)

260.15 hinderance] injury, hurt (sb 1 obs)

260.28 to his hand] ie, that he might consult it

260.32 publish] bring to public notice (v 3b obs)

261.15 oddes ... odde] difference ... unequal ('Odds' sb 2; 'Odd' a 7 obs)

261.23–5 with fethers ... like friends] Perhaps a play on Tilley B393 'Birds of a feather will flock together'; one of many images of birds and flying.

261.25–6 pay their price with their pastime, and mend their faire with their praye] ie, with both their labour and the results of their labour, they redeem the expense of their cost to those hiring them (and add to their diet with the things they catch) ('Mend' v 4)

261.28 swimme] glide (v 5)

262.8 rowling] wandering, travelling ('Roll' v^2 12a; 'rowling residence' is a paradoxical phrase for the state of the teacher who never stays for long in one place). For some background on the problem of teachers never staying long in one place, and dropping out of the profession as soon as a living was obtained, see introduction, xxiii–xxxiv.

262.9 fretished] chilled (v^1; see 59.7)

262.10 *swallow*] Tilley S1025 'One swallow makes not summer'; the reference to 'that foolish fellow,' who steps out too early to follow the early swallow, is not explained in Tilley or in Erasmus *Adagia* in LB 2:299C–F trans CWE 32:124 'Una hirundo non facit ver.'

262.28 incontinently] immediately (adv^2 arch)

263.1 appointment] ordinance or decree of what is to be done (sb 6)

263.14 stoppes] obstacles (sb^2 7 obs; with an additional musical sense)

263.20 beyond all crie] to a certainty (see 181.29–30 note)

263.29–30 set backward] made to repeat a year ('Set' v 141 'set back' does not give this meaning)

264.18 *sparing* of *expenses*] On the cost of books, Spoudeus in Brinsley's *Ludus Literarius* comments: 'But it is a great charge to poore men, to provide so many bookes as may seeme necessary' (312). If textbooks cost on the average

6d to a shilling each (Brown *Elizabethan Schooldays* 52; books usually sold for 1/2 d a sheet unbound according to Johnson 'Notes on English Retail Book-Prices' 89), boys in the senior forms of many schools would have had to pay as much as 10s for new books, a large sum when one considers that their masters' annual salary was only 20 times that amount. Of course, books were traded, handed on, or sold second-hand, so many boys would have paid much less. Besides their own texts, boys were often required to contribute to the school library; the boys of St Paul's (technically speaking a 'free school') were made to pay a shilling each in 1582–3, and the resulting total ('about £9') amounted to less than a third of what was spent that year on dictionaries and other classroom helps (Baldwin *William Shakspere's Small Latine* 1:422–3).

A survey of the vast Elizabethan textbook business is given by Baldwin (*William Shakspere's Small Latine* 1:494–531; see also Bennett *English Books and Readers 1558 to 1603* 167–79), but he does not say much about books imported from abroad, of which there must have been a huge number (Simon *Education and Society* 316). Baldwin mentions no anthologies of the kind recommended by Mulcaster (especially at 265.2ff), though there were certainly many collections of *sententiae, parabolae,* and the like, and a number of books containing selected passages from an individual author, such as Cordier's (englished) construe of Cicero's letters called *Principé Latina* (1575).

Textbook publishing was a monopoly controlled by a few printers, and one of the chief profiteers was Vautrollier, Mulcaster's printer – an irony, seeing that Mulcaster was opposed to the practices of textbook publishers in particular and monopolists in general.

264.28 an overflush of bookes] The number of books produced annually grew rapidly during the 1570s and 1580s; according to the indexes in volume 3 of the revised *STC*, the number of imprints in the year 1560 was 172; in 1570, 264; in 1580, 298; and in 1590, 353.

264.29 growes chargeable to] becomes increasingly the responsibility or the fault of ('Chargeable' a 5 obs; there seems to be double sense here in that the printers are 'responsible' for the 'overflush of bookes' and that they 'charge' more money for them, as well as the more obvious sense that they bear greater charges for the books that are unsold)

264.30 *Juvenall*] Probably referring to Satire 1.17–18: 'stulta est clementia, cum tot ubique / vatibus occurras, periturae parcere chartae' (it is a foolish clemency when you jostle against poets at every corner, to spare paper that will be wasted anyhow) and the rest of the poem, which attacks various contemporary writers and literary fashions.

264.31 he is marde that comes lag] ie, he who comes last is prevented (from writing by the overflush of books) ('Mar' v 1 obs; 'Lag' sb[1] or a 1)

264.31–2 some few leaves be occupied] This supports the contention by Bolgar

'Classical Reading' that the listing of an author or text in Elizabethan school statutes rarely meant reading the author completely.

264.35 those of the meaner sort, whose children maintain schooles most] That children who attended schools were not by and large from wealthy or privileged families is certainly true from Mulcaster's experience. See introduction, lxv–lxvi and notes, for a breakdown of the social background of his students.

265.23–4 They that assigne *grammer* maisters wherein to travell] Most school statutes that instruct the master to teach particular authors do not go on to specify works, so that a master of a senior form could select his material from (for instance) anywhere in the works of Ovid, Horace, Virgil, and Persius for poetry and Caesar, Sallust, and Valerius Maximus for history, not to mention a wide choice of books for oratory and 'humanitie' (if one takes the statutes of Norwich, 1566, as being fairly typical; see Baldwin *William Shakspere's Small Latine* 1:415–17). In other words, the range of selection was vast, and it seems unlikely that a boy would finish much more than a single work, or even one book of a work, unless he read ahead on his own (see Bolgar 'Classical Reading in Renaissance Schools'). Mulcaster's advice that anthologies of important passages be used instead of collected texts seems remarkably sensible.

From what he says in the following passage, Mulcaster seems to have a low opinion of historians and poets, except in so far as they supply matter or art to the orator. His idea of history is certainly that of a rhetorician, although his understanding of the concept of 'circumstances' gives his historical asides and interpretations a curiously modern air; some of the changes in historical writing of the time, especially its increasing 'sense of anachronism,' are discussed in Ferguson 'Circumstances and the Sense of History in Tudor England,' which unfortunately does not comment on the rhetorical nature of the term 'circumstances.' Mulcaster's idea of poetry is that it is a form of oratory; his own poetry was always occasional and usually epideictic.

265.31 vaines] dispositions ('Vein' sb 14; see also 11 with specific literary sense)

265.34 actes and monumentes] A play on the title of John Foxe's *Actes and Monuments* (first published London: John Day 1563, as a translation of the author's *Rerum in ecclesia gestarum ... digesti ... commentarii* which first came out in Strasbourg in 1564). Also known as Foxe's *Book of Martyrs,* this would have been the work of 'history' best known to Mulcaster's English readers. Mulcaster taught Foxe's son Samuel at Merchant Taylors'.

265.38 list] inclination (sb[4] 2; the words 'list' and 'leisure' were often found together)

265.39 after meates] of after eating ('Meat' sb 4b)

268.8 a fabulous veele] A common way of talking about the allegorical function of poetry. Cf Sir John Harington: 'the men of greatest learning and highest within the auncient times did of purpose conceale these deepe mysteries of learning, and, as it were, cover them with the vaile of fables and verse for sundrie causes' (Preface to his translation of Ariosto, *Orlando furioso* [1591] in G. Gregory Smith ed *Elizabethan Critical Essays* 2:203). Also, Sir Philip Sidney: 'there are many mysteries contained in Poetry, which of purpose were written darkly, lest by profane wits it should be abused' (*Apology* ed Shepherd 142 with a note on the topos by the editor).

266.14 *Platoes* whole penning] Plato, who forbade the study of poetry in his ideal commonwealth, is here used to exemplify the poet of eloquence. This ironic reversal was used also by other Elizabethan authors, most notably Sidney, who said of Plato that 'of all philosophers he is the most poetical' (*Apology* ed Shepherd 128). Plato's eloquence is commended by Quintilian 10.1.81. Mulcaster's reference to Plato's saintly eloquence may be from Quintilian, or from Erasmus' 'Convivium religiosum,' for which see 75.30 note.

266.16 his] Cicero's, in *De oratore* 1.16.70 and 1.34.154.

266.22 *Horace*] *Epistles* 2.1.126–7: 'os tenerum pueri balbumque poeta figurat, / torquet ab obscenis iam nunc sermonibus aurem' (the poet fashions the tender, lisping lips of childhood; even then he turns the ear from unseemly words). The moral value of Horace's poetry, mentioned in the next sentence, was one of the principal claims for his work's being taught in the Elizabethan schools. Mulcaster's pupils were examined in the *Odes* by Alexander Nowell in 1572. Brinsley (1612) considered Horace a difficult author for schools, even for senior boys, and recommended the use of a commentary to help students in their construing (*Ludus Literarius* 122). Elyot preferred Horace to Ovid (*The Boke Named the Governour* 1.10 ed Croft 1:67–8). Ascham, however, proclaimed 'nihil Horatio doctius' – no one more learned than Horace (*Whole Works* ed Giles 2:180). See also Baldwin *William Shakspere's Small Latine* passim, especially 2:497ff.

266.29ff *Apollinarius* ...] Shortly after the beginning of his reign in Constantinople, Julian the Apostate prohibited Christians from studying and teaching the Greek classics. Apollinarius (bishop of Laodicea and an important philosopher) and his father, also named Apollinarius, outwitted the Emperor by rewriting large sections of the Bible in dialogues and verses, using correct classical styles, 'to the ende the christians shoulde not be ignorant and unskilfull in any rare gifte that excelled among the Gentils' (Eusebius, Socrates, and Evagarius *The Auncient Ecclesiasticall Histories* trans M. Hanmer [1576] 307 [from Socrates Scholasticus *Ecclesiastical History* 3.1]). Mulcaster has, however, altered the story slightly; Socrates is quite explicit that Apollinarius the son wrote dialogues, not verses.

(Curiously, he gets the story right his *Cato Christianus*, sig O4r, where the prose envoi 'Cur à pietate Christiana, & carmine inchoanda puerorum disciplina' tells the same story from Sozomenus.) Also opposed to the Emperor's injunction were Basil, bishop of Caesarea, and Gregory of Nazianzus (for whom see Socrates 4.2 trans Hanmer 334–5). The *Ecclesiastical History* of Socrates Scholasticus (fifth century AD) was continuation of the work by Eusebius, and was often printed with it. Sozomen or Sozomenus (fifth century AD) also wrote a history of the church (covering the years 324 to 439) which runs parallel to, and now and then supplements, the work of Socrates; his additions are often given in notes of the editions of Socrates.

267.5–6 poeticall furie] The *furor poeticus* was a technical term in Platonic and Neoplatonic philosophy for the 'divine instinct' which was the poet's source of genius (it is mentioned at the beginning of Puttenham's *Arte of English Poesie*, for which see G. Gregory Smith ed *Elizabethan Critical Essays* 2:3). The notion was rejected by Sidney *Apology* ed Shepherd 130 and 142. Mulcaster seems suspicious of this 'rapt inclination,' and treats poetry as a branch of prose rhetoric.

For contemporary attitudes towards verse-writing as a skill to be learned by children, compare Elyot *The Boke Named the Governour* 1.10 ed Croft 1:68–9: 'And if the childe were induced to make versis by the imitation of Virgile and Homere, it shulde ministre to hym moche dilectation and courage to studie: ne the making of versis is nat discommended in a noble man: sens the noble Augustus and almost all the olde emperours made bokes in versis.' On this subject there are Brinsley *Ludus Literarius* 190–8; Baldwin *William Shakspere's Small Latine* 2:380–416.

267.10 *Quintilianes* rule] 1.8.4: 'Cetera admonitione magna egent, in primis, ut tenerae mentes tracturaeque altius, quidquid rudibus et omnium ignaris insederit, non modo quae diserta sed vel magis quae honesta sunt, discant.' (There are other points where there is much need of instruction: above all, unformed minds which are liable to be all the more deeply impressed by what they learn in their days of childish ignorance, must learn not merely what is eloquent; it is even more important that they should study what is morally excellent.)

268.3 stomake] resent, be offended with ('Stomach' v 1c obs)

268.9 pinches] strictures (sb 1b obs only citation)

268.16 pinch] bite, snap at (v 4 obs)

268.19 so the height of their argument overtop not their power to farre] ie, in so far as they do not promise more than they can perform ('overtop' means 'excell, surpass' v 2b first citation)

268.23 it] ie, adverse criticism

268.23–4 thing, (as it is in deede) naturally, and] Modern repunctuation might read: 'thing, as it is indeed, naturally and'

268.26 verie] ie, at the very time

268.29 warranting] assurance (on the part of the would-be reformer) (vbl sb from 'Warrant' v 7)

268.33 blindnes] Cf the proverbial Tilley S206 'Who so blind as he that will not see?'

268.34 misconsture] misconstrue (a common variant spelling; see 'Misconstrue' v; and *Elementarie* sig 2C1v 'Misconster')

269.5–6 hit ... misse] Cf Tilley H475 'Hit or miss.'

269.9 schoole *ordinaunces*] Whether the rules of schools were ever posted publicly may never be known, but there are several instances of schools where the parents and children had to agree to certain articles as a condition of entry (Stowe *English Grammar Schools* 130–2). One of the most common requirements was that the child miss no more than a certain number of days in the year (ibid 133–4; Brown *Elizabethan Schooldays* 89–92). At Merchant Taylors' a boy who missed more than three weeks was to be expelled; the statutes go on to say: 'And this is good to be shewed to his friends, or other that offer him at his first presenting into the schoole' (Draper *Four Centuries* 248).

269.13 condiscent, to] agree to ('Condescend' v 5b obs)

269.19–20 the *prevention* to have fourmes equall] the precaution or anticipating plan to maintain a clear difference in the advancing levels of instruction (as discussed above, especially 263.18ff; 'Prevention' 4 b obs first citation 1600)

269.34–5 *occasions* ... to play, which be now very many] Boys attended school for six days of the week, with one or two afternoons off for play or to attend classes out of school, in music, writing, Hebrew, or whatever. The Merchant Taylors' School statutes permitted only one remedy or 'leave to play' a week, except if there were 'one or more hollydayes in the weeke,' in which case the remedy was forbidden (Draper *Four Centuries* 248). In most schools, boys were let off for all principal saints' days and holy days, though usually they were required to attend church in the morning. Finally there were breaks between each of the quarters of the school year, sometimes as long as two weeks per break, so that the boys would receive as many as eight weeks off in the year (Brown *Elizabethan Schooldays* 92–6). For complaint about holidays, compare Brinsley: 'For schooles, generally, doe not take more hinderance by any one thing, then by over often leave to play. Experience teacheth, that this draweth their [ie, pupils'] mindes utterly away from their bookes, that they cannot take paines, for longing after plaie, and talking of it' (*Ludus Literarius* 301).

269.39 *punishment*] Although Mulcaster comments on corporal punishment elsewhere in *Positions* (see introduction, lxiv–lxv, for reports of his severity), this passage is his most extensive reflection on the subject. He is strongly in favour of beating and the use of fear in the classroom, though only for 'lewdnesse' and 'negligence,' not for 'learning,' and he concludes his comments here with the important qualification that 'ever the maister must have a fatherly affection, even to the unhappyest boye, and thinke the schoole to be a place of amendment' (275.33–5). In his general approval of corporal punishment, Mulcaster is close to the opinion of other teachers of the age as for instance in the detailed chapter 'Of execution of justice in schooles by punishments' in Brinsley *Ludus Literarius* 286–96. Roger Ascham, who never taught school, was a strong opponent of beating, as is shown in the Preface to his *Scholemaster*; Mulcaster, though opposed to beating for natural disability in a boy, has, however, little accord with those 'that write most for gentlenesse in traine' (272.10). Aspects of corporal punishment are described in Brown *Elizabethan Schooldays* 124–32 and Stowe *English Grammar Schools* 140–5. There is also Henry Barnard's history of 'School Punishments. The Strap – Rod – Ferule – Birch' in his *English Pedagogy – Old and New* and Schnucker 'Puritan Attitudes towards Childhood Discipline, 1560–1634.' Lawrence Stone describes and comments on corporal punishment in *Family* 163ff. Pollock *Forgotten Children* qualifies the general and oft-repeated view that children were grossly mistreated in the early modern period: in home and school discipline 'brutality was the exception rather than the rule' (199). A quasi-anthropological explanation for classroom beating is found in Ong 'Latin Language Study as a Renaissance Puberty Rite.'

270.2–3 *rod* may no more be spared] Following the biblical injunction 'Spare the rod and spoil the child' (from Proverbs 13:24; also Tilley R155).

270.7 the private] ie, the private, or domestic, situation.

270.7 *birchely*] This personified form not in *OED*. Birch was the usual means of punishment; Brinsley says for 'greater faults' 'give three or fowre jerkes with a birch, or with a small redde willow where birch cannot be had' (*Ludus Literarius* 288). The 'stripes' or 'jerks' or blows would be applied to the buttocks, often naked (the 'sides' are named by God, suggests Bartholomew Batty *The Christian Mans Closet* 26r, specifically to receive such punishment). 'The threat'ning twigs of birch' (Shakespeare *Measure for Measure* 1.3.23–7) were bound in a bundle, and in this form were flexible yet strong; they would sting, even cause bleeding on bare buttocks, but not cause bruising or fracture ('For as the common Proverbe is: *Byrch breaketh no bones*,' says Robert Cleaver in *A Godlie Forme of Householde Government* 266). 'Lady Birch' is the common expression for a form of punishment given by males to males; presumably punishment by a (symbolic) female to the male buttocks would intensify the humiliation. The ferule, not named here as a punishment by

Mulcaster, was another device used by schoolmasters; this straight rod had at its end a flat surface or plane, within which was a small round hole. It would raise an immediate welt on the skin when applied to the hand or, as was often the case, to the mouth of the boy.

270.8 gest] guest

270.11 will match some men] ie, the misery felt by the boy will be as great to him as the misery of a much severer punishment will be to a man

270.20 frantike] raging mad (a A 1) Indeed, there are many instances of schoolmasters becoming half-crazed with fury towards their charges. See Bernard 'School Punishments.'

270.31 bear away the bell] prevail (Tilley B275 'He bears away the bell' means 'he carries away the prize'; in this case, the boy will prevail against the master because his too fond or too easily swayed parents have interceded)

270.34–5 a *catalogue* of schoole faultes] Mulcaster's idea of a list of faults and their appropriate punishments does not seem to have been commonly held, though the statutes for Oundle (1566) have the following clause: '*Item*, to cause the Scholars to refrain from the detestable vice of swearing, or Ribauld words, be it ordered, for every oath or Ribauld word spoken in the School or elsewhere, the Scholar to have *three stripes*' (Carlisle *Concise Description* 2:218). The statutes for Sandwich (1580) list the following offences: 'everie absence from Church or from such assemblies, and everie unreverent behaviour at any time, to be sharply punished ... pride, rybawdrie, lying, pyckinge and blasphemynge to be sharplie punished' (Carlisle *Concise Description* 1:604).

270.36 picking] stealing (vbl sb[1] 2a) In a fully normalized text, '*false* witness' and 'picking' would be italicized, as they are part of a series.

270.37 *tardies*] Earliest *OED* citation for 'tardiness' is 1605; 'tardies' may be Mulcaster's variant spelling or may be an error for 'tardines.'

270.38 *Xenophon*] *Cyropaedia* 1.2.6: 'For as a matter of course, boys also prefer charges against one another, just as men do, of theft, robbery, assault, cheating, slander, and other things that naturally come up; and when they discover any one committing any of these crimes, they punish him.'

271.2 stripes] strokes or blows (of the birch) (sb[2] 2)

271.7 beyond crye] to excess ('Cry' sb 17b obs)

271.8 monitours] Then as now many schools had a system of monitors (or prefects), usually senior boys (such as the seventh-formers at Eton, called prepositors) or boys elected by their classmates on a regular rotational basis (as described by Brinsley *Ludus Literarius* 272–4); see Brown *Elizabethan Schooldays* 117–19. In the understaffed schools, the master would need to share his power to maintain order.

271.11–13 And if ye correcte ... that must go home to prove beating without cause] ie, If you punish the boy – and you must do so if your monitor or school prefect is to be worth anything, indeed you must do so if you wish to maintain control in the school – then the boy must be able to establish absolutely to his parents that his punishment has been undeserved (if he is to enlist parental support). (This paraphrase may be wrong; a difficult sentence because of the unclear status of the word 'that.')

271.15 starting hole] means of evasion ('Starting-hole' obs 2; in the non-figurative sense, 'hole in which a hunted animal takes refuge,' from 'Start' v 6 'to escape')

271.17 To tell tales out of schoole] Proverbial; Tilley T54 'To tell tales out of school.'

271.20–1 *apopthegme* in either *Plutarch, Aelianus*, or *Erasmus*] Apophthegms ('that is to saie, prompte, quicke, wittie and sentencious saiynges, of certain Emperours, Kynges, Capitaines, Philosophers and Oratours' according to the title page of Udall's translation of Erasmus' *Apophthegmes* [1542]) were as much studied in the Elizabethan grammar school as proverbs, *sententiae* (to which they are closely related), and epigrams. Plutarch's 'Sayings of Kings and Commanders' in *Moralia* 172–94 was said to be a kind of textbook prepared for Trajan and may have been based on the author's *Parallel Lives*; it was often used in the Renaissance classroom. Claudius Aelianus' Greek *Varia historia* was also used as a collection of apophthegms; it had been translated by Abraham Fleming as *A Registre of Hystories* (1576). Erasmus' *Apophthegmata* (1531), modelled on Plutarch, went through many editions in the sixteenth century. Short sayings also made up the 'small Cato' that preceded the distichs or 'large Cato,' in its combined form perhaps the most popular of all sixteenth-century textbooks. But what Mulcaster is getting at here is the kind of sly verbal jousting exemplified in the anecdote of the 'banns,' given in the introduction, lxv.

271.27 graffed] grafted

271.29 in rearward] ie, the last thing to appear, slow to show itself (as well as a pun on the nature of the punishment)

271.30 grate ... of] fret ... about, be upset ... because of ('Grate' v^1 does not have this sense)

271.36 round] uncompromising (a 13b obs)

272.7 reward] ie, punishment (an irony)

272.16 curifavour] currying or seeking favour, ingratiation ('Curryfavour' obs 2 only citation)

272.17 harp on the harder stringe] Proverbial; Tilley S936 'To harp upon one string'; cf 208.22.

272.29 last staffe] final resort (not in *OED* sv 'last' or 'staff'; there is a play here on 'staff' as 'rod')

272.32 witnesse] beare witness (v 2)

272.39 best common weale] Plato *Republic* 7.536E: 'Do not ... keep children to their studies by compulsion but by play.'

273.11–12 slavish ... to be bet] Plato *Republic* 7.536E: 'a free soul ought not to pursue any study slavishly.' In the following syllogistic argument, Mulcaster seems to have no qualms about turning Socrates' words into a defence of beating.

273.18 point] describe the qualifications of ('Appoint' v 14–15, in the sense of 'equip' or 'prepare') Mulcaster argues correctly that although Plato and Scorates are careful to describe the qualities of the learner, they say comparatively little about the qualities of the teacher.

273.19 Censores] A 'censor' is probably a director of education (or *archos*) described in Plato *Laws* 6.765Dff.

273.27 it is not enough to name the man] ie, it is not enough just to require a 'good master'; one must go on to specify what qualities make up a good master

273.29 caveat] precaution ('Caveat' sb 4 obs first citation 1596 [Spenser])

273.32 *Xenophon*] See *Cyropaedia* 1.3.16–17 for the story of Cyrus' judgment in the case of the two coats (274.5ff) and his subsequent punishment. *Anabasis* (literally 'journey, expedition'), book 3 and following, tells how Xenophon himself took charge of the Greek mercenaries after the death of Cyrus II the Younger and led them back from Assyria to the Hellespont.

273.34 *Tullie*] Cicero *Ad Quintum fratrem* 1.1.23: 'Cyrus ille a Xenophonte non ad historiae fidem scriptus, sed ad effigiem iusti imperii' (The great Cyrus was portrayed by Xenophon not in accord with historical truth, but as a model of just government), a theme picked up by many writers, eg Sidney *Apology* ed Shepherd 110–11.

274.4 *Socrates* his schoole] After Plato, Xenophon was the best-known pupil of Socrates, as is related in the life of Xenophon by Diogenes Laertius *Lives* 2.48–59.

274.18–19 Slight considerations make no artificiall anatomies] weak thoughts, inadequate reflections, do not lead to skilful analyses ('Artificial' a 6 obs; 'Anatomy' 10)

274.21–2 rime ... reason] Cf Tilley R98 'Neither rhyme nor reason.'

274.30 hard head] dullard, one not easily moved ('Hardhead' 1)

275.7 thousandes under my hand] For the number of Mulcaster's students, see introduction, lxv.

275.14 in the least paucitie] ie, at the very least ('Paucity' 1 and 2 first citation 1650: 'smallness')

275.19 pretence] false allegation (against beating) (sb 5 first citation 1608)

275.29 Leave nothing to had I wist] Proverbial; see above 225.27 note.

275.31 *Solon*] Diogenes Laertius *Lives* 1.59: 'On being asked why he had not framed any law against parricide, he [Solon] replied that he hoped it was unnecessary.'

275.36 misses] wrongs, offences (not necessarily intentional, of that boy who is at school to be corrected) or, possibly, mistakes ('Miss' sb[1] 3 obs or sb[1] II 3 obs)

275.37–8 yeares ... alonenesse] In the few Elizabethan school statutes specifying the age of the master, the minimum requirement ranges from twenty-six to thirty years of age. At Merchant Taylors' and St Paul's the master might be either single or married; some few schools required him to be single. See Stowe *English Grammar Schools* 57–8. 'Alonenesse' in the sense of 'celibacy' is not found in *OED*.

276.3 constantnesse] constancy, firmness (sb obs cited)

276.3 constantnesse ... an ancker] Mulcaster draws constancy (usually symbolized by staff, column, rock, or bull) and hope (anchor) together in this image; de Tervarent *Attributs et symboles* 44, 107, 323, and 370, and see the note for 29.31 above.

276.7 curious] cautious, particular (a 2 b obs)

276.12 sunne] Tilley S984 'The sun sees all things and discovers all things'; cf Erasmus *Parabolae* in LB 1:607Eff trans CWE 23:241f, and see above, 191.37 note, for the schoolmaster as the sun.

276.16 evidently] distinctly (adv 1 obs)

276.20 take a pyrre at some toy] start up in a sudden fit of ill-temper at some idle fancy or whim ('Pyrre' only citation; 'Toy' sb 4 obs)

276.33 uncharmed] not fortunate, not blessed (ppl a first citation 1592)

276.34 meter] ie, verse ('Metre' sb[1] 3a), or metrical prose

276.34 president] I have been unable to trace the 'precedent,' which may be a classical (Greek or Latin) tag, in verse or metrical prose, expressing the notion that 'if the private is uncared for or abused, the public will suffer.'

276.38 proverbe] Tilley M247 'Man is either a god or a wolf to man' (and M245 'Man is a wolf to man,' from the well-known Latin proverb 'Homo homini lupus,' in Erasmus *Adagia* in LB 2:55D trans CWE 31:115).

277.2 *Plinie*] *Historia naturalis* 7.1.1: 'natura magna, saeva mercede contra tanta sua munera, ut non sit satis aestimare, parens melior homini an tristior noverca fuerit' (great nature ... asks a cruel price for all her generous gifts, making it hardly possible to judge whether she has been more a kind parent to man or more a harsh stepmother).

277.4 rempare] rampart, solid defence ('Rampire' sb 2)

277.5 *Horace*] *Odes* 3.3.1–8, especially 7–8: 'Si fractus inlabatur orbis / impavidum ferient ruinae' (Were the vault of heaven to break and fall upon him [ie, the man tenacious of purpose in a righteous cause], its ruins would smite him undismayed).

277.26 first of *conference*] A possible source for the idea of regular conferences may be J.L. Vives *De tradendis disciplinis* 2.2 and 2.4 (in *Opera omnia* 6:278, 292 trans Watson 62 and 82), where the author recommends regular meetings of teachers: 'Four times a year let the masters meet in some place apart where they may discuss together the natures of their pupils and consult about them.' And: 'Every two or three months let the masters meet together, and deliberate and judge with paternal affection and grave discretion concerning the minds of their pupils ...'

277.27 cooplementes] pairs ('Couplement' obs 2a first citation 1588)

278.19–20 love thy neighbour] Matthew 22:39

278.23 thine] ie, thy opinion

278.28 in respect of their persons] ie, as they are beings in themselves, and not in relation to the wishes we may have for them (even though Mulcaster goes on to define them in relation to others)

278.32 purtracte] portrait ('Purtract,' a variant spelling)

278.38 mammering] state of doubt or hesitation (vbl sb obs 2)

279.5 advertisemente] notice (sb 4 obs)

279.17–18 angrie nature is an eager monster] Not in Tilley or *ODEP*.

279.18 overthwart] perverse, contentious (A a 3)

279.20 convenient] appropriate (a 4b obs)

279.21 redresse] put (the matter) right again (v^1 7b obs)

279.35 shed] shedding (an unusual shortened form, an example of apocope; not in *OED* sv 'Shed')

280.11 forge] utter falsely (v^1 4, a modern sense)

280.11 halt] play false ('Halt' v^1 5 obs). Halting (or 'limping') Vulcan was god of the forge: perhaps there is a play on this classical allusion?

280.11–12 *Zenophon*] Anecdote in *Cyropaedia* 3.1.1–2.24 (The preferred spelling is 'Xenophon' elsewhere, and this form may be a misprint, or an acceptable alternative.)

280.17 defect] ie, his (previous) failure (sb 2)

280.27 listes] boundary, limits (ie, to which the parent may hope to trust the master) (sb^3 8 obs, often plural). The phrase (and personification) 'shew hope her listes' sounds proverbial, but is not in Tilley or *ODEP*.

281.7 common companies] public companies, or guilds (unlike the professions of law and medicine and unlike various trades, such as the Merchant Taylors for whom Mulcaster worked, teachers had no common organization)

281.32 hart] man of courage ('Heart' sb 15)

281.34 engrosing] buying in large quantities to obtain a monopoly ('Engrossing' vbl sb 1) Mulcaster here shows a deep distrust of monopolies and so reflects an opinion common to many of his contemporaries. 'Engrossing' also referred to 'the amalgamation of two or more farms into one' (Thirsk

'Enclosing and Engrossing' 201) and was a technique of monopolization that accompanied enclosure (for which, see above 186.2–3).

281.35 forestauling] buying up of goods beforehand ('Forestalling' vbl sb 2)

281.35 intercepting] preventing (the free flow of goods) (vbl sb first citation 1598)

281.36–7 crie out of] protest loudly against (v 21b obs)

281.38 pointed] appointed ('Point' v² obs 2)

281.39–282.2 reason ... retinew ... hoste] ie, Reason's 'retinew,' which consists of 'authorities,' does not need to be called upon to prove this obvious point (about the use of 'conference' for good applications, even though we object to it for its bad uses). It is not entirely clear who Reason's 'hoste' is. Perhaps it is pure logic. That is, if something is utterly obvious by the pure light of reason, there is no need to to prove the point by additional argument, and certainly no need to quote authorities on the matter. Not in Tilley or *ODEP*.

282.25 limitable] (a; first citation)

282.29–31 The best and most heavenly thinges be both most certaine, and most constantly certaine] Other Tudor reflections on order and degree are found in Elyot *The Boke Named the Governour* 1.1 ed Croft 1:3) and Spenser *Faerie Queene*, throughout the 'Two Cantos of Mutabilitie.' Mulcaster has introduced a topos or commonplace to support the argument for order and certainty in schools and school curricula. There is a chapter on 'Order' in Tillyard *The Elizabethan World Picture* 7–15 that has influenced many late twentieth-century readers of Elizabethan literature. In it Tillyard cites other writers, including Shakespeare, on 'order' and 'degree,' and claims that the Elizabethans 'saw' the world according a particular structure. Yet it should by now be clear that for Mulcaster the 'certain' exists only tenuously within normal human existence. We can argue for orderly behaviour from the extra-normal 'order,' but our existence is too caught up in the confusing and sometimes contradictory 'circumstances' of the everyday. He questions the Platonic ideal, even though he now and then argues from it – as he does here – for an order (or *ratio*) to regulate behaviour. When order is followed 'mutabilitie is everie daye endaungered' (283.1–2).

283.34 will make his own proufe his fairest president] ie, will prove from his own instance, will demonstrate by his own example; any household that doesn't realize this is not a good example (or, perhaps, lacks a good example because it doesn't have such a well brought up young man within it) ('Proof' sb 5 obs; 'Precedent' 4b obs; 'president' in line 36 has the modern sense of 'precedent' as 'example')

284.3–4 to enter the Church with children upon *holydaies*] This is one of Mulcaster's few reflections upon the religious instruction of the young, a topic of major concern in the period. The statute requiring orderly church attendance of boys at East Retford (1552) is typical of many of the school orders of the period: 'The Schoolmaster and Usher of the said School ... shall command and compell their Scholars to come and hear Divine Service in the Parish Church ... every Sunday and Holiday' (Carlisle *Concise Description* 2:281; for a calendar of other statutes on this subject, see Watson *English Grammar Schools* 45–9; see also Brown *Elizabethan Schooldays* 64–7). Episcopal injunctions were also emphatic on church attendance, as much to ensure religious conformity of the masters as to have the scholars instructed in pious doctrine (Simon *Education and Society* 324–5). Often masters were required to examine their pupils in Sunday sermons (ibid 329), and techniques in the note-taking of sermons are described by Brinsley (*Ludus Literarius* 255–8). 'The Religious Teaching of Children' is discussed in chapter 6 of Wood *The Reformation and English Education* 135–82, especially 167–8.

284.15 regiment] ruling, governing (sb 4)

284.19 stayed yearde] fixed yardstick, such as one finds in shops selling cloth (or 'flexible stuffe')

284.19–20 *Bladders* and *bullrushes*] As is suggested here, swimmers used inflated bladders and bullrushes to help them learn to swim (Orme *Early British Swimming* 51 [rushes, in Plautus] and 132 [bladders]). ('Bullrush' not listed under 'Bull- ')

284.32–3 rouling ... rewled] moving in a disorderly fashion ... ordered ('Rolling' vbl sb[2] II)

284.36 revolt] draw back (from the decided course of action) (v 2b obs)

285.2 *Emperour* of all] Although God 'changeth the times and seasons' (Daniel 2:21), He did say 'I am the Lord: I change not' (Malachi 3:6). See 282.29–31 note.

285.10 prime] spring season (sb[1] 7; or possibly merely 'first stage of development' sb[1] 6)

285.17–18 in no case be altered] See 228.2–3 note.

285.22–3 with procession] in due order (sb 2b is not quite the same)

285.31 accidentarie] accidental, non-essential (in the logical sense; 'Accidentary' a obs 2)

285.32 Such a supplie hath justice in positive lawes by equitie in consideration, as a good chauncellour to soften to hard constructions.] ie, discretion allows for exceptions in the rule of 'certainty,' just as justice has additional room beyond the formally imposed law through the exercise of equity in interpreting (the Lord Chancellor could, by considering things the law did not normally cover, modify an overly severe interpretation of a lower court which had applied the 'positive law')('supply' sb 7 obs meant 'supplement or appendix to a literary work')

285.38 *Brutus*] The famous and probably legendary story of how Lucius Junius

Brutus, the early Roman consul, discovered his sons' treacherous alliance with Tarquinius and how he condemned his sons to death is told by Dionysius of Halicarnassus *Roman Antiquities* 5.7–8, Livy 2.4–5, and Plutarch 'Publicola' 3–7 in *Lives* 98–100.

286.9 putting to] sprouting, growing (vbl sb[1] 2 first citation 1615)

286.25 the present execution must follow the particular] ie, the ends of educational reform which I am now outlining may only be reached after the particular means have been dealt with

287.8 have ... wishe] The several uses of 'have' and 'wish' may be a play on the proverb 'Better to have than wish' (Tilley H214).

287.11 sentence] opinion (sb 1 obs)

287.15 moane] complain of, or pity (v 1 or 2)

287.18 aphorismelike] See 47.30 note.

287.21 precisenesse] severity (sb 2b obs)

287.29 conferred] gathered (v 1 obs)

287.30 common sense] The 'sensus communis' was the inner faculty which sorted out the data presented by the five senses (E. Ruth Harvey *The Inward Wits* 43–4). He has taken his principles and checked them against his well ordered common sense. (In this statement one can see the modern meaning of 'common sense' beginning to take shape.)

287.31–3 And besides these, some reason doth lead me very probable to my selfe, in mine owne collection, what to others I know not, to whom I have delivered it, but I must rest upon their judgement.] ie, besides reading, experience, custom, and common sense, some reason also directs me, reason very demonstrable to myself in my own way of thinking, but probable or not to others I do not know, and they must decide ('Collection' 5 obs)

288.9 motion] instigation, prompting (sb 7 obs)

288.9–10 in rate] in sharp reproof (sb[2] and v[2] 3)

288.11 countenaunce an affection so well quallified] ie, approve of my restrained attitude or state of mind ('Countenance' v 5b first citation 1590; 'Affection' sb 5; 'Qualified' ppl a 5 first citation 1599).

288.14 robe] ie, the role of a counsellor of state or of a lawyer, or the counsellor's office itself (sb 2)

288.18–19 never hitherto daring to venture upon the print] See 3.13 note.

288.19 raine] rein

288.27 contentation] satisfaction (sb 2 obs)

289.4 chippinges] parings of the crust of a loaf of bread (vbl sb 2a obs); ie, his arguments chop the material pretty finely, but maybe this fine arguing is better than leaving it whole, and letting the reader do the chopping

289.12 maine] main subject, chief matter (sb[1] 6 first citation 1602; 'main' sb[3] 2 also meant 'match' or 'contest,' and that sense is clearly being played with here)

289.17 sillie] trifling (a 2b first citation 1587)

289.30 primitive] first (in the sense of 'basis') (sb form of 'Primitive' a 3, as found in the title of *Positions*)

289.38 quoated out] noted down ('Quote' v 5 obs)

290.13 if] as though

289.15 But how have I delt in them.] The syntax would seem to require a question mark, but the sentence can be read as a declarative introduction to the following sentences: ie, 'But how I have dealt in them [I shall now go on to say].'

290.16 awaye with] tolerate (adv 16)

290.20 remove] ie, either from the school, or perhaps from one form or level within the school to another

291.5 partible] capable of being divided (a)

291.6 prerogative] superiority (sb 2b obs)

291.10 pesture] overcrowd ('Pester' v 2 obs)

291.16 limitation of certaineties] ie, the setting down of statutory requirements and responsibilities as discussed above in chapter 43

291.28 translate the crime] ie, instead of seeing themselves as criminals for seeking education, maidens will accuse their accusers as wrongdoers for preventing them from obtaining the education they deserve

291.30 fantasticallnes] capriciousness (sb 4 first citation 1583; this passage cited in *OED* under sense 2, 'eccentricity, oddness,' but sense 4 seems preferable, as the meaning should accord with the adjective 'fantasticall' in line 31)

292.11–12 in the cloudes] in the realm of fantasy or unreality (sb 9b first citation 1649, and cf Tilley C444 'To speak in the clouds,' to speak incomprehensibly)

292.16 rowme] ie, room (miscorrected from 'rowmeh' to 'rowmh')

292.23 repetition] renewal (of their readerships) (sb 4 first citation 1597)

292.34 construction] interpreting (of his words, as the reader might interpret a legal document) (sb 9; see above 285.33 note)

292.36 healthing] furthering or imparting of health (vbl sb 1 only citation)

293.1 abide the tuch] withstand the knock or blow (or an attacker against these positions) ('Touch' sb 4)

294.1 *To the courteous reader.*] Here Mulcaster asks his readers to go through the book and make appropriate corrections, a common request of the time. In only a few copies have early readers actually penned in these changes. I have left the list of errors as he has them, with the original page numbers. The table of variants, which follows immediately, shows all these corrections and many more made to the text.

294.3 distinctions] marks of punctuation (sb 1b obs)

Bibliography

PART 1 THE WRITINGS OF RICHARD MULCASTER

Note: Fuller information about many of the publications in part 1 may be found in part 2, the list of works cited that follows. For convenience I add information regarding certain of the reprints and transcriptions of these works.

1559 [Attributed] *The Quenes Maiesties Passage through the Citie of London to Westminster the Daye before her Coronacion*. London: Richard Tottell 1558 [ie, 1559] *STC* 7589.5. Another edition, *The Passage of Our Most Drad Soueraigne Lady Quene Elyzabeth* ..., appeared the same year (*STC* 7590). Mulcaster certainly wrote a book describing the pageant (Baskervill 'Richard Mulcaster') but the relationship of this to the printed text is unclear.

Reprinted: 1) 1604, *STC* 7592 and variant [1604], *STC* 7593; 2) Nichols *Progresses ... of Queen Elizabeth* (1823) 1:38–60; 3) Arber ed *English Garner* 4 (1882) 217–47; 4) Pollard ed *Tudor Tracts* (1903) 365–95; 5) in facsimile Osborn ed *The Quenes Maiesties Passage* (1960); 6) Kinney ed in *Elizabethan Backgrounds* 7–39 (with full textual discussion, though nothing on attribution)

1561 [Attributed] Verse speeches by David, Orpheus, Amphion, Arion, Topas, in a pageant for Sir William Harper, Merchant Taylor, the new Lord Mayor. Merchant Taylors' Books 7, 12a–13a. Because the speeches are in the same style as those in the 1568 pageant, Robertson and Gordon *Calendar of Dramatic Records* xxxiv argue that it is 'not unlikely' that Mulcaster was also the author of these speeches; of course, Mulcaster may have been imitating the style of the 1561 speeches, so the claim is open to doubt.

Transcribed: 1) Sayle *Lord Mayors' Pageants* (1931) 38–9; 2) Robertson and Gordon *Calendar of Dramatic Records* (1954) 42–3

1568 Verse speeches by St John and four boys, in honour of Sir Thomas Rowe, Merchant Taylor, the new Lord Mayor. Merchant Taylors' Books 7, 22b–23a. Mulcaster is named as the author in a contemporary document; see Sayle *Lord Mayors' Pageants* (1931) 48.

Transcribed: 1) Sayle *Lord Mayors' Pageants* (1931) 53–5; 2) Robertson and Gordon eds *A Calendar of Dramatic Records* (1954) 48–9

1573 Verses beginning 'Si quis in hoc genere est liber vtilis, vtilis hic est' in John Baret *An Alvearie or Triple Dictionarie, in Englishe, Latin, and French* London: H. Denham 1573. *STC* 1410. Sig *4v. The poem is headed 'Richardus Moncasterus.'

1575 Verses beginning 'Jupiter è summi, dum vertice cernit olympi' read to the Queen on her visit to Kenilworth in 1575. Mulcaster is named as author by Gascoigne in his description of the pageant. The early printing is no longer extant.

Reprinted: 1) Gascoigne *A Briefe Rehearsall* in *The Whole Woorkes* (1587) *STC* 11638 sig A3v (in the last series of signatures); 2) Gascoigne *Princely Pleasures ... at Kenilworth Castle* (1821) 10; 3) Gascoigne *The Princelye Pleasures at the Courte of Kenelworth ... 1575. Imprinted at London, by Rychard Ihones ... 1576* (1821) 4 (transcribed in DeMolen PH D diss [1970] 279 from this text and not from the preceding one as claimed, and translated 200); 4) Gascoigne *Complete Works* ed Cunliffe (1907–10) 2:95

1575 Verses entitled 'In Musicam Thomae Tallisii, et Guilielmi Birdi' in Thomas Tallis and William Byrd *Cantiones, quae ab argumento sacrae vocantur, quinque et sex partium ...* London: T. Vautrollier 1575. *STC* 23666. Sig A3r. The six parts are discantus, tenor, contra tenor, bassus, superius, and sexta pars, and the poem is printed in the preliminaries to each part. It is signed 'Richardus Mulcasterus.'

Reprinted, with translation, in Boyd *Elizabethan Music* rev ed (1967) 286–9

1577 Verses entitled 'Emanueli Demetrio hom*ini* verè amico' in *Album amicorum Emanuelis de Meteren* Bodleian Library ms Douce 68 fol 38. Signed 'Richardus Mulcaster' and dated London 1577. The last two lines of the poem are found, also in Mulcaster's hand, on the fly-leaf of the album.

Transcribed by DeMolen PH D diss (1970) 281.

1578 Verses on the death of Henry Dow: 'Qualis in Autumno judex Academia, certe / Nobilis in primo palmite gemma fuit.' These appeared on a brass plaque, formerly in Christ Church Cathedral, Oxford, and one of two erected in the memory of Henry Dow. He studied under Mulcaster at Merchant Taylors' School, entered Christ Church in 1576, and died there in 1578. On this brass, in addition to the lines by Mulcaster, are distichs by Dow's three brothers and his two tutors (John Rainoldes and John Horden). The upper brass is still in the cathedral (though not in its original place); the text of the lower brass, which is lost, was transcribed by Anthony Wood some time before 1695 and is quoted in his *History and Antiquities* ed Gutch [1786] 3:484.

1580 Verses entitled 'De τετραγλώττῳ Barretti Alueario' in John Baret *An Alvearie or Quadruple Dictionarie, Containing Foure Sundrie Tongues: Namelie, English, Latine, Greeke, and French* ... London: H. Denham 1580. *STC* 1411. Sig A4v. The poem is signed 'Richardus Mulcaster.'

1581 Autograph letter from Mulcaster to Abraham Ortelius. Dated 24 April 1581. Formerly in the possession of Dr Arthur Freeman and now in a private collection. Microfilm in British Library, Department of Manuscripts M/457.

Transcribed: 1) Hessels ed *Ecclesiae Londino-Batavae archivum* 1 (1887) 249–52; 2) DeMolen PH D diss (1970) 263–5

1581 *Positions Wherin those Primitiue Circumstances Be Examined, Which Are Necessarie for the Training Vp of Children, Either for Skill in their Booke, or Health in their Bodie* ... London: Thomas Vautrollier 1581. *STC* 18253; Alston 10:18–19. *STC* 18253a has 'Thomas Vautrollier for Thomas Chare' on the title page.

Reprinted: 1) ed Robert Hebert Quick, London and New York: Longmans, Green, and Co 1887, 1888; 2) anthologized in James Oliphant ed *The Educational Writings of Richard Mulcaster (1532–1611) Abridged and Arranged, with a Critical Estimate* Glasgow: James Maclehose and Sons 1903, a modernized abridgment; 3) ed Richard L. DeMolen, New York: Teachers College Press, Columbia University 1971 (Classics in Education 44), a modernized abridgment; 4) in facsimile, as *The Training Up of Children* Amsterdam: Theatrum Orbis Terrarum and New York: Da Capo Press 1971 (English Experience 339); 5) in facsimile, with commentary, in Barker PH D diss (1982).

1582 *The First Part of the Elementarie Which Entreateth Chefelie of the Right Writing of Our English Tung* ... London: Thomas Vautrollier 1582. *STC* 18250; Alston 6:462.

Reprinted: 1) ed E.T. Campagnac, Oxford: Clarendon Press 1925 (Tudor and Stuart Library); 2) anthologized in James Oliphant ed *The Educational Writings of Richard Mulcaster (1532–1611) Abridged and Arranged, with a Critical Estimate* Glasgow: James Maclehose and Sons 1903, a modernized abridgment; 3) in facsimile, Menston: Scolar Press 1970

1582 Verses entitled 'In Christophori Oclandi Elisabetham' in Ocland *Εἰρηναρχία siue Elizabetha* ... London: C. Barker 1582. *STC* 18775a (issued as part of *Anglorum praelia* which is *STC* 18772.5). Sig A4r. Signed at end 'Richardus Mulcaster'

1583 Verses entitled 'In *τετραγλωττίαν* doctissimi Claudij Holibandi, aliâs Desainliens: Richardus Mulcaster' in Claude Desainliens *Campo di Fior or else the Flourie Field of Foure Languages* London: T. Vautrollier 1583. *STC* 6735. Sig *3v

1593 Letter to Sir John Puckering from Mulcaster, holograph, c 4 September 1593, concerning the prebend of Yatesbury. British Library Harleian ms 6996 fol 35 (there is another incomplete copy, in a contemporary hand, in Additional ms 4160 fol 201 [97]).

Reprinted in facsimile, in part, by Greg et al *English Literary Autographs* 3:72; transcribed in DeMolen PH D diss (1970) 266

1595 Prose dedication 'To the curteous reader' in Victorinus Strigelius *A Third Proceeding in the Harmonie of King Dauids Harp: That is to Say, a Godly and Learned Exposition upon 17. Psalmes* ... trans Richard Robinson. London: Valentine Sims 1595. *STC* 23361. Sig A4v.

1598 Two poems 'In nauales Richardi Hakluyti commentarios' and 'Eiusdem in eundem' in Richard Hakluyt *The Principal Nauigations, Voyages, Traffiques and Discoueries of the English Nation* ... London: G. Bishop, R. Newberie, and Robert Barker 1598. *STC*. Vol 1 sigs 2*3r and 2*3r–v respectively. In the new edition of volume 1 in 1599 (*STC* 12626), the poems occupy the same signatures. The first poem is signed 'Rich. Mulcaster.'

For Mulcaster's involvement in subsequent history of editions, see Quinn ed *The Hakluyt Handbook* 312 and 591 n; poems summarized in Watson 'Hakluyt and Mulcaster.'

1599 *Poemata*. 12° listed in Lowndes *The Bibliographer's Manual* rev ed Bohn (1861) 1628 and Hazlitt *Hand-book* (1867) 404, based on description in the catalogue of the sale of the Benjamin H. Bright collection at Sotheby's in March/April 1845 (British Library Mus Bibl III 8º 516 [6]), item 4611 (bound after *Pugna porcorum* Antwerp 1533). Not traced.

1599 *Catechismus Paulinus*. The first edition of this work may date from this year; it was entered to T. Stirrop on the Stationers' Register on 6 November; the copy in the St Paul's School library, printed by F. Kingston, may be this first edition, though it lacks the title page (see *STC* rev ed Addenda and Corrigenda 18249); a later edition of 1601 listed below.

1600 *Cato Christianus, In quem conijciuntur ea omnia, quae in sacris literis ad parentum, puerorumque pietatem videntur maxime pertinere* London: Valentine Sims nd. The work is dated from the end of the epistle dedicatory 'Londini. Mensis Maii sexto, anno Domini 1600' after which 'Richardus Mulcaster.' *STC* rev ed 18249.5

See Barker and Chadwick 'Preface to *Cato Christianus*'

1601 *Catechismus Paulinus, In usum Scholae Paulinae conscriptus, ad formam parui illius Anglici Catechismi qui pueris in communi precum Anglicarum libro ediscendus proponitur* London: excudebat Iohannes Windet, impensis Mattheae Law 1601. *STC* 18249. Mulcaster's name appears at the end of the epistle dedicatory, sig A5v, with the date 'Nouemb. 17. An. 1599.'

1603 *In mortem serenissimae Reginae Elizabethae. Naenia consolans. Hoc solo officio potui me ostendere gratum*. London: for Edward Aggas 1603. *STC* 18251. This long poem is signed '*Ri: Mulcaster*' at the end (sig B2v).

1603 *The Translation of Certaine Latin Verses Written vppon her Maiesties Death, Called a Comforting Complaint* ... London: for Edward Aggas 1603. *STC* 18252. This long English poem is a translation of the preceding item, and is signed 'R.M.' (sig B2v).

1603 [Perhaps by Mulcaster] 'Oratio habita, et ad Regem, et coram Rege prae schola Paulina,' 'a latine Oration ... *Viua voce* deliuered to his Grace, by one of maister *Mulcasters* Schollers, at the dore of the free-schole fownded by the Mercers' in Thomas Dekker *The Magnificent Entertainment: Giuen to King Iames ... the 15. of March. 1603* London: T.C. for Tho. Man the Younger 1604. *STC* 6510. Sigs H1v–2v. The oration is found in English in the 2nd ed of London: Edward Allde for Thomas Man 1604 (*STC* 6511) and in Latin in the 3rd ed London: E. Allde for Thomas Man the Younger

1604 (*STC* 6513). There is also an edition of Edinburgh: T. Finlayson 1604 (*STC* 6512).

Reprinted (with full textual commentary and information regarding later editions) in Dekker *The Dramatic Works* ed Bowers 2 (1955) 291–2 (with translation 293–4). If this composition was indeed written, as seems likely, by one of Mulcaster's scholars, he might have had a hand in its composition.

1604 Copy of letter to Peter Junius, 13 May, requesting assistance in a suit to the king. Bodleian Library Smith ms 77 fol 397

Transcribed by DeMolen PH D diss (1970) 269

1605 Autograph letter to Sir Julius Caesar, Master of Requests, 25 November, on behalf of his wife's sister Mrs Wheteneall. British Library, Lansdowne ms 161 fol 25 (24)

Printed in partial facsimile in Greg et al *English Literary Autographs* 3:72 and transcribed by DeMolen PH D diss (1970) 270 (the outer fold, omitted from DeMolen's transcription, has, in Mulcaster's hand: 'To the right worshipfull *Sir* Julius Caesar Knight *Master* of Requests to his *Maiestye*' and a note in another hand summarizing the letter).

PART 2 WORKS CITED

Note: All quotations and translations from classical authors, unless otherwise noted, are from the Loeb Classical Library (Cambridge, Mass: Harvard University Press; London: William Heinemann, various dates); references are generally given to standard text divisions, not to Loeb page numbers, though volume and page numbers are sometimes added for convenience.

The best general list of books on education for Mulcaster's period is still that of Joan Simon in George Watson comp *The New Cambridge Bibliography of English Literature* 1:2381–418.

Adams, H.M., comp *Catalogue of Books Printed on the Continent of Europe, 1501–1600 in Cambridge Libraries* 2 vols. Cambridge: University Press 1967

Addy, John 'A Further Note on the Episcopal Licensing of Schoolmasters' *Church Quarterly Review* 160 (1959) 251–2

Aelianus, Claudius *A Registre of Hystories* ... trans Abraham Fleming. London: for T. Woodcocke 1576 (*STC* 164)

– *Varia historia* ed Mervin R. Dilts. Leipzig: B.G. Teubner 1974

Aetios of Amida *The Gynaecology and Obstetrics ...* trans [from the Latin edition of Cornarius, 1542] James V. Ricci. Philadelphia and Toronto: Blakiston 1950
Agrippa, Cornelius *A Treatise of the Nobilitie and Excellencye of Woman Kynde* trans David Clapham. London: T. Berthelet 1542 (*STC* 203)
Allen, C.G. 'The Sources of "Lily's Latin Grammar": A Review of the Facts and Some Further Suggestions' *The Library* 5th ser 9 (1954) 85–100
Allen, D.C. *Mysteriously Meant: The Rediscovery of Pagan Symbolism and Allegorical Interpretation in the Renaissance* Baltimore and London : The Johns Hopkins Press 1970
Allen, J.W. *A History of Political Thought in the Sixteenth Century* 1928; London: Methuen 1960
Alston, R.C., comp *A Bibliography of the English Language from the Invention of Printing to the Year 1800 ...* Leeds: For the Author 1965–
Ames, Joseph, and William Herbert *Typographical Antiquities ...* 3 vols. London: Payne 1785–90
Anders, H. 'The Elizabethan ABC with the Catechism' *The Library* 4th ser 16 (1935–6) 32–48
Andrewes, Lancelot *XCVI Sermons* ed William Laud and John Buckeridge. 5th ed. London: G. Bedell and T. Collins 1661 (Wing A3142a)
Arber, Edward, ed *A Transcript of the Registers of the Company of Stationers of London; 1554–1640 A.D.* 5 vols. London: Privately Printed 1875–94
Archambault, Paul 'The Analogy of the "Body" in Renaissance Political Literature' *Bibliothèque d'Humanisme et Renaissance* 29 (1967) 21–53
Ariès, Philippe *Centuries of Childhood: A Social History of Family Life* trans R. Baldick. New York: Alfred A. Knopf 1962
Aristophanes [See headnote to this list]
Aristotle [See headnote to this list]
Ascham, Roger *English Works: Toxophilus, Report of the Affaires and State of Germany, The Scholemaster* ed W.A. Wright. Cambridge: University Press 1904
– *The Schoolmaster (1570)* ed L.V. Ryan. Ithaca, NY: Cornell University Press for the Folger Shakespeare Library 1967
– *The Whole Works* ed the Rev Dr Giles. 3 vols in 4. London: John Russell Smith 1864–5
ASD = Erasmus *Opera omnia* (1969–) [See below]
Aulus Gellius [See headnote to this list]
Avicenna *Liber canonis* Venice 1507; rpt Hildesheim: Georg Olms 1964
Babb, Lawrence *The Elizabethan Malady: A Study of Melancholia in English Literature from 1580 to 1642* East Lansing, Mich: Michigan State College Press 1951
Bailey, Richard W., ed *Early Modern English: Additions and Antedatings to the Record of English Vocabulary 1475–1700* Hildesheim and New York: Georg Olms 1978

Bakeless, J.E. *The Tragicall History of Christopher Marlowe* 2 vols. Cambridge, Mass: Harvard University Press 1942

Baldwin, T.W. *Shakspere's Five-Act Structure: Shakspere's Early Plays on the Background of Renaissance Theories of Five-Act Structure from 1470* Urbana: University of Illinois Press 1947

– *William Shakspere's Petty School* Urbana: University of Illinois Press 1943

– *William Shakspere's Small Latine & Lesse Greeke* 2 vols. Urbana: University of Illinois Press 1944

Ball, W.W. Rouse *A History of the Study of Mathematics at Cambridge* Cambridge: University Press 1889

Banister, John *The Historie of Man* ... London: J. Daye 1578 (*STC* 1359)

Baret, John *An Alvearie or Quadruple Dictionarie, Containing Foure Sundrie Tongues: Namelie, English, Latine, Greeke, and French* ... London: H. Denham 1580 (*STC* 1411)

– *An Alvearie or Triple Dictionarie, in Englishe, Latin, and French* ... London: H. Denham 1573 (*STC* 1410)

Barkan, Leonard *Nature's Work of Art: The Human Body as Image of the World* New Haven and London: Yale University Press 1975

Barker, William 'Richard Mulcaster's *Positions* and Girolamo Mercuriale's *De arte gymnastica libri sex*' 199–207 in A. Dalzell et al eds *Acta Conventus Neo-Latini Torontoniensis* Binghamton NY: Medieval and Renaissance Texts 1991

–, and Jean Chadwick 'Richard Mulcaster's Preface to *Cato Christianus* (1600): A Translation and Commentary' *Humanistica Lovaniensia* 42 (1993) 323–67

Baron, Hans 'The *Querelle* of the Ancients and the Moderns as a Problem for Renaissance Scholarship' *Journal of the History of Ideas* 20 (1959) 3–22

Barrow, R.H. *Plutarch and His Times* London: Chatto and Windus 1967

Bartlett, Kenneth 'The Decline and Abolition of the Master of Grammar: An Early Victory of Humanism at the University of Cambridge' *History of Education* 6 (1977) 1–8

Baskervill, C.R. 'Richard Mulcaster' *Times Literary Supplement* (15 August 1935) 513

Bateman, Stephen *A Christall Glass of Christian Reformation* London: J.Day 1569 (*STC* 1591)

Battenhouse, R.B. *Marlowe's 'Tamburlaine': A Study in Renaissance Moral Philosophy* Nashville, Tenn: Vanderbilt University Press 1941

Batty, Bartholomew *The Christian Mans Closet. Wherein is Conteined a Large Discourse of the Godly Training Up of Children* ... trans William Lowth. London: Thomas Dawson and Gregorie Seton 1581 (*STC* 1591)

Beaumont, Francis *The Knight of the Burning Pestle* ed S.P. Zitner. Manchester: Manchester University Press 1984

Becon, Thomas *The Worckes* 3 vols. London: J. Day 1560–4 (*STC* 1710)

Benndorf, Cornelie *Die englische Pädagogik im 16. Jahrhundert wie sie dargestellt wird im Wirken und in den Werken von Elyot, Ascham und Mulcaster* Vienna and Leipzig: W. Braumüller 1905; rpt London: Johnson Reprint 1965

Bennett, H.S. *English Books & Readers 1558 to 1603 Being a Study in the History of the Book Trade in the Reign of Elizabeth I* Cambridge: University Press 1965

Bentley, Thomas *The Monument of Matrones* ... London: H. Denham, 1582 (*STC* 1892)

Bergeron, David M. 'Elizabeth's Coronation Entry (1559): New Manuscript Evidence' *English Literary Renaissance* 8 (1978) 3–8

– *English Civic Pageantry 1558–1642* London: Edward Arnold 1971

Bernard, Henry 'School Punishments. The Strap - Rod - Ferule - Birch' in *English Pedagogy - Old and New* ser 2 as *Education, the School, and the Teacher in English Literature* 2nd ed. Hartford, Conn: Brown and Gross 1876

Berry, Boyd M. 'The First English Pediatricians and Tudor Attitudes toward Childhood' *Journal of the History of Ideas* 35 (1974) 561–77

Berry, Lloyd E. 'Thomas Charde, Printer and Bookseller' *The Library* 5th ser 15 (1960) 57–8

Besant, Walter *London in the Time of the Tudors* London: Adam and Charles Black 1904

Besso, Marco *Roma e il Papa nei proverbi e nei modi di dire* Rome: Fondazione M. Besso; Florence: Leo S. Olschki 1971

Bèze, Theodore de *Confessio Christianae fidei* London: T. Vautrollier 1581 (*STC* 2006.2)

The Bible. Geneva: R. Hall 1560 (*STC* 2093)

Binns, J.W. *Intellectual Culture in Elizabethan and Jacobean England: The Latin Writings of the Age* Leeds: Francis Cairns 1990

Boccaccio, Giovanni *Concerning Famous Women* trans G.A. Guarino. New Brunswick, NJ: Rutgers University Press 1963

– *Forty-six Lives* ... trans Henry Parker, Lord Morley, ed Herbert G. Wright. London: Oxford University Press 1943 (Early English Text Society os 214)

Bolgar, R.R. *The Classical Heritage and Its Beneficiaries from the Carolingian Age to the End of the Renaissance* Cambridge: University Press 1954

– 'Classical Reading in Renaissance Schools' *Durham Research Review* no 6 (September 1955) 18–26

Boswell, John *The Kindness of Strangers: The Abandonment of Children from Late Antiquity to the Renaissance* New York: Pantheon 1988

Bourne, William *A Booke Called the Treasure for Traveilers* ... London: for T. Woodcocke 1578 (*STC* 3432)

Bowers, Fredson *Elizabethan Revenge Tragedy 1587–1642* Princeton: Princeton University Press 1940

Boyd, M.C. *Elizabethan Music and Musical Criticism* Rev ed. 1962; Philadelphia: University of Pennsylvania Press 1967

Bradbrook, M.C. 'St. George for Spelling Reform! Social Implications of Orthography – Cheke to Whythorn; Mulcaster to Holofernes' *Shakespeare Quarterly* 15.3 (Summer 1964) 128–41

Bradwardine, Thomas *Geometria speculatiua* ... Paris: I. Petit 1511

Brailsford, Dennis *Sport and Society: Elizabeth to Anne* Toronto: University of Toronto Press; London: Routledge and Kegan Paul 1969

Brewer, Charlotte 'The Second Edition of the *Oxford English Dictionary*' *Review of English Studies* ns 44, no 175 (1993) 313–42

Brinsley, John *Ludus Literarius* ... London: T. Man 1612 (*STC* 3768) rpt Menston: Scolar Press 1968

Broughton, Hugh *An Explication of the Article κατῆλθεν εἰς ᾅδου* ... 2nd ed. London [ie, Middleburg?]: n pr 1605 (*STC* 3863)

– *Works* ... London: N. Ekins 1662 (Wing B4997)

Brown, J. Howard *Elizabethan Schooldays: An Account of the English Grammar Schools in the Second Half of the Sixteenth Century* Oxford: Basil Blackwell 1933

Brunoni, W. 'Il "De arte gymnastica" di Gerolamo Mercuriale visto da un educatore fisico' *Romagna Medica* 8 (1956) 459–66

Buckley, William *Arithmetica memorativa* ... London: T. Marshe 1574 (*STC* 22252 [part of John Seton *Dialectica*])

Buisson, F. *Répertoire des ouvrages pédagogiques du XVIe siècle* 1886; rpt Nieuwkoop: de Graaf 1962

Burton, Robert *The Anatomy of Melancholy* ed Thomas C. Faulkner, Nicholas K. Kiessling, Rhonda L. Blair, et al. Oxford: Clarendon Press 1989–

Busacchi, Vincenzo 'Gerolamo Mercuriale nel 350° anniversario della morte' *Romagna Medica* 8 (1956) 417–30

Byrne, M. St Clare 'Anthony Munday's Spelling as a Literary Clue' *The Library* 4th ser 4 (1923–4) 9–23

–, and Gladys Scott Thomson '"My Lord's Books": The Library of Francis, Second Earl of Bedford, in 1584' *Review of English Studies* 7 (1931) 385–405

Caelius Aurelianus *On Acute Diseases and On Chronic Diseases* ed and trans I.E. Drabkin. Chicago: University of Chicago Press 1950

Camden, Carroll *The Elizabethan Woman ... 1540 to 1640* Houston, New York, London: Elsevier Press 1952

Camden, William *Epistolae* ed Thomas Smith. London: R. Chiswell 1691 (Wing C361)

– *Remaines, Concerning Britaine* ... London: John Legatt for Simon Waterson 1614 (*STC* 4522)

Carlisle, Nicholas *A Concise Description of the Endowed Grammar Schools in England and Wales* 2 vols. London: Baldwin, Craddock, and Joy 1818

Carruthers, Mary *The Book of Memory: A Study of Memory in Medieval Culture* Cambridge: Cambridge University Press 1990

Case, John *Apologia musices tam vocalis quam instrumentalis et mixtae* Oxford: J. Barnesius 1588 (*STC* 4755)

– [attributed] *The Praise of Musicke* Oxford: J. Barnes 1586 (*STC* 20184)

Castiglione, Baldassare *The Book of the Courtier* trans T. Hoby. London: J.M. Dent 1928 [Apparently follows the trilingual edition of 1588, *STC* 4781]

Celsus, C. [See headnote to this list]

Chambers, E.K. *The Elizabethan Stage* 4 vols. Oxford: Clarendon Press 1923

Charlton, Kenneth 'Ages of Admission to Educational Institutions in Tudor and Stuart England: A Comment' *History of Education* 5 (1976) 221–6

– *Education in Renaissance England* London: Routledge and Kegan Paul; Toronto: University of Toronto Press 1965

– '"Not Publike Onely But Also Private and Domesticall": Mothers and Familial Education in Pre-Industrial England' *History of Education* 17 (1988) 1–20

– 'The Professions in Sixteenth Century England' *University of Birmingham Historical Journal* 12 (1969) 20–41

– 'The Teaching Profession in Sixteenth- and Seventeenth-Century England' 24–61 in Paul Nash ed *History and Education: The Educational Uses of the Past* New York: Random House 1970

Chew, Samuel C. *The Crescent and the Rose: Islam and England during the Renaissance* New York: Oxford University Press 1937

Churton, Ralph *The Life of Alexander Nowell, Dean of St. Paul's ...* Oxford: At the University Press for the Author 1809

Cicero, M. Tullius [See headnote to this list]

Clair, Colin 'Thomas Vautrollier' *Gutenberg Jahrbuch* (1960) 223–8

Clarke, M.L. *Classical Education in Britain 1500–1900* Cambridge: University Press 1959

C[leaver], R[obert] *A Godlie Forme of Householde Government: For the Ordering of Private Families, According to the Direction of Gods Word* London: F. Kingston for T. Man 1598 (*STC* 5383)

Cleland, James *The Institution of a Young Noble Man* (1607) ed Max Molyneux. 2 vols. New York: Scholars' Facsimiles and Reprints 1948 [Reproduces *STC* 5393]

Clement, Francis *The Petie Schole with an English Orthographie ...* London: Thomas Vautrollier 1587 (*STC* 5400) rpt Leeds: Scolar Press 1967

Clement of Alexandria *Christ the Educator* trans Simon P. Wood. New York: Fathers of the Church 1954

Cliffe, J.T. *The Yorkshire Gentry from the Reformation to the Civil War* London: University of London Athlone Press 1969

Clode, Charles M. *The Early History of the Guild of Merchant Taylors of the Fraternity of St. John the Baptist, London ...* In 2 parts. London: Harrison and Sons 1888

Close, A.J. 'Commonplace Theories of Art and Nature in Classical Antiquity and in the Renaissance' *Journal of the History of Ideas* 30 (1969) 467–86

– 'Philosophical Theories of Art and Nature in Classical Antiquity' *Journal of the History of Ideas* 32 (1971) 163–84

Comparetti, Domenico *Vergil in the Middle Ages* trans E.F.M. Benecke. London: Swan Sonnenschein and Co. 1895

Complete Peerage. See Gibbs, (Hon) Vicary.

Cooper, Charles Henry, and Thompson Cooper *Athenae Cantabrigienses* 3 vols. Cambridge: Deighton, Bell, and Co [et al] 1858–1913

Cooper, Thomas *Thesaurus linguae Romanae & Britannicae* ... London: T. Berthelet for H. Wykes 1565 (*STC* 5686) rpt Menston: Scolar Press 1969

Cooper, Rev Wm. M. [pseudonym for James Glass Bertram] *Flagellation and the Flagellants: A History of the Rod in All Countries from the Earliest Period to the Present Time* New ed. London: William Reeves nd

Corte, Claudio *The Art of Riding, Conteining Diverse Necessarie Instructions* trans T. Bedingfield. London: H. Denham 1584 (*STC* 5797)

Cressy, David 'A Drudgery of Schoolmasters: The Teaching Profession in Elizabethan and Stuart England' 129–53 in Wilfrid Prest ed *The Professions in Early Modern England* London: Croom Helm 1987

– *Education in Tudor and Stuart England* London: Edward Arnold 1975

– *Literacy and the Social Order: Reading and Writing in Tudor and Stuart England* Cambridge: Cambridge University Press 1980

– 'School and College Admission Ages in Seventeenth-Century England' *History of Education* 8 (1979) 167–77

Croll, Morris *Style, Rhetoric and Rhythm: Essays* ed J. Max Patrick et al. Princeton: Princeton University Press 1966

Cruttwell, Patrick 'Physiology and Psychology in Shakespeare's Age' *Journal of the History of Ideas* 12 (1951) 75–89

Cuming, G.J. *A History of Anglican Liturgy* 2nd ed. London: Macmillan 1982

Curtis, Mark 'The Alienated Intellectuals of Early Stuart England' *Past and Present* 23 (November 1962) 25–43

– 'Education and Apprenticeship' *Shakespeare Survey* 17 (1964) 53–72

– *Oxford and Cambridge in Transition 1558–1642: An Essay on Changing Relations between the English Universities and English Society* Oxford: Clarendon Press 1959

Cyprian, St *Treatises* trans R.J. Deferrari et al. New York: Fathers of the Church 1958

CWE = Erasmus *Collected Works* [See below]

Dal Piaz, Stelvio, and Alda Paoletti *Un ginnasiarca dell'età elisabettiana 'Richard Mulcaster'* Arezzo: D. Badiali 1967

Davies, W.J. Frank *Teaching Reading in Early England* London: Pitman 1973

Dee, John [See Euclid *The Elements*, below]

Dekker, Thomas *The Dramatic Works* ed Fredson Bowers. 4 vols. Cambridge: University Press 1953–61

DeMolen, Richard L. 'Ages of Admission to Educational Institutions in Tudor and Stuart England' *History of Education* 5 (1976) 207–19

– 'Four of Richard Mulcaster's Last Publications' *Papers of the Bibliographical Society of America* 66 (1972) 291–3

– 'Richard Mulcaster: An Elizabethan Savant' PH D dissertation University of Michigan 1970 [= PH D diss]

– *Richard Mulcaster (c.1531–1611) and Educational Reform in the Renaissance* Nieuwkoop: de Graaf 1991

– 'Richard Mulcaster: An Elizabethan Savant' *Shakespeare Studies* 8 (1975) 29–82

– 'Richard Mulcaster and Elizabethan Pageantry' *Studies in English Literature* 14 (1974) 209–21

– 'Richard Mulcaster and the Elizabethan Theatre' *Theatre Survey: The American Journal of Theatre History* 13 (1972) 28–41

– 'Richard Mulcaster and the Profession of Teaching in Sixteenth-Century England' *Journal of the History of Ideas* 35 (1974) 121–9

– 'Richard Mulcaster's Philosophy of Education' *Journal of Medieval and Renaissance Studies* 2 (Spring 1972) 69–91

Desainliens, Claude [or Holiband] *Campo di Fior or Else the Flourie Field of Foure Languages ...* London: T. Vautrollier 1583 (*STC* 6735)

Diogenes Laertius [See headnote to this list]

Dionysius of Halicarnassus [See headnote to this list]

DNB = Stephen, Sir Leslie, and Sir Sidney Lee, eds *The Dictionary of National Biography* Rev ed. 21 vols. Oxford: Oxford University Press 1908–9 *Supplement January 1901–December 1911* ed Sir Sidney Lee. 3 vols in 1. 1912; rpt Oxford: Oxford University Press 1920

Dolmetsch, Mabel *Dances of England and France from 1450 to 1600 with Their Music and Authentic Manner of Performance* London: Routledge and Kegan Paul 1949

Domenichi, Lodovico *The Nobility of Women* trans William Bercher [ie, Barker] ed R. Warwick Bond. London: Roxburghe Club 1904

Dorsten, J.A. van *Poets, Patrons and Professors: Sir Philip Sidney, Daniel Rogers, and the Leiden Humanists* Leiden: University Press for the Sir Thomas Browne Institute 1962

– *The Radical Arts: First Decade of an Elizabethan Renaissance* 2nd ed. Leiden: University Press for Sir Thomas Browne Institute 1973

Draper, F.W.M. *Four Centuries of Merchant Taylors' School 1561–1961* London: Oxford University Press 1962

Dufour, Antoine *Les Vies des femmes celebres* [1504] ed G. Jeanneau. Geneva: Droz 1970

Duhamel, P. Albert 'The Ciceronianism of Gabriel Harvey' *Studies in Philology* 49 (1952) 155–70

Durling, Richard J. 'A Chronological Census of Renaissance Editions and Translations of Galen' *Journal of the Warburg and Courtauld Institutes* 24 (1961) 230–305

E[llis], H[enry] 'Biographical Anecdotes of Richard Mulcaster' *Gentleman's Magazine* 70 (1800) 419–21, 511–12, 603–4

Elyot, (Sir) Thomas *The Boke Named the Governour* ed H.H.S. Croft. 2 vols. London: Kegan Paul, Trench, and Co 1883

– *The Castel of Helth* ... London: T. Berthelet 1541 (*STC* 7644) rpt New York: Scholars' Facsimiles and Reprints nd

– *The Defence of Good Women* London: T. Berthelet 1540 (*STC* 7657.5)

Emden, A.B. *A Biographical Register of the University of Oxford to A.D. 1500* 3 vols. Oxford: Clarendon Press 1957–9

– *A Biographical Register of the University of Oxford A.D. 1501 to 1540* Oxford: Claredon Press 1974

Emmison, F.G. *Elizabethan Life: Morals and the Church Mainly from Essex Archidiaconal Records* Chelmsford: Essex County Council 1973

Erasmus, Desiderius *Apophthegmes* ... trans N. Udall. London: R. Grafton 1542 (*STC* 10443)

– *Collected Works of Erasmus* gen ed J.K. McConica. Toronto: University of Toronto Press 1974– [CWE]

– *Declamatio de pueris statim ac liberaliter instituendis* ed J.-C. Margolin. Geneva: Droz 1966

– *The Education of a Christian Prince* trans Lester K. Born. 1936; rpt New York: W.W. Norton 1968

– *Opus epistolarum* ed P.S. Allen, H.M. Allen, and H.W. Garrod. 11 vols with index. Oxford: Clarendon Press 1906–58

– *Opera omnia* Amsterdam: North Holland Publishing 1969– [ASD]

– *Opera omnia* ... ed J. LeClerc. 10 vols in 11. Leiden: vander Aa 1703–6 [LB]

–, et al *Varij lusus pueriles ex D. Eras. M. Corderio, & L. Viue separati in gratiam puerorum*. Paris: M. David 1555

Euclid *The Elements of Geometrie* ... trans Henry Billingsley and preface by John Dee. London: J. Daye 1570 (*STC* 10560)

Eusebius, Socrates, and Evagarius *The Auncient Ecclesiasticall Histories* ... trans M. Hanmer. London: T. Vautroullier 1576–7 (*STC* 10572)

Farr, W.C., et al *Merchant Taylors' School: Its Origin, History and Present Surroundings* Oxford: Basil Blackwell 1929

Feingold, Mordechai *The Mathematicians' Apprenticeship: Science, Universities and*

Society in England, 1560–1640 Cambridge: Cambridge University Press 1984

Fenton, Geoffrey, trans *A Forme of Christian Pollicie Gathered Out of the French* London: H. Middelton for R. Newbery 1574 (*STC* 10793a) rpt Amsterdam and New York: Theatrum Orbis Terrarum and Da Capo Press 1972 (English Experience 454)

Ferguson, Arthur B. 'Circumstances and the Sense of History in Tudor England: The Coming of the Historical Revolution' 170–205 in *Medieval and Renaissance Studies* ed John M. Headley. Chapel Hill: University of North Carolina Press 1968

Ferguson, F.S. 'Relations between London and Edinburgh Printers and Stationers (–1640)' *The Library* 4th ser 8 (1927) 145–98

Ferguson, W. Craig *Pica Roman Type in Elizabethan England* Aldershot: Scolar Press 1989

Feuillerat, Albert, ed *Documents Relating to the Office of the Revels in the Time of Queen Elizabeth* Louvain: A. Uystpruyst 1908 (Materielen zur Kunde des älteren Englischen Dramas 21)

Feyerharm, W.R. 'The Status of the Schoolmaster and the Continuity of Education in Elizabethan East Anglia' *History of Education* 5 (1976) 103–15

Finney, Gretchen 'Vocal Exercise in the Sixteenth Century Related to Theories of Physiology and Disease' *Bulletin of the History of Medicine* 42 (1968) 422–49

Firmicus Maternus, Julius *Matheseos libri VIII* ed W. Kroll and F. Skutsch. 2 vols. 1897; rpt Stuttgart: Teubner 1965

Flynn, Vincent Joseph 'The Grammatical Writings of William Lily, ?1468–?1523' *Papers of the Bibliographical Society of America* 37 (1943) 85–113

Forster, Leonard *Janus Gruter's English Years: Studies in the Continuity of Dutch Literature in Elizabethan England* Leiden: University Press and London: Oxford University Press, for Sir Thomas Browne Institute 1967

– 'The Translator of the "Theatre for Worldlings"' *English Studies* 48 (1967) 27–34

Foster, Joseph *Alumni Oxonienses: The Members of the University of Oxford, 1500–1714* ... 4 vols. Oxford: Parker and Co 1891–2

Fraser, Antonia *A History of Toys* London: Weidenfeld and Nicolson 1966

French, Peter *John Dee: The World of an Elizabethan Magus* London: Routledge and Kegan Paul 1972

Friedman, Alice T. 'The Influence of Humanism on the Education of Girls and Boys in Tudor England' *History of Education Quarterly* 25 (1985) 57–70

Fuller, Thomas *The History of the Worthies of England* ... London: J.G.W.L. and W.G. (for Thomas Williams) 1662 (Wing F2441)

Galen *A Translation of Galen's Hygiene (De Sanitate Tuenda)* trans Robert Montraville Green. Springfield, Ill: Charles C. Thomas 1951

– *Opera omnia* ed C.G. Kühn. 20 vols in 22. Leipzig: Car. Cnoblochius 1821–33

Gardiner, Dorothy *English Girlhood at School: A Study of Women's Education through Twelve Centuries* London: Oxford University Press 1929

Gascoigne, George *The Complete Works* ed John W. Cunliffe. 2 vols. Cambridge: University Press 1907–10

– *Princely Pleasures ... at Kenilworth Castle* London: J.H. Burn 1821

– *The Princelye Pleasures at the Courte of Kenelworth ... 1575. Imprinted at London, by Rychard Ihones ... 1576* London: F. Marshall 1821

– *The Whole Woorkes ...* London: Abel Ieffes 1587 (*STC* 11638)

Gaster, M. 'Virgil and the Bread' *Times Literary Supplement* (4 September 1937) 640

Gebert, Clara *An Anthology of Elizabethan Dedications and Prefaces* Philadelphia: University of Pennsylvania Press 1933

Gentleness and Nobility Oxford: Oxford University Press 1950 (Malone Society Reprint)

Gibbs, (Hon) Vicary, et al, eds *The Complete Peerage of England Scotland Ireland Great Britain and the United Kingdom by G.E. C[okayne]* 12 vols. London: The St Catherine Press 1910–59

Gibson, Strickland, ed *Statuta antiqua Universitatis Oxoniensis* Oxford: Clarendon Press 1931

Gilbert, Allan H. 'Martin Bucer on Education' *Journal of English and Germanic Philology* 18 (1919) 321–45

Gilbert, (Sir) Humphrey *Queene Elizabethes Achademy ...* ed F.J. Furnivall. London: N. Truebner 1869 (Early English Text Society es 8)

Gilbert, Neal W. *Renaissance Concepts of Method* New York: Columbia University Press 1960

Goldberg, Jonathan *Writing Matter: From the Hands of the English Renaissance* Stanford: Stanford University Press 1990

Gosson, Stephen *The Schoole of Abuse ...* London: Thomas Woodcocke 1579 (*STC* 12097) rpt ed Arthur Freeman. New York and London: Garland Publishing 1973

Gower, Lord Ronald Sutherland *The Tower of London* 2 vols. London: George Bell and Sons 1901–2

Grafton, Anthony, and Lisa Jardine *From Humanism to the Humanities: Education and Liberal Arts in Fifteenth- and Sixteenth-Century Europe* London: Duckworth 1986

Graham, T.H.B. 'The Family of de Mulcaster' *Transactions of the Cumberland and Westmorland Antiquarian and Archaeological Society* ns 18 (1918) 110–24

Gratarolus, Guilielmus *A Direction for the Health of Magistrates and Studentes ...* trans T. N[ewton]. London: W. How for A. Veale 1574 (*STC* 12193a)

Great Britain. Privy Council *Acts of the Privy Council of England* ed J.R. Dasent ns 5 (1554–6). London: Eyre and Spottiswoode 1892

Greaves, Richard L. *Society and Religion in Elizabethan England* Minneapolis: University of Minnesota Press 1981
The Greek Anthology [See headnote to this list]
Green, Henry, and James Croston, eds *The Mirrour of Maiestie ... 1618* Manchester and London: A. Brothers and Trübner and Co 1870 (Holbein Society 3)
Greene, Thomas M. 'Roger Ascham: The Perfect End of Shooting' *ELH: A Journal of English Literary History* 36 (1969) 609–25
Greg, W.W. *A Companion to Arber ...* Oxford: Clarendon Press 1967
– et al *English Literary Autographs, 1550–1650* 3 vols. London: Oxford University Press 1925–32
– and E. Boswell *Record of the Court of the Stationers' Company 1576 to 1602 from Register B* London: Bibliographical Society 1930
Gregory IX (Pope) *Decretales ...* Rome: In aedibus populi Romani 1584
Grieg, C. Margaret 'The Identity of E.K. of the Shepheardes Calender' *Notes and Queries* 197 (1952) 332–4
Gruner, O. Cameron *A Treatise on the Canon of Medicine of Avicenna Incorporating a Translation of the First Book* London: Luzac and Co 1930
[Guy de Chauliac] *Guydos Questions ...* London: T. East 1579 (*STC* 12469)
Hakluyt, Richard *The Principal Navigations, Voiages, Traffiques and Discoveries of the English Nation ...* 3 vols. London: G. Bishop [et al] 1598 (*STC* 12626)
Hale, George *The Body Politic: A Political Metaphor in English Renaissance Literature* The Hague and Paris: Mouton 1971
Harris, H.A. *Sport in Greece and Rome* London: Thames and Hudson 1972
Harrison, John, and Peter Laslett *The Library of John Locke* 2nd ed. Oxford: Clarendon Press 1971
Harrison, William *Harrison's Description of England in Shakespeare's Youth ... A.D. 1577, 1587* ed F.J. Furnivall. Part 1, book 2. London: N. Trübner for the New Shakespeare Society 1877
Hart, (Mrs) E.P. *Merchant Taylors' School Register 1561–1934* 2 vols. London: Merchant Taylors' Company 1936
Harvey, E. Ruth *The Inward Wits: Psychological Theory in the Middle Ages and the Renaissance* London: Warburg Institute, University of London 1975
Harvey, Gabriel *Ciceronianus* ed H.S. Wilson and trans C.A. Forbes. Lincoln: University of Nebraska 1945
– *Marginalia* ed G.C. Moore Smith. Stratford-upon-Avon: Shakespeare Head Press 1913
– *Pierces Supererogation or a New Prayse of the Old Asse ...* London: J. Wolfe 1593 (*STC* 12903) rpt Menston: Scolar Press 1970
– *Rhetor; vel duorum dierum oratio de natura, arte, et exercitatione rhetorica* London: H. Binneman 1577 (*STC* 12904)

Hasler, P.W. *The House of Commons 1558–1603* 3 vols. London: HMSO 1981 (History of Parliament)

Haugaard, William P. *Elizabeth and the English Reformation: The Struggle for a Stable Settlement of Religion* Cambridge: University Press 1968

Heal, (Sir) Ambrose *The English Writing-Masters and Their Copy-Books 1570–1800: A Biographical Dictionary and a Bibliography* Cambridge: University Press 1931

Heninger, S.K., Jr *Touches of Sweet Harmony: Pythagorean Cosmology and Renaissance Poetics* San Marino, Cal: Huntington Library 1974

Heron, Haly *The Kayes of Counsaile. A Newe Discourse of Morall Philosophie (1579)* ed Virgil B. Heltzel. Liverpool: University Press of Liverpool 1954

Hessels, J.H., et al, ed *Ecclesiae Londino-Batavae archivum* 3 vols in 4. Cambridge: University Press 1887–97

Hexter, J.H. 'The Education of the Aristocracy in the Renaissance' 45–70 in his *Reappraisals in History* London: Longmans 1961

Hill, Georgiana *Women in English Life from Medieval to Modern Times* 2 vols. London: Richard Bentley 1896

Hippocrates [See headnote to this list]

Hoeniger, F. David *Medicine and Shakespeare in the English Renaissance* Newark: University of Delaware Press; London and Toronto: Associated University Presses 1992

Hollander, John *The Untuning of the Sky: Ideas of Music in English Poetry 1500–1700* Princeton: Princeton University Press 1961

Homer [See headnote to this list]

Hoole, Charles *A New Discovery of the Old Art of Teaching Schoole, in Four Small Treatises ...* London: J.T. for Andrew Crook 1660 (Wing H2688) rpt Menston: Scolar Press 1969

Horace [See headnote to this list]

Horne, David H. *The Life and Minor Works of George Peele* New Haven: Yale University Press 1952

Howell, Wilbur Samuel *Logic and Rhetoric in England, 1500–1700* Princeton: Princeton University Press 1956

Huarte de Navarro, Juan *Examen de Ingenios. The Examination of Mens Wits ...* trans R[ichard] C[arew]. London: Adam Islip for Richard Watkins 1594 (*STC* 13890) rpt New York and Amsterdam: Da Capo Press and Theatrum Orbis Terrarum 1969

Hughes, Paul L., and James F. Larkin, csv *Tudor Royal Proclamations* 3 vols. New Haven and London: Yale University Press 1964–9

Hull, Suzanne W. *Chaste, Silent and Obedient: English Books for Women 1475–1640* San Marino: Huntington Library 1982

Humphrey, Lawrence *The Nobles or of Nobilitye ...* London: Thomas Marshe 1563

(*STC* 13964) rpt Amsterdam and New York: Theatrum Orbis Terrarum and Da Capo Press 1973

Hunter, G.K. 'The Marking of *Sententiae* in Elizabethan Printed Plays, Poems, and Romances' *The Library* 5th ser 6 (1951) 171–88

Hurstfield, Joel *The Queen's Wards: Wardship and Marriage under Elizabeth I* London, New York, Toronto: Longmans, Green and Co 1958

The Institucion of a Gentleman London: T. Marshe, 1555 (*STC* 14104) rpt Amsterdam: Theatrum Orbis Terrarum; Norwood, NJ: Walter J. Johnson 1974 (English Experience 672)

Isaac, F.S. 'Elizabethan Roman and Italic Types' *The Library* 4th ser 14 (1933–4) 85–100 and 212–28

– *English Printers' Types of the Sixteenth Century* London: Oxford University Press 1936

Isocrates [See headnote to this list]

Jahn, Robert 'Letters and Booklists of Thomas Chard (or Chare) of London, 1583–4' *The Library* 4th ser 4 (1923–4) 219–37

Jardine, Lisa 'Humanism and Dialectic in Sixteenth-Century Cambridge' 141–54 in R.R. Bolgar ed *Classical Influences on European Culture A.D. 1500–1700* Cambridge: University Press 1976

– 'The Place of Dialectic Teaching in Sixteenth-Century Cambridge' *Studies in the Renaissance* 21 (1975) 31–62

Jenkins, Gladys 'A Note on the Episcopal Licensing of Schoolmasters in England' *Church Quarterly Review* 159 (1958) 78–81

Johnson, Francis R. *Astronomical Thought in Renaissance England: A Study of the Scientific Writings from 1500 to 1645* Baltimore: Johns Hopkins Press 1937

– 'Notes on English Retail Book-prices, 1550–1640' *The Library* 5th ser 5 (1950–1) 83–112

– 'Thomas Hood's Inaugural Address as Mathematical Lecturer of the City of London (1588)' *Journal of the History of Ideas* 3 (1942) 94–106

Jones, John *The Arte and Science of Preserving Bodie and Soule in Healthe, Wisedome, and Catholike Religion* ... London: H. Bynneman 1579 (*STC* 14724)

– *The Bathes of Bathes Ayde* ... London: W. Jones 1572 (*STC* 14725)

Jones, R.F. 'Richard Mulcaster's View of the English Language' *Washington University Studies* 13 (1926) 267–303

– *The Triumph of the English Language: A Survey of Opinions Concerning the Vernacular from the Introduction of Printing to the Restoration* Stanford: Stanford University Press 1953

Jonson, Ben [*Works*] ed C.H. Herford and P. and E. Simpson. 11 vols. Oxford: Clarendon Press 1925–52

Joseph, (Sister) Miriam *Shakespeare's Use of the Arts of Language* New York: Columbia University Press 1947

Josephus *Autobiographie* ed and trans André Pelletier SJ. Paris: Société d'Edition 'Les Belles Lettres' 1959 (Collection Budé)

– [For other works, see headnote to this list]

Joubert, Laurent *Treatise on Laughter* trans Gregory David de Rocher. University, Alabama: University of Alabama Press, 1980

Judson, A.C. *The Life of Edmund Spenser* Baltimore: The Johns Hopkins Press 1945

Junius, Adrianus *The Nomenclator, or Remembrancer* ... trans John Higins. London: R. Newberie and H. Denham 1585 (*STC* 14860)

Justinian *Codicis Dn. Iustiniani ... libri XII* Antwerp: Christopher Plantin 1575

Justinus, M. Junianus *Epitoma historiarum Pompei Trogi* ed O. Seel. Stuttgart: B.G. Teubner 1972

Juvenal [See headnote to this list]

Kelso, Ruth *Doctrine for the Lady of the Renaissance* Urbana: University of Illinois Press 1956

– *The Doctrine of the English Gentleman in the Sixteenth Century, with a Bibliographical List of Treatises on the Gentleman and Related Subjects Published in Europe to 1625* Urbana: University of Illinois Press 1929 (University of Illinois Studies in Language and Literature 14)

Kempe, William *The Education of Children in Learning* London: T. Orwin for J. Potter and T. Gubbin 1588 (*STC* 14926) rpt in Pepper ed *Four Tudor Books on Education*

Kinney, Arthur F., ed *Elizabethan Backgrounds: Historical Documents of the Age of Elizabeth I* Hamden Conn.: Archon Books 1975 (*The Quenes Maiesties Passage* 7–39)

Klähr, Theodor *Leben und Werke Richard Mulcaster's, eines englischen Pädagogen des 16. Jahrhunderts* ... Dresden: von Bleyl und Kaemmerer 1893 (diss, University of Leipzig)

Koelbing, Huldrych M., et al *Beiträge zur Geschichte der Lepra* ... Zurich: Juris Druck und Verlag 1972

Kocher, Paul H. *Science and Religion in Elizabethan England* 1953; rpt New York: Octagon Books 1969

Labalme, Patricia H., ed *Beyond Their Sex: Learned Women of the European Past* New York: New York University Press 1980

Lanham, Richard A. *A Handlist of Rhetorical Terms: A Guide for Students of English Literature* 2nd ed. Berkeley: University of California Press 1991

La Primaudaye, Pierre de *The French Academie* ... trans T. B[owes]. London: Edmund Bollifant for G. Bishop and Ralph Newbery 1586 (*STC* 15233)

– *Académie françoise* ... Paris: G. Chaudière 1577

Lausberg, Heinrich *Handbuch der literarischen Rhetorik: Eine Grundlegung der Literaturwissenschaft* 2 vols. Munich: Max Hueber Verlag 1960

Leach, A.F., ed *Educational Charters and Documents 598 to 1909* Cambridge: University Press 1911

Leader, Damian Riehl 'Grammar in Late Medieval Oxford and Cambridge' *History of Education* 12 (1983) 9–14

LeFanu, W.R. 'Thomas Vautrollier, Printer and Bookseller' *Proceedings of the Huguenot Society of London* 20 (1959) 12–25

Lehmberg, Stanford E. *Sir Walter Mildmay and Tudor Government* Austin: University of Texas Press 1964

LeRoy, Louis *De la vicissitude ou variété des choses en l'univers* ... Paris: Pierre l'Huilier 1576

– *Of the Interchangeable Course, or Variety of Things in the Whole World* ... trans R. A[shley]. London: C. Yetsweirt 1594 (*STC* 15488)

Lewis, C.S. *English Literature in the Sixteenth Century Excluding Drama* Oxford: Clarendon Press 1954

Liddell, Henry George, and Robert Scott *A Greek-English Lexicon* rev Sir Henry Stuart Jones et al. With a supplement. Oxford: Clarendon Press 1968

Lily, William, and John Colet [attributed] *A Shorte Introduction of Grammer* ... London: R. Wolfe 1549 (*STC* 15611) rpt Menston: Scolar Press 1970

Lincoln's Inn, London *The Records of the Honorable Society of Lincoln's Inn. The Black Books. Vol. II. from A.D. 1586 to A.D. 1660* London: Lincoln's Inn 1898

Linthicum, M. Channing *Costume in the Drama of Shakespeare and His Contemporaries* Oxford: Oxford University Press 1936

Livy [See headnote to this list]

Lodge, Thomas [Reply to Gosson's *Schoole of Abuse*] [London]: n pr, nd (*STC* 1926) rpt in Stephen Gosson *The Schoole of Abuse* ed Freeman

Lohr, Charles H., SJ 'Medieval Latin Aristotle Commentaries Authors: Robertus-Wilgelmus' *Traditio* 29 (1973) 93–197

Lomazzo, Paolo Giovanni *A Tracte Containing the Artes of Curious Paintinge Carvinge Buildinge* ... trans R. H[aydocke]. Oxford: J. Barnes 1598 (*STC* 16698)

Lowndes, William Thomas *The Bibliographer's Manual of English Literature* ... 6 vols. Rev ed Henry G. Bohn. London: Henry G. Bohn 1857–64; rpt [in 8 vols] Detroit: Gale Research 1967

Lucian [See headnote to this list]

Lupset, Thomas *The Life and Works of Thomas Lupset with a Critical Text of the Original Treatises and the Letters* ed J.A. Gee. New Haven: Yale University Press 1928

Lupton, J.H. *A Life of John Colet, D.D.* ... rev ed London: George Bell and Sons 1909

– 'Richard Mulcaster' in *DNB* (1894)

Lupton, Thomas *A Persuasion from Papestrie* ... London: H. Bynneman 1581 (*STC* 16950)

Lyly, John *The Complete Works* ... ed R. Warwick Bond. 3 vols. Oxford: Clarendon Press 1902

Maclean, Ian *The Renaissance Notion of Woman: A Study in the Fortunes of Scholasticism and Medical Science in European Intellectual Life* Cambridge: Cambridge University Press 1980

Maddison, Francis, et al, ed *Essays on the Life and Work of Thomas Linacre c. 1460–1524* Oxford: Oxford University Press 1977

Magoun, Francis Peabody, Jr *History of Football from the Beginnings to 1871* Bochum-Langendreer: Verlag Heinrich Pöppinghaus 1938 (Kölner Anglistische Arbeiten 31)

Mallet, (Sir) Charles E. *A History of the University of Oxford* 3 vols. London: Methuen 1924–7

Manning, Percy 'Sport and Pastime in Stuart Oxford' 83–135 in Rev H.E. Salter ed *Surveys and Tokens* Oxford: Clarendon Press 1923 (Oxford Historical Society 75)

Manning, R.J., and Alastair Fowler 'The Iconography of Spenser's Occasion' *Journal of the Warburg and Courtauld Institutes* 39 (1976) 263–6

Manschreck, Claude *Melanchthon: The Quiet Reformer* New York and Nashville: Abingdon Press 1958

Marcel, R. '"Saint" Socrate patron de l'humanisme' *Revue internationale de philosophie* 5 (1951) 135–43

Margolin, J.-C. 'L'Idée de nature dans la pensée d'Erasme' 9–44 in his *Recherches Erasmiennes* Geneva: Droz 1969

Markham, Gervase *Countrey Contentments, in Two Bookes* ... 2 parts. London: I.B. for R. Jackson 1615 (*STC* 17342)

Marlowe, Christopher *The Poems* ed Millar MacLure. London: Methuen and Co 1968

– *Tamburlaine the Great in Two Parts* ed Una Ellis-Fermor. London: Methuen and Co 1930

Marrou, H.-I. *A History of Education in Antiquity* trans George Lamb. London: Sheed and Ward 1956

Martial [See headnote to this list]

Mason, John E. *Gentlefolk in the Making: Studies in the History of English Courtesy Literature and Related Topics from 1531 to 1774* Philadelphia: University of Pennsylvania Press 1935

Master Broughtons Letters ... London: John Wolfe 1599 (*STC* 3864)

Maxwell-Lyte, H.C. *A History of Eton College (1440–1910)* 4th ed London: Macmillan 1911

Mazzini, Giuseppe *Jeronimo Mercuriale (1530–1606) y su 'De arte gymnastica'* Santiago, Chile: Imprento 'Cultura' [Boletin de Educacion Fisica] 1940

McConica, J.K., ed *The Collegiate University* vol 3 of *The History of the University*

of Oxford gen ed T.H. Aston. Oxford: Clarendon Press 1986
– 'Humanism and Aristotle in Tudor Oxford' *English Historical Review* 94 (1979) 291–317
McDonnell, (Sir) Michael F.J. *The Annals of St Paul's School* London: Privately Printed for the Governors 1959
– *A History of St. Paul's School* London: Chapman and Hall 1909
– *The Registers of St. Paul's School 1509–1748* London: Privately Printed for the Governors 1977
McKerrow, R.B. *A Dictionary of Printers and Booksellers ... 1557–1640* 1910; London: Bibliographical Society 1968
– *Printers' and Publishers' Devices in England and Scotland 1485–1640* London: Chiswick Press, for the Bibliographical Society 1913
McLean, Antonia *Humanism and the Rise of Science in Tudor England* London: Heinemann 1972
McMullen, Norma 'The Education of English Gentlewomen 1540–1640' *History of Education* 6 (1977) 87–101
McPherson, David 'Ben Jonson's Library and Marginalia' *Studies in Philology* 71.5 (December 1974)
Melanchthon, Philipp *Selectarum declamationum ... tomus primus* [etc] 4 vols. Strasbourg: n pr 1559–60
– *Werke* ed R. Stupperich. 9 vols. Gutersloh: Gerd Mohn 1951–75
Menander [See headnote to this list]
Mercuriale, Girolamo *Arte ginnastica* trans Ippolito Galante. Rome: Banco di San Spirito 1960 [rpt of *De arte gymnastica* 1601 in accompanying volume]
– *De arte gymnastica libri sex* Venice: Giunta, 1573 [Other editions consulted are those of Venice: Giunta 1569; Paris: Du Puys 1577; Venice: Giunta 1587; Venice: Giunta 1601]
Meteren, Emanuel van *Album amicorum Emanuelis de Meteren mercatoris Antuerpianj* ... Bodleian Library, ms Douce 68
Michaud, J.-F. *Biographie universelle* 2nd rev ed. 45 vols. Paris: Delagrave et Cie 1843–
Millican, C.B. 'The Northern Dialect of *The Shepheardes Calender*' *ELH* 6 (1939) 211–13
– 'Notes on Mulcaster and Spenser' *ELH: A Journal of English Literary History* 6 (1939) 214–16
– *Spenser and the Table Round: A Study in the Contemporaneous Background for Spenser's Use of the Arthurian Legend* Cambridge, Mass.: Harvard University Press 1932
Milton, John 'Of Education' ed D.C. Dorian 357–415 in *Complete Prose Works* 2 [1643–1648] ed E. Sirluck. New Haven: Yale University Press 1959
– *Poems* ed John Carey and Alastair Fowler. London: Longman 1968

Montaigne, Michel de *Oeuvres complètes* ed A. Thibaudet and M. Rat. Paris: Gallimard 1962

Moore, Philip *The Hope of Health* ... London: J. Kingston 1565 (*STC* 18060)

Moran, Jo Ann Hoeppner *The Growth of English Schooling 1340–1548: Learning, Literacy, and Laicization in Pre-Reformation York Diocese* Princeton: Princeton University Press 1985

More, Thomas *Utopia* ed E. Surtz, SJ, and J.H. Hexter in *Complete Works* 4. New Haven and London: Yale University Press 1965

Morgan, John *Godly Learning: Puritan Attitudes towards Reason, Learning, and Education, 1560–1640* Cambridge: Cambridge University Press 1986

Morrice, Thomas *An Apology for Schoolmasters* ... London: B. Alsop for R. Fleming 1619 (*STC* 18170)

Mortimer, Ruth, comp *Harvard College Library Department of Printing and Graphic Arts Catalogue of Books and Manuscripts Part II: Italian 16th Century Books* 2 vols. Cambridge, Mass.: Belknap Press at Harvard University Press 1974

Motter, T.H. Vail *The School Drama in England* London, New York, Toronto: Longmans, Green and Co 1929

Mulcaster, Richard [All works and editions of works by Mulcaster are given in part 1 of this bibliography]

Mullinger, J.B. *The University of Cambridge* 3 vols. Cambridge: University Press 1873–1911

Nashe, Thomas *Works* ed R.B. McKerrow. Rev ed by F.P. Wilson. 5 vols. Oxford: Basil Blackwell 1966 [first published in Oxford 1904–10]

Nelson, William 'The Teaching of English in Tudor Grammar Schools' *Studies in Philology* 49 (1952) 119–43

Nevinson, J.L. 'Emanuel van Meteren, 1535–1612' *Proceedings of the Huguenot Society of London* 19.4 (1953–9) 128–45

Newcourt, Richard *Repertorium Ecclesiasticum Parochiale Londinense* ... 2 vols. London: B. Motte for C. Bateman [et al] 1708–10

Newton, John *School Pastime for Young Children: or The Rudiments of Grammar* ... London: Robert Walton [1669?] (Wing N1068–9; issued in two parts)

Nichols, John, comp *The Progresses and Public Processions of Queen Elizabeth* ... New ed. 3 vols. London: John Nichols and Son 1823

Norden, Eduard *Die antike Kunstprosa vom VI. Jahrhundert v. Chr. bis in die Zeit der Renaissance* 2 vols. 2nd ed. Leipzig and Berlin: B.G. Teubner 1909

Norman, Philip 'Sir John de Pulteney and His Two Residences in London, Cold Harbour and the Manor of the Rose, Together with a Few Remarks on the Parish of St. Laurence Poultney' *Archaeologia* 57 (1901) 257–84

Northbrooke, John *A Treatise Wherein Dicing, Dauncing, Vaine Playes or Enterluds ... are Reproved* London: H. Bynneman for G. Bishop [1577] (*STC* 18670)

[Nowell, Alexander] *Christianae pietatis prima institutio, ad usum scholarum Latine scripta* London: Stationers' Company 1610 (*STC* 18719)

Ocland, Christopher *Εἰρηναρχία siue Elizabetha* ... London: C. Barker 1582 (*STC* 18775a; also part of Ocland's *Anglorum praelia* 1582, *STC* 18772.5)

ODEP = *Oxford Dictionary of English Proverbs* 3rd ed rev F.P. Wilson. Oxford: Clarendon Press 1970

O'Day, Rosemary *Education and Society 1500–1800: The Social Foundations of Education in Early Modern Britain* London and New York: Longman 1982

OED = *The Oxford English Dictionary* ed James A.H. Murray et al. Corrected re-issue. 13 vols. Oxford: Clarendon Press 1933

Oldham, J.B. *A History of Shrewsbury School* Oxford: Blackwell 1952

Ong, Walter J., SJ 'Latin Language Study as a Renaissance Puberty Rite' *Studies in Philology* 56 (1959) 103–24

– *Ramus and Talon Inventory* Cambridge, Mass: Harvard University Press 1958

– *Ramus, Method, and the Decay of Dialogue: From the Art of Discourse to the Art of Reason* Cambridge, Mass: Harvard University Press 1958

Oribasius *Oeuvres* ed and trans C. Daremberg, U.C. Bussemaker, and A. Molinier. 6 vols. Paris: Imprimerie Nationale 1851–76

Orme, Nicholas *Early British Swimming 55 BC–AD 1719* Exeter: University of Exeter 1983

– *Education and Society in Medieval and Renaissance England* London and Ronceverte: Hambledon Press 1989

– *English Schools in the Middle Ages* London: Methuen 1973

– 'Schoolmasters' in C.H. Clough ed *Profession, Vocation and Culture in Medieval England* Liverpool: Liverpool University Press 1981; rpt Orme *Education and Society* 49–71

Orpen, P.K. 'Schoolmastering as a Profession in the Seventeenth Century: The Career Patterns of the Grammar Schoolmaster' *History of Education* 6 (1977) 183–94

Osborn, James M., ed *The Quenes Maiesties Passage* New Haven: Yale University Press 1960

Ovid [See headnote to this list]

Paige, Donald 'An Additional Letter and Booklist of Thomas Chard, Stationer of London' *The Library* 4th ser 21 (1940–1) 26–43

Palliser, D.M. *The Age of Elizabeth: England under the Tudors 1547–1603* London and New York: Longman 1983 (Social and Economic History of England)

Paoletti, Italo *Gerolamo Mercuriale e il suo tempo: studio eseguito su 62 lettere e un consulto inediti del medico forlivese giacenti presso l'Archivio di Stato di Parma* Lanciano: Cooperativa Editoriale Tipografica 1963

Paradise, N. Burton *Thomas Lodge: The History of an Elizabethan* New Haven: Yale University Press 1931

Parker, Clement C. *Compendium of Works on Archery* Philadelphia: G.S. MacManus 1950

Parks, George B. 'Pico della Mirandola in Tudor Translation' 152–69 in E.P. Mahoney ed *Philosophy and Humanism: Renaissance Essays in Honor of Paul Oskar Kristeller* New York: Columbia University Press 1976

– 'William Barker, Tudor Translator' *Papers of the Bibliographical Society of America* 51 (1957) 126–40

Parmentier, Jacques *Histoire de l'éducation en Angleterre: les doctrines et les écoles depuis les origines jusqu'au commencement du XIXe siècle* Paris: Perrin 1896

Partee, Morriss Henry 'Sir Philip Sidney and the Renaissance Knowledge of Plato' *English Studies* 51 (1970) 411–24

Pauly, A.F. von *Paulys Real-Encyclopädie der classischen Altertumswissenschaft* ed G. Wissowa. Riehe 1, 24 vols; Riehe 2, 19 vols; Suppl, 15 vols; Register. Stuttgart: J.B. Metzlerscher et al 1893–1980

Pausanias [See headnote to this list]

Peacham, Henry, the Elder *The Garden of Eloquence* ... London: H. Jackson 1577 (*STC* 19497)

Peacham, Henry, the Younger *The Compleat Gentleman* ... London: Francis Constable 1622 (*STC* 19502)

Pepper, Robert D. ed *Four Tudor Books on Education* Gainesville, Fla.: Scholars' Facsimiles and Reprints 1966

– 'Francis Clement's *Petie Schole* at the Vautrollier Press, 1587' *The Library* 5th ser 22 (1967) 1–12

Petroski, Henry *The Pencil: A History of Design and Circumstance* New York: Alfred A. Knopf 1990

Philo Judaeus [See headnote to this list]

Piccolomini, Aeneas Sylvius (Pius II) *De liberorum educatione* ed and trans Br Joel S. Nelson. Washington, DC: Catholic University of America Press 1940

Pico della Mirandola, Giovanni *Conclusiones sive theses DCCCC* ed Bohdan Kieszkowski. Geneva: Droz 1973

Pienaar, W.J.B. 'Edmund Spenser and Jonker Jan van der Noot' *English Studies* 8 (1926) 33–44 and 67–76

Pigman, G.W., III 'Versions of Imitation in the Renaissance' *Renaissance Quarterly* 33 (1980) 1–32

Pinchbeck, Ivy 'The State and the Child in 16th Century England' *British Journal of Sociology* 7 (1956) 273–85 and 8 (1957) 59–74

– and Margaret Hewitt *Children in English Society Vol. I: From Tudor Times to the Eighteenth Century* London: Routledge and Kegan Paul 1969

Plato [See headnote to this list]

– *Opera* ed I. Operinus. Basel: I. Valderus 1534

Pliny the Elder [See headnote to this list]

Pliny the Younger [See headnote to this list]
Plutarch [See headnote to this list]
Pollard, A.F. *Tudor Tracts 1532–1588* Westminster: A. Constable 1903
Pollock, Linda *Forgotten Children: Parent-Child Relations from 1500 to 1900* Cambridge: Cambridge University Press 1983
– *With Faith and Physic: The Life of a Tudor Gentlewoman Lady Grace Mildmay 1552–1620* London: Collins and Brown 1993
Powell, Chilton Lathem *English Domestic Relations 1487–1653 ...* New York: Columbia University Press 1917
The Prayer-book of Queen Elizabeth 1559 ... ed William Benham. Edinburgh: John Grant 1911
Prest, Wilfrid R. *The Inns of Court under Elizabeth I and the Early Stuarts 1590–1640* London: Longman 1972
Proclus *Commentaire sur la République* trans A.J. Festugière. 2 vols. Paris: Vrin 1970
– *A Commentary on Euclid's Elements* trans Glenn R. Morrow. Princeton: Princeton University Press 1970
– *... In primum Euclidis elementorum librum commentariorum ... libri IIII* ed Franciscus Barocius. Padua: G. Perchacinus 1560
– [See also Plato *Opera* ed Operinus]
Prothero, G.W. *Select Statutes and Other Constitutional Documents Illustrative of the Reigns of Elizabeth and James I* 4th ed. Oxford: Clarendon Press 1913
Quinn, D.B., ed *The Hakluyt Handbook* 2 vols. London: Hakluyt Society 1974
Quintilian [See headnote to this list]
Rashdall, Hastings *The Universities of Europe in the Middle Ages* rev ed by F.M. Powicke and A.B. Emden. 3 vols. Oxford: Clarendon Press 1936
Read, John *Through Alchemy to Chemistry: A Procession of Ideas and Personalities* London: G. Bell 1961
Recorde, Robert *The Pathway to Knowledg, Containing the First Principles of Geometrie ...* London: R. Wolfe 1551 (*STC* 20812)
Renwick, W.L. 'Mulcaster and Du Bellay' *Modern Language Review* 17 (1922) 282–7
Rhazes (Muhammed ibn Zakariya al-Razi) *Opera* Lyons: imp J. de Ferraris 1511
Ricchieri, L. [Caelius Rhodiginus] *Lectionum antiquarum libri triginta ...* Postrema editio. Paris: Apud haeredes Andreae Wecheli, Claudium, Marnium, et Ioannem Aubrium 1559
Ricci, Seymour de *English Collectors of Books & Manuscripts (1530–1930) and Their Marks of Ownership* 1930; rpt New York: Burt Franklin 1969
Riginos, Alice S. *Platonica: The Anecdotes Concerning the Life and Writings of Plato* Leiden: E.J. Brill 1976
Ringler, William 'The Immediate Source of Euphuism' *Publications of the Modern Language Association* 53 (1938) 678–86

Roberts, Thomas *The English Bowman* London 1801; rpt East Ardsley, Wakefield, Yorks: EP Publishing 1973

Robertson, Jean, and D.J. Gordon, eds *A Calendar of Dramatic Records in the Books of the Livery Companies of London: 1485–1640* London: Oxford University Press 1954 (Malone Society Collections 3)

Robinson, Charles J. *A Register of the Scholars Admitted into Merchant Taylors' School* London: for the Editor 1882

Robinson, (Rev) Hastings, ed and trans *Original Letters ...* Cambridge: University Press 1846 (Parker Society)

– ed and trans *The Zurich Letters ...* Cambridge: University Press 1842 (Parker Society)

Robinson, Richard, trans *The Auncient Order, Societie and Unitie Laudable, of Prince Arthure ...* London: J. Wolfe 1583 (*STC* 800)

Rodger, Alexander 'Roger Ward's Shrewsbury Stock: An Inventory of 1585' *The Library* 5th ser 13 (1958) 247–68

Rose, Paul L. *The Italian Renaissance of Mathematics: Studies on Humanists and Mathematicians from Petrarch to Galileo* Geneva: Droz 1975

Rowse, A.L. *The Elizabethan Renaissance: The Life of the Society* London: Macmillan 1971

Russell, K.F. 'A Checklist of Medical Books Published in English before 1600' *Bulletin of the History of Medicine* 21 (1947) 922–58

Ryan, Lawrence V. *Roger Ascham* Stanford: Stanford University Press 1963

Sadoleto, Jacopo *Sadoleto on Education: A Translation of the 'De Pueris Recte Instituendis'* trans E.T. Campagnac and K. Forbes. London, etc: Oxford University Press 1916

Sammut, Alfonso *La fortuna dell'Ariosto nell'Inghilterra elisabettiana* Milano: Editrice Vita e Pensiero 1971

Sarton, George *The Appreciation of Ancient and Medieval Science during the Renaissance (1450–1600)* Philadelphia: University of Pennsylvania Press 1955

Sayle, R.T.D. 'Annals of Merchant Taylors' School Library' *The Library* 4th ser 15 (1934–5) 457–80

– *Lord Mayors' Pageants of the Merchant Taylors' Company in the 15th, 16th & 17th Centuries* London: Printed for Private Circulation 1931

Schäfer, Jürgen *Documentation in the 'O.E.D.': Shakespeare and Nashe as Test Cases* Oxford: Clarendon Press 1980

– *Early Modern English Lexicography* 2 vols. Oxford: Clarendon Press 1989

Schmid, Karl Adolf, ed *Geschichte der Erziehung vom Anfang an bis auf unsere Zeit* 5 vols in 7. Stuttgart 1884–1902; rpt, in 10 vols, Aalen: Scientia Verlag 1970

Schnucker, Robert V. 'Puritan Attitudes towards Childhood Discipline, 1560–1634' in Valerie Fildes ed *Women as Mothers in Pre-Industrial England:*

Essays in Memory of Dorothy McLaren London and New York: Routledge 1990 pp 108–21

Schüling, Hermann *Bibliographie der psychologischen Literatur des 16. Jahrhunderts* Hildesheim: Georg Olms 1967

Schulz, Herbert C. 'The Teaching of Handwriting in Tudor and Stuart Times' *Huntington Library Quarterly* 6 (1942–3) 381–425

Scott, Izora *Controversies over the Imitation of Cicero as a Model for Style and Some Phases of Their Influence on the Schools of the Renaissance* New York: Teachers College Columbia University 1910

Seaborne, Malcolm *The English School: Its Architecture and Organization 1370–1870* Toronto: University of Toronto Press 1971

Seneca the Younger [See headnote to this list]

Shakespeare, William *Much Ado about Nothing* ed J. Dover Wilson. Cambridge: University Press 1953

Shakespeare's England ed Sidney Lee. 2 vols. Oxford: Clarendon Press 1916

Shaw, A.E. 'The Earliest Latin Grammars in English' *Transactions of the Bibliographical Society* 5 (1898–1900) 39–65

Sheppard, H. Fleetwood 'Flowers of Anecdote' *Notes and Queries* 11 (1855) 260

Shorey, Paul *'Φύσις, Μελέτη, 'Επιστήμη'* *Transactions and Proceedings of the American Philological Association* 40 (1909) 185–201

A Short-Title Catalogue of Books Printed in England, Scotland, and Ireland and of English Books Printed Abroad 1475–1640 comp A.W. Pollard and G.R. Redgrave. London: Bibliographical Society 1926; rev ed by W.A. Jackson, F.S. Ferguson, and Katharine F. Pantzer. 3 vols. London: Bibliographical Society 1976–91 [*STC*]

Shuger, Debora K. *Sacred Rhetoric: The Christian Grand Style in the English Renaissance* Princeton: Princeton University Press 1988

Shumaker, Wayne *The Occult Sciences in the Renaissance: A Study in Intellectual Patterns* Berkeley, Los Angeles, London: University of California Press 1972

Sidney, (Sir) Philip *An Apology for Poetry or The Defence of Poesy* ed Geoffrey Shepherd. 1965; rpt Manchester: Manchester University Press 1973

Siegel, Paul N. 'English Humanism and the New Tudor Aristocracy' *Journal of the History of Ideas* 13 (1952) 450–68

– 'Milton and the Humanist Attitude toward Women' *Journal of the History of Ideas* 11 (1950) 42–53

Siegel, R.E. *Galen's System of Physiology and Medicine: An Analysis of his Doctrines and Observations on Bloodflow, Respiration, Humors and Internal Diseases* Basel and New York: S. Karger 1968

Simon, Joan *Education and Society in Tudor England* Cambridge: University Press 1966

Sinz, William 'The Elaboration of Vives's Treatises on the Arts' *Studies in the Renaissance* 10 (1963) 68–90

Smith, G. Gregory, ed *Elizabethan Critical Essays* 2 vols. London: Oxford University Press 1904

Smith, G.C. Moore 'Spenser and Mulcaster' *Modern Language Review* 8 (1913) 368

Smith, Hallett 'Tamburlaine and the Renaissance' 126–31 in *Elizabethan and Other Essays in Honor of G.F. Reynolds* University of Colorado Studies Series B, vol 2, no 2 (October 1945)

Smith, Roland M. 'Spenser's Scholarly Script and "Right Writing"' 66–111 in D.C. Allen ed *Studies in Honor of T.W. Baldwin*. Urbana: University of Illinois Press 1958

Smith, (Sir) Thomas *De Republica Anglorum* London: H. Midleton for G. Seton 1583 (*STC* 22857) rpt Menston: Scolar Press 1970

Socrates Scholasticus [See Eusebius, above]

Sonnino, Lee A. *A Handbook to Sixteenth-Century Rhetoric* London: Routledge and Kegan Paul 1968

Spenser, Edmund *Faerie Queene* ed J.C. Smith. 2 vols. Oxford: Clarendon Press 1909

– *Minor Poems* ed E. de Sélincourt. Oxford: Clarendon Press 1910

Spufford, Margaret 'The Schooling of the Peasantry in Cambridgeshire, 1580–1700' 112–47 in Joan Thirsk ed *Land, Church, and People: Essays Presented to Professor H.P.R. Finberg* Reading: Museum of English Rural Life 1970 (*Agricultural History Review* 18 [1970] supplement)

Starkey, Thomas *A Dialogue between Reginald Pole and Thomas Lupset* ed Kathleen Burton. London: Chatto and Windus 1948

STC = *A Short-Title Catalogue* (above)

Stern, Virginia F. *Gabriel Harvey: His Life, Marginalia and Library* Oxford: Clarendon Press 1979

Sterry, Wasey *The Eton College Register 1441–1698* Eton: Spottiswoode, Ballantyne & Co 1943

Stockwood, John *A Sermon Preached at Paules Crosse ... the 24. of August. 1578 ...* London: H. Bynneman for G. Bishop nd (*STC* 23284)

Stone, Lawrence 'Ages of Admission to Educational Institutions in Tudor and Stuart England: A Comment' *History of Education* 6 (1977) 9

– *The Crisis of the Aristocracy 1558–1641* Oxford: Clarendon Press 1965

– 'The Educational Revolution in England 1560–1640' *Past and Present* 28 (July 1964) 41–80

– *The Family, Sex and Marriage in England 1500–1800* London: Weidenfeld and Nicolson 1977

– 'Social Mobility in England, 1500–1700' *Past and Present* 33 (April 1966) 16–55

Stone, Lilly C. 'English Sports and Recreations' 427–79 in L.B. Wright and V.A.

LaMar eds *Life and Letters in Tudor and Stuart England: First Folger Series* Ithaca, N.Y.: Cornell University Press for the Folger Shakespeare Library 1962

Stopes, Charlotte Carmichael 'Sixteenth Century Women Students' *Transactions of the Royal Society of Literature* 2nd ser 25 (1904) 151–81

Stow, John *A Survey of London Reprinted from the Text of 1603* ed C.L. Kingsford. 2 vols. 1908; Oxford: Clarendon Press 1971

Stowe, A. Monroe *English Grammar Schools in the Reign of Queen Elizabeth* New York: Columbia University Press 1908

Strabo [See headnote to this list]

Strauss, Gerald *Luther's House of Learning: Indoctrination of the Young in the German Reformation* Baltimore and London: Johns Hopkins University Press 1978

Strigelius, Victorinus *A Third Proceeding in the Harmonie of King Davids Harp ...* trans Richard Robinson. London: V. Sims 1595 (*STC* 23361)

Strutt, Joseph *The Sports and Pastimes of the People of England from the Earliest Period ...* rev and enlarged J.C. Cox. London: Methuen 1903

Strype, John *The Life of the Learned Sir John Cheke, Kt. ...* London: John Wyat 1705

Stubbes, Philip *The Anatomie of Abuses ...* London: Richard Iones 1583 (*STC* 23376)

Sturgess, H.A.C. *Register of Admissions to the Honourable Society of the Middle Temple ...* London: For the Honourable Society of the Middle Temple by Butterworth 1949

Sturm, Johann *A Ritch Storehouse or Treasurie for Nobility and Gentlemen, Which in Latine is Called Nobilitas Literata ...* trans T. B[rowne]. London: H. Denham 1570 (*STC* 23408)

Suaudeau, René, and C. Suaudeau-Deterne *La Renaissance de la gymnastique médicale du XVe au XVIIe siècle et le 'De arte gymnastica' de Mercurialis* Clermont-Ferrand: Librarie Queyriaux [Institut d'Education Physique de Clermont-Ferrand] 1943

Suetonius [See headnote to this list]

Tallis, Thomas, and William Byrd *Cantiones, quae ab argumento sacrae vocantur, quinque et sex partium ...* London: T. Vautrollier 1575 (*STC* 23666)

Tate, W.E. 'The Episcopal Licensing of Schoolmasters in England' *Church Quarterly Review* 157 (1956) 426–32

Taylor, A.C. 'Virgil and the Bread' *Times Literary Supplement* (28 August 1937) 624

Taylor, Archer *The Proverb* Cambridge, Mass: Harvard University Press 1931

– 'The Proverb "The Black Ox Has Not Trod on His Foot" in Renaissance Literature' *Philological Quarterly* 20 (1941) 266–78

Taylor, E.G.R. *The Mathematical Practitioners of Tudor and Stuart England* Cambridge: University Press for the Institute of Navigation 1954

Tempest, N.R. 'Some Sources for the History of Teacher-Training in England and Wales' *British Journal of Educational Studies* 9 (1960) 57–66

Tervarent, Guy de *Attributs et symboles dans l'art profane 1450–1600: Dictionnaire d'un langage perdu* Geneva: Droz 1958–9

Terzi, M., and W. Ronchi 'Ginnastica medica e medicina sportiva nell'opera di Gerolamo Mercuriale' *Romagna Medica* 8 (1956) 449–58

Textor, I. Ravisius *De memorabilibus et claris mulieribus: aliquot diversorum scriptorum opera* Paris: S. de Colines 1521

Thirsk, Joan 'Enclosing and Engrossing' 200–55 in Thirsk ed *The Agrarian History of England and Wales Volume IV 1500–1640* Cambridge: University Press 1967

Thomas, I., trans *Selections Illustrating the History of Greek Mathematics* [Loeb edition; see headnote to this list]

Thomas, Keith 'Children in Early Modern England' 45–77 in Gillian Avery and Julia Briggs ed *Children and Their Books: A Celebration of the Work of Iona and Peter Opie* Oxford: Clarendon Press 1989

– 'The Double Standard' *Journal of the History of Ideas* 20 (1959) 195–216

– *Man and the Natural World: A History of the Modern Sensibility* New York: Pantheon 1983

– 'The Meaning of Literacy in Early Modern England' 97–131 in Gerd Baumann ed *The Written Word: Literacy in Transition* Oxford: Clarendon Press 1986

– 'Numeracy in Early Modern England' *Transactions of the Royal Historical Society* 5th ser 37 (1987) 103–32

Thomas-Stanford, Charles *Early Editions of Euclid's Elements* London: Bibliographical Society 1926

Thompson, Craig R. 'Schools in Tudor England' 285–334 in L.B. Wright and V.A. LaMar eds *Life and Letters in Tudor and Stuart England: First Folger Series* Ithaca, NY: Cornell University Press for the Folger Shakespeare Library 1962

– 'Scripture for the Ploughboy and Some Others' 3–28 in D.B.J. Randall and G.W. Williams eds *Studies in the Continental Background of Renaissance English Literature: Essays Presented to John L. Lievsay* Durham, NC: Duke University Press 1977

– 'Universities in Tudor England' 335–82 in L.B. Wright and V.A. LaMar eds *Life and Letters in Tudor and Stuart England: First Folger Series* Ithaca, NY: Cornell University Press for the Folger Shakespeare Library 1962

Tilley = Tilley, Morris Palmer *A Dictionary of the Proverbs in England in the Sixteenth and Seventeenth Centuries ...* Ann Arbor: University of Michigan Press 1950

– *Elizabethan Proverb Lore in Lyly's 'Euphues' and in Pettie's 'Petite Pallace' with Parallels from Shakespeare* New York: Macmillan 1926

Tillyard, E.M.W. *The Elizabethan World Picture* London: Chatto and Windus 1943

Travitsky, Betty S. 'The New Mother of the English Renaissance (1489–1659): A Descriptive Catalogue' *Bulletin of Research in the Humanities* 82 (1979) 63–89

– 'The "Wyll and Testament" of Isabella Whitney' *English Literary Renaissance* 10 (1980) 76–94

Tuck, J.P. 'The Latin Grammar Attributed to William Lily' *Durham Research Review* 1.2 (September 1951) 33–9

– 'The Use of English in Latin Teaching in England in the Sixteenth Century' *Durham Research Review* no 1 (July 1950) 22–30

Turler, Jerome *The Traveiler* ... [from the Latin]. London: W. How for A. Veale 1575 (*STC* 24336)

Turner, William *A Booke of the Natures and Properties, as well as of the Bathes in Englande as of Other Bathes in Germany and Italy* [*STC* 24351 found in] *The Seconde Parte of William Turners Herball* Collen: A. Birckman 1562 (*STC* 24366)

Tztetzes, John *Book of Histories* [in I. Thomas trans *Selections* above]

Ulmann, Jacques *De la Gymnastique aux sports modernes: histoire des doctrines de l'éducation physique* 3rd ed. Paris: Vrin 1977

Vasoli, Cesare *La dialettica e la retorica dell'Umanesimo: 'invenzione' e 'metodo' nella cultura del XV e XVI secolo* Milan: Feltrinelli 1968

Vegetius Renatus, Flavius *The Foure Bookes ... Briefelye Contayninge a Plaine Forme, and Perfect Knowledge of Martiall Policye* ... trans John Sadler. London: Thomas Marshe 1572 (*STC* 24631)

Vegius, Mapheus *De educatione liberorum et eorum claris moribus libri sex* ed Srs Maria W. Fanning and A.S. Sullivan CSJ. 2 vols. Washington, DC: Catholic University of America 1933–6

Venn, John, and J.A. Venn, comps *Alumni Cantabrigienses: A Biographical List of All Known Students, Graduates and Holders of Office at the University of Cambridge, from the Earliest Times to 1900* Part 1, in 4 vols, to 1751; part 2 in 6 vols, from 1752 to 1900. Cambridge: University Press 1922–54

Vergil, Polydore *De rerum inuentioribus libri octo* Basel: M. Isingrinius 1540

Vickers, Brian *Francis Bacon and Renaissance Prose* Cambridge: University Press 1968

Virgil *Bucolica, Georgica, Aeneis* ... Venice: A. Pincius 1536

– [See also headnote to this list]

Vitruvius [See headnote to this list]

Vives, Juan Luis *De anima et vita libri tres* Basel: R. Winter 1538; rpt Turin: Bottega d'Erasmo 1963

– *In pseudodialecticos: A Critical Edition* ed and trans Charles Fantazzi. Leiden: E.J. Brill 1979

– *On Education: A Translation of the 'De Tradendis Disciplinis'* trans Foster Watson. 1913; rpt Totowa, NJ: Rowman and Littlefield 1971

– *Opera omnia* ed Gregorio Mayans y Siscar. 8 vols. Valencia: Benedictus Montfort 1782–90; rpt London: Gregg 1964

Vives, Juan Luis *Tudor Schoolboy Life: The Dialogues of Juan Luis Vives* trans Foster Watson. 1908; rpt London: Frank Cass and Co 1970

– *A Very Frutefull and Pleasant Boke Called the Instruction of a Christen Woman* trans Richard Hyrde. London: T. Berthelet 1529 (*STC* 24856) (edited, and somewhat abridged, by Watson *Vives and the Renascence Education of Women*, below)

Vos, Alvin 'The Formation of Roger Ascham's Prose Style' *Studies in Philology* 71 (1974) 344–70

Walker, Thomas Alfred *A Biographical Register of Peterhouse Men ... Part I 1284–1574* Cambridge: University Press 1927

Wallis, P.J. *Histories of Old Schools: A Revised List for England and Wales* Newcastle upon Tyne: Department of Education, University of Newcastle upon Tyne 1966

Watson, Foster *The English Grammar Schools to 1660: Their Curriculum and Practice* Cambridge: University Press 1908; rpt London: Frank Cass and Co 1968

– 'Hakluyt and Mulcaster' *Geographical Journal* 49 (1917) 48–53

– *Richard Mulcaster and his 'Elementarie'* London: For the Author 1893 (reprinted from *Educational Times* [1 January 1893])

– *Vives and the Renascence Education of Women* London: Edward Arnold 1912

Watson, George, comp *The New Cambridge Bibliography of English Literature* vol 1 [600–1660]. Cambridge: University Press 1974

Webster, John *The Complete Works* ed F.L. Lucas. 4 vols. London: Chatto and Windus 1927

Weigall, Rachel 'An Elizabethan Gentlewoman. The Journal of Lady Mildmay, circa 1570–1617 (Unpublished)' *Quarterly Review* 215 (July and October 1911) 119–38

Weinstock, Horst *Die Funktion elisabethanischer Sprichwörter und Pseudo-sprichwörter bei Shakespeare* Heidelberg: Carl Winter / Universitätsverlag 1966

Weiss, Roberto 'Pico e l'Inghilterra' 1:143–52 in *L'opera e il pensiero di Giovanni Pico della Mirandola nella storia dell'Umanesimo* 2 vols. Florence: Istituto Nazionale di Studi sul Rinascimento 1965

West, Michael 'Spenser, Everard Digby, and the Renaissance Art of Swimming' *Renaissance Quarterly* 26 (1973) 11–22

Whitaker, William *Ad rationes decem Edmundi Campiani iesuitae ... responsio* London: T. Vautrollier, imp T. Chardi 1581 (*STC* 25358)

Whitelocke, (Sir) James *Liber Famelicus* ed John Bruce. London: Camden Society 1858 (Camden Society 70)

Wiener, Leo 'Richard Mulcaster, an Elizabethan Philologist' *Modern Language Notes* 12 (1897) 65–70

Williams, Franklin B., Jr *Index of Dedications and Commendatory Verses in English*

Books before 1641 London: Bibliographical Society 1962
Wilson, (Rev) H.B. *The History of Merchant-Taylors' School from Its Foundation to the Present Time* London: F.C. and J. Rivington [et al] 1814
Wilson, H.S. 'Gabriel Harvey's Orations on Rhetoric' *ELH: A Journal of English Literary History* 12 (1945) 167–82
Wilson, K.J. 'Ascham's *Toxophilus* and the Rules of Art' *Renaissance Quarterly* 29 (1976) 30–51
Wilson, Thomas *Arte of Rhetorique 1560* ed G.H. Mair. Oxford: Clarendon Press 1909
– *The Rule of Reason* ... London: Richard Grafton 1551 (*STC* 25809)
Wing, Donald G. *Short-Title Catalogue of Books Printed in England, Scotland, Ireland, Wales, and British America and of English Books Printed in Other Countries 1641–1700* 3 vols. 1945–51; 2nd ed New York: Modern Language Association 1972–88
Wood, Anthony à *Athenae Oxonienses* ... [1691] ed Philip Bliss. 2 vols. London: F.C. and J. Rivington [et al] 1815
– *The History and Antiquities of the Colleges and Halls in the University of Oxford* ed John Gutch. 3 vols. Oxford: Clarendon Press for the Editor 1786
Wood, Norman *The Reformation and English Education: A Study of the Influence of Religious Uniformity on English Education in the Sixteenth Century* London: George Routledge and Sons 1931
Woodfill, Walter L. *Musicians in English Society from Elizabeth to Charles I* Princeton: Princeton University Press 1953
Wright, Herbert G. *Boccaccio in England from Chaucer to Tennyson* London: University of London Athlone Press 1957
Xenophon [See headnote to this list]
Yates, Frances *The Art of Memory* London: Routledge and Kegan Paul 1966
Zwingli, Ulrich *Certayne Precepts* ... trans R. Argentyne. Ipswich: A. Scolocker 1548 (*STC* 26136)

❧ Index

Most of this index is to the headings in the commentary, but all names in *Positions* and some subjects are added for the convenience of the reader. References without line numbers are to the text; those with line numbers indicate that besides a passage in the text there is also a note in the commentary. The headings are indexed in modern spelling, except for a few old spelling variants. An asterisk shows where the commentary adds to or questions the first edition of the *Oxford English Dictionary*. Proverbs are indicated by '(prov).' A few additional references have been given to the introduction (in roman numerals).

abate 91.14
abce 42.4
absolute: (perfect) 28.32; (mere) 226.35
absoluteness 241.23
Academy of Plato 236.23, 248.35–7
accident 24.12, 41.37–8
accidentary 285.31
account 24.34
Achilles as a runner 96.8
acts and monuments 265.34
Adam, old (prov) 204.19
Adam's rib 171.35
admiration 137.19
advertise 236.12
advertisement 231.19, 279.5
advisedly 166.6
advisedness 166.9
advisement 202.19
Aelian 270.21
Aesculapius 106.27
Aetius on running 96.29
affection: a tyrant 34.5; 129.16; 189.22 is blind (prov) 254.24–5; overrules reason 255.14–15; 288.11
affections 90.27
affiaunce 22.5
aggravation* 15.13
agues, quartan 66.17
air, freedom of 225.36
alchemist 205.35
Alexander the Great: a runner 96.8; his horse Bucephalus 168.14, 199.37; Hephaestion, his favourite 201.18–20; teacher should think each child an 234.37; even Philip his father had to get him a good teacher 273

alien (v) 190.20
aliening 208.22
alledger 21.30
allow 16.22
almain-like* 81.27
aloneness 171.16
Amata 87.18
Anacreon 175.28–32
anatomies 274.18–19
anchor: of hope 29.31; constancy an 276.3
anciency 200.8
animals 'naturally appointed for mans use' 105.1
Annicerus, school of 248.35–7
answer 112.1
antecedent 164.15
Antiochus 117.17–19
antiquary* 134.2–3
Antyllus 67.23
apaid 15.22
Apelles, exemplary painter 46.11, 47
apes 206.3
aphorism: and style xlv, lvi n 1; 'flat and stearne' 47.30; 260.13; 287.18
Apollinarius, father and son, rewrite the Bible in classical verse 266.29
Apollo 106.35, 214
apophthegm 271.20–1
aposteme 66.16
apotherapeutic 63.8
appendents 229.15
apple, show a child an (prov?) 162.32
applied 211.25
appoint 257.25–7
appointment 263.1
appose 134.4
apprenticeship 255.31
archery (shooting): 106–9; background 106.32; in Crete, Cyprus, Indian islands 107.13–14; the Balearic islands 107.16; compared with hunting 107; types of 108; and knights of Prince Arthur 108.24–5
Archimedes 244.20
Ariosto, Ludovico 174.29–30
Aristarete 182.34–7
Aristippus: 243.32; school of 248.35–7
Aristophanes: on riding 103.1–2; on wealth 195.10
Aristotle: his *Physics* and method 18.20; on 'discretion' in reason 22.37; as an 'authority' 24; on writing and drawing 46.21; on benefits of singing 68.24–5, 69.1; on the crying of children as an exercise 74.8; on running 96.32; on running in summer 98.26–9; on exercise in summer 120.34, 121.19–20, 124.35–6; on exercise after meals 121.25; on difference between men and women 172.35; as the 'Philosopher' on justice 129.38; on practical wisdom 136.4; on the need for a large middle class 207.27; his logic understood by study of mathematics 243.11 n; on commentaries or 'helps' 243.16; on the age to study philosophy 244.37; his precepts exemplified by Plato 245.16–17; as leader of the Peripatetics 248.35
armball 111.38 *See also* ball games
armour, dancing in 81.4
arrest 30.22
art (or 'method'): 'artificiall principles' xviii–xix; terms of 17.12; 'art weyeth the matter abstract' 114 (114.5–6); the limits of, for the teacher 136. *See also* method
Arthur's knights, Prince. *See* archery
artificial 274.18–19

as 34.23
Ascham, Roger: 'a cunning Archer, and a skilfull maister' 108.16; the title of his *Scholemaster* regretted 238.37
Asclepiades 52.28
aspectable 46.3
ass: stalled for an 52.28; desires lion's skin (prov) 205.30–1; bewrayed by his ears (prov) 205.36;
assay (sb) (1) 33.31, (2) 86.32
Assuerus 201.18–20
assurance 234.15
Athenaeum 226.10
Athenaeus 226.6
auditory of two or three boys 189.34–5
audits 225.23
Augustus, Caesar: his soldiers to walk 90.6; walking in sand one of his remedies 93.25; used a running leap as cure 99.17; his horse's infirmity spied by Virgil 172.8; 244
authorities: alledging of 21.16; on their use to support arguments 23–7; two sorts of 23.19; citation of, as a form of rhetoric 26; their ideal claims 27–8
Avicenna on reading aloud 70.25; on walking after meals 121.25
avoid 56.11, 73.1
avoided 130.6
away with (v) 118.38, 290.16
awreaked 218.6

Bacis 175.28–32
Balearic islands 107.16
ball games 109–13 (109.7)
ballast: (ballase) 32.15; (ballast) 100.30
band, in 135.16
bank, again the 100.14
bar, to the 24.21
bare head 171.30
Barozzi, Francesco 243.37
Basil, St 266.29
bastard (v) 147.37
bastard (a) 167.4
bastarded 201.5
bastardize 195.38
bayard, blind (prov) 168.9
bear the bell (prov) 61.36, 270.31
beating: RM's attitude towards lxiv–lxv; wrong for the very young 36.14; too much dulls the child 45; weeping as an exercise 74–6; and the humours of negligence 72, 74.32; absence of tears shows a 'verie shrewd boye' 74; necessary, despite Socrates 75–6; general discussion of 269–75; and necessity of the rod 269.39 n; and Lady Birchely 270.7 n; affection important 275.33–5; that it is 'slavish' to be beaten 273.11–12
beggar, a prince (prov) 150.24–5
bell. *See* bear the bell (prov)
belly-cauls* 106.9
bembix (Greek) 87.22
bend, or break (prov) 147.14
beseeming* 180.26
bet 173.13
bettership* 187.38
bewray 16.1
Bible: St Paul on 'learning' 141.5–6; Adam's rib 171.35; spare the rod 270.2–3; love thy neighbour 278.19–20; God is emperor of all 285.2
bid ho. *See* ho
biled* 84.32
billow drives on another, one (prov) 254.35–6

Birchely, my lady. *See* beating
bit ... bridle 49.5
bladders for swimming 101.17, 284.19–20
blaze 255.23
blindness (prov) 268.34. *See also* affection
blush, first 17.15
boarding abroad 223.16–17, 224
Boccaccio, Giovanni 174.29–30
body: xviiff; 38, and soul 51–2; 'lumpish and earthy' 51.21–2; health of 52; and exercise 53; wise mind and healthful 53.9–10; the four elements of 53 (53.22); instrumental parts of 53–5 (53.34); change in 54–5; place of exercise 55; need for appropriate exercise 56; diet and clothing of the young the parents' business 56; RM's emphasis will be on exercise for health 57; the basic considerations of health and exercise 57–9; exercise of different kinds of 115–19; the 'body' of the state 139.7–8. *See also* exercise
boiling 121.33
bolden 135.30
bones, make no (prov) 247.16
book (v)* 152.6
book, lighten the 162.39
Book of Common Prayer ('nature and property') 42.7
booking* 147.31
book-maintenance* 152.2
bookmen* 147.5, 228.7
books and schoolbooks: 265–7; cost of 264.18; too many 264.28; rarely read right through 264.31–2
booted 256.35
borough 211.23
boughs 248.21
bounder 258.24
bowelled 160.21
bows 248.21
brad (bred) 187.32
Bradwardine, Thomas, archbishop 243.16
brag 258.4
brain 58.27
brains, to beat one's (prov) 249.25
brake, in 152.34
brambly 93.16
braved 82.7
breath 55.16
breathing: as exercise 76–9; is beneficial 76–9 (76.20); dangers of improper 77–8; proper methods of 78–9
bremer 196.4
bridle (prov) 30.29
bridled 238.26
broad 163.2
Broughton, Hugh, estimates RM's learning lx
brust 45.3
Brutus, L.J., condemns his sons to death 285.38
Brutus, Marcus Junius 175.28.32
Bucephalus. *See* Alexander the Great
Buckley, William 239.12
bulk 59.11
bull, bear the (prov) 79.14
bullrushes* (used for swimming) 284.19–20
burdenous 61.13
bursars 165.4
butt 144.29

Caelius Aurelianus: on speaking aloud 67.17; on reading aloud 70.6

Caesar, Julius: as swimmer 101.36–8; a learned general 202.7–9; seeks the 'great pontificate' 218.26
Caius, John, employer of RM? lx
Callimachus (sculptor) 99.39
Callimachus (poet), on the spinning top 87.22
calling and discovering hours 145.19–20
calling* 181.8
campish 75.36
canker (prov) 256.22
canvass out (v) 86.31–2
canvass* (sb) 142.36
captain (a) 126.4
captain* (sb) 253.32
carcass 121.11
cared for 95.23
carriages* 179.15–16
case altered (prov) 228.2–3, 285.17–18
cask, empty (prov) 177.36
casting 71.32–3
casual 195.37
casualty 146.21–2
casualty 55.6
catarrh 59.2–3
caterpillars 163.27–8
Catilinary* 67.13–14
caul 79.9
caveat* 273.29
Celsus, Cornelius, on benefits of reading aloud 70.3
censors 273.19
certain, in 141.3
certainty, defined and discussed 282–4 (282.29–31)
cestus* 112.25
chafe 105.23, 124.22
chafed 97.38
chancel have a minister ..., if (prov?) 246.13–14
Chard, Thomas lxxix
charge, give 189.15
charge 220.2
chargeable 264.29
chariest 39.27
check (sb) 16.1, 21.28, 64.23
check (v) 30.22
cheery* 127.2
cheese is scraped 194.39–195.1
cheironomia (Greek) 83.6
Cheke, (Sir) John 239.3
cherish 99.31
children: abilities and psychology defined xvii–xx; when to send them to school 27ff; important to consider their body and mind together 27–36; before schooling (nurse, milk, friends, etc) 28; their parents, ideal and real 28–31; time for school outlined in general terms 31; their 'ripeness' not tied to one time 31; types of 31–3, 142; their need for physical exercise 34–5; always stirring 35; wrong to beat very young 36.14; their 'naturall abilities' 37; their soul before their body 38 (see also soul); psychology of 38–9; that they be taught in an orderly manner 42; that what they are taught is appropriate for their age 42; health of 56.8–9; on voluntary learning of 75–6; physical education of (see body; exercise); differences of, recognized by teacher's 'discretion' 136; environment of their city 137.4–5; their clothing 137.6–7; which ones are to attend school 137ff; exposure and destruction of 140.27; of rich and

children (cont'd)
poor 143–4; how to restrain numbers of seeking school 145ff; their obedience a good sign 153–6; qualities of, as learner 154.21, 156; where they are to learn 222–9; when they are to learn 229–30; trickery of lxv, 270.20–1; their need for 'certainty' at school and at home 282–3; need for regular attendance and 'certainty' at church 284
chimney does not smoke (prov?) 129.36
chippings 289.4
Chiron 106.27
choice* (a) 28.13
choice* (sb) 28.8
choler 122.3
chopped 228.15
Cicero: RM claims his style to be Ciceronian liv–lvi; as an 'authority' 25; his orations as a form of physical exercise 67.13–14; on Pontius the Samnite 162.8; the 'eloquentest oratour' praises poets 266.16–18; Cyrus the 'paterne of the best Prince' 273.34
cinquepace 80.39
circumstance: xlvii–xlviii; lvii n 7; 1.3; its force and nature 21–3; and discretion 22–4; and 'truth' 24; and authorities 24; to be considered with exercise 64, 113–14
clattering commended to cloakbag 71.25
clear by the breath 94.14
Clement of Alexandria on wrestling 83.32
clipper 157.17
clipping 168.26
cloakbag, and clattering 71.25
close (sb) 226.2
clothing: thin 56.21; slight ('single') 98.24; changing, after exercise 137; 'frise' 155.10; 'happing' 228.12
clouds, in the* (prov) 292.11–12
clowns 148.22
cloyed 78.15
coat of arms 200.7
cobbler (prov) 166.38
cockering 30.11–12
cockhorse 142.35
cods 79.9
coeliac disease 66.19–21
cognisance 186.15
collection, common 165.32–3
collection 287.31–3
collegianer 165.3
colloquies 237.4
collusions 238.7
colour, upon any 155.34
colour 163.6
commend 199.37
commodious 84.37
commoditie 4.27, 31.2, 67.6, 95.21
common sense 287.30
common (a) 187.29, 281.7
communicants* 185.8
communicate (a) 193.36
communicate (v) 185.6
companies 281.7
comparisons, odious (prov) 154.35–6
compendium 255.11
competent 125.24–5
complaint 33.4
complexion 28.6
compound 18.8
conceit (idea) 3.10–11; (opinion) 4.22; (notion) 17.25; (disposition) 70.11

conceiver 32.33
concent* 49.4
concoction 121.33
condescend 269.13
conduit 57.28
conference: between parents and teachers on which children to attend school 157–9; between parents and neighbours 277–9, 277.26; between teachers and neighbours 279; between parents and teachers 279–8; between teachers 280–1; its general good 281
conference (comparison) 193.8–9
conferred 287.29
confession 18.14, 188.23
confirm 80.32–3
consequence: (conclusion to syllogism) 3.27, 164.15; (order, succession*) 43.4, 173.24–5, 245.2, 253.27
consequent 164.15
conserve (sb) 74.29
considerate 29.23, 150.20
constantness 276.3
construction 292.34
contentation 288.27
continuance 232.30
contrary (oppose) 150.6; (contradict) 115.32, 232.6
control 21.27
controller 19.35
controlment 191.11
conusance 241.27–8
convenient 279.20
conveyances 201.15
Corinth 226.7
Cornelia 183.15
coronell (colonel) 216.8
corrosive 178.20–1
couch 130.30
counsellor (prov) 249.8
countenance (sb): (favour) 3.8; (appearance) 232.30, 256.10; (reputation) 19.12, 238.35
countenance (v): (pretend*) 165.26–7; (approve*) 288.11
counterbranches 185.1
countermatch 146.29
counterreceipt* 95.25
couplements 277.27
courteous 114.34
covert (a)* 89.29
covert (sb) 88.31
cowghe (cough) 70.25
Cratinus, father of Irene 182.34–7
creature* 82.36
credit 3.9
Crete 107.13–14
crudities 66.32
cry, beyond 181.29–30, 271.7, 263.20
cry ho. *See* ho
cry out of 281.36–7
cryptoporticus (Latin) 93.34
cumber 42.26
cumbersome 148.33
cumbred 66.32
Cupid: Diana the huntress avoids 104.25; as sign of the power of archery 107
cure 39.37
curious: (attentive) 192.3; (cautious) 276.7
current* 24.13
curryfavour 272.16
cursedly 228.7
cursitor 159.26
customary 165.7
cybistic* 112.25
cypherlike* 147.34
Cyprian, St, criticizes gladiatorial combat 86.7

Cyprus 107.13–14
Cyrus. *See* Xenophon
Cyzicus, home of Iaia 182.34–7

dainty (wary) 20.6; (scarce) 143.21
dancing: 59.4; as an exercise 79–83; background to 79.27; debate over 79–80; in armour 81.4; and 'desire' 82; its relation to music 82–3; with hand 83.6
dastard 101.4
daunter 218.21
daws 166.31, 208.16
daylight, burn (prov) 175.9
deer in the herd, a special 145.16–17
decretals of Gregory 227.20
defect: (deficiency*) 54.30; (failure) 280.17
defluxions 97.17
degrees and buildings by patches, things grow by (prov?) 247.4–5
Delphi 214
Demetrius 'taker of cities' 244.23
democracy 154.4–7
Demosthenes: walked uphill as exercise 93.2
deposing 224.35
desert 192.34
desultory 219.29
devise 19.37, 46.17
devisor 240.9
devotion 87.27
Diana 104.25
difference, a private 187.13–16
digested 249.13
Diogenes Laertius 226.7, 248.39–249.1
Dionysius the tyrant, visited by Plato 209.11
Dionysius of Halicarnassus 244.26, 285.38
dipnosophist 134.2–3
discursory* 60.25
discus* 112.25
dispose 70.2
dissolve 94.21
distemperature 54.7
distempered 92.3
distilling humours 59.2
distinctions 294.3
distraction 130.24
divinity, college for 241, 245
doltry 206.1
domestically* 158.25
doubling 167.15
down bank 76.3
drams (drachmas) 216.1
drawing: as part of elementary xxi–xxii; 45–7 (45.28g); equipment for 45; utility of 46; and writing 46; setting of colours unnecessary 46; lewd paintings hid by curtains 49.25
dreggy 70.1
drift 17.18
dropsy 66.13
dryness of the body 34.28–9, 54.23
dumpish 32.31
dunghillry 205.38
dustbox 45.32
duty 102.25–7

each-where 133.30
eachway* 128.7
eager (a) 70.11
eager (v) 208.15; 225.8
eagering 84.33
ear, turn a deaf (prov) 144.25
edged out 84.18
education (and schooling): uniformity of, and general situation in England xv–xvi; nature, art, and

use xviii–xx; curriculum at Merchant Taylors' lxii–lxvi; religion in xvi–xvii, 132; whether all should receive it 137ff (138.38); that too many seek it 139.24; of rich and poor 143.24; all desire their children learned 146.20; limitations set by necessity including law and lack of employment 146ff; those to be admitted to be chosen by qualities 153–7; master and parents together to admit students 157–9; admission to school also controlled by admission to colleges, preferment to degrees, and available livings for the educated 159–68; private and public, with public defended xxix–xxx, 185–93 (186.1–2); 'education' defined 186; making the 'private public' 192.15; schools 'overcharged with too many' 192.25; location of school 222–9; hours of school 224.3, 229–30 (230.3); admission of new boys 232.12–13; and danger of haste 253–8; uniformity in 259–62, 267; order and 'dispatch' 262–4; sparing of expenses by reforming textbooks 264–7; curriculum in 265.23–4; schoolbooks in 265–7; school orders or 'faultes' to be published 269–75 (269.9, 270.34–5); holidays 269.34–5; punishment in 269–75; use of 'monitors' 271.8; bringing of children to church 284.3–4

See also beating; children; elementary program; gentleman, education of; nobleman, education of; language; mathematics; parents; schoolhouse; teacher; universities; women, education of

education, physical: *See* exercise

Edward VI 239

effectual 132.8, 240.30

eleemosynary* 248.16

elementary program: xxi–xxii; and the grammarian 18–19; importance of beginning at right time 19; this program the starting point for the 'positions' 20; program outlined 41–50 (*see* reading, writing, drawing, music); how long children to remain, and danger of haste 253–8. *See also* education

elements, four 53.22

elephantiasis 66.19

Elizabeth, Queen: as patron of RM lxviii; RM's dedication of *Positions* 3–5 (3.1); that she need not read all this book 4.9; as 'Lion' 4.10; as the Tenth Worthy 175.20; praised 181.36; a precedent for not travelling 212; praised 221; many schools erected in her reign 226.18; 239; 292

embase 80.13

embasement 80.14

embasing 50.6–7

embassages 213.3–4

enable 3.7

enclosure 186.2–3

end, middle 148.4

enduement* 218.11

enforce 130.2–3

enforcing* 73.38

enform 40.6

English. *See* language

engraff 187.12

engrossing 281.34

enhance 228.3

enough, beyond 196.9

ensign 204.21
entertain 30.2
entertained 35.12
entertainment 232.13g
entitled 17.18
entrails* 60.28
entrances 225.38
entreat 18.23
enure 18.6
epilepsy 66.29
equity 285.32
Erasistratus 52.28–9
Erasmus 270.21
erected 1.9
erection 222.31–2
Esther 201.18–20
Euclid: and the 'method' of geometry 18.10ff; copy of given to RM by Cheke 239.16–20; 243 (243.16)
Eurydice 'the Epirote' 183.16
events: but foolish masters (prov) 150.21–3; 182.3
evidently 276.16
execution 142.10; 192.27
exercise: and physical education xxiff; benefits of xxiii; general considerations 51–9; divisions of discussion 59–60; types of exercise (athletical, martial, physical) 61–2; defined 62; derived from the Latin *exercitus* 62.8; defined 62.33; degrees of (preparative, postparative, gymnastic) 63; types of, within doors (*see* speaking aloud; singing; reading aloud; talking; laughing; weeping; breathing; dancing; wrestling; fencing; top), and without doors (*see* walking; running; leaping; swimming; riding; hunting; shooting; ball-playing) 63; these notes on, for all ages 112; circumstances in 113–14; nature of 114–15; of places for 119–20 (119.22, 120.8–18); of time for 120–3, 124; the 'end of exercise' 123; quantity of 123–6; manner of 126–8; training master and 128–37; exercises to be held in the same place as learning 221; exercise and eating 229.28
exhalation 102.12
exhibition 256.29
exposition 140.27
exquisite 28.15
exulceration 91.38
eye, the paragon sense 44.10
eye might behold (prov?) 166.27

faint 104.30
fainting 57.33
falling* 102.8
falling evil* 91.12
falling sickness 66.29
fancy 27.4, 129.16
fantastical 21.1
fantasticalness* 291.30
fast 229.36
fastness 39.2
fatal (v) 196.35–6
fault of man makes thing seem filthy 49.32–3
feathers, foreign (prov) 166.25–6
feathers ... like friends (prov?) 261.23–5
feebled 114.19
fellonly 169.9
feltered 211.23
fencing: 85–7 (85.6); some forms too violent 85
fet 40.38
fetch 162.36

fetchers 164.10
Figulus, P. Nigidius 244.17
fine 22.13
fined 43.1
fineish 78.3, 237.8
fines (fineness) 28.4
fingering 162.13
fining 22.37
fire (prov) 142.11–12
fire (prov) 142.29–30
Firmicus, Julius, Maternus 244.18
fish in troubled water (prov) 139.35–6
fit in 147.8
fleame (phlegm) 66.17
fleet 32.13
fleeter 25.16
fleeting 139.32
flidge 237.20
flix 100.24 *and see* 'flux'
flourish 181.19
flowered (floored) 119.23
flux 92.2
fly ere they be feathered (prov) 247.38
fog 61.13
foil 153.5
fond 191.10
fondness 254.4
fool ever laughing (prov) 73.1
fool can weep 73.2
football 111. *See also* ball games
forborne 188.8
force 237.30
foregoer 38.36
foreign* 28.8
foreign air 58.12
foreign ... fit (various senses) l
forestalling 281.35
forewardly 155.5
forge (v) 280.11
form 248.8
forslow 158.16
forstall 166.23
fort is surrendered (prov?) 44.7–8
forth, so 205.2
forthink 159.6
fortune (v) 256.5
fortune's frown (prov) 39.32–3
foundation 17.31
frank 108.25
frantic 70.13, 270.20
fray 39.39, 182.32
freeze 70.1
fremd 240.26
fretished 262.9
fretishing 59.7
friend and foe (prov) 86.33
frieze 155.10
fronting 211.38
frosts, fair blossoms and nipping (prov) 145.9
Fuller, Thomas, his biography of RM lxx–lxxi
fumes 99.30
furniture 52.6
furor poeticus (Latin) 267.5–6
furthwith 16.1

galancy 174.3
Galen: Asclepiades and Erasistratus confuted 52.28–9; medical theories outlined 53.22; on benefits of singing 68.24–5; his 'rule' on choosing exercises 88.34; on running 97.3; cited on leaping 100.21; on horse-racing of the Romans 103.9; on hunting 105.16; on the newborn of the Germans 109.17; on how to quiet infants 114.24; his praise of his country 118.9; on exercise in summer

Galen (cont'd)
121.11, 121.19–20; on the seeds of disease 125.38; on kupos 126.20–1; as translated by Linacre 126.20–1; on the trainer 126.29; on the soul and the body 130.21; his *Thrasybulus* 133.24; on natural diseases 172.11; on education of physicians 241.24, 252.15
Galetes (or Galestes) 201.18–20
gall 15.19
galled* 84.32
galliard 81.28
Gallus, G. Sulpicius 244.17
gaming 61.9
garnished 171.23
gay 172.25
gaying 242.22
gaze, give the 33.13
gear 44.25
geason 171.4–5
generosus (Latin) 199.11
gentleman, education of xxviiiff; 184–221; to be the same as the common 193–4; wealth no criterion 194–6; professions of 202–5; why so many desire to be a gentleman 205–6; curriculum outlined 206–7; and drawbacks of travel 208–17; gentleman to be 'pacifike most, and warlike but upon defense' 218. *See also* education
geometry, origins of 244.31
Germanicus Caesar, helped by riding 103.33
gest (guest) 270.8
gig 87.26
girls, education of. *See* women, education of
glass to gaze on 162.32
glister 199.36
Gnato 219.2–4
go through 194.12
goodman 179.19
goulfe (gulf) 139.28
government, kinds of 154.4–7
graffed (grafted) 271.27
gramercy 219.8
grammar-books 5.8–9
grammarian 17.31
grate* 271.30
grater 149.10
grave 67.30
gravel 104.6
Gregory IX, pope, on support for schoolmasters 227.20
Gregory of Nazianzus, St 266.29
grief 93.8
grines (groin) 103.24
gross (a) 52.26, 58.20, 59.17
groune (grown) 136.27
gymnasium 226.13

had I wist (prov) 225.27, 275.29
Hadrian, emperor 90.6, 226.10
Hagar, as learning 242.37
hair, again the (prov) 72.18
haled 61.31
hallow 106.3
halt 280.11
halteres 112.25
hand is his heart, in whose (prov?) 221.11
hand, on the mending (prov) 66.18
hand over head (prov) 233.14
happing 228.12
hardhead 274.30
harding 31.24
harp on harder string (prov) 272.17
harping on one string (prov) 208.22
harvest 120.23

Harvey, Gabriel xxxv, lvi, lviii n 25
haste, danger of 253–8
haste is a foe (prov) 19.18
haste, to post 19.6
haste, posting 253.8
haste with waste (prov) 256.6
hasting 31.24
have ... wish (prov) 287.8
haviour 55.23
hawking up 91.12
head, of a 106.20
head 176.17
healthing 292.36
heart: (organ) 58.13; (man of courage) 281.32
heat, 'ingenerate' or natural 35.28, 69.33
heat, thicken the natural 66.3
height, of the 65.6
Heliodorus on hunting 104.25
helps 243.16
Henry VIII and the Latin grammar 5 (5.8–9)
Hephaestion 201.18–20
Heraclitus, as patron of weeping 74.36
herbour (arbour) 94.28
herbs, studied by Persian women 182.18
Hercules 214.1–3
Hermaeum 226.10
Herodicus 117.17–19
Hesiod, on the silencing of disease 125.36–7
hide their heads 241.14
hidebare* 49.6
hindrance 260.15
Hippocrates: on running 98.14, on running in winter 98.26–9; praises his own country 118.9; more exercise in winter 121.4, 124.35–6; does not deny exercise in summer 121.19–20; no exercise on empty stomach 122.8; no exercise on full or empty stomach 229.28
Hippolytus 104.26
history in the curriculum 265–6
hit ... miss (prov) 60.12–13; 269.5–6
ho: (bid) 79.25; (cry) 123.30
holidays at school 269.34–5
holpen 250.12
holy (wholly) 195.25
Homer: on Achilles as runner 96.10; on hunting 104.25; as the 'greeke poet' 247.29
honested 151.12
Hoole, Charles, and *Positions* xxxvi–xxxvii
hope at anchor 29.31
Horace: on riding 103.6; as the 'poet' 133.1; on the horse that forfeited its liberty 161.4; advises that quantity of syllables be taught 266.22; on a resolute mind 277.5
Horatius Cocles, P., as swimmer 101.36–8
horse-racing of the Romans 103.9
Hortensia 183.15
hostel (or college 'hall') 250.31
hours, calling and discovering 145.19–20
house has odd master, old (prov?) 205.10–11
house is his castle (prov) 222.7
house 223.16–17
huddled up 109.6
humour* 104.24
humours: general definition 53.22; 'superfluous' 35.20–3; 'roaming' 86.24
hunter, the hungry 107.30
hunting 104.22

hurling 58.18

Iaia (Lala) 182.34–7
ill will be ill 140.11–12
imbrew 40.6
immanity 85.30
impatronize* 194.34
impeached 15.18
impeachment 18.8
impression, first (prov) 249.9
improportionate 150.3
incident 40.2–3
incommodity 67.6
incontinent 54.30
incontinently 262.28
inconvenience (prov) 162.3–4
Indian islands 107.13–14
indifferent 240.20
indiligence 171.24
indivisble 136.21
infer 117.13
inflation 94.14–15
injury (v) 191.19
install 165.22
institute 90.11
instrumental parts 53.25
intend 122.16
intercepting 281.35
Irene 182.34–7
ischiatica 97.19
Isocrates 218.30
Isthmos 214

Jack a gentleman (prov) 195.1–2
jogging 70.13
Jonson, Ben, owned *Positions* xxxvi
Josephus: his own nobility 204.37; praised Philo 242.33
juice 86.22
Julian the Apostate: patron of Oribasius 67.24; bans the classics 266.29
jump 115.26
Jupiter: has silenced sickness 125.36–7; his temple at Olympus 214.1–3
justiciary 207.24
Justinian, on support for schoolmasters 227.27–8
Juvenal: on horse-racing of the Romans 103.9; on honesty 228.11g; on too many writers 264.30

kakocheirotechnos (Greek) 100.1
kernel 238.4
kind 209.15
kolon (Greek) 86.27
krikos (Greek) 87.13
kunikon spasma (Greek) 97.16

labour and love being lost (prov) 167.6
labour is the conqueror (prov) 240.16–17
Lacedemonian women 172.4
ladder, leap the (prov) 167.15–16
Laelia 183.15
lag 264.31
Lala (Iaia) 182.34–7
lamb and the lark (prov) 229.38
language: RM's defence of English xlviii–xlix; the qualities of English xlix; proverbs and apophthegms li; Latin and English 16–17 (16.38), 41–3 (42.35); Latin to be taught where actually needed 148; training in 148.16–17; language, college for 236–7, 242; all learning will be brought to one language 238.12; too much attributed to languages 238.17; things

over words 238.28–9; word given according to property of thing 242.10–11
Latin (v) 17.7
latinists, parents no 16.38
Latinus 103.3
laughing: as physical exercise 72–3 (72.4); and weeping compared 75
law, college for 241, 245 (245.21)
law, positive 285.32
lay 116.20
lead (prov) 142.29–30
leaf, turn a new (prov) 152.2–3
Leander as swimmer 101.9
leaping 98–100 (98.30)
lease 32.1, 185.14, 250.4
leesing 27.26
legacy 103.4
leisure 52.18
Lent, the time for tops 87.7–8
leprosy, Egyptian 66.19
let 16.10, 37.31
lewd 191.2
liberty keeps the keys (prov?) 31.4–6
lice 211.23
life spirit* 58.29
lightly 34.24, 208.17
lightness 49.9
lightsomeness 157.22
likest 64.31
Lily's grammar 5.8–9
limitable 282.25
Linacre, Thomas, translator of Galen 126.20–1
-ling 32.29–30, 38.6, 151.21–2, 180.22, 254.22
lining 182.21
lion, paw of (prov) 4.10
list (sb): (inclination) 265.38; (limit) 280.27
list (v): (choose) 50.31; (incline to) 67.16
livery 53.8
living 139.31–2
livings (scholarships) 247.37
livings: advancement to, to be controlled 167–8
Livy, on Brutus 285.38–286.1
loated 149.15
loath 88.37
loftiness 154.35
logical help to chop (prov) 183.6
London: and archery 108.25–6; streets of 137
losels 206.7
love and labour being lost (prov) 167.6
lowlings 180.22
Lucian: depiction of Solon on cock-fights 85.34
lungs 58.8
Lycaeum 236.23
lying spirit 145.18

machance 80.17
Machaon 106.27
Maecenas Messius, his silence 71.30
maim 144.20
main (sb)* 25.32; 289.12
making up 45.8
mammering 278.38
man is a wolf or god to man (prov) 276.38
manuary: (trade) 46.14; (one who works with hands) 198.4
mar 264.31
mark 159.14
market, mar the (prov) 143,33; 255.17
Martia 182.34–7
Martial: on horse-racing of the Romans 103.9
massive 221.7

massy 132.32
master, second (usher) 258.7
mathematical 18.10
mathematics: 46.14; college for 237–44; teaching of 237.12 n; attitudes towards 237.24–5; and the study of logic 243.11
mean (a) 32.33
mean (sb): (instrument) 55.37, 68.28; (moderation) 56.8; (condition) 96.39
mean (v) 56.8;
mean, in a 108.1
mean, makes the 217.14–15
meaning 16.23
many (a) 229.4
meany (sb): (dependants or flock) 207.29; (assembly) 248.11
measure 124.5
meat, but not for mowers (prov) 181.34
meats, after 265.39
medicine (physic), college for 241, 245
medicine, galenic theory outlined 53.22. *See also* exercise
mediocrity 28.29; 55.27; 181.26
meet with 118.14
Melanchthon, Philipp, and his 'Miseries of Schoolmasters' 259.3, 276
memorandum* 112.28
memory: a treasury 39.2–4; technique, using Muses 190.3
menalty 178.25
Menander 195.17
mend 261.25–6
Merchant Taylors' School: building 228.23–4, 228.36. *See also* Mulcaster, Richard
merchantable 20.2
Mercuriale, Girolamo: RM's use of xxivff; his life and works xl n 40; as source for chapters 6 through 35 (see commentary passim); marginal reference to 79.14; first named as source 134.11
mere (a) 180.27; 200.22
mere (adv) 155.25
mere (sb) 101.22
Meteren, Emmanuel van, a friend of RM lxvii
method: discussed 18; defined 18.1; mathematics and 18.10; the 'braunching, order, and method' used for exercise 59–60 (60.6). *See also* art
metre 276.34
Micon, father of Timarete 182.34–7
militare 80.4
Milo: immoveable 61.29; his breathing exercise 79.14
milt 96.29
minced 63.19
minister 196.13
mischief (prov) 162.3–4
misconsture (misconstrue) 268.34
misliker 254.26–7
mislotted* 142.37–8
misses 275.36
mistiming 81.17
Mithridates as a hunter 105.35
moan 287.15
moan (v) 52.23
moan (sb) 80.20
moaned 33.5
mock-mathematicals 241.13
moil 28.2
moist (v) 94.8
moisture 32.21–2
monarchy: wit best suited for 153; and other forms of government 154.4–7; 'best kinde

of government' 285
monitors 271.8
moon, above the (prov) 237.29
moonish 178.11–12
Moses learned in Egyptian mathematics 243 (242.37, 252.7)
mostwhat 16.37, 140.2
mostwhere 34.3
mother to truth 257.12
mother, matter, *mater* 252.20–1
motion 288.9
Mulcaster, Richard: birth and early years lixff; his learning lx; and Quenes Majesties Passage lx and lxiin 11; as headmaster of Merchant Taylors' School lxff; his attitude towards beating lxiv–lxv (*see also* beating); his pupils lxv–lxvi; his learned friends lxvii; later career lxii, lxviii–lxix; his various church livings lxviii; at St Paul's School lxix; Fuller's biography of lxx–lxxi; his writings listed 453ff; *Positions* his first time in print 3.13, 6 ('prima tessera'), 288.18–19; his years of teaching 16.3, 228.29; his school building 228.3–4; his number of students lxv, 275.7. *See also Positions*
murdered 222.34
mure up 77.18
Muses: to 'muse' at 122.31; as memory device 190.3
music: as part of elementary xxi–xxii, 47.7; divided into voice and instrument 47; praise of 47 (47.37–8); the eye of the ear (prov) 47.9; a medicine from heaven 47.19; where practised 48; for soul and body 48; arguments against 48–9; music, number and soul 48–9; musicians' care for their limbs 50.22; on singing as exercise 68–9; and dancing 82–3; haste in training for 258; need for parental discipline in 258
muster 232.30
mutability 282.29–31. *See* certainty

narrowly 29.4
Nashe, Thomas, on *Positions* xxxv
national 211.2
natural (sb) 142.33, 181.20, 204.1
natural heat. *See* heat, natural
natural name 187.4–5
natural philosopher 18.18
nature and nurture 29.18–19
nature and property 42.7
nature, as 'natural abilities' xviii–xx
nature: mother or stepmother 277.2; an eager monster (prov?) 279.17–18
naughty 66.13
naule (awl) 167.2
ne (nor) 155.33
Nearchus, father of Aristarete 182.34–7
nearest, dearest (prov?) 178.19–20
neating 230.8
necessity is the spur (prov?) 191.6
necessity (need) is imperious mistress (prov) 139.37–8
needle 180.2
Nemea 214.1–3
Neptune 6, 144.8–9, 214.1–3
Nero 220.27, 226.10
Newton, John, and *Positions* xxxvii
niggardish 37.37
nimbling 67.26
nip 94.17
nobilis (Latin) 199.11

nobleman, education of xxviiiff; 184–221; nobility defined and discussed 197ff (196.4–5)
nonsuite* 177.11
nosethrills (nostrils) 102.6–7
notorious 46.14–15
nurture, nature 29.18–19
nuzzled 58.1, 164.33

obsequious 154.37
occasion is bald (prov) 30.37
odd 155.2, 189.16
oddness 189.16
odds 22.17, 261.15
of (off) 141.31, 234.2
offend 124.18
officer 53.2
officious* 4.15
Offley, Hugh 108.34
ointed 127.21
oligarchy 154.4–7
Olympus 214.1–3
onlyest 42.1
open 193.2
or 243.1
order: in education 262–4; and certainty 282.29–31
ordinance 152.20
ordinarily 83.4
ordinary (a): (customary) 33.13, (methodical) 52.15–16
ordinary (sb) 118.5–6
ordinate 153.24
Oribasius: on loud speaking 67.24; on running in winter and summer 98.26–9
overflush 141.14
overlaid 244.25
overreaching 122.7–8
overshot 176.21
overthwart 279.18
overtop 269.19
overtreat 27.10
overtreated 137.17
overweening* 187.39
ox, the black (prov) 144.5

pace* 82.20–1
pad 209.38
painting. *See* drawing
pair 104.15
Palaemon, Q. Remmius, a boastful schoolmaster 164.17–18
palaestra 83.25, 226.13
palsy-like 80.29–30
Panathaenaicum 226.10
pancrace* 112.25
pancratical ... wrestling 84.5–6
pant 66.37
papbones* 73.36
Papirius the runner 96.8
parability 110.14
parable 88.35
parents: generally not latinists 16.38; nature of 28–31; too fond 30.11–12, 34.5; to judge child's readiness for school 31; yet advice from teacher must be sought 33–4, 36; their negligence 35; their 'mannering' of the young 40; to be bound more to country than to child 146ff; to decide with master which children to attend school 157–9; their peevishness 263; discipline of home and school to be similar 272; the 'displeased parent' 276; their conference with neighbours 277–9; their conference with teachers 279–80; need for child's 'certainty' at home 283
partialities 103.10
partible 291.5

party 15.20
passage* 60.3
passenger 108.3
patient 15.20, 117.34
patrimony 146.24–5
patronage, common 3.10–11
Paul, St. See Bible
Pausanias 226.6
pearcher 29.9
pearing (appearing) 39.15
peevish 50.6–7
peised 61.30
pencil 45.30
penny: good silver (prov) 19.33–4; allow a (prov?) 150.25; the loss of a (prov?) 179.39–180.1
pension, put to 250.4–5
perfect (v) 59.35
perfect (sb) 167.37
perfection: unattainable 28–31; the perfection of Socrates 75–6
perilous 149.10
perish 55.24
pert 254.21
pertling 254.22
perug 211.24
pester 291.10
pestering 139.16
petaur* 112.25
pettiness 19.39
pettiship 180.23
petty 5.23
pewkishness 66.10
Philippic* 67.13–14
Philo: on benefits of singing 68.24–5; on the perfect number ten 175.21; on the soul 218.13; on Hagar (school–learning) and Sarah (wisdom) 242.37
philosophy, college for 241,244–5 (244.36–7)
Philostratus 226.7
phonaskoi 65.5
physic-like 69.7
picked 25.17
picking 270.36
pickler 56.20
Pico della Mirandola, Giovanni, his theses 248.13
pierce 195.34
pinch (sb) 268.9
pinch (v): (find fault with) 168.32; (snap at) 268.16
pine (v) 55.23
pipes 57.29, 74.8, 189.38
pitch 211.30
pith 17.21, 54.20
place (in an argument) 20.19
plain 90.9
plat (v) 59.25
plat (sb) 28.25
Plato: as an 'authority' 24; on arithmetic and geometry 44.29–30; on benefits of singing 68.24–5; his *Laches* on courage 86.9; on the left and right hand 88.8, 171.31; on walking as exercise for soldiers 90.1; that women exercise as well as men 100.12; on the need for doctors themselves to suffer disease 106.30; his Prodicus confused for Herodicus 117.17–19; on the qualities of the guardians 143.2; Proclus' commentary on, and comparative virtue of men and women 172.27g; as traveller 209.11; on Socrates in prison 213.10; his *Laws* on travel summarized 213–17 (213.18); on school building of Sparta 226.6; rejects pupils without geometry 237.36; on study of mathematics

Plato (cont'd) 237.27–8, 242.29, 242.36, 243.31, 245 (245.12); as example of Aristotle's precepts 245.16–17; his Academy 248.35–7; taught for more than fifty years 249.1–2; and poetry 266.14; on punishment 272.39, 273.12

plausible 156.17

Pliny the elder: practised reading aloud 70.23; on the silence of Maecenas Messius 71.30 on gladiators 86.6; on Callimachus the sculptor 100.2; on horse-racing of the Romans 103.9; on women artists 182.34ff; nature a better mother, or bitterer stepdame 277.2

Pliny the younger: on his uncle's reading aloud 70.23; on Roman horse-racing 103.11; on Spurinna 117.17–19

Plutarch: on Demosthenes and walking 93.2; on the silencing of disease 125.36–7; on women 174.11–12, 175.27; his epistle to Trajan 174.21; ps–Plutarch on Eurydice 183.16; on Alexander's favourite 201.18; on Sulla 202.7; on Julius Caesar 218.26; apophthegms in 271.20–1

Plutus 195.10

ply 184.15

Podalyrius 106.27

poetry: reciting of, as exercise 68; hunting and 104; in the curriculum 265–7; low opinion of 265.23–4; as 'fabulous veele' 268.8; Plato and 266.14; 'poetical fury' 267.5–6; teaching of verse–writing 267.5–6

point (sb) 27.11

point (v) 176.37, 273.18, 281.38

poise 92.32

policy 24.32; 68.26; 202.25

pontificate, great 218.27

Pontius the Samnite 162.8

poorlings 151.21–2

port is repentance 82.12

port 168.31

Porus, his 'dog' 199.37

Positions: publication lxxix; printing lxxx; accuracy of text lxxxi; proof-correction and variants in lxxx–lxxxii; variants and corrections listed 295–303; copies listed 303–4; as a preface to a series xxxviii n 2, 159, 229, 287 *See also* Mulcaster, Richard

positions: the term explained xiv–xv, 1.1; why they must be outlined methodically 17–21; summarized 20–1; 288

positive 20.20

post over 129.15

posting (on a horse) 104 (103.23, 104.17)

posting haste 19.5, 253.8

postparative 63.4–5

praise at parting (prov) 22.10

prating 177.34

prattling 177.34

preacher, unlearned 142.13–14

prease ('press' and 'praise') 82.12–13

preasing (pressing) 253.11

precedent 17.35, 117.21, 283.34. *See also* president

precise 80.23

preciseness 287.21

preferment 224.15–16

pregant women long for unripe fruit 253.19

prerogative 56.36, 291.6

presidency* 175.33
president: (precedent) 17.35, 276.34; (presiding patron*) 106.35; (one in charge) 215.36. *See also* precedent
pretence* 275.19
pretend 144.28
prevent 138.24
prevention: (stopping*) 141.34–5; (precaution*) 269.19–20
price 238.24
price (prize) 85.12
price, in 63.1
priests on the bridge as the Pope passes, make not all (prov?) 166.37–8
prime 285.10
primitive (a) 1.2–3
primitive (sb) 289.30
primitively* 20.16
prince, education of 220–1 (220.6)
principle 135.5
private education. *See* education
private 181.7
privating 188.37
problematory 134.2–3
proceeders 239.31
process* 232.10
procession, with* 285.22–3
Proclus: commentary on Plato 172.27g;, commentary on Euclid 243.37
Prodicus 117.17–19
profess 18.26
profession 53.14, 68.12
professions: the divine 202–4; the lawyer 204–5; the physician 205
prohemes 67.19
proof 283.34
properly 50.39
property 54.20
property, nature and 42.7
proportion 48.20–1
Protogenes 244.23
prove 145.6
proyn (prune) 19.13
psychology of children. *See* children
Ptolemy 201.18–20
public education. *See* education
publish 260.32
puffer up 187.37
pugillate* 112.25
pull down 71.34–5
pulse, arterial 55.16
puniship 43.33
punishment, corporal. *See* beating
purchaceable* 105.19–20
purchase (v): (gain) 95.21; (plunder) 201.13
purpose, of 195.34
purtracte (portrait) 278.32
push (sb): (swelling, boil) 126.17; (ambitious effort*) 187.18
putforths* 205.27
putting to 286.9
pyrre 276.20
Pythagoras: on music, number, and the soul 49; as traveller 209.11; 245.11

qualified* 288.11
qualify 138.22
qualifying 37.14–15
quartan agues 66.17
questuary* 72.14
quickling* 32.29–30
quicksilver 219.23
quintessence 208.17
Quintilian: as an 'authority' 25; on 'fault of man' 49.32–3; on the teacher not knowing all 164.11; on the learning of a private student 188.18–19; on the teacher of two or

Quintilian (cont'd)
three boys 189.34–5; on joining private with public 191.23; teacher like the sun 191.37; on public schooling 192.10; teacher to think each child an Alexander 234.37; young children should study the morally sound as well as the eloquent 267.10
quite (v) 211.7
quoiting 112.26
quotation marks 15.12g
quoted out 289.38

raine (rein) 288.19
range 22.29
rarely* 5.13
rate, in 288.9–10
ravening 122.7–8
rawness 66.32
reach 128.1
reading: as part of elementary xxi–xxii; teaching of 41.15–16, 41.34–6; English before Latin 41–2; aloud, as exercise 59.14, 69.24; instruction in 143.21–3
reaping, image of 16.21
rearward 271.29
reason and rote 42.29
reasty 32.30
rebating 54.28
rebound 32.16
receipt: (capacity) 39.4; (place for storage) 242.8
reckless 124.24, 144.4, 210.17
reclaim 136.9
recoiling 48.10
redress 279.21
referendary* 4.15
reformation 247.19
reft: (taken away) 49.28; (deprived) 255.33
refuse* 157.17
regiment 284.15
rehearsal 15.11
rein, give the (prov) 252.18
relish* 108.22
remiss 84.10
rempare 152.25; 277.4
renown (v) 218.7
rent 228.6
renting 79.4
repair 232.24
repairers get the pence (prov?) 134.23
repentance: 'hath repulse' 46.18; 'be her port' 82.12
repetition 292.23
repulse is a miserable strip 167.38–168.1. *See also* repentance
reseant 157.6
resemble 213.27
residence 77.23
residentiary* 217.13
resolutely 18.6
resolution 73.27
resolve 20.4
resolved on* 135.31
resolved 66.22
resort 188.19
respects* 248.17
revenge 35.9
revolt (v) 284.36
Rhazes, cited on hunting 105.32
rhetoric: and authorities 26 (26.25)
rhyme ... reason (prov) 274.21–2
riddance 44.23
ride post 104.17
ridge 161.5; 245.13
ridgebone 110.33
riding 59.8, 102–4, 102.28
rifting 66.11
rig 100.4

ring out all in 146.19–20
ripe, rotten (prov) 253.13
road 29.32
roam 139.29
roaming humours 86.24
robe 288.14
rock of marble (prov?) 247.15
rod beats them, their own (prov) 237.32
rolling: (wandering) 262.8, (moving in disorderly fashion) 284.32–3
Roman Catholic church: favoured Latin 41–2; a harbour for the educated 151.35–6
room 139.29
rote and reason 42.29
round: (energetic) 108.14; (uncompromising) 271.36
roundly 258.1
rowme (room) 292.16
ruck 58.3
rudiments 240.22–3
ruff 76.9
rules of school to be posted 269.9, 270.34–5
running 58.39, 95–8 (95.26)

sad 80.27
sadly 60.28
sadness, in good 28.14–15, 107.6
sail, bear a 181.8
sail, under 241.2
salve: (heal) 56.30, 136.19, 255.14; (make good) 140.4
sanguinary 86.3–4
Sappho 175.28–32
Sarah, as learning 242.37
saturity 81.29
sauciness, unsweetening with (prov) 156.10
Scaeva, M. Caesius, as swimmer 101.36–8
scare crow* 153.9
schiomachia 85.17
scholarships in university 247.37
school points 24.34
schoolhouse, ideal 225–6 (225.36); location of 223.7, 228 (228.27); description of building 228–9
schoolmaster. *See* teacher
schools erected in Elizabeth's reign 226.18
scouring 19.8–9
scrape 251.24
scurf 66.19
seat: (placement in the body) 116.29; (foundation) 134.7
seek 62.9
seem is less than to be, to 167.8
Semiramis 175.28–32
Seneca, on benefits of reading aloud 70.7
sense, common 287.30
sentence 287.11
service 141.22–3
Servius 175.28–32
Sesostris 175.28–32
set backward 263.29–30
set over* 225.25
severed: (set apart) 41.1–2; (separated) 205.35
shadowish 86.29
shed 279.35
shifters 139.30
ship of state (prov) 240.1
shooting. *See* archery
shooting at the mark (image) 59.30
show for a shadow (prov) 180.24
shrew 112.6
shrews have dined (prov) 158.1–2
shrike (shriek) 132.21
shrink 123.28

shuffle up cards 206.8
Sibyl 175.28–32
Sicily, Plato's travel to 209.11
sillily 130.35
silly: (helpless) 29.27; (defenceless) 213.10; (trifling*) 289.17
similary parts 53.25
similitudinary 240.35
simply 60.30
sinews 57.26
singing 68.8
single 98.24
sinisterly 209.7
Siren 49
sitter by 190.9
sklender 32.28
sleight 101.4
smack 148.20
smally 193.6
Smith, Thomas 108.38
smoky substance 77.10–11
snuff (v) 143.29
snuff (sb) 188.4
sober 80.27
Socrates: on voluntary learning by the young 75.19; 'Socratical saints' 75.30; Aristophanes against 103.1–2; would not disobey law of Athens 213.10; and mathematics 237.27–8, 243; 'the wisest maister' and mathematics 239; logic the backbone of mathematics 245.12; that it is slavish to be beaten 273.12; teacher of Xenophon 274.4. *See also* Plato
Socrates Scholasticus 266.29
soilth 224.29
Solon: in Lucian on cock-fights 85.34; a traveller 209.8; on parricide 275.31
sook (soak)* 127.22
sooth 79.14–15
soothe 22.7
sort 49.39
soul: xviiff; qualities of learner's 38 (38.31–2); and body 51ff, 129–32; its authoritative part in Philo 218.3. *See also* children
soulish 58.29
soureth not the mean 15.24–5
sovereign 65.16
Sozomenus 266.29
Spartan women 99.39
speak finely, reason wisely (prov) 238.19
speaking aloud 59.11, 65.11
spelling, teaching of 41.15–16
Spenser, Edmund, a pupil of RM lxvii
Speusippus 249.1–2
spirit 57.29
spoil 140.27
sports. *See* exercise
spreed 47.36
spring (v) 140.26–7
spring (sb) 146.19
spur, upon the 32.27
Spurinna, Vestricius 117.17–19
squaring 150.13
staff, last* 272.29
staff, set down (prov) 227.37–8
stage, forced to the 26.11
staid 202.19
staidest* 81.27
stake, tied to the (prov) 190.17–18
stamp 255.38
stand upon 196.24
standing 209.23
standings* 111.25
stant* 227.15
starting-hole 271.15
statary 198.26

state 191.11
statuary 46.13
stay (sb): (control) 23.38; (delay) 38.7–8
stay (v): (support) 23.14, 55.36; (pause) 38.7–8; (bring to a halt) 136.37
stayed (a) 22.24
staying (ppl a) 69.30
steam (v) 92.21
stifle 55.22
still (v) 32.25, 165.10
stir 35.17
stirring 221.3
Stoa 236.23
stomach (v) 268.3
stomach (sb) 210.25
stomaching 154.25
stone gathers moss, rolling (prov) 159.27–8
stops 263.14
store (sb) 135.14, 255.17
Strabo 244.26
strain out 209.35
strainable 114.34
strait (v) (keep ill supplied) 55.23; (confine) 77.26, 127.9, 202.29; (constrict) 90.22
strait (a) (narrow) 116.27; (severe) 225.23
strangeness 255.15
stretchers 57.26
strigil 127.26
string 57.25
strip 167.38–168.1
stripes 271.2
stripping 168.38
stroke, strike the 232.31
strout (strut) 92.18
strutting (swelling) 78.33; (thrusting) 91.24
stuff (v) 34.23, 55.22
stuffing 219.1
style 257.29
subaltern 130.24
subdivident 198.5
substance 24.13
subtle (v)* 59.15
Suetonius: on Augustus and his cure by sand 93.25; on Augustus and his cure by leaping 99.17; on Germanicus Caesar and riding 103.33
suffer 89.12
sufficiency 234.38
Suidas 226.7
Sulla, L.C. 202.7–9
sun (prov) 276.12
supererogatory 144.14
superlative* 185.13
supposal 25.16
surveyor 80.23
swaddling the chest 77.34
swallow (prov) 262.10
sway 92.31
sweet, sour a (prov) 5.25
sweet and sour 51.8–9
swim, he knows neither letters nor to (prov) 100.34–5
swim (v) 261.28
swimming 100–2, 100.31, 284.19–20
swimming (ppl a) (affected with dizziness) 80.36
swinge, bear all the 154.7
swinge 52.11, 76.3
syllabe 43.2
symposiac 134.2–3

taches 210.18
taint* 170.31
talents 173.35
tales out of school, to tell (prov) 271.7

talking and silence as exercise 71–2
Tamburlaine 218.3
Tanaquill 175.28–32
tankard-bearer 142.34
tardies (tardiness?)* 270.37
tarried the pulling and hung the full harvest (prov?) 219.21
teachers: general discussion xxxiii–xxxiv, 230–5; to teach the young manners 39–40 (40.2); to follow order in instruction 42; of physical exercise 128–37; to possess great skill 134–5; their need for 'discretion' 135; to choose, in consultation with parents, which children are to attend school 157–9; of their boarding of pupils 223–8; their need for better pay xxxiv, 227–8 (228.6, 232.13g, 234.2), 232–3, 276; immunities for 227.24; licences for 228.18; elementary 231–2; elementary often the meanest 231.37–232.1; whether one teacher can handle all elementary subjects 233.32; grammar 233–5; requirements for good 234.14; a college to train the grammar masters 235ff (235.9–10, 245.33–4); age of 275 (275.37–8); marital status of 275–6 (275.37–8); 'teachers life is painful' 276; and the 'displeased parent' 276; to confer with neighbours 279; to confer with parents 279–80; to confer with other teachers 280–1
temper, in 78.29
temperature 54.3, 69.9, 118.36
tempered 53.37
ten, the 'absolute number' 175.21
tenants in the house of several lords, two (prov?) 130.10–11
tender 170.15
tendering 127.37
Terence, Gnatho and Thraso of 219.2–4
term, in 206.38
tetters 91.29
Theodorus Asinaeus 172.27g
thermae of Nero 226.10–11
Thraso 219.2–4
threaped upon 24.32
thrid 90.31
thronged 65.24
Tiberius, emperor 103.33
Tibur 226.10
ticklish* 155.29
Timarete 182.34–7
timber 178.8
timbered 148.3
time: to tarry 241.25; digesting 241.33; discretion the daughter of 241.26–7
timely 19.6
Timon of Athens* 176.38
title: (section of book) 4.9, 8.1; (matter) 59.35
tofore 107.19
tooth and nail (prov) 169.30–1
top 87–9 (esp 87.3)
touch, abide the 293.1
toward 22.2
towardness 39.19
toy* 159.14
toy 276.20
toyousness 180.30
traine 3.5
trance 213.3
translate 228.17
travail (sb) 3.13
travail (v): (cause to work) 106.4; (study) 218.35
travel (travail) 3.13, 106.4, 218.35

travel: disapproved of, as part of education of gentleman 208–17 (208.6); defined 210 (210.4–5)
trochos (Greek) 87.13
troll 254.37
truantry 224.9
truth, mother to 257.12
truth, not dependent on authorities 26–7
Turkish captivity 141.9
turn (sb)* 69.12
turn (sb) 229.1–2
tutor, role of 231.32
twenty things 224.29
twist 97.36
two (too) 155.5

unbewitched 196.3
uncharmed* 276.33
under minus* 144.2
under means 252.16
under-travailer 108.32
undershining 176.14
underteacher 226.35
unequal* 126.11
unfriends 213.12
uniformity in teaching 259–62 (259.29)
universities: admissions into colleges, to be controlled 160–5; graduation to be controlled 165–7; location of colleges 222; the 'masters' of 235.19–20; appropriation of lands of 236.1; proposal to reorder by professions (languages, mathematics, philosophy, divinity, medicine, law) 236–47 (236.24, 241.20); logic and rhetoric in 241.37–8; necessity of the proposed colleges 242ff; the seventh college, for training masters 245–6; proposal to sort students of like years into like rooms 247; proposal to improve support for students 247–8; need for better teachers within universities 248ff
unlikely 166.27
unproved 37.30
unracked 43.1
unwieldiness 57.27
unwieldy 52.32
urinals 182.16
urine, sharp 112.15
use (or habit) xix
use (sb): (employment) 185.23; (customary practice) 229.33
usher, role of 226–7 (226.35). *See also* second master, underteacher
utterable 208.38

valetudinary* 115.20
valiancy 136.11, 201.34
valure 175.23–4
vantage (advantage) 107.31
vanting (vaunting) 130.29
varicose veins 100.16
Varro, M.T., as father of Martia 182.34–7
vaulted 228.36
Vautrollier, Thomas lxxix
Vegetius Renatus, cited on walking 90.3
veins, varicose 100.16
veins 265.31
venture, at a 212.39
Verrine* 67.13–14
very 123.14
vessel of weakness (prov) 178.22
Virgil: compares Amata to a spinning top 87.18; on riding 103.3; as judge of horses 172.8; on the Roman genius for government 244.12

virtue (prov?) 199.32–3
virtue, private 192.33
Vitruvius 244.19
Vives, Juan Luis 256.15
voluntary 258.5–6
vowed 158.38
vyage (voyage) 211.19

wailing women 72.14
waker 118.35
walk 72.3
walking 89–95 (89.3)
walking rooms 89.28
wall, thrust to (prov) 228.10
wanne 32.15
war-master* 134.2–3
ward 167.20
warrant(sb) 101.35
warrant (v): promise) 17.19; (keep safe from) 101.33,
warranting 268.29
warrious 210.35
waste 55.13
watchman, blame the (prov?) 254.31
water (prov) 142.11–12
water-bearer 142.34
waters, deep (prov) 164.28–9
wave (prov). *See* billow
wax, work like 35.4
way, one right 260.4
weal or woe (prov) 171.16
wealthlings 151.21–2
weather fair when shrews have dined (prov) 158.1–2
weather 9.23
weeping, as physical exercise 74
well (sb) 64.16
welter 144.32
whether (weather) 9.23
Whitelock, (Sir) James, a pupil of RM lxiv
wholesome (v)* 94.36
whoresons 162.22
will, in way in (prov?) 84.33–4
Will: to stop (prov) 30.30; a good boy (prov) 39.29; think that well, bid (prov) 148.5–6
wind 94.17
windcourse* 84.30–1
windwork 65.16
wiseman 22.16
wite 32.11
witness (v) 272.32
women, education of xxxff, 169–84; exercise to be the same (Plato) 100.12; both male and female to be educated in body and mind 137–8; 'naturally the male is more worthy' 138; education of women an 'accessory' 138; logical proof why girls should learn 169–70; presence in elementary and grammar schools 169.26; custom allows girls learning 170–1; women celebrated for learning 170.36–7; Greek and Roman paragons 171.1–3; men owe women learning 171–2; women are naturally 'toward' 172–6; the 'end' and the 'circumstances' of their learning 176ff; curriculum 178–9; the importance of their 'needle' 180.2; 'how much' 180–3; male teachers 'frame them best' 184; women 'counterbraunches' to men 185; their education defended further 291–2
woodish* 104.28
workmanship 182.14
world to see (prov) 254.3
Worthies, Nine 175.20
wrest 25.7

wrestling 83–5
wring (v): (twist) 25.7; (harm) 123.27; (suffer) 165.13; (distress) 195.21
wring to the wall (prov) 168.31–2
writing: as part of elementary xxi–xxii; 43–5 (43.13); writing and speech 43; origins uncertain 43–4; teaching of 44; reading and writing the two basic skills 44–5; the English hand first 45.20–1; relation with drawing 46

Xenophon: his portrayal of the sour centurion in *Cyropaedia* 74.37; on hunting 105.3; Persian ordinance on who may attend school 147.36; schoolroom commodious in 229.12; copy of, given to RM by Cheke 239.16–20; masters of Cyrus old men 246.22; on listing of school faults 270.38; Cyrus, 'paterne of the best Prince' was beaten 273.32; Cyrus confers to discover truth 280.11–12
*xystum** 226.13

yard, stayed 284.19
yeaxing 92.13
youngling 38.6

www.ingramcontent.com/pod-product-compliance
Lightning Source LLC
LaVergne TN
LVHW010445080826
844660LV00027B/1221